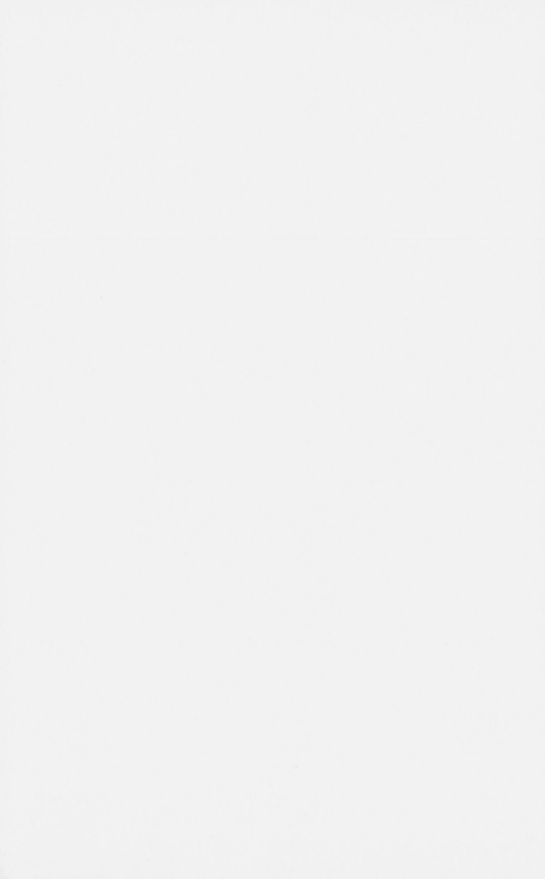

KINGS IN
THE NORTH

KINGS IN
THE NORTH

The House of Percy in British History

Alexander Rose

Weidenfeld & Nicolson

LONDON

First published in Great Britain in 2002
by Weidenfeld & Nicolson

A CIP catalogue record for this book
is available from the British Library.

ISBN 0 297 81860 0

Typeset by Selwood Systems, Midsomer Norton

Printed in Great Britain by Butler & Tanner Ltd,
Frome and London

Weidenfeld & Nicolson

The Orion Publishing Group Ltd
Orion House
5 Upper Saint Martin's Lane
London, WC2H 9EA

Contents

Acknowledgements   vii
Author's Note   ix
Family Tree   x
Introduction   1

 1. The First Northerner   17
 2. When Christ and his Saints Slept   44
 3. The End of the Line?   72
 4. Sir Richard Percy, the Northerners and Magna Carta   79
 5. Sir Henry Percy and the Barons' War   94
 6. Great Captain   111
 7. The Border Baron   142
 8. Henry Percy IV and the Outbreak of Peace   167
 9. Henry Percy IV and the Conquest of Scotland   198
10. The Closing Years of Henry Percy   234
11. Adventures Abroad   251
12. Inexorable Ascent   297
13. The Fall of the Percys, 1377–1408   322
14. A Good and Faithful Servant   367
15. A Safe Pair of Hands   378
16. Mutual Assured Destruction   400
17. Recovery and Disaster   414
18. Bird in the Bosom   435
19. Percy Restored   443
20. Kings in the North   461
21. The Rise and Fall of the North   471

    Epilogue   487
    Notes   491
    Select Bibliography   539
    Index   555

Acknowledgements

It remains a necessary pleasure in life to thank the people who aided the writing of a book.

I must mention Emily Bearn, Nicholas Boys-Smith, Adrian Brettle, Adrian Carr, Chris Champion, John Coldstream, Ian Farrow, Charlene Fern, David Gardner-Roberts, Marc-Henri Glendening, Dean Godson, Paul Goodman, Jane Hall, Daniel Hannan, Neil and Anna Hitchin, Duncan Jackman, Emma Jarvis, George and Maya Jonas, Jaroslava Korpanec, Edward Lipman, Virginia McMullan, Athena Malpas, Sean Ramsden, Duncan Reed, Andrew Roberts, Maxwell Rumney, Melissa Seckora, Douglas Smith, Zara Steiner, Graham Stewart, Christine Stolba and Lynn Sweet.

And also my colleagues at Canada's *National Post*: Kenneth Whyte, Hugo Gurdon, Martin Newland, Isabel Vincent, Tim Rostron, Terence Corcoran, Andrew Coyne, Rebecca Eckler and the Editorial Board (Natasha Hassan, Ruth-Ann MacKinnon, Neil Seeman, Ezra Levant, Peter Taylor, Jonathan Kay and John Williamson).

I am especially indebted to Marcella Munro, Laura Ingraham, John O'Sullivan and David and Danielle Frum for a truly astounding amount of advice, sustenance and, of course, friendship.

This book is about a family. It could never have been written without the unstinting support and encouragement of my own, on both sides of the Atlantic: my grandparents, Professor John and Fay Rose, the late Elsie Kaplow, and Mordechai and Mildred Kaplow; my parents, Professor Paul Lawrence and Susan Rose, and siblings, Olivia, Zoë and Ari; as well as John, Judith, Michael and Jessica Rose; and Wendy, Adam and Audrey Krat.

I must also thank the librarians of Cambridge University Library; the University of London Library; the Robarts Library at the University of Toronto; the Institute of Historical Research (London); the Pennsylvania State University Library; the Library of Congress; the British Library; and Georgetown University Library.

Great and belated thanks must go to His Grace the Duke of

Northumberland; my agent, Georgina Capel of Capel & Land; my original editor at Weidenfeld & Nicolson, Rebecca Wilson; and Weidenfeld & Nicolson's publishing director Richard Milner. It was Andrew Maxwell-Hyslop who first informed W&N that the manuscript was somewhat more expansive than originally expected, and then heroically undertook the task of editing it. Celia Levett did a quite extraordinary job of copy-editing the entire text. I need also thank Francine Brody, who uncomplainingly dealt with a thousand last-last-minute changes, as well as Douglas Matthews, who compiled a very difficult index indeed.

A last word of acknowledgement, I think, should be extended to those obscure Victorian and Edwardian antiquarians who diligently devoted decades to compiling volumes of documents from medieval fragments, chronicles and records. Without their efforts, our knowledge of the Middle Ages would be sparse indeed.

Alexander Rose
Washington, DC
3 February 2002

Author's Note

Although the surname was originally spelt 'Perci', I have followed convention in referring to the English form, 'Percy', throughout the text (except in the case of quotations) to prevent confusion.

Medieval chronicles and later historians spell the names of the early Percys in various ways: that is, Jeffrie, Geoffrey, Jeffrey. I have tended to keep to the versions used by the writers.

Although the mark was not used as currency in medieval England (no coins known as marks were ever circulated there), both the mark and the pound were used as measures of account. The mark, which was accepted throughout western Europe, was equivalent to eight ounces of silver or two-thirds of a pound (13s 4d or 66.66 pence).

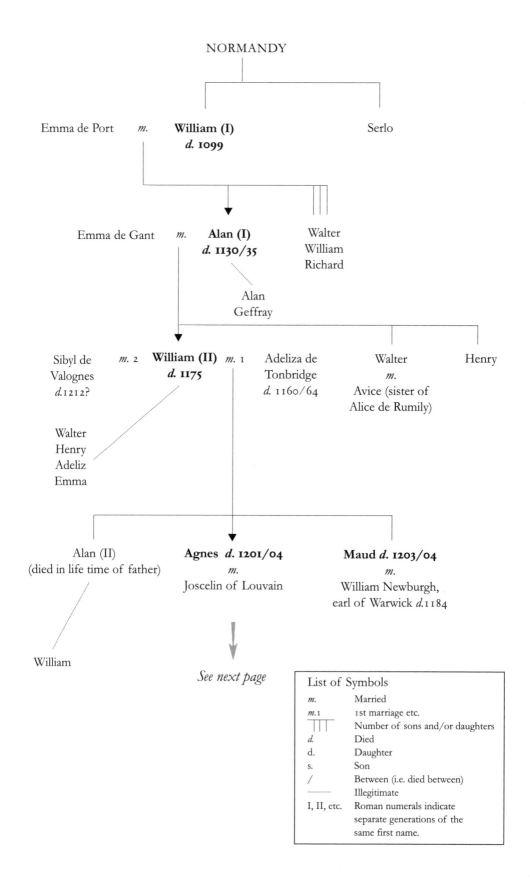

NORMANDY

Emma de Port   m.   **William (I)**   Serlo
                      d. 1099

Emma de Gant   m.   **Alan (I)**   Walter
                      d. 1130/35   William
                                            Richard

                              Alan
                              Geffray

Sibyl de   m. 2 **William (II)** m. 1 Adeliza de   Walter   Henry
Valognes   **d. 1175**   Tonbridge   m.
d.1212?   d. 1160/64   Avice (sister of
                                                             Alice de Rumily)

Walter
Henry
Adeliz
Emma

Alan (II)   **Agnes d. 1201/04**   **Maud d. 1203/04**
(died in life time of father)   m.   m.
                                        Joscelin of Louvain   William Newburgh,
                                                                 earl of Warwick d.1184

William

                                        See next page

List of Symbols

m.	Married
m.1	1st marriage etc.
⊤⊤⊤	Number of sons and/or daughters
d.	Died
d.	Daughter
s.	Son
/	Between (i.e. died between)
....	Illegitimate
I, II, etc.	Roman numerals indicate separate generations of the same first name.

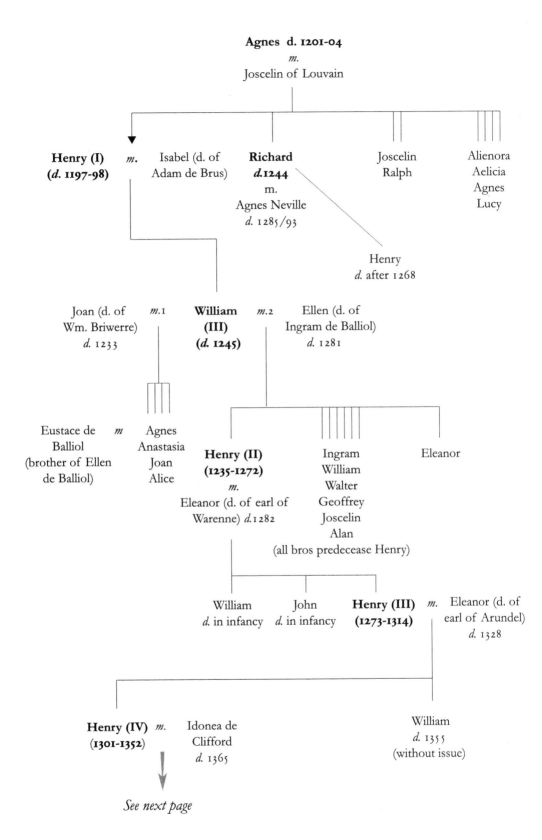

Agnes d. 1201-04
m.
Joscelin of Louvain

Henry (I) *m.* Isabel (d. of **Richard** Joscelin Alienora
(d. 1197-98) Adam de Brus) *d.1244* Ralph Aelicia
m. Agnes
Agnes Neville Lucy
d. 1285/93

Henry
d. after 1268

Joan (d. of *m.1* **William** *m.2* Ellen (d. of
Wm. Briwerre) **(III)** Ingram de Balliol)
d. 1233 **(d. 1245)** *d.* 1281

Eustace de *m* Agnes **Henry (II)** Ingram Eleanor
Balliol Anastasia **(1235-1272)** William
(brother of Ellen Joan *m.* Walter
de Balliol) Alice Eleanor (d. of earl of Geoffrey
Warenne) *d.*1282 Joscelin
Alan
(all bros predecease Henry)

William John **Henry (III)** *m.* Eleanor (d. of
d. in infancy *d.* in infancy **(1273-1314)** earl of Arundel)
d. 1328

Henry (IV) *m.* Idonea de William
(1301-1352) Clifford *d.* 1355
d. 1365 (without issue)

See next page

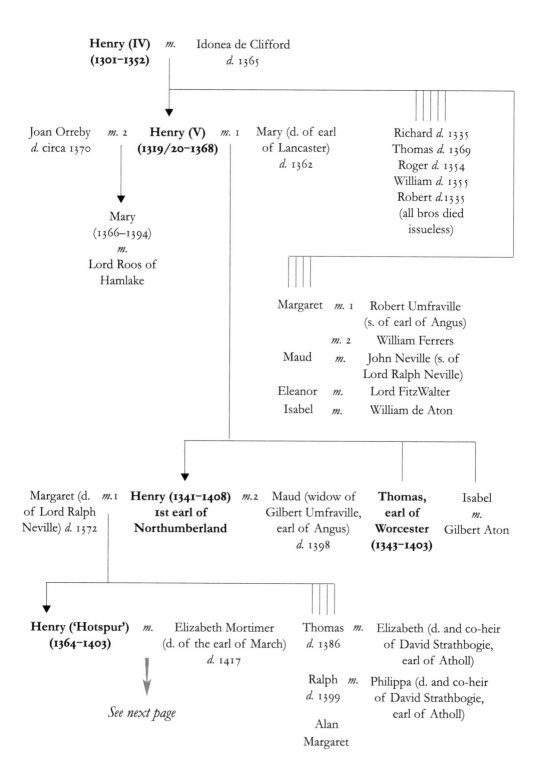

Henry (IV)   *m.*   Idonea de Clifford
(1301–1352)   *d.* 1365

Joan Orreby   *m.* 2   **Henry (V)**   *m.* 1   Mary (d. of earl   Richard *d.* 1335
d. circa 1370   **(1319/20–1368)**   of Lancaster)   Thomas *d.* 1369
                                      d. 1362   Roger *d.* 1354
                                                  William *d.* 1355
                                                 Robert *d.*1335
              Mary   (all bros died
        (1366–1394)   issueless)
             m.
       Lord Roos of
         Hamlake

                               Margaret   *m.* 1   Robert Umfraville
                                             (s. of earl of Angus)
                                        m. 2   William Ferrers
                               Maud   *m.*   John Neville (s. of
                                            Lord Ralph Neville)
                             Eleanor   *m.*   Lord FitzWalter
                               Isabel   *m.*   William de Aton

Margaret (d.   *m.*1   **Henry (1341–1408)**   *m.*2   Maud (widow of   **Thomas,**   Isabel
of Lord Ralph   **1st earl of**   Gilbert Umfraville,   **earl of**   *m.*
Neville) *d.* 1372   **Northumberland**   earl of Angus)   **Worcester**   Gilbert Aton
                                         d. 1398   **(1343–1403)**

Henry ('Hotspur')   *m.*   Elizabeth Mortimer   Thomas   *m.*   Elizabeth (d. and co-heir
(1364–1403)   (d. of the earl of March)   *d.* 1386   of David Strathbogie,
                          d. 1417   earl of Atholl)
                                      Ralph   *m.*   Philippa (d. and co-heir
                                      d. 1399   of David Strathbogie,
       See next page   earl of Atholl)
                                      Alan
                                     Margaret

See next page

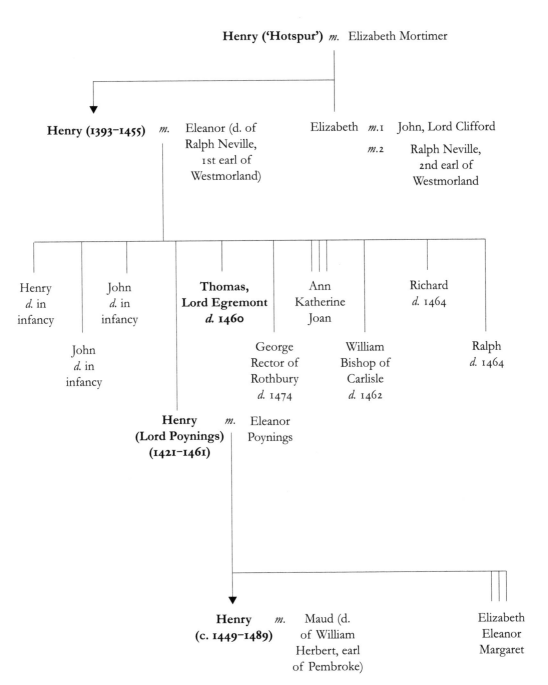

Henry ('Hotspur') *m.* Elizabeth Mortimer

Henry (1393–1455) *m.* Eleanor (d. of Ralph Neville, 1st earl of Westmorland)

Elizabeth *m.1* John, Lord Clifford
m.2 Ralph Neville, 2nd earl of Westmorland

Henry *d.* in infancy

John *d.* in infancy

John *d.* in infancy

Thomas, Lord Egremont *d.* 1460

Ann
Katherine
Joan

Richard *d.* 1464

George Rector of Rothbury *d.* 1474

William Bishop of Carlisle *d.* 1462

Ralph *d.* 1464

Henry (Lord Poynings) (1421–1461) *m.* Eleanor Poynings

Henry (c. 1449–1489) *m.* Maud (d. of William Herbert, earl of Pembroke)

Elizabeth
Eleanor
Margaret

This book is dedicated to
my parents and grandparents.

The North, the South and Scotland

The Northerners

In 1377, some eleven generations after his Norman ancestor stepped ashore in England and made his way to the North, a Percy was created earl – the earl of Northumberland – by King Richard II. He also held one of the four great offices of state – that of marshal of England – and was the closest confidant of John of Gaunt, that son, uncle and father of kings. This Percy, too, was himself a king: the King in the North, guardian of the Anglo-Scottish frontier.

In that tumultuous place, the Westminster-based, Southern king's writ hardly ran. In Percy country, there was Percy law backed by a Percy army paid for by Percy money. Without a Percy magnate in charge, English kings would find themselves beset by successive Scottish crises. At other times, it would be the Scottish kings who found themselves preyed upon. Indeed, the earl's grandfather and father had brought half of southern Scotland under their dynasty's sway.

Yet, thirty-one years later, this Percy, now silver-haired, penniless, landless, titleless and loathed as a traitor, would end his life face down in bloodied snow with a pathetic Northern army of smiths, tailors, falconers, countrymen, mercers and artisans, following him loyally to his doom. Ignominiously, Percy's head would be mounted atop London Bridge, his corpse quartered and then pickled in a mixture of cloves, cumin and anise. His limbs were tossed into sealed sacks and despatched to the four corners of the Percys' Northern kingdom. An immortality, at least, was conferred on Northumberland and his son, 'Hotspur', by Shakespeare.

Even at the height of their glory, however, the Percys were different from the grand lords of Southern England. They were, to put it bluntly, Northern. If anything, they had more in common with the Scots across the Border than with people living below the Humber, let alone in London. Indeed, one Southern chronicler of the time, upon hearing Percy angrily abuse a fellow peer 'in the manner of his people' confused his rough Northern accent with that of a Scot. 'His people' – Northerners, it seemed, were regarded as quite a separate breed even then. Nowadays, of course, they still are. To Southerners, the North is a gruff, poor, grim, gritty, slightly backward, alien, cold, soggily sentimental, violent place populated either by pale young men wearing T-shirts in the middle of winter or recalcitrant yokels.

When the earl and his Northern retinue travelled to London, locals would stare at the foreigners. The Northerners were poorer and rougher, and it showed. Northern soldiers, overdressed for the warmer climate, sweatily clanked through the streets carrying older-style weapons and outmoded armour; even the earl's warhorse was a feeble creature compared to the splendid steeds favoured by Southern magnates. The Northerners were permanently wary and clannish: a product, no doubt, of the Anglo-Scottish frontier, where their lives, wives and property had been, since the Conquest, at almost constant risk from Scottish raids. To them, the last man standing between Northerners and destruction was not the faraway king, but a Percy. He was their commander, their protector, their judge and their sheriff.

'English' History

'British history', as it is usually conceived, is not even English history, but English Southern history.[1] London is inevitably the focal point in every sense: politically, militarily, culturally, economically and socially. Short shrift is given to Scottish or Northern affairs; many people, for instance, can recite the names of at least some famous English kings and great battles, but few, I imagine, know much about the medieval Scottish kings or are aware just how long the Anglo-Scottish wars lasted. Yet, for centuries, those obscure Scottish kings played a central role in Southern English history. For instance, the Hundred Years War, which was fought between England and France, was actually a triangular war, the Scots comprising the third side, a second front and a first-class menace. For centuries, as well, it was regarded almost as a rite of passage for English kings to undertake the conquest of Scotland and establish English paramountcy over what they regarded as a 'breakaway' region. The Scots, for their part, believed it was their divine mission to dish the English by any means necessary and hurl them over the Border for good. As for the Northerners, they were caught in the crossfire.

When I, a half-American and half-British historian (of decidedly Southern English bent), set out to write this book, I wanted to redress the balance and, additionally, illuminate these darkened aspects of the Middle Ages. I had no political or personal axe to grind; after all, the sum total of my experience of the North and Scotland had been visits to my grandparents in Lancashire, a week in Northumberland, a weekend in Edinburgh and the discovery of Newcastle Brown Ale. Over the course of actually writing it, I moved cities four times and changed countries three times, but one verity remained with me: the North was different.

Whilst 'national character' is a term that has long fallen out of fashion, the historian John Le Patourel once observed that 'there can be no doubt that to most English people "The North of England" does mean something… The people of the North are generally supposed to have certain characteristics; and although there are many dialects in the North, in the popular idea of what a dialect is, it is not usually thought to be a nonsense to talk of "northern speech", or, for that matter, of northern habits of mind and northern attitudes.'[2]

Curious people of the late nineteenth century liked to standardise and quantify and calculate things, all things. In 1888, confident that intelligence and ability could likewise be scientifically measured, Arthur Conan Doyle – creator of the rationally minded Sherlock Holmes – once analysed the Victorian great and good, and discovered that 'the lowlands of Scotland, Aberdeenshire, Dublin, Hampshire, Suffolk, London, Devonshire, Gloucestershire and Berkshire' were, in that order, 'the divisions of the kingdom which have during the last twenty or thirty years produced the most plentiful crop of distinguished citizens'. The 'mental nadir' of the country, unfortunately, lay in western Ireland. Of the five Northern counties – Northumberland, Cumberland, Durham, Lancashire and Yorkshire – Conan Doyle found that 'the proportion of celebrities to the total population is low as compared with many other districts of England'. In particular, 'Northumberland produces men of a practical turn [and] there are no poets and few authors in her records.'[3]

Some years later, Havelock Ellis, seeking a 'comprehensive view of the men and women who have chiefly built up English civilization' over the last 1000 years, dissected the *Dictionary of National Biography* and concorded with Conan Doyle. Of the Northern half of England, Ellis observed that 'in proportion to its size, [it] has not produced many men in purely intellectual fields'. Indeed, 'its children have usually been more remarkable for force of character than for force of intellect. Their stubborn independent temper involves an aptitude for martyrdom.'[4]

Passing over the profoundly unscientific nature of these scientifically derived – if alarmingly accurate – conclusions, an investigation of these idiosyncrasies necessarily means examining the contribution of the North – the English Badlands – to the defence, and sometimes defiance, of the realm, as well as revealing its unique characteristics. Only then can the

House of Percy, the hereditary warrior-kings in the North, be properly understood in their rightful context.

The Dismal Geography of the North

To a certain extent, natural geography can play a mighty role both in forming the constitution of a given region's inhabitants and, more concretely, in shaping that region's history. The North of England is certainly no exception. Nowhere else, says one historian of the early North, 'structure[d] the opportunities for human endeavour, whether peaceful or warlike, with less subtlety'.[5] But where, exactly, was the North? There is no clear-cut, one-size-fits-all answer, as its borders shifted back and forth during the formation of the United Kingdom.[6] Nevertheless, we should bear in mind that the region remained 'an autonomous political and cultural unit corresponding generally to our *prima facie* notion of the North of England, though varying considerably in territorial extent'.[7] In this respect, the North is rather like Bordeaux, Tuscany or the American South.

All are agreed that the four former Border counties – Northumberland, Durham, Cumberland and Westmorland – are definitely in the North.[8] Lancashire and Cheshire are usually counted (the latter less often); the River Trent may be a rarity,[9] but the inclusion of Yorkshire is sometimes disputed. The latter, in particular, is regarded, like the past, almost as a different country, although 'the Vale of York and the East Riding were socially far more closely akin to the Midlands, of which they are a geographical extension, than they were to the wild dales of Northumberland, or even to the valleys of the West Riding.'[10] In size, Yorkshire was nearly equal to the combined areas of the four Border counties plus Lancashire, and contained two-thirds of their total population, thereby making, in 1377, a Yorkshireman out of every ten Englishmen.[11] Although the richest and the most crowded of its geographical brethren, Yorkshire could not compete with her Southern rivals since 'in general all counties north of the Wash failed even to double their lay wealth between 1334 and 1515 at a time when the others had, on average, enjoyed a threefold increase.[12] Compared to frontiersmen standing guard in Border counties, who were mired in poverty and outlawry and threatened nightly by Scottish raids, Yorkshiremen slept soundly. But they always dozed with one eye propped open in case that raid turned into an invasion. Whilst its land was relatively prosperous and was ideally placed on a direct highway to courtly London – and safety, if push came to shove – on balance Yorkshire always remained part and parcel of the North.

Yorkshire, moreover, was 'the southern limit of a militarised zone prepared for defence in depth against Scottish invasion'.[13] Towns such as
York and Beverley 'were called upon to provide mounted archers or
hobelars [lightly armed but mounted infantrymen], far more often than
southern towns'.[14] No small surprise to find, then, that an air of the Wild
West tinged Southern perceptions of the North, with Yorkshiremen
classed as Northerners, but not unspeakably so (and anyone was better
than the cut-throats and brigands infesting Tynedale and Redesdale),

The North, then, should be divided into an Inner Core and Outer
Perimeter. The former consists of Yorkshire, of course, and portions of
Lancashire, but the Outer Perimeter comprises the four Border counties,
the ones initially expected to blunt Scottish attacks. This proud bloc, virtually an independent nation-state ruled by warlords and bishops and
studded with ancient powers, unwritten rights and leftover privileges – a
'region of gaps, discontinuities and *lacunae* in which the king's writ did not
run' – was a medieval relic of the kingdom of Northumbria.[15]

Northumbria's southern border had proceeded from the swift-flowing
Humber, its mouth gaping eight miles wide and even thirty-five miles
inland, still a mile across, making the river England's most effective
natural obstacle. Nennius, an early historian of the Britons, was so
impressed that he referred to it as 'the Humber sea'.[16] Ermine Street, one
of the three main Roman passages to upper Britannia, ran from London
to Lincoln before abruptly halting at the Humber. Until the Middle Ages,
no army, if facing even moderate opposition, could force a crossing. To
get around it, the Romans laid down a second road branching west off
Ermine Street a few miles outside Lincoln. This skirted the additional
obstacle of the flat, marshy land surrounding the Humber river system ('a
barrier hardly less effective than the estuary itself')[17] and passed through
Doncaster and Pontefract before arriving at Tadcaster. Here, like Gaul,
it was split into three. The most easterly road ended in York, about
fifteen miles away; the northern, converted into Dere Street, continued
through Yorkshire and Northumberland to Edinburgh; and the westerly
traversed the Pennines, which run like a spine up the country, into
Lancashire.

From the Humber, Northumbria's border curved just under Sheffield,
followed the existing division of south Yorkshire and Derbyshire, crossed
the Pennines and continued up to the Ribble river. Depending upon hap-
penstance and a Northumbrian king's aptitude for war, the Border
sometimes shifted down to the peat-moss bogs of the Mersey.[18]

The Humber was the key for keeping and becalming the North. Hold
and cross the Humber and you controlled York, as well as the rivers
Derwent, Ouse, Aire, Don and Trent. Control these in conjunction with

the Ribble–Mersey area, and any enemy approaching from the south was shunted into a narrow corridor between the Humber's swamps and the Pennine foothills. A defending army could simply wait for the enemy to arrive.

Small wonder that, almost from the very beginning of British history, a distinct and often bellicose 'them-and-us' attitude arose between those dwelling above and below the Humber. Soon after their great invasion, the victorious – but cautious – Romans sliced their new province into a number of military and administrative divisions. Using ancient tribal borders, they designated York as the capital of their northern territories, collectively named Britannia Inferior, and commanded by a praetorian governor. To the south lay Britannia Superior, headed by a consular governor in London, an altogether higher posting.[19] Hence, the eventual establishment of two archbishoprics, northern and southern, based at Canterbury and York.

Between the Roman withdrawal from Britain in the early fifth century, and the middle of the seventh century, waves of Angles and Saxons overran the country. Again, the Humber acted as an unbridgeable moat. By the eighth century – the heyday of the kingdom of Northumbria – the Venerable Bede, writing his *Ecclesiastical History*, commonly referred to those Angles above the Humber as 'Northanhymbri'. He even dignified them with the title of 'nation'. There was little, if any, friendly contact, or trans-Humbrian empathy, with Angles living in the southern kingdom of Mercia; even the word itself was related to the Old English word, *mearc* – 'boundary' or 'march'.[20] Bede, for his part, Latinised it to Mercii for the purpose of describing the multitudes entrenched south of Northumbria and west of Suffolk.[21] So, 'the most important fact in the history of the earliest English kingdoms is the clear distinction which was maintained for more than two centuries between the peoples established respectively north and south of the Humber.'[22]

Between the boundary fencing off Mercian from Northumbrian, and the fluid Anglo-Scottish border, lay three natural regions – the eastern and western coastal plains, and the uplands – that together comprised the North. The two coastal plains were separated by the Pennines, which, from the Mercian border, rippled north up to the Tyne gap (a thin but vulnerable strip of land between Carlisle and Newcastle, which mirrored Hadrian's Wall and, more recently but less romantically, the A69) and divided 'the westward-looking west from the eastward-looking east'.[23] After this topographical interval, a second range of hills merged into the southern highlands of Scotland. These, at an almost perpendicular angle to the Pennines, ran from western Galloway to Lothian, Tweeddale and the Lammermuirs in the east.

To the seaboard and valleys west of the Pennines, then, came the Norsemen after their extended visits to the Western Isles and Ireland. During the ninth and tenth centuries, the Danes, on the other side of this barrier, mingled with the Angles and conveniently maintained links with their colleagues on the Continent.

The west coast plain, a poor and moist place, extended from the Mersey's bogs through western Lancashire, coastal Cumberland and the Vale of Eden to Galloway. Piercing its heartland was the Lake District, 'the highest and wildest area in Northern England.'[24] The eastern plain, a vaster, lavisher region, began in the Vale of York, included eastern Durham, crossed the Tyne, and enclosed Northumberland and Tweeddale before breaking at the Lammermuirs and reappearing in Lothian. Once a Scottish aggressor had either evaded or destroyed the northern defences, the eastern plain, with its relatively rich pickings, lay exposed. If the Scots were waylaid by the English or Northumbrian force, it was quite easy to escape over the hills into Cumbria before finding a route back into Scotland. Likewise, however, Scottish war-bands could sweep in a south-easterly curve through Cumbria directly into the heartlands of the North.

What Cumbria lacked economically, it therefore made up for strategically. Cumbria had evolved alongside Northumbria following the Roman withdrawal, but remained primarily confined to the Clyde valley. As the Northumbrian kingdom's political and cultural health declined in the late eighth and ninth centuries, a reinvigorated Scots-dominated Cumbria expanded into the basins of the rivers flowing into the Solway Firth. In its prime, Cumbria stretched from the Clach nam Breatann (Britons' Stone) in Glen Falloch, above the head of Loch Lomond – near the current northern border of Strathclyde and the Central region – to the Rere or Ray Cross.[25] The latter, a stump still visible beside the Roman road from Scotch Corner to Appleby (also known as the A66), was very close to the intersection of north Yorkshire, Durham and Cumbria.[26]

By the tenth century, however, the eclipse of Cumbria was plain to see, and in 945, Edmund, the king of Wessex, committed Strathclyde to Malcolm I, king of the Scots, on a vague condition of vassalage. The natives soon threw out their overlords – until 1018, after which the land remained firmly in Scottish hands until 1092.

Alarmed that the Scottish king could now lodge on his own land within two days' ride of York, the Norman conquerors set about pushing the Scots back to where they came from. First, in 1080, Guy de Balliol was given upper Teesdale. About ten miles east of Rere Cross he built Barnard Castle, so blocking the obvious route from Cumbria into Northumbria, and protecting Dere Street, the vital communications and military artery to the Norman South. Second, King William Rufus, the son of William the Conqueror, crossed the Pennines, took possession of Carlisle and built a castle there. Splendidly situated at the Solway, about nine miles south of what, by 1157, would be counted the Anglo-Scottish border, it shielded the western entrance of the Tyne gap from any Scottish invasion aimed at penetrating Northumbria.

With the western defences in place, the Normans and their successors, the Angevin kings, turned to the equally threatening routes from the northeast. Before the far-flung kingdoms of Bernicia and Deira coalesced into a greater kingdom of Northumbria, the Bernicians' northern frontier reached as far as the Firth of Forth and enclosed Lothian.[27] Here, it struck against the aggressive new Scoto-Pictish kingdom united by Kenneth mac Alpin in the mid-ninth century. On one side, 'to a king of Scots it was natural to look for expansion and booty to the south – far more profitable than anything he could find to the north and west'.[28] On the other, 'once the main impetus of Scandinavian invasion and settlement had slackened, it was inevitable that Saxons advancing northward should meet Scots advancing southward. It was simply a question of when, where, and upon what terms.'[29]

At first, Lothian would be the battleground, before shifting back permanently to the Tweed. Tired of an expensive, faraway war – he would be the first, but by no means the last – King Edgar ceded Lothian in 973 to King Kenneth of the Scots, in return for the latter promising to behave in future. According to the foremost historian of the Anglo-Scottish border, this cession was 'recognition by a powerful but extremely remote south-country king of a long-standing *fait accompli*'.[30] By the time the Normans arrived, Lothian had been well and truly annexed to Scotland.

The Lothian–Tweed problem would dog English kings until the Treaty of York of 1237, which set into stone the Anglo-Scottish border. Not only did they have to contend with hungry Scots kings who felt that large portions of the North fell within their sphere of influence, but also with rebellious Northern barons keen to assert their autonomy from the English centre whilst simultaneously keeping the Scots at bay. It has been said that 'the history of Anglo-Scottish relations during the hundred years or so [and longer] after 1066 is just not comprehensible save against the background of a Scottish ambition to expand further into the old kingdom of Northumbria'.[31]

Spending so long on a few simple borders may appear inordinate, but as the North sprawled across the strategic no-man's-land between two aggressive kingdoms, and was also mesmerised by its own proudly independent history, it was inevitably cursed with rebellion, rapine, invasion, outlawry, plague and poverty. 'This emphasis,' one author has tellingly surmised, 'on the negative aspects of Northern geography is essential for an understanding of the history of the lands beyond the Humber.'[32] And, it might be added, it is essential for understanding the history of the House of Percy, so closely was it entwined within this most reluctant province of the king's England.

'A nasty, short, brutish and proud existence'

Its dismal geography certainly 'made parts of the North economically backward, but that backwardness was intensified by centuries of war'.[33] The hard facts of a – literally – borderline existence moulded the Percys and their followers, but what was it like, this existence? How did their slightly more genteel Southern cousins perceive these rough and violent frontiersmen?

A relatively prosperous estate of the Percys in Cumberland was described for the Crown in 1570, a mostly peaceful time, as 'consyst[ing] most in wast grounds and ys very cold hard and barren for the wynter'. It 'bredyth tall men and hard of nature, whose habitaciouns are most in the valleys and dales...they have but little tillage, by reason whereof they lyve hardly at ease, which makyth them tall of personage and hable to endure hardnes when necessyte requyryth.'[34] Around the same time, on his tour of the North, the historian William Camden observed that 'the very carcasses of the inhabitants' appeared to have been hardened by this 'rough and barren' land. Wandering the wastes, 'you would think you see the ancient nomads, a martial sort of people'.[35]

Nevertheless, one anonymous sycophant rapturously described the Percy lands:

> *In wholesome aire amidd the mouth*
> *of Cocke and Darwent streames I stande:*
> *whose flagg of fame hathe borne great name*
> *throughout Britania pleasant Lande.*
> *Whose statelie hills to starrie skies*
> *have hoysed up their haughtie heades:*
> *whose Dounes and valeis couched fyne*
> *of chattell yearelie thousands breades.*[36]

Edenic perhaps for poets, but the reality was 'wasts and mountaynes',[37] relieved by 'vast tracts of barren and empty moorland'.[38] Even in 1832, when William Cobbett rode through Northumberland on one of his cantankerous 'Rural Rides', he observed that 'the country generally speaking, is very poor land, scarcely any trees at all; the farms enormously extensive, only two churches, I think, in the whole of the twenty miles [between Morpeth and Alnwick, seat of the Percys]'.[39] Algernon Charles Swinburne enjoyed a rather more elevated view:

> *Between our Eastward and our Westward sea,*
> *The narrowing strand*
> *Clasps close the noblest shore fame holds in fee,*
> *Even here where English birth sets all men free —*
> *Northumberland!*[40]

Romanticism and cruelty, bloodied glory and notionless blood-feuds, martyrdom and treason – all meshed bizarrely in the North, much to the bemusement and horror of Southerners. It was believed that, like Homer's doomed Trojans, the Northerners had fallen foul of the gods. Only divinely vengeful wrath visited upon them could possibly explain their travails. Of the arrival of the Vikings in York in 867, Asser, Alfred the Great's Welsh biographer, noted that 'a great dispute, fomented by the devil, had arisen among the Northumbrians, as always happens to a people which has incurred the wrath of God',[41] while the twelfth-century author of the *Gesta Stephani* concluded that 'the root and origin of all evil arose in that part of England called Northumbria to produce plunder and arson, strife and war'.[42] 'The north', pithily claimed another chronicler three centuries later, was 'whence all evil spreads'.[43]

A deep tinge of madness, a bold hint of 'otherness', were associated with Northerners. After defeating Richard III at Bosworth in 1485, the new king, Henry VII, set off for York in order to 'keep in obedience the folk of the North, savage and more eager than others for upheavals'.[44] The 'rude people of the north' were 'more superstitious than virtuous, long accustomed to frantic fantasies', at least compared to civilised Southerners like Richard Layton, writing in the sixteenth century.[45] In one recent commentator's apposite words, Northerners were derided for 'haughtiness, being perfidious and perverse, overripe for rebellion, and ... ferocious[ness]'.[46]

Northern alienness was further exacerbated by their near-incomprehensibility. Those living in York were so accursed with a 'scharp, slitting, and frontynge and unscharpe [accent], that we southerne men may that longage unnethe understande'.[47] This was probably because Yorkshiremen had 'much intercourse with the Danes, and intermarried with them, and became like them in speech'.[48] The Northerners were so backward that, at the turn of the fourteenth century, 'a man of London

...had a Bible in English of northern speech, which was seen by many men and it seemed two hundred years old.'[49] Chaucer, at home amid Richard II's court, gently mocked his student in 'The Reeve's Tale' by making him speak with a pronounced Northern accent. To this, our greatest medieval poet, the North was the back of beyond.[50]

Many found it unbelievable that anyone had settled there in the first place. Geoffrey of Monmouth's *History of the Kings of Britain*, written around 1135, wonderingly remarked: 'It was a frightful land to live in, more or less uninhabited, and it offered a safe lurking place to foreigners. Indeed, by its very geographical position it lay open to the Picts, the Scots, the Danes, the Norwegians and anyone else who came ashore to ravage the island.'[51] Why live up north, added another chronicler, when there was 'better corne londe, more peple, more noble citees, and more profitable havenes' down south? Moreover, 'the men of the south beeth esier and more mylde; and men of the north be more unstable, more cruel and more unesy.'[52]

One could almost envisage these savage inhabitants as beasts; in 1550, Sir Robert Bowes, reported to the marquess of Dorset that those residing in North Tynedale 'were wild and misdemeanoured people much inclined to disorder and given to theft, and must be kept continually in dread of justice under their keepers'.[53] A rather good precedent existed for permanently inspiring this 'dread of justice': the notorious insolence of the Northerners towards their rulers, or 'keepers', in the South.

Northern rebelliousness was well entrenched by the middle of the tenth century. One revolt was caused 'by a suggestion made to [a local magnate] by the Northumbrians, that their country has been wont to have a king of its own and to be tributary to none of the south Angles'. From that day until the thirteenth century (when the Scottish wars of Edward I diverted their attention), the Northerners 'griev[ed] through want of a king of their own, and of the liberty they once enjoyed'.[54] A foretaste of what lay in store for the unsuspecting Normans was the deposition of Edward the Confessor's tyrannical Earl Tostig by the Northumbrian thegns in 1065 (see Chapter 1). According to William of Malmesbury, the rebels gave an ultimatum to Edward: 'averring that they were a people free born and freely educated, and unable to tolerate the cruelty of any prince...[if the king wished] them to be obedient he should appoint Marcher [Earl Morcar, a Northern scion] the son of Elfgar to preside over them, who would experience how cheerfully they could obey provided they were treated with gentleness.'

In 1069, William the Conqueror, infuriated by the murder of a number of his appointed earls, decided to break Northern separatism once and for all by his Harrying of the North (see Chapter 1), the relentless violence of which horrified even seasoned contemporary observers like Orderic Vitalis, born in England but raised in a Norman monastery. After that, there was no more open rebellion in Yorkshire, although Norman officials were open game. During the 1070s, for instance, William's sheriff of Yorkshire found it prudent to travel with a small army for protection.[55]

Northerners did not want independence but, rather, strong military leadership in the North, provided by Northerners. With no especial territorial quarrel with those living below the Humber, they reserved their ire for the Scots. A Northerner's overriding concern was the protection of his life and livelihood, and unwarranted Southern interference on the frontier obstructed their own princely warriors – such as the Percys – from appeasing these concerns by bludgeoning the Scots occasionally. Whenever a king sought to impose his will on the Northumbrians, they rose against him. The system, such as it was, worked most harmoniously during the times of the Wardens of the Marches, when a local warlord, usually a Percy, was appointed by the king, got on with the job and turned a profit at the same time.

Apart from the obvious dangers of rebellion, cross-Border raids constantly menaced Northern stability. From small, irritating beginnings in the eleventh century, when Malcolm III's Scots raced through the new Norman lands, plundering, burning churches and enslaving the young, these raids culminated in the organised offensives of Robert Bruce and his successors in the fourteenth century. At first, the furthermost English defences were virtually useless against 'rapid cross-border strikes and deep-penetration guerrilla raids'. The Normans' failure to modernise the ancient Northern fortresses left the forward areas 'locked in immobility' and unable to be centrally organised. Castles had been built, but 'were singularly ineffective, easily isolated, surrounded and bypassed'.[56]

By the fourteenth century, harsh experience had taught lessons. The Border was heavily militarised, and was studded with hundreds of pele towers – 'cramped, strictly and starkly utilitarian structures with stone walls seven to ten feet thick' – suitable for small-scale defence and early warning.[57] The requirement for mobile forces that could range swiftly and hunt down Scots stragglers or ruffians was met by lightly armed and mounted hobelars – a Cumbrian innovation – and mounted archers. Castles protected livestock and civilians in the event of a serious invasion. But when the inhabitants of Bamburgh in 1316 took their dismantled shacks into the castle for safe keeping because the Scots were near, the garrison charged such exorbitant rates for storage that they complained of being caught 'between the enemy on the one side and the constable [of the castle] on the other'.[58]

Robert Bruce's highly organised 'surprise' raids, developed between 1311 and 1323, were intended 'to compel the inhabitants of the northern counties to buy truces with money or supplies, generally corn...though of course if money or supplies were not forthcoming devastation quickly followed'.[59] It was the worst of coincidences that amid this gangsterism, the North was suffering from a run of harvest failures and livestock plagues, thereby making it impossible for tenants to pay off this Scottish protection racket.

The Bruce was neither charitable nor sympathetic. The North was razed. The yearly tithes income for Holy Island collapsed from £202 before 1296, to only £21 in 1326. Between 1299 and 1316, the average annual tithes income for the lands around Norham was £162; it had fallen to less than £2 by 1319.[60] During these years, huge swathes of Westmorland, Cumberland and Northumberland were so efficiently devastated that they could not pay any taxes. In Annandale, the fighting was so heavy in 1317 that 'no man nor beast was left between Lock Maben and Carlisle', which are about twenty-five miles apart on today's main road between Carlisle and Lockerbie (the latter is very close to Loch Maben, modern Lochmaben).[61] A generation later, a Scottish raid utterly destroyed twenty-four villages in north Northumberland, followed in 1346 by the same number along the Tyne and Derwent.[62] On the other hand, an English raid of 1544 burnt 192 villages, towers, farmsteads and parish churches; 403 Scots were killed and 816 taken prisoner. Nearly 10,000 head of cattle, 12,500 sheep and 1300 horses were stolen (or perhaps returned to their rightful owners), as well as grain and other goods.[63] Those deprived of land and possessions turned to banditry, adding to the anarchy. In the South, wagers were made 'whether thieves or true men [did] most abound' in the upper reaches of England.[64] Outsiders found it incredible, but despite the interminable warring and the blood-feuds spilling over generations, there was continuous cross-Border contact. Families intermarried, traded and worked with each other. Southerners were always suspicious of this 'intercommuning', reinforcing the perception that Northerners were an untrustworthy breed apart.

An alternative set of rituals and customs governed the actions of the fighting barons, whose heroic exploits engendered a corpus of 'Border Ballads' – medieval equivalents of Homer's *Iliad*, with its even-handed praises of Greek and Trojan martial prowess. Ballads such as 'The Battle of Otterburn' and 'Chevy Chase' portrayed an enclosed, Mafia-like society of 'intensely personal relationships, a small-scale world, a world of private feud and personal vendetta'.[65] Reflecting the essential sameness of Scottish and Northern societies, the customs of their aristocracies are almost identical. The ballads, with their mutual grudging admiration for the foe's talents and virtues, helped create a shared conviction that Scoto-Northern society possessed an identity and culture distinct from anywhere else. Yet, the 'Border', once an Anglo-Scottish *zone* with its own codes and ways of life, was gradually transformed into a jurisdictional and strategic boundary *line* between Scotland and England – an 'instrument of national separation'.[66] Thus, 'the ballads emphasise the rigid political separation of the two aristocracies and societies and describe how it is sealed in blood. But at the same time they seek to perpetuate the idea of one frontier society in the sphere of skills and values, a common adherence to local rather than national patriotisms.'[67]

The Percys and Writing History

If I could inject a personal note, from the beginning I knew how I did *not* want to write this book. I did not want to write a Percy hagiography. There is a famous, and understandable, tendency of biographers to identify with their subjects; with aristocratic subjects in particular, this tendency can lead to whitewashing of their more dubious actions. I wanted to write a clear-eyed history of the early Percys. In this respect, the very alienness of the Middle Ages was both a help and a hindrance.

A help because the distance of time and place allows a biographer to maintain his objectivity and sense of perspective. A hindrance because that same distance, combined with the obscurity of the Percys for at least the first three centuries of their time in England (let alone their prehistory in Normandy and Denmark), entails minutely scouring medieval documents such as land-deeds, wills, chronicles and official records to find even the briefest mention of a given Percy's name. Gradually, by accumulating a skeletal list compiled from these sources, some pieces fall into place and a fuzzy picture of a Percy's movements and actions emerges. Now, it would have been a simple task to write a biography based on these humdrum facts: 'Percy did this, and then he did that, and two years later he was here,' and so forth through each and every Percy's life.

But of cardinal importance, I thought, was to supply the rich, lustrous background of British history to this desiccated biographical foreground. I wanted to present the grander sweep of five centuries' worth of historical events and ideas not only alongside, but intertwined with, the long, slow arc of one family's saga over the course of more than a dozen generations. It was a matter of employing the microcosm of the House of Percy to highlight the macrocosm of the Middle Ages.

Thus began the tortuous process of discovering *why* and *how* a Percy was present at a battle, or bought lands in a particular location, or attended a royal council meeting in London on a given date. I wanted to *explain*. To take just two quick instances, it was all very well to narrate that one Percy bought a castle for such-and-such a price, but I wanted to explain how on earth he managed to raise the financing, whom he went to for the loan and how the medieval banking system worked. Then there was the marriage market. Any genealogical table can inform you that Lord ABC married Lady So-and-So and had four children; but it is far more significant to explain how these marriages were arranged, who gained by them and why these networks of kinship mattered politically, financially and strategically.

One advantage of this rather laborious method – as poor old Weidenfeld & Nicolson discovered when the manuscript was somewhat longer and a little later than expected – is that history, to me at least, turns more interesting when one is deeply familiar with the characters involved. Many general histories are just that, general. Diplomatic treaties, the dates of coronations and the outcome of battles are picked out from a bird's-eye view. But if one can intersperse these needful facts with the worm's-eye of a particular Percy, who happened to have played a role in negotiating a treaty, or participated in a ceremony at Westminster Abbey, or commanded a knightly division in the field, then impersonal history becomes personal. The key, of course, is to maintain a balance between foreground and background: too much emphasis on colour results in a non-biographical History of Britain, but too much biographical detail loses the general historical context. I have tried to keep this balance.

Even then, a biography dealing with medieval subjects presents special problems. I did not, for instance, find any likenesses of medieval Percys. I have little or no idea what they looked like, nor do I know for certain their temperaments or beliefs (although occasionally, a chronicle will observe that one was 'grey-bearded' or 'implacable'). How to get round this obstacle to the biographer?

My solution, such as it is, was to make some reasonable suppositions about their characters and motivations based on the isolated snippets I had as well as taking into account what others around them were thinking and doing. Thus, knowing that one particularly rebellious Percy who had come to grief had willed but a single book to his youngest daughter, who had been married off to some nonentity, might yield some insight if I described what the book was about while keeping in mind his fate. Since books in the Middle Ages were quite rare things, it would make sense if a baron commissioned copies of books he particularly admired, books that spoke to him, and passed them on as a kind of 'message' to his children. For instance, surely it is indicative that Queen Isabella, the murderous wife of Edward II who had an affair with the Flashmanesque paramour Mortimer, possessed an inordinate fondness for dreadful, bodice-ripping, chivalric romances of heroic derring-do?

On a broader level, medieval nobles were men of fidelity and principle combined seamlessly with a staggering degree of self-interest. Thus, while they far preferred loyalty under rightful majesty to anarchy or rebellion, they were capable of renouncing their oaths of fealty if the king or overlord did not pay enough attention to their subjects' interests. There were always factions and petty jealousies, but unfortunately it is extremely difficult to determine exactly an individual Percy's politics. For this reason, it was necessary to make some judgement using such yardsticks as his ranking in a listing of barons, or his signature on certain documents, or the posts to which he was appointed by his superiors, or his presence in particular places at key times, or the degree of his marital and territorial ties with magnates mightier than himself. Owing to the occasional paucity of sources singling out early Percys for mention, I sometimes assumed that if he was identified with a certain clique or group, his movements and beliefs pretty much coincided with whatever the leader of that clique or group was doing and thinking. Such is the way of politics.

Moreover, the Percy connection with the North provided numerous clues. Kings who allowed them to get on with the job and paid them on time were adored, but those monarchs who interfered by appointing Southern or courtly placemen to traditionally Percy offices or, worse, sought to make peace with Scots at the expense of their Northern barons, could usually expect trouble.

This explains why the Percys are always 'present' even if they are not actually mentioned in the narrative. As increasingly prominent members of the power elite, they are always intimately affected by, and are frequently participants in, the great affairs of state.

This book is about power: the mechanics of how a family acquired, kept, augmented and lost it, and the background to why it all happened.

Alexander Rose
Washington, DC
24 November 2001

CHAPTER ONE

The First Northerner

William de Percy, Baron of England and Soldier of God

The Unknown Scion – Mainfred the Dane and Normandy

William de Percy was the first of that name to depart for England from Normandy in the eleventh century and was most likely the first to bear the surname, 'de Percy'.

Using such toponymic surnames to indicate hereditary land tenure was a recent Norman invention. First, the land was procured. Then, a son inherited it and began using the prefix 'de', or 'of'. Finally, when the lands and title passed to his son, the surname became a family name and title. During the 1040s and 1050s, it was almost *de rigueur* among the landowning and warrior class to assume such names, mainly to protect their claims to lordship.[1]

Where is Percy? It is commonly believed that the Percy family 'held the *château* of Percy near Villedieu, in what is now the arrondissement of St Lô, department of La Manche; together with great estates in both Lower and Upper Normandy'.[2] Thus, the 'great' Percy estates were in the Cotentin – the far West of Normandy – the implication being that the Percys were top-drawer nobles many decades, even centuries, before the Norman Conquest of England. The truth is a great deal more interesting.

Let us find who these Percys really were. Blessed with documents and hearsay now lost to us, Sir William Dugdale's *Baronage of England*, compiled in 1675, judged that 'this antient and right Noble Family, do derive their descent from *Mainfred de Perci*. Which *Mainfred* came out of Denmark into Normandy, before the adventure of the famous Rollo thither; and had issue *Geffrey*, who accompanied *Rollo* into those parts'.[3] He gave little credence to the *Metrical Pedigree of the Percyes*, an early sixteenth-century work compiled by William Peeris, a clerk and priest attached to the Percys' household.[4] Peeris, whose livelihood depended on his patrons' indulgence, compiled a vividly poetical history of the early Percys to whose romanticism successive historians have succumbed.

For instance, Gerald Brenan in 1902 combined Dugdale's rather skeletal outline with Peeris's ornamentation to propose a tentative but ultimately specious pedigree of the pre-Conquest Percys, as follows:

MAINFRED; [paraphrasing Dugdale] 'who came out of Denmark into Normandy, before the advent of Rollo;' he begat:

GEOFFREY; associate of Rollo; baptized at Artois, A.D. 912; he begat:

WILLIAM, Sieur de Percy, governor of South Normandy, and Comte de Caux; slain by Hugh Capet; he begat:

GEOFFREY II, Comte de Caux, Sieur de Percy, &c; he begat:

WILLIAM II, Comte de Caux and de Poictiers, Sieur de Percy; he begat:

GEOFFREY III, Comte de Caux and de Poictiers, Sieur de Percy, &c; reputed father of William de Percy, who settled in the North of England, and of Serlo de Percy, Abbot of Whitby.[5]

Nevertheless, one painstaking genealogist of the great Northumberland families has slightly overstated the case when he dismisses Peeris's *Pedigree* (and all pedigrees flowing from it) as 'a romantic account of the early Percys ... made up from his own imagination'.[6] It can be argued that there are isolated nuggets of truth hidden amid the exaggerations. Certain facets of Peeris's *Pedigree* may have passed down verbally through generations of the family before being written down by the clerk. Thus, there are jarring incidents where Peeris skips the romance and focuses intently on exact historical details. In so doing, Peeris surprisingly – given the fairly crude Renaissance sense of the past – exhibits some mastery over obscure facts and what happened six centuries before. The *Pedigree* specifies that

> *This noble & valiant Duke Rollo of holy Baptisme*
> *received the necessary Sacrament ...*
> *& L[or]de Jeffrey P[er]cy w[i]th devout intent*
> *To receive the same grace was glad & content*
> *& of ffrance Arch Bishop of Reine [Rouen]*
> *They received Christendome & Baptizacon.*[7]

In another example, and this is extremely rare in such old familial histories, the founder of the dynasty, strangely, is not given pride of place in the battle honours; instead, Peeris claims, the son overshadowed the father.

> *The name of the Lord P[er]cy w[hi]ch was associate to the*
> *forenamed Duke Rollo was called Jeffrie P[er]cie*
> *A right valiant knight gracious & fortunate*
> *whose father named Mainefreed was fallen unto fate.*[8]

So, based on these scraps of information, what do we know of the earliest Percys? Let us start with 'Duke Rollo', for what he was doing and what was happening is of crucial importance. He has now been identified as Rolf, the errant son of the Norwegian, Rögnvald, earl of Möre. Exiled by the king for having raided the bay where Oslo now stands, Rollo (the Latinised form of his name), according to a Norwegian chronicle, 'afterwards crossed the sea to the Hebrides, in the British Isles, and from there went south-westward to France, where he harried and possessed himself of a great earldom [called Normandy]'.[9] It used to be thought that Rollo reached the Seine in 876, but recent evidence indicates that he arrived in Gaul between 905 and 911.

At that time, the kingdoms of England – Northumbria, Mercia and Wessex – were in turmoil as Norwegians and Danes raided the coasts with impunity during the late eighth and early ninth centuries. Their first target was the defenceless monastery of Holy Island off the Northumbrian coast in 793. Throughout western Europe, the sight of the Norse longships, yellow and black shields menacingly draped along their sides, was soon followed by the stripping of altars glistening with gold and gems, and the destruction of manuscripts. Monks, if healthy, were taken as slaves. By the 840s the pirates reached the Seine. Having ransacked Rouen, by 885–6 they were besieging Paris. After the siege, despoiling, looting, ravaging and burning all the while, the Vikings ranged 'by horse and foot... killing babies, children, young men, fathers, sons and mothers'.[10]

Eventually the Norsemen, wishing to settle down to enjoy their new wealth, planted themselves in Ireland and the western areas of the North.[11] The Danes, however, preferred the area round the North Sea and the English Channel, which allowed them to launch hit-and-run raids on the southern and eastern coasts of England and northern Europe, while remaining close to home, hearth and safety. In 865, a Danish 'Great Army' landed in the East of England and virtually annexed the North. Within fifteen years, Mercia and Northumbria had collapsed, and a Danish landowning class imposed itself on the native English peasantry.

In 878, after defeating the Anglo-Danes marching southwards on Wessex, Alfred the Great forced a treaty (and baptism) on Guthrum, the Danish leader. The Danes retired into the almost-autonomous area of 'Danelaw', whose boundary ran diagonally along Watling Street and the Thames, thereby dividing England between Northern Danes and Southern Saxons. Subsequently, the Danish armies grouped around fortified centres known as *burhs* (the Five Boroughs of Lincoln, Leicester, Stamford, Nottingham and Derby), mirroring the Wessex–Danelaw border.[12] It was Edward the Elder, Alfred's successor, who began to absorb Danelaw into Wessex, a task completed *to a limited extent* by Edward's son, Athelstan, thereby establishing a unified kingdom of England.

But the patina of unity barely concealed divisions between those living above and below the Humber. For many centuries afterwards, the North remained 'different' from the South. The Scandinavians had introduced their own law, agriculture, money, measurement and personal nomenclature into their new territories. Frank Stenton, the foremost authority on Anglo-Saxon England, admirably summed up the situation: 'we begin to discern two races in pre-Conquest England, differing in language, law, and social order, held together by little more than common acquiescence in the rule of a king whose authority was narrowly limited by custom.'[13]

These developments lay in the future. Back in 896, however, the veteran Danish army crumbled away under Alfred's pressure. Danes with some capital settled down in England,[14] but according to the *Anglo-Saxon Chronicle* (a quasi-official journal of record), 'those [Danes] who were without money got themselves ships and went south across the sea to the Seine'.[15]

The Mainfred – probably a bastardisation of the Danish name Manni – mentioned in the Percy histories was probably one of those retired pirates. Upon leaving his native Denmark for adventures overseas, he joined his fighting host in Northumbria and pillaged far and wide, up into the land of the Scots and the Picts, and down into Wessex's outskirts. Alfred's victory over Guthrum brought a temporary halt to his activities, and by 896 a dispirited Mainfred decided it was high time to leave England.

He imposed lordship upon a small holding of land, probably on the coast in the Pays de Caux, north-west of Rouen. He was not alone. According to David Bates, 'place-names containing an Anglo-Saxon element in the Pays de Caux [at this time] suggest the immigration of Scandinavians who had lived for a considerable period of time in England.'[16] Few of these recent Scandinavian immigrants were peasants: indeed, the Percys' ancestor, Mainfred, was probably the leader of a small, none-too-successful Danish war-band. By inventing the title, 'count of Caux', to please his Percy master, Peeris may have been embroidering a belief that the family hailed from that area. This inflation of the Percy pedigree followed a medieval tradition, once described by Sir Steven Runciman as the 'glamour of names'. For example, the ancient Caucasian family of Bagration claimed descent from King David and Queen Bathsheba, and irritated their neighbours by referring to the Holy Virgin as Cousin Mary.[17] Restricting one's lineage to the 'Comtes de Caux and de Poictiers' seems modest compared to the claims made elsewhere.[18] Indeed, many Danes believed they were descended from Antenor, who had escaped from the burning remnants of Troy.

Many of these Danish rovers arrived in Normandy before, or at the same time as, Rollo. Having landed in Gaul between 905 and 911, Rollo forced terms upon Charles the Simple, king of the West Franks, after the battle of Chartres on 20 July 911. The treaty of St-Clair-sur-Epte granted Rollo's Norwegians territory in the lower Seine, the Pays de Caux and the city of Rouen (in other words, upper Normandy), *thereby bringing Mainfred within the orbit of Rollo's new duchy.* In exchange, Rollo and his followers would renounce their pagan ways.

The eleventh-century 'official historian' of the Norman dukes, Dudo of St Quentin, states accordingly that Rollo and many companions were baptised by Franco, archbishop of Rouen, in 912.[19] Peeris's *Pedigree* also alleges that 'L[or]de Jeffrey P[er]cy' of 'ffrance [hence Franco] Arch Bishop of Reine [Rouen] ... received Christendome & Baptizacon'. These lords dragooned their followers into converting; ferocious punishments followed refusal or reversion.

Peeris also remarks, before telling of Jeffrie's baptism that 'Mainefreed was fallen unto fate'. Perhaps he refused baptism, so Rollo executed him. But Jeffrie seems to have converted, and was accepted by the new regime. A Henrician pre-Reformation chaplain, presenting a laudatory pedigree to his master, may have whitewashed Mainfred's embarrassing paganism.

By 924, after participating in several battles, Rollo had acquired lower Normandy, including the Bessin (around Bayeux) and Maine up to the River Vire. In 925, the Seine 'Normans' ravaged the territory of Beauvais and Amiens, and in the north-east, Rollo built the fortress of Eu. Many of its 1000-strong garrison were soon slain in a siege.[20] Whether they included Rollo is unknown, but he was certainly dead by 927, 'end[ing] a career which, judged by its later consequences, must be ranked among the most momentous in medieval history'.[21] The young Jeffrie – that 'right valiant knight gracious and fortunate', in Peeris's words – probably participated in these small wars.

Normandy's western frontiers were finally decided in 933, when Rollo's successor, William Longsword, acquired the Cotentin and the Avranchin.[22] These additions, together with the settlements of 911 and 924, created the duchy of Normandy – but the Pays de Caux lands had fallen under Rollo's purvey in 911, so making Mainfred and Jeffrie among the area's earliest foreign inhabitants. But they were not great barons; 'sire' better indicates their distinctly middling status. And so the Percys would stay for another six generations.

The Norman Conquest and the Northern Rebellions

The Percy line actually originated in Calvados, in the village of Percy-en-Auge, very close to Mézidon, in the bishopric of Lisieux. This village straddled the Seine, about a hundred miles from the Danish strongholds in the Pays de Caux.[23] How or when the family arrived in the region remains unknown. It is most likely that William de Percy's father obtained the Calvados lands through a dowry (his parents remain unidentified), necessitating a move from the family's Pays de Caux stamping ground sometime between 1025 and 1035. Our William was probably an eldest son (his younger brother, Serlo, will be discussed later) who inherited the family's modest property after his father's death. He was in his early thirties at the time of the Conquest, when he assumed the name 'de Percy'.

Until relatively recently, Percy was thought to be a 'Companion of the Conqueror' – one of those magnates who personally accompanied Duke William of Normandy across the Channel in 1066, which implies the Companion's aristocratic status and blood-kinship to the duke in the 'Old Country'. Every Anglo-Norman family worth its salt later jostled for inclusion in the list; subtle, and sometimes not so subtle, pressure was applied to the chroniclers to accommodate yet another name on the slenderest evidence. Hence the extraordinary variation in numbers as medieval and Tudor genealogists compiled their Rolls. Estimates ranged from 149, 'over and besides the great numbers of knights and esquires', to Holinshed's 1577 figure of 629 Companions.[24] In 1866, twenty-four square metres of stone in the church at Dives were engraved with the names of the presumed Companions (now cut to 485),[25] and in 1931 a similar catalogue was erected at Falaise.

In reality, there is express evidence of only thirty-two Companions, and certainly no more than fifty.[26] Although mentioned in most earlier Rolls, William de Percy was not a Companion, but he (and Hugh d'Avranches, of whom more below) did indeed accompany the Conqueror – only he arrived in early *December 1067*, when the duke returned to England after celebrating his conquest back in Normandy.[27] An ancient document of Whitby Monastery (refounded by William de Percy in the late 1070s) states that 'memorandum quod anno domini millesimo sexagesimo septimo, Hugo comes Cestrensis, et Willielmus de Percy venerunt in Angliam, cum domino Willielmo duce Normannorum conquestore'.[28] Crossing the Channel that winter, the keen lord of Percy and his friend impressed the young but immensely powerful Hugh d'Avranches, the future infamous earl of Chester – colourfully known as the grotesque 'Hugh the Fat' or the rapacious 'Hugh Lupus' (Wolf). Percy's friend was Robert, son of Humphrey of Tilleul-en-Auge, a village about five miles south-east of Percy-en-Auge. Humphrey was an original Companion, having left his son in Normandy.

The uppity Norman duke may have been crowned King of the English, the lawful heir of the Confessor, on Christmas Day 1066, but he was not master of all he surveyed. The Conquest was not a revolution, but an evolution. By late 1067 and throughout 1068, the North witnessed open rebellion and native insolence. The king sought men of fighting age to subdue the obnoxious Yorkshire and Durham Danes, with whom de Percy would have felt no nostalgic kinship; Normans were now more Frankish than the Franks.[29] Whilst those safe in Southern England could indulge in political intrigue (like Odo of Bayeux, the Conqueror's half-brother and the earl of Kent), Normans hoping to become barons in the new empire could expect a free hand to make their names fighting the Scots and 'pacifying' the *Nordanhymbri*.

William de Percy's whereabouts are unrecorded between his arrival in December 1067 with the Conqueror and 1070, when he was engaged on the rebuilding of York Castle after its destruction by said Danes. So where was he, and what was he doing? Almost certainly he participated in William the Conqueror's notorious Harrying of the North. This explains his presence in York in 1070, and his charitable intercession on behalf of a rebellious Northumbrian earl, Cospatric, at Christmas of that year.

To understand Percy's probable course of action, we need to return to 1055, when the Danish earl of Northumbria, Siward, died. Earls of Northumbria and York were normally either of the native house of Bamburgh or northern Anglo-Scandinavians. To rein in the North, the royal House of Wessex gave the earldom (earldoms at that time were not strictly hereditary) to the Southern-based Tostig (brother of the future, doomed King Harold) instead of to Cospatric, the leading Bamburgh representative, or Waltheof, Siward's son.

When King Malcolm III of Scotland began raiding, Tostig upset the Northumbrians by signing a peace treaty. He upset them still more by signing another after Malcolm had pillaged his way throughout the North in 1061 while Tostig was travelling to Rome. Tostig, furthermore, allowed Malcolm to keep Cumberland,[30] ignoring the strategic implications of Malcolm's new Cumbrian headquarters at Stainmore being only two days' ride from York.

Tostig then assassinated Cospatric, the eldest surviving Bamburgh claimant to the earldom. He also raised taxes in order to pay the army with which he protected himself, and he corruptly administered justice. Yorkshiremen and Northumbrians, with some reason, rebelled.

In March 1065, the insurgents broke into York, murdered 200 of the (again) absent Tostig's bodyguards, captured his treasure and weapons, declared the earl outlawed and invited Morcar, earl Edwin of Mercia's younger brother, to take Tostig's place. Morcar accepted, then threatened the South by ravaging Northamptonshire. King Edward the Confessor and Harold, his brother-in-law, fearing Northern wrath, consented to Tostig's permanent deposition.

Tostig then sailed up the Humber with an invasion fleet, but was driven back by Morcar. After escaping to Malcolm III's court, he was contacted by King Harold Hardrada of Norway, then planning a full-scale conquest of England from Yorkshire.

In the late summer of 1066, Hardrada collected Tostig, disembarked 300 shipfuls of Vikings on the Humber and stormed York while Harold, now king, and Morcar were in the South awaiting Duke William's imminent invasion. Morcar raced north, and gathered an army with Edwin of Mercia, but the earls were routed (though they managed to escape) by Hardrada at Fulford Bridge, just outside York, on 20 September 1066. Rushing to Tadcaster four days later, King Harold decisively defeated the jubilant Scandinavians at the battle of Stamford Bridge. Tostig and the ambitious Hardrada were killed, and only twenty shipfuls of Norwegians sailed home that day. The punishment that Harold would have exacted on his treacherous Northern subjects, had he won the battle of Hastings scarcely three weeks later, is a matter for conjecture.

Now, however, it was left to William the Conqueror to confront Northern rebelliousness. As William Kapelle observes, 'as king, William inherited all the problems of northern government that had been created before his arrival, but he lacked the necessary knowledge, if not the will, to deal with them.'[31] He needed to find an acceptable candidate as earl of Northumbria. William's failure to make the right choice caused him serious difficulties and contributed to one of the North's darkest hours. For centuries afterwards, the kings of England would be faced by similar dilemmas in the North.

Appointing Copsig, who was a Northerner but also Tostig's former chief henchman, as earl of Northumbria probably seemed a good idea just before King William departed for Normandy in February 1067. But with William absent, Copsig attempted to kill Osulf, the new scion of the House of Bamburgh. Osulf escaped, recruited an army, and a month later surprised Copsig. Copsig headed for the local church, probably St Cuthbert's in Norham. Respecting the law imposing outlawry and forfeiture on whoever pursued a feud inside a church,[32] Osulf set fire to it, forcing Copsig into the open where he was killed.

Such murderous shenanigans were not music to William's ears. His royal authority had been flouted, his mercenaries required payment, his Normans wanted land and now his most promising tax-extractor was dead. Luckily, then, Osulf was himself killed in the autumn of 1067 by an outlaw. Returning from Normandy in December 1067 (with William de Percy) owing to the disastrous rule in his absence of earl-bishop Odo (his half-brother), the king sold the earldom to Cospatric, the new head of the House of Bamburgh.

In the spring of 1068, 'the king was informed that the people in the north were gathered together and meant to make a stand if he came.'[33] After Cospatric launched a rebellion to establish a Bamburgh ruling dynasty above the Humber, William moved cautiously to Warwick and Nottingham, where he built castles and collected men. Meanwhile, a handsome, eloquent spendthrift, Edgar the Ætheling – a sixteen-year-old royal prince who had an alarmingly good claim to the English throne and was the brother of the future Queen Margaret (later St Margaret) of Scotland, wife of Malcolm III – had escaped William's control and was heading north.[34] Faced by Christendom's most formidable warrior, Edgar and Cospatric fled to Scotland. In mid-1068, William reached York and quickly raised a castle – on the site of what is now Clifford's Tower – and the Northern rebellion fizzled out. Yet the instigators remained at large, armed and dangerous.

Bamburgh rule in the North having failed, William chose Norman officials instead and garrisoned York Castle with 500 men under William Malet. Richard fitz (son of) Richard assumed his duties as constable of Yorkshire. In the winter of 1068, William's chosen earl, Robert de Comines, was ordered to bring Durham to heel. Robert entered the city with 700 men who plundered and pillaged at will. It was too easy, thought Bishop Aethelwine, whose warning of a Northumbrian trap was ignored. Later that night – 28 January 1069 – as the Normans, some dripping with looted gems, sprawled drunkenly around the city, the Northumbrians rushed the gates, slaughtered all but one or two survivors and burnt the church in which Robert was hiding. When he emerged, he was butchered. (This tactic appears to have been a Northern speciality.)

The rebels, now joined by Cospatric and Edgar, lured Richard fitz Richard away from his Castle and murdered him. Then they besieged William Malet in York, now the last Norman stronghold above the Humber. Unlike the half-baked 1068 affair, the 1069 revolt seriously threatened the Norman Settlement.

Marching north, William surprised the rebels at York before the castle fell, and put them to flight. Even after building a second castle in York, later known as the Old Baile, in only eight days and entrusting it to the steady William fitz Osbern, the closest Companion of the Conqueror, William still faced rebellion. The leaders and their followers were in the hills, awaiting his eventual departure for the South. As a precaution, William sent Queen Mathilda back to Normandy in case his empire completely collapsed.

In the autumn of 1069, things went from worse to still worse. The rebels had communicated with Swein, king of Denmark, who also harboured ambitions to be king of England. After the Danish fleet had plundered its way up the Humber, Cospatric and Edgar met the Danes outside York and, in late September 1069, burnt it. Those in the city were either massacred or enslaved, although Malet and the few survivors succeeded in fleeing for the South. To all intents and purposes, Norman power above the Humber had been extinguished.

But it was a Pyrrhic victory, for with York burnt, there was nowhere to shelter for the encroaching winter. Twice William defeated lost Danish war-bands searching for a winter base. In desperation, the Danes made an agreement with William: they could forage along the coasts, but promised to leave for ever come the spring of 1070. The king now confronted his main problem: the Northern rebels who had redispersed to the hills on hearing of the Danish surrender.

Previously, the Normans had stayed in their castles and waited for an attack. William now followed the rebels' tactics and sent his men into the hills and vales of the Pennines to hunt down the insurgents. In his wrath, he also gave instructions to exterminate the general population and waste the entire land. The systematic ruthlessness and bloodletting of the 'Harrying of the North' is without parallel in British history. In Yorkshire alone, thousands of peasants were massacred and entire villages were wiped out. William then proceeded methodically through Durham, southern Northumberland and west across the Pennines into Cheshire, smiting by the sword what torches could not sear. Even Orderic Vitalis, born in England but raised in a Norman monastery, was shocked:

[William] commended that all crops and herds, chattels and food of every kind should be brought together and burned to ashes with consuming fire, so that the whole region north of the Humber might be stripped of all means of sustenance. In consequence so serious a scarcity was felt in England, and so terrible a famine fell upon the humble and defenceless populace, that more than 100,000 Christian folk of both sexes, young and old alike, perished with hunger. My narrative has frequently had occasion to praise William, but for this act which condemned the innocent and guilty alike to die by slow starvation I cannot commend him.[35]

The consequences were horrifying:

> some peasants sold themselves into slavery to avoid starvation. Others joined the bands of outlaws that formed in the free zone and plundered villages that had escaped the Normans. Many starved to death; according to Symeon of Durham, the roads and huts of the North were littered with decaying bodies that spread diseases among the living. There is even evidence ... that wolves came down from the hills to feast on the bounty of William the Conqueror.[36]

At the end of 1069, William held a macabre Christmas ceremony in the blackened husk of York, with 'all the visible paraphernalia of his kingship to symbolise the legitimacy of the continuing slaughter'.[37] Early in the New Year, William reached the Tees, where he heard of the cowed Cospatric's submission. Yet there was no execution, an act of forgiveness partly attributed to the counsel of William de Percy, who interceded on Cospatric's behalf. Indeed, Cospatric was restored to the earldom of Northumbria, probably to prevent him forging a new alliance with Malcolm. Satisfied that Cospatric held a ruined realm unenviably placed between the potentially aggressive Scots and the Norman North, the king returned in the depths of a terrible winter to York, where work commenced on rebuilding castles.

Percy's pleading directly with the king indicates that he had proven himself in battle and ability since his arrival two years before as a minor baron. What can be deduced from the few known facts of Percy's whereabouts during those two years? First, there is no record of him owning land in the South. Therefore, he did not tarry long below the Humber after stepping off the boat in December 1067. When the rebellion of 1068 broke out and William marched north, one can reasonably assume that Percy was in his train. During the campaign, the castles of Warwick, Nottingham, Lincoln, Huntingdon, Cambridge and York were raised, giving young Percy ample opportunity to act as a deputy to one of the constables; not at York, however, for he was obviously not among Malet's garrison slaughtered in September 1069.

So, between mid-1068 and the winter of 1069–70, Percy was standing guard somewhere in the Humber region. When William began the Harrying, Percy participated; no eleventh-century Norman stood aside from his king's business. In January 1070, he was present at Cospatric's submission, which means he travelled up to the Tees and back down to York with William. Thereafter, he was engaged upon the rebuilding of the York castles, acting as custodian, his experience from 1068 being much in demand.

It is also known that he participated in the Conqueror's expedition to Scotland in 1072.[38] After 1070, Yorkshire, administered by Norman sheriffs, was virtually added to the royal demesne, with Cospatric holding Northumbria as a kind of buffer zone. Malcolm III, however, wanted to isolate Northumbria, so that summer he invaded Teesdale through Cumberland, intending to waste the North Riding and cut Cospatric off from Norman support. Should Cospatric switch sides – an idea to which he was never averse – Scotland could annex Northumbria. But after Malcolm's forces turned north and attacked Durham, the infuriated Cospatric attacked Cumberland and recovered the booty Malcolm had stolen from Teesdale. In revenge, Malcolm allowed his men to kill or enslave any Northerner they captured. As a calculated insult to William, he also offered safety to Edgar the Ætheling (his new brother-in-law), currently cooling his heels at sea as a pirate.

William was unable to come north as he needed to suppress the English rebels (including the former earl Morcar) under Hereward the Wake and the remnants of King Swein's fleet at the Isle of Ely in Cambridgeshire. It had been a long siege, made enormously difficult by the swampish Fens.[39]

In the summer of 1072, William steeled himself for another Northern confrontation. He advanced up the east coast with an army, which included William de Percy, in order to obtain seaborne supplies (there was little left with which to feed an army in Yorkshire). However, Malcolm decided to negotiate at Abernethy. He recognised William as his overlord, bound over Duncan, his eldest son, as hostage (see below) and exiled the incorrigible Ætheling, who now found refuge in Flanders.

By the Abernethy agreement, William had rendered Cospatric dispensable. He retracted Cospatric's earldom, charging him with murdering Norman officials in 1069 and with fomenting rebellion. Cospatric too fled to Flanders, and was replaced by Waltheof, the son of a rival native earl. After fighting alongside the Danes during the storming of York in September 1069, Waltheof had submitted to William, who prudently married him to Judith, daughter of William's half-sister, Adelaide. In 1075, Waltheof expelled William's tax-collectors and, goaded by Malcolm, invited the Danes to join him in open rebellion. But when the Danish fleet did not arrive, Waltheof capitulated. William imprisoned him for a while (during which he daily recited 150 psalms), and beheaded him on 31 May 1076 after Judith testified to his treachery. The Conqueror never forgave twice, and Waltheof had doubly betrayed his favours. The only Englishman executed by King William, Waltheof enjoyed a posthumously glorious reputation as a Northumbrian martyr.[40]

Malcolm then broke the Abernethy treaty. He invited back from

Flanders both Cospatric (whom he made earl of Dunbar in the strategically placed Lothian) and the unfortunate Edgar. The latter accepted Malcolm's invitation, but it did not escape his brother-in-law's notice that Edgar was a spent force with no credibility. Malcolm therefore counselled him to make his peace with William. In Normandy, William greeted Edgar with great pomp, allowed him a daily stipend of one pound of silver, gave him some estates in Normandy and kept him under very strict supervision.

After the Conqueror died in 1087, six weeks after sustaining an internal wound when his horse stumbled, his empire was divided, following Norman custom, between his two sons: William Rufus received England, and Robert Curthose became duke of Normandy.

Malcolm renewed the Treaty of Abernethy with William Rufus in 1091, and was promised the restoration of Cumberland. However, Rufus had no intention of returning such a strategic piece of land, and in any case Malcolm marched south in the summer of 1093 to overrun Northumberland. But this time the new earl of Northumbria, Robert de Mowbray, was ready and waiting south of the river Aln. As the Scots crossed, Mowbray's army attacked. Most of the invaders – including Malcolm and his heir, Edward – drowned or were killed as they tried to surrender. It was a fatal lesson in perfidy to a most perfidious monarch.[41]

In the meantime, the feckless Robert Curthose – who had fallen in with Edgar – sought to launch an invasion of England from Normandy, prompting an invasion of Normandy itself by Rufus. The two brothers reached a settlement when Robert agreed to expel Edgar and confiscate his estates. Edgar ended up, as usual, in Scotland. In 1093, following Malcolm's death, Edgar plotted with William Rufus to seize the Scottish throne from Malcolm's brother, Donald Bane. In 1097 the Ætheling, with William's help, deposed him, taking the precaution of blinding him. The late Queen Margaret's son, Edgar (the Ætheling's nephew in other words), was then placed on the throne. It was his sister, 'Good Queen Maud', who would marry William Rufus's successor, Henry I, the only son of the Conqueror to be born after the Conquest.

The Ætheling was riding high. But his first successful coup made him overconfident, and after falling out with William Rufus, he was again exiled. This time he travelled to the Mediterranean and ended up commanding a fleet manned by the Byzantine Emperor's crack, axe-wielding Varangian Guard (in which also served numerous dispossessed Anglo-Saxon nobles). In 1106, he would return to Normandy and take up arms with his old comrade, Robert Curthose, in a rebellion against Henry I. Following his capture at the battle of Tinchebrai, Edgar finally decided to call it a day and retired. He died soon after, penniless, unmarried and childless.[42]

William de Percy and the Keeping of the Peace

What of William de Percy after the Scottish expedition of 1072? It is at this time that the paths of Percy and Hugh d'Avranches again crossed. After arriving with Percy in 1067, Hugh participated in the Harrying of the North as well as a number of battles. He may have first cast eyes on Cheshire, 'scarcely less ruthlessly devastated than Yorkshire', during the Harrying.[43] He may have been in charge of suppressing Cospatric's revolts. If so, then Percy may have been attached to his retinue.

Cheshire, strategically positioned on the Mercian–Welsh border, saw many disturbances before, and after, 1066. In 1070, only William's energetic intervention prevented the Mercians from allying with the Welsh to overthrow Norman rule.[44] Within a year, determined the West should not follow the chaotic North, William created a palatine (that is, virtually autonomous) earldom at Chester, vested with vast emergency powers and such towering resources that, if need be, the Welsh might be crushed.[45]

It was to this earldom that Hugh d'Avranches was elevated, where he rapidly stood apart from his fellow earls in military, legal and economic power if not in rank. His almost viceregal position may be gleaned from the Conqueror's words to him at the bestowal of earldom: 'Tenere ita libere ad Gladium, sicut ipse Rex tenebat Angliam per Coranum [To hold as freely by the Sword, as the King himself held England by the Crown].'[46]

Owing to the Harrying, Cheshire was poor, sparsely populated by terrified peasants and unproductive. So the earl was given expanses of rich land outside the area, most notably, for our purposes, in Yorkshire. In the first twenty years of his reign, the Conqueror settled almost a quarter of the land in England upon only eleven of his vassals; Hugh was one of these. By 1087, the earl was receiving more than three times the income from his manors outside Chester as from Chester itself.[47]

This larger-than-life figure was, Dugdale simply noted, 'a fat Man'. Even his cook held two manors of him, signalling that he was a gourmand.[48] The earl was 'a great lover of Worldly Pleasures, and Secular Pomp; profuse in giving, and much delighted with Enterludes, Jesters, Horses, Dogs and other like Vanities; having a large attendance of such persons, of all sorts, as were disposed to these sports'.[49] 'Such persons' included great men like Anselm, the future archbishop of Canterbury, who was his confessor. Yet jolly Hugh the Fat (who eventually become so unwieldy that he could barely crawl) was also feared for his predatory ravaging of the North. He even wasted his own lands to provide more space for hunting and hawking.

The first connection – through land – between Hugh and Percy comes in 1074 when the earl disposed of his cliff-hanging estate in Whitby (Yorkshire), including its ruined abbey, sacked by William's men in 1070. This, as well as eighty-six lordships in Yorkshire and thirty-two in Lincolnshire, Percy held as tenant-in-chief or undertenant (usually of Hugh) by the time of the Domesday Survey, at which point Percy held nearly a quarter of his Yorkshire fief of Hugh.[50]

As part of the Norman settlement, the Conqueror imported feudalism, bringing about a massive tenurial reformation (importantly, it was not a *revolution*, for feudal elements already existed in Anglo-Saxon England). This marvellous administrative mechanism forced Norman, and later English, society into a framework of contracts, which gradually evolved through custom into the rule of law.

Since time immemorial, successful warriors had been awarded land. During the reign of the Norman dukes, such awards came with a price: a 'fief ... was granted to a vassal not as a simple reward but as an earnest of favour, valuable, profitable, and *conditional* upon the performance of future service ... In turn the great vassals of emperor, king, or prince granted fiefs to their own vassals.'[51] Norman expansion was fuelled by the potential acquisition of land, and William's task was aided by the near-disappearance of the Anglo-Saxon noble class. The cream had fallen with Harold at Hastings or fighting the Norwegians in the North; others fled abroad or to Scotland, leaving their possessions behind. Those left cast in their lot with the invaders or were hunted down in the aftermaths of the revolts.[52] William's redistribution of territory created a happy following of Normans, linked to the king and his tenants-in-chief through personal ties of lordship and loyalty.[53] In England, whose half-subjugated population of one and a half million were dominated by a small Norman military aristocracy, feudalism was crucial to William's political power.

The king was suzerain of the land: all his subjects held their estates in return for military service and an oath of fealty. He, in turn, assumed the onerous responsibilities and burdens of kingship, so making a medieval king roughly no more than *primus inter pares* (first among aristocratic equals), although this was really only in theory. Thus, Hugh d'Avranches was indebted to provide William with a certain number of knights, and therefore Hugh might 'subinfeudate' (or 'sub-let') his lands to tenants, who would contribute a negotiated proportion of his requirements. And so the hierarchy descended: the tenants-in-chief would enfeoff their own vassals, so that all England was held directly or indirectly of the king, everybody owing somebody higher up knightly or other service. The system also worked in reverse; those below you were owed protection and cheap land. At its grandest scale, then, feudalism joined the lowliest serf with the king of England. Percy, for example, might be subinfeudated to provide, say, five well-armed, well-schooled knights – the *servitia debita* for magnates great and small, usually worked in multiples of five or ten – whenever Hugh or the king called a fighting host drawn from all his barons. At royal level, William was 'owed' 5000 knights by his vassals for the defence of the realm if necessity required.

The number of knights' fees, as the obligations were termed, to be extracted from an estate was negotiated between tenant-in-chief, tenant, subtenant and so on. Sometimes a tenant failed to provide his quota, and by 1100 'scutage', or financial commutation for personal service, was permitted; otherwise a free knight willing to serve for pay, or a dispossessed one hoping to regain his lost fief, might be found.[54]

The North needed innovative tenants-in-chief and undertenants, although few wanted devastated manors – several of which were sometimes packaged together to form an 'honour' – when lush Southern land beckoned. In 1086, for example, there were about 250 tenants overall in Yorkshire, but in Essex, Norfolk and Lincolnshire combined (a similar size to Yorkshire) there were 1620. More worryingly for royal administrators, of about 180 lay tenants-in-chief nationally (the rank from which Norman officials such as sheriffs were recruited), only 2 per cent resided in Yorkshire.[55] Percy, for instance, was custodian of York Castle for a time, and deputy sheriff under Hugh fitz Baldric. However, the relative independence and power available to those undertaking Northern duty offered glittering opportunities for ambitious men like William de Percy.[56] In many ways, the military aristocracy, which William and Hugh introduced into Yorkshire, was a parvenu aristocracy packed with new men.

In 1086, Percy controlled land in Yorkshire valued at £54 16s, but it had been worth nearly twice that modest figure before the Harrying.[57] Many of his manors were severely devalued, with maybe a couple of hapless villeins and a plough to their name. In some places, Percy did his utmost to repair the damage: Seamer of 1066, for instance, was home to only three ploughs' worth of land: by 1086, Percy had imported fifteen villeins and a priest, and had given them another two ploughs and a church. The manor doubled in value to £4.[58]

Despite being the thirteenth-largest, and sixth-wealthiest, tenant-in-chief in Yorkshire, Percy was a landholder of distinctly local stature. A fellow Yorkshire tenant-in-chief and neighbour was count Alan the Red, whose vast Honour of Richmond enclosed 199 manors (almost a shire), with at least another 300 outside its limits.[59] Nevertheless, counting up the number of manors or calculating the acreage in a fief can be misleading. Manors ranged from small farms worth a few shilling to villages bringing in more than £100 a year. The acreage might include sturdy husbandmen and cattle ploughing fertile fields or scorched earth and slain peasants. All things considered, Percy's fief had not fared so badly, being worth 60 per cent of its 1066 value; the average drop among Yorkshire lay tenants-in-chief was 56.2 per cent. Of the twenty-six tenants-in-chief, of whom most lived outside the county, twenty-three suffered 'negative equity' in Yorkshire.[60] Most calamitously, Hugh's Yorkshire lands had fallen in value from 5200 shillings (£260) to a laughable – if it weren't so tragic – 210 shillings (nearly £11) in the twenty years' interval since the Conquest, which might explain his disinclination to do anything but hunt on them.[61]

The total annual worth of all rural land in England in 1086 was about £73,000. Of this, the ten shires of Wessex south of the Thames contributed £32,000, and the three East Anglian shires about £12,950. And what about blasted Yorkshire, where Percy held his fief? Together with harried Lancashire, this enormous area was worth a mere *£1200*, only two-thirds of what William required to remunerate his few minor officials and personal servants ('King's Serjeants'). On a *national* scale, Percy's modest estate of £55-odd places him firmly within the famous definition of a 'Class E' (that is, the lowest type) barony, along with ninety to one hundred other tenants-in-chief.[62] Another 'second-rank' baron, Judhael of Totnes, received lands in Devon valued at £163 ('Class D'), or three times as much as Percy's, which illuminates the plight of the Northern landholder compared to a Southerner of similar status.[63] By way of comparison, a 'Class A' magnate like Hugh of Chester received an annual income of some £900, whilst the Conqueror reserved £17,650 per annum for the support of the Crown and royal house.[64] Still, the fact that Hugh and King William trusted the young Percy with so much relatively worthless, but strategically located, land illustrates their faith in him. He was just the kind of man needed to guard the North, and put the fear of the Conqueror into its inhabitants.

Chief among Percy's Yorkshire estates was Topcliffe (probably granted in 1070–1), where, with William's licence, he raised a castle sometime after 1072–4.[65] Other Yorkshire lands of Percy's in Whitby, Tadcaster, Wheldrake and Spofforth were extensive,[66] but Topcliffe remained the family's principal residence – serviced by nearly fifty peasants, a mill and a nice church – until the purchase of Alnwick Castle in the early fourteenth century.

Early Norman castles differed somewhat from our romantic Gustave Doré-tinged imaginings of soaring towers and roaring fireplaces;

Norman lords would have been nonplussed by legendary Camelot or the Castle of Otranto. Topcliffe, in fact, was a typical example of a Norman motte-and-bailey castle. A forty-five-foot-high artificial hillock (motte) was surmounted by a timber stockade forty feet in diameter. There were probably one or two small timber turrets as well. The motte was connected by a narrow steep bridge to a horseshoe-shaped great court (bailey). The bailey at Topcliffe enclosed about an acre, and was also protected by a wide ditch and timber ramparts, pierced with a bridge that could be raised or lowered across the outside ditch.

Architecture gives a clue to the habits and manners of the time. Norman barons, as one Edwardian observer quaintly put it:

> were not exactly the sort of people one would now-a-days ask to dine with us. Take the roughest and most brutal Durham pit-lad you can find, invest him with absolute and uncontrolled authority, and you would have a very fair sample of the Norman baron of the time... In those days it was not fashionable to wash, handkerchiefs were unknown, common decency, not to speak of privacy, was conspicuous by its absence... The virtue of no girl or young married woman with any pretensions to good looks was worth a moment's purchase; it was an acknowledged perquisite of the ruling classes to take what they chose in this line. The revolting cruelties practised upon prisoners... proves clearly enough how brutal, bestial, and horrible were those days. Nor were the women any better than the men. It is recorded that a high-born Norman lady would relieve the tedium of a long day, when her lord was out hunting, by having an unoffending servant – male or female – stripped and soundly thrashed in the courtyard... The Norman barons had their redeeming features; they were at least men. They had to be, for it was a case of the survival of the fittest, and the castles they erected reflect the brutality of the builders.[68]

Norman castles were not built to protect the inhabitants and their flocks and herds from attack; only the English and the Danes had lightly fortified some towns for communal defence. In Normandy, fortresses protected the individual lord, and were imported into England after 1066 to overawe the populace and impose the king's peace. Before the Conquest, English nobles lived in two-storeyed timber houses encircled by a hedge or low stockade, which was fine for warding off wolves but presented no great obstacle to rampaging Normans. As the outstanding symbols of feudalism, the castles raised across William's England proclaimed the Norman triumph.

In the wild North, moreover, the chain of motte-and-bailey castles were used as forward operational bases against outlaws and rebels.[69] Percy's military aptitude shone through in his chosen site: Topcliffe occupied a brilliant strategic position about ten miles north-east of the Yorkshire city of Ripon. A short distance to the east of the fortress there was a junction of two streams – the Swale and Cod Beck – between which a natural ridge rose above the swamp. Built on that ridge, Topcliffe was, in effect, a highly defensible island.

Ten miles north was Northallerton, another Norman stronghold, and then Richmond; twenty miles south lay Tadcaster and, beyond that, Pontefract. Moreover, south-east of Topcliffe was York. What was the significance of all this? First, these fortresses were placed alongside the Great North Road from the south that skirted the Humber marshes at Pontefract and split into three at Tadcaster. One road led to York; the second continued along the Northumbrian–Cumbrian border past Topcliffe and Richmond (near Scotch Corner), crossed into Lothian and ended near Edinburgh; the third headed east into Lancashire. These roads were William's foremost lines of communication and supply to the North, and these new castles defended them.

Not all Norman castles were the same. Richmond and Pontefract, in particular, were castleries: land and power concentrated for specific strategic reasons.[70] Count Alan the Red's power base surrounding Richmond commanded the Stainmore Gap, frequently used by the Scots to raid Yorkshire from Cumbria. Ilbert de Lacy's huge fee of Pontefract stretched from the Pennine foothills to the fens on either side of the River Aire.[71] Thus, the two main eastern invasion-routes through the Pennines were blocked. Moreover,

> their lords … possessed formidable judicial powers that included infangthief [jurisdiction over a felon apprehended within the manor's limits], the right to have a gallows, the right to the goods of condemned fugitives, the assize of bread and ale, and the return of writs except for pleas to the crown. These gave a baron the effective policing powers he needed to combat outlaws and robbers, probably the principal day-to-day function of these fees.[72]

Topcliffe was an outlying post between these two virtual provinces, and was detailed to police the Wensleydale region, which was overrun with cut-throats and desperate men fleeing from the Harrying. Percy was to lead his knights and mercenaries into the Pennines and exterminate ruined Englishmen, not only for the good of Norman authority north of the Humber, but also to prevent the harassment of his own peasants by their countrymen.

The Home Life of William de Percy

At sometime, probably in the mid-1070s, Percy wedded Emma de Port, the daughter or niece (possibly illegitimate) of another young lord with moderate possessions in Normandy who did very well out of the Conquest.[73] Perhaps he spied out the land ahead of time on a brief visit: the New Minster at Winchester tantalisingly records that one of its pre-Conquest benefactors was a certain Hugh de Port.[74]

Hugh de Port's overlord in both Normandy and England was the Conqueror's half-brother, Odo, bishop of Bayeux and earl of Kent. 'To be a reliable subordinate of the earl-bishop was the golden passport to success for many Normans in England', judges one historian of the Conquest.[75] For Hugh de Port it certainly was, for by 1086 he was the greatest lay tenant in peaceful Hampshire, a world away from the rough-house Northern frontier. In Percy's eyes, the union brought him some safe wooded land with a mill in Hambledon (in Hampshire), worth a useful £4.[76]

Sadly, that is all we know about Emma de Port; like most medieval women, she fades uncomplainingly into the background after marriage. There is one interesting rumour about her that, unfortunately, previous Percy family biographers have taken as Gospel truth.[77] A chronicle of the early Percys, compiled by a monk of Whitby Abbey hundreds of years after the events, states that 'William, Lord Percy, the fyrst Founder of Whitbye [married] Emma of the Porte, which Emme fyrst was Lady of Seamer besides Skarburgh [Scarborough], afore the Conquest, and of other landes, William Conqueror gave to Syr William Percy for hys good Service, and he wedded hyr that was very heire to them, in discharging of his conscience.'[78] William Peeris likewise confirmed that 'into the Boreall [that is Northern] parts hee [William] willed him to resort/ a noble Lady caused him to marry named Em de Porte'. [79] In other words, 'Emma of the Porte' came from Seamer and was a native Anglo-Saxon heiress. Some sources even add that she was the daughter of the Cospatric for whom Percy had interceded with William.[80]

In this reading, Percy is a merciful and kind Norman lord who inter-married and wished to settle down in his adopted country. A tale even grew up that Percy acquired a nickname – 'cognomento Asgernuns' – an older form of *aux gernons* or *à les gernons*. In other words, he affected whiskers or a moustache in the Saxon style; Normans were usually clean-shaven, with cropped hair. At this distance, it is impossible to tell whether this was a contemporary description or whether it dates from long after his death. However, when it is considered that the House of Percy later became 'Kings in the North,' these medieval traditions were probably invented to distinguish the family artificially from other rapacious or alien Norman overlords.

First, less picturesquely, the Domesday Survey states that Percy 'holds Ambledune [Hambledon in Hampshire]. He received it with his wife.'[81] This manor adjoined the estates of Hugh de Port, the Norman, and moreover, the land descended in the Percy family until as late as 1242–3. In addition, Hugh held land in Isleham and Snailwell in Cambridgeshire, which Emma de Port later bestowed on Whitby Abbey.[82] Second, Emma was the most common Norman name, not an Anglo-Saxon one. Third, why would William give a Saxon bride to one of his tenants-in-chief? Fourth, it was exceedingly rare for a Norman of Percy's generation and rank to intermarry with a Saxon. Such unions occasionally occurred between knightly tenants or foreign mercenaries in Norman service and local women, but certainly not a daughter of a native Northern earl. When Henry I of England married Edgar the Ætheling's niece, Eadgyth, sister of the king of Scots, in 1100, strictures began to be relaxed among the aristocracy. Even so, she changed her name to the respectably Norman Matilda (or Maud).[83] Only by the 1180s was intermarriage so common that a contemporary remarked 'it can scarcely be decided who is of English birth and who of Norman'.[84]

Percy himself disappears from the official records between the Domesday Survey of 1086 and 1096, when he donned the Red Cross and left for the Holy Land on the First Crusade. Nevertheless, an intriguing story arose about this enigmatic baron. According to an anonymous monk writing in the early twelfth century, Percy emerges as an over-determined and over-resolute character. At the time, every prudent Norman, before he left his threshold for a journey of even a single night, crossed himself, recited a paternoster and offered a prayer to St Julian for protection of his person, his chattels and properties against ghostly and other foes. Percy unerringly observed this custom, but his success in England had caused him to become arrogant. He began to ignore St Julian, saying to his worried chaplain in jest as he left for a tour of his estates, 'What need we further of St Julian and his petty hospitality? Tonight we shall sleep in our own houses. Why ask for what is our own?' The chaplain pleaded with Percy to offer the prayer, but his master, irritated, cried, 'Who hinders you to pray as you will? Only let me be and do not trouble us with your prayers.' Hardly had the party travelled half a mile from Topcliffe but they saw it in flames. After an uncomfortable night in his peasants' hovels, Percy's band left the next morning for Tadcaster, but discovered that all his granaries and barns had burnt down in the night. Again, they sheltered in a hovel, Percy's mood decaying by the hour. When the chaplain timidly reminded him of what happened to those who ignored St Julian, he was sharply dismissed. His servants began to take bets, whispering to each other, 'See which wins, the saint or Sir William.' In the morning, they made for York, only to find that Percy's mansion there had been blown down by a furious wind. At daybreak, Percy set off for Nafferton to visit his wife and infant son Alan, but arrived just in time to witness his house burning down and his family, intoxicated by the smoke, being carried to safety. Only then did Percy finally regain his humility and offer prayer. Following yet another miserable night in local accommodation, Percy crossed the Humber into Lincolnshire, where he met his reeve. The man told him that he had received the letter sent five weeks before, commanding him to store in readiness provisions for 300 or 400 men, along with food for their horses and hounds. Bemused – for he had authorised no letter to be sent – Percy turned to his notary and chamberlain, who shook their heads at this marvellous occurrence. The chaplain then appeared and delivered a sermon berating Percy for thinking himself mightier than a saint. A huge feast ensued: Percy regretted the error of his ways, his fortune had been saved and, best of all, his wife and son joined him, both having made a rapid recovery. Although the story has been patently embroidered, the author's familiarity with Percy's estates is quite remarkable, leading one to conclude that at some point fire did consume a number of his properties.[85]

The Death of William de Percy

The First Crusade of 1096–9 launched in reaction to Muslim encroachments into Europe and Islam's seemingly inexorable expansion, was either an exercise in savage fanaticism or a monument to the highest ideals of devotion, bravery and sacrifice.

In March 1095, legates of the beleaguered Byzantine Emperor Alexius I Comnenus arrived at a papal council in Piacenza, pleading to Pope Urban II for military aid against the Seljuk Turks,[86] who had overrun the Anatolian peninsula and were threatening Constantinople. Coinciding with the Pope's concerns that the Peace and Truce of God was dissolving under the internecine warfare of the European princes, the message struck a chord.

Imagine this knightly bellicosity channelled into a Holy and Just War against the Infidels: Jerusalem a Christian kingdom; the Holy Sepulchre – the Tomb of Christ himself – glimpsed! A galvanised Urban travelled throughout Europe, persuading princes and tyrants alike that their sins would be redressed if they launched a Holy War. On 27 November 1095, the Pope reached Clermont, high in central France; his audience of thousands, gathered in an immense field outside the city, included archbishops, nobles, clerks, priests and peasants. He spoke of Turkish abominations: how 'it amused them to kill Christians by opening up their bellies and drawing out the end of their intestines, which they then tied to a stake. Then they flogged their victims and made them walk around and around the stake until their intestines had spilled out and they fell dead upon the ground.'[87]

'Let those,' concluded the pontiff, 'who are accustomed to wantonly wage private war against the faithful march upon the infidels in a war which should be begun now and be finished in victory. Let those who have been robbers now be soldiers of Christ...Let nothing delay those who are going to go.'[88] Righteous anger seized the princes and peasants, and a cry of *Deus Vult* – God wills it! – erupted. Many pledged to go there and then; garments were rent into the shape of crosses and sewn onto shoulders or breasts.

First to leave, in April 1096, was the People's Crusade, 30,000 strong, led by Peter the Hermit, which slaughtered and pillaged its way to Constantinople before being massacred in Anatolia by Sultan Qilij Arslan. Few survived. Christendom had been blooded. The next 'crusade', led by the petty lord Emich of Liesingen, never got beyond Hungary after perpetrating massacres of the Jews in Cologne and Mainz.

The contingents of the Christian princes began to gather in Constantinople soon after. Duke Robert Curthose's Anglo-Norman army of 1000 knights and more infantry arrived in the winter of 1096–7. William de Percy personally accompanied Duke Robert, who had mortgaged Normandy to his brother, William Rufus, for a three-year loan of 10,000 silver marks (around £6600) to pay for the expedition.[89] Raymond IV, count of Toulouse and marquess of Provence, followed in April 1097, with 1200 knights and 8800 soldiers. Next was the fierce Bohemund, prince of Taranto and disinherited son of Robert Guiscard, the Norman conqueror of southern Italy, much to Alexius's consternation, as 'the mention of his name occasioned panic'. His 500 knights, which included many experienced Italian nobles and his nephew, Tancred, were the crack cavalry of Europe. There was also Duke Godfrey de Bouillon's force of 8000 Lorrainers.

Percy's preparations for the Crusade help explain his perplexing attachment to the rebellious Duke Robert. Before he left, Percy confirmed his generous gifts to his beloved Whitby Abbey in case he should not return. Yet for nigh on twenty years, the abbey had been embroiled in controversy.

In the late 1070s, Reinfred, a Benedictine monk and a former knight in Percy's host who had participated in the Harrying, beseeched Percy to refound the ruined religious house, which Percy gladly did. The manor of Whitby was then a desert worth a risible £3 (in 1066 it had been valued at £112); of the ancient monastery sacked by the Danes in 867 nothing could be salvaged; for 200 years, the seabirds had flown through the blank lancets of walls fiercely lashed by wind and sand; masonry lay shattered everywhere.

Soon after his installation as prior, Reinfred was replaced by one of the monks, Stephen, much to Percy's displeasure. In spite of Stephen's rapid restoration of the abbey, Percy began to cause trouble over its charter, by which the abbey held its lands from him. 'Repenting of his liberality', Percy tried repeatedly to banish Stephen.

Making complaint to the king, Stephen and those monks who support-ed him were allowed to make habitable the deserted monastery of Lastingham, but still Percy continued to harass them. Finally, Stephen appealed to William for a second time. William ordered Percy to reinstate the banished monks, which Percy ignored. In a fait accompli, he had already given the priorship of the abbey to Serlo, his brother from Normandy. But with the question of the abbey's charter still unresolved, the two brothers soon disagreed over Percy's interference with the abbey's workings. The atmosphere was further poisoned by Percy's gift of some Whitby lands to a faithful retainer, Ralph de Everley. At this final insult, Serlo appealed to the new king, William Rufus, who bluntly ordered Percy to return the lands and desist from further interference. Again, Percy ignored a royal instruction and marched on the abbey, driving Serlo and his monks into the wilderness.

Now threatened with excommunication, and in disgrace at the king's court on the eve of his departure for the Holy Land, Percy reinstated the land to the abbey and allowed Serlo to return. Piety and contrition are in evidence here (renunciation of disputes with churches over doubtful rights was common among Crusaders preparing to leave), but Percy may have received cash for healing the twenty-year rift.[90] Crusading, after all, was expensive.[91] Duke Robert, feeling cheated by his brother's succes-sion to the English throne, gladly took on disgruntled Anglo-Normans who, like Percy and Odo of Bayeux, had fallen out with their king.[92]

It was an absolved man, then, who marvelled at the splendours of imperial Constantinople in the spring of 1097, after a long journey by way of Norman Italy and the Adriatic. 'It was a city of gleaming wealth and far-reaching influence, with a dozen splendid palaces and three hundred churches, with great gardens and vast public places where the paving stones were slabs of marble and hundreds of bronze statues stood on marble pedestals ... Sometimes the doors of palaces and churches were made of solid silver.'⁹³ The anonymous *Gesta Francorum* breathlessly described the sophistication that put the coarse Normans to shame.

> Frequent voyages bring to the citizens at all times necessities in abundance. Cyprus, Rhodes and Mytilene, and Corinth and innumerable islands minister to this city. Achaia, Bulgaria and all of Greece likewise serve the city and send to it all their choicest products. Moreover the cities of Romania in Asia and Europe, and also the cities of Africa never cease sending donatives to Constantinople. Greeks, Bulgars, Alans, Cumans, Pigmatici, Italians, Venetians, Romans, Dacians, English, Amalfitans and even Turks and many gentiles, Jews and proselytes, Cretans, Arabs and people of all nations come to this great city.⁹⁴

Constantinople was spiritually dazzling as well, housing as it did the church of the Virgin of the Pharos, a reliquary for the grave-clothes of Christ, pieces of the True Cross, the Crown of Thorns, the Nails and the Holy Lance, the Mantle and the Robe of the Virgin. These symbols buttressed the emperor's divine authority; regarded as the thirteenth Apostle, he gloried in the title, *en Christo Autocrator* – 'Autocrat in Christ' – and for the Byzantines was almost the incarnation of Christ himself. His power eclipsed that of any European king, prince or duke, a sobering reminder to any petty Norman baron used to pushing his villeins around.

At the end of April, the imperial navy ferried the Christian armies into Asia Minor. Their first objective was Nicaea, the capital of the Seljuk Sultan sixty miles south-east of Constantinople. With the Sultan absent from the city, Nicaea was taken on 19 June 1097 after a short but fierce siege.

A week later, with Bohemund and Robert of Normandy in the vanguard, and the Lorrainers a day's march behind, the Crusaders set off south towards Dorylaeum. Somewhere ahead, the Sultan was massing legions of mounted bowmen. On 1 July, the Turks charged down from the hills against the vanguard on the plain of Bathys, 'howling like wolves and furiously shooting a cloud of arrows'. The ensuing battle of Dorylaeum would be the first clash between Crusaders and Turks. Initially the Turks held the advantage. Heavily outnumbered, the European kings had never before encountered swirling hordes of cavalry shooting from the saddle, and the Crusaders suffered many dead before Bohemund ordered his infantry to protect the non-combatants and women whilst the knights dismounted. Messages were sent to the second army, and before the end of the day, the Franks and Lorrainers had reached the camp. With their cohorts re-formed, the knights charged. Mounted archers, a useful lightning-strike force, were no match against an armoured assault. The Turks broke and fled.

Bolstered by their victory but desperately thirsty as the Turks had poisoned the wells, the Crusaders pushed on through the scorched countryside towards the legendary city of Antioch, the first bishopric of St Peter, awaiting liberation from the Infidel. After four months, the main army stood outside its gates on 20 October 1097, where they remained in a state of siege until the night of 3 June 1098, when Bohemund and his men scaled the Tower of the Two Sisters, unlocked the gates and took the city by surprise. While the infantry ran through the streets looting and killing many Christians by mistake, 'the knights, who were experienced in the business of warfare, continued to seek out and kill the Turks'.[95]

But in a city that was empty of provisions and too large to defend properly, the Crusaders found themselves besieged by the relief force of Kerbogha, the Turkish ruler of Mosul, who had promptly settled in the Crusaders' abandoned camps. On 28 June 1098, six orderly divisions of knights and infantry clanked into line facing Kerbogha, who was playing chess in his pavilion. Spurring their emaciated horses (the night before, the knights had fed their steeds their own dole of grain), the heavy cavalry, led by Duke Robert Curthose, Hugh the Great and the count of Flanders, slammed into the Turkish army. After some desultory arrows, the archers fled. Their horses' weakness preventing a pursuit, the Crusaders ransacked the Turkish camp, in which they discovered gold, silver, robes, fresh horses, magnificent turbans and food. 'In regard to the women found in the tents of the foe the Franks [a general term for Crusaders] did them no evil but drove lances into their bellies.'[96]

The Crusaders then rested for four months. After quarrelling with his fellow commanders, Bohemund stayed behind when the army headed south, naming himself prince of Antioch. Following the beautiful coastal road through Lebanon and Palestine, past ancient Tyre, Acre and Haifa, they descended from Mount Carmel to Caesarea and thence Jaffa, where they turned inland for the ascent to Jerusalem.

On 7 June 1099, the Crusaders stood at the tomb of the Prophet Samuel on the 900-foot summit of Montjoie – the Joyous Mountain[97] – and glimpsed the honey-coloured walls of the world's holiest city, shimmering in the heat-haze nine miles to the south.

However, the Turks had wasted the surrounding area; wells were poisoned, trees had been felled so there was no shade and the harvest had been burnt. In the camps, one Crusader recalled, sandstorms whipped faces and the heat was so deadening that in the Pool of Siloam at the foot of Mount Zion:

> Those who were strong pushed and shoved their way in a deathly fashion through the pool, which was already choked with dead animals and men struggling for their lives, and in this way they reached the

rocky mouth of the fountain…Those weaker ones sprawled on the ground besides the pool with gaping mouths, their parched tongues making them speechless, while they stretched out their hands to beg water from the more fortunate ones.[98]

William de Percy, now aged about fifty, succumbed neither to Turk nor Northumbrian, but to the strangling heat and a burning thirst in the siege of Jerusalem. According to the memorialists of Fountains Abbey and Whitby Abbey, Percy died 'within sight of Jerusalem': 'Denique nobilissimus Willielmus de Perci Ierosolimam petens, apud locum qui vocatur Mons Gaudii, qui est in provincia Ierosolimitana, migravit ad Dominum, ibique honorifice sepultus est.'[99]

One final, poignant word on the crusading experience, which stands just as well for William de Percy:

His abiding memory would have been of a continual hunt for provisions. The chances were that within a year his horses and pack animals had died. So when he had fought, he had fought on foot, and when he had marched, he and his surviving servants had had to carry his arms and armour in sacks across their shoulders. Even before they left Europe crusaders had begun to pass from reality into unreality, slipping into a dream world from which they did not escape until they returned home, a world in which for much of the time they were homesick, starving, diseased and exhausted…a world in which acts of unspeakable cruelty were committed against the backdrop of a night sky glittering with comets, auroras and shooting stars, and in which Christ, Our Lady and the saints appeared to them in visions, and the ghosts of their dead returned to comfort and encourage them, and to assure them that death in such a holy war was martyrdom.[100]

Jerusalem was successfully stormed on 15 July with the aid of siege engines, an innovation in crusading warfare. Robert, duke of Normandy, entered the city with his men at about noon, the hour Christ had died on the Cross. The fleeing Saracens were cut down and dismembered, and the survivors cornered. 'Nearly ten thousand were beheaded…None of them were left alive. Neither women nor children were spared.'[101]

Godfrey de Bouillon was chosen Prince of Jerusalem, but reigned for only a year before the emir of Caesarea poisoned him. In September 1099, having fulfilled his vows, Robert Curthose prepared to return to Normandy (and to his rebellious ways). In his contingent travelled the faithful Ralph de Everley, to whom Percy had given the lands of Whitby. He buried his master's heart in the chapter-house of Whitby Abbey.[102]

CHAPTER TWO

When Christ and his Saints Slept

The Anarchy of King Stephen and the
Making of William Percy II

'Wherever we turn, the politics of Stephen's reign seem to dissolve into family history.'[1]

'The fact that landed property descended by inheritance was enough to make the barons of England expert genealogists.'[2]

'The mind boggles at the analysis of human motivation that can result from a long, hard evening spent in front of a well-developed family tree.'[3]

History tells us little of William de Percy's four known sons, the eldest of whom, Alan, inherited his property by 9 January 1100.[4] Alan spent a great deal of time consolidating his estates, and extracting what income he could from blasted lands still recovering from the Harrying of the North. Following a new family tradition, he confirmed his father's gifts to Whitby Abbey, and even made several additional ones.[5] His younger brother, Walter, is a shadowy figure and nothing is known of him; another brother, William, became canon of York. The youngest, Richard, married Adeliza, widow of Walter de Argentom.[6]

The rein of Henry I (1100–35) was a socially mobile one. The courtiers (or *curiales*), made of new English money, surrounded the wily king, much to the disgruntlement of the old Norman magnates to whom the traditionally minded Conqueror had granted English territory.[7] Still, Henry spread his largesse diffusely enough to avoid any noble rebellions in the last thirty-three years of his reign.[8] As a king who clearly mixed business with pleasure, Henry was aided in this task by the brilliant employment of fourteen of his (acknowledged) twenty-one illegitimate children, whom he married off in a complicated network of allegiances with the great and the good, both in England and abroad.

Alan de Percy was, of course, a relatively new man himself, but his modest Northern estates precluded him from any real involvement with the court. No royal offices came his way, and his mother's family do not seem to have helped ease him into the higher Norman aristocracy, despite the fact that his uncle, Henry de Port, frequently attended the king's court.[9] Perhaps the courtly Southern Ports regarded the Northern Percys as their embarrassing country cousins.

As the scion of a strictly middling Yorkshire family, Alan's marriage prospects were limited to the North, preferably into a local clan with strategically situated estates in Yorkshire. When in pursuit of aristocratic women, Normans sniffed around for money or position, but their basic – and basest – instincts were heightened to fever pitch by the potential acquisition of land.[10] Alan sought, and found, a marriage through which he succeeded in allying with a Northern family of higher rank and controlling assets outstripping his own.[11] His wife was Emma, daughter of one of the twenty richest secular barons of the Norman Settlement. Gilbert de Gant was not quite a magnate but nor was he a *curiale*.[12] Nevertheless, the Gants were a force in Northern, rather than national, politics.

Alan's claim to her hand was aided by the fact that his father and Gilbert were not only veterans of the wars but also officials in the Conqueror's administration of the North. Sometime between 1086 and 1095 Gilbert's Lincolnshire estates were augmented by a large grant in the East Riding of Yorkshire. Although he himself was not 'old Norman money', Gilbert had married Alice, daughter of Hugh de Montfort II, the constable of Normandy before 1066, and in England and Normandy for some time thereafter. Such 'lateral marriages', however, 'carried little potential for social mobility unless the bride's father, brother, or nephew made significant social gains after the wedding'.[13]

In this respect, Alan had chosen tolerably well; Gilbert had fathered at least ten children. From this pool of latent talent, a younger son – Robert – would find favour with Henry I's successor, King Stephen, as chancellor *circa* 1140 and dean of York. Gilbert's eldest son and heir, Walter (who died in 1139), would fight at the side of Alan's son, William de Percy II at the battle of the Standard. Walter's son and heir was Gilbert de Gant II, who would be created earl of Lincoln by King Stephen *circa* 1147–48.[14] Nevertheless, during the Anarchy that followed, the Gant connection would trouble William de Percy as he tried to decide which side to fight on (see below).

Emma's *maragitium*, or the portion of the family property she received on marriage, consisted of about 2400 acres around Hunmanby in the East Riding of Yorkshire, then worth about £3 (but worth £12 in 1066),[15] which included the berewicks of Wold Newton, Staxton and Ganton.[16] Of prime importance to Percy was location. These lands were situated near Semer, Nafferton, Foston on the Wolds, Snainton, East Ayton and other manors all belonging to the Percy family. In this coastal, potentially fertile corner of Yorkshire, Alan de Percy was methodically organising a highly concentrated dynastic protectorate.

Alan died sometime between 1130 and 1135, and Emma seems to have followed him in late 1135. His son and heir was William Percy II, who had two younger brothers of whom little of interest is known. More pertinently, there were three bastards, one of whom – Alan – would face his legitimate sibling across the field of battle.

William Percy's Family

To ambitious men of action, the blast of war resounds with opportunities. When William Percy II succeeded his father, Alan, around 1135, he seemed destined for a wholesome life, tending to his estates and marrying a well-off Yorkshire lass. But less than a month after Henry I had breathed his last, a period known as the Anarchy, lasting nigh on twenty years, erupted. During it, by dint of brilliant marriage and happy circumstance, Percy would catapult himself into the front rank of Northern politics.

William Percy's career perfectly exemplifies how a lord could master an array of excruciatingly complex, and frequently conflicting, relationships of kinship and property in order to survive – and thrive. In a world where there were few permanent friendships but even fewer diehard enmities, only a baron's interests reigned eternal.

Early medieval England was steeped in feudalism, but was governed by kinship. Not only were politics dominated by men to whom the most service was owed, but society was arranged hierarchically according to ties of blood. Merit and ability, of course, had their place, but few men reached the commanding heights of power and wealth without a fortuitous marriage into a great or rising family. Kinship and feudalism, then, were two sides of the same coin.

So, a man's *maragitium* was a present with strings attached: technically the lucky bridegroom held the land as a feudal tenant of his father-in-law. For instance, the estates encircling Hunmanby, which Alan de Percy had received from Gilbert de Gant, helped cement the alliance between their families.[17] Family ties that were conceived as 'close' comprised the lord's grandparents, parents, uncles, aunts, brothers- and sisters-in-law, siblings, children, grandchildren, nephews, nieces and first cousins, but inevitably there were times when the duties of feudalism and the interests of family clashed.

With this in mind, in his mid-twenties, Percy married Adeliza de

Tonbridge, daughter of Richard fitz Gilbert de Clare II by Alice, sister of Ranulf I, earl of Chester.[18] This alliance is more momentous than it might at first appear from the roster of names.

First, the Clares were a family related to the Conqueror's grandfather.[19] Its scion Richard de Clare acted as regent of England in 1075, for which service he was granted one of the largest fiefs in the realm, centring around Clare in Suffolk and Tonbridge, so making him Surrey's richest landowner.[20] Owning rich swathes of Essex and Kent as well, Richard absorbed manors in Huntingdonshire and Hertfordshire through marriage. At the Domesday Survey, his estate was valued at £873 (compared to William de Percy I's at £55), making him the sixth-wealthiest layman in England.[21] It was his grandson, another Richard, who married Alice, sister of Ranulf I of Chester, so elevating the Clares from great courtiers into a family affiliated with an earldom. Richard and Alice's son, Gilbert, was finally granted the coveted earldom of Hertford by King Stephen *circa* 1138. In 1152, Gilbert died unmarried, but his nephew, Richard, earl of Hertford, would rule the House of Clare for four decades.

The Clares seem to have been unique in that both senior and cadet branches gained earldoms (the junior acquired that of Pembroke in 1138),[22] and neither died barren. As a result, their dynastic alliances over the course of a century multiplied exponentially. By 1130, remarkably, no fewer than five Clares were tenants-in-chief of the Crown simultaneously.[23]

So, summing up this complex welter of family relationships, William Percy's new brother-in-law was Gilbert earl of Hertford, whilst his uncle-in-law was earl of Pembroke. But one additional kinsman is of some interest here: Gilbert de Gant II, his mother's nephew – Percy's cousin – who in 1149 would be created earl of Lincoln. That's three earls linked to the Percys through one marriage.

What of Percy's mother-in-law's side? When Hugh d'Avranches died in 1101, the great earldom of Chester passed to his only (legitimate) son, Richard, aged but seven. He later married Maud, granddaughter of the Conqueror, and both he and his wife drowned in 1120. His closest relative was Ranulf le Meschin, then a French *vicomte*, who accordingly succeeded to the title. A confirmed advocate of checks and balances to keep overmighty magnates overawed, Henry I had allowed Ranulf to take control of all the Chester estates, but requested that he surrender Cumbria, including Carlisle.[24] This Ranulf I of Chester did, and with singular good grace. The avuncular new earl took as his wife the twice-widowed Countess Lucy – her surname and exact provenance are uncertain – who already had a son named William de Roumare (born about 1100) from her second marriage. The heir-presumptive to the earldom of Chester, however, was Ranulf and Lucy's son, Ranulf II, born *circa* 1105. The half-brothers, William de Roumare and Ranulf II – an enigmatic character widely considered to be either lounging at your feet or lunging at your throat – regarded Henry I's demand to relinquish Cumbria as royal extortion.[25] In 1129, when his father died, Ranulf II was granted the earldom and continued to view Cumbria as rightfully his.

Why was Henry I so concerned with diminishing Chester's empire? It was always dangerous for a king to interfere with his magnates, yet Henry evidently felt it was worth the risk. When Ranulf I inherited the earldom, it meandered from the heart of the palatinate, Chester itself and Cumbria through Leicestershire, Nottingham and Derbyshire down to, as Henry noted, the family's gigantic Lincolnshire estates. As such, it encompassed a third of the English realm in a thick buffer zone separating the South from the North.[26] At either end – in Yorkshire/Cumbria and Lincolnshire – the earls were busy sealing their dominance with marriage alliances.

The king intended to solve a potential problem with a two-pronged approach. First, having gained control of Cumbria – a bone of contention with the Scots ever since Malcolm III had lost it in 1092, Henry donated it to David I, their king, and titled him earl of Cumbria. At the time, Henry was married to David's sister and had helped raise the young David in England. David had already been granted the English earldom of Huntingdon, but giving him Cumbria as well would help ensure a friendly border. Second, Henry assiduously promoted the Beaumont family in the Midlands to act as a counterbalance.[27] Between the Scots and Beaumonts, the earls of Chester could hopefully be kept in their box, but Ranulf II's dogged refusal to recognise Henry's cession of Cumbria boded ill for the future.

The Succession

In 1120, the well-laid plans of succession for many noble families were thrown into disarray when the *White Ship*, crowded with heirs to lands and wealth, capsized. Younger sons and obscure cousins – like *vicomte* Ranulf, for instance – suddenly found themselves in unanticipated receipt of terrific inheritances. For a horrified Henry I, however, the disaster threatened his kingdom's stability: his only legitimate son, William the Ætheling (so named to signal that his parents had united the Norman and Saxon royal houses), was among the drowned, leaving his detested nephew, William Clito, as heir-presumptive. Sensing an opportunity and smarting from a military defeat inflicted by Henry the year before, King Louis VI of France promptly made Clito count of Flanders and married him to his queen's half-sister. These actions were doubly dangerous to Henry, for when he died England would fall under the sway of France, not Normandy; if he lived, a French invasion of England could be launched from the Flanders ports. Whatever happened, the dissolution of the *regnum Norman-Anglorum* looked imminent.

There was one trick left – and Henry played it. He married his daughter Matilda, widow of the German Emperor Henry V, to Geoffrey V, count of Anjou, the hereditary enemy of the Normans.[28] Anjou was fast expanding by 1100, and for Henry a new and strong Anjou–Normandy alliance could push Louis onto *his* back foot.

Next, at Christmas 1126, Henry politely but firmly requested his barons and bishops to swear fealty to Matilda as his rightful heir – on condition that he did not himself produce a son. (His wife having died in 1118, Henry married Adeliza de Louvain – we shall hear more about her in Chapter 3 – within a few weeks of the *White Ship* disaster.) This they duly did but after Clito's fortuitous death by blood-poisoning in 1128, they started looking for an ideal male candidate as Henry's successor.

This was Stephen, born *circa* 1096, the son of the count of Blois and Chartres, and of Adela, daughter of the Conqueror – an impeccable pedigree. He was also on good terms with the king, unlike the Empress Matilda's Angevin husband. (Matilda was informally known as the 'Empress', even though, not having received the imperial crown from the Pope, she officially remained 'Queen of the Romans'.) Grants of land made Stephen one of the richest men in England, but he owed everything to Henry's largesse, including his wife Matilda, the daughter of Count Eustace III of Boulogne – the area through which all English wool passed. As the English economy depended heavily on the cloth trade, having Stephen in place ensured that the tariffs remained low and that mercantile interests were appeased.[29]

So, economically speaking, Stephen was preferable to Empress Matilda, but the problem of the oath of loyalty still niggled. Even before the old king had died, the barons and churchmen whose finances depended on trade were being forced to choose between self-interest and allegiance to their oath. Most chose the former, especially when Stephen arrived from Boulogne at breakneck speed only a few days after the ailing Henry I died on 1 December 1135. Owing to an ill-timed spat between her husband and Henry, Matilda was delayed in Anjou; Stephen meanwhile was greeted rapturously by the burghers of London and 'elected' king. Then he dashed to Winchester, where the bishop – Henry of Blois, his older brother – had deftly secured the support of Roger of Salisbury (the justiciar, or controller, of the government of England) and William de Pont d'Arche, who oversaw the royal treasury.[30] To make his claim complete, Stephen needed to be anointed king by the archbishop of Canterbury, who was threatening to uphold the oath of loyalty. A man reassuringly named Hugh Bigod conveniently vouchsafed that Henry, on his deathbed, had announced that Matilda should remain in Anjou and Stephen should reign. Although the evidence was dubious – Bigod was absent when the king died – the archbishop had his get-out clause for the oath and subsequently anointed Stephen king on 22 December.

King David I of Scotland was furious: his niece, the Empress, had had the crown ripped out of her hands and his royal kinsman's dear wishes had been flouted. Immediately, he invested Carlisle and overran Northumberland and Newcastle, ominously receiving 'from the chiefs and nobles of that locality views and pledges of fidelity to his niece, the Empress'.[31] Yet these promises were forgotten when Stephen marched to Durham at the head of a hastily hired mercenary army and forced David to parley. Stephen temporarily purchased David's acquiescence to his regal fait accompli by guaranteeing the earldom of Huntingdon for David's son, Henry, and recognising David's control of Cumbria.[32]

Learning that Cumbria – *his* Cumbria – had cravenly been signed away to the Scots by a politically inept king, earl Ranulf II of Chester exploded when David was treated with honour at Stephen's court. At a feast the earl strutted out, followed by the archbishop of Canterbury, who was livid that David had been seated at the king's right hand, his customary place.[33]

Stephen was now confronting the same harsh realities of patronage that had so bedevilled Henry I and William Rufus. Whereas the Conqueror was fortunate enough to possess a blank chart of his kingdom – a tabula rasa – allowing him to dispense large tracts of land as he thought fit and creating magnates *ex nihilo*, his successors were constrained by the feudal system of land settlement. All the geographical blanks had by now been filled, and rewarding one faithful baron implied that another would accordingly be disappointed, disenchanted or disinherited – a kind of medieval zero-sum game.

There were three ways, however, that the later Anglo-Norman kings could redistribute land in favour of their followers: escheat, forfeiture and alienation. Regarding the first, a plenitude of noble heirs prevented much land automatically reverting to the king after the death of a barren baron. As for the second, thirty-three years of Henrician peace had allowed only occasional forfeitures of estate as punishment for rebellion.[34] The combination of these two factors left kings with little option but to alienate portions of their private assets – the royal demesne or *terra regis* – to their followers. The result was that 'the stock of royal lands was dwindling faster than it was being replenished [through escheat or forfeiture]'.[35] In 1130, the value of alienated land was about £41, but by 1154 it would balloon to £2451.[36]

An additional catch was that every time a king alienated his personal lands, he gained an adherent but he also diluted his own royal power as the realm's wealthiest landholder. Forced to rely increasingly for military support on their bloated followers, weakened kings were frequently prey to assaults by magnates with a grudge.

Nevertheless, the glitter and the pomp of the moment disguised the rot seeping underneath. Stephen's Easter court of 22 March 1136 was attended by almost all of the Norman and English bishops, and nearly all of the nobles, including William Percy. As far as Stephen was concerned, all was well: the Empress was a spent force confined to Anjou, David was an ally (of sorts) and the Scots had been appeased at Ranulf II's expense.

The battle of the Standard, 1138

The cordial relationship that had existed between Kings David I and Henry I is a puzzling one. David, according to chroniclers, was a humble ruler renowned for his charity and piety,[37] while Henry sometimes appears to be nothing less than moody, rapacious, sexually bestial and unforgiving.[38] Yet David, the youngest son of Malcolm III – a man not famed for his love of the Normans – named his heir in honour of the English king, and was proud to be earl of Huntingdon.

As a boy, David had lived at the court of William Rufus whilst his brother, Edgar, reigned in Scotland.[39] In the sophisticated South, David shrugged off his Scottish rusticity, acquired polished Norman manners and imbibed a great deal about modern Norman military tactics and cutting-edge feudalistic notions of land tenure.

Two events transformed him from being a teenaged knight on 'work experience' to a worthwhile contact in Henry I's watchful eyes. By taking David's sister, Eadgyth (renamed Matilda – evidently a popular aristocratic name at the time), as his wife, Henry instantly became his brother-in-law and protector. A few years later Alexander, another of David's brothers (whom he loathed), became king; as the former was childless and likely to remain so, David was next in line. Once David was crowned, Henry could rely upon him to keep the Northern peace while he dealt with his troublesome Continental dominions.

The benefits of having a self-appointed guardian soon became apparent. In his will, King Edgar had bequeathed south-west Scotland and south Lothian to David, pieces of land that Alexander only relinquished when David appeared at the head of an English army provided by Henry. The south-west, however, straddled the Anglo-Scottish frontier zone, and *traditionally* enclosed 'English' Cumbria, then held by the earls of Chester, 'but in Scottish eyes it was and remained an integral part of an ancient kingdom which had passed into the hands of the kings of Scots as long ago as the middle of the tenth century'.[40] Moreover, Durham and Northumberland fell naturally within David's Lothian sphere of influence.[41] Indeed, through his marriage to a daughter of Earl Waltheof – executed by the Conqueror for rebellion – David enjoyed a strong claim to the earldom of Northumbria.

In 1124, Henry's plans reached fruition when David was crowned king of the Scots. Thanks to his years in the South, his sway in the North and his well-known desire to 'feudalise' Scotland, David acted as a magnet for hopeful younger sons and gentlemen-adventurers, who were attracted to his armies, castles and territories, all of which were crying out for knights and administrators.[42] One of these was a certain Alan de Percy, one of William Percy II's bastard brothers, who rose high in David's gleaming military machine and was granted land in Roxburghshire in the Borders.[43]

William Peeris's chronicle of the Percy family tells of another illegitimate son named Geffray (known as Gaufrid in Scottish charters). To this 'right noble man ... David king of Scotland gave Hedon, & Oxencambe w[hi]ch bee in Scotland'.[44] Oxencambe is now called Oxnam – a town outside Jedburgh (in Scotland) and seven or eight miles from the Border; Heiton ('Hedon') lies near Kelso, about six miles from the Border. We now know that Alan was also granted land in those two areas of Roxburghshire. From the late 1140s, moreover, we can place Henry, yet another brother of William Percy II, but legitimate this time, who held lands in Roxburghshire gifted by King David. Grants by Alan and Geffray/Gaufrid to Whitby Abbey were confirmed by King David himself.[45]

From this evidence we can surmise that the Percy family enjoyed extensive cross-Border links, the senior line staying in the North and the younger, mostly illegitimate, sons departing to seek their fortune in the service of King David. It is important to point out now, for the sake of future reference, that these Scottish lands did not descend back to the senior line, for by the end of the thirteenth century, the Percys 'did not belong to the group of Anglo-Scottish landowning families who held estates both in England and Scotland'.[46] Indeed, Hedon later belonged to the Colville family.[47]

More generally, by the end of David's reign, the whole of southern and central Scotland (with the exception of Galloway) had been parcelled out among his new tenants in lordships great and small.[48] He was the first Scots king to issue his own coinage and to institute administrative reforms, like sheriffdoms, which were coming into vogue across the Border. David's goal was to shove Scotland out of the Dark Ages into the light cast by the twelfth-century renaissance (see below), but such an unexpectedly arduous task required more than just a few years. Ultimately, the process took a little more than a century.

During that span, while English and Scottish feudalisms appeared to be converging in a legal sense, there was a growing awareness of national separateness, culminating in the great medieval wars between the two essentially different countries sandwiching the North. Thus, after 1066 the Normans adhered to the notion of *kingship*, according to which they were personally bound to the present leader, rather like a wandering band of warriors voluntarily following a chieftain. In the English case, the king remained a king of the Normans only if his great barons *consented* to his rule, but by the end of the thirteenth century, the king was the king by divine appointment, which bestowed the *authority* to rule. Thus, the intimate relationship of king-*ship* evolved into a concept of king-*dom*, which doubly referred to the territory over which the king reigned and those living within its borders. In other words, the phrases 'kingdom of England' and 'kingdom of the English' became synonymous, allowing not only a detached geographical meaning, but also indivisibly incorporating king, lords and commoners – the 'English' – into a nation-state.

North of the Border, the equivalent expressions, 'kingdom of Scotland' and 'kingdom of the Scots', were never used before the 1150s. By the end of the century, however, they were commonplace. Just as an English geographical and national consciousness was being moulded, the 'kingdom of Scotland' was 'a unifying concept … bringing together east and west, Lowlands and Highlands [as well as] culturally and racially, for the sense of *regnum Scotie* was identical for the native population and the Anglo-Continental incomers alike.'[49]

While David focused on Normanising Scotland into modernity, Stephen was not allowed the time to reflect carefully about his Northern – Scottish policy, owing in part to his preoccupation with Normandy and the South. In January 1138, annoyed at his Scottish counterpart's continuing politicking on the Empress Matilda's behalf, Stephen broke his previous agreement and refused to grant the earldom of Huntingdon to David's son, Prince Henry, or to confirm the king's right to Cumbria. Provoked, David raided Northumberland and Durham, but was easily forced back across the Tweed by Stephen.

In August of that year, David struck again across the border, hoping to stir the Northern barons into rebellion against Stephen whilst realising his dream of a greater Scotland: that is, a kingdom enclosing all of England north of the River Humber, including Lancashire and Cumbria.[50] But this time David had misjudged the mood of the North-East and Yorkshire (although not of the Cumbrians, who fought on behalf of the Scots), for the Northern barons were understandably suspicious of a Scottish army marching through Yorkshire claiming to 'liberate' them from Stephen's allegedly iron rule. Directed by an elite guard of 200 Norman nobles, this army – the largest force hitherto summoned by a Scottish king – comprised archers and spearmen dragooned by their native leaders from all the provinces of Scotland. It was a disparate bunch, disciplined through cruelty, made up of Islanders, Lowlanders, Picts, Scots, Gaels and the notoriously rapacious Galwegians, that joined with David on the great expedition.

Despite numbering 26,000 men (according to one contemporary observer, and surely a vastly exaggerated figure), the Scottish 'common army' still suffered the same weakness that had bedevilled Malcolm III: its soldiers worked for booty, not pay. This made it cheap to run, but it was no match against Europe's most highly trained and heavily armed knights in pitched battle. Draw the Scots into combat, so the Normans had gleaned from their Border experiences, and you will break them.[51]

The Scottish commanders were aware of this strategy, but held a trump card: the advantage of short supply lines. For Stephen, on the other hand, the North lay hundreds of miles from his bases in the South-East. An expensive army of mercenaries tramping up there would be exhausted, so the Scots believed, and after they had played cat-and-mouse with him in the hills and vales, Stephen would surely negotiate. But, unbeknown to the hubristic David, he would be faced by an army of Northern barons and their feudal levies independently scratched together by Thurstan, the venerable Archbishop of York.

Two of David's Northern friends with large estates spanning the Border, Bernard of Balliol and Robert de Brus (who was on friendly terms with Alan de Percy),[52] had pleaded with him to call off the invasion if they entreated Stephen to grant Prince Henry the earldom(s) once promised. When the king refused, they regretfully withdrew their homage to him and took up arms.[53]

The Anglo-Scottish war of 1138, which culminated in the battle of the Standard, was essentially a territorial war where father and son, brother and brother, fought on opposite sides. William Percy II's illegitimate brother, Alan de Percy, fought for the Scots, just as did one of Robert de Brus's sons. Many families were split by the decision of illegitimate sons and brothers to side with David because they believed he would grant them the lands of their defeated relations.

The Battle of the Standard is one of the greatest – yet unheralded – battles in British history, the first major collision between the nascent kingdoms of England and Scotland, both inexorably intent on occupying the same limited area known as the North. In the eleventh century, the protagonists had been, more or less, equally matched: the Conqueror and Malcolm III were each strong, ruthless kings, but with the Scots riven by ancient hatreds and William's hold on Yorkshire tenuous, the outcome of any possible showdown was always uncertain. By the twelfth century, however, Henry I's reign as *rex pacificus* had accelerated his kingdom's economic, political and intellectual development. With the advent of the nailed horseshoe and the collar harness, horses – instead of ponderous oxen – were yoked to heavy ploughs, making agriculture more efficient. These improvements, in tandem with the three-field system of crop rotation, significantly expanded both the supply of food and the population, which flowed in large numbers into the booming cities and market towns. Administered by the new permanent bureaucracy, these were places where commerce was oiled by money, not by the disappearing barter system. Aided by such cosmopolitanism, a proto-renaissance emerged, stimulating an interest in antiquity and prompting the application of logic to theological problems. The first translations into Latin – the intellectual's Esperanto – of the lost Greek texts of Plato and Aristotle, the tracts of Jewish mystics and the treatises of Arab scientists appeared relentlessly throughout the century.[54] Such highbrow fare was not confined to the donnish; their practical influence can be detected even in the comical picture of a beetle-browed, hunting-obsessed Henry I, studying the habits of stags so intensely that he could tell the size of any one's antlers just by looking at its hoofprint.

Beginning with William of Malmesbury, English historians had heaped contempt on Scotland, contrasting its savageness with civilised Norman society. In no other sphere was this contrast more pronounced than in warfare. The Scots were not thought capable of chivalry: an evolving code of values shared by an aristocratic warrior class in order to regulate the intensity of violence (among other things), the first instances of which occur in the late eleventh and twelfth centuries.[55] After battle, the code stipulated, vanquished knights and defeated kings were to be treated humanely and honourably as prisoners held for ransom – a practice altogether more civilised and profitable than the blood-lusty massacres and mutilations committed by the Scots. To the increasingly 'progressive' Anglo-Normans, who had only recently themselves dispensed with such unsavoury bestiality, only the Scottish enthusiasm for slave-raiding was more repugnant than their love of wanton butchery. Thus, whereas the eleventh-century *Anglo-Saxon Chronicle* calmly described Malcolm III's slaving as 'carrying off people into captivity' – as if this sort of thing was commonplace – a mid-twelfth-century writer denounced the same raid of 1070 rather more stridently: '[Malcolm] commanded them no longer to spare any of the English nation, but either to slay them all or drive them away under the yoke of perpetual slavery...Old men and women were either beheaded by swords or stuck with spears like pigs destined for the table...Babes were tossed high in the air, and caught on the spikes of spears...Malcolm watched all these things without pity; merely ordering his slave-drivers to make haste.'[56]

So, in 1138, we have a Normanised king surrounded by a Norman warrior-elite invading the North for feudal reasons at the head of a Dark Age army intent on ravaging and enslaving. Small wonder that across the Border, David lost control of his men. The Scots, lamented Orderic Vitalis, 'spared no one, killing young and old alike, and even butchered pregnant women by savagely disembowelling them with their swords'. At another place, cried Richard of Hexham, that execrable army 'slew a multitude of children together, and having collected their blood into a brook which they had previously dammed back, they drank the mixture, of which the greater part was pure blood'.[57] By all accounts, David was horrified at the atrocities unleashed on the population he wished to rule.

With David threatening York, Archbishop Thurstan assumed his viceregal powers and summoned all those willing to defend the Church and the North. Among the fifteen barons who answered the call were William Percy II; his uncle, Walter de Gant – by now 'an old man nigh unto death'; Robert de Brus and his son, Adam; Bernard of Balliol; and William le Gros, count of Aumale and lord of Holderness.[58] Thurstan, 'a man of great firmness and worth, animated them by his counsel and exhortations...not to allow themselves through cowardice to be prostrated at one blow by utter savages'.[59] Forming a division of heavy cavalry, the total *servitium debitum* of these fifteen barons was at least 375 knights (many landless knights would also have been present).[60] Compared to David's guard of 200 knights, the Anglo-Norman superiority in arms immediately becomes apparent.

The Norman army gathered at Thirsk, a few miles north-east of William Percy's castle in Topcliffe, which lay alongside the most direct route to York, and then marched to Cowton Moor – open ground near the road about four miles north-west of Northallerton. If the Scots wanted to storm York, they would be forced to do battle.

There the Normans planted their famous jerry-rigged standard, composed of a ship's mast fixed on a low, four-wheeled carriage.[61] At the summit was lashed a silver pyx of the Blessed Host, and on the descending crossbars were fastened the banners of St Peter of York, St Wilfred of

Ripon, St Cuthbert of Durham and St John of Beverley – four of the major Northern towns and their saints. At the mast's base, a priest carved this diehard distich:

> *Dicitur a stando standardum, quod stetit illic,*
> *Militiae probitas vincere sive mori.*
> (Standard, from stand, this fight we aptly call:
> Our men here stood to conquer or to fall.)

Once the troops had rallied round the standard, the horses were tethered a short distance away: no man would flee on horseback this day. The archers were placed in the front rank; behind them stood the spearmen and lancers protected by mailed knights each wearing forty pounds of iron. Surrounding the standard was the bodyguard. Priests in their vestments girded the soldiers' morale with prayer before the Bishop of Orkney declaimed one of the great military speeches of the Middle Ages. Intending to bolster the Anglo-Norman conviction that they, like the Greek warlords at Troy, were sackers of cities while the boorish Scots merely ransacked villages, the bishop cried: 'Gallant France fell beneath your arms; fertile England you subdued; rich Apulia flourished again under your auspices; Jerusalem renowned in story, and the noble Antioch, both submitted to you.'[62]

As the Scots formed up, tribal rivalry took precedence over an effective order of battle. Thanks to his Norman schooling, David wanted to place his armoured soldiery and bowmen in the vanguard to blunt the Norman archers' salvos. The Galwegians, shock-troops who fought naked, immediately complained that their traditional position in the front line had been usurped. Their earl of Strathearn cried – in suspiciously fanciful language: 'Oh king! That thou hast committed thyself to the will of the Gauls, when none of them with their arms shall surpass me in battle to-day though I wear no armour!' At which Alan de Percy caustically rejoined, 'Thou has spoken the word which this day thou mayst not be able to perform with thy life.' To calm the friction between Normans and natives, David foolishly listened to this Ajax instead of his Norman Ulysses and he put the Galwegians at the front. Behind them, in one wing, the Cumbrian spearmen and knights were commanded by his son, Prince Henry; another wing comprised his Lowlanders and the men of Aberdeenshire, with the Norman and Scottish cavalry in the centre.[63]

On the morning of 22 August 1138, the blare of Scottish horns signalled the attack. Raising three howls, the terrifying Galwegians surged forward, drumming their spears on their shields as the English archers loosed their volleys: 'the arrows flew like the densest rain, rushing into the breasts of those who stood in the way, sticking into their faces and eyes.' The confused survivors blundered into the Norman ranks but their weapons could not penetrate the enemy's covering mail. One crazed Galwegian – at least – could be seen 'bristling all round with arrows, and nonetheless brandishing his sword and in blind madness rushing forward [to] smite a foe [and] lash[ing] the air with useless strokes'. Soon afterwards, the remnants of the Galwegian regiment crumbled and fled. Alarmed that some of his own men were defecting, Prince Henry charged, but many of the Cumbrians were cut down with lances and spears after the initial shock sent the Normans reeling. Henry and some of his companions barely managed to escape, but it was too late to save the day, and the rest of the Scottish army was put to flight only two hours after sounding the first charge.

Surprisingly, the Norman cavalry did not pursue those fleeing, but followed their standard to York to give thanks for their victory. Over the next few days, parties searched the roads and woods for Scottish stragglers, killing any they found. A large number starved to death during the arduous trek back home. The enmity that existed between the tribes and those they called the 'English' resurfaced in the aftermath of defeat: the Scots and Galwegians preyed on the Cumbrians, and vice versa.

Over fifty knights were taken prisoner, including David's chancellor, William Cumin, a descendant of the Conqueror's murdered earl of Northumbria, Robert de Comines.[64] Of David's proud bodyguard of 200 Norman knights, barely nineteen brought back their armour, and still fewer their horses, to Carlisle.

It is clear that Alan de Percy survived the carnage, for in 1152–3 he donated some land to Whitby Abbey.[65] There is a very slim possibility that he was still alive in 1176, when a gift was made by a Walter de Denton to Sallay Abbey. Among the witnesses is 'Alano de Hedona'.[66] Alan was a fairly common Norman name, it is true, but *this* Alan could be the by now very frail son who was given land in Heiton (originally 'Hedon') by David fifty years before. Alternatively, Alano de Hedona could be either his, or his brother Geffray's son, named after his long-dead grandfather. We shall never know, but more fruitfully we can note that William Percy witnessed Alan's gift to Whitby Abbey – Cain sometimes buried his enmity with Abel in the land above the Humber. It is a telling illustration that affection and hatred, as well as property, politics and family, acted as the five variables governing Northern–Scottish relations for centuries.

In 1138, however, the North had won the day. Thousands of Scotsmen died on Cowton Moor, but Norman casualties were negligible, the only noble death being that of William de Lacy.[67] After the rout,

Stephen travelled north and created William le Gros, whose gallantry had been conspicuous, earl of York. In actuality, this title conferred vice regal powers so that the holder controlled the finances, the military resources and the justice system of the whole of Yorkshire, just like a provisional governor. Between 1138 and 1150, Stephen created no fewer than twelve earls almost randomly, signalling that he distributed titles whenever he was faced with a regional crisis – a sure sign of weakness. Contemporaries frequently remarked upon Stephen's easygoing, amicable demeanour, but also noted that his episodes of tough-mindedness were often mistimed. By way of comparison, a strong, ruthless king like Henry I created few earls (there were only seven in 1135), and hardly any of those held real power.[68] But a little independence can be a dangerous thing. As Stephen's centre slowly collapsed during the coming Anarchy, some earls, including William of York, realised that they could offer the local barons an alternative 'centre'.

In other troubled regions of England during the Anarchy, there were two sides to choose from – the king's or the Empress's – but only in the hapless North would there be no fewer than five earls, two kings, a prince of Scotland and a duke of Normandy forming and dissolving alliances as they battled for supremacy. It is a sterling example of how markedly distinct were Northern–Scottish politics compared to national-Southern politics. And, due in part to his conflicting familial, tenurial and personal ties, William Percy II was right in the thick of it for more than a decade.

The Northern Anarchy and William Percy II

During the 1140s, Stephen left the earl of York in charge of his affairs in the North.[69] Naturally, the earl was granted possession of the king's alienated wapentake, hundredal and soke manors in Yorkshire, which were inevitably among the key strategic centres of power.[70] By 1140, York exerted total control over territory stretching from Holderness on the Humber all the way up the east coast to Middlesbrough (and twenty miles inland). However, there were two small but highly significant wapentakes on the coast – Turbar and Hunthow – held by William Percy's cousin, the very young Gilbert de Gant II, which inconveniently prevented Holderness and York's coastal lands further north from connecting neatly in the middle. There are another two immediately noticeable details about the configuration of the earl's acquisitions. First, the vast majority of William Percy's manors (such as Seamer and Topcliffe) are situated within York's zone of control, except for Wold Newton, Staxton and Ganton, which had been part of Emma de Gant's *maragitium* to Percy's father.[71] These fell within Gilbert's wapentake of Turbar, which also included the castle of Hunmanby. Second, in the centre of Yorkshire, York owned the enormous wapentake of Burghshire; adjoining this to the north was the Honour of Richmond, and to the west, the land of Craven, both rich potential prizes. Whilst William Percy held 17,400 acres of Craven, stretching twenty-five miles north to south,[72] Richmond at this time was held by Count Alan the Red's grand-nephew, Alan III, who had been created earl of Richmond by Stephen in 1136.[73] Overlooking the traditional Scottish invasion routes from the north and Cumbria, Richmond was now a domain administered by an earl of equal rank to York. Alan, who remained the king's staunchest ally in Yorkshire throughout the Anarchy,[74] was Gilbert de Gant II's uncle.

The potential conflicts of interest would have been frighteningly apparent to a rather nervous William Percy. In terms of family, his rightful place was at the side of his cousin Gilbert and, by extension, Earl Alan. On the other hand, his feudal ties and the new balance of power dictated that he pay homage to the earl of York. It was a question of geography versus genealogy.

In 1140–41, feeling confident as the king's confidant, York determined to annex Turbar and Hunthow. In direct opposition to Stephen's wishes, however, he built a castle at Bridlington, the main port of Hunthow, and secured the castles of Driffield, Scarborough and Pickering.[75] A glance at any road atlas reveals clearly that York had single-handedly sealed off Hunmanby from outside relief. Making his intentions aggressively clear, York began building Galclint Castle – specially designed and stocked for *siege* warfare – in Willerby, a parish only five miles west of Hunmanby. Willerby, strikingly, is in the midst of the Percy lands at Seamer, Wold Newton, Ganton and Staxton. York's plans temporarily came to naught when Alan of Richmond daringly scaled the walls of Galclint Castle at night and drove out the earl.[76]

In retaliation, York turned his attention to neighbouring Burton held by Adam de Brus II, then only an infant but a distant relative of Earl Alan, who, just as pertinently, also held lands in the area. York forcibly betrothed young Adam to his sister, Agnes (who was already married). The actual marriage – if it ever occurred – did not take place until after 1151, when her first husband, William de Roumare II, died (the significance of her first marriage will become clear). For his pains, York took whatever he wanted from the Brus fee: namely, the castle of Danby and various other manors. Soon afterwards, King Stephen was forced to visit the North and cancel a jousting tournament in order to prevent his two earls of York and Richmond coming to blows.[77]

These were the first shots of the vendetta. York and Richmond also vied for control of the bishop of Durham's lands in Howden, Welton and Northallerton. Richmond eventually emerged from the struggle controlling the roads to the city of York, so it was with good reason that he was rumoured to be capable of the 'greatest cruelty and craft', and possessed of extreme truculence and cunning.[78] If he stormed York itself, Earl William was finished.

For Percy, these were extremely dangerous developments. Topcliffe was equidistant between Thirsk and Ripon, and it would only be a matter of time before the two lords crushed him beneath their combined weight. Soon after, firing a warning shot across Percy's bows, Richmond broke into the church at Ripon and wasted the estate.

One explanation of Richmond's fury is that Percy had chosen geography over genealogy by plumping for York sometime between 1139 and 1141. A great deal of the latter earl's activities occurred on, or in close proximity to, Percy land, but Percy had made no complaints. After all, as William of Newburgh pointedly observed, the earl of York was 'more truly king beyond the Humber than King Stephen'.[79]

Where was Stephen? How had such a calamitous state of affairs arisen in the North? We must backtrack slightly to 1138 – the 'official' outbreak of the Anarchy – and consider the Empress Matilda's campaign to gain the Crown. Despite her absence from England, Matilda's party was not altogether weak: David I, as we know, fought her corner; there were barons who surreptitiously stayed true to her cause; and her husband was capable of causing Stephen immense trouble across the Channel. In June of that year, moreover, her powerful, resourceful and respected but illegitimate half-brother (Henry I fathered some twenty bastards), the 48-year-old Earl Robert of Gloucester, renounced his fealty to Stephen and handed over the Norman territories of Bayeux and Caen to Geoffrey of Anjou, Matilda's husband. Then, William d'Aubigny, the second husband of Henry I's widow, Queen Adeliza, invited the Empress and Robert to land at Arundel, in Sussex. By the end of September 1139, the latter two and a force of 140 knights were quartered safe and sound in England. For the remainder of that year and throughout 1140, Stephen and his friends were faced with an irritating series of rebellions, skirmishes, sackings and sieges from Cornwall to East Anglia.[80]

Because these uprisings diverted Stephen from a considered Scottish policy in the aftermath of the battle of the Standard, the resulting Treaty of Durham (1139) was a godsend for David. Stephen was desperate to avoid yet another war on yet another front, and so David and Prince Henry got more than they could have possibly dreamt – all the lands they had held before 1138 (excepting the castles of Newcastle and Bamburgh), with Prince Henry created earl of Northumbria. The Northern barons were permitted to pay homage to the Scottish royal house while remembering their oaths to the king of England – a confusing stipulation, which recognised the distinctly Northern problem of cross-Border familial and tenurial ties. And for all this – the present counties of Northumberland, Durham, Cumbria and Lancashire north of the River Ribble – David and Henry merely had to hand over five hostages and pledge their undying good faith and peaceful intentions. To stunned Northern royalists, it seemed that Stephen had abandoned them to the tender mercies of either the earl of York or King David.

By this treaty, Stephen loosed two more actors into the crowded theatre of Northern power-politics and skulduggery: David, whose ambitions stopped only at the Humber, and Ranulf II, the implacable earl of Chester. As his rightful patrimony of Carlisle and Cumberland had (again) been signed away to the Scots, he and his half-brother, William de Roumare, rebelled. But they did not join the Empress's party, thereby exhibiting the slipperiness of twelfth-century barons faced with conflicting tenurial and familial ties. A baron who was against Stephen was not necessarily for Matilda. Likewise, it cannot be said that the barons were utterly untrammelled by scruples in the pursuit of their own ends. In a feudal society, they unquestioningly accepted the principle of a hierarchy over which a strong king extended his protection in return for service and loyalty. But when King Stephen appeared to be putting the interests of the Scots before defending the North as king-protector, they naturally made their own security arrangements with neighbouring earls, high-ranking kinsmen, the Empress and sometimes the king of the Scots. Ranulf, moreover, was infamous for calculated inconstancy (he changed sides up to seven times during the civil war),[81] and his complete indifference to the Empress's Angevin cause mocked his own father-in-law, Robert of Gloucester (the earl had married his daughter, yet another Matilda, before 1135). William de Roumare, it is worth mentioning, had his own grudge against David and Prince Henry. After the Scottish king had invaded England in 1138, a brand new earldom was given to Roumare. Following the Treaty of Durham, however, the earldom was absorbed into Prince Henry's domain, leaving Roumare essentially jobless.[82]

Now in semi-rebellion, the half-brothers decided to settle an old score. Having failed to ambush Prince Henry en route to Scotland, they sent their wives to call upon the wife of the Royalist constable of Lincoln Castle. When an unarmed and unarmoured Ranulf dropped by to pay his regards, he and the three knights who had accompanied him overcame the guards and opened the gate to let in Roumare's men.[83]

Stephen, although furious, reacted cautiously. He placated Roumare by making him earl of Lincoln and rewarded Ranulf lavishly with administrative and military powers over Lincolnshire, all indications that the brothers continued to accept the general authority of Stephen except where their own interests were concerned.

In early 1141, however, Stephen treacherously laid siege to Lincoln Castle, but not before Ranulf had escaped to Chester and appealed to Robert of Gloucester. Immediately, they marched south 'with a dreadful and unendurable mass of Welsh', hoping to catch the king lingering at Lincoln.[84] Stephen knew that his army was outnumbered but he decided to fight.[85] To this end, the king summoned his great captains to Lincoln, including Gilbert de Clare (earl of Hertford) and, surprisingly, the warring earls of Richmond and York. Contemporary chroniclers, however, cast doubts on their enthusiasm for the coming battle – and they were right to do so. Many of them, including York and Richmond, deserted the moment (if not before) it looked as if the king was about to lose. As Henry of Huntingdon observed with no little understatement, 'perceiving the impossibility of supporting the king, [they] deferred [their] aid for better times'.[86] For Stephen, it was a disaster; he was captured, as were many of his remaining baronial supporters, including Gilbert de Gant II.

But with Stephen safely in fetters, the Empress mistakenly took her time – five months – wending her way to London to claim the Crown. Persuading a city that had supported Stephen through thick and thin to accept an Angevin dynasty required tact and diplomacy, two virtues unfortunately absent from the Empress's meagre arsenal of attributes. Instead, she demanded a colossal sum of money to recoup the costs of fighting for the Crown. When the merchants complained,

> she, with a grim look, her forehead wrinkled into a frown, every trace of a woman's gentleness remove from her face, blazed into unbearable fury, saying that many times the people of London had made very large contributions to the king, that they had lavished their wealth on strengthening him and weakening her, that they had previously conspired with her enemies for her hurt, and therefore it was not just to spare them in any respect or make the smallest reduction in the money demanded.[87]

The detested Empress fled on the eve of her coronation when Stephen's Queen Matilda arrived with an army and the citizens rang the bells to welcome her into Westminster. The Empress marched to Winchester, but her underprepared army was crushed.[88] She herself escaped by the skin of her teeth, leaving the luckless Robert of Gloucester as prisoner.

On 3 November 1141, a mere thirty-two weeks after the stunning capture of the king, Stephen was exchanged for Robert and the civil war continued as if nothing had happened.

Although a newly released Stephen chased the Empress to Oxford, he was unable to smash the rebels. Whenever the king stormed an enemy castle, Earl Robert would forcibly acquire one of his own. The opposing sides were finely balanced, and so, between 1142 and 1147, according to the *Gesta Stephani*, 'England began to be troubled in many different ways; on the one hand to be very hard pressed by the king and his supporters, on the other to be most violently afflicted by the Earl of Gloucester... but always and everywhere to be in a turmoil.'[89]

It was not until late 1147 that the stalemate finally eroded. Robert of Gloucester died and, feeling unable to continue the war without her brother, the Empress sailed for Normandy (which Geoffrey of Anjou had captured in the meantime) in January 1148. She never returned to England and died in 1167. But in the meantime the struggle for the mastery of the North, and the throne, continued.

Ignoring the exemptions detailed in the Treaty of Durham, Prince Henry of Scotland insolently took control of Newcastle and Bamburgh; David transferred his principal court, mint and offices of administration to Carlisle, and implanted his favourite Scottish barons throughout Cumbria. By 1141 at the latest, David dominated northern Lancashire as well.[90] Through intermarriage and feudal ties, David and Henry expected to annex Yorkshire peacefully from the east and north.

Percy nimbly adapted to the earl of York's newest competitor as a matter of survival. Of the Percys' Yorkshire estates, fully one-third – including Topcliffe – were close to David's new lands. Worryingly, David's nephew, William fitz Duncan, was married off to the immensely rich Alice de Rumilly, who held nearby lands in Cumbria (the Honour of Copeland) and Yorkshire (Skipton).[91] If the Scots did turn aggressive, the Percy fee would inevitably be the first to be wasted.

Percy's new neighbour occasioned grounds for grave disquiet. In 1138, William fitz Duncan had infamously led an expedition of Picts into Cravenshire. According to Richard of Hexham: 'Sparing no rank, no age, no sex, no condition, they first massacred... children... in the sight of their relatives, masters in sight of their servants, and servants in sight of their masters, husbands before the eyes of their wives... And finally, these brutal men... when tired of abusing these poor wretches like unto animals, made them their slaves, or sold them for cattle to other barbarians.'[92]

Seeking to safeguard his property (and himself, perhaps) from a similar fate, Percy persuaded his younger brother, Walter, to marry the twice-widowed sister of Alice de Rumilly sometime in the late 1140s. Two other arranged marriages of this time exhibit similar signs of self-preservation. First, that of the earl of York and Cecily, the absurdly young daughter of William fitz Duncan and Alice de Rumilly.[93] Second, the marriage of York's sister, Agnes, to William de Roumare II, son of Ranulf's half-brother, which took place sometime after 1145.[94] The earls of York and Chester had, it seems, come to terms: York allied himself with a north-western lord with the aim of squeezing the hated Richmond, while Chester acquired a friend useful for eventually pushing the Scots out. Any alliance between two such opportunist men surely could not last long. The ever-subtle York, for his part, made sure to maintain his loyalty to Stephen, even as Ranulf's relationship with the king continued to erode.

As for Percy, he had, through luck or guile, for the first time secured a great deal of protection as a result of these marriages. He had extended his family's ties into the Scottish royal house; he was newly related to, and not just a tenant of, the earl of York; and lastly – and this could be a blessing or a curse – he was a kinsman to Ranulf of Chester, 'a man of reckless audacity, ready for a plot, not to be depended on in carrying it out, rash in battle, careless of danger, with designs beyond his powers, aiming at impossibilities.'[95]

What does all this marital activity add up to? Put briefly, the Northern (vicious) circle was gradually being squared. For a decade, the earl of York, Ranulf of Chester and King David had been at each others' throats in the North. By the late 1140s, however, the warring factions were coalescing. The only fly in the ointment was the simmering feud between Ranulf and David over Cumbria. Even though David had tried to placate the earl by marrying his nephew to Ranulf's cousin, Alice de Rumilly, the relationship was too distant for comfort, especially given Chester's unpredictability. Yet, even supposing David magnanimously surrendered Cumbria, Ranulf had by now widened his demands to lay claim to the whole of northern Lancashire as well.[96]

In 1145, the slippery earl finally submitted to Stephen with tearful humility and made a pact of peace. Delighted, Stephen granted him the Honour of Lancaster and all the land between the Ribble and the Mersey. There was a small catch, however, because 'the honour of Lancaster if not south Lancashire was in David's hands in 1146; but now Ranulf was entitled to take over the whole if he could'.[97] Stephen's view was that Ranulf of Chester and David could fight themselves to a standstill for the next few years.[98]

But Chester's enemies at court – and there were many – were horrified: once Ranulf had dealt with the Scots, he would turn his army on them. They whispered to the king that Ranulf was planning some dark deed of treachery, so Stephen tested Ranulf's fidelity by requesting that he return the castles of Coventry and Lincoln and hand over hostages to ensure his future loyalty.[99] When Ranulf bridled at these demands, Stephen arrested him for treason and fettered the earl in irons. Chester was not freed from his squalid confinement until 28 August 1146, when he finally assented, but he immediately 'burst into a blind fury of rebellion, scarcely discriminating between friend and foe'.[100]

Ranulf's private war against Stephen continued throughout 1148, but there was a crucial development in May 1149, when the Northern earls and King David finally combined to form a coalition against Stephen under the impetus of Henry Plantagenet, the sixteen-year-old son of Empress Matilda and the dying Geoffrey of Anjou.

As the imminent heir to the duchy of Normandy, Henry of Anjou was keen to win his spurs fighting Stephen, and wished to receive a knighthood from King David. He landed at Carlisle, his presence providing a standard around which the nobility of the North, including Percy, could rally. It was there that Earl Ranulf did homage to David and surrendered his claim to Carlisle. 'It was agreed between them, that instead of Carlisle he should have the lordship of Lancaster, and Earl Ranulf's son should marry one of the daughters of Henry, son of the king of Scotland.'[101] Recompensing David for his munificence towards Ranulf, Henry Plantagenet promised him that when he became king, the area 'inter Twedam et Tynam' would be unconditionally Scottish for ever.[102] Afterwards, Henry Plantagenet, Ranulf and David planned an attack on York – 'a tiny royal island amidst a hostile sea'[103] – by gathering their forces in Lancaster and advancing through friendly Cravenshire and Topcliffe. As the great army approached York, Percy was assigned the task of harassing York and the countryside from his castle at Wheldrake, a few miles south-east of the city.[104] But when Stephen invested York with a powerful force of knights, Percy was cut off. Facing a protracted siege, the grand alliance decided to divide and confront the king with at least three threats in different places. Believing the trio's insurgency had fizzled out, Stephen turned his attention to Percy's annoying castle in Wheldrake, and destroyed it with the willing aid of the citizens of York. He then moved towards Salisbury, intending to scorch the earth from there to Devizes (where Henry Plantagenet was holed up).

This was Ranulf's opportunity to attack Lincoln, a major diversion that allowed him to settle the score with Gilbert de Gant II, who faced an equally opportunistic assault in the North when the earl of York destroyed his castle at Hunmanby, seized the family's priory of Bridlington and confiscated the Gant estates in the area.[105] To all intents and purposes, the coup eliminated the Gant family from the East Riding of Yorkshire.[106]

In the meantime, Henry Plantagenet escaped to the Continent; following his father's death, he received the title of duke of Normandy and gained control of Anjou. In a brilliantly dextrous move, Henry (aged nineteen) bagged Eleanor (who was thirty or so), the newly divorced wife of King Louis VII. The two seemed to understand each other quite well. For Eleanor, Henry was a potential king of England; for Henry, Eleanor was duchess of Aquitaine, the massive principality in south-western France. Merge the two together, and you have an empire. First, however, Henry needed to gain England and, fortunately, he now had the resources to raise a formidable invasion force.

When the young duke eventually stepped ashore at Wareham in January 1152 no battle of annihilation awaited him; instead the king and the duke (now recognised by Pope Eugenius III as Stephen's lawful heir, on the grounds that Stephen had obtained the throne by perjury) shadowed each other across the country. In August, the two armies finally faced each other across the Thames at Wallingford: 'wherefore the leading men of each army, and those of deeper judgement, were greatly grieved and shrank, on both sides, from a conflict that was not merely between fellow countrymen but meant the desolation of the whole kingdom'.[107] There was no dramatic showdown: Stephen's beloved Queen Matilda had died only three months before and he was tired of war and its betrayals. He let himself be persuaded by his brother, the bishop of Winchester, to accept an honourable peace and to open negotiations with Henry to arrange the succession, from which Stephen's sons were to be excluded. Prince Eustace sullenly provoked Henry, but died (conveniently) soon after, while Stephen's other son, the earl of Surrey, took his compensation and retired to his estates.

At Christmas 1153, the Treaty of Winchester, framed by Archbishop Theobald and the efficient bishop of Winchester, was accordingly promulgated. According to Robert de Torigni, 'the king first recognised the hereditary right which Duke Henry had in the kingdom of England; and the duke graciously conceded that the king should hold the kingdom all his life ... An oath was taken that those landed possessions which had fallen into the hands of intruders should be restored to the ancient and lawful possessors who had them in the time of the excellent Henry [I].'[108]

For the first time in England, the Crown was to pass – now and henceforth – by *hereditary right* to the heir with the best hereditary claim. Until then, whichever prince could attract the support of the most influential magnates in the realm through merit, promises, knavery or luck, had been able to raise himself to the throne. The assembled barons accepted the changes, even though the treaty stipulated the return of all 'ancient and lawful possessions' to their original owners. Now that the children of tenants-in-chief and undertenants had a lawful right to inherit the family estates, the king, as the nation's landlord, could no longer disinherit any man's heir at will and without reason.

Previously, the noble caste had suffered from such volatility: of the 193 baronies that were in existence between 1086 and 1135, only fractionally more than half (52.9 per cent) had successfully descended in the male line, including Percy's.[109] For the barons, then, any legalistic reform that increased the chances of male descent and so ensured continuity was a welcome one, especially since many barons already considered that their lands belonged to them by *custom*. After 1153, the Norman system of feudal tenure, whereby baronial tenants *held* their land by the king's grace, began evolving into a modern Anglicised (and Angevin) concept of hereditary *ownership* by a right enshrined in law.[110]

If a baron owned his 'property' (itself a new concept) by dint of heredity, then surely his own tenants – and in turn their subtenants – were granted the same right? According to what came to be called 'bastard feudalism' they were; thus, barons desperate for good service competed to alienate their demesne lands to tenants who sought good lordship *on their terms*. After 1135, for instance, Percy was obliged to grant away more than 60 per cent of his demesne lands to retain the allegiance of his vassals.[111] To put this massive transfer into perspective, at the end of King Stephen's reign, the Percy family held about 160 manors; a century later, they retained only six in demesne.[112] Just as the Norman kings had discovered at the baronial level, unless you subsequently obtained offices, privileges and favours for your men, when the land ran out, so did your vassals.

The erosion of pure feudalism weakened the personal relationship between a baron and his vassals, the more capricious of whom realised that they could play one landlord against another in return for privileges and patronage. Much of the time, the conversion of a previously feudal relationship into a commodity exchange was an ugly sight, and legal disputes between lords and tenants occurred with ever-increasing frequency (one lord even brought twenty tenants to court simultaneously); occasionally, it escalated into violence or simply boiled down to a compromise.[113] During Henry II's reign, as a consequence, numerous tenants transformed themselves into a wealthy and increasingly influential 'gentry' based on newly acquired property. By the beginning of the thirteenth century, 'honours seem to have lost much of their political and social significance', and money, rather than tenure, was the measure of a man.[114]

Back in the 1150s, however, it was well known that the deliberately vague injunction in the Treaty of Winchester to return disputed land would be honoured more in the breach than the observance. After all, adhering to strict interpretation instead of expediency would have meant that David must return Northumberland and Cumbria, a requirement contradicting Henry's pledge to King David in 1149. Henry was saved from any possible embarrassment by the deaths of Prince Henry and King David in 1152 and 1153 respectively, leaving the latter's delicate grandson, Malcolm 'the Maiden' IV in charge. In 1157, the young man was obliged by Henry to hand back Northumberland and Cumbria, thereby erasing David's gains. After the death of William fitz Duncan in 1153/4, Henry, now determined to make the North English, deprived the Scots of their Cumbrian and Cravenshire footholds. The benighted King Stephen died at Dover on 25 October 1154, aged nearly sixty. Two months later, Henry II was crowned and elegantly styled himself *Rex Angliae, Dux Normanniae et Aquitaniae et Comes Andegaviae.*

In the prevailing post-Anarchy atmosphere of forgive and forget, Earl William of York compensated his old foe, Gilbert de Gant, for the damage he had inflicted on the priory of Bridlington, and when Henry II visited the North in 1155, the earl returned his Yorkshire empire to the royal keeping.[115] Henry was intent on ushering in an era of royal centralisation, and reining in local potentates was a first step in that direction. In return, Count William (he had lost the Stephen-bestowed title of earl) was allowed to keep his other lands for life.[116]

More troubles might have followed from too many heirs chasing too few honours, but a most fortuitous run of deaths had unburdened Henry II of potential claimants, troublemakers and competitors: Robert of Gloucester (1147), Queen Matilda (1152), Prince Henry of Scotland (1152), Prince Eustace (1153), King David (1153), Gilbert de Gant (1156) and, thankfully, Ranulf II of Chester. He was poisoned in 1153 by a former vassal whose fief was sought by the eternally ambitious earl.

The inclination to lay old antagonisms aside, moreover, benefited William Percy and his heirs. The risks he had run throughout the Anarchy had eventually paid off in the late 1140s, and his gains were guaranteed with the succession of Henry II. He had adapted to the exploding confusion of conflicting tenurial, familial and political ties, and had successfully managed to reconcile genealogy with geography.

But how well had this hard-faced man done out of the war? He had done remarkably well. The most telling illustration we have is the *Cartae Baronum* of 1166, a sort of 'Domesday Book II' commissioned by the efficient Henry II for military and tax purposes. The inquest required, among other things, information as to how many knights – or alternatively, how much their fees were worth, thus allowing for 'fractions of knights' – each tenant-in-chief had enfeoffed on their honours at the death of Henry I – known as the 'old feoffment' – and how many had been enfeoffed since then – the 'new feoffment'. It appears William Percy had twenty-eight knights of the old feoffment, and had added 8.4 in the meantime (plus another 7.5 knights' fees derived from the family's various subtenancies), making an increase of about 57 per cent.[117] By way of comparison, in 1166 there were twenty-six Yorkshire tenants-in-chief whose average increase was about 21 per cent.[118] Although the number of knights enfeoffed is not an absolute index of wealth, the figures show that by 1166 Percy had risen to become the seventh-greatest tenant-in-chief in Yorkshire and a Northern baron of senior, but not pre-eminent, standing.

Now, in Professor Hollister's words, 'any magnate who had enfeoffed 100 or 150 knights on his estates by 1135 must have been, to say the least, comfortably well off'. The only Yorkshire landholder close to fitting this description in 1135 was Roger de Mowbray, with eighty-eight knights enfeoffed. This implies that a weighty tenant-in-chief based exclusively in Yorkshire, or the poor North, such as Percy, was very small beer compared to those magnates with lands scattered over a large number of counties, especially Southern ones. If we update William Corbett's system of measuring wealth, a picture emerges of Percy's national ranking in the mid-twelfth century:

- Class AA, 'supermagnates' such as Stephen of Blois and Robert of Gloucester with about 300 knights each.
- Class A, consisting of eight lay magnates, including Ranulf II and the head of the Clare family, with 100 to 200 fees each.
- Class B, consisting of twelve lay magnates with between sixty and ninety fees each.
- Class C, consisting of about thirty lay magnates between thirty and sixty knights' fees.[119]

In Chapter 1 it was shown that at the time of the Domesday Survey William Percy I was placed firmly in Class E, the very lowest, and most common, baronial status. His grandson, it seems, had succeeded in propelling the family into the lower ranks of Class C in the midst of civil war. It was at this level, however, that the law of diminishing returns prevented any significant improvement in the future. There was not much more room to expand in Yorkshire; to achieve truly national stature, the Percys required estates further afield than the Humber.

There remains little more to be said about William Percy II, except that in the early 1160s his wife died. Sometime between 1164 and 1166,

Percy married Sibyl de Valognes, widow of Robert de Ros, baron of Wark (Northumberland) and Helmsley (Yorkshire, about fifteen miles East of Topcliffe). Sybil was not quite the spectacular catch that Adeliza had been (although she brought Leconfield, in Humberside, as a dower), but in the less hectic days of Henry II's reign it is interesting that Percy chose to marry a woman linked to a steady but Class E Yorkshire family associated with the former earl of York.[120] Nothing tangible is known of Sybil's parentage, although she is in some way related to a well-off tenant of Percy's named Geoffrey de Valognes who died in 1169, probably at a young age. Perhaps she was his sister.[121]

When he died, of unknown causes, it was William Percy II's misfortune that, with the exception of four children born to unknown mothers (to put it delicately), he left no male issue to continue the Percy line.

CHAPTER THREE

The End of the Line?

Agnes and Maud Percy

When William Percy II died between Michaelmas and Easter 1175, he left two legitimate daughters, Maud and Agnes, and an inheritance crisis. William's only son, Alan Percy II, had predeceased him sometime in the 1160s, leaving a bastard grandson named William, who could not be sole heir to the family estates. With no other male claimants alive the situation was grave, but at least the Percy properties would not escheat to the Crown, for by this time the Henrician laws of inheritance assumed that, in the absence of a son, an eldest daughter and her husband had an automatic right to claim.[1] By custom, provision was also made for younger sisters, although the eldest had a right to the chief property; in Percy's case, this was Topcliffe.[2] Still, if William Percy II, the last male Percy of pure Norman lineage, went to his deathed disappointed that the Yorkshire estates carved out by his ancestors were now to be divided, he must have been relieved that his daughters were safely married to men of indisputably noble, even royal, blood.

Agnes appears to have been the elder because she inherited Topcliffe. In 1154, with the Anarchy over, she had married Joscelin of Louvain, the son of Godfrey 'Barbatus' VII, duke of Lower Lorraine (and previously count of Louvain) and his second wife, Clementia, the daughter of William I, count of Burgundy.[3] Whence this sudden, upper-class Continental connection? Joscelin had maintained close relations with his half-sister, the dowager queen of England, Adeliza, the second wife of Henry I. As part of her dower following the death of Henry I in 1135, Adeliza was granted the great fief of Arundel in Sussex, and soon after married William d'Aubigny. It was they who invited the Empress Matilda to land at Arundel in 1139.

Joscelin first set foot in England in the late 1140s, a couple of years before Queen Adeliza died in 1151, and he attended her funeral at Reading Abbey. He became acquainted with the young Agnes Percy over the next three years, and married her in 1154. Gerald Brenan, a previous biographer of the Percys, claims that sixteen-year-old Agnes was a maid of honour at King Henry's fashionable court, where Joscelin met her.[4] Less romantically, perhaps, we know that soon before Adeliza's death, William d'Aubigny gave Joscelin the Honour of Petworth in Sussex, which was part of his Arundel lands.[5] Illustrating the family's close ties with the Angevins, Henry Plantagenet, then still duke of Normandy, confirmed d'Aubigny's gift in 1154, probably to mark the occasion of Joscelin's marriage.[6]

A rumour, which persisted throughout the later Middle Ages and can even be found reproduced in modern geneaological compilations, is that William Percy II persuaded Joscelin to take the name of his wife to preserve the proud Percy name. It is also supposed that Joscelin amiably agreed but stipulated that he was to keep his paternal coat of arms. This is pure fantasy. First, there is no record of a 'Joscelin Percy' in any document; whenever Joscelin appears, he is invariably titled *Jocelinus frater Adelide regine* (Joscelin, brother of Queen Adeliza) or *Jocelinus de Luuain*, even many years after his marriage.[7] In short, Joscelin – the brother of a queen of England and son of a duke – never changed his name, nor would a mere Yorkshire baron presume to direct that he do so. We know, however, that Joscelin and Agnes's children later voluntarily adopted the surname Percy. Perhaps there was an unwritten agreement that the boys took their mother's 'English' name and not the 'foreign' moniker of Joscelin.

Second, regarding the paternal coat of arms that Joscelin wished to retain:[8] in contemporary accounts, his House's arms are described as 'feld Ore, a Lyon Rampant azure' – the famous 'Blue Lion' of Brabant and, later, the Percys (the first and fourth quarters of the arms borne by the Percy dukes of Northumberland since 1766 is 'field Or, a lion rampant azure'). Yet, no coat of arms is known for Joscelin's family until fully half a century after his father's death, and even then it is 'sable, a lion rampant'. No Blue Lion. A possible solution to this conundrum begins with the *Whitby Chartulary*, which began the rumour in the first place. It remarks at one point that 'of right the Lord Percy shold be Duke of Brabant, though they be no[t] so in dede'. Joscelin's father was Godfrey 'Barbatus', duke of Lower Lorraine and former count of Louvain; but several centuries ago somebody, understandably, confused Barbatus with another Godfrey, Joscelin's half-brother, later the count of Brabant. Crucially, it was *his* ruling House's emblem that is thought to have been a Blue Lion. In any case, the first time that a Blue Lion appeared on *any* Percy shield was in the reign of Edward I, more than a hundred years after Joscelin's marriage.[9] In fact, Joscelin probably bore the arms of five fusils – a typical Flemish device originally based on a wooden spindle which, in its heraldic form, looks like an elongated lozenge – although here we enter a minefield,[10] since it has been claimed that the first William de Percy's arms were 'Field azure, five mill pykes [fusils] or'.[11] Who bore what when remains uncertain; but certainly no one carried the Blue Lion at this date. One interesting side-effect of this confusion is that in the eighteenth century, Sir Hugh Smithson, the founder of the present line of Percys, claimed the dukedom of Brabant through his wife's descent, but received the dukedom of Northumberland as a compromise.

Even stripping away the encrusted myths of the Middle Ages, the marriage of Joscelin and Agnes is worthy of remark, for it heralds the arrival of the Percys on the national stage. Although the family still held Hambledon in Hampshire through the *maragitium* of Emma de Port in the eleventh century, this was a very insignificant manor compared to the rich Honour of Petworth. A local lord could only achieve magnate status by diversifying his holdings into a number of counties, preferably safe Southern ones like Sussex. Petworth itself was assessed in the 1166 *Cartae Baronum* at 22.5 knights' service (Hambledon was merely one knight's service), compared to the entire Percy fee's assessment of about 43 knights. Mysteriously, the same survey shows Joscelin holding 5.5 knights' fees in Yorkshire – probably a wedding present from his Percy father-in-law.[12]

If Percy successfully extended his talons into Sussex thanks to Joscelin, then he also cleverly expanded them into the Midlands through his younger daughter's marriage to William Newburgh, the earl of Warwick, a singularly colourless individual of whom we know next to nothing. We are left in the dark as to the date of Maud's marriage, except that it was 'before' 1175. It was Warwick's second marriage, and he left no children before dying on 15 November 1184 in the Holy Land.[13]

So it was that when William Percy II died, the grand Percy honour was divided almost equally between Joscelin and Warwick in April 1175. Maud, countess of Warwick, and her husband received twenty knights' fees and, among other things, the demesne estates of Tadcaster, Spofforth and parts of Craven. Joscelin and Agnes were given twenty-three knights' fees and Topcliffe, Hambledon and Seamer, the most ancient of Percy demesne possessions. Whitby Abbey and much forest land were to be shared.[14] Little more can be said of this sad partition of a Yorkshire barony, tended and defended by the sword for a century. Nevertheless, the Percys had enjoyed a good innings considering the frighteningly high extinction-rate among baronial dynasties.[15]

What happened to Maud and Agnes? In many respects, their lives ran in parallel: their husbands died within four years of each other (Joscelin of natural causes in 1179/80). Maud herself died between 1203 and 13 October 1204, and Agnes between 1201 and 13 October 1204. These coincidences, and the almost equal division of the Percy Honour, inspire us to wonder whether the two girls were twins, Agnes being the first-born.

It seems likely that Agnes enjoyed that rarity among dynastic alliances – a deep devotion to her husband. She makes frequent reference to her widowhood and prays for her late husband's soul in nearly all of her charters.[16] Contrast this with the charters of Maud's dating from after her husband's death in 1184: only two pray for the earl (and even one of those was dutifully drafted when the poor man was still alive).[17] Moreover, Agnes bore Joscelin four boys and four girls (no danger of the Percy name dying out now), but William and Maud remained childless. Agnes also seems to be the kindly sister, ensuring the livelihood of an illegitimate nephew with a generous grant of land.[18] Maud, on the other hand, made the ghastly Richard Malebisse, a ringleader off the 1190 massacre of the Jews at York, a direct tenant of her half of the barony at Wheldrake.[19]

On Joscelin's death his eldest son, the newly knighted Sir Henry Percy, assumed the lordship of Petworth. By all accounts a generous man, Henry confirmed grants to Reading and Fountains Abbeys and even gave the priory of St-Lô in Rouen the Hambledon property, which was of sentimental, if not great monetary, value.[20] He married Isabel, daughter of Adam de Brus II, baron of Skelton, Yorkshire, an honour that in 1166 could lay claim to fifteen knights' fees.[21] On Henry Percy's wedding day, he and his wife received the village of Kirk Levington, near Middlesbrough.[22] In return for the land, Percy and his heirs were required, every Christmas Day at Skelton Castle, to lead the lady of the castle from her chamber to the chapel for Mass, and then escort her back to her chamber and take meat with her before withdrawing.[23] This pleasant, if curious, ritual survived until the Reformation.[24] Mysteriously, Henry 'crossed the sea' during 1197 on the king's service – he may have participated in a battle against the French – but died soon after his return (probably of lingering wounds), thereby predeceasing his mother.[25]

He left an infant son, William Percy III. As the sole great-grandson of William Percy II, this boy was heir to the *entire*, reunited Percy Honour – after the death of his frail grandmother and childless great-aunt, of course. One can easily imagine the angry disappointment of his uncle, Sir Richard Percy, the *second* son of Agnes and Joscelin, at little William's sudden appearance. If Sir Henry had died childless, then Sir Richard would have inherited everything. Nevertheless, William III would only achieve his age of majority *circa* 1214, leaving plenty of time for his Uncle Richard to take matters into his own hands.

The result is a perfect example – hitherto unrecognised – of a legal problem known as the *casus regis*, named after the dispute over the succession to Richard the Lionheart. By August 1186, John, the fifth and youngest son of Henry II, was second in line after Richard for the throne and possession of the Angevin domains stretching from Northumberland to the Pyrenees; Henry II was in his fifties (and would die in 1189); his two eldest sons, William and Henry, were dead; Richard was unmarried; and in that same month his fourth son, Geoffrey of Brittany, died. So, if the Crusade-loving Richard died without leaving a son, the Crown would automatically pass to John. But early in 1187, to John's horror, Geoffrey's wife Constance gave birth to Arthur of Brittany, who stood higher in the royal pecking order than the king's youngest son. Suspicious of his disappointed brother's motives, Richard spirited Arthur far away from John and publicly named him as his heir should he die without issue. He then departed to the Holy Land.

Arthur's succession was thereby assured except that his father had died *before* Henry II. Could a son who predeceased his father be described as his 'heir'? And if Geoffrey had never been *formally* designated as Henry's heir, then Arthur's claim was invalid despite Richard's acclamation. So who was Richard's closest heir: the youngest son of Henry II, or Henry II's under-age grandson? It was a moot question and it was the *casus regis*.

Ranulf Glanvill, the greatest medieval authority on the laws and customs of England, put the two points of view thus:

> Some have sought to say that the younger son is more rightly heir than such a grandson, on the ground that since the eldest son did not survive until the death of his father he did not survive until he was his heir; and therefore ... since the younger son survived both father and brother, he rightly succeeds to his father. Others, however, have taken the view that such a grandson ought in law to be preferred to his uncle; for, since that grandson was born to the eldest son and was heir of his body, he ought to succeed to his father in all the rights which his father would have if still alive.[26]

Glanvill's opinion was simply that 'the position at the present day as between uncle and grandson is that the party in possession will prevail',[27] an ambivalent judgement asserting might over right similar to one of equally masterful, if callous, resignation uttered by William Marshal in support of John's succession: 'the son is nearer the land of his father than the nephew is'.[28]

John grasped the ambiguities of the *casus regis* perfectly and set about courting the nobles with his argument that he, of course, was rightful heir. Following Richard's death in France from an arrow in April 1199, John was crowned king on 27 May, but Arthur, now a pretender, remained at large in France. Three years later, John succeeded in having Arthur confined to the tower at Rouen. To 'neutralise' his dangerous nephew, he ordered the warden, Hubert de Burgh, to castrate or blind his prisoner, an instruction at which the jailer baulked. Soon after, Arthur disappeared from the tower and was never seen again.

With this ugly episode in mind, we return to Sir Richard Percy, coincidentally faced with exactly the same tricky problem at exactly the same time as John. Mindful of the royal feud, Isabel de Brus, little William Percy III's mother, transferred the child into the custody of William Briwerre in April 1200 to protect him from the potential threat posed by his predatory Uncle Richard.

Briwerre was a courtier-minister favoured by King John. As sheriff of Devon and a baron of the Exchequer he turned a tidy profit holding the wardships of not only William Percy III but a number of other under-age heirs. Also a lord in Buckinghamshire and Somerset, he was a protector with royal connections based at the other end of the country, far from Richard Percy.[29]

Richard may have been of an acquisitive nature, but before painting him as an illegal usurper of his nephew's fortune and title as previous biographers have done,[30] it should be borne in mind that, according to the laws of the day, he had a perfect right to claim the Percy fee. After all, had not the king done the same? Yet, on 13 October 1204, acting on instructions issued by the royal government, the sheriff of Yorkshire perpetuated the division: Briwerre would control the late countess Maud's moiety (her half of the partitioned barony) until his charge William Percy III achieved his majority *circa* 1214, whilst Richard received his mother's moiety.[31]

That settlement should have ended the matter, but mutual antagonism ignited over three decades of bitter legal disputes – including writs flying between the parties, the imposition of fines, tit-for-tat accusations, reversal of judgements and various subterfuges – which ended only when Sir Richard died, aged over eighty, in 1244. For instance, in 1214, as his first act as a responsible adult, William Percy III needlessly demanded five manors from Richard, including Topcliffe, claiming that his uncle had dispossessed him of them. In May 1218, with King John dead, the two warring kinsmen forged a new agreement over the division of lands; it was virtually the same as the one Maud and Agnes had amicably drafted decades before.[32] Inevitably, more legal infighting and harassment soon erupted, and a new arbitration of 24 August 1219 was torn up.[33] Two years later, William III opened another suit against Richard, which was still in progress in 1233.[34]

On 6 July 1234, King Henry III intervened and ordered that the affair be ended in his presence. He instructed the two miscreants from on high that the terms of the original settlement stood – permanently.[35] It is said that Richard and William III agreed to keep the estates divided during Richard's lifetime, but after his death, with a small exception (Settle, in Ribblesdale, which he gave to his illegitimate son),[36] his lands were to be handed to his nephew. This arrangement was merely to salve Richard's *amour propre*: he had twice married but had fathered no legitimate children and his two younger brothers were both dead, so his estates would have descended to William III anyway. Nevertheless, this arrangement reunified the once-proud Percy fee. William III died only a year after Richard, although it must have given him a welcome sense of satisfaction knowing that he had outlived the old curmudgeon.[37]

The troublesome *casus regis* gradually faded away and, by Edward I's reign, had disappeared from the law books. The question that perplexed Glanvill – can property ascend to an older generation (the uncle) or does it fall gravitationally to the descendants (the nephew)? – was resolved. Physics prevailed. The inheritance overwhelmingly descended to the younger generation. Thus if William Percy III had lived in 1304 instead of 1204, he would have been able to recover the land from his Uncle Richard.[38]

CHAPTER FOUR

Sir Richard Percy, the Northerners and Magna Carta

The only historical document of European civilisation that is discussed more often than Magna Carta is the New Testament. As the Great Charter, the first Statute of England, it remains the cornerstone of the Anglo-American political and legal system. Alongside the Bill of Rights and the Petition of Right, declared Lord Chatham in 1770, Magna Carta is the Bible of the English Constitution.[1] Perhaps surprisingly, the Great Charter of liberties was actually a workaday, practical document hewn from six months' worth of hard bargaining, and it closely – but not exclusively – reflects noble concerns. Its genius, however, lies in its adaptability to new conditions, and the manifold interpretations buried deep within its disarmingly simple words.

Sir Richard Percy and his Legal Problems

In the previous chapter's closing pages, Sir Richard's thirty-year struggle with his nephew over the Percy inheritance was outlined. Now this needs to be seen in a wider context, for this Percy would play a major role in the drama surrounding Magna Carta.

To recap, in 1204, with Agnes and Maud dead, Richard and William Percy III each received approximately half of the Percy estates. As William III was under age, his moiety was controlled by William Briwerre, one of King John's ultra-loyalists. For Richard Percy, losing the Countess Maud's share was a 'staggering blow to [his] expectations and pride',[2] for his claim as an uncle to the whole inheritance was perhaps stronger than that of his young nephew. However, he should have counted himself lucky to receive even this tidy sum, for Briwerre could have used his court connections to acquire everything, were it not for the *casus regis* – always nagging at John's suspicious and nervous mind. Given Richard Percy's penchant for dogged bloody-mindedness, had he, as an uncle, been deprived of land, uncomfortable questions would inevitably have surfaced about the right of John, another uncle, to the throne. So, allowing Richard Percy his moiety was intended by John to keep him quiet, royal connivance thereby allowing Briwerre to milk whatever profit he could out of his youthful ward, albeit one with only half of a great estate.

But Richard, born *circa* 1160, had patiently waited for forty-five years as the dutiful second son, only to be cheated at the last moment. Frustratingly, however, there was little he could do about it, at least for the moment: tangling with Briwerre meant acrimony with the king, and John could additionally unleash the Exchequer hounds onto him. Richard would be fined backbreaking amounts for small infractions and would lose any hope of preferment or offices; any debt he held of the king would be immediately enforced. These were tangible dangers. Many had fallen foul of King John; few emerged unscathed, especially after 1204.

In this year John lost his Normandy inheritance to Philip Augustus of France, and the consequences flowing from John's fruitless attempts to get it back over the next decade helped fuel the civil war against the king.[3] If John had quickly regained Normandy all would have been well, but for ten years he vainly wasted tens of thousands of pounds of his barons' money before their livid eyes.

Adding to baronial discontent, as well as that of the newly propertied (but heavily taxed) gentry, was the spiralling rate of inflation from 1180 onwards, as tons of silver extracted from the new mines in Tuscany, the Tyrol and the Meissen flowed into the economy via the cloth and wool trade. Inevitably, the rise in prices (reaching 100–200 per cent, between 1200 and 1220), in combination with heavier and more frequent taxes, affected the ability to pay of many families whose wealth was based on land let out at fixed rates, especially those who had incurred large fines for various transgressions or had simply overspent.[4] The most common way of sorting out immediate financial difficulties was to take out loans from the Jews.

After a few weeks' grace, interest would be charged at the standard rate of twopence per pound per week, and a defaulting borrower's lands would be held in mortgage.[5] Usually, the system worked efficiently and fairly, and in the North especially there was 'a vast and sophisticated traffic in bonds between Jews and Christians'. Many of the wilier ecclesiastical corporations and religious houses such as Durham enthusiastically bought up unredeemed mortgage bonds at a large discount, thereby building up their estates quite cheaply at the expense of their Christian flocks.[6] A large number of clerics actually preferred to deal with the Jews rather than with the official papal bankers. As Bishop Robert Grosseteste explained:

I accept a loan of a hundred marks for a hundred pounds: I am compelled to give a written paper and to sign the same, in which I acknowledge to have accepted a loan of a hundred pounds, to be paid at the year's end; and if you should wish to pay the pope's usurer the money lent you within a month, or some time less, he will not receive any less than the full hundred pounds, which terms are more oppressive than those of the Jews; for when you return to a Jew the money he has lent you, he will receive it with a good grace, and with only interest commensurate with the time the money has been lent.[7]

If all did not go well, however, resentful debtors identified the king and the Jews as the twin causes of their travails; William of Newburgh once described the Jews as the *regiis foeneratoribus* (royal usurers),[8] a possibly ironic phrase meaning that the king 'accounted as revenue whatsoever property the Jews … had in their possession'.[9] As the great jurist Bracton wrote, 'The Jew can have nothing that is his own, for whatever he acquires, he acquires it not for himself, but for the King.'[10] In effect, the Jews were imagined by the Crown as cash cows to be milked that could also be flogged off cheaply, for they relied on the capricious authority of the king to conduct business without harassment. Richard the Lionheart, in particular, was not averse to sharp practice. The largest debt owed to any Jew in the twelfth century was 6400 marks (about £4224), borrowed by nine Cistercian abbeys from Aaron of Lincoln. Newly crowned and running into liquidity problems concerned with funding the Third Crusade, Richard enterprisingly appropriated the debt and discounted it down to 1000 marks (around £660), strictly payable in cash to himself.[11]

Before 1204, John had raised tremendous sums by selling offices and land, settling taxes at a cash discount, pardoning barons of interest due to *debita Judaeorum*, accepting large 'fines' (voluntary contributions to buy the king's benevolence) to escape the taxman's hard-eyed assessment of baronial assets, and encouraging them to pay 'scutage' instead of performing military service. Regarding 'scutage', according to the original tenet of feudalism men held land in return for knightly service to their lord, but under the Angevin kings, substituting cash for service was a burgeoning market, helped by absurdly easy rates for the king's friends. Thus, a baron who was required on paper to provide forty-five knights might be favourably assessed to pay for the equivalent of five. In turn, the king hired mercenaries to fight his battles, and the baron used his bonus of forty knights' fees to buy privileges, speculate, indulge in litigation or fine heavily for John's continued attention.

After the loss of Normandy, this freewheeling atmosphere changed.

To pay for the continuing war, John relentlessly tightened the financial screws all over the kingdom. The distant North, which hitherto had avoided the Exchequer's close scrutiny, looked especially promising. Despatched from London, John's bean-counters were so efficient that they raised more than three times the Northern revenue received in 1199.[12] Penalties and amercements for minor transgressions rocketed. Thus, whilst in 1201, Alan of Thornton, a chief forester, was fined 100 marks (around £66) for 'keeping his forest badly', William Cornborough was amerced 1000 marks (about £660) for the same offence in 1209 (he died in jail, unable to pay the debt).[13] More ominously, any debts incurred of the Jews stretching back to 1186 – which had traditionally escheated to the Crown on their death – became immediately payable on John's orders in 1207. After that year, the Exchequer seized lands and property of those who could not pay.[14] These 'veterans among debtors' should obviously have paid off their loans years before, but John had previously pardoned them if they served on the Continent.

John was, moreover, determined to control the debts of *all* Jews. Debtors had to compound whatever was owed to the Jews directly with him and in 1210 he further imposed on the latter group an awesome one-off penalty of 66,000 marks (almost £44,000) for 'administrative reasons'. When one Jew had the temerity to object, John ordered that one tooth a day be extracted until he paid his due; after a week, John received his money.[15] More inventive ways of feeding the royal cash machine followed. A tax levied at the rate of one thirteenth of incomes and personal property 'of all classes, lay and clerical, feudal and non-feudal' yielded £60,000 in 1207, and a national customs system, the first of its kind, brought in £5000 in two years.[16] Many knights, barons, churchmen and small freeholders were unpleasantly surprised at the scale of the demands.

In 1204, the Angevin tradition of excusing and pardoning was increasingly replaced by penury and despair. One of the barons who later rebelled against John, Peter de Brus (Richard Percy's brother-in-law), faced bills totalling £2923 in 1208. He paid off a portion, and the Exchequer consolidated the debt to £1235 on strict condition that he submit £330 immediately, followed by two yearly instalments of £400, a real strain for a middling baron when £500 annually amounted to an 'exceptional baronial income'.[17] The £6800 debt that Nicholas de Stuteville had inherited from his father led him to lease or sell nearly all the family's property.[18]

But the king's friends were left alone. Instead, privileges, confiscated lands and pardons showered down upon them. For example, John de Lacy was pardoned £2800 in debts on 5 March 1214. Resentment spread from the North at such blatant favouritism, aimed both at the king personally and at the very arbitrariness of his rule.

Richard Percy was one of the very few barons who stood aloof from this casino culture, perhaps because before 1204 he had very little with which to gamble. Then, when he finally had some money after his aunts died, John began his clamp-down on debtors, which Percy may have regarded as an omen not to get involved. So never once did Richard Percy bother to fine with the king for office. His consolidated debts in 1211 amounted to just £31 6s 8d, a figure so trivial that it was ignored by even the keen bookkeepers at the Exchequer.[19]

His position was very similar to that of Eustace de Vesci, a Yorkshire landowner and baron of Alnwick in Northumberland. Like any Northern lord, Vesci retained strong links with the Scots (he held a barony there as well), and married a daughter of William the Lion, the Scottish king (1143–1214). Vesci parsimoniously kept his debts to an easily manageable 300 marks (nearly £200), and made only one offer for land (at 100 marks, or £66).[20]

The Rebellion

In the summer of 1212, determined to retake Normandy and the lost Angevin lands in France, John began preparations for the biggest military campaign in English history until that time by launching a detailed inquiry into the barons' terms of tenure and the amount of military service owed. For the barons, this foreshadowed yet another 'contribution' from their diminishing coffers, possibly the largest so far. But on 16 August, John learnt of a baronial plot to assassinate him.

The evidence pointed to widespread Northern involvement. Marching from London to hunt down the conspirators, John reached Durham by 3 September 1212. But the assassins faded away, with the exception of Eustace de Vesci, who fled to Scotland. Believing he had scared the Northern barons into submission, John headed south in November and continued his invasion preparations.

In the summer of 1213, John had to postpone his war when, breathtakingly, six Northern barons refused to serve, provide knights or pay scutage for the expedition. They claimed there was no ancient feudal obligation to fight anywhere but the historic homeland of Normandy. Other Angevin lands, they said, were an Angevin's problem – England should not be exploited for John's extravagances. Who were these six intractable barons, all of whom, no doubt, had been involved in the plot to kill the king? *Richard Percy*, Eustace de Vesci, Peter de Brus, Roger de Montbegon, Robert Grelley and William de Mowbray.[21]

Leaving aside his plan to avenge this act of Northern insolence, John nevertheless raised just enough money – thereby alienating even more barons – to set sail in February 1214. But at the battle of Bouvines on 27 July, King Philip crushed the weak English army, and by October John faced a brewing crisis at home among his discontented barons, who were tired of his financial transgressions and expensive antics abroad.

By the spring of 1215, in alliance with a large number of knights, there were no fewer than thirty-nine barons in revolt. Half, remarkably, were Northerners. Another twelve, led by Robert fitz Walter and Earl Richard de Clare, were based in East Anglia.[22] The Northerners, especially, were strengthened by intimate ties of kinship, cross-ownership and friendship, but, even so, these close-knit webs of Normans were eroding alongside the disintegration of pure feudalism. Since the accession of Henry II, capital had gradually replaced the family or property as the link between king, nobility and knightly tenants. This trend accelerated under John, when loyalty became a commodity to be traded on the open market.

Originally, the tenant held land of his lord in return for his fidelity and knightly service. But when the land's monetary value exceeded its intangible 'loyalty' value, there ensued a greater degree of subinfeudation, or sub-letting, among more and more tenants. Everyone skimmed the difference between the under-assessed 'loyalty' rent you paid for your land, and the market-derived rent you received for it. Thus, while the simple lord–tenant relationship still existed in principle, in practice nearly all knightly tenants had tenurial links with more than one lord. The result? As it was difficult to be loyal both to oneself and to more than one lord, knightly tenants dispensed with feudal military obligations and switched their loyalty to their neighbourhood, usually the shire. In time, these 'knights of the shires' would proceed to a Parliament of commoners as representatives of their territorial area. Importantly, however, in the North there had been far less erosion of traditional feudal bonds than in the South.

Returning to 1215, of paramount importance to the autonomously minded Northerners and the knights, then, were the unceasing raids on their purses by po-faced, ill-bred officials. In the days of the Norman kings, the barons' clerks told them, the king was *primus inter pares* – 'first among equals' – and he gladly sought the wise counsel of his tenants-in-chief. But the Angevins, and especially Richard and John, had designated themselves grand autocrats, and were clearly constructing a centralised, bureaucratic government machine tolerating no dissent.

So when a humiliated John returned from France in the autumn of

1214, the Northerners insisted that he adhere to the Coronation Charters of Henry I and Stephen, in which those kings undertook to maintain the ancient Anglo-Saxon laws, liberties and customs of Edward the Confessor (canonised, pointedly, in 1161, one of his redeeming features being that he remitted taxes),[23] which had been upheld by the Conqueror. Henry I, his physician once said, feared high taxes so much that he was tormented by nightmares of outraged clerics, knights and peasants rising against him.[24]

To the barons' minds, in the Confessor's idyllic realm it was pertinently laid down that 'the king is to provide just judgement with the advice of the magnates. He is to take nothing except by right of reason, by the law of the land and the judgement of a court. Officials are to maintain the just and ancient constitutions of the realm.'[25] The new baronial demand pointed a gun directly at the heart of the Angevin settlement. John was being compared, literally – and unflatteringly – to a saint.

Stalling, John situated his imported mercenaries in several royal castles and prepared for civil war. To isolate the hard-core rebels, he cordially summoned the barons to a council in London on 6 January 1215. There, although infuriated at the demand by Richard Percy, Eustace Vesci and Robert fitz Walter that he confirm their ancient Northern liberties, John wished to appear conciliatory and so postponed a final decision until Easter at Northampton.[26] In the meantime, he gained Pope Innocent III's goodwill and protection by proposing a Crusade (a master stroke that automatically put him and his possessions under divine protection); in return, Innocent, the ecclesiastical arbiter of European quarrels, warned the barons that they risked excommunication if they ignored tra- ditional monarchical prerogatives and hindered John's preparations for a Crusade. This Roman diktat might have persuaded the waverers that, despite his fiscal demands, the king held the moral high ground against needlessly intransigent Northerners – except that the papal letters did not arrive until the end of April.[27] By that time, the rebels had decided to renounce their fealty to John. They too could play the 'moral card': Robert fitz Walter, the rebel leader, assumed the overblown title of 'Marshal of the Army of God and Holy Church', perhaps reflecting the barons' lofty conception of their own crusade for freedom against tyranny. When, on 12 May, John ordered that the rebels' lands be confis- cated, he was too late. The barons had marched. Five days later, London's over-taxed citizens happily opened their gates to the rebels.

With his capital under rebel control and alarmed at the number of baronial defections from the royalist party, John sought a temporary concord with the rebels, although he was cunningly aware that there was still one trick up his sleeve: any charter granting the barons' demands, especially one extorted by threats, could be annulled by the Pope. The two sides agreed to meet in a Surrey meadow on the Thames, almost surrounded by water, called Runnymede.[28] On 15 June, John was presented with a rough preliminary agreement called 'The Articles of the Barons'.[29] Immediately afterwards he petitioned Innocent to render void the agreement, a breach of faith that the Northern barons had foreseen, as they themselves had no desire to appear as armed insurrectionists forcing the king to issue a charter under duress in exchange for their loyalty. They knew full well that without proof that Magna Carta was a 'freely given grant in perpetuity', it could be instantly annulled. Hence the cautious touches that characterised Runnymede were designed to counter John's subsequent argument that the charter was coerced from him. Thus, on 19 June 1215, after three days of bargaining over the Articles, both sides met under canvas at Runnymede, where the barons renewed their homage to the king and exchanged kisses of peace *before* an 'agreed draft which stated the terms of settlement precisely' was read out and all swore an oath on a holy relic to uphold it.

The picture of a glowering John personally signing an 'original' Magna Carta is misleading, if colourful. John, a king, would never have personally negotiated or signed anything – such matters being beneath his dignity – and it was one of his senior Chancery staff who sealed the documents with wax.[30] Formal, sealed copies of this draft – the beautifully precise and balanced Magna Carta proper, with the imprint of royal clerks overseen by Stephen Langton,[31] the archbishop of Canterbury and a rebel sympathiser – were made nearly a week later. Finally the rebels appointed a committee of the 'Twenty-Five Barons' (probably those best versed in affairs of state), including Richard Percy, Eustace de Vesci, Roger de Montbegon and William de Mowbray (all members of the original six Northerners who refused to pay the scutage in 1213–14), to ensure that John abided by his promises.[32]

The Northerners played such a central role in the rebellion partly owing to John's close interest in the lands north of the Humber. His father had only made occasional flying visits to the North, and Richard travelled but once as far as Nottingham. John, however, toured the North virtually every year that he reigned; indeed, he knew it 'better than any king since the ancient rulers of Northumbria' and his objective, as always, was extracting profit. Each time he left in his wake a trail of ransoms, amercements, fines and inquiries. In York, for instance, as the citizens had not met him at the gates or billeted his crossbowmen, they had to pay £100 for these transgressions.[33] The absence of John certainly made Northern hearts grow fonder.

For John, however, the semi-autonomous Northern barons had

enjoyed their wide-ranging liberties and privileges (such as the right to a gallows) for far too long. As he saw it, the frontier's rickety administrative, financial and judicial machinery needed modernising to align it with the centralised Southern system controlled by the king and his agents. In objective terms, the North was being exploited no more than anywhere else, but to barons unused to being exploited at all, John's annual arrival heralded a new wave of tyranny. They also took umbrage at John's attempts to break the cosy Anglo-Scottish bonds of kinship and tenure; he suspected (rightly) that the frontier zone was a hotbed of subversion and uncertain loyalty to the English Crown. The king was interfering in business traditionally left to the barons, who dealt with distinctively Northern problems – like the Scots – in the feudal Norman manner inherited from their forefathers. It was from the North, therefore, that the first sounds of dissent were heard.

Ironically, whilst the Northern rebellion was the 'last and bitterest manifestation of the old, of Norman feudalism'[34] against the shock of the new, slightly more progressive, system, it resulted in Magna Carta, the motor that propelled parliamentary government into being.

Magna Carta

The Great Charter of 1215, which was later revised, is a manuscript comprising sixty-three chapters. Some had a purely contemporary relevance, such as Article 23, which directs that 'no vill or individual shall be compelled to make bridges at river banks'. Others, such as Article 33 – 'all fish-weirs shall be completely removed from the Thames' – today aid in regulating navigation on that river. Of eternal interest, however, is the group concerned with general principles of law and government. Chief among these is Article 39: 'No free man shall be arrested or imprisoned or disseised [that is, dispossessed] or outlawed or exiled or in any way victimised, neither will we attack him or send anyone to attack him, except by the lawful judgement of his peers or by the law of the land [*per legale iudicium parium vel per legem terrae*].'

A 'free man' – *liber homo* – of the 1200s was not Everyman, but it did include everyone who was not a serf, so lending the term a wide currency,[35] although it is anachronistic to claim that Magna Carta was fuelled by any real democratic drive. Even so, John had once greeted the men of Kingston-upon-Thames, who in the Conqueror's day had been mere villeins, as *liberi homines*.[36]

Regarding the concluding phrase – 'the lawful judgement of his peers or by the law of the land' – the barons did not mean trial by jury, but rather according to 'due process of law'. The free men of England, in other words, were to be protected from 'extralegal or illegal treatment by the king [who] was to be bound by the law in his dealings'.[37] The king, it seemed, was not above the law, but was subject to the same law governing his nation. It was during Edward III's reign that a 1354 Act of Parliament clarified the wording of Article 39 to read that 'no Man, of what Estate or Condition that he be' shall be subject to arbitrary diktat by his governors.[38]

Magna Carta was a contract spelling out the rights and obligations of lord and vassal, ruler and ruled. It was the genesis of the contractual theory of government, which reached its apogee in the terrific clashes between Parliament and Crown in the seventeenth century.[39] In Article 61, for instance, Magna Carta condoned the ancient right of the ruled to rebel against an unjust and tyrannical king, but expressed it in the language of a contract. The barons cast the Article's terms in their own interest – they really 'aimed at legalising baronial resort to force without risking forfeiture of their lands as rebels' – but it was easily adaptable to general application.[40] For instance, the threat to 'distrain and distress' the king if his transgressions were not corrected would often be cited during medieval baronial rebellions and was later employed to bring Charles I to trial.

If the barons threatening to seize the king's 'castles, lands, possessions' if John broke the contract was not intolerable enough, even more so was the committee of twenty-five barons monitoring John for any deviation from the Articles. In appointing this watchdog committee, the rebels went too far. Many of their moderate supporters were frightened off by the concordant diminution of royal rights.[41] Sensing an opportunity to split the barons' ranks, John pleaded with the Pope that the rebels were stamping on his divinely ordained monarchical powers. Innocent III, annoyed that men like Richard Percy had haughtily ignored his previous warning, annulled Magna Carta in his Bull of 24 August, calling it 'shameful' and 'illegal' and 'impairing [the king's] rights and dignity'.[42] Soon after, a renewed round of civil insurrection erupted between the hardline barons and the revivified royalists, such as Earl Ranulf III of Chester, Ranulf II's grandson and the last male of the line. By January 1216, John held the upper hand, principally owing to the Twenty-Five's clumsy decision to invite the French and the Scots to join them, which not only inspired a further flurry of baronial defections to the king in the name of English solidarity but demonstrated that the rebels could no longer claim to represent the 'community of the realm'.

In September 1216, King Alexander II of Scotland – crowned two years before, he was the great-grandson of David – reached Dover, where he rendezvoused with the rebels and the French Prince Louis, who had advanced a very dubious claim to the throne. Apart from areas in the North and East Anglia, the rebels were locked within the South-East. John controlled the West and the Midlands, and each week saw valued knights and barons draining away to the royalists, including every prelate, abbot and great magnate in the realm.

Then, on the night of 18/19 October 1216, John, already a sick man, colourfully (if allegedly) died of a surfeit of peaches and new cider while campaigning in East Anglia. Hastening his death was the news that his baggage-train, transporting his treasure and royal regalia, had disappeared in the bottomless quicksands of the Wash (which is why Henry III was crowned with a golden circlet instead of John's crown, 'adorned with precious stones, topped with a cross and seven flowers').[43]

John's death should have renewed the rebels' hopes of final victory, but the efficient William Marshal, earl of Pembroke, supported by the conciliatory new Pope, Honorius III, ensured that John's nine-year-old son smoothly succeeded to the throne as Henry III. Marshal had previously acted as the royal agent during the Magna Carta negotiations and perceived that the barons' bellicosity was spurred by personal hatreds of John and his habits, not his son or the monarchy itself. No one, moreover, wanted a return to the nineteen long winters of Stephen's anarchic reign. Therefore, Marshal reasoned, moderation on the Charter question would diffuse baronial anger (as well as divide the bitter-enders from the make-peacers). In collusion with the Pope, the council that ruled in Henry's name redrafted Magna Carta – with some strategic revisions, such as the omission of the 'security' clause initiating the Twenty-Five – in November 1216, attracting a number of barons back into the fold.

By now Prince Louis's campaign was running out of steam, and the French, Scottish and English cohorts were bickering. After Marshal bloodlessly put to flight the French and baronial forces at Lincoln on 20 May 1217, more than 150 barons and knights (including several of the Twenty-Five) had submitted to the king. The indomitable Richard Percy appears to have been undaunted by these misfortunes; only a week before the battle of Lincoln, the king ordered that his lands be given to William Percy III,[44] who had scrupulously sided with the royalists along with his political mentor, and now father-in-law, William Briwerre (he had married Briwerre's daughter, Joan). After that, Richard had little to lose by taking one last throw of the dice but, perhaps fortunately, Louis surrendered with honour on 12 September after a tremendous sea battle. Marshal wanted Louis out of the country before he caused any more trouble, so the terms were lax and the confiscated lands and chattels of the barons were returned to them (Richard Percy's were returned on 2 November).[45] Nevertheless, peace reigned uneasily. Some diehard rebels like Richard Percy had 'itchy trigger-fingers'. Therefore, on 4 October Marshal forbade a tournament because, as the royal letter ran, 'our tranquillity is still slight and can easily be disturbed'. Playful duels, and a profusion of weaponry and liquor, mixed with the inevitable personal slights that accompanied these events, could suddenly explode into another civil war.[46]

Within a few years, all the fight had gone out of even the most intransigent rebels like Richard Percy and, after further revisions, the definitive legal version of the Great Charter, 'with the most objectionable clauses omitted [including the "security" clause] or replaced', was issued in 1225 and confirmed by the minor, Henry III, of his free will.[47] With nine of the Twenty-Five barons dead, the survivors solemnly witnessed its confirmation alongside the great loyalist magnates, so marking a final reconciliation.[48] However, some technicalities again prevented Magna Carta from being unquestionably adopted, and throughout the years 1234–7 it was a 'time of definition and law-making' in a series of new Great Councils composed of magnates, prelates and judges who 'combined to solve problems which affected English social life from top to bottom'. The Great Council may not have been a 'national assembly' such as a Parliament, but these *feudal* assembly members, as they said themselves, 'wish[ed] to keep in mind the common welfare [*utilitas*] of the whole realm and not to burden the poor'.[49] Thus, first on the list of the Great Council's concerns was the welfare of the 'community of the realm', a tremendously important phrase and concept with its origins in Magna Carta.

The 'community of the realm' is the *nation*. In its thirteenth-century sense, the 'nation' as 'community' was virtually synonymous with the *regnum*, the kingdom of the English, of which the king himself was a part. As merely a part, the king's power could be limited by the actions of other parts of the corporate community, such as the barons, the knights and other free men lower down the scale. Just as the Crown claimed certain rights and functions, then so did all individual free men possess certain rights and functions, but the barons collectively were thought to represent the community's interests by acting as intermediaries. The genesis of the parliamentary idea is discernible, but so too is the base of the English common law – the *lex terre* ('law of the land') – literally common to all.

That was one view, the baronial argument so to speak. But officials and Chancery clerks advanced an alternative interpretation of the *regnum*: that the kingdom was a 'royal possession, that *area* which the rule of their master, as king, pervades.'[50] In the king's eyes, the kingdom as a geo-graphical and administrative entity belonged to him – *regnum nostrum*. Those who lived in it were his subjects. Thus, as was described in Chapter 2, the earlier Norman identification of the 'kingdom of England' with the 'kingdom of the English' was already splitting, leaving an ideo-logical, political and constitutional gulf between king and barons (as representatives).

Between 1234 and 1237 the Great Council (of which the aged Richard Percy was a member) concentrated on reconciling real grievances with the great principles of Magna Carta. In February 1234, because the rights of the baronial tenants echoed those of the king's tenants, it was agreed that a tenant could appoint an attorney to represent him in court, even if he was bringing a suit against his own lord. Similarly, the council decided on 23 January 1236 that until he was convicted no man could be deprived of his lands or chattels. Another important decision concerned what is sometimes called the Statute of Merton. Roman canon law stipulated that a child whose parents married after his birth was legitimate. The bishops sought confirmation of this, thus aligning canon law with English common law. But the council refused: a child born out of wedlock, even if the parents married subsequently, must continue to be legally defined as illegitimate.[51]

The distinction was crucial: the Great Council predicted a terrible res-urrection of the succession of inheritance problems that had so plagued the twelfth-century if the heirs to baronies (or the eldest sons of dying men) were suddenly supplanted by their once-illegitimate siblings. The practical consequences on the Percy fee of this refusal to change the law will shortly be seen.

These debates eventually ironed out the inconsistencies inherent in any document drawn up hastily during a war. Hence it was not until January 1237 that Magna Carta was confirmed in a binding and unexcep-tionable form, and then only after a dispute over the costs of Henry's marriage and his debts. The barons accused him of ignoring the Great Charter's strictures on obtaining the 'common counsel of the realm'; besides, his finances were not their problem. Taken aback, Henry re-confirmed the grants and liberties of Magna Carta – even though he had done so already during his minority.

By this time, the only surviving barons of the Runnymede Twenty-Five were John de Lacy, Richard de Muntfichet and Richard Percy, the last warmly portrayed by the chronicler, Matthew Paris, as the grand old man of English politics whose unbending views commanded respect. Once, during a meeting of the barons at the king's palace to complain about the imposition of a tax, they left the chamber to confer. The young loyalist Gilbert Basset, a close associate of Henry III, whispered, 'My lord king, send someone to attend this discussion with your barons.' Overhearing, Richard Percy, whose ideas about baronial–royal relations never changed, roared, 'What a thing to say, friend Gilbert, are we aliens and not also the king's friends?'[52] They were left alone.

That Magna Carta confined itself to *limiting* royal power rather than *usurping* it entirely provides a key to its longevity. There was nothing revolutionary about the Charter; despite outward appearances, it was a baronial exercise in compromise and moderation. Its moderateness stems from the barons' collective recognition of the king's right to levy amercements, accept fines for office, call upon his vassals for military service and administer justice through the royal courts. But in return, the barons wanted to draw a legal line between acceptable and unacceptable use of regal powers.

Sir Richard Percy and his Legal Problems Revisited

The grand backdrop to the litigation between Richard Percy and his nephew over the Percy inheritance has been described. Furthermore, Richard's and King John's mutual antipathy suggests that this litigation was not entirely unrelated to Richard Percy's resistance to the king's authoritarianism.

The first suit was pressed by William Briwerre, acting in William's name as his ward, in 1212, just after John had caught wind of the Northern baronial plot to kill him. Up to then, Richard had escaped relatively unscathed, apart from the lawsuit, which he lost as a matter of course. However, to dispossess Richard by granting his moiety to his nephew was politically impossible when John had so recently avoided being assassinated; back would come all those unpleasant questions about John's right to the throne after his nephew's mysterious death. Here, the *casus regis* was Richard's shield against Angevin oppression.

In 1214, following the Northern barons' refusal to pay scutage or fight in France – an insult John could not let pass – William Percy (who had reached his majority) launched a second suit in which he claimed five manors from Richard. This case, commented M. J. Vine, 'has something of the nature of harassment of his uncle'.[53] That William Percy assiduously sought the king's favour by volunteering to fight in France in 1214 and sided with him in the post-Magna Carta civil war is no surprise.[54] William Briwerre had also kept his finger in the Percy pie by marrying him to one of his five daughters.[55] Without Magna Carta, William would surely have gained the whole Percy fief in return for his sterling service to John. As it was, nephew and uncle thereafter loathed each other. As we have seen, the legal hostilities lasted until 6 July 1234, when Henry III ordered that the feud be terminated.

This seemingly innocuous date assumes fascinating importance when three factors are considered. First, William Percy III's wife, Joan Briwerre, died in mid-1233, leaving him with four daughters and an unenviable dilemma. If William predeceased Richard Percy, the latter's claim to the whole estate would be strengthened, yet if William survived Richard, the moiety would be quartered between his daughters and their husbands – an ever-diminishing financial repetition of the division between Agnes and Maud. So, Henry III wished to clear up the matter once and for all after William's widowerhood. William, however, desperately wanted a son to frustrate Richard and keep his moiety intact. Hence the haste with which he married his second wife, Ellen, the very young daughter of Ingram de Balliol and the granddaughter of the chamberlain of Scotland, in late 1234 or very early 1235, the year that his son and heir, Henry Percy, was born (followed by six brothers, to ensure at least one survived to outlive the hated Richard Percy). William III may have met Ellen de Balliol a few years earlier when his daughter, Agnes, married her brother, Eustace.[56]

Second, the year 1234 marks the beginning of the Great Councils on harmonising the community of the realm with the king, the end being the final vindication of Magna Carta. At such a time, a symbolic figure like Richard Percy should have been setting a better example to others, and pressure was accordingly applied to both sides to come to terms.

Third, the council's decision to retain the division between legitimate and illegitimate children explains the reversion of the entire Percy fee to William Percy III on Richard's death in 1244. If the council had changed the law, Richard's illegitimate son, Sir Henry Percy (who died after 1268),[57] might have gained control of his father's moiety, which would doubtless have prolonged the painful legal battles into the next generation.

As it turned out, this Sir Henry, evidently a decent soul, bequeathed the manor of Settle in Yorkshire, which Richard Percy had given him as a consolation prize,[58] to William Percy III's eldest son and eventual heir, another Sir Henry Percy, in 1260.[59] The long rupture of the fathers was sealed by their sons and the Percy inheritance was reunited after nearly a century of turmoil.

CHAPTER FIVE

Sir Henry Percy and the Barons' War

William Percy III's son Henry serves admirably as a microcosm of greater events swirling around him. He was present at every major battle during Montfort's rebellion and a participant in the proto-Parliaments that regularly took place, yet his name rarely appears in the history books or the chronicles. He obviously possessed the rank, treasures and connections appropriate to his status as a Percy, but he consistently blended into the background, perhaps because he followed magnates far more powerful and wealthy than he, thereby escaping the notice of the monkish scribes recording the politics of the day. Alternatively, Henry may have taken after his father rather than his uncle and, following a youthful fling with rebellion, matured into a respectably colourless, middling baron who followed the orders of his betters. This does not mean, however, that he is uninteresting. Throughout his life, he associated with a court faction, as opposed to his uncle's adherence to the rustic Northern baronial group. As a successful, if unremarkable, satellite of greater bodies, moreover, this Henry Percy smoothed the path for the arrival of his son and his descendants on the national stage.

Henry Percy's Friends

Henry Percy was born in 1235, four years before the eldest child, named Edward, of Henry III and his young queen, Eleanor of Provence. When Percy's father died a decade later, the boy came into the custody of the king in stylish London while royal agents administered the Percy estates. Four years afterwards, Henry had found his own clerks to manage his inheritance and he paid the considerable sum of £900 to the Exchequer to release his land, allowing him to marry his choice of bride.[1] Between February and June 1257, Percy came of age and was knighted.[2] Soon after, summoned to the king at Bristol, he was given command of a small force in the rearguard (where he could do the least harm) of an army marching into North Wales. Percy's performance was competent enough for him to be summoned for further service in 1258, 1260 and 1263.[3]

Besides garnering invaluable military experience in Wales, Percy fell in with other nobles of his own age there. Foremost among these of course was Prince Edward, but there was as well John de Warenne, earl of Surrey (usually called Earl Warenne), born four years before Henry Percy.[4] These headstrong youths ushered Percy into an exalted political group, which included the (Welsh) Marcher lords Roger Clifford and Hamo l'Estrange, as well as Henry of Almain (son of Richard, earl of Cornwall, the king's younger brother).[5]

At court, two coteries vied for the king's favour, a sign of the rising factionalism during Henry III's weak rule.[6] The first comprised the queen's recently arrived relations from Savoy. One, Peter, was given the Honour of Richmond in 1240, and his brother, Boniface, was elected archbishop of Canterbury in 1241.[7] Opposing them were the king's half-brothers by his mother's second marriage. They came from Poitou and were known collectively as the Lusignans after their father, Hugh de Lusignan, lord of Valence.[8] They arrived in England after the Savoyards, but rapidly established themselves as rivals. Hence, William de Valence married the widow of the earl of Pembroke; Aymer, his brother, was elected to the bishopric of Winchester in 1250; and two others, Guy and Godfrey, received many favours from Henry III. As Professor Prestwich points out, the Poitevins were not as able a group as the Savoyards 'but their ambition and ruthlessness made them extremely dangerous'.[9]

Between 1254 and 1258, Edward was under the wing of the starchy Peter of Savoy, but then, persuaded by Earl Warenne, William de Valence's most steadfast ally, he changed sides. Valence, for his part, gladly lent the prince money to subsidise his exorbitant spending. Despite the financial inducement, throwing in one's lot with the Lusignans was not the most diplomatic of moves as by now they were almost universally loathed for their bullying and arrogance. In 1252, for example, Valence and Aymer despatched a Poitevin gang into Archbishop Boniface's palace at Lambeth to steal his money, silver plate and jewels. The Lusignans had also antagonised the realm's most powerful magnates, such as the earls of Leicester, Hereford and Gloucester, by taking them to court over land and rights. At one point, the fiery earl of Leicester (Simon de Montfort) snarled at Valence, 'You must know without a shadow of a doubt that you will lose your castles or your life.' This from a man famed for keeping implacably to his word.[10] Valence may have suffered some uncomfortable nights awaiting Leicester's revenge, but he knew that friendship with Prince Edward protected him for the foreseeable future.

The Politics of Henry's Reign

What had caused this bitterness and factionalism? The years between 1234 and 1258 are sometimes known as the era of Henry's 'Personal Rule', when, unintentionally aided by a slew of (natural) deaths in the 1230s and early 1240s, he controlled the government.[11] In 1241, for instance, there were so many mortalities that Matthew Paris remarked, 'And so, alas, the nobility of England passed, day by day.' By 1245, William Percy III and Richard Percy had died. Most spectacularly, Ranulf III of Chester's heir, John the Scot, himself died without issue in 1237 and so the realm's greatest palatinate and one of the last relics of the Norman Conquest passed to the Crown.[12] Granted to Edward in 1254, to this day the title 'earl of Chester' is a dignity retained by the sovereign's eldest son.

As the old guard faded away, Henry was left with a youthful, inexperienced court. Back in January 1236, when Henry married Eleanor of Provence, he was twenty-nine years old, and all his most important nobles (with one exception, Humphrey de Bohun IV, the earl of Hereford, aged thirty-five) were younger than he. Richard of Cornwall, and the earls of Arundel, Norfolk, Oxford, Warwick and Winchester were all in their twenties, and the earls of Devon and Gloucester were minors.

Another young man at court had a name that would in time eclipse that of any other thirteenth-century noble: Simon de Montfort. In the summer of 1231, he had charmed the earl of Chester (who had held custody of the Montforts' Leicester honour since 1215) into agreeing to relinquish it. In August, Henry III generously granted half the honour to Montfort. Although he was not ceremonially belted an earl until 1239, Montfort immediately adopted the title on assuming his moiety and enjoyed flaunting it about when the king was not looking. One of Montfort's first acts as titular earl was to try to expel, for no discernible reason, the Jews of Leicester. His swaggering pride and provocative actions tellingly provide a foretaste of what tumult Montfort was capable of.

To ensure harmony and reduce criticism of the influx of foreigners, Henry arranged a web of marriages between Savoyards, Lusignans and English houses. For instance, Earl Warenne married William de Valence's sister, and Valence married Joan, the heiress to the county of Pembroke. The heirs to the earldoms of Gloucester and Derby, Gilbert de Clare IV and Robert de Ferrers III, married two of the king's Lusignan nieces (Gilbert de Clare, it was said, could not abide his wife; decades later, he would coldly disinherit his children by her). On the other side, the earl of Lincoln, Edmund de Lacy and John de Vesci (the ultimately childless grandson of the rebel Northerner, Eustace de Vesci) were married off to the queen's Savoyard second cousins.[13]

But Henry's love-scheme backfired when what had once been minor 'personality conflicts', restricted to courtly circles, widened to include new in-laws and their kin. In 1258, these simmering feuds would eventually burst into a baronial war. With that in mind, a glance at Edward's activities – and those of his friends – in these years would be illuminating, especially as they relate to Henry Percy's decision to align himself temporarily against the king.

Edward's Party

By 1258, the young nobles of Henry's Personal Rule had grown up, as had their sons. Measuring a regal six foot two inches (hence his familiar name, 'Longshanks'), Edward's appearance commanded attention. Clean-shaven was his face but 'a sinking, or dip, between the chin and under-lip, was very conspicuous. Both the lips were prominent; the nose short, as if shrunk... there was an unusual fall, or cavity, on that part of the bridge of the nose which separates the orbits of the eyes.'[14]

In 1254, on his fifteenth birthday, Edward was granted gigantic estates in Ireland, Gascony, Wales and England. He was also knighted and was married to Eleanor, daughter of Alphonso X of Castile. The only thing which Edward lacked, and it rankled, was an actual title. All his friends had one. Moreover, he was forbidden to alienate any of his land to potential allies, as Henry wanted to protect the ever-shrinking royal demesne.[15] To prevent the formation of a dangerous Edwardian clique of flatterers, Henry appointed competent Savoyards, or their associates, as Edward's officials.[16] But by 1258 Edward was favouring the Lusignan party, who let him do as he liked. He was also attracting his own circle: chancers like himself who sought to make their fortunes, such as Henry of Almain (his cousin), Earl Warenne, Roger Clifford, Hamo l'Estrange, Robert Burnell (later, Edward's greatest chancellor) and Roger Leyburn.

For our purposes, the most striking omission from Edward's party is Henry Percy. Although, of course, friendly with Edward, he was then closely associated with the most powerful nobleman in England, Richard de Clare IV, earl of Gloucester, under whom he served in Wales in 1257 and probably 1258. Even by the standards of the day, Gloucester's loathing for the Lusignans (especially William de Valence) was exceptional and must have placed Percy firmly in the pro-Savoyard camp. By mid-1258, determined to destroy the Lusignans, the earls of Gloucester, Leicester and Norfolk, plus four other major lords, swore an oath to form a league against them (as we shall see).

They could count on the rank-and-file baronage, which overwhelmingly backed the 'Establishment' party of the Savoyards against the Lusignan upstarts. How many smaller barons, such as Percy, had personally suffered attacks by the Lusignans is unknown. Their support of the Savoyards may have been heavily contingent on their hold on the powers of patronage. Such mercenary instincts may explain why the more roguish, raffish Lusignans inspired greater loyalty (Earl Warenne would remain ever-steadfast) and had drawn Edward into their orbit. As for the king, he was losing control of his baronage.

A Shot Across the Bows: the Baronial Movement of 1258

Henry's attempts to reimpose his legal authority failed disastrously. In 1254, he had accepted the Pope's bizarre offer of the throne of Sicily to his second son, Edmund, in return for paying £100,000 into the papal coffers and sending an army to conquer the kingdom. Knowing that a Great Council would never grant the resources he needed – he possessed neither money nor army, let alone a transport navy – Henry postponed summoning one until April 1258 (by this time, Pope Alexander IV was sounding out the European courts for another taker).[17]

On 28 April, now in a hurry, the king requested aid for the invasion of Sicily from a council of his most eminent prelates and greatest magnates at Westminster, but was taken aback by the strident unenthusiasm of the Savoyard faction (which controlled the council). As far as the barons were concerned, the whole plan was not only a self-evidently stupid idea, it had also made them the laughing stock of Europe. Sicily was a folly, a fiasco, a giant white elephant. The council, nevertheless, promised to 'debate' it for three days. Fortunately, we possess an eyewitness account of the proceedings:

> On the third day, as the third hour approached, noble and vigorous men, earls, barons and knights went to the court at Westminster, armed in excellent fashion ... However, they placed their swords at the entrance to the king's hall, and, appearing before the king, saluted him as their lord king in devoted manner with fitting honour. The king was immediately disturbed in mind, and uncertain why they had come

armed. He said, 'What is this my lords, am I, wretched fellow, your captive?'

The earl of Norfolk reassured Henry, 'No, my lord, no! But let the wretched and intolerable Poitevins and all aliens flee from your face and ours as from the face of a lion, and there will be glory to God in the heavens, and in your land peace to men of goodwill.' Norfolk then revealed to the king that the barons wished for him – and Edward, pointedly, given his recent political affiliations – to adhere to 'our counsels'. What did this adherence involve? asked Henry, to which Norfolk replied: 'Together with your son and heir Edward, swear on the Gospels that, without the consent of twenty-four prudent men of England to be chosen ... you will impose no ... unaccustomed yoke [for example tax] ... and that you will not delay handing your royal seal [symbolising executive power], through the counsel of the foresaid [twenty-four], to a discreet man whom they will provide.'

Thus, later that day, 'the king ... seeing that he was not able to put the matter off any further, along with Edward his son and heir, *although the latter was unwilling* [italics added], swore on the Gospels ... and commended everything to their counsel [that is, of the twenty-four] ... and approved all things which they wished to be done.'[18] On 2 May, after detailed negotiations, a royal letter recording the king's oath omitted the requirements not to levy tax without counsel and to hand over the seal; instead, the king and the magnates would each select twelve men to serve on the council of twenty-four. Furthermore, in exchange for dropping the tax-and-seal clauses, the king and Edward had to concede that 'whatever shall be ordained on this matter [the reform of the realm] by the twenty-four ... we will observe inviolably'. To sweeten the insult, the magnates promised that 'they will do their best, in good faith, to ensure that a common aid shall be granted to us by the community of the realm' in order to save the Sicilian deal.[19] Note how the nobles carefully pledged to 'do their best' but did not affirm that aid would be granted. However, Edward swore no oath to uphold the revised wording.

In Oxford, on 11 June 1258, king and magnates met in a 'parliament' to draw up concrete reform proposals and announce the members of the twenty-four. Elected for the king, among others, were the stalwarts Henry of Almain, Earl Warenne, Guy de Lusignan and William de Valence. The baronial side featured the usual suspects of Montfort, Gloucester, Hereford, Hugh Bigod, Peter de Montfort and Hugh Despenser. The outcome was a written constitution of sorts called the 'Provisions of Oxford', which laid down that a privy council of fifteen would 'devise a general programme of legislative and administrative

reform'.[20] That privy council would be appointed by four representatives
– two each from the baronial and royal halves of the twenty-four – to rule
in tandem with the king, who had to clear anything that affected the
'community of the realm' with the privy council. Additionally a justiciar
(Hugh Bigod, brother of the earl of Norfolk) was appointed to oversee
the renovation of justice, despite his non-existent legal experience.[21] The
barons were determined to stamp out the Lusignan bias of the courts.

There remained unfinished business with the Lusignans. During the
Oxford Parliament, William de Valence had not faded into the background. On one fiery day, Valence accused Gloucester, Leicester and
other leading barons of plotting treachery with the Welsh; only the king's
personal intervention prevented Leicester from striking Valence. After
dealing with the legislative and administrative reforms, the magnates,
according to the chronicler Matthew Paris, claimed that Henry had
'exalted his uterine brothers [the Lusignans] in a most intolerable fashion,
as if they had been native born, contrary to the right and law of the
kingdom'. It was at this point that the league of seven major lords led by
Gloucester, Leicester and Norfolk – and including Peter of Savoy, Hugh
Bigod (the justiciar and brother of Norfolk), John FitzGeoffrey and Peter
de Montfort (no relation to Simon, although a close ally) – combined to
destroy the Lusignan ascendancy. Get rid of the Lusignan boys, the
thinking went, and England could return to good, sound government and
the rule of law. All came to Oxford fully armed and fully prepared to go
to war if the king bull-headedly backed his half-brothers.

The Seven cleverly dressed up their attack as a means of improving
Henry's financial position. They forwarded a fiercely anti-alien 'Petition
of the Barons',[22] the gist of which was the return of 'all the lands, holdings and castles alienated from the Crown by him [the king]' as William
de Valence, 'since coming to England in 1247 … had received far more
land from the king than anyone else'. Now facing ruin,[23] the Lusignans
heroically told the Parliament that 'by the death and wounds of Christ …
they would not surrender the castles, lands and wardships given them by
the king'. To which Simon de Montfort urbanely replied, 'Well, either
you give up your castles or you lose your head.'[24]

The Lusignans had one trump left: Edward. Irritated at being dictated
to, towards the end of June Edward provocatively announced new
appointments for Geoffrey and Guy de Lusignan. But the privy council
reiterated that no one could be appointed without *its* permission, plus, of
course, royal consent, it added as something of an afterthought. Early the
next month, realising the game was up, Valence, Aymer, Geoffrey and
Guy fled to Winchester, where on 10 July they surrendered. On that same
day, forsaking his Lusignan cronies, Edward took his oath to the

Provisions of Oxford. On 14 July 1258, the four Lusignans sailed across the Channel into exile.

Where did this leave the leading actors? King Henry had been buffeted, but the magnates, who proclaimed their loyalty repeatedly, had been careful not to alienate him. The vast majority of moderate barons, moreover, could resume their place by his side. After his Lusignan flirtation, Edward remained something of a loose cannon, but it was hoped he would grow bored with dilettantish politicking and return to his duties as heir. On the reformers' side, Gloucester and Leicester remained in control, although the latter was becoming dangerously fixated on the constitutional problem, whilst Gloucester recognised that with the inflammatory Lusignans purged, compromise could bring tranquillity.

Henry Percy was in Gloucester's entourage, and it can be inferred that he was among the moderate reformers. There is no record of any connection between Percy and the Lusignans, nor of any legal disputes between them. Therefore, if Percy did not have any *personal* enmity towards the Lusignans, why is he numbered among Gloucester's moderate reformers? First, he was barely past the age of majority and the baronial reform movement ('Remember the Provisions of Oxford!') was a seductively idealistic one. Second, although Henry Percy was the rebellious Richard Percy's nephew, he was also son of the ultra-loyalist William III. This 'mixed blood' helps to explain Henry's disinclination to decide whether he was really a loyalist royalist or a firebreathing Montfortian rebel.

The Iron Pact and its Aftermath

At the end of July 1258, a fortnight after abandoning the Lusignans, Edward met Gloucester and his brother William de Clare, evidently because he had come to terms with the cause of moderate reform. However, a terrible occurrence of food-poisoning (one reason why infants drank wine was that it was less deadly than water) marred the occasion. Both of the Clares fell sick, and William died in agony shortly afterwards. As for the earl, his hair fell out, and his fingernails and toenails, after rotting, snapped off. Gloucester's steward was subsequently hanged for poisoning his masters. Curiously, he happened to be Edward's tenant, so the prince took control of his lands.[25]

Fortunately, Gloucester did not believe Edward was involved and, once he recovered, concluded a pact of mutual support with the prince on 14 March 1259. But a pact against whom? Strikingly, since their alliance against the Lusignans, Gloucester had grown disenchanted with Montfort, whose descent into outright radicalism threatened to overturn the new status quo. In February 1259, for instance, at a Parliament where the barons were discussing the Provisions of Oxford, Gloucester expressed some doubts about some of the clauses, whereupon Montfort furiously exclaimed (and the earl of Hereford nodded in agreement), 'I hate to live with such changeable and treacherous men. We have sworn to do these things.'[26] For Montfort, anyone who dared question his will or The Cause was a traitor and his mortal enemy. Such blind rectitude, and the bizarre assertion that Henry III was an Oriental-style autocrat, did not endear him to moderates like Henry Percy. There were whispers about the earl of Leicester's own tyrannical tendencies.

What Edward gained from the pact is unclear. Surprisingly, he had more in common with Montfort (leaving aside some of Leicester's more unbalanced views) than with Gloucester. Thus, fewer than eight months after his pact with Gloucester against Montfort, Edward switched sides again. Gloucester had been more trouble than he was worth, and the two had almost come to blows over some competing land claims in the West of England. On 15 October 1259, Edward swore an oath to give aid and counsel to Montfort.

At the time, an Edward–Montfort combination was a natural fit. A treaty under negotiation with the French proposed that Henry III, who had given up on the possibility of ever regaining the Angevin lands lost by his father, renounce his sovereign rights in Normandy, Maine, Touraine and Anjou, and accept vassal status in Aquitaine, which meant performing homage to the French sovereign.

A word on Aquitaine. Confusingly, the English sometimes used the term 'Gascony' interchangeably with Aquitaine. Most of Gascony, a former duchy, passed to the dukes of Aquitaine in the eleventh century, which in turn was joined to France when Eleanor of Aquitaine wed Louis VII in 1137. Her subsequent marriage to Henry II of England in the 1150s set the stage for a long struggle between England and France for possession of Aquitaine/Gascony.

While the French terms were not terrific, for Henry an appeased King Louis IX might potentially make a useful ally against Montfort. Indeed, the only English negotiator to oppose the treaty strenuously was Montfort, for his wife (Eleanor, sister of Henry III) refused to surrender her claims in Normandy. Gloucester, another negotiator hoping to manage English decline in a temperate manner, was furious with Leicester's obstruction, and backed the treaty equally strenuously.

If the treaty was agreed, however, Edward's territory of Gascony would lie exposed to eventual French annexation, but Louis IX refused to conclude negotiations without Eleanor's renunciation. So, keeping on Montfort's good side was, therefore, a matter of the greatest importance for Edward. The Treaty of Paris (1259) was eventually sealed when it omitted the clauses requiring the countess of Leicester to renounce her claims. Edward bitterly blamed Gloucester for the treaty's success.[27]

Although the Gloucester–Edward pact was dead, it exerted a lasting impact on Percy. As he was listed as one of Gloucester's supporters,[28] the pact had naturally brought him into contact with the far less stuffy – and vastly more flashy and knavish – 'set' surrounding Lord Edward: caddish men like Earl Warenne, Henry of Almain, Roger Clifford and Philip Basset (a future justiciar, of all things). It was time to switch horses, in other words, and when the pact eventually dissolved, Percy calculatingly stayed in Edward's entourage. It proved a wise choice: Gloucester would die in 1262, and Percy was edging towards the royalists at exactly the right time.

By the spring of 1260, Henry III, worried by reports of Edward's feud with Gloucester, summoned the barons and their entourages to London, stipulating that they be escorted by the knights they owed under their feudal obligations.[29] Although the gathering of so many armed men could turn dangerous, Henry aimed to awe the feuding barons with a display of his regal power to convoke a feudal host. The barons remained, theoretically at least, his vassals, which they seem to have forgotten. And Henry Percy, given his association with the errant Edward, was one of those summoned.[30]

Londoners were nervous. Two armed retinues were descending upon them, but Richard of Cornwall sensibly allowed only their leaders into the city. It was in late April that Henry, through the agency of Cornwall and the archbishop of Canterbury, reconciled Edward and Gloucester. They even promised to relinquish their rival claims on each other's land. During the spring of 1260, then, the whip-hand of royal authority was gradually reasserting itself in the country.

Until November, that is. In the meantime, Edward amused himself at foreign tournaments (his performance was unspectacular by all accounts), but he was again falling into bad habits. Visiting Paris at the end of November 1260, he succumbed to the fatal Lusignan charm and, against the council's express order, returned to England in the spring of 1261 with William de Valence, granting him lavish favours.[31]

Edward's shucking of council authority coincided with his father's successful effort to overthrow the watchdog baronial government and rid himself of the tiresome Provisions of Oxford.[32] Henry complained that the council had lately gone too far by appointing a new justiciar, chancellor and treasurer against his wishes; that the barons had stripped him of 'his power and royal dignity, so that no one carries out his orders'; that the councillors were corrupt and incompetent; that brigandage was rising, tenants were worse off than before, and castles and manors were falling into disrepair. He also claimed that 'by the counsel of a certain man [Montfort] Edward had been seduced from his father's friendship and obedience'.[33] His envoy in Rome accordingly obtained a papal bull on 13 April 1261, absolving the king and others from their oaths, and in June Henry formally rejected the Provisions of Oxford.[34] Steeling himself for baronial resistance, Henry strengthened the Tower of London's defences, but the barons – agreeing with Gloucester that the radicals had needlessly provoked the king by enforcing the Provisions to the *exact* letter – remained silent.[35] Montfort did not. Declaiming heroically that 'he preferred to die without land than ... depart from the truth', Montfort stormed out of the chamber and left the country for the following year, during which he returned only once – when the king was in France – to remind the barons ominously that 'the Provisions made at Oxford [must] be held in all things'.[36]

During Montfort's absence, Queen Eleanor – a devoted, sometimes overprotective mother – was not enamoured with the company Edward had been keeping.[37] In late February 1262, after hearing the latest court gossip, she told her son that Roger Leyburn, his old friend and the man entrusted with his finances, had been misappropriating funds. When Leyburn had his own lands appropriated, a split developed between Edward and his supporters, such as Henry of Almain, Earl Warenne, Roger Clifford and Henry Percy, with the prince suspecting that he had been used. With Montfort abroad sulking, Gloucester dying, his friends snubbed, Edward was drawing very close to his father in 1262–3. Henry even kindly granted him all the revenue derived from the Jews for three years to help him out of his chronic financial woes.[38]

National affairs appeared to be stable, moreover, and Henry was daily strengthening his mastership of the royal government. The baronial flurry of idealism was disillusioned, with its king over the water. But below the placid surface, the government was collapsing. Henry was in France after July 1262 discussing the Treaty of Paris with Louis IX and visiting shrines to satisfy his pietistical urges (Edward was named after the Confessor, and the noble edifice of Westminster Abbey was then rising under royal command). In his absence, Prince Llywelyn ap Gruffydd of Gwynnedd had rebelled and was crashing his forces against the Anglo-Welsh border. It was at this time that Percy was again called up for service in Wales. At court some sixty councillors, courtiers and officials were dying of an unknown disease (including Ingram Percy, Henry's brother).[39] The nineteen-year-old Gilbert de Clare IV, having taken over from his father the earldom of Gloucester, had fallen prey to Montfortian radicalism and was stirring up sedition in the West Country. Taxes lay uncollected, and men everywhere were settling old scores because Henry's new justiciar was unsure what to do.

Then, in the spring of 1263, Montfort returned to England, intending to lead a resurgent baronial movement. Young Gloucester and other leading Marcher lords of Wales met him at Oxford – a nice touch – and all solemnly promised to restore the Provisions or die trying. It was a bloodless revolution; on 15 July 1263, the unnerved Henry, much to Edward's disgust, caved in and reinstituted them.

By August, however, Henry had belatedly realised that, despite the Montfortian bluster, his rhetoric was all mouth and little trouser. After all, scarcely a noble of the first rank, apart from Gloucester, supported Montfort, and most barons were lukewarm about the whole affair. So during the summer a secret campaign was launched to secure the baronage's permanent fidelity. In the wake of each little rebellion or upset over the past several years, barons on the losing side often had parcels of land confiscated as punishment; Henry now authorised the return of these. On 14 August, as a result, Percy received the lands confiscated during his 'rebellious phase'.[40] By the year's end, over 100 property restorations had been ordered, and Montfort could only watch his followers being lured away, although the younger nobles tended to stick with him.[41] Simultaneously, Edward courted his estranged friends like Warenne, Almain, Percy and even the disgraced Leyburn.

Neither side was confident enough to launch a civil war and, unprecedentedly, they selected Louis IX of France as an arbitrator.[42] Montfort had high hopes of a victory, but his baronial proctors confused Louis with a bewilderingly complex argument and bored him with a dense analysis of the administrative details on a clause-by-clause basis,[43] so losing sight of their strongest point: namely, whether Henry had illegally broken his oath to uphold the Provisions and rule in co-operation with the council. The king on the other hand (supported by Henry Percy and the other royalist and Edwardian barons) [44] addressed Louis as a fellow monarch, stirringly denounced the Provisions and called for a return to the political conditions of 1258, in which the king would govern guided by the principles of Magna Carta. In his 'Mise of Amiens' – the award of judgement – on 23 January 1264, Louis accepted the royal case and annulled the Provisions of Oxford.[45]

The Montfortians refused to accept the judgement. Royalists and rebels girded for battle, and in early April 1264, the king, accompanied by Henry Percy, surrounded the baronial forces in Northampton.[46] Within two days the royalists had stormed the castle, killing or taking prisoner over half of Montfort's total force; baronial resistance in every Midlands castle and town crumbled.

After accompanying the king at Northampton, Henry Percy was holed up in Rochester Castle, part of a detail assigned to cut the line of communication between London and Dover, a major baronial stronghold. The garrison commander was Edward's supporter, Earl Warenne (Percy being one of his lieutenants). Montfort and Gloucester laid siege to Rochester in mid-April. The baronial army carried the city and breached the outer bailey, but a valiant defence of the great keep by Roger Leyburn frustrated a rebel victory.

When Montfort's scouts reported that Henry and Edward were marching towards Dover, he was obliged to break off the siege. (On 28–9 April, the king relieved Rochester, and its garrison – including Percy – joined his army). The loss of the Midlands had been a terrible blow; unless Montfort acted, the royalists would surely win as castle after castle slipped from his grasp. Aware that Henry was resting his army at Lewes (in Sussex) before clanking onwards, Montfort decided on a pitched battle. Dr Carpenter strikingly points out that, regarding battles, 'not a single person on either side in 1264 had ever been in one'.[47] A tournament was the closest anyone had come. The last battle – a large skirmish, really – had been Lincoln in 1217. Montfort's gamble reveals a man who, despite his overweening arrogance and self-righteousness, possessed a fearsome confidence.

On 13 May at Lewes, the Montfortians formally withdrew their homage and fealty to the king. This meant war and there was no going back.[48] The royalists had the preponderance of knightly cavalry (about 1500 compared to Montfort's 500) and lightly armoured foot soldiers. However, after a night march the rebels located themselves on the plateau of a 400-foot hill just north-west of the castle and priory of Lewes. Any attacker would be obliged to charge up a slope, partly erasing the cavalry's offensive advantage.

The royalist battle order comprised three divisions: the first, commanded by Edward, the ever-lurking William de Valence and Earl Warenne, on the right; the second, under Richard of Cornwall and Henry of Almain, in the centre; and the third, the king's, on the left. Henry Percy and the corps of Northern lords were part of Cornwall's cohort. The rebels were also grouped into three divisions, but Montfort commanded a central reserve in the rear from where he could observe the entire battlefield. Facing Edward were volunteer Londoners – dismissed by Matthew Paris as 'bran-dealers, soap-boilers and clowns' – on foot and armed with bows and slings; opposite Cornwall was Gloucester's division; and Montfort's sons (Henry, Simon and Guy) were on the right, opposing the king.

When the London division – the weakest limb of Montfort's army –
began ambling down the hill, Edward charged his cavalry, put the entire
cohort to flight and irresponsibly kept going for three or four miles when
he should have wheeled and maintained contact with the main body of
the army. As it was, he had no idea what was happening on the battlefield. In partial mitigation, however, as he returned, Edward pounced on
a coach decked out with Montfort's standard and accompanied by a
heavy guard. Unfortunately, in the mêlée, some *royalist* Londoners
imprisoned in an iron cage were killed.

With the entire royalist right gallivanting about the countryside,
Gloucester seized the moment and attacked the now-vulnerable centre
under Cornwall and Almain as it started up the steep slope. Ordering his
bowmen to fire from a distance, Gloucester so disordered the division
that Cornwall was forced to hide in a local windmill, although his son and
some survivors found their way to the king. Henry Percy, and others,
were not so fortuitous; the *Chronicle of Dover* names Percy as one of those
'confessedly panic-struck' by the barrage and violence. It was in this condition, perhaps an early form of shell-shock, that Percy and the earls of
Hereford (a former Montfortian) and Arundel yielded to Gloucester.[49]

With Cornwall routed (soon to surrender) and Edward's whereabouts
still unknown, Montfort's sons and Gloucester joined forces with
Montfort's fresh reserve and clashed against Henry's last division in
Winterbourne Hollow. Many of Henry's nobles were slaughtered or died
from their wounds. The king 'was much beaten by swords and maces and
two horses were killed under him' before being spirited to the priory by
his bodyguard, leaving Montfort supreme in the field but not yet the
victor.[50]

By the late morning, Edward returned to find the royalist forces in disarray. After rallying what was left of them, he was attacked by Montfort
whilst Earl Warenne, William de Valence and Guy de Lusignan lit out for
Pevensey and escaped to the Continent.[51] With the remainder of the
army, Edward joined his father in Lewes Priory. Two days later, the
priory capitulated, the king surrendering his sword to Gloucester and
agreeing to uphold the Provisions of Oxford. In return, Montfort
promised arbitration on the most objectionable clauses of the Provisions,
a pledge he ignored once Henry, Edward and Henry of Almain were in
his custody. By evenfall on 15 May, Simon de Montfort, earl of Leicester,
was master of England.

It was a precarious mastership, however. Edward and Almain's rank
prevented their execution; and as part of the settlement, Edward's friends
– Roger Mortimer, Hamo l'Estrange, Roger Clifford and Roger Leyburn
– had been freed. The troublesome Lusignans and Warenne were still at

large, and splits were developing within the baronial leadership. Montfort's most powerful ally, Gilbert of Gloucester, was worried by Leicester's megalomania – never restrained, it was rampant after the Lewes victory – and favouritism towards his sons. In April 1265, when Montfort's new alliance with Llywelyn up Gruffydd threatened his Welsh territories, Gilbert began collaborating with Edward's friends, most of whom also possessed lands in the March. Montfort's diplomatic situation was worse still: the Pope condemned him; the king of France was displeased at his disobedience; and the queen was planning an invasion from Flanders. And finally, in May 1265, the Lusignans and Earl Warenne landed at Pembroke, hoping to join forces with the Welsh Marchers.

On 28 May, confined in Hereford, Edward was allowed to exercise on his guards' horses. Having exhausted all those available but one, he leapt upon it and galloped away, cheerfully shouting over his shoulder as he departed, 'Lordings, I bid you good day. Greet my father well, and tell him that I hope to see him soon.' Finally breaking with Montfort, Gloucester had planned the escape (his brother was among the guards) and Edward met him at Ludlow, with Mortimer and the other Marchers, followed soon after by Valence and Earl Warenne.[52]

There followed two months of manoeuvring in the West until both sides converged a mere four miles apart at Evesham, near Worcester, on 4 August 1265.[53] From the start, it was not an equal fight, and the royalists knew it. Montfort's son Simon had been defeated by Edward at Kenilworth some thirty miles away on 2 August, although Montfort was ignorant of this and believed his son's reinforcements were imminent. Montfort's barber, an expert at recognising heraldic insignia (every army had one), saw Simon's banners advancing towards them in the distance, delighting the rebels. But these were the banners captured by Edward. Climbing the bell-tower of Evesham Abbey to confirm Simon's approach, the barber discovered Gloucester, Edward and Mortimer closing on the small rebel force from three directions. Panicking, he shouted to Montfort, 'We are all dead, for it is not your son as you believed.' In a splendid example of nonchalant arrogance, Montfort marvelled in self-congratulation, 'By the arm of St James, they are advancing well. They have not learned that for themselves, but were taught it by me.'[54] Above him, a thunderstorm was gathering.

Montfort seized the initiative and hurled his cavalry in a wedge at the heart of Edward's division. The royalist lines held, and the wings curved inwards, pinching off Montfort and his cavalry (as well as the captive Henry III, who had been haplessly dragged along) from the foot soldiers following behind, who fled. The thunderstorm had broken, and the rain spattered on the encircled remnants of the rebel forces, turning the ground into mud, as slippery as priests. Outnumbered by at least six to one, their horses cut from beneath them, the young Montfortian barons sank quickly. The king, unrecognisable beneath his borrowed armour, was wounded in the shoulder and only avoided being impaled by crying, 'I am Henry of Winchester your king, do not kill me.' As Edward rushed to his father's aid, a dismounted, lonely Simon de Montfort was seized from behind by unknown assailants and stabbed to death.

A word on casualties. Contemporaries were startled at the profuse bloodletting of Evesham, one calling it a 'murder'... for battle it was none'.[55] Yet, of Montfort's barons, only thirty or so were killed, a minute figure compared to the slaughterhouses of future ages. At Lincoln in 1217, only two or three barons had died, and at Lewes, fewer than a dozen. Early medieval warfare was fairly safe for those who carried armour (as opposed to the anonymous infantry). A person of note, once bested, customarily surrendered. 'To kill him was a very deliberate act,' comments Dr Carpenter. 'It probably meant getting him on the ground, pulling off his helmet and stabbing him... Normally things never got that far... At Evesham the key difference was that no surrenders were accepted.'[56]

Politically, Montfort's murder was necessary; as the constitutionalist William Stubbs judged, 'It may have been best for England that he lived no longer. He was greater as an opponent of tyranny than as a devisor of liberties.'[57] The fate of his corpse, however, was gratuitously repellent. His limbs were cut off before he was beheaded and his testicles were delicately balanced on his nose and placed in his mouth. As a souvenir, his head was sent to Roger Mortimer's wife, although it remains a mystery what she did with it. Doubtless she was wary of opening parcels in future. It was thanks to the victory at Evesham, however, that Henry Percy and his fellow barons, held captive since Lewes, were released.[58]

The Last Years

Afterwards, the estates of leading rebels were distributed to royal supporters. However, at the end of October 1266, to comb over old hatreds, the rebels were permitted to buy back their land, the price varying from the annual rent up to seven times that, contingent on their degree of involvement in the civil war.[59] This 'Dictum of Kenilworth' reconciled the rebels with the new regime, which had finally dispensed with the Provisions of Oxford. The rebel John de Vesci, who was captured at Evesham and whose barony of Alnwick in Northumberland would feature in the Percy family's story, had rebelled yet again when his lands were seized. After surrendering to Edward, he paid 3700 marks (just under £2500) for Alnwick, a sum which Vesci must have considered fair, for he later became one of the prince's closest allies.

By the end of 1267, peace and order had been restored. As for Sir Henry Percy, on 8 September 1268 he married Eleanor, the daughter of his old comrade-in-arms, Earl Warenne, and his wife Alice, the uterine sister of Henry III, and, of course, the full sister of William de Valence and the Lusignans. Percy was by now a confidant (and kinsman through marriage) of Lord Edward, soon to be crowned king. Sadly, Percy did not live to see the coronation where he would have enjoyed a place of honour. Neither did Henry of Almain, assassinated in a church by Guy and Simon de Montfort in March 1271 for the mutilation of their father's corpse – even though he was absent at Evesham.[60] On leaving the church after Henry's murder, Guy declared: 'J'ai fait ma vangeance.' So dreadful was the killing that Dante, in the *Inferno*, portrayed Guy submerged up to his throat in boiling blood, shunned even by other murderers. William de Valence died peacefully in 1296, and is buried in a monumental tomb in the Chapel of St Edmund in Westminster Abbey.

Eleanor bore Percy three boys: William, John and Henry. The first died in infancy, a common occurrence.[61] The second, born in 1270, suffered the same fate.[62] This left Henry Percy III, a son his father never knew, for he was born on 25 March 1273, nearly seven months to the day after his father died of unknown causes on 29 August 1272, aged only thirty-seven. His birth saved the Percys from extinction, for all six of Sir Henry's brothers were dead by that year, leaving behind no legitimate children. Eleanor died about a decade later (there is an unsubstantiated rumour that she married a Scottish lord's son),[63] as did the boy's grandmother, Ellen de Balliol, in November 1281.[64] Thus, in his teens, Henry Percy III was left an orphan without any close relatives except his grandfather on his mother's side, Earl Warenne.

CHAPTER SIX

Great Captain

Sir Henry Percy III versus the Scots

Today the Percys are inextricably linked to Northumberland, but from William Percy's arrival in 1067 until the earliest years of the fourteenth century, the family was Yorkshire through and through with a touch of Sussex. Since Magna Carta the Percys had preferred Petworth, where this chapter's Henry Percy was born, to the North. The battles pockmarking Henry III's reign were fought in the South or the Midlands, and the quiet rule of the Scottish kings, Alexander II and Alexander III, had also contributed to this shift of focus. But Edward's dangerous obsession with Scotland brought the Percys back to the North.

The period from December 1217 to March 1296 is a 'record of unbroken peace' in Anglo-Scottish affairs, and 'relations were probably as intimate and productive as relations between medieval states could ever become'.[1] In 1221, Alexander II had married Henry III's sister, sparking a succession of alliances between the two neighbouring aristocracies. The cross-kingdom networks were revived to an even greater degree than those existing at the time of David I and Henry I.

The Border was still retained 'as a basic jurisdictional, administrative and strategic boundary, although movement across it was fluid. Always at the back of any king's mind, however, was the niggling problem of three Northern counties: namely, Cumberland, Westmorland and Northumberland. The Scottish kings, from ancient times, had nursed a claim to them, but by the thirteenth century its legitimacy was growing ever more tenuous.[2]

Alexander II's resurrection of the Northern claim in 1237 was clearly for tradition's sake. Alexander knew he could not succeed in prising the North from London's grip, and he proved content to quitclaim the counties in perpetuity for lands worth £200 annually in Northumberland and Cumberland, to be held of the English Crown. From these negotiations resulted the Treaty of York (1237), an 'amiable compromise between equals' accepting Scotland's 'separate status as an independent kingdom'.[3]

'Border' is something of a misnomer, denoting as it now does a dotted line on an Ordnance Survey map. The medieval conception of the Border was of 'a tract of territory separated in some senses from the countries on either side of it ... a frontier of a peculiar kind'.[4] In fact, men knew it only when they saw it, its trail following dykes and ditches and turning corners at tall trees, cairns and other landmarks. Scottish and English conceptions of the exact boundary in their area usually conflicted, just as one eye perceives a slightly different image from the other; in 1245, for example, sheriffs and knights from either side, dispatched to settle a border dispute, almost fought a battle over where *precisely* it lay.[5]

Before the outbreak of the Anglo-Scottish Wars, the Borderers rubbed easily alongside each other. Shortly afterwards, this peaceful(ish) tract of territory was divided into general Scottish and English 'Marches', the term denoting an entity with its own military and judicial jurisdiction acting somewhat autonomously from central authority. Although the Scottish and English *states* recognised the Border, to the local communities that line was a fuzzy one. These 'two halves of a singular society ... acquired distinctive mechanisms for defence and the making and maintaining of truces, similar habits of raiding and a shared culture of valour. They were societies organised for war.'[6] Given these exceptional circumstances and the distance from London, the chief of the North – usually called a warden – drew his authority directly from the Crown, not Parliament; 'the region placed under his control was therefore necessarily withdrawn from the ordinary administration of the kingdom'.[7] A warden generally enjoyed sweeping powers to keep his March safe and free. Sometimes, however, the temptation to believe oneself independent of London, to be a King in the North in one's own right, proved too heady to resist – with dreadful results. These events lay in the near future, but it is worth noting in passing how greatly English aggression altered life on the Anglo-Scottish border.

In 1249, Alexander II died, and was succeeded by his son by his second marriage, Alexander III, then aged nearly eight. Until he turned twenty-one, in September 1262, Scotland would be ruled by a regency of magnates and prelates. In 1251 Henry III secured the marriage of Alexander to Princess Margaret, his daughter (and a few scant months older than her husband), before a glittering gathering of English and Scottish nobles at York. The boy looked on him as his adopted father and Henry appointed himself the Scottish king's 'supreme adviser',[8] so keeping the kingdom – and its factions – on an even keel.[9] A daughter was born at Windsor in February 1261, followed by two brothers, both of whom died early in the 1280s. As for the queen, she predeceased her husband in 1275.

Alexander's one daughter, Margaret, married King Eric II of Norway and bore another Margaret, known to us as the 'Maid of Norway'. After her mother and uncles died, this sickly three-year-old child was heiress to the throne of Scotland. In 1285, desperate for a sturdy male successor, Alexander, now forty-four, remarried after a decade of bachelorhood. His bride was the youthful Yolande of Dreux. But less than six months later, Alexander snapped his neck in a riding accident as he rushed to spend the night with her.[10]

Properly speaking, the earls, barons and prelates of Scotland should have assembled at Scone to proclaim the Maid of Norway their queen. But there were problems. Queen Yolande may have been pregnant with Alexander's child. If a son was born, then the Maid's claim – as a grand-daughter – would be nullified. If a daughter, the picture muddied, as a younger daughter outranked the daughter of an elder daughter by right of degree – as some argued. Truth to tell, nobody was quite sure of the answer. Amid this confusion, some nobles argued that a grown man should be king, particularly in the context of King Edward I's violent annexation of Wales in the early 1280s; the Englishman, crowned in 1274, was turning out less amicable than his father.

Chief among these nobles was Robert Bruce, the fourth lord of Annandale in western Scotland and a descendant of the Anglo-Norman Robert de Brus granted land in Annandale by David I.

This Bruce was the son of the *second* daughter of David, the youngest of King David I's three grandsons. By way of comparison, Alexander III was the grandson of King David's second grandson (King William 'the Lion', 1165–1214). Indeed, at one point, Bruce had been the man nearest to the royal line, and was declared heir to the throne in 1238 – briefly. In that year, Alexander II was childless and not yet married to his second wife (the mother of Alexander III). The moment Alexander III was born, of course, any chance of succeeding was snatched away. Consoling himself, Bruce married a daughter of the earl of Gloucester, so entering 'the small circle of the greatest aristocratic families of England'. During the Barons' Wars, Bruce aligned himself with Henry and Edward. However, in 1286, Scotland beckoned, for 'in the uncertain state of the law of succession to the throne, it is not impossible that the Scots mag-nates should have declared their preference for a man rather than a woman'.[11]

There was one more joker in the pack: John Balliol II (born in 1249), an Anglo-Scottish noble descended from the Norman Guy de Balliol, lord of Bywell in Northumberland. By this time, however, the Balliols were lords of the fortress of Barnard Castle in County Durham (it blocked any invasions above Richmond from Cumbria into

Northumbria). John's father had married Dervorguilla, the *eldest* daughter of David, the youngest grandson of King David. This made her Robert Bruce's cousin, and additionally brought the Scottish lordship of Galloway.[12] Later, the distinction between Balliol's descent from the *elder* daughter, and Bruce's from her *younger* sister, would assume a monumental importance.

Notwithstanding the family connections, rivalry abounded, for Annandale and Galloway lay adjacent to each other, although this aggressiveness was relatively recent. Moreover, Bruce's son and heir, another Robert, married the Scottish countess Marjorie of Carrick and, *jure uxoris*, became earl of Carrick. Thus, Balliolite Galloway was hemmed in from the north by Carrick (its ancient territorial enemy), and from the east by Annandale.

These factors and actors coalesced at the baronial gathering of 28 April 1286, and set the stage for the momentous events of 1291–2. Gambling that Queen Yolande would produce a girl, both the 76-year-old Bruce and Balliol advanced their claims. Until a child was born, the assembly decided to elect six guardians to govern Scotland and act as trustees for the Crown. These six were carefully chosen to prevent civil war. Three came from the Highlands, and three from the South; one earl, bishop and baron supported each claimant, to ensure a balance.

Then began the tense wait for Yolande's baby, due in November 1286. But no child appeared. What had happened? It is possible the queen lost her child through miscarriage in early August and was then secretly prevailed upon to go through with the deceit. Perhaps, at the last moment, a male baby would be procured from some maid in trouble and placed on the throne of Scotland. Whatever the reason, three guardians beseeched Edward I's counsel and protection, for civil war seemed inevitable 'unless Edward's authority could be invoked to hold Bruce in check'.[13] Leading this appeal were William Fraser (bishop of St Andrews), Alexander Comyn (earl of Buchan) and John Comyn (lord of Badenoch), who together comprised the Balliol group of guardians.

Bruce was preparing for a clash in the winter of 1286, probably aided by Irish troops. He, the Macdonalds, Dunbars and Stewarts (including his own tame guardian, James Stewart, whose lands were enormous),[14] joined forces with two Ulster magnates and their allies at Turnberry on 20 September 1286 and swore to reserve their fealty to 'who will obtain the kingdom of Scotland by reason of the blood of the late King Alexander according to the ancient customs hitherto approved and used in the kingdom of Scotland' – cautious language, in case Yolande had a son. The 'ancient customs' refers to Bruce's recognition as heir in 1238, excluding at least three females who were then nearer by line to Alexander II.[15]

Which brings us to Edward's reply to the Scottish request for intervention in the autumn of 1286. Unfortunately, nothing was written down, possibly owing to the sensitive nature of the request, but we can understand his dilemma. Edward, always a stickler for legal procedure (especially if it suited his interests), would have believed that the Maid, until the outcome of Yolande's pregnancy was known, was the rightful queen. And happily, from his point of view, a weak queen was far preferable to a strong king in Scotland. Bruce's lands, moreover, were situated alarmingly close to Cumberland and Westmorland, and a renewed claim to the Northern counties might result. On the other hand, extending English support might suck Edward into a Scottish civil war. It is, therefore, likely that Edward provided advice and agreed to quieten the March. But extending protection, for the moment, was out of the question.

This holding tactic prevented civil war until 1289. Even the king of Norway was persuaded that Scotland was safe enough to allow his daughter, the Maid, to be inaugurated queen. Now a plan emerged, probably instigated by the guardians, for the Maid to marry Edward of Caernarvon, Edward's five-year-old heir.

The Scots, the English and the Norwegians met at Salisbury. In the resulting Treaty of Birgham it was agreed that Queen Margaret should arrive in Scotland by 1 November 1290. Had an heir been born of the proposed marriage, the Crowns of England and Scotland would have been united 300 years before James I of England and VI of Scotland.

That is not to say that the Scots desired a Great British superstate. They were well aware that Edward was one of the most predatory monarchs to stalk the Middle Ages, and they too could foresee the day when Edward of Caernarvon and Margaret would have a prince. Therefore the guardians ensured that the Treaty of Birgham clearly laid out the Scottish terms. In the words of Professor Barrow,

> The treaty envisaged two feudal kingdoms ... ruled separately though in harmony by a king and queen respectively [Caernarvon and Margaret], whose sovereignties would remain distinct. The Scottish kingdom was to remain, as the Scots had stipulated, separate, free in itself and without subjection ... [Moreover] no parliament dealing with Scottish affairs was to be held outside Scotland, and there was to be no taxation of the Scots except for Scottish needs.[16]

For Edward, these terms were fair enough; with his son married, the English king would be entitled to intervene in Scottish affairs when necessary, but he displayed a characteristic high-handedness in his subsequent actions. On the day he ratified the Treaty of Birgham, he announced the appointment of the shady bishop of Durham, Anthony

Bek (of whom more later), as his 'lieutenant' of Scotland in a letter to the guardians that was 'unmistakably Edwardian in its mixture of courteous legality and thinly veiled menace'. Bek's task was to 'reform and set to rights the ... realm in conjunction with the remaining guardians', who were to 'be obedient to him and put yourselves at his bidding'.[17]

Then Scotland experienced its greatest disaster so far. On her voyage from Norway to meet her husband, six-year-old Margaret died, extinguishing the Scottish royal dynasty. Nonetheless, a king must be had, and Balliol and Bruce prepared for a showdown. Sensing trouble, William Fraser (the Balliol-supporting bishop of St Andrews) wrote desperately to Edward on 7 October 1290, asking him to come north and prevent bloodshed. Between September 1290 and May 1291, a number of earls, on Bruce's behalf, alluded to a proposal to submit the problem of succession to Edward for his judgement.[18]

The idea for this, however, probably emanated from the English side: Edward, or his advisers, remembered that Henry III and Montfort had asked Louis IX of France in 1263–4 to arbitrate on the Provisions of Oxford. But this case was vastly different, for it would raise the unsettling matter of the exact feudal relationship between two states, England and Scotland.

On many occasions, the English had claimed that the king of Scotland held his realm as a vassal of the king of England. Yet there was no '"correct" answer to the question whether Scotland was feudally subject to England, [nor] one which is equally true for all periods of the Middle Ages'.[19] Sometimes it was, and sometimes it was not. Some English kings insisted upon homage, others did not. Edward was one who did. The seeds of the problem were sown when William Rufus gave military aid to Duncan II and Edgar in 1094 and 1097, actions that were easily interpreted as those of a feudal superior. Then, the homages uttered by Malcolm 'the Maiden' IV to Henry II could also be seen as signifying vassal status. More concretely, in 1174 Malcolm's brother, King William 'the Lion', foolishly invaded England and was captured.[20] In the resulting Treaty of Falaise, Henry II forced from William a written statement of Scotland's subjection to the English Crown. However, fifteen years later, Richard I of England's 'studiously vague' Treaty of Canterbury may or may not have restored the pre-1174 status quo by appearing to say that William was released from his obligations to be liegeman for Scotland, but not for the lands he held in England of the king.[21]

The ambiguity and contradictions of the Anglo-Scottish situation are reminiscent of the modern conundrum over Taiwan's international status. Thus, in 1235 Pope Gregory IX reminded Alexander II that his father (William 'the Lion') 'did liege homage and swore fealty ... and you ... and your successors, and the earls and barons of Scotland, are bound to offer the same'.[22] But in 1251, Pope Innocent IV informed Henry III that while Alexander III was his 'liegeman and has done you homage' *for lands in England*, Scotland itself was a 'kingdom of another sovereign'.[23] Alexander III certainly believed that he owed nothing to Edward for his kingdom, but happily acquiesced in paying homage for his English possessions, such as Huntingdon. In 1278, at Westminster, Alexander told Edward: 'I become your man for the lands which I hold of you in the realm of England for which I owe you homage, *reserving the right of my kingdom* [italics added]'.[24] Moreover, the Treaty of Birgham explicitly stated that Scotland was to remain an independent state without subjection to England.

It was upon this background that Edward drew in the spring of 1291. He laid down his terms forthrightly at Norham in Northumberland on 5 May: if the guardians, earls, prelates and barons wanted him to choose their king from among the potential claimants, they must publicly acknowledge his feudal suzerainty of Scotland. To ensure Scotland's permanent subjection, Edward insisted on being styled *Superior et Directus Dominus*, or a 'sovereign lord endowed with overriding authority'. The Scots nimbly sidestepped the issue. They pointed out that only a king, not his advisers, could decide on such a momentous step.

In early June, some hard bargaining produced a compromise, slightly weighted in Edward's favour. Homage would be given to the English king, and sovereign lordship granted, but only if Edward maintained Scotland's traditional laws and liberties, kept the relics and charters of Scottish royalty in a safe place, did not delay proceedings, and restored the realm to the new king within two months of making his decision. The penalty for default on any of these terms was £100,000, to be paid to the Holy See for a Crusade. It was a sum 'so astronomically large as to be symbolic rather than realistic'.

As a result, on 13 June 1291, the guardians – now merely deputies – and the Scottish community of the realm swore fealty to King Edward I of England as their 'superior and direct' lord. The claimants had done so a week earlier.[25] Thus was Edward not a disinterested arbiter but a judge granted the authority to make a binding decision, and he let the claimants know that he was their lord paramount at every stage.

So began the 'Great Cause', the lawsuit for the Scottish Crown. On 2 August, at Berwick, the claimants presented their declarations of intent to Edward, whereupon he had these sewn up inside a sack and the proceedings were adjourned until 2 June 1292 to allow the claimants time to assemble their cases. There is no space here, unfortunately, to detail the 'thrilling phases of claims and counterclaims, precedents, answers and arguments, minutes, procurations and notarial notes of the sundry sessions'.[26]

Put briefly, of the fourteen claimants who tried their luck, only Bruce (now known as 'the Competitor') and Balliol merit attention.[27] To aid his deliberations, Edward announced that 104 'auditors', plus himself, should be appointed, a body 'modelled with conscious archaism on the *centumviri*, the court of 105 used under the Roman republic to settle questions of succession to property', as well as hereditary succession.[28] Twenty-four auditors were to be members of the English council, with forty each nominated by Balliol and Bruce. Of the two, Balliol's men were indubitably more representative and authoritative than Bruce's.

On 5 and 6 November 1292, after all the claims had been sifted through, the auditors agreed with Edward that 'the [claimant] remoter in degree lineally descending from the first-born daughter [Balliol] was to be preferred to the one nearer in degree issuing from the second daughter [Bruce]'.[29] Thus, on 17 November, the court awarded Scotland to John Balliol.[30] There was no question of Edward fixing the result; by all accounts, he was scrupulously fair in his deliberations. Anyway, Balliol was indisputably the rightful king according to the traditional laws of primogeniture. Think of it as a Scottish version of the *casus regis*.

Edward immediately extracted repeated oaths of homage and fealty from King John, who was enthroned on St Andrew's Day (30 November) 1292 on the seat of royalty above the Stone of Destiny at Scone, considered the national Palladium.[31] No more ambiguity. The new king bent down and said in French: 'My lord, Lord Edward, lord superior of the realm of Scotland, I, John Balliol, king of Scots, hereby become your liegeman for the whole realm of Scotland.'[32] On 3 January 1293, the Scots began to comprehend what Edward's conception of being 'lord superior' entailed: he forced Balliol to nullify any previous agreements made with the guardians, like the Treaty of Birgham guaranteeing sovereignty. It was clear, in hindsight, that Edward had been intent on annexing Scotland since June 1291. Now he had.

Henry Percy and the Invasion of Scotland

Percy was uninvolved in the affairs laid out above, except in one sense, indirectly. His grandmother was Ellen, daughter of Sir Ingram de Balliol and William Percy III's second wife. She was also distantly related to King John. This family connection would assume great importance during the Anglo-Scottish wars.[33]

As we saw at the end of the previous chapter, young Henry Percy was left orphaned, and bereft of any close relatives apart from his maternal grandfather (Earl Warenne). In 1293 he succeeded to the Percy fortune and lands, but it was in 1294 that Percy truly came into his own. Three events mark this year as especially interesting: first, he married; second, he adopted the Lion as the heraldic symbol of the House of Percy; and third, he warred.

The *Chronicles of Alnwick Abbey* state bluntly that 'this Henry had to wife, Eleanor, daughter of the Earl of Arundel'.[34] At the same time, he changed his arms; Percy is the first private person in England whose personal Herald King of Arms is known. His name was Walter Marchis, and he later transferred to the royal household (Edward I also found the mechanisms of chivalry absorbing).[35] To have one's own herald so young bespeaks in Henry Percy an abiding interest in genealogy as well as a somewhat immodest desire to mark his dynasty's, and his own, achievements. Marchis and his master influenced each other regarding the change of arms. As we saw previously, the story of William Percy II forcing Joscelin de Louvain to change his name but allowing him to keep his family's arms (the Blue Lion of Brabant on a gold shield) is a myth – although it must have enjoyed some currency at the time. It was actually the Percy under consideration here who adopted the 'or, a lion rampant azure'. Until then the arms of Percy had been five fusils in fess – or five elongated diamonds displayed in a bar across the central third of the shield.[36] So why the change of arms?

Joscelin was the brother of the Dowager Queen Adeliza, the widow of Henry I, who later married William d'Aubigny, earl of Arundel. For generations, the Arundels had sported a golden lion on a red field ('gules, a lion rampant or'). In consultation with Walter Marchis, Percy adopted the famous lion to emphasise his ancestors' royal pedigree and to promote his kinship, through his new wife Eleanor, with the grand old earls of Arundel. As for the blue and gold, Earl Warenne's coat of arms was 'chequy or and azure' – a chessboard pattern with alternate blue and gold squares.[37]

Percy's new arms, therefore, honoured his mother's family, his very much alive and influential grandfather, and the man he regarded as the founder of the second Percy dynasty, Joscelin de Louvain (*leeuwen* is Flemish for lion). It also promoted his rather well-worn royal connection. The Blue Lion of the Percys was a compromise shedding light on the scale of Henry Percy's ambitions and the warmth of his relationship with his grandfather.

Soon after his nuptials, Percy was summoned for military service in Aquitaine (see below), but was instead blooded in Edward's December 1294 expedition into Wales to put down a revolt. Percy, it seems, accompanied Warenne to be introduced to his father's (and grandfather's) old acquaintance from the Barons' Wars, King Edward.[38]

The Welsh campaign of 1294–5 provided ideal experience for green soldiers, such as Percy, who would later fight in the Scottish theatre. Placed in the king's headquarters, Percy saw how to victual and support a war machine consisting of thousands of specialised workmen and tens of thousands of infantrymen, cavalry, esquires and camp-followers. It was only in the field that youthful warriors could imbibe the qualities of command. Operationally, he learnt how to attack and defend castles, march his companies across fields at night and plan three-pronged assaults against the enemy. He also witnessed the growing importance of archery in pitched battle. From that moment on, there would be few moments in Henry Percy's life not devoted to the warlike arts.

Soon after the end of the Welsh rebellion in the spring of 1295, Percy travelled to Scotland with his grandfather, who may have been a Surrey earl but was also an old Scotland hand. Warenne had been involved in the marriage negotiations between Prince Edward and Queen Margaret. It was no coincidence that John Balliol had married his daughter along the way, making the wily earl the father-in-law to the new king of Scotland.[39] Warenne, owing to the need to have someone in the North in case there was a Bruce-inspired emergency across the Border, had recently been appointed by Edward custodian of the counties beyond the River Trent and the castle of Bamburgh. On 18 October 1295, however, he was despatched to Scotland on the king's service. On his way there, no doubt, he brought his grandson up to speed on Scottish affairs.[40]

What had happened to require Warenne's presence? In 1293, Edward had flexed his muscles by humiliatingly summoning Balliol to Westminster and threatening to confiscate three of his castles during a small legal dispute. There, Balliol was treated 'like a defaulting debtor' and judged to be in 'contempt of court' for daring to answer back.[41] Fortunately for Balliol, Edward was diverted by threats to his duchy of Aquitaine, which he held as a fief of the French Crown (see Chapter 5).

On 19 May 1294, Philip IV of France had confiscated Aquitaine, followed by Edward renouncing his homage as duke on 24 June. Summonses for military service were circulated during that month (including one for Henry Percy) ordering the feudal levies to be at Portsmouth on 1 September. Similarly, Balliol's personal presence, as well as that of ten earls and sixteen barons of Scotland, was commanded. 'Here was "superior and direct" lordship with a vengeance,' comments Professor Barrow, for no king of Scotland had performed overseas military service since Malcolm IV travelled to Toulouse with Henry II in 1159. While the Scottish nobles forced Balliol to prevaricate, the Welsh (also having received Edward's demands) revolted in September 1294; this explains why Percy found himself in Wales rather than Aquitaine that year.[42]

In the spring of 1295, Philip undertook secret negotiations with the

Scots to form a potentially hostile northern front to counter Edward's courting of Germany, Spain and the Low Countries. By early July 1295, the Scots, impatient at Balliol's indecisiveness, elected a council of twelve (four bishops, four earls and four barons) to take control of the government and send envoys to France. In late October 1295, a treaty between France and Scotland committed them to wage war on Edward simultaneously, so marking the first appearance of the 'Auld Alliance' which would dog English kings for centuries.[43] The Scots Parliament and the (more reluctant) king ratified the treaty and the decision was taken to call out the feudal host of Scotland by 11 March in accordance with the treaty's terms.

Revealingly, the Bruces – the aged 'Competitor' had died, and his son had succeeded to the lordship of Annandale, while his grandson, later King Robert I, was confirmed as earl of Carrick – were deaf to the rising Anglo-Scottish din. Expecting Edward to smash Balliol for his disobedience, the Bruces, still panging for the throne, believed it would descend to them – if they kept their noses clean. To this end, they refused to comply with the Scottish summons, and even went so far as to refer to Balliol as the 'former king of Scotland'.[44]

It is difficult to say which side went to war first. The Scottish ratification of the treaty was technically a declaration of war, but it had been Edward who, hearing of the Scottish embassy to France, on 16 October 1295 ordered that all the goods and lands of Scotsmen in England be seized (so explaining Warenne's journey to the North on 18 October 1295).[45]

In any case, the Scottish Wars of Independence had begun. Accordingly, on 5 April 1296, Balliol, who evidently had not forgotten his dressing-down at Westminster three years before, issued a virulent renunciation of his homage to Edward: 'Now you have come to the frontiers of our realm in warlike array, with a vast concourse of soldiers, and with an army openly assembled...We cannot any longer endure these injuries, insults, and grievous wrongs, nor these hostile attacks, nor can we remain in your fealty and homage, which, be it said, were extorted by extreme coercion on your part.'[46] Edward's reaction upon receiving this incredible letter goes, dismayingly, unrecorded, but John Balliol, as it proves, was no mere puppet, but an unsatisfactory king occasionally capable of a great measure of dignity.

The Conquest of Scotland and Henry Percy

Near the end of March 1296, Edward laid siege to Berwick, the richest and largest town in Scotland.[47] At almost the same time a large body of Scottish infantry forded the Solway and attempted to storm Carlisle

Castle, but retreated back into Annandale after a single day. In the east, Edward had chosen easier pickings: Berwick was ringed only by a ditch and a timber palisade. On the morning of 30 March, Edward knighted several especially favoured young nobles, including Henry Percy.[48]

By girding himself with a sword, the essential ceremony associated with knighthood, Percy was happily undertaking an expensive business: he would also have to buy a surcoat, gambeson (a padded waistcoat), mail hose and gloves, and chain mail for both man and horse. On top of that, expertly hewn arms had to be purchased. Then, a specially bred warhorse (each costing anywhere between £40 and £80 or more) whose spine was capable of bearing such an enormous quantity of armour was required. By way of comparison, a lightly padded trooper's horse cost only £5.[49]

Soon afterwards, the English attacked and Berwick fell within the day. Edward ordered that no man be spared, for the merchants and artisans of the town had stupidly set 'themselves on the heights, bared their breeches and reviled the king and his people'. Others gamely attacked the king's fleet, whilst the womenfolk, 'bringing fire and straw, endeavoured to burn the ships'. According to the chronicles, there were so many corpses (11,060 according to one – exaggerated – early estimate) by the end of the massacre that they had to be chucked into the sea, thrown down wells or buried in deep pits by the survivors, whom Edward paid a penny a day to perform the gruesome tasks.[50]

Hoping to draw Edward south into England, the earls of Mar, Ross and Menteith led a raid into Northumberland, pausing only to burn some schoolboys alive in the church at Hexham.[51] Nevertheless, even as the Scots wasted and pillaged, Edward remained at Berwick, squarely intent on importing English officials to make it his administrative and financial headquarters for the final conquest of Scotland.[52] By mid-April, the three Scottish earls had returned northwards and blockaded themselves in the castle of Dunbar – the seat of the earl of Dunbar, one of Edward's loyal Scots and a descendant of Earl Cospatric of Northumbria in 1068, who was currently lodging with Edward at Berwick. Unbeknown to the earl 'with the blak berd', his wife was a secret Scottish loyalist and had ordered the garrison to unbar the castle gates for the earls.[53]

Annoyed at this feminine perfidy, Edward sent a small force, which included Percy, under the command of Earl Warenne to spy out the land around Dunbar before he unleashed his main army. On 27 April, as he prowled around the castle walls, Warenne received an unpleasant shock: he saw a Scots army (although not the feudal host led by King John Balliol) approaching rapidly. Leaving behind his junior officers (commanded by Percy) to keep the garrison occupied, Warenne took the rest of his cavalry to engage the Scots on a hill to the west. The Scottish cavalry, charging forward without waiting for the footmen, were cut to pieces by Warenne's troops. The battle, or rather skirmish, of Dunbar was a rout, although only one senior Scottish noble was slain and four knights were captured (one English knight lost his life).[54]

It was an ebullient king, then, who travelled to Dunbar the next day to congratulate Warenne, Percy and his officers. Later that day, the castle surrendered and the great prize of three earls, seven barons, twenty-eight knights and eleven clerics fell into English hands.[55] Edward was so jubilant that he even granted the Scots foot soldiers safe-conduct to wherever they wished to go.[56] After this victory, Percy was counted among the most trustworthy, resolute and efficient of Edward's commanders.[57]

The rest of Scotland's fortresses fell rapidly: James Stewart surrendered Roxburgh; Edinburgh held out for a week before opening its gate; at Stirling, the greatest strategic castle in Scotland, the garrison fled, entrusting the keys to the bemused porter. All the while, Balliol's army was retreating northwards, unwilling to meet Edward in a pitched battle. The king doggedly followed it up the eastern coast and reached Elgin at the end of July 1296. Throughout that month, Balliol had vainly tried to submit several times but was ignored by Edward, demonstrating his obsession over the subjugation of Scotland. When Edward finally agreed to treat with Balliol, the latter was brusquely directed by Edward's negotiators (Bishop Anthony Bek and Earl Warenne) to resign his kingdom, break his seal and renounce the Franco-Scottish treaty.[58] To add insult to injury, Edward publicly stripped Balliol's coat of arms from its tabard before sending him to the Tower of London. Following Balliol in disgrace southwards were nearly 100 earls, barons and knights captured during the campaign.

One final act demonstrated that Edward was now not merely feudal overlord but conqueror. He ordered the removal from Edinburgh to London of the Scottish regalia, a mass of plate, records and archives, jewellery and relics (including the Black Rood of St Margaret, 'the holiest and most venerated relic in Scotland'). The Stone of Destiny, 'on which the kings of Scots ha[d] been enthroned since time immemorial', was ravished from the abbey church at Scone and placed in Westminster Abbey.[59] The Stone, embedded deep in romance, prophecy, record and chronicle, was returned to Scotland by the rather less imposing figure of John Major in 1996.

That summer, Edward, spending barely a night in each town or castle he visited, triumphantly toured his new imperial possession, returning to Berwick on 22 August to hold a Parliament on the future government of Scotland. All those attending what has been called the first 'Union Parliament' were, depending on their allegiances, either proudly or painfully aware that Edward the Conqueror had vanquished an independent kingdom in fewer than five weeks.[60]

During the Parliament, Edward appointed Earl Warenne the first lieutenant, or keeper, of the province. When he handed over the Scottish seal of government to the earl, Edward mirthlessly observed, 'A man does good business when he rids himself of a turd.' Serving alongside Warenne was the obese and unpopular Hugh Cressingham as treasurer, and Walter of Amersham as chancellor. Soon after arrived the apparatus of English administration, including justices, sheriffs, clerks and escheators (officials overseeing the Crown's feudal rights and revenues).

As reward for his sterling service in Wales, Berwick and Dunbar, Percy was appointed on 8 September 1296 to what amounts to the governorship of the huge territory of Galloway and Ayr. This was a very tough assignment, for that area was a potential hotbed of pro-Balliol insurrection.[61] His headquarters was at Carlisle Castle, where Percy could not only keep a watch over his patch – stretching from south-western Scotland to Cumberland – but also liaise with his fellow wardens in the North, such as Robert Clifford, who stood guard in Westmorland.[62]

Clifford is interesting because he and Percy hailed from almost identical backgrounds and worked together for a number of years on the Border. Amazingly, the two of them were the same age, both born around March 1273. As fast friends, Percy and Clifford would unite their families by arranging for Percy's son and heir to marry Clifford's daughter, Idonea. The Cliffords were an ancient Welsh Marcher family, but Robert's father had married Isabella de Vipont of Appleby (in Westmorland), so explaining his connection with the North at this time. Robert Clifford was also present at the battle of Dunbar and waited alongside Percy at the castle whilst Warenne chased the Scots.[63]

For the next year, Percy and Clifford could afford to relax. Luckily, the elder Bruce (son of the Competitor), for the moment, was hardly a danger. He had pitifully beseeched Edward for the Crown after the battle of Dunbar, only to be greeted with a fine example of Edward's mercilessly dry humour, spoken with his slight lisp: 'Have we nothing else to do but win kingdoms for you?' a remark which induced guffaws from the English warlords present.[64] Soon afterwards, having established his new government, Edward departed Scotland on 16 September to prepare for the war against France.

He left prematurely; the conquest had been *too* easy and many of his official were not up to the task of government. Warenne loathed the climate so much that he preferred to spend his time on his Yorkshire estates (for his health, he claimed). Hugh Cressingham, Warenne's treasurer, who was despised by the Scots, seemed to go out of his way to insult the natives.[65] Around them, the demoralised Scots barons and bishops, such as James Stewart and Bishop Robert Wishart, were secretly forming an embryonic resistance.

A young man, William Wallace, soon came to the fore. Although William was not a knight, the Wallaces were an originally knightly family once from Shropshire, but now based in Paisley, the heartland of Stewart's fief. Wallace, therefore, was fairly highly placed in Stewart's feudal retinue. As Paisley bordered on Galloway and Ayrshire, any Stewart–Wallace movements would have to be dealt with by a Percy–Clifford combination.

Wallace was not 'the democratic leader in a war of precocious proletarian nationalism' depicted in the movie *Braveheart* ('Freedom!'). In fact, the Scots were intensely conservative, and Wallace in turn was far more conservative than many of Scotland's great magnates. Whilst the film portrayed Wallace as a commonsensical common man with no time for nobles, kings or factions – only Scotland and his (fictional) murdered wife, a victim of the (also fictional) 'right of the first night' – in reality Wallace was devoted to King John Balliol's claim. 'Utterly fearless, violent but not lacking in compassion, possessed of a certain grim humour [and blessed with an] extraordinary singleness of mind and purpose ... he was not a revolutionary either in politics or as a soldier.' A fine guerrilla fighter (but Bruce was finer) and a fair general on the battlefield (but no match against Edward's brilliance), his singleness of mind, impressive as it may have been, compelled in Wallace a constricting lack of imagination.[66]

In May 1297, Wallace murdered the English sheriff of Lanark, and was joined by Stewart, Bishop Wishart, Sir William Douglas and the earl of Carrick (the young Robert Bruce and future king). Bruce's decision to throw in his lot with the Scots, rather than trail after his father vainly begging Edward for scraps, marks his first independent action. Whilst Wallace's little band ran rings around the English near Glasgow, and Andrew Murray (the son of a prominent baron) rose in the Highlands, Percy and Clifford decisively tackled his four compatriots at Irvine, halfway between Ayr and Paisley, in June 1297,[67] after being given free rein by Edward 'to arrest, imprison, and justify all disturbers of the peace in Scotland'.[68] Percy and Clifford brought their cavalry to face the Scottish foot, whereupon Stewart and Douglas, but not Bruce, asked for terms. After wasting a month negotiating (so allowing Wallace plenty of time to wreak havoc in central Scotland), they finally submitted to the two English warlords on 7 July 1297.[69]

In late July, Hugh Cressingham wrote a series of panic-stricken letters to Edward regarding the state of affairs in Scotland (the king had bluntly asked why his treasurer had not sent dues and taxes owed by the Scots). Of great interest here is the frequent mention of Percy in laudable terms, showing that Percy was rapidly establishing himself as among the most formidable and capable of Edward's warrior-administrators. The crushing of Stewart at Irvine while the other English leaders were chasing shadows was an accomplishment that would not have evaded Edward's eye.

According to the letters, Cressingham, then in Bolton in Northumberland waiting for Warenne to bother showing up, was desperately recruiting 300 cavalry and 10,000 infantry, for he intended to mount an expedition into southern Scotland to put down the insurrection. The night before he intended to leave, Percy and Clifford arrived with the news that they had already pacified the whole of southern Scotland. Cressingham, however, still wished to hunt down Wallace (then hiding in Selkirk forest) and Murray, 'but it was determined that no expedition should be made until the earl's [Warenne's] arrival; and thus matters have gone to sleep, and each of us went away to his residence'.[70]

While Warenne tarried, Cressingham wrote another letter to the deputy treasurer in London, begging him to send the £2000 promised by the king. The reason he needed the money was that his infantry was deserting because 'not one of the sheriffs, bailiffs or officials of the Lord King ... can at this time raise a penny of the revenues ... on account of a multitude of different perils which daily and continually threaten them'.[71] Two weeks later, Cressingham explained to Edward himself why no expedition against Wallace and Murray had yet set out: 'by far the greater part of your counties of the realm of Scotland are still unprovided with keepers [because of] death, sieges, or imprisonment; and some have given up their baillywicks, and others neither will nor dare return; *and in some counties the Scotch have established and placed* [their own] *bailiffs and ministers* [italics added].' He promised that 'the earl [Warenne], Sir Henry de Percy, and Sir Robert de Clifford ... will (as he ought) take pains to do what is for your honour and profit with the greatest of haste that may be'.[72] Despite Cressingham's assurances, by the end of the summer, Andrew Murray had ejected the English from Moray and from the land between Elgin and Aberdeen (it would remain entirely English-free until 1303), and he had joined Wallace to march on Edinburgh and Berwick.

We can only imagine Edward's impotent rage at Warenne's inactivity during the imminent collapse of English power north of the Tweed. From France, Edward fired off a furious rebuke to his lieutenant, ordering him to bring Wallace and Murray to battle. At long last Warenne began recruiting thousands of infantry, including many Welshmen, and summoning his lords and their mounted men-at-arms.

Meanwhile, there was intelligence that Wallace and Murray had camped on the north bank of the Forth with – more or less, and probably many less – 10,000 poor commoners armed with spears. Blocking their path south stood mighty Stirling Castle, 'the key which would unlock the two halves of Scotland'.[73] Warenne and Cressingham, as well as, of course, Percy and Clifford, marched in good cheer to intercept the rebels at Stirling.[74]

A word on geography. The Scots were brilliantly situated (Wallace was no mean tactician) on the south-west-facing slope of the Abbey Craig, a mile north of a narrow bridge that crossed the Forth half a mile from the castle on the other side. The bridge was at the western curve of a deep horseshoe in the river; within that horseshoe of land lay soft, perhaps marshy, ground unsuitable for the English heavy cavalry. On the morn of the battle on 10 September, Warenne overslept whilst his officers fretted outside his tent. It did not bode well for the elderly earl's chances. Noticing with alarm that the bridge could only accommodate two horse-men abreast at a time, Sir Richard Lundie suggested a flanking attack on the Scots, using a ford farther up the river. As the earl dithered, Cressingham urged an immediate attack, volunteering himself to lead the troops over the bridge while the cavalry waited until they were deployed on the other side to provide cover. Warenne agreed to this brave, if ludi-crous, plan. For a short time, Cressingham's Welsh foot crossed Stirling Bridge unmolested by the Scots waiting on the hill. When Wallace judged that enough men had crossed, he launched his spearmen against the bridge, thereby turning the horseshoe into a noose, and leaving Cressingham's terrified infantry surrounded by unfordable water on three sides. The English commanders and barons, ensconced across the water in Stirling Castle with their cavalry, could only watch in powerless shock as Cressingham's men were massacred. Nevertheless, they fought bravely in the hand-to-hand combat that followed; one casualty was Andrew Murray, thus leaving Wallace leader of the Scottish resistance. As for Cressingham, he was flayed and his skin was carved into small pieces as souvenirs for the exultant Scots; it is said Wallace made a sword-belt out of it.

After witnessing Cressingham's fate, Warenne entrusted the defence of Stirling Castle to a number of luckless senior knights and rode like the devil with his commanders to Berwick. In itself, Professor Barrow com-ments, the battle of Stirling Bridge was not decisive, 'but it would be dif-ficult to exaggerate its importance in the struggle for Scottish independence. It is hard to convey the sheer shock of it.' The impossible had happened: not only had a 'cavalry army of gentlemen-professionals been defeated by an infantry army of peasant-amateurs' but in a bitterer blow still, 'an English army had been defeated by the Scots'.[75]

With the English reeling, Wallace raided the North of England during

October and November 1297. As Langtoft cried: 'In Northumberland the madmen have begun/To burn and destroy both houses and corn.'[76] But while Wallace's savage raids may have terrified villagers and clerics, he was unable to capture any castles (apart from the weakly held Stirling). All of them were manned by garrisons that easily repulsed Wallace's Lowlanders, rogues and the uncontrollably murderous men of Galloway. Percy, commanding Carlisle Castle, fought off a Scottish assault without much trouble.[77] After Stirling Bridge, the Scots under Wallace never again won a victory against the English in open battle.

During the winter, in preparation for a major Scottish campaign, summonses went out for a levy of 30,000 infantry to muster at Newcastle on 6 December 1297.[78] Of these, about 18,500 eventually turned up, a good average.[79] In December, contracts of service were also agreed with Percy, Warenne and the earls of Norfolk, Hereford, Warwick and Gloucester. Percy contracted to provide fifty men-at-arms and horses for payment of £769 3s 4d, about half as many as the most powerful earls in the land, the total being 500 heavy cavalry.[80] In Edward's absence, Warenne, amazingly, was appointed captain of the forthcoming expedition.[81] Despite his defeat, Warenne did possess military experience stretching back to the Barons' Wars, which was more than could be said for the rest. Moreover, there were perhaps few willing to take the job. A month before his army was destroyed at Stirling Bridge, when Edward was growing impatient with Warenne's reluctance to quell the rebellion, Edward proposed to Brian FitzAlan that he himself take Warenne's place. 'I do not think that I in my poverty can...keep the land in peace to your profit or honour, when such a nobleman as the earl [Warenne] cannot well keep it in peace for what he receives from you,' replied FitzAlan diplomatically.[82] Warenne was, at best, Edward's second choice for command.

Knowing Edward was keeping an eye on his performance, Warenne managed to relieve Roxburgh and Berwick before Christmas,[83] but received notice in February 1298 to desist until Edward arrived in person from Flanders. In the meantime, Wallace was granted a knighthood. When Edward reached York in early 1298, he prepared for a long, arduous campaign; for the next six years, the common law courts and the Exchequer were based there. By calling up welsh contingents, Edward's army surged to 26,000 infantry and 2,000–3,000 disciplined cavalry. As nearly half his foot infantry were Welsh – they being of doubtful loyalty, Edward spent an inordinate amount of time arranging fair and prompt payment – the king relied on his cavalry to smash Wallace. These horsemen comprised knights fighting for pay and contingents brought by the earls, barons and the militant prelate, Anthony Bek. Evidence of Edward's determination arises from his words to Sir John Marmaduke, a singularly ferocious killer: 'You are a bloodthirsty man, I have often had to rebuke you for being too cruel. But now be off, use all your cruelty, and instead of rebuking you I shall praise you.'[84]

Assembling at Roxburgh on 25 June, the army advanced through Scotland to the Forth. But the Welsh were already causing trouble. When Edward sent 200 tuns of wine to cheer them up, a drunken brawl erupted and several English priests were murdered. To bring the Welsh to their senses, Edward ordered his knights to charge the foot soldiers, killing eighty. As the Scots were nowhere to be found, English morale plunged and Edward considered returning home. Then scouts reported that Wallace was hidden in Callendar Woods near Falkirk, a mere fifteen miles away. Immediately, Edward marched his dispirited and hungry army west to Falkirk, spending the night just east of Linlithgow.

As the sun rose on 22 July 1298, the Scots glimpsed the glint of English steel across the narrow Westquarter Burn separating the armies.[85] Edward may have been cruel on occasion but he understood the drudgeries of war and wanted the men and horses fed before fighting. His earls, however, wisely prevailed upon him not to delay. The English formed up into four 'battles', or brigades, of cavalry, with the archers lined up behind armed with the longbow – a weapon that would come to dominate warfare for the next two centuries. The longbow lent the English (or, rather, the Welsh) foot a devastating superiority in firepower over the Scottish spearmen. Averaging six feet in length, the bow had a draw weight of anywhere from sixty to ninety pounds and its operator could *accurately* launch twelve arrows per minute at distances up to 220 yards (if elevated, the longbow could achieve considerably greater distances, but its killing power diminished).

From our point of view, the cavalry battles are of primary interest. On many maps of the battle, only three brigades are shown: the first (or vanguard) on the left, under the earls of Lincoln, Hereford and Norfolk; the second on the right flank, under Anthony Bek; and the third (or 'King's Battle') in the centre, commanded by Edward and including Clifford.

That leaves the mysterious fourth, the reserve, and it was in this small but potentially deadly brigade of veterans that Henry Percy, Warenne and the earls of Gloucester, Arundel, Oxford and Pembroke were placed. There are some illuminating family connections in this group: Percy was married to Arundel's daughter, and Arundel's son would later marry Warenne's granddaughter, her mother being the daughter of the earl of Oxford. Pembroke, because of his later importance, also requires some comment. Aymer de Valence had inherited the title from his father, the loathed Lusignan William de Valence, in 1296. In an instance of heavy medieval irony, owing to his towering height and paleness, he was nastily nicknamed 'Joseph the Jew'. He and Percy were well acquainted with one another, as their fathers had been, and were very distantly related. Evidence for this order of battle comes from the Falkirk Roll of Arms, a heraldic catalogue of those present, compiled by Percy's aforementioned private herald.[86]

On the Scots side, Wallace had invented (or, more likely, brilliantly employed) a 'schiltrom', a tight circle, crammed with 1500 spearmen, in which the front ranks knelt with their twelve-foot spears held upwards at a 45° angle while those behind pointed their weapons directly forward at chest height. Surrounding each schiltrom – of which there were four – was a palisade of sharpened wooden stakes roped together, giving a hedgehog effect. Any cavalry smashing into the schiltrom would be torn to pieces. Between the schiltroms, Wallace placed his Selkirk bowmen under Sir John Stewart (brother of James Stewart); behind this formidable line were the nobles' valuable cavalry, hoping to charge Edward's infantry once the inevitable cavalry offensive had been repulsed. It is not known whether Robert Bruce was there, but he was certainly not waiting alongside Edward I: another detail that *Braveheart* got hopelessly wrong.

As the first two English brigades rolled forward, Wallace declaimed to the schiltroms: 'I have brought you into the ring: now see if you can dance.' The first circled to attack Wallace's right, whilst the second, under Bek, rode east, making for his left. The third and fourth held back as the flaw in Wallace's deployment became apparent. The English commanders ignored the schiltroms and aimed directly at the bowmen between them, who stood no chance against the mail-clad knights. Almost to a man, from Sir John Stewart downwards, the bowmen were slaughtered. The Scottish horse, 'disgracefully', reared in panic and fled the field.

Leaving the schiltroms untouched, the first and second pulled back and waited for the Welsh archers to open fire with a rain of arrows. Gaps quickly appeared in the spearmen's ranks, and the schiltroms contracted into an ever smaller space. Just as the other two brigades overwhelmed the schiltroms, Edward led the third in a fearsome attack on the rear. The Scots losses were horrific with many thousands cut down or drowned in the nearby loch. Wallace, however, escaped and fled north. On the English side, infantry losses amounted to about 2000 dead and hundreds of horses slain, yet only two men of rank were killed (the masters of the English and Scottish Templars). Falkirk was Edward's greatest victory, and spelt the end of Wallace's guardianship of Scotland. From then on, Wallace would be a guerrilla, not a general, and it would be another sixteen years before a Scottish army dared take the field against the English.

The year 1299 was a bountiful one for Henry Percy, now home from the wars. On 6 February, he acquired a formal 'barony by writ' when

Edward summoned him to Parliament. He thus became the first Lord Percy, or Lord of Topcliffe.[87] Before 1299, the Percys had held the barony of Topcliffe as feudal lords, and were courteously referred to as 'baron' – unless they were dubbed knights. At this time, a 'baron had no specific legal functions or privileges, and the term did not denote a precise economic rank'.[88] The vast majority of the 'barons', or tenants-in-chief – some 3000 of them – were knights, squires and serjeants, but at the other end of the scale existed the wealthiest lay landholders in the country. This 100 or so landed elite comprised two groups. At the top were the earls, barons summoned by writ, rich knights and ministers, who together 'served on the King's Council, performed the higher functions of law and administration, led his forces in war, and whose wealth and power covered the kingdom as a whole'. Below them were the knights and gentry who ran local institutions and drew their wealth from one, or at most two, counties.[89] Percy's promotion from 'rich knight' to 'baron summoned by writ' shows both that he had joined the landed elite and that Edward planned to devolve onto him baronial, not knightly, responsibilities. His receipt of the writ of summons to become a peer of Parliament propelled him, therefore, into the ranks of the truly consequential. And so the Percy title may be said to date from 1299, although such a privilege was not at this time a strictly hereditary one. Without some evidence of wealth, wisdom or prowess, a peer's heirs were unlikely to receive similar writs of summons. The increasingly obsolete feudal baronage was a far more liquid body than many give it credit for. Indeed, it would not be until the mid-fifteenth century that the distinction between an aristocrat and a gentleman was firmly demarcated.

In the same year of Percy's ascension, Robert Clifford was summoned and created Lord Clifford,[90] indicating that Edward was justly rewarding two of his favourite commanders. Being asked to attend Edward's Parliaments was an unmistakable signal of royal favour. During Edward's reign, the attendance of shire and borough representatives (that is, knights and burgesses) to parliaments was regularised and writs were also issued to archbishops, bishops and earls. Official members of Edward's council, such as the chancellor, treasurer and judges, were nearly always present. For our purposes, the list of lay magnates that Edward compiled is of the greatest interest. According to Professor Prestwich, 'the king was looking to men whose advice he valued, and whose local power and authority he could not ignore. There was something of a concentration of men who held estates on the borders near Wales and Scotland, a natural reflection of their military importance.'[91]

The genesis of modern Parliament is discernible in Edward's assemblies, with one important difference: Parliament possessed no independent existence, and could be summoned only at the king's will and in his presence at a place of his choosing, usually Westminster. Notwithstanding Edward's periodic nastiness (for example, his expulsion of the Jews in 1290), he was a remarkably efficient lawgiver, preferring to promulgate legislation by statute, which avoided the 'imposition of arbitrary notions from above', whilst concentrating practically on 'known grievances', 'problems which came up in courts', 'correcting wrongs' and 'improving the efficiency of royal justice'.[92] He had, evidently, learnt something from Montfort's rebellion.

Edward's Parliament may have discussed affairs of great importance and consented, on behalf of the community of the realm, to grant taxes, but it was the king's council (later known as the privy council) that gave Edward 'the expert advice and assistance he needed if the country was to be governed effectively'. Comprising a mixture of high officials and experts, the king's council also brought on board Edward's most trusted military advisers, such as the earls of Lincoln and Hereford, as well as Henry Percy, who was invited in September 1305.[93] From 1299 onwards, however, Edward listened carefully to Percy's advice, especially on military affairs. In July of that year, for instance, Percy, Clifford and a select band of Border warriors were bid to York to discuss with the king Scottish strategy over the coming years.[94]

It was in 1299, also, that Henry Percy became the first Percy to own land in Scotland since the illegitimate sons of Alan de Percy in the early twelfth century. In February of that year, Percy received from Edward all the estates in England and Scotland of a recently deceased very distant relative – the childless Ingram Balliol – as a share of the spoils.[95] Being something of a patriot, Ingram had specifically directed that his estates pass to a Scottish cousin, Ingram Umfraville.[96] Both Ingrams had, however, become involved in the Scottish rebellions, and Edward had no compunction about giving Balliol's land to Percy (nor had he any about accepting them). Thus, Percy acquired the manors of Foston in Leicestershire and Wharrington-upon-Tees in Durham, as well as the barony of Urr in Galloway and Red Castle in Angus, two of his old stamping grounds.[97] Even when Ingram Umfraville, as Bruce's enemy, changed sides and loyally stood with Edward I (and later, Edward II at the 1314 battle of Bannockburn), Percy did not hand Urr and Red Castle to their rightful owner. Edward's kindness, however, was never engagingly altruistic; rather than merely serving as a royal appointee, Percy now had a vested interest in the conquest of Scotland. The next six years would see him becoming a significant Scottish landowner. He even temporarily managed to pick up Bruce's earldom of Carrick, as we shall see.

Judging by the number of military summonses he received, Percy spent the next year quelling Scottish subversion or patrolling Galloway and western Scotland. In July 1300, he travelled to Carlisle in preparation for the king's summer expedition into Scotland. The army was even equipped with a French herald (Percy's had been headhunted by Edward), hired to sing of the inevitable triumph of English arms and men. Unfortunately, little exciting happened during the campaign, apart from the successful, if brief, siege of Caerlaverock Castle by the English. The sprawling 'Song of Caerlaverock', composed by a herald desperate for something glorious to relate, includes pen-portraits of the English bannerets.

Clifford, for one, seems to have been a handsome devil: 'If I were a young maiden, I would give him my heart and person.' Warenne (under whom Percy, as usual, served) is praised:

> *John the good Earl of Warenne*
> *Of the other squadron held the reins*
> *To regulate and govern,*
> *As he who well knew how to lead*
> *Noble and honourable men*

and so on in similar vein until:

> *And he had in his company*
> *Henri de Percy, his nephew* [sic],
> *Who seemed to have made a vow*
> *To rout the Scots;*
> *A blue lion rampant on yellow*
> *Was his banner very conspicuous.*

Even among his contemporaries, Percy's Blue Lion and his determination to subdue Scotland elicited comment.[98]

From Caerlaverock Castle (entrusted to Clifford), the army marched westwards into the heart of Galloway and Ayrshire, along the way putting to flight a small force of Scots thanks to Warenne's re-formed fourth brigade. Nevertheless, the infantry's enthusiasm for the fight was eroding rapidly and thousands deserted. Edward saw that the campaign was growing futile and circled back to Carlisle in September. Later that month, Percy, still based there, led a raid across the Border.[99]

Subsequently, we lose track of Percy's movements between 1301 and 1303, apart from frustratingly fleeting glimpses of his whereabouts and activities. Wherever he was, Percy was in high favour; in October, he was fondly referred to in a Chancery document as a 'King's cousin'.[100] His son and heir was born, the most likely date and place being 6 February 1301 at Leconfield, near Beverley in Humberside.[101] We know that Percy sent a letter to the chancellor from Leconfield on 17 November 1301.[102] He seems to have stayed there for quite a while, tending to the management of his estate, for 'a medieval estate was ... the equivalent of a major industrial enterprise today', says Professor Prestwich, and 'although magnates had councils to assist in the process of management, and ... officials from stewards and receivers down to humble bailiffs and reeves, regular supervision by the lord was required'.[103] And as Percy had been away at the wars for many a year, a formidable backlog of Things To Do had accumulated. An obscure entry in *The Percy Chartulary*, a compilation of deeds and legal documents, notes that Henry Percy was engaged in granting a half-acre of land at Nafferton (not far north of Leconfield), part of the Percy fief since the Domesday Book, to the local abbot and convent at the end of January 1301.[104] Percy cultivated an intense interest in this area, and his wife probably lived at Leconfield, not Topcliffe. Thus his son was born away from the family's Domesday residence, perhaps because Leconfield was well away from the dangers of the Border and the popular raiding-routes to York. Henry Percy was never averse to breaking with tradition.

As Percy recovered from the rigours of Border life, the political situation in Scotland had altered drastically. Pope Boniface VIII had begun taking a keen interest in the Scottish cause, and Scottish agents in Rome soon persuaded him that Edward had extorted oaths of fealty from Balliol through fear and force.[105] Balliol, now exiled in Burgundy, moved to France under the wing of King Philip the Fair, Edward's mortal enemy, who pledged a French army to restore his throne. Thus, it was in early 1302 that a sulking Robert Bruce, terrified lest a resurgent King John Balliol sought to exact his revenge for the Bruces' opportunism, submitted to Edward in return for a promise that, first, he would not be disinherited, and second, 'the king will support him in his right and defend him, so far as a lord should do for his vassal'.[106] Nevertheless, the Franco-Balliol alliance collapsed after the Flemings defeated the French in July 1302. Following an Anglo-French peace treaty in May 1303, Edward could turn again to Scotland and Wallace, who had meanwhile returned to the fray.[107]

On 20 January 1303, Percy was again summoned for military service and 'enjoined to place himself, with horses and arms, and all his forces, under the command of Johannes de Segrave, the King's Lieutenant in Scotland'.[108] Percy must have concluded his business in Nafferton before hurrying up North to rendezvous with Segrave in mid-February. Once there, three brigades of cavalry mounted a foray into Scotland, but on 24

February John Comyn and Simon Fraser defeated this force at Roslin, just south of Edinburgh. A number of the first brigade, including the wounded Segrave and perhaps Percy, were captured, but, luckily, their fellows in the second squadron rescued them.[109] The English had come within a hair's-breadth of having a substantial proportion of their horse smashed on a routine mission. The skirmish illustrated the dangers of sending cavalry into action without infantry protection.

In the meantime, Edward was making preparations for yet another major offensive, eventually taking with him rather fewer heavy cavalry than in 1300. Percy accompanied him throughout the year, which ended with the king reaching Dunfermline on 5 November 1303. There he rested for the winter, whilst his Irishmen fought the Scots on the Clyde. A raid led by Segrave and Clifford managed to rout Wallace in Lothian, forcing the guerrilla leader to escape into the hills.[110]

Utterly disheartened by Bruce's craven defection, Balliol's impotence, Philip the Fair's untrustworthiness and Wallace's run of ill-luck, the majority of Scottish nobles capitulated to Edward on 9 February 1304 at Strathord, north of Perth – but not unconditionally. It is said that Percy played a major part in the negotiations.[111] He was certainly in Edward's presence at this time; two weeks later he asked the king to appoint a few knights to investigate the murder of a Peter de Lound by unseen hands.[112] The nobles, headed by Sir John Comyn of Badenoch (the inveterate insurrectionist and former guardian who had humiliated Segrave at Roslin), demanded that there be no disinheritances or reprisals and that prisoners be exchanged free of ransom. Edward was not the kind of king to accept 'conditions' when his enemies were on their knees, but was hamstrung by the fact that many Scottish estates had already been granted to his English followers. Remembering the post-Evesham Dictum of Kenilworth of 1266 (see Chapter 5), he permitted some forfeited lands to be redeemed on a sliding scale, usually two or three times the annual value. But in Ingram Umfraville's case, he stipulated *five times* its value. This deliberately unaffordable price was no coincidence, for Henry Percy had held Umfraville's lands since 1299.

Because William Wallace had begun to exert an unhealthy obsession on Edward's ageing mind, the king forbade giving safe-conducts to Stewart, Umfraville, Fraser and a few others until they themselves rid him of the accursed terrorist. They had until mid-January 1305 to hand Wallace over, and Edward would 'watch to see how each of them conducts himself so that he can do most favour to whoever shall capture Wallace, with regard to exile or legal claims or expiation of past misdeeds', as a royal clerk helpfully noted for the records.[113]

Cognisant that he could trust the word of Scottish nobles about as far as he could throw them, in April 1304, Edward left his winter quarters at Dunfermline and made preparations for a lengthy siege of the last symbol of rebellion, the fortress of Stirling, commanded by the young Scotsman, Sir William Oliphant. Percy's status at this time is indicated in the rosters of earls, barons and bannerets who accompanied Edward. Both at Dunfermline and at the forthcoming siege Percy appears seventh. After the six earls, then, he was the highest-ranking baron.[114] He also dined with the Prince of Wales on three occasions in February of 1304.[115]

Edward intended to make a spectacular example of the castle's stalwart defender. The parts of three great siege engines, or catapults, were dragged to Stirling, and Robert Bruce helpfully provided a few more. As for Percy he and the prince stripped the neighbouring churches of their roofs for the lead needed to make the counter weights ('provided always that the churches be not uncovered over the altars,' added Edward thoughtfully to his instructions), and battalions of carpenters were drafted to construct the engines in sight of the defenders. In their spare time, the workmen built an elaborate shelter for the queen so that she could watch the fight with some degree of comfort. One order of Edward's stands out: he told his lieutenant to provide a 'horseload of cotton thread, one load of quick sulphur, and another of saltpetre'. These combined to produce an explosive gunpowder, which, when poured into earthenware pots and set aflame, was an innovation known as 'Greek Fire'. From May onwards, fiery pots and rounded stones were hurled into the castle. On 20 July, Oliphant offered an unconditional surrender, but Edward refused until he had experimented with his new toy, a gigantic trebuchet called 'Warwolf' which had taken five master carpenters and fifty men months to complete. It was only four days later that Edward allowed the shaken defenders to leave. The king, somewhat surprisingly, was merciful to his abased enemies after informing them, 'You don't deserve my grace, but must surrender to my will.' An exception was made for an English traitor found skulking among the ruins.[116]

Amid the triumphal crash of Scotland, one jarring note, momentarily muted, sounded: the death of Robert Bruce's father on 21 April, ensuring that 'the earl [of Carrick] was now, accordingly, in his own eyes, and in the eyes of many in Scotland, the rightful King of Scots'.[117] Even as Edward enjoyed the irony of watching Bruce's catapults cripple his fellow Scots, Carrick had sneaked away and was at Cambuskenneth intriguing with Bishop Lamberton, an indefatigable patriot and ally of Balliol and Wallace. On 11 June 1304, the two men entered into a pact of mutual friendship and co-operation. From then until Lent 1305, Bruce disappeared, knowing that Edward was growing frailer and weaker, and planning his eventual return.

The campaign that led to the siege of Stirling was the last in which the doughty 75-year-old Earl Warenne participated. He died soon after and was buried before the high altar of Lewes Priory.[118] Percy and a man who would soon play a large part in his life, Guy Beauchamp (earl of Warwick) were among the mourners.[119]

The remainder of 1304 and much of 1305 were quiet and peaceful. On 3 August 1305, wonderful news spread among the English garrisons north of the Tweed: William Wallace, asleep in the arms of his latest paramour, had been captured near Glasgow by Sir John Menteith, who received land worth £100 for his initiative. As Menteith and his band were Scots, Wallace was handed over by his own countrymen. Wallace's doom was dreadful, yet the man 'had not conducted his campaigns according to the chivalric codes of the day, and there was no reason why Edward should have treated him with compassion or respect'.[120] Even so, Edward's retribution was needlessly dire. Brought to London in late August, Wallace was bound to a cart and dragged to the elms of Smithfield before the mob. On the scaffold, Wallace was hanged until on the cusp of death, disembowelled and beheaded, the first time such an execution was used. His heart and entrails were burnt, and his corpse cut into quarters. Leaving the head hoisted above London Bridge, the parts were displayed in Newcastle, Berwick, Stirling and Perth as a warning to those who dared flout Edward the Conqueror's will.[121]

Tended by his surgeons, the king realised that he would soon follow his nemesis Wallace to the grave, and wanted to leave a stable empire for his heir, Edward of Caernarvon. To this end, he had learnt the lesson of the past bloody decade. If, as a despot, he tightened the screws, the surviving Scottish nobles clustered closer together and talked of rebellion. It was far more statesmanlike to draw the nobles in voluntarily and give them a stake in maintaining the status quo of English rule. Thus, at a Lent Parliament in 1305, at which Percy was present, Edward actually deigned to ask Bruce – the king was unaware of his double game – and two other leading Scots for their advice on the future running of Scotland. They said that ten representatives should attend the next Parliament and help draw up a new constitution. Accordingly, in September Percy was directed to treat with the Scots representatives concerning the government of the 'land' – Edward no longer referred to it as a 'realm' – at Westminster.[122]

There, the Parliament of Scots and Englishmen promulgated an ordinance which appointed many Scottish sheriffs and constables (although the strategically crucial Lowlands remained in English hands) and handed half of the regional justiceships to locals. Interestingly, apart from Bruce, Wallace's captor, Sir John Menteith, was the only Scot to be given charge of a castle (this 'expert in betrayal' would later surrender it to Bruce).[123] The English offices of lieutenant, chancellor, controller and chamberlain were to remain intact, but a Scottish council of twenty-two earls, bishops and barons was established to 'advise' the lieutenant. In other words, despite the ordinance, 'Scotland was once more what she had been in 1296, a conquered country [and now not even a kingdom] ... governed by the foreign officials of a foreign king'.[124] Yet in five months, the ordinance, and the chance of lasting peace, would be a dead letter.

In early February 1306, before Edward's officials had taken up their posts, Bruce invited Sir John Comyn (the diehard Balliol supporter who had played an infinitely more heroic role in the war so far than the conniving Robert Bruce) to the Greyfriars' church at Dumfries. Without his support, Robert Bruce's secret pact with Bishop Lamberton, also a Balliol man who had made the magnificent leap to the Bruce camp, would come to naught.[125]

On the night of 10 February, the two met at the church's high altar. Bruce confided to Comyn his plans to mount a rebellion against Edward and crown himself king of Scotland. Comyn demurred, for such a plan meant disclaiming John Balliol as the rightful king. Angry words were exchanged; and Comyn called Bruce a traitor. Bruce, sacrilegiously, drew his dagger and slashed Comyn, leaving him for dead on the bloodied flagstones below the altar. As the admiring biographer of Bruce rhymed of this sordid deed: 'with a knyff ... hym reft the lyff'. Hurrying away from his murder in the church, Bruce was obliged to return to finish the grisly job when he heard that the Franciscans had succeeded in reviving the victim.

Now, Bruce had to act fast. With good fortune, it might be possible to present a fait accompli to Edward. Within two weeks, Bruce had seized five of the castles guarding the Firth of Clyde, thereby protecting his Irish supply lines, but Galloway, being Balliol country, remained aloof and Lothian was defended by the heavily garrisoned fortresses of Roxburgh, Stirling, Edinburgh and Berwick.

Until 25 March 1306, Bruce was little better than a charismatic murderer, but on that day – the tenth anniversary of the war's outbreak – in the presence of three bishops and four earls he was crowned king at Scone Abbey. On his head was placed a golden coronet, and he was garbed in borrowed episcopal robes and vestments (the royal ones having been brought to London by Edward along with the Stone of Destiny.

In the meantime, Edward had not remained impassive. One of his first acts was to strip Bruce of his earldom of Carrick and grant it to his good and faithful servant, Percy, now one of the leading landlords in Scotland. Then, on 5 April, royal messengers sped north to deliver Edward's orders to Aymer de Valence and Henry Percy, whom he appointed his two senior commanders in Scotland and the Marches. Valence was to take charge of the East March – that is, Yorkshire, Northumberland and Lothian – and Percy was promoted to virtual gauleiter of the West March, the 'Capitaneus' of Lancashire, Westmorland, Cumberland and Galloway.[126] Edward directed them 'to burn and slay and raise dragon', a terrifying phrase that referred to the Dragon banner, the rarely flown signal that no quarter would be given,[127] and swore 'ful stalwartly,/that he suld drawyn and hangit be' the Bruce.[128] As his generals mustered their local troops (Valence had sixty men-at-arms, and Percy thirty-five),[129] the king wended his way slowly north. But he was in no shape to lead an expedition and decided in October to rest at Lanercost Priory, overlooking Hadrian's Wall, about ten miles north-east of Carlisle.[130]

The campaign began in the east, when Valence secured Perth, routing Bruce and his army at Methven on 19 June 1306 – 'Sum woundyt, and sum all ded:/The grass woux off the blud all rede [The grass grew red with blood],' according to the poet Barbour – and forcing the new king to flee west with a few hundred men into the mountainous Drumalban territory, which divided Perthshire and Argyll. When they ventured to Dalry, south-west of Glasgow, Percy intended to make a raid 'to grieve the King's enemies as much as he can', but was finding recruitment difficult without money.[131] Percy eventually mounted the raid and his men defeated the Scots again, but the rump, including Bruce, escaped. Percy felt that he had come within an ace of capturing Bruce, only to be let down by his demoralised men's exhaustion, caused by administrative incompetence and unwillingness to send funds. He discharged a furious rebuke to Sir James de Daliegh, the quartermaster at Carlisle, 'marvel[ling] greatly that he has not sent him the victuals for the sustenance of his host as he charged him, and commands him at his highest peril and as he values the king's honour, to send these with the utmost despatch'.[132]

After Bruce's wife, now queen, and female members of the royal household had been captured trying to escape to Norway, and with Bruce's rebellion in tatters, Edward raised his own dragon. In the summer's fighting, tens of Scottish nobles had fallen into English hands; Edward aimed to terrorise Scotland into submission by ridding it of its entire military class. Gone were the halcyon days of inviting the Scots to be stakeholders in the English enterprise.

The earl of Atholl was the first earl in 230 years to be executed. When it was quietly pointed out to Edward that the earl was his distant kinsman, the Conqueror remarked that Atholl should then be hanged from a higher gallows than the others, after which he was to be beheaded and burnt. Simon Fraser was drawn, hanged and decapitated, his head stuck on a pole next to that of William Wallace. At least twenty others were hanged on 4 August 1306. Any man accused of aiding or abetting the Bruce at any time was executed.

Edward's punishment of the captured women is peculiarly perverse. Whilst the queen was treated leniently (but her appointed servants had to be elderly and were ordered never to crack a smile), Bruce's sister, Mary, and the countess of Buchan were jailed in custom-made, latticed timber-and-iron cages placed on the turrets of Roxburgh and Berwick castles. It is said that Edward picked up the idea from the Italians, in whose country this kind of punishment was fairly common. Originally, Edward wanted Bruce's adolescent daughter, Marjorie, to be caged at the Tower of London, but relented. He released her, as well as Bruce's other sister, Christina, into the safe custody of Henry Percy.[133]

Bruce himself remained at large, his whereabouts unknown. He seems to have to gone to ground in Ireland over the winter of 1306–7. In February or March 1307, Percy, then commanding the 300-man garrison at Turnberry Castle in Carrick, received a bloody nose when Bruce and his companions took his troops by surprise, killing many in their beds. For this coup, Master John Barbour raised a cheer, which is here translated: 'In the castle Percy heard the noise and cry of the slaughtered men outside in the barracks, and so could those with him, and they were all terrified, but none was so brave as to issue forth to rescue them from the Scots.'[134]

Soon afterwards, a raiding party led by two of Bruce's brothers was ambushed; one was killed and the other was hanged and beheaded in Carlisle. For months afterward Percy

> *with a full sympill cumpany,*
> *In Turnberyis castell lyand;*
> *For the king Robert sua dredand [was so feared],*
> *That he durst nocht ysche out to fair [that Percy daren't sally out].*

Once reinforcements arrived, Percy summoned a council with his knights, most of whom were itching for a fight. Sir Roger St John proposed that the English should wait in Turnberry while Percy and an escort slipped through the enemy lines into England to ask for assistance and further instructions. Percy successfully crossed the Border soon after, but the Barbour chronicle remarks that he stayed away for a suspiciously long time because he so 'dred the kyngis mycht [feared Bruce's might]'. Before ascribing a yellow streak to Percy, we should remember that Marjorie and Christina remained his prisoners, making it unlikely that Bruce, especially with his blood up, would be lenient should Percy fall into his hands.[135]

In the spring, hoping that Bruce was cornered in Carrick and Galloway, Percy rejoined Clifford and Valence, and together they planned to lure the fugitive into decisive battle. By this time, the three commanders had Edward breathing down their necks, for on 11 February 1307 they each received an ironic letter from the king, asking why Bruce's head had not yet been brought to him and commanding them 'to write distinctly and clearly ... the news of the parts where he is, the state of affairs there, and the doings of himself and ... how he and they have arranged further proceedings. For he suspects from his silence that he has so over-cautiously conducted matters that he wishes to conceal his actions.'[136] Privately, Edward mentioned to his treasurer that 'he hears they have done so badly that they do not wish him to know'.[137]

Bruce had hidden in the impenetrably wild country of Galloway. English contingents that pierced the interior and hunted him with 'sleuth-hound' and horn were being destroyed by his outlaws. In early May 1307, Bruce jumped Valence's force at Loudoun Hill, about four miles east of Kilmarnock. Fighting on a narrow front, so barring the English cavalry from delivering a flank attack, the Scots put Valence to flight and reversed the rout of Methven. This, and his initial raid on Turnberry, illustrates Bruce's new guerrilla strategy. He avoided pitched battles except when he wanted them: 'speed, surprise, mobility, small-scale engagements, scorched earth and dismantling of fortresses – these were to be the hall-marks of his campaigns' until 1314.[138]

Edward's three most experienced and senior commanders had finally failed him through overcaution. Disappointed, he called a feudal muster at Carlisle and set out for Scotland to deal with Bruce himself, but the fearsome *Scottorum Malleus* ('Hammer of the Scots', although the epithet was only carved onto his tomb during the reign of Elizabeth I) died aged sixty-nine on 7 July 1307 at Burgh-by-Sands, before he had even crossed the Border.

CHAPTER SEVEN

The Border Baron

Lord Percy versus Edward II and the Scots

In 1307, Henry Percy was in fine fettle, with Edward I's peevishness over the failure to capture Bruce forgotten in the aftermath of the grand old man's death. What was he like, this Percy? Unlike his arthritic, black-gummed, hobbled labourers and their similarly afflicted wives, Percy, like most tolerably well-nourished nobles, stood anywhere from five foot six to five foot ten (any taller or shorter would have elicited comment in the chronicles). When not campaigning, his diet included beef, pork and mutton as well as herrings (a dozen for a penny), eels and salmon. Ducks, chicken, eggs (but little milk) and bread also featured prominently; he drank Rhineland and Gascony wine and especially ale; a good number of Englishmen habitually walked around slightly sozzled, which might explain some of the era's endemic violence. Apples and pears were a staple, with pomegranates as a treat. On special occasions there were foreign exotica such as sugar and rice, but at royal feasts were served boars' heads burnished with silver, peacocks and swans on golden plat-ters and exquisite pastries. Dentistry then being in its infancy, his teeth would have been ground down to the flat.

His body would have exhibited the tell-tale ailments of the martially engaged. Falls from horses and the clatter of swords upon his armour left a painful catalogue of fractured ribs, stretched tendons, worn joints and sprains. His muscled right arm was longer than the other from wielding heavy swords and lances since he was a youngster. Unlike the peasants, he spoke a U-dialect of French.[1]

Apart from briefly rebelling against the king – as described in this chapter – Percy was unswervingly loyal to the Crown, particularly to the person and legacy of Edward I. Percy had very firm ideas about what made a king a king; the man who fell short of this ideal may have contin-ued to receive his fealty, but not unconditionally. In Percy's eyes, Edward I perfectly combined the manly art of kingship with the Crown, but his son was a weakling with a taste for foreign favourites.

Percy was a soldier first and last. As the Scottish chroniclers and later historians do not spit out his name with malice, Percy clearly avoided a reputation for rapaciousness or undue inclemency towards the subdued. A number of contemporary observers, however, alluded to his angry ruthlessness in war and his unbending sense of honour. The chronicler of Alnwick Abbey said that 'he would not suffer injury from any one, without a heavy punishment' and that 'this Henry so gallantly command-ed his servants, that they were feared in the whole realm'.[2] Even William Wallace's faithful chaplain, John Blair, admitted that Percy was 'True, and ay of great avail,/Sober in peace, and cruel in battail'.

Notwithstanding his (relative) restraint, Percy had no doubts about the Scottish crusade and spent most of his life fighting for English master-ship. He had also gambled heavily by becoming a substantial landowner across the Border and accepting the earldom of Carrick after Edward I stripped the disgraced Bruce of it in 1306. Thus, any royal disinclination to prosecute the war would be immensely disappointing; Edward I's manic single-mindedness in this respect effortlessly raised his stature in Percy's eyes, but Edward II's lack of interest and incompetence would prove the death of Henry Percy.

Intensely ambitious for his descendants, his purchase of Alnwick Castle (described below) shows admirable foresight for the destined Percy ascendancy in the North. Likewise, his early alteration of the family's arms bespeaks a man determined to pass on a memorable symbol of Percy greatness. He also took immense care to move his wife and child to a safer part of Yorkshire than Topcliffe, where they would have been vulnerable to a Scots raid. During Edward's I's reign, Percy was regarded as a wise head on sound shoulders, a resolute, trustworthy, clubbable fellow and a welcome addition to the king's personal council. After his mentor's death, Percy, while still respected, had to accept that he and his friends were identified as part of the gruff, starchy Old Gang by Edward II's glittering courtiers.

The New Regime

On his deathbed at Burgh-by-Sands, suffering from dysentery, Edward I urgently summoned the earls of Lincoln and Warwick, Robert Clifford and Aymer de Valence, to witness his last command. These men, like Percy, were the lions under Edward's throne; it is hard to imagine that they might ever hear a word said against their revered sovereign. Percy, however, was not present; with Clifford, Valence and the others away, he was left in charge of southern Scotland.

Guy de Beauchamp, as earl of Warwick, was a cultivated aristocratic ruffian of good breeding and better reading; around thirty-eight years old, he had served in Scotland since 1298, where he had fallen in with the late Earl Warenne, Aymer de Valence and Henry Percy.[3] Edward I's old Scotland hands, it seems, were part of a very small world.

The earl of Lincoln, Henry de Lacy, was the oldest of the ten or so English earls. Born in about 1250, he had uncomplainingly fought whenever King Edward sent him. No mean diplomat, he also handled delicate matters, such as royal marriages and treaty negotiations. His two sons died while drunk (one drowned in a well, the other fell off the ramparts at Pontefract), so he arranged for the king's younger brother, Edmund 'Crouchback' of Lancaster, to hold his lands upon his death, a signal mark of respect and loyalty to Edward, who repeatedly promoted him. At Falkirk and Caerlaverock, Lincoln commanded the vaunted first squadron, the vanguard. He had also acted as the prince's protector in Scotland, and it was as a personal friend of Edward I, and grandfatherly companion of the prince, that Lincoln was called to the king's bedside in July 1307.[4]

At Burgh-by-Sands, the king 'prayede them, oppon the faithe that they to him owede, that they shulde make Edward of Carnaryuon, Kyng of Engeland, his sone... and that they shulde nought suffre Piers of Gaveston come ageyn into Engeland [some of the language has been modernised]'. The next morning he died gasping in his servant's arms, his last words being: 'Have mercy upon me, Almighty God!'[5]

Who was this hateful 'Piers of Gaveston', and why did he provoke such hostility in Edward I that he summoned his captains out of the field when the noose was tightening around Bruce? Piers Gaveston, born in Gascony, was the son of a leading baron of Béarn named Arnaud de Gabeston with connections to Edward I in the 1270s.[6] Piers, his father and his two brothers served Edward I in Scotland during the 1298 Falkirk campaign and the 1300 expedition. In the latter year, the king arranged for Gaveston to transfer into the Prince of Wales's household as one of his squires. Gaveston's martial ability and famously fine manners doubtless persuaded Edward I that his somewhat disappointing son might learn something from the Béarnais. By August 1303, Gaveston, the young prince's favourite, was riding high in Edward I's esteem.

During Edward's winter sojourn in Dunfermline in 1303–4, the prince stayed at Perth with Gaveston, where the future king and his charming, bitchy friend entertained the gruffer English earls and barons, such as Percy. After the fall of Stirling, prince and favourite returned to England. In late May 1306, Edward, Gaveston and 266 other young men were knighted, perhaps the largest congregation of knights ever, at Westminster.

Soon afterwards, Sir Piers and his royal patron returned to Scotland to help hunt down Bruce, who had disappeared after his rout at Methven. In October 1306, with Percy, Clifford and Valence crying out for extra manpower in Galloway, the king was furious to hear that the prince and Gaveston had held a tournament in direct contravention of Edward's order banning – on pain of death – such amusements during wartime. Edward stormed that he wanted the young knights executed, but he relented and in January 1307 those who had participated were pardoned, barring one – Sir Piers Gaveston. By the end of April, Edward decreed, Gaveston was to be banished to Gascony.[7]

Then at Lanercost, the king had been informed of the prince's relationship with Gaveston, which far exceeded that normally expected of just good friends. We can be fairly, if not definitely, certain that the relationship was a somewhat homosexual one, and for the moment, luckily, the secret was confined to baronial gossip. The revelation of a homosexual Prince of Wales would humiliate such a virile king as Edward (eighteen children by two wives, of whom Edward was the youngest but only surviving son, apart from two half-brothers). Edward of Caernarvon would be a laughing stock among the baronage and a usurper like Simon de Montfort might emerge. Furthermore, the relationship jeopardised the prince's long-arranged marriage to Isabella of France, eldest daughter of the upright Philip IV – who had recently destroyed the Templars by accusing them of institutionalised sodomy. With these fears uppermost in his mind, Edward beseeched Lincoln, Warwick, Valence and Clifford to ensure a safe succession in July 1307 and to keep Gaveston at arm's length.

Other worries about the prince plagued Edward in his last days, particularly his son's alarming disposition towards favouritism. Edward had always spread his patronage far and wide so that few could complain and allies could always be found in an emergency; but the prince put all his eggs into Gaveston's basket, placing flattery and friendship above political calculation. Worse still, he regarded Scottish affairs as a bore and military service as a chore. The problem was that the poor prince was so *unkingly*, preferring rowing, swimming, fine clothes, games and rustic crafts to defending the realm. According to the chronicler Higden, making a concealed dig at the prince's sexual predilections, 'undervaluing the society of the magnates, [Edward] fraternised with buffoons, singers, actors, carters, ditchers, oarsmen [and] sailors'. The stories about Edward eventually filtered 'downstairs'; a messenger in the king's household was jailed briefly for making a crack about the prince.[8] And the Scots composed bawdy ditties lampooning the prince, which English infantry stationed across the Border could hear their supposedly defeated enemies sing in the night.

An account, taken from a reliable chronicler, sheds light on the king's exasperation with his worthless son. In early 1307, the prince asked his father to make Gaveston count of Poitou: 'You wretched bastard,' the king erupted, 'do you want to give away lands now? You who never gained any?' And with that he tore out clumps of the prince's hair and threw him out of his chamber.[9]

Contemporaries worried that when the prince was not being apathetic, melancholic, or hysterical, he was giving himself over to wantonness and passing his time in voluptuous excess, all in the company of Gaveston. It seemed that Edward II would be the first king of England who was not a man of kingly business.[10]

Edward's ad hoc council did its best in the circumstances: Edward of Caernarvon duly succeeded his father, but promptly summoned Sir Piers back and elevated the former squire to the earldom of Cornwall, a gift worth the titanic figure of £4000 per annum. By way of comparison, Henry Percy's annual income from his estates was approximately £900.[11] This record-breaking rise caused consternation among the other earls, but no man wanted to be the first to make an enemy of a new king.

Percy may have grumbled, but he had far more worrying matters nagging him. On 25 August 1307, Edward II departed Scotland and did not return for another three years. Quite unthinkingly, he refashioned his father's military organisation in Scotland; the effective Valence was replaced by the ineffectual John of Brittany, and Clifford was 'promoted' to marshal of England (in which post he was responsible for organising billeting and sentry duty), a tiresome post that he surrendered less than a year later when another Scottish emergency arose.[12] Percy was relieved of his command, and told to return home. But on 18 October 1307, he was hurriedly directed to 'repair to Scotland with all his forces, for the defence of the country, as well as of his own possessions [that is, Carrick, Urr and Red Castle].'[13] He was too late.

In that month, stunned at the sudden disappearance of Percy, Clifford and Valence, Robert Bruce had escaped from the Galloway hinterlands and marched northwards across the mountains with 3000 men – many more recruits joined him later – to Inverness and Loch Ness.[14] In November he pushed eastwards to Elgin and razed Buchan, leaving the Highlands a shambles by shattering loyalist Scottish nobles and expelling the English. Galloway and Argyll still lay undefeated, but Bruce would surely return south.

In mid-August 1308 he did. Defeating the pro-Balliol/Comyn Argyllsmen, Bruce then raided Northumberland with impunity through Lothian. Colonial Scotland was slipping through Edward II's muscleless fingers. On 22 August 1308, Percy again received a military summons and sped to one of the English castles in Galloway.[15] The Northumberland raids had been a diversion for a savage assault on Galloway by King Robert's only surviving brother, Edward Bruce, who turned to the chain of castles linking the territory with Carlisle: namely, Lochmaben, Caerlaverock, Dumfries, Dalswinton, Tibbers, Loch Doon (King Robert's own island fortress) and mighty Ayr. It was around these that Percy and the newly arrived Clifford organised the defences so effectively that none fell until at least 1309. (A couple even held out until 1313.) Nevertheless, by the autumn of 1308, the three great heartlands of Anglo-Balliolism – Buchan, Argyll and Galloway – were overrun with Bruce's troops. However, centred around the castles of Stirling, Edinburgh, Roxburgh, Jedburgh and Berwick, the English grasp on the south-east, in Lothian especially, remained apparently unshakeable.[16]

In March 1309, Bruce insolently summoned his first Parliament, at which the vast majority of the community of the realm was represented. And what was Edward II's reply to an affront his father would never had tolerated? He sent the new earl of Gloucester (whose sister – and niece of the king – had been married off to Gaveston in November 1307) to the Scottish court and made a truce to last until 1 November.

Apart from boredom, one reason for Edward II's appeasement of the Scots was that England had teetered on the brink of civil war for nearly two years. One annalist observed that there were 'two kings in one kingdom', referring to Edward and Piers Gaveston, who now controlled the flow of lush patronage and favours in his friend's name. He was accused of manipulating ecclesiastical appointments and taking bribes. Those earls and magnates outside Gaveston's racket were angered at having to pay for their privileges. Their ill-humours were not salved by Gaveston's supercilious victory at a tournament held at Wallingford on 2 December 1307. There, he and his side – 'all the younger and more athletic knights of the kingdom' – unhorsed the earls of Arundel, Hereford and Warenne (the grandson of Earl Warenne) and unsportingly trod them under foot. In turn, his humiliated antagonists complained that Gaveston had led 200 knights into the field instead of the agreed sixty.[17]

The first visible, and alarming, sign of rebellious discontent arrived on 31 January 1308. A letter – the 'Boulogne Agreement' – ominously distinguished between fealty to the person of the king and that due to the Crown, and declared the barons' determination to uphold the rights of the Crown. As for the king, they merely wished to preserve his honour, but Gaveston was dragging his name into disrepute. The leaders of this coalescing anti-Gaveston faction are indicated in the letter's signatories. The moderates included Anthony Bek (bishop of Durham) and the earl of Pembroke (Valence), who wished to warn Edward of discord looming within the peerage. Implacably opposing Gaveston were Edward I's other 'lions', the earls of Lincoln and Warwick, and Robert Clifford, as well as new enemies like Hereford and Warenne.[18] Percy's sympathies are impossible to know for he was uneasily watching Bruce's successes. However, all his friends were deeply involved in the anti-Gaveston campaign. He *probably* ascribed Edward's unwillingness to oppose Bruce's remorseless march towards his hard-won possessions in Galloway to Gaveston's malign influence.

What Percy saw of Gaveston when he travelled down to Westminster for the coronation of Edward II on 25 February 1308 would not have been encouraging.[19] Rumours that Edward loved Piers far more than Isabella, his twelve-year-old queen, had reached his French in-laws' ears, no doubt via the disgruntled earls.[20] Following a French threat to boycott the ceremony, there was a week-long delay until Edward sullenly agreed to clip Gaveston's wings.[21] Nevertheless, during the coronation, the king obnoxiously raised Gaveston above the other earls by permitting him to carry the crown of St Edward, as opposed to the lowlier duties of bearing swords, gilt spurs, royal vestments and the chalice.[22]

The banquet that followed came close to ending in murder. Piers entered the hall sporting a flashy outfit of imperial purple trimmed with pearls, and beckoned the king to join him at his seat. One earl, livid at the favourite's presumption, drew his sword but was restrained by his fellows. The queen's relatives and foreign dignitaries were shocked at Edward's preference for Piers over Isabella's company and haughtily departed the feast. For stiff-necked soldiers like Percy, his abiding memory of the banquet (apart from a possible discussion of his Blue Lion with the duke of Brabant, another guest) would have been disgust at Gaveston's foppery and Edward's meekness.

Ten days after the coronation, the nobles congregated at Westminster for a Parliament. There, Lincoln angrily proposed that Edward agree in writing to get rid of Gaveston, an indignity to the king's authority that was opposed by Thomas, the earl of Lancaster (Edward's cousin) and which Hugh Despenser (a 'hateful' baron who, 'more from a desire to please [the king] and a lust for gain than for any creditable reason, had become an adherent of Piers', according to the Monk of Malmesbury) bravely attacked, despite jeers from the assembly.[23] A few hours later, Edward stupidly announced that he would postpone such matters until Easter, thereby giving the (correct) impression that he was reneging on his pre-ceremony pledge to keep Gaveston in check. Between then and Easter, Edward surreptitiously prepared for war, munitioning and repairing his castles, and replacing those such as Clifford, who had signed the Boulogne Agreement, with Gaveston's friends.[24] Percy, lacking royal patronage, had not yet shown his colours, despite his close friendships with Lincoln and Clifford. In the middle of March 1308, then, he was appointed to the constableship of Scarborough Castle in an effort to bring him onside. Very mysteriously, however, the order was 'cancelled' but he was permitted to reside there temporarily. Had Percy perhaps refused the offer and decided to stay belligerently neutral for the time being?[25]

On 28 April 1308, when Parliament met again, the earls came armed. They were also powerfully supported; nearly all of the barons were circumspectly anti-Gaveston, and only two earls – Lancaster and Richmond (another royal cousin) – were undeniably royalist. Barons such as Despenser and William Latimer stood up for Gaveston but the aggrieved queen, prompted by Philip IV and his brothers, offered support against her husband. There are confirmed reports that the French king was at this time engaged in talks with the earls and even sent Lincoln £40,000 to finance a rebellion.

At the Parliament, Lincoln developed the 'doctrine of capacities', which had blurrily appeared in the Boulogne Agreement – and before that, in Magna Carta, arguing that 'a higher duty is owed to the Crown than to the person of the king. It is the magnates' professed duty to maintain the estate of the Crown, even if this should mean disobedience to the king in the event that the estate of the Crown should be diminished.' Therefore, as Gaveston was usurping the Crown estate through patronage, he was necessarily a traitor (the fact that Lincoln himself was in semi-treasonous contact with Philip was omitted from the speech). The implication that nobles, selflessly acting in the Crown's interest, might depose mere kings forced Edward's hand. On 18 May 1308, he agreed that Gaveston would again be sent into exile, his lands reverting to the Crown.[26] Gaveston's sojourn abroad would not be unpleasant; the king craftily ensured that his income would remain £4000, the same sum as he had drawn from the earldom of Cornwall.[27]

In fact, exile meant Ireland, with Edward appointing him his lieutenant on 16 June 1308.[28] The earls were understood to have acquiesced, just to get Gaveston out of the country. Finding his apparent neutrality useful, they even nominated Henry Percy as one of their representatives to witness the king seal Gaveston's letter of appointment.[29]

Nevertheless, Edward did not forget those who lent their support, explicitly or implicitly, to the uppity earls. Soon afterwards, Percy and Clifford were ordered to defend what was left of English Scotland from Robert Bruce, a deliberately thankless task, as they had to provide their own troops without royal support.[30]

From the day Piers left, the king plotted for his return, showering gifts, promises and blandishments on the earls,[31] a task made infinitely easier by the fractious Gaveston's absence. The natural inclination of the nobles was always to gravitate towards the Crown, like sheep to the shepherd. Only the most overmighty subjects could afford to strike poses of haughty independence. As we saw earlier, magnates almost always pursued rebellions with restraint and pulled back from anarchy, ultimately preferring the rule of law to unbridled licence. The well-informed monkish observer of the life of Edward II advanced a difference explanation: 'See how often and abruptly great men change their sides... The love of magnates is as a game of dice, and the desires of the rich like feathers.'[32]

The king soon ensured the young earl of Gloucester's loyalty (he never lost the friendship of Richmond, the only earl never to change sides) by granting him swathes of, sensibly enough, Gloucestershire. When the respected Lincoln, formerly the most dangerously vocal opponent of Gaveston, stood alongside his sovereign, Warenne, Hereford, Arundel, Oxford, Warwick (Lincoln's accomplice) and Pembroke also made their peace.

Of these mention must be made of the brutal and disreputable Earl Warenne, whom Lincoln and Lancaster – who was married to Lincoln's daughter, Alice de Lucy[33] – soon grew to hate (Percy seems to have avoided him like the plague). The young earl of Hereford, Humphrey de Bohun, who had sauntered about elegantly dressed during the siege of Caerlaverock, was married to one of Edward's sisters. For a few years they were friends, but the touchy earl possessed a certain independence of mind and action.[34]

The earls of Arundel and Oxford are shadowy figures, but on the whole they were committed members of the baronial camp at this stage. Through his wife, Percy was Arundel's brother-in-law and the two became acquainted up in Scotland when Arundel undertook his first military service after being knighted on 22 May 1306 (he was summoned as earl six months later). He was still bitter at being unhorsed by Gaveston in the Wallingford tournament in December 1307.[35] His maternal grandfather, the earl of Oxford (Robert de Vere), was slightly younger than the ancient earl of Lincoln but had only inherited his title in 1296.[36]

The canny Warwick, although wary of Edward's motives, allowed him the benefit of the doubt for the time being.[37] It was the earl of Lancaster – magnate of magnates, the 'wealthiest earl in the world' and Warwick's godfather[38] – who experienced the most profound shift in allegiance. From defending Edward after the coronation debacle, he broke away to form, for the moment, a one-man opposition. In the hierarchy of earls, it was not, however, altogether 'one man, one vote'. If anything, Lancaster was the man, so he had the vote.

Through escheats, inheritances and forfeitures, the earls of Lancaster had swallowed the lands (and the titles) of the earldoms of Leicester, Derby and Salisbury, and in a few years would digest Lincoln as well. As he held a goodly part of Edward's realm, his defection was, therefore, of no little consequence. The 31-year-old Thomas, the earl of Lancaster and Henry III's grandson, is generally regarded as a coarse, unscrupulous, violent man swollen with the pride of his birth – and indeed he was. Nevertheless, these character defects masked his genuine commitment to good government.[39] Lancaster had perceptively sensed that the king's suspiciously sudden deference to the earls was only to lull them into approving Gaveston's return. Then Gaveston would soon be up to his old tricks again, but Lancaster was loath to rescue Edward for a second time. For the next two years, Lancaster refused to witness Edward's charters or take advantage of his blandishments.

At the Westminster Parliament of April–May 1309, Edward predictably tested the waters by asking whether Gaveston could return, which, after some horse-trading, was eventually agreed. On 27 June 1309, the newly reinstated earl of Cornwall exultantly stepped ashore in England.

Within a few months, Lancaster was proved right: Gaveston had reverted to form. He made no secret of his disdain for most of his fellow earls, for whom he invented all sorts of offensive nicknames. Warwick was called 'Black Cur', then considered a grave and treacherous insult. When this tag was reported to the said earl, he calmly replied: 'If he call me a dog, be sure that I will bite him so soon as I shall perceive my opportunity.' As for Lancaster, he was sneered at as a 'Churl'.

Some of the earls realised their mistake; others threw in their lot with the king. In October 1309, Warwick, Arundel and Oxford joined with Lancaster in refusing to attend a Parliament at York simply because of Gaveston's presence. In February 1310, they were joined by Hereford and a reluctant Pembroke, who would move back to his 'moderate' position between the camps. Lincoln, too, sought to remain aloof from the factions, but Gloucester and Warenne fell in alongside the ever-loyal Richmond by siding with Edward.

When a Parliament finally – and momentously – convened, on 27 February 1310, Edward was presented with a devastating indictment of his government. Accusations ranged from extortion to corruption – singling out Gaveston. Unsurprisingly, given their Scottish interests, the earls were incensed by Edward's unwillingness to do anything about King Robert and the lost kingdom of Scotland. They reiterated their humble duty to safeguard the Crown's majesty, and stridently asked Edward's permission to establish a committee composed of prelates, earls and barons to set the kingdom to rights. Edward knew perfectly well that this 'request', if refused, was a prelude to civil war, but was equally worried about the threat to Gaveston if Lancaster packed the committee with his yes-men. Caught in an impossible situation and after prevaricating for a little more than a fortnight, Edward reluctantly granted the earls' wishes on 16 March.

Lord Percy and the Alnwick Castle Business

What was Percy doing at this time? After witnessing the king seal Gaveston's appointment as lieutenant in Ireland in mid-1308, Percy again tried to hold back Bruce's attack on Galloway, but he was back in England by the end of the year. King Robert's first Parliament in March–April 1309 bespoke one inevitability in Percy's eyes: a great war between the states must ensue – there were simply too many vested interests in Scotland for Edward to ignore, Gaveston or no Gaveston.

Another consideration may have played upon his mind. Yorkshire was too cramped for an ambitious baron to expand his empire. Topcliffe, for instance, was hemmed in by chunks of the great earls' estates. With the prospective resumption of the Anglo-Scottish war, the real action had shifted northwards to the Borders, where capable warlords were lacking and land was plentiful. Two of his friends were similarly inclined: Clifford had transported himself from South Wales and Warwick had bought Balliol's Barnard Castle and estates from the Crown in 1307.[40] Previously, Percy had been a Yorkshire baron who served in the Marches; if he moved north, he might become a Marcher lord who summoned Yorkshire barons.

Moreover, as a lower-ranking peer and a former member of the king's council, Percy may well have nursed hopes of a real, English earldom; his family went back to the Conquest and he associated with many of the earls as a near-equal. But, relegated to Yorkshire, he could never acquire the income, status and estates that launched men into the hierarchical stratosphere. However, if he voluntarily placed himself in the line of fire, a grateful king might reward him with titles, lands and offices.

Whilst musing over these delightful thoughts as he pored over his accounts, Percy was presented with the perfect opportunity to realise them in the summer of 1309. In 1297, the last lord of the castle, manor and barony of Alnwick in Northumberland – William Vesci – had died without lawful issue, leaving the estate in limbo. Because he had spent so much time in the West, Percy might have preferred a Cumbrian barony, but castles rarely came onto the market and beggars could not be choosers. In any case, perched midway between his Yorkshire lands and his Scottish acquisitions, Alnwick would make a useful base.

William Vesci was the direct descendant of the Vesci who had fought alongside Sir Richard Percy in the struggle for Magna Carta. Before he died, however, William Vesci allegedly entrusted Anthony Bek, the wily bishop of Durham, with the Honour of Alnwick to be held for his *illegitimate* son, William Vesci of Kildare. It is usually thought that the notoriously greedy Bek treacherously sold Alnwick to Percy.[41] Others, however, implicitly whitewash Bek of any wrongdoing: the *Chronicle of Alnwick Abbey*, written in 1377 with the aid of some of the original documents, innocuously notes that 'Lord Henry Percy purchased the barony of Alnwick'.[42] Did Bek defraud Vesci of Kildare?

A concord exists between Bek and the senior William Vesci, dated 29 October 1295, which states plainly that Vesci's Yorkshire and Lincolnshire manors should pass to his illegitimate son, but Alnwick and its appurtenances were to remain with Bek and his heirs.[43] Therefore, it seems the bishop was within his rights to sell Alnwick to Percy.

However, that concord was only a non-binding draft; a final contract always needed to be registered with the Exchequer. And here is the problem. Vesci of Kildare did receive the promised Yorkshire and Lincolnshire manors, because a copy dealing with that conveyance is lodged in the official records.[44] When it comes to the *baronio, castro, manerio et villa d'Alnewyck*, however, we are not so fortunate. Although Bek sold Alnwick, no document acknowledging his *original* ownership is lodged in the records for Northumberland, merely an undated and hurriedly written *private* copy of the final contract.[45] Perhaps a dying William Vesci had handed Alnwick to Bek *temporarily* in trust for Vesci of Kildare, but the bishop surreptitiously altered the non-binding concord of 29 October 1295 so that Alnwick would be his. Bek, obviously, never registered a final, official contract with the Exchequer because there wasn't one; if anyone bothered asking questions, he could base his claim on the fraudulent draft of October 1295. Perhaps the Alnwick conveyance was perfectly above board, but the lack of official confirmation is mysterious, to say the least.

Further shrouding the truth are some subsequent events regarding these estates. William Vesci of Kildare died at the battle of Bannockburn (see below), and his Yorkshire and Lincolnshire lands, after Chancery clerks had combed the records for an heir, passed to Gilbert Aton, whose distant relative was a Vesci.[46] Gilbert subsequently claimed Alnwick, but on 2 December 1323 confirmed Percy's son's ownership. In return, Aton received 350 marks (about £230) from the younger Percy, whose daughter married Aton's son (see Chapter 11). These transactions can be interpreted in two ways. If Bek *had* defrauded Vesci of Kildare, and therefore Alnwick was rightfully part of Aton's inheritance, Percy's son gave Aton a choice between a lengthy and expensive court case or a respectable out-of-court settlement. But if Bek was innocent and Aton was blackmailing Percy's son with the threat of a suit, then the latter may have paid the 350 marks to shut him up.[47]

There is little advantage in condemning or condoning the somewhat murky business surrounding the purchase of Alnwick Castle. A question mark must be placed over Henry Percy's involvement in any fraud on Bishop Bek's part. The forgery, if it happened, of the agreement occurred a decade before Percy's purchase, yet did he know that he was buying possibly stolen goods? Probably not, but keep in mind that Henry Percy was not averse to slippery property dealing: he had, as we saw in Chapter 6, refused to return the baronies of Urr and Red Castle in Scotland to their rightful owner, a distant relative of his.

By buying Alnwick, Percy was taking an enormous risk, but the rewards were commensurate. His annual income was £900, but the yearly revenue from the Alnwick estates was estimated at about £475, thereby increasing his income by slightly over 50 per cent. The £4666 purchase price – a fair one, equalling ten years' income (the average) from the estate – was a different matter. Percy needed outside assistance to pay Bek, and therefore did as other Englishmen did: he took out a loan with Italian merchant bankers, obtaining £2666 (4000 marks) from the Lombard society, the Bellardi of Lucca, through their London agent, John Vanne, in Lombard Street in the City.[48]

There are no records of any interest paid on this debt, but it would be strange if there were. After Henry III had banned usury in 1240 in a moment of godly self-righteousness, various schemes were dreamt up to get around it. By 1270, on top of repaying the principal in instalments, the merchant bankers would charge for 'damages' (that is, fines for late repayment of the principal on absurdly short schedules, sometimes only a month) and 'expenses' incurred as a result of the loan; amazingly enough, these invoices coincided with the repayment timetable. In general, however, the merchant bankers were lucky if they ever received the principal in full. As the acerbic monk of Malmesbury observed: 'the English race excel other nations ... in pride, in guile, and in perjury ... a very great kind of guile ... is common in England; I speak of those who accept a loan and fail to pay the debt on the appointed days.'[49] Percy's firm, for example, a fairly small one, which advanced the Crown £7493 between 1298 and 1307, only saw £4021 of that repaid. So why did bankers lend so unquestioningly to England and European crowns and nobles?

Where the Italian companies excelled was in taking advantage of extremely favourable exchange rates to transfer credit, so that the profits dwarfed the losses caused by slack repayments – provided the instalments were paid in London, and thence exchanged abroad through the bankers' agents. In a single transaction, for instance, the Frescobaldi instantly made £666 by manipulating the difference between official and unofficial exchange rates on a loan of £7000.[50] Knowledge of international high finance among English nobles being rudimentary, to say the least, we can confidently assert that men like Henry Percy had no idea what was going on or why Mr John Vanne of the Bellardi Company so courteously insisted that the instalments be paid through his offices in the City.

As Percy's income was now in the region of £1400 per annum, his debt load was not unduly heavy, and was considerably lightened by his acquisition of the wardship of an heir in his minority in 1310, annually worth £170,[51] and by his appointment as custodian of the see of Durham following Bek's death in 1311, bringing him another £200 per annum.[52] These additional monies, even after the Bellardi had taken their cut, left Henry Percy wealthy enough to refurbish his castle's defences.

The castle of the Lord of Alnwick (and, it was hoped, future earl of Northumberland) was to form the cornerstone of Percy power in the North and stand as a warning to the Scots. Displaying the strategic foresight of his ancestor, William de Percy, who had chosen the brilliantly situated Topcliffe, Percy's Alnwick would be almost impervious to attack thanks to its natural defences. It was raised on a peninsular bluff, and directly to the north wound the River Alne, while to the south and east there was the ravine of the Bow burn. On the west side stood the main gate, before which was cut a deep ditch, making the site almost an island.

From the eleventh century, Alnwick had been a motte-and-bailey castle with a stone keep. By Percy's day, castle-building had moved on to concentric defences. Basing his stronghold's design on Edward's futuristic castles at Caernarvon and Conwy, and drawing on his early experiences in Wales, Percy added a heavily fortified barbican to defend the gateway, rounded towers (square ones were vulnerable to mining and battering at their corners) at the enfilading angles of each stretch of the curtaining walls, a watery moat, an indispensable well, a portcullis, a drawbridge and eight semicircular bastions to the keep.[53]

Percy had chosen an ideal time to buy. Owing to the Gaveston trouble down south, a series of flimsy truces brought peace to the Border between February 1309 and March 1310. The first Lord of Alnwick, however, gambled heavily on war showering him with opportunities and, shortly after, his risk was to pay off handsomely.

The Storm Breaks

During that same March 1310, Edward II agreed to the election of twenty-one 'Lords Ordainers' to set his realm to rights.[54] These twenty-one included eight earls variously drawn from the moderate, anti-Gaveston and courtly factions, with a slight bias towards the Lancastrian adherents.[55] Pembroke and Lincoln were of the first group (sympathisers with Lancastrian concerns, although they were more concerned with ensuring stability than destroying Gaveston); Lancaster, Hereford, Warwick and Arundel were of the second; while Gloucester, Warenne and Richmond stood for the status quo.

Hoping to split the Ordainers, Edward II decided to launch a Scottish campaign in June 1310, a month before he accepted their preliminary ordinances regarding governmental reform. Normally the earls would have turned out in force to fight the Scots, but in the end only Gaveston, Gloucester, Richmond and the warlike Warenne (Lincoln was appointed regent in the king's absence) accompanied Edward on this ill-starred campaign. The others refused, claiming they were too busy working on their reforms. Irritated at his subjects' hauteur, Edward disregarded the ordinances already in force and appointed Gaveston justice of the North and keeper of Nottingham Castle. At this, Lincoln threatened to resign and the Ordainers were 'much disturbed and enraged'.

Until the spring of 1311, there is little to record by way of English military success in Scotland: Bruce cleverly refused to fight and his men hid in the marshes and mountains; Gaveston and the other earls tramped around the country pointlessly; and money drained from the Exchequer. Other developments, moreover, were dogging Edward. On 6 February 1311, the earl of Lincoln died, thereby removing a moderating influence from the Lords Ordainers, and his lands and title descended to his son-in-law, the earl of Lancaster. On his deathbed, the aged Lincoln revealed his true colours to the hot-headed Lancaster, who he thought needed a calming, calculating ally against the king: 'he cleped Thomas [of Lancaster] to him, and comaund him to stand with the rite of the reme, and that he schuld be governed be the council of [Guy] erl of Warwick.'[56]

Remembering these ringing words, Lancaster travelled north to the River Tweed to swear fealty to the king for the fifth of his earldoms but refused to leave English territory to do so. Following a period of exchanging glares across the river, the king crossed over with Gaveston, a humiliating spectacle. Even then, Lancaster pointedly ignored Gaveston in his greetings.

For the duration of the Scottish campaign, Percy and Clifford had served in the army – not everyone could afford to turn a blind eye to a royal summons. In early May 1311, Gaveston, who enjoyed teasing starchy underlings, gave Percy command of 200 knights at Perth, a promotion that went unappreciated as 200 horse and no infantry in a town surrounded by aggressive Scotsmen looked like a death sentence. He was directed to stay there until Michaelmas.[57] More alarmingly still, however, the king was making preparations to withdraw from Scotland to hold a Parliament, leaving Percy isolated in the North. In mid-August of that year, following a savage raid across into Northern England by Robert Bruce, Gaveston and his friends accordingly retired across the Border to the safety of Bamburgh Castle.

Percy evidently succeeded in fighting his way out of Perth, because he was in London on 5 October. Meanwhile, the Lords had read their completed Ordinances to Edward on 16 August. Chapter 20 called for Gaveston to be sent into perpetual exile both from England and from all English possessions abroad. Edward, miserable, offered to agree to everything else if just that one condition was retracted. However, in the face of baronial solidarity, Edward ultimately accepted the forty-one Ordinances in full, probably hoping to let Gaveston slip back into the country when the excitement had died down. About five weeks later, the Ordinances were published in St Paul's churchyard in the presence of Arundel, Lancaster, Hereford, Oxford, Pembroke and Warwick. And on 5 October, the Ordinances were read out to the people of London in the same place by Gloucester, Henry Percy, the chancellor, the treasurer and other members of the king's council.

Almost at once Edward daringly flouted the letter of the Ordinances, if not their spirit. As soon as Gaveston left England for the Low Countries, the king duly took back his lands but handed them over in trust to Gaveston's loyal officials, so that they should be ready for Piers's return.

Flushed with success at finally being rid of Gaveston for ever, the earls overplayed their hand by decreeing that his friends and partisans should also leave the court. 'At this the king's anger knew no bounds ... so out of hatred for the earls he recalled Piers, swearing as he was wont on God's soul that he would freely use his own judgement.'[58] Whether Gaveston wanted to leap back into the lion's den is uncertain, but he secretly arranged to meet Edward in York in early January 1312.[59] On 20 January his lands were returned, the first sure indication to the earls that Gaveston was back. The two men stayed at York, for Gaveston's wife was in the last stage of pregnancy and could not be moved.

Edward girded himself for war by purging Lancastrian sympathisers from positions of power. For instance, on 6 March, Percy was ordered to hand over Scarborough Castle, over which he was custodian, to Robert de Felton.[60] Percy ignored the order. A week later, a second, brusquer order commanded him to surrender the castle to William Latimer, a Gaveston loyalist, and his archers. Percy absconded but left his retainers in possession of the castle, who proceeded to hold it against the royal forces. For his cheekiness, Percy was imprisoned briefly. After meekly submitting to the king, he was released and reluctantly pardoned.[61] Already suspicious at Percy's presence in London reading out the Ordinances, Edward now definitely knew which side Percy was on. He had conceived an intense dislike towards this particular Northern baron.

By March 17, Gaveston, no less, was ensconced in Scarborough Castle. Edward, it seems, had wanted Percy out in order to establish a refuge, even a possible redoubt, for his favourite. Meanwhile, Edward treacherously contacted Robert Bruce – with whom he was technically at war – about a safe haven for Gaveston in Scotland in return for recognition of King Robert's claims to the throne and a permanent peace. Referring to Edward's blatant dismissal of the ordinances, Bruce replied bluntly: 'How shall the king of England keep faith with me, since he does not observe the sworn promises made to his liege men? ... No trust can be put in such a fickle man.'[62]

The opposition was gathering steam – Gloucester and Warenne had sniffed the wind and switched sides – and Lancaster was chosen, unsurprisingly, as leader of the baronial forces, which he divided into regional commands.[63] Percy (fresh from his display of defiance towards Edward and Gaveston) and Clifford were put in charge of the March. Pembroke and Warenne were delegated the key task of capturing Gaveston. Why Pembroke and Warenne? It was a strange choice and the first indication that they were being set up by their fellows for a bigger game.

By April, king and favourite were in Newcastle, but the arrival of an army under Lancaster, Percy and Clifford forced them to scurry back to the better-defended Scarborough.[64] (Pembroke and Warenne were still down south.) In their haste to escape, Edward and Gaveston left behind their own men and a trove of gold and jewels. When the hunters stormed Newcastle, and stumbled across Gaveston's treasures, their eyes could never before have beheld such opulence. Room after room, like Tutankhamun's tomb, was crammed with wonderful things, all evidence of Edward's fondness for his favourite. Rings garnished with sapphires and diamonds; gold buckles studded with emeralds, rubies and pearls; forty goblets and eighty plates of silver: these were just a small sample of the hundreds, even thousands, of items. Crowning the booty was a colossal ruby encased in gold worth at least £1000 – a sum approaching Percy's annual income. Small wonder that Lancaster, Percy and Clifford spent no fewer than four days cataloguing and valuing the hoard, which eclipsed the fabled treasure King John lost in the Wash.[65]

More disturbingly – or perhaps not – Gaveston had abandoned his wife and baby daughter in Newcastle, leaving them to the mercy of Lancaster and his two lieutenants. Leaving Gaveston to hold Scarborough the king hared for Gaveston's old haunt at Knaresborough to raise local recruits, whereupon Percy and Clifford, now finally joined by Pembroke and Warenne, besieged Scarborough. Lancaster, strangely, left for the South immediately afterwards. On 19 May, partly thanks to Percy's intimate knowledge of the castle defences, Gaveston and his starving garrison (including a lord named Henry Beaumont – we shall meet him later) surrendered and made terms.[66]

The vigilantes took matters into their own hands. After Gaveston's surrender, Percy, Warenne and Pembroke solemnly pledged to guarantee his safety until 1 August, by which date it was hoped that some national agreement would be hammered out. Such were the almost suspiciously easy terms of this offer, that if no concord was reached by 1 August, Gaveston would be returned to Scarborough Castle.[67] As a further token of good faith, the honest Pembroke pledged his estates on carrying out his promise to guarantee Gaveston's life. By 26 May, the three earls had taken Gaveston to York, to await Lancaster's arrival. But Lancaster never showed up, a development as odd as his sudden departure for the South at the beginning of the siege of Scarborough. It is here that the story, including Percy's role in it, clouds darkly.

Mysteriously, Pembroke was persuaded to escort Gaveston to a place of greater safety in the South in early June, leaving Percy and Warenne in York. On 9 June 1312, they stopped at Deddington in Oxfordshire for a rest. While Pembroke was visiting his wife at nearby Brampton, Warwick and his men surrounded the inn where Gaveston was staying. Warwick cried out: 'Arise traitor, thou art taken.' Seeing that the guardsmen assigned to his 'protection' stood motionless with their arms kept sheathed, Gaveston was forced to dress and descend. Stripping the disgraced Gascon of his knight's belt, Warwick lumbered him onto a nag and, 'with blaring trumpets … and the horrid cry of the populace' in the background, threw him into prison. 'He whom Piers called Warwick the Dog has now bound Piers with chains,' ironically commented a contemporary.[68]

Clearly, Gaveston's capture was a conspiracy from which Pembroke, and probably Warenne were excluded. On hearing of Gaveston's imprisonment, poor Pembroke rushed in panic to the nearby earl of Gloucester and beseeched him for help, not only because he was worried about

Piers's fate, but also because his own lands had been pledged to his safety. Gloucester's crushing reply is illuminating: *'He* [Warwick] *did this with our aid and counsel*; and if, as you say, you have pledged your lands, you have lost them anyhow. It only remains to advise you to learn another time to negotiate more cautiously [italics added].'[69] It is not recorded whether Pembroke thanked him for the lecture.

A few days later, most of the earls and some other magnates met at Warwick. Gaveston's execution was beyond debate; there was more concern with its method. Uncomfortably cognisant that they were setting a precedent in being the first earls in history to murder one of their own in defiance of the king, those present insisted on a cumbrous protocol to make the affair 'look proper'. In so doing, the earls, unwittingly, jolted one step closer to two centuries of self-mutilating aristocratic turbulence, which would sweep away many of these, and other, ancient baronial houses. Eventually, they judged that Piers should not be hanged as a common thief nor drawn as a traitor. Instead, as a nobleman of sorts he was to be decapitated – the gentleman's preferred exit.

On 19 June 1312, Warwick led Gaveston forth from the filthy prison to Kenilworth, the property of the earl of Lancaster. There, he handed him over to the waiting earl, who 'took upon himself the peril of the business, and ordered Piers, after three terms of exile, as one disobedient to three lawful warnings, to be put to death'.[70] Warwick then withdrew to his nearby castle, and the other earls and onlookers retreated a safe distance away.

Gaveston prostrated himself in front of Lancaster, begging for mercy – to no avail. The killing party then departed for Blacklow Hill, on whose summit Lancaster shoved Gaveston into the arms of two Welshmen, 'one of whom ran him through the body and the other cut off his head'.[71]

Finale

The assassination of Piers Gaveston was a planned, orderly affair. The question is, when Percy and Warenne stayed in York whilst Pembroke escorted Gaveston south, did they know that this would be Piers's last journey? Like the earls at Kenilworth who left the scene before Thomas of Lancaster murdered Gaveston, were they preparing their alibis in advance? Judging by Warenne's later actions (see below), he, like Pembroke, was unaware of what was to happen. In April, he, a former friend of Gaveston, and a confirmed moderate, Pembroke, had been specifically chosen by the other earls to capture Gaveston so as to put him at his ease, yet it was Lancaster, Percy and Clifford who originally cornered him at Scarborough. Gaveston, no doubt, might have fought much harder at the castle had Lancaster (who left quickly) or the warlike Warwick been waiting outside its walls.

We shall never know exactly when the plot was hatched; Gaveston had been captured at Scarborough on 19 May and he reached the inn at Deddington on 9 June, which gave the leading conspirators ample opportunity to meet and decide what was to be done with him. Even so, the earls had gathered as early as April, and in the following months Lancaster and Percy were in constant contact. Lancaster had then left Scarborough, a castle in the heart of the Percys' eastern fiefdom, and he never returned to York, even after Gaveston had been taken prisoner. He was obviously waiting in the South with the other earls, waiting for word from Percy that Gaveston had left Yorkshire. Who had persuaded Pembroke that the South, where earls lurked, was so much safer for Gaveston than being under armed guard in York?

Edward was at first 'saddened and grieved very much' upon hearing of Gaveston's death, and then furious. He 'decided to destroy those who had killed Piers'. In mid-July he summoned his loyal advisers and enquired what he should do. By then, Pembroke and Warenne had detached themselves from the baronial camp because of the shoddy way they had been treated by the conspirators, and they urged the king to declare outright war on the other earls, whom they now called traitors.[72] Cooler-headed counsel, however, argued that civil war would hand Robert Bruce a golden opportunity to invade Northumbria. The Scots, taking advantage of the chaos, had recently been launching raids into Northumberland, Cumberland and Westmorland. Bruce had already come close to taking England's pride, Berwick; by October, Roxburgh and Edinburgh castles had been razed, and Bruce's army was besieging Stirling.[73]

As usual, the Scottish problem came second to Edward's personal desires, and he inclined heavily to Pembroke and Warenne's view for the moment.[74] Levies were accordingly commanded to be raised, castles were fortified and the mayor of London agreed to shut the city's gates against the earls.

Two weeks after the meeting, on 28 July 1312, Edward II singled out one man for punishment by ordering the escheator to 'take into the king's hand the land and goods of Henry de Percy'.[75] A couple of days later, the sheriff of Yorkshire was directed to arrest Percy and hold him under armed guard. The other miscreants were, of course, well known to the king, but Edward was warning the earls of imminent and dire retribution, and he used Percy as an example.[76]

As the baronial forces under Lancaster, Warwick and Hereford approached London for a reckoning with Edward, the earl of Gloucester, platitudinous but forked-tongued (as Pembroke had lately discovered), mediated between the two sides. Gloucester told Edward that 'they are your friends whom you call enemies... Whatever they do is for your benefit.' At this the king raised a quizzical eyebrow, musing sadly that 'there is none who is sorry for me: none who fights for my right against them'. He was convinced that Lancaster, 'who might have been content with five earldoms without seizing others', had stolen Gaveston's treasure and Edward felt that he should be tried for theft and condemned to death for robbery with violence. Paranoia gripped his mind: 'It is very likely that they do not wish to have any consideration for me, but to seize the crown and set up for themselves another king.'

The earls reacted by energetically asserting their ultimate loyalty to the Crown, protesting 'that it had never entered their heads to wish to set up another king'. If the king 'treats his earls and barons with the regard that is their due', then 'we will obey him as king, we will serve him as lord'. Lancaster added that he had never 'carried off' Gaveston's goods; in fact, 'having made an inventory of everything, ordered them to be kept to the king's use'.[77]

Any thoughts the earls had ever entertained about deposing the king soon vanished, because on 13 November 1312 Queen Isabella gave birth to a 'handsome and long-looked-for son' whom the king named Edward. After the celebrations came more negotiations, the king being especially concerned with the recovery of Gaveston's abandoned treasure. The earls advanced a set of proposals known as the *Prima Tractorio*, in which they offered to submit to the king and seek his pardon, to provide 400 men-at-arms for the next Scottish campaign, and, lastly, to return the treasure. In exchange, they directed that the Ordinances be maintained and that Percy be freed and have his lands returned. Moreover, Gaveston must be publicly declared by Edward to be a *commun enemy du roi et du rouime*, a request that the king resolutely refused.

In late December, Pembroke and Edward's long-time acolyte Lord Despenser, representing the king, and Hereford and Clifford the barons, reached a provisional settlement (the ringleaders, Lancaster and Warwick, were still required to assent to it) which omitted the Gaveston problem temporarily. First on the list was the release of Henry Percy and the return of his lands and goods, an order that Edward authorised two days before the agreement was signed.[78] The erring earls were also to be pardoned for their offences against Gaveston at the next Parliament, to be held in mid-March 1313, and they would do their utmost to help pay for another Scottish war. The earls, the most rebellious of whom held lands in Scotland, were far keener on fighting Robert Bruce than Edward. Indeed, from the king's point of view, the provisional settlement was a favourable one: it did not mention the Ordinances and it stipulated that Gaveston's treasure was to be returned on 13 January 1313 at St Albans. In the event, Lancaster changed his mind and refused to hand over the jewels unless Edward acknowledged that Gaveston was a felon and accepted the Ordinances.[79]

Although they honourably returned the treasure on 23 February after consulting with the freed Percy and Clifford, Lancaster and Warwick refused to confirm the December treaty because they believed it white-washed Gaveston. Advised by the canny Despenser that the other earls were growing impatient and wanted peace, Edward, deliberately height-ening the tension between the earls, left for France in May. In September 1313, Gloucester persuaded the hardline Lancaster and Warwick to accept a final settlement with or without the indictment of Gaveston, and so on 14 October the earls submitted to the king. They received his pardon through clenched teeth – on both sides, no doubt. Henry Percy was pardoned two days later for his association with Lancaster and 'par-ticipation in the death of Gaveston'.[80] Exactly a month later, Percy duly received his receipt from the king for the return of Gaveston's treasure.[81]

Neither side was fully satisfied with the truce, the barons least of all. Lancaster, in particular, still felt aggrieved that Edward had evaded affirming Gaveston's treachery and his beloved Ordinances. It was a fatal obsession with a dead Gascon and the English constitution that bewitched this violent but, according to his lights, honourable, noble, which would lead to his own execution less than a decade later.

As for Percy, although by rights he should have received back all of his confiscated lands, his association with Lancaster proved rather expen-sive. While Percy was locked up, King Robert took advantage of his antagonist's ironical discomfort (Percy, acting on Edward I's order to keep her in safe custody, had jailed Bruce's daughter years before). Sometime before October 1313, King Robert granted the earldom of Carrick, as well as Urr and Red Castle to his brother, Edward Bruce, the man who had raided Galloway in 1308. Percy's son would seek to recover these lands, a quest described in the following chapter.

Bannockburn

Peace, of a sort, had broken out between the king and his barons. Edward had so far escaped performing penance for Gaveston's felonies, but at the cost of accepting the baronial desire for a more 'forward' policy towards the Scots. This led to the battle of Bannockburn in June 1314, one of the most decisive clashes in British history.[82] Limited space, unfortunately, will be devoted to the battle, because Henry Percy was not present.[83]

Having said that, Percy had never disobeyed a summons before, so why would he do so now? Edward was, after all, mounting a major expedition; if it was successful, Percy might win back the earldom of Carrick, and regain Urr and Red Castle. On the other hand, Percy was highly disgruntled after being jailed and stripped of his estates and income. Moreover, Edward's Scottish campaign of 1310–11, in which he had loyally participated, had been a complete waste of time and money. Nothing suggested that the planned 1314 expedition would not be the same. Ignoring a summons was not unheard of; plenty of barons had done it before if the timing was inconvenient. Percy, more honourably, evaded military service on a point of principle, although personal disaffection also influenced his decision to abstain.

Percy was not making a lone stand: five earls – Warwick, Lancaster, Arundel, Oxford and Warenne (now recovered from his irritation with the other earls) – refused to serve personally with Edward in 1314. Instead, they sent the bare minimum of knights and men-at-arms under their feudal obligations, a paltry sixty men. Gloucester, Pembroke, Hereford and other barons made up the deficit with nearly 900 mounted soldiers of all types.[84] Hereford, who had always backed Lancaster, was in this case acting as constable of England, which explains his dutiful presence. If Percy refused to attend personally, he probably sent the three knights feudally due from Alnwick.

Nevertheless, Clifford, a man not terribly keen on Edward but not as deeply involved as Percy, went. Before he left for Scotland Clifford arranged with Percy and Warwick that they should act as the administrators of his property in case he should fall in battle.[85] Clifford's cautious desire to entrust his estate on behalf of his under-age son with two great friends is quite touching.

From the beginning, the campaign's chances of ultimate success were not auspicious. Adhering scrupulously to the Ordinances, the boycotting earls said 'that it would be better for all to meet in Parliament and there unanimously decide what ought to be done'. Edward, wanting to restore some kingly lustre, replied that he did not want to wait for a Parliament, to which the earls retorted forthrightly that 'they would not fight without Parliament, lest it should happen that they infringed the Ordinances'.[86] In this, Lancaster and his allies followed Clause 9 of the Ordinances, which stated that the king must not 'undertake any war without the common consent of his baronage, and that in Parliament. If he does otherwise, and summons his service for such an enterprise, the summons shall be null.' Edward had avoided apologising for Gaveston (Clause 20), and they would not permit him to scorn a clause as important as Clause 9 with its Magna Carta antecedents.

But Edward's household officials advised him 'to demand their due service ... and set out boldly for Scotland'.[87] This would split the baronial ranks and highlight the earls' petulance at the time of a great patriotic war. This explains the refusal of the five earls mentioned about to attend the king personally; Percy, as a supporter of the Ordinances, could not in all conscience fulfil his service in a war which, lacking parliamentary consent, he and the rebel earls regarded as illegal. Despite repeated summonses, he stayed resolutely at Alnwick.[88] The abbot of Meaux observed that many nobles similarly disobeyed the summons for Bannockburn.[89]

The battle was a rout, a catastrophe, the Falkirk of the English. At least thirty-seven English lords and bannerets lay sprawled on the field, dead. They included Gloucester, Robert Clifford and Hereford's nephew, Sir Humphrey Bohun (his skull broken in half by Bruce's battleaxe), the marshal of Ireland, the steward of the king's household and, perhaps conveniently for Percy, William Vesci of Kildare. Another 500 knights were captured. The king was forced to flee, leaving behind his shield, possessions, clothing and arms, as well as the privy seal. Had he been captured, the staggering ransom that he commanded would have paid Scotland's debts many times over. It is inconceivable that Bruce would have released him without extracting English recognition of his Crown and Scottish independence. As it was, the captured Hereford was exchanged for not only Bruce's queen but his daughter Marjorie, his sister and the bishop of Glasgow to boot.

As for Percy, with English power in Scotland suddenly collapsed, he received an emergency summons from Edward a few days after Bannockburn to get to Newcastle post-haste.[90] Simultaneously, 362 knights and small landholders were called for personal military service. The list was addressed to Lancaster, instructing him to bring these men, and Percy's name was placed at the top.[91] If the Scots pushed home their advantage by invading *en masse*, and there were to be a last-ditch defence of the North, it would be left to these scratch forces to provide it. In the event, Bruce instead launched a series of smaller-scale raids, not an army.

During the Bannockburn campaign, what had Percy been doing? For the most part, guarding his Alnwick estates against Scottish predators, who, since 1311, had been sent by Robert Bruce to ravage the North, especially Northumberland and Durham.[92] Periodic truces were arranged between the raiders and inhabitants on payment of 'blackmail' (a tribute exacted from farmers and small tenants by freebooting Border chiefs, in return for protection or immunity from plunder). This official protection racket shook down the aforesaid tenants as well as walled towns, ecclesiastical benefices, convents, manors and even whole counties. The Percys, however, do not appear to have succumbed to Bruce's thugs and as a result their lands were repeatedly raided. On Alnwick Castle's estates alone, between Michaelmas 1314 and Michaelmas 1315, the agricultural lands lost 4.1 per cent of their value. By 1316 the deficit had risen to 16.5 per cent, and by 1317, to 28.6 per cent. The next year hardly any rents could be collected and in 1319 only the castle itself and some coal mines were untouched.

These early years foreshadowed the devastation wreaked by the Scots all over the North during the next decade or so. By the death of King Robert I, hero of Bannockburn and 'saviour' of Scotland, about £20,000 – far more than the king of England received in taxes – had been violently extracted from some of the poorest and most vulnerable people in the country. English barons were no saints, either, yet for the most part their violence had hitherto been confined to their Scottish counterparts. It was Robert Bruce who 'erected the murderous neighbourly strife of the Border into an instrument of national policy'.[93] It was to become a fact of life on the Marches and a double-edged policy that hurt the Scots just as painfully as it did the English for the next 250 years.

Sometime between 2 and 10 October 1314, Henry Percy died at Alnwick Castle, aged just forty-one.[94] Nothing is known of the manner, or causes, of his early death but I would venture to suggest that he was fatally wounded during an encounter with a band of these Scots freebooters. It would indeed be fitting if this man, who lived by the sword, died also by one, singularly so were it wielded by a Scotsman.

CHAPTER EIGHT

Henry Percy IV and the Outbreak of Peace

Near a Border frontier, in the time of war,
There's ne'er a man, but he's a freebooter.[1]

At his father's death in 1314, Henry Percy IV was a few months short of
his fourteenth birthday, not quite old enough to be allowed unleashed
freedom, but equally not young enough to require constant supervision.
During his minority, therefore, the king appointed Sir John Felton to
look after Alnwick and the Northumberland estates,[2] the archbishop of
Canterbury was granted wardship of Petworth and Roger Damory supervised the Percy manor of Foston in Leicestershire. Percy's mother controlled the family's Yorkshire lands.[3] She settled in the ancient Percy
heartland of Seamer until she died in 1328. According to William Peeris's
Chronicle, Eleanor

was a constant Lady honourable and wise.
A fair tyme of life was graunte her in this world to dwell
At Semar, a new Chapell the said Lady did devise,
And caused it to bee built in right costly wise.[4]

Edward II's choice of Felton as trustee is interesting. Until 1314, he had
been a youthful knight in the royal household, which by now resembled
an elite military corps. His family's loyalty was beyond question. In 1312,
at the height of his insubordination to the king, Percy had refused to
hand over Scarborough Castle to his father, Robert Felton. By the time
of his Alnwick trusteeship, Felton was attached to the service of Hugh
Despenser the Younger, whom we shall meet again. Clearly, Edward
wanted someone trustworthy to keep an eye on young Henry Percy until
he reached his majority to ensure that he did not fall into Lancaster's
clutches, as his father had.

We do not know the date of Percy's marriage to Idonea, the daughter
of the late Lord Clifford, but his first son was born *circa* 1319–20, so the
ceremony probably took place a year or so after his lands and rents were
smoothly returned to him on 13 November 1318.[5] This dynastic alliance

must have been long planned by their respective fathers and the couple were well suited – by the standards of the day, at least – both being about the same age and status. Although Percy's father had rubbed along with Eleanor, his wife, he had spent so much time in Scotland that only two boys were born (Sir William Percy, the younger brother, would die childless in 1355). Although Henry Percy IV was clearly affectionate towards Idonea – at least compared to the number of his peers who loathed their spouses and were cursed with childless marriages – having no fewer than six sons and four daughters by her, childlessness and early death afflicted the Percys in the male line (for his daughters' marriages, see Chapter 9). Excepting his heir apparent, another Henry, two of his sons predeceased their father and left no children, one became bishop of Norwich (no offspring there, one hopes), and the remaining two died within a year or so of their father.[6] Again, apart from the eldest, no male Percy married.

The dynasty would come within a hair's breadth of extinction. Already the family were bucking the odds: of 136 barons summoned to Parliament between 1295 and 1300 (which figure includes the late Henry Percy III), fully thirty-six lines were extinct by 1325. By 1500, only sixteen – including that of Percy – of the original class of '1295–1300' would still be in existence.[7] The House of Percy was establishing itself as a member of a diminishing, but genealogically exclusive club.

The End of the Earl of Lancaster

Between 1315 and 1321, we hear little of Henry Percy. He probably spent his time defending his estates from the insolent predations of the Bruce's Scots,[8] as well as hunting down such English bandits as Sir Gilbert Middleton's notorious gang of renegade knights. Percy was also troubled by the Europe-wide famine of 1315–17, which hit the North particularly hard.[9] One well-informed monk heard that 'in Northumbria dogs and horses and other unclean things were eaten. For there, on account of the frequent raids, work is more irksome, as the accursed Scots despoil the people daily of their food.'[10] As part of a belt-tightening regimen, the council even ruled that nobles could not have more than two meat courses at dinner, although earls were allowed an extra one if they so wished.[11]

Despite being the youngest participant and not yet a knight, Percy attended a hastily arranged council of war among fifty Northern barons in Doncaster in April 1315 to decide what to do about the Scots, but little seems to have been settled.[12] No help from London was forthcoming, even though Lancaster was now effectively running the country as chief councillor in the chaotic aftermath of Bannockburn. Various plans to avenge the defeat came to naught because Lancaster and Edward simply refused to co-operate with each other. 'Whatever pleases the lord king the earl's servants try to upset,' complained a monkish observer, 'and whatever pleases the earl the king's servants call treachery.'[13]

Time was on Edward's side, as he well knew. Rumours spread that Lancaster was incompetent, and that his allies were disappearing whilst the royal party was regaining strength (the earl of Warwick had died in August 1315). Indeed, the obstreperous earl who clung to his beloved Ordinances was increasingly regarded as a bore by the younger generation. Percy, for one, would have been bemused by his father's allegiance to Lancaster; as he was a child at the time, the Gaveston brouhaha was inexplicable to him. He may have heard the name of the sainted Edward I uttered by his father on any number of occasions, but he belonged to a different, fusty era. All Henry Percy cared about was getting rid of the damned Scots who sacked his villages, and, in his eyes, it was Lancaster who was obstructing the king from ruling effectively. There were also disturbing rumours that 'Robert Bruce, when he devastates the district of the March, has now for many years left the earl's [Lancaster's] estates untouched.'[14] We can assume that Percy would have taken a dim view of Lancaster's alleged treasonous activities. For example, the value of Percy's Yorkshire lands had collapsed by £400 to almost nothing 'on account of the destruction therein by the Scotch rebels'.[15]

There was a crux in Lancaster's worsening relations with the king in 1317. Lancaster was worried by the rise of a clique of new royal favourites, who made no bones about their desire to be rid of him. Following the earl of Gloucester's death at Bannockburn with no surviving male successor, his lands had been partitioned between three co-heiresses, who quickly became the most sought-after women in England. The eldest was married to Hugh Despenser the Younger, and the other two (one being Gaveston's widow) were given to the former household knights Hugh Audley and Roger Damory (one of Percy's trustees), in early 1317. Along with William Montague, the new steward and father of the future earl of Salisbury, these creatures of Edward's whim not only formed a dangerous combination of quasi-magnates but were the nucleus of an ultra-loyalist Edwardian faction.

It was these men who, at a meeting of the council at Clarendon on 9 February 1317, accused Lancaster of plotting with the Scots. By now, the unstable Earl Warenne had fallen in with the favourites, and it was probably during the council that they planned the abduction of Lancaster's wife, a mortal insult calculated to drive the earl into rebellion.[16] In May, she was duly kidnapped and one of Warenne's knights publicly announced that he had slept with her before her marriage ('she is said to have acknowledged the truth of his story, and so disgraced herself before the whole world').[17]

Lancaster threatened not to attend any future Parliaments until these evildoers were expelled from the king's household. 'He also asks that he may without offence take vengeance and such satisfaction as he can get for the wrong done to him,' a signal that he wanted a private war with Warenne. Edward told Lancaster that he would never expel his household on a mere earl's command. If Lancaster wished to avenge his wife's abduction, 'let him seek a remedy in law only'. A meeting between king and earl was arranged, but Lancaster's spies warned him that the king 'would either have his head or consign him to prison'.[18] When Edward gathered troops at York, the obvious target was Lancaster's stronghold at Pontefract. However, the ever-emollient Pembroke persuaded them to settle things peacefully, although Lancaster did seize Warenne's Yorkshire castles as punishment.[19] The rest of the baronage, now returning to the king's side like sheep to the shepherd, did nothing.

Sensing he was isolated, Lancaster made terms with the king in the Treaty of Leake (in Yorkshire) on 9 August 1318. Lancaster was pardoned, and saw the three favourites – Montague, Audley and Damory – removed from the court. Despenser the Younger, however, was promoted to chamberlain. In return for a disavowal of civil war, Lancaster received the lands of his arch-enemy, Warenne, in North Wales and Yorkshire. According to one chronicler, Warenne 'cut his losses to escape a greater danger', and lay low to avoid Lancaster or one of his assassins.[20]

Percy was uninvolved with these high politics, and in 1318 was primarily concerned with is own survival. In the summer of 1316, the Scots had penetrated as far as north Yorkshire. The raiders – usually led by the 'douchty of deid' Sir James Douglas (whose family would become the Percys' hereditary enemies) or Thomas Randolph, the newly created earl of Moray – were draining Northumberland dry of money, swine and wine by stealing anything that moved (anything that didn't was burnt). Moray was a striking figure in an era of striking figures. According to Master John Barbour, 'he wes of mesurabill stature,/ and portrait weill at all mesure,/ With braid visage [broad face], plesand and fair.' He was pleasant company – 'debonar' and 'solacius' – and valued loyalty and honour above all else.[21]

Douglas dealt the English a crushing blow on the night of 1 April 1318. Owing to the treachery of Peter de Spalding, an English burgess of Berwick, the Scots clambered over a pre-arranged part of the town wall.

After some street fighting, the first outpost of Edward I's empire fell. The castle itself held out for another three months before being starved into surrender. With the loss of Berwick, not a single English soldier remained in Scotland.[22]

During the three-month siege, the Scots had also tightened the noose around Alnwick; the castles of Wark, Mitford and Harbottle were successfully stormed, leaving Percy's fortress as one of the few major castles left intact in Northumberland. Hoping to draw Percy out of his lair, Douglas razed the areas surrounding Northallerton, Ripon and Topcliffe; for good measure, he returned to Scotland via Craven, which he devastated, again denting Percy's pocket, and his pride as well.[23]

His courage fortified by having put Lancaster back in his place, Edward decided to instil some order into the North. Summoning a respectable force of 8000 men at Newcastle in June 1319 (including Lancaster, following the Treaty of Leake), the king marched to recover Berwick. The quotas they brought to the campaign give some indication of Percy's standing among the Northern lords. While Thomas Wake, Gilbert Umfraville and Ralph Neville – all men destined to play a significant role in the future – each brought forty knights, Percy was escorted by eighty, the largest of the Border complements.[24]

In the midst of the Berwick siege, a Scottish turncoat alerted Edward that Douglas and Moray were intent on cutting the English supply lines behind them in Yorkshire, and that Douglas even intended to abduct the queen at York. In disgust, Edward was forced to raise the siege, whisk his unbeloved queen to Nottingham and return south to the Trent. Douglas, teasingly, merely rode to Westmorland, waited until the harvest was brought in and burnt it.[25]

At Christmas of that benighted year, the English arranged a two-year truce with the Scots lasting until 1321. Edward bargained out of exhaustion, but Robert Bruce, then seeking the Pope's support for recognition of his kingship and Scotland's independence, wanted to be seen earnestly seeking peace. (Thus, his subordinates conducted raids to pressure the English while Bruce 'plausibly denied' knowledge of them.)

On 6 April 1320 the earls and barons of Scotland addressed a secret letter, famously remembered as the 'Declaration of Arbroath', to Pope John XXII. After cataloguing Edward I's misdeeds, the Declaration stated that 'from these countless evils we have been set free ... by our most valiant prince, the lord Robert' and accordingly 'have made him our prince and king'. Similar to many medieval courtly documents in its combination of propaganda and very shaky historical justification, the Declaration is distinguished by its unswerving forthrightness, a far cry from the pathetic supplications of the 1290s to Edward's overlordship.

In a rhetorical display lifted from Sallust's *Catiline* (medieval barons may have been thugs, but never mindless thugs), the nobles cried that 'we will never on any conditions be subjected to the lordship of the English. For we fight not for glory, nor riches, nor honours, but for freedom alone, which no good man gives up except with his life.'[26] One may dismiss this as mere political eyewash, but the Scots have consistently sung of the value of freedom and the subjection of thraldom. The fourteenth-century biographer of Robert Bruce and his times, Master John Barbour, devoted passages to these themes in language redolent of the Book of Proverbs: 'A! fredome is A noble thing! ... A noble hart may haiff nane else.'[27] Whereas, in the days of Henry I and David I, amicability had existed between the two distinct governments, Edward's obsessive legacy of forced annexation resulted equally in a Scottish fixation with full and sovereign independence.

This appeal to the Pope had its desired effect. He beseeched Edward to come to terms with the Scots, although he diplomatically refrained from calling Bruce a 'king'. However, Edward had more serious problems. The Northern nobles were again questioning Lancaster's activities. Some said that Robert Bruce had friends in high places – a tilt at the earl – for it was alleged that at the siege of Berwick none of Lancaster's retinue had assaulted the walls. James Douglas, it seems, had passed unscathed through the earl's lands on his return journey to Scotland (the one where Percy's estates were blasted). It was asserted, on still scantier evidence, that Lancaster had received £40,000 from Bruce to let him alone. The king, of course, listened to, and even encouraged, these slanderous words; during the siege, for instance, he had remarked to his favourites: 'When this wretched business is over, we will turn our hands to other matters. For I have not yet forgotten the wrong that was done to my brother Piers.'[28]

But Lancaster could wait. Civil war was rumbling in Wales, where Edward was deceitfully encouraging the younger Despenser to empire-build at the expense of his fellow Marcher lords (including the earl of Hereford, the two Roger Mortimers – uncle and nephew – and Roger Clifford – Percy's relative and the son of the Clifford who was killed at Bannockburn). The Marchers made common cause and wrecked Despenser's territory of Glamorgan.[29] Envisaging the Marchers as the spearhead of an attack on royal power and favouritism, Lancaster allied himself with his old comrade, Hereford, and his Welsh party.[30] On 24 May 1321, he called a council at Pontefract Priory, hoping to fuse the Northern baronage (he considered himself their natural lord) with the Welsh Marchers. And it is here that Percy enters the story, albeit briefly.

Percy attended that seditious meeting, as did all the Northern barons who were invited.[31] He listened attentively to the declamations and declarations that filled the chapter-house, but in the end decided that Lancaster [was too hot a firebrand for his liking, quite apart from his suspected treachery]. His suspicions were confirmed a month later, when the rebels – now known to us as the 'Contrariants' – swore 'to banish, persecute, condemn, and perpetually disinherit the Despensers, father and son'.[32] Lord Despenser the Elder had been Lancaster's and Hereford's personal bugbear since the days of Gaveston, and the fact that his destruction was of prime concern persuaded many Northerners that the rebellion was really about deposing the king. In Percy's case, he refused all contact with his father's old confederates from the Pontefract council onwards.

A shrewd decision. The Contrariants marched on London in July and demanded that Edward hear their complaints; if he refused, they declared they would 'set up another ruler to do justice to all and humble the pride of the guilty and stiffnecked'.[33] At this point, the conciliatory Pembroke intervened. A magnate with a Welsh palatinate threatened by Despenser's empire-building, he persuaded an understandably reluctant Edward to receive the Contrariants.[34] At their meeting, they accused Despenser the Elder and the Younger 'of evil counsel; of conspiracy and falsehood; of being a destroyer of the people, a disinheritor of the Crown, an enemy of king and kingdom'.[35]

Backed into a corner, on 19 August 1321, Edward assented to exile both Despensers, thinking that, as he had with Gaveston, he could recall them when the rebels' anger had cooled. The Elder accepted his sentence gracefully, but his more intemperate son turned to piracy and 'became a sea-monster, lying-in-wait for merchants as they crossed his path. He was master of the seas, their merchandise and chattels, and no ship got through unharmed.' Soon afterwards, he boarded a great Genoese vessel, killed its crew and stole more than £5000 in treasure.[36] Edward III would later pay 8000 marks (or £5280) in compensation to the ship's owners for Despenser's criminal enterprise.[37]

Edward, as he had successfully done during Gaveston's periodic exiles, split Lancaster's fragile coalition. He recruited other earls, including Pembroke, Warenne, Arundel and, very usefully, his two young half-brothers, the earls of Kent and Norfolk. These disparate individuals cleaved to the king after the Contrariant Sir Bartholomew Badlesmere haughtily refused admittance to the queen at Leeds Castle in Kent. Pembroke, a starchy stickler about these things, was especially offended by Badlesmere's denigration of royal privilege. This unlucky castle garrison suffered the first infliction of martial law to internal discord; after its surrender, Edward executed every last man. Henceforth, 'opponents of

the king could seriously expect to lose their heads if they were defeated'
in war.[38] The demon loosed by Lancaster atop Blacklow Hill in 1312
would eventually take its toll of noble blood.

Next, Edward cut off the Mortimers from Lancaster's fragmentary
Northern forces by blocking them into Wales. The two men saved their
heads by surrendering without a fight, but Hereford escaped and
sheltered with Lancaster.

Lancaster called another private counter-Parliament to assemble at
Doncaster on 29 November 1321. Percy, of course, along with 106 other
barons, received an invitation to attend, but kept away, as did nearly all of
his peers, on the direct orders of Edward.[39] Their refusal was prompted
by Edward's usual tactic of buying support from his neutral barons. By a
remarkable coincidence, Percy was suddenly offered his father's old custodianship of Scarborough Castle less than a month later, on Christmas
Day.[40] In the meantime, Edward bullied the clergy into declaring that
Lancaster's forceful proceedings against the Despensers were illegal, and
thus void.[41]

The 'Doncaster Petition', which emerged from Lancaster's counter-
Parliament, was doomed. The earl presented himself as a Simon de
Montfort-like guardian of the public interest. He asserted the right of
worldly baronial control over a divinely ordained king, just as Montfort
had, and he preached rebellion against the king. He had forgotten,
however, that Pope Innocent III in 1215 had annulled Magna Carta as
'lessening unduly and impairing [the king's] rights and dignity'.[42]
Likewise, in 1264, King Louis IX had dismissed Montfort's Provisions of
Oxford because they detracted from the gravity of monarchy. Lancaster's
unduly forthright petition inspired the same reaction – with a twist.
Edward militantly defended his royal prerogative and dignity, for as
feudal overlord only he had the right to summon Parliament. He then
recalled the Despensers from exile, quoting Magna Carta and his own
coronation oath (a rather shaky tactic, considering how often he had
broken it) as the legal justification.

Whilst Lancaster was engaged in Doncaster, Edward had issued a general
military summons, telling his barons to send their troops to Coventry,
thence to advance northwards, by the end of February 1322. Owing to a
Scottish incursion, Percy was delayed in Yorkshire and could not make the
deadline.[43] In a way, this was fortunate, because in the interim Lancaster had
left Doncaster and was besieging the royal castle of Tickhill, about five miles
south. Percy's orders were changed: he was to take his levy, 'attack and
pursue' Lancaster and aid in raising the siege.[44] Having hotfooted it to
Tickhill, whose garrison was shaken but otherwise cheerful, Percy was
bemused to discover that Lancaster and Hereford had disappeared.

They had in fact given up the siege and pushed sixty miles southwards to Burton-on-Trent, where they blocked the road and bridge before Edward had arrived from Coventry via Lichfield (where the recently returned Despensers met him). Apart from some minor skirmishing, the two sides did not meet in battle; instead, the Lancastrians were panicked into retreating the seventy-five miles to Lancaster's Pontefract stronghold, when a royal detachment of cavalry, led by the Despensers, Pembroke and Arundel, unexpectedly appeared on their flank.[45] As Edward chased them, Percy's brigade waited at Tickhill until it could rejoin the main army as it passed east of Sheffield in early March. Had Percy dined with the king and his commanders, he would have been interested in the latest news: soon after he left Coventry, Edward had easily taken Lancaster's castle at Tutbury. There, king's clerks, sifting through Lancaster's papers, found secret correspondence proving the earl's treachery. In December 1321, it seems, his agents had negotiated with Percy's arch-enemy, Sir James Douglas, and even more shockingly, Roger Clifford – a *Clifford*, of all people – had met with the earl of Moray. A draft treaty promising mutual aid between Robert Bruce and Lancaster was also uncovered during a search of the castle records.

By this time, Lancaster had realised that his damning correspondence was in the king's hands. He decided he would barricade himself in Pontefract and try to persuade the king that the correspondence was forged, which it indeed may have been, although it's rather doubtful. At this display of trimming, the Welshman Clifford – 'a man of great strength', according to the Lanercost chronicler, but a 'knave', in Barbour's words – drew his sword and swore to kill the earl if he did not make a run for the deep North with the rest of them. Their planned destination was the most northerly of Lancaster's castles, the coastal fortress of Dunstanburgh in Northumberland, a mere seven miles or so from Alnwick. There, the dejected rebels hoped to hold out until Scottish reinforcements could arrive (a forlorn hope: Bruce far preferred an English civil war to an Anglo-Scottish war). Lancaster acceded reluctantly to what might be called, with some justice, peer pressure.[46]

On 16 March 1322, pursued by the royal forces, Lancaster and Hereford flew past York until abruptly halted at Boroughbridge in Yorkshire by a detachment blocking the north side of the only bridge spanning the River Ure. Beyond the Ure lay the North and safety.

The small force was commanded by Sir Andrew Harclay, an extraordinarily enterprising young knight who had served in the Scottish wars since 1304, mainly under the late Lord Clifford although the older Percy knew him. Since Bannockburn, as sheriff and 'Sovereign Arrayer of Forces' in Carlisle he had attacked Scots raiders as they passed into

Cumbria. Posting his few knights and more numerous pikemen on the northern edge of the bridge with the archers behind them, Harclay deployed the rest of his pikemen in a schiltrom a short distance away at a ford. Evidently, his years on the Border had allowed Harclay to pick up a knowledge of Scottish tactics.

The battle of Boroughbridge, although more realistically a skirmish, was an epochal event in medieval warfare, marking the passing of offensive cavalry-power in favour of defensive archery. Boroughbridge was the direct forerunner of Crécy and Agincourt. Indeed, the very fact that Harclay's knights dismounted to fight was a revolutionary development.

Lancaster decided to take his cavalry across the nearby ford, smashing the schiltrom and swinging around Harclay's flank. Hereford and Clifford would assault the rickety bridge, but this had to be on foot. The Contrariants never foresaw the havoc that Harclay's archers would wreak. Before Lancaster could approach the ford, his cavalry had sustained such enormous losses that the attack petered out. Meanwhile, Hereford and Clifford had charged the enemy, but Hereford was mortally speared in the 'fondement' (buttocks) by a 'thef, a ribaulde' skulking beneath the bridge 'so that his bowailles comen out there'. Alongside him fell his standard-bearer and a number of other knights. As for Clifford, he was wounded several times by pikes and arrows but survived.[47]

Losing so fearsome an earl as Hereford caused morale to collapse. The next morning most of Lancaster's army had deserted. The royalist forces approaching rapidly from the south detached hunting parties to capture any ringleaders among the deserters. Percy was temporarily given the safe custody of Lancaster's confiscated castle at Pickering, which was fifteen miles west of Seamer – an area he knew backwards and where his tenants would gladly hand over strangers. His special orders were to 'pursue and arrest adherents of Lancaster' throughout Yorkshire.[48] Back at Boroughbridge, by midday on 17 March the rebel leadership, including more than a hundred knights, had surrendered to Harclay.

A couple of days later, at Pontefract – Lancaster's favourite fortress – Edward confronted the manacled prisoners, many still raggedly attired in pieces of armour and vividly coloured tunics. They knew what to expect: dispossession and disgrace followed by an opportunity to buy back their lands at inflated prices, as had occurred in the Dictum of Kenilworth in 1266, and later in Scotland. Some might be comfortably exiled for a few years – the established and civilised way of doing things – but certainly not executed. They ought, however, to have recalled the merciless fate of the Leeds Castle garrison.

On 20 March, Lancaster appeared before a small commission of his peers. The earl was not tried under the *common* law and was disbarred from speaking in his own defence according to the strange procedures of *martial* law, which was employed if the king had previously unfurled his banners against a foe, as was held to have happened in Lancaster's case. When this occurred, the two sides were conceived to be at war and common law was suspended. In fact, Edward had *not* flown his royal banners. He had wanted to, but the younger Despenser dissuaded him because he feared being tried under the same conditions should the king lose the imminent battle.[49]

To Edward, these fine distinctions were eyewash, and his blindness in these matters manifested itself in the tyranny staining his reign's last years. His first victim was Lancaster, the forthright, if clumsy, upholder of the Ordinances of 1311. Lancaster was sentenced to death and damned without reply, the first time that an earl, let alone a member of the royal family like Lancaster, had received such a punishment for high treason. This now encompassed the crime of rebellion against the king, who himself personified the realm and its subjects. To rise against him was to betray the people.[50]

Lancaster 'mounted on some worthless mule was led to the place of execution. Then the earl stretched forth his head as if in prayer, and the executioner cut off his head with two or three strokes.'[51] One hopes the axeman was berated for his incompetence, but for Edward, it was just punishment for Lancaster's murder of Gaveston on Blacklow Hill.

The earl's noble blood prevented the infliction of a more excruciating death; others were not so lucky. On the same day as Lancaster was executed, twenty-four of his baronial and knightly followers, including Clifford, were drawn and hanged at their own castles. (The 'drawing' referred to being dragged, feet first, bound on a hurdle to the place of execution. Thus, the order of the words should be, 'drawn, hanged and quartered', although in this case the bodies were not disembowelled.) The rest were imprisoned on starvation rations, as were their wives and children. Edward even jailed Lancaster's mother-in-law, the ancient countess of Lincoln.

The Fall of Edward II

After enjoying the bloodbath, Edward travelled to York, where he ennobled the victor of Boroughbridge, Sir Andrew Harclay, as no less than earl of Carlisle.[52] 'Sir Andrew was the first commoner who, without influence or interest, had raised himself to such eminence by his own efforts in the field,' demonstrating Edward's propensity for accelerated promotions into the thinning ranks of feudal earls, whose numbers had more than halved from the twenty-three in existence in 1154. His father, for instance, had never created any new earldoms for the men who faithfully served him, although perhaps he should have.[53]

During his stay at York, Edward knighted young Percy, both for his sterling service in the Contrariants' rebellion and because he planned to employ him soon on the Border.[54] As a Knight of the Bath, Percy received from the King's Wardrobe scarlet robes, and a tunic and cloak for his vigils.

During the period of the two-year truce arranged with Bruce in December 1319, Edward had opened tentative negotiations with the Scots. In March/April 1321, the English proposed a twenty-six-year ceasefire to avoid the tricky question of recognising Bruce's *de jure* kingship, as opposed to his *de facto* hold on the office. Needless to say, it was rejected. Instead, to pressure Edward into relinquishing his claim to overlordship, Bruce loosed Moray and Douglas across the Border shortly after the truce expired at the end of December 1321. Simultaneously, Bruce had encouraged Lancaster to continue his rebellion by dangling promises of aid. The scheme had backfired: with the Contrariants defeated, Edward could devote his full energies to Scotland.

First, however, he intended to tie up loose ends. Summoning Parliament in York in early May 1322 – which Percy attended – Edward's regality was restored by the 'Statute of York', which annulled the Ordinances of 1311 on the grounds that they wrongfully impeded royal power.[55] The king could again appoint his own councillors and declare war without the prior consent of Parliament. Yet, the knightly representatives of the shire, who had appeared intermittently during Edward I's Parliaments, became more prominent, which was reflected in the Statute's concluding clause. This spoke of the necessary 'assent of the prelates, earls and barons, *and the community of the realm*, as has been the custom in times past [italics added]'. Only ten years previously, such a phrase would have been synonymous with the peerage; by 1322, however, the 'community of the realm' was being identified as the 'Commons'. By the end of Edward's reign, the Commoners were being integrated into the official legislative process, marking the evolution of Parliament into a House of Lords and a House of Commons. The 1322 Parliament also witnessed the elevation of the elder Despenser to the earldom of Winchester. Like his son, Despenser was highly unpopular, but with Edward's stock at its peak, there were no dissenting voices.

Reinvested, finally, with sovereign power, Edward issued a general military summons on 11 May for a Scottish campaign, and Percy obediently went to Newcastle.[56] He had been ordered – a very tall order indeed

– to bring 'all his tenants, men, horsemen and footmen' between the ages of sixteen and sixty.[57] Unsurprisingly, the expedition was doomed to failure, and it was the last Edward would ever undertake across the Border. Owing to his ruthlessness towards the Contrariants, who included many veterans of Scottish campaigns, Edward's officers, including Percy, were inexperienced in conducting large-scale military operations.

In early August, the cumbersome English army of 22,000 men – mostly unpaid Southern levies, but including Harclay's 3500 crack Cumbrians – ground into Edinburgh, but were confronted neither by Scotsman nor obstinate castle. Bruce had already burnt the harvest and shepherded the livestock north of the Forth. After desultorily sacking Holyrood Abbey, they encountered a lone lame cow in Lothian, prompting Earl Warenne to quip (out of Edward's hearing) that it was 'the dearest beef I ever saw; surely it has cost a thousand pounds or more!' Famine and dysentery brought heavy, and needless, deaths; to complete Edward's misery, James Douglas ambushed a lagging brigade, killing many men.[58]

By early September, the stricken army had straggled back to England, its leaders thoroughly disenchanted with Edward's incompetence so soon after Harclay's triumph against the Lancastrians.[59] Percy had a week's brief respite before being summoned again for Scottish service. He was directed to 'leave a sufficient force' for defensive purposes at Alnwick and place himself and his 'entire *posse*' under the command of a *Scotsman*: the Strathbogie earl of Atholl, the new *custos* of the Northumberland March.[60]

David of Strathbogie (b. circa 1290)was yet another conspicuous character thrown up during the Anglo-Scottish wars. His father, the earl of Atholl, had supported the Bruces in the Great Cause of 1291–2, but his son married a daughter of John Comyn of Badenoch – murdered by Bruce in 1306 – after which Strathbogie defected to the English but changed sides again in 1312. He was appointed constable of Scotland by Bruce, but after Strathbogie betrayed him on the eve of Bannockburn, Bruce stripped him of his comital title and gave his lands to loyalists. A man who valued kinship over kingship, Strathbogie's hatred of the Bruces intensified when he discovered that the King's brother, Edward Bruce, having seduced his sister, had then deserted her for the earl of Ross's daughter. In future, there would be a line of 'pretender' Strathbogie earls of Atholl, and he was courteously referred to by this title in England.[61] During Edward III's reign, Strathbogie's son would play a significant if inglorious role in the renewed Anglo-Scottish war.

Percy was none too pleased with not only being passed over for promotion but by being expected to serve under a distinctly slippery Scot.

Judging by a waspish rebuke he received from the king in late September, the diva-ish Percy had gone off sulking. Pointing out that a small Scots force had recently 'entered the March, and, after infesting the neighbourhood of the castles … doing mischief, and, what is worse, taking ransoms and hostages from his subjects', Edward noted that this force had 'got away without challenge or damage from the garrisons'. The lethargy shown by Percy and his lieutenants was to their 'dishonour and shame'. He was 'astonished that among them they have not proper scouts and espial, and delay to harass the enemy. Wherefore he commands them … to see and do better.'[62]

Edward had been perfectly right to criticise Percy's attitude; the raid's purpose had been to assess the Northern defences and to discover any gaps in the chain of castles. Within a few days of Edward's letter, Bruce and a massive band of soldiers crossed the Solway, from where he could move through the Pennines via the Vale of Eden in Yorkshire, and threaten either Durham or York. By early October it was appallingly apparent he had chosen the latter. Edward was then relaxing at Rievaulx Abbey with Queen Isabella, about fourteen miles east of Northallerton, and Bruce was mounting a guerrilla raid to capture him. If this weren't bad enough, Percy faced ruin when spies reported on 12 October that Bruce had actually reached Northallerton. From there the route to Rievaulx ran directly through the Percy heartland of Topcliffe, now about to become a war zone. Percy gained permission from Strathbogie to leave Alnwick and sped to Topcliffe in order to join the local emergency forces being gathered by the wizened, loyalist earl of Richmond, John of Brittany, rousing himself from retirement for one last battle.[63]

The English intercepted Bruce at Old Byland on Scawton Moor, just outside Rievaulx, but were outflanked whilst fending off a frontal assault by Douglas and Moray. Richmond himself was captured and was held prisoner for two years (there was bad blood between him and Bruce) after his knights broke ranks and fled. Percy and his forces, it seems, retreated to Topcliffe and frantically readied its meagre and dated defences. By an amazing stroke of luck, these were not needed, for Bruce was in too much of a hurry to waste time pillaging.

Hearing the battle raging, Edward and Isabella had escaped from Rievaulx with only minutes to spare. Edward, 'being ever chicken-hearted and luckless in war',[64] again abandoned his treasure, instruments of government and baggage to the Scots (as he had after Bannockburn), amplifying the humiliation of being defeated in battle within his own kingdom. Rushing to Bridlington, with Bruce, Douglas and Moray in hot pursuit, Isabella left for the South by ship whilst Edward returned to York with the earl of Pembroke. Bruce wisely avoided a siege. His men were equipped for hit-and-run tactics, not a prolonged encampment in enemy territory. Just for good measure, however, Bruce hastened to Beverley, near the Humber, and prised blackmail from its citizens before returning home in triumph. The now-forgotten battle of Old Byland and the preceding expedition damaged Edward's authority far more than Bannockburn. Indeed, many participants in the 1322 'campaign' would come to hound Edward in future.[65]

Unsurprisingly, Northerners were edgy for the remainder of the winter, when the wispiest rumour that the Scots were coming could provoke general flight. The Border commanders were on virtually twenty-four-hour alert. In November, for instance, Percy received a panic-stricken order to 'assemble as many men-at-arms as he can, over and above his usual train, and to be ready to proceed against the Scots in case of invasion'.[66] A fortnight later, after the alert died down, there was another call to arms.[67]

In this tense atmosphere, allusive of the Blitz in that the huddled population could do little but wait for the bombs, or the Scots, to fall, the actions of Sir Andrew Harclay illuminate the changes in the North after Edward I's death. Whereas the senior Henry Percy or any other old Scotland hand would never have sought peace with their enemies, even when their lands were at risk, the new Northerners were far more politically flexible. The failures of Edward II, who lacked his father's military virtuosity and air of terrifying majesty, obliged Northern barons to keep an eye out for their own individual and collective interests. For those in the front line, the Anglo-Scottish wars could no longer be viewed as a zero-sum equation of English paramountcy and Scottish thraldom; in the modern Northern arena, survival demanded pragmatism.

Harclay, according to a Northern chronicler, shrewdly

> perceived that the King of England neither knew how to rule his realm nor was able to defend it against the Scots ... he feared lest at last he [the king] should lose the entire kingdom; so he chose the lesser of two evils, and considered how much better it would be for the community of each realm if each king should possess his own kingdom freely and peacefully without any homage, instead of so many homicides and arsons, captivities, plunderings and raidings taking place every year.[68]

The phrase 'the lesser of two evils' admirably summarises the Border mentality.

On 3 January 1323, Harclay travelled to Bruce at Lochmaben and negotiated a peace treaty without Edward's knowledge. In exchange for the payment of £27,000 to the Exchequer over ten years, Harclay recognised Bruce's kingship and Scotland's sovereignty. He also arranged the marriage of Bruce's male heir with whomsoever Edward chose from the English royal family.[69]

When the king, stunned, heard of Harclay's unauthorised enterprise, Harclay was brusquely summoned to Knaresborough to explain himself. The earl pleaded that he had brought peace to the Border, but on 1 February his arrest was ordered for treason. At the subsequent hearing, Harclay claimed that Northerners, from the meanest to the mightiest, 'were not a little delighted that the King of Scotland should freely possess his own kingdom on such terms that they themselves might live in peace'.[70] This extraordinary sentiment marks the reawakening of the almost schizophrenic, uniquely Northern phenomenon of dual allegiance, created by the real dangers of living so far from London and so close to Edinburgh. In practical terms, the Northern barons, their tenants and the local merchants were realising that their existence depended on choosing 'the lesser of two evils'. Not too far into the future, a distinctively Northern sensibility, even patriotism, would emerge under Percy leadership.

Sir Anthony de Lucy was entrusted with Harclay's arrest. His entry into Carlisle Castle was delayed by his having to kill the porter who tried to bar the inner gate,[71] and this allowed Harclay to destroy his copy of the treaty. It is only through the greatest good luck that we know its contents, as the copy held by the Scots also vanished. Only in the nineteenth century was a copy discovered in, of all places, a *Codex Diplomaticus* formerly belonging to the Episcopal See of Bergen in Norway.[72]

On 3 March, Harclay was degraded from his earldom by having his sword taken and he was divested of his knighthood by the striking off of his gilt spurs. Afterwards, he was dragged by horse to the gallows, where eloquently 'he explained to all men the purpose he had in making the aforesaid convention with the Scots'. He was hanged, beheaded, disembowelled and quartered; his head was spiked at the Tower of London, and his limbs distributed among the castles of Carlisle, Newcastle, Bristol and Dover. It was an act calculated to warn Northerners harbouring similar ideas of the inevitable penalty of treason.[73]

The irony of Harclay's terrible doom was not lost on those same Northerners two scant months later when Edward and Bruce made a peace treaty – of sorts. In May, Edward tactlessly addressed his opening letter to the 'people of Scotland' and omitted mentioning Bruce's name. The Scottish monarch was more amused at Edward's churlishness than offended by the slight. Ostentatiously replying as 'Robert, by God's grace king of Scotland', Bruce referred to Edward's 'very strange way of speaking'. Nevertheless, this hiccup was passed over, and Percy was chosen as one of the hostages (along with the Northern Lord Thomas Wake) to stay at Bruce's court whilst his counterpart, the earl of Moray, went to London as a Scottish ambassador, whose safety Edward guaranteed (on Percy's life).[74]

Eventually, a thirteen-year truce was concluded at Bishopthorpe, a mile or two south of York, at the end of May, at which Percy was present.[75] Although the talks reduced Border friction (no new castles or pele towers, used to sound the alarm if the Scots appeared, would be built on either side, for instance), they ultimately foundered on Edward's refusal to recognise Bruce as a fellow king and his unwillingness to return the Stone of Scone.[76] Duplicitously, moreover, Edward recalled the former King John Balliol's son, Edward Balliol, from Brittany, hoping to install him as a puppet-king once the forty-nine-year-old Bruce was dead (the latter was showing signs of *la grosse maladie* – leprosy – the disease that would kill him.[77]

One clause, inserted at Bruce's insistence, particularly displeased some Northern barons by abrogating any claims by Englishmen to Scottish lands and titles.[78] At a stroke, Percy's claims through his father to Urr, Red Castle and the earldom of Carrick were erased. Likewise, two other Northern loyalists, Henry Beaumont (who nursed a claim to the earldom of Buchan through his wife) and Thomas Wake, were left out of pocket.[79] The fiery Beaumont made such a commotion about this in a council meeting that Edward ordered him to leave his presence.[80] The two later became reconciled, outwardly at least. Whilst Percy was more diplomatic than Beaumont, he was angry about Edward's casual negation of his valuable claims, especially considering his losses in the last few years through raiding.

The Northern barons saw Bishopthorpe as an abandonment of the North. Apart from bursts of kingly interest in the future, the North was 'left to the mercy of the Scots, the king's over-mighty subjects and its own devices'.[81] The Northern baronage would have to sort out Northern problems for much of the Middle Ages.

No sooner was Edward's famished Exchequer belching its satisfaction at the thousands of pounds it was saving as part of the Anglo-Scottish 'peace dividend' than the king almost blundered into another war, this time abroad, with his brother-in-law, the new king of France, Charles IV. The *casus belli* was the homage of Edward, king of England, owed the French Crown for Aquitaine (used almost interchangeably with 'Gascony'). Charles had attended Edward's coronation in 1308, and had not been pleased with what he saw of his antics with Gaveston, especially because Queen Isabella was his sister. He was also very aware of Edward's habitual backsliding on his duties.

Charles IV was determined that his brother-in-law was not going to backslide out of this one. According to the Treaty of Paris made by Henry III and Louis IX in 1259, Edward owed fealty to the Capetian kings of France for the duchy. By this, Henry surrendered his claim to the territories lost by King John – namely, Normandy, Anjou, Maine, Touraine and Poitou, all of which had comprised the Angevin empire – but retained his lands and title as duke in return for paying homage as a vassal of the French king.

Accordingly, Charles politely requested Edward to come to France to perform his service *in person* and kneel before him. It was only thanks to the soothing abilities of Pembroke, who had connections with the French court, that prevented affairs coming to a head initially. That great earl Aymer de Valence unfortunately died in 1324, and the only other Anglo-French magnate of comparable status was the earl of Richmond, a member of the ruling house of Brittany but currently languishing as Bruce's prisoner.

The political situation in Aquitaine, however, deteriorated. Fights began breaking out between English and French administrators, culminating in Charles's threat in February 1324 to seize the duchy. Summoning an expeditionary force in the summer, the English despatched a fleet carrying eighty-three baronial contingents, but owing to adverse winds, it did not arrive until mid-October. Then, when they landed, the barons found no money or food awaiting them, and there were riots between townspeople and soldiers.

Percy was not aboard. In March 1324 Percy had been released from his constableship of Scarborough Castle. Despite appearances, this was no mark of royal disfavour; instead he was promoted to keeper of the coast of Yorkshire on 23 July 1324, a time when the arrival of a French invasion fleet looked imminent.[82] Whilst these duties excused him from the original muster for the expeditionary force, his turn came at the end of December.[83] He was to assemble at Portsmouth in mid-March of 1325, but a month before the deadline the order was cancelled when it was decided to send Queen Isabella on a mission to assuage her brother's anger.[84]

Isabella was 'pleased to visit her native land and her relatives, delighted to leave the company of some whom she did not like', the odious Despensers heading that particular list.[85] Once she began work, however, a peace treaty emerged. On the question of homage, Charles relented and allowed the thirteen-year-old Prince of Wales to perform the ritual instead of his father. In September 1325, embassy affairs being completed, Edward instructed Isabella, now twenty-nine, to return to England with the prince. But she mysteriously ignored the command; in Paris, she was embarking on an affair of her own.[86]

It never dawned on Edward that his queen had quietly been conspiring against him since the end of 1322. Brought together by a shared detestation of the Despensers, a powerful band of nobles had secretly clustered around Isabella. Pre-eminent among them were Henry, currently earl of Leicester and the brother and heir of Lancaster, and the king's own half-brothers, the earls of Kent and Norfolk. Kent, at the moment, was staying in Paris along with the queen's ecclesiastical allies – the bishops of Winchester and Norwich, who just happened to have been her two ambassadorial escorts. Also joining them was Henry Beaumont, the Northern baron who had never forgiven Edward for signing away his claim to the earldom of Buchan at Bishopthorpe in 1323. He had escorted the young prince to France, and there informed the queen about the anti-Edwardian mood in the North. Percy's name is certain to have come up in Beaumont's intelligence briefing.

Percy's loyalism at this time was under severe strain. Although Edward had regularly promoted him, his arc of ascent had not exactly been stellar – being 'Keeper of the Sea-Shore' was not quite in the same league as 'Warden of the Marches', a post still held by Strathbogie – besides which, he had recently lost his claims to what he regarded as his rightful Scottish possessions, wrenched from Robert Bruce's hands by his father. Then there was a recent letter from Edward, starchily reminding him 'to be more careful in granting safe conducts to the Scots to come into England'.[87] In sum, he was dissatisfied, but not actively so, with the regime; he would be ripe for recruitment, but only if Edward looked likely to topple. Following his secret meetings with the queen, Beaumont headed home and circumspectly began sounding out his fellow Northerners.

The most dangerous of all the conspirators was Sir Roger Mortimer of Wigmore, the jailed Contrariant who in 1323 had made an audacious escape from the Tower of London when friends drugged his guards.[88] A rope-ladder over the walls and a fast horse to the next ship leaving for France completed the adventure. Isabella evidently liked the waggish and caddish cut of his jib – which made a pleasant change from discussing basket-weaving with her husband – and love, or something else, was in the air.

Isabella, revealingly, had a taste for books of the sort much favoured at the time: chivalric romances and romantic histories. Her favourite story was that of Aimeri of Narbonne, who struck his wife, Lady Ermenjart, to the ground when she remonstrated with him for sending her seven sons into the world to seek their fortune. One of them defended his mother, but Ermenjart was delighted with her husband's stern reproof. She allayed her son's temper, saying that God would 'bless the arm which has so well recalled me to myself. What I said was folly ... Do what you will.' Hokey, middlebrow stuff, undoubtedly, but Mortimer's macho derring-do was redolent of Aimeri's compelling brutality. (As later events would show, Isabella herself rarely shied away from violence.)[89]

Charles IV, however, despite his dislike of Edward, disliked adultery still more, and requested Isabella, Mortimer and the prince to leave France. He was especially wary of Mortimer, whose Flashmanesque qualities did not exclude murderousness. Lately, two of his captured agents had confessed to an extraordinary Mortimer-inspired scheme to assassinate Edward and the two Despensers by means of the dark art of necromancy and £35 paid to a magician from Coventry who specialised in pushing pins through wax figures of the intended victims.[90]

The group made their way to Hainault (in modern Belgium) where its count, William II, was charmed by Isabella's offer of her son, the heir to the kingdom of England, as husband to his daughter, Philippa.[91] He was so charmed, in fact, that he paid for an invasion force of Hainaulters (700 men-at-arms and 800 foot) under Mortimer's command.[92] The royal rebels landed at Harwich in Suffolk on 24 September 1326, taking Edward completely by surprise. Four days later, he promised pardons to all who would desert Mortimer and, moreover, put a price of £100 on his head, dead or alive.[93] Despenser the Elder was not so optimistic: hearing of Isabella's small force, he cried, 'Allas, Allas! We be all bitraiede; for certes with so litil power she nad neuer comen to londe, but folc of this lande were to her consentede.'[94]

The invaders were assured of a warm welcome. London, the key to the kingdom since the time of the Empress Matilda, hated Edward for his interference in its civil affairs and frequent impositions of taxation. It would become the bulwark of Isabella's invasion. In the country at large, Edward had been faced with constant acts of sabotage and small-scale insurrection since the execution of Lancaster, who enjoyed a posthumously romantic reputation among the populace. Edward's savage punishment of the Contrariants led to their relatives rising against him, joined by former Lancastrians who had survived the purge. Most of Wales and the Welsh Marches, for example, were no-go areas for royal officials owing to the guerrilla attacks of Contrariants lately stripped of their lands. When assailants set upon one such official in Gloucestershire, they tore out his eyes, broke all his limbs and stole the account books he was taking to the Exchequer.

Things were no better in the North. Percy was commissioned 'to pursue and arrest disturbers of the peace who join together to make raids by day and night, commit robberies, imprison people until they make ransom, go to fairs and markets and take goods without paying for them, beat those who will not be of their party, and waylay merchants'.[95] England, in short, was plunging into chaos.

If Edward had immediately decided to rid himself of the notoriously avaricious but miserly Despensers, he might have cooled the ardour of his barons and perhaps even the rogue Contrariants. This was the same man, however, who recalled Piers Gaveston three times.

The Despensers, slightly more politically astute than their king, were quietly making preparations in case the worst came to the worst. Hugh the Younger, for example, secretly withdrew the enormous sum of £2000 from his accounts with the Bardi and Peruzzi, the private Italian bankers, into which he had been funnelling the expropriated wealth of Contrariants. He had also squirrelled away the proceeds of his brief but highly profitable stint as a Channel pirate. In addition, Edward had granted him lands worth £7000 annually plus goods valued at about £3000.[96]

To repel the invasion, the English defences were organised quickly. The regional commanders included Winchester and Leicester, Lancaster's brother, in the central and northern Midlands respectively; and the king's elder half-brother, the earl of Norfolk, was in charge of Essex, Hertfordshire and East Anglia, the most crucial areas of all. Arundel controlled Lincolnshire, but his deputy was the second husband of Alice de Lucy, Lancaster's widow, making his true allegiance murky. The North was given to Warenne, with Percy acting, in an unglamorous capacity, as his deputy chief surveyor of the array, with personal responsibility for the East Riding.[97] An uncompromising order was communicated to the Northern commanders: 'Magnates having castles and fortresses in those parts should stay there for the defence of those parts.'[98]

At the invasion's outset, the two most important earls, Norfolk and Leicester, switched sides, as had earlier been arranged in France. Isabella's tiny army of 1500 was soon swelling to appreciable proportions. Secret Contrariants and their retinues flocked to the earl of Norfolk.[99] Edward and the Despensers seemed to have had no inkling that many apparently loyal officials, like Richard Perrers (sheriff of Essex) for instance, had been conspiring with the Contrariant underworld for years. In early October, Isabella, Mortimer and Leicester moved west to assemble at Dunstable, just outside Luton, before entering London in triumph. Edward, however, had fled the city and was streaking towards Wales, accompanied by an Exchequer official carrying £29,000. He reached Gloucester, where he tried to buy the support of the Welsh lords, Gruffyd Llywd and Rhys ap Gruffyd.

Isabella followed him, and was joined at Gloucester by the Northern musters led by Percy, Wake and Beaumont, 'the most formidable military group left in England and their junction with Isabella gave her overwhelming strength'.[100] Their tardiness in joining Isabella suggests that the three colonels took stock before deciding to throw their weight behind the queen. Beaumont had connections with her circle, and perhaps his promises of rewards finally persuaded the other two to desert Edward. It was a terrible risk they ran. Isabella's success was by no means assured, and the fate of the Contrariants reminded them of the penalty for choosing the wrong side. It was unlikely that the three men, in particular Percy, *hated* Edward II as Lancaster once had; certainly, they were angry at him for selling their Scottish possessions down the river, but whether they intended usurping a divinely ordained king is another question. Others, like Leicester or Mortimer, had appreciable personal grievances against Edward, but for Percy and the two Northerners the Despensers had to be deposed, for it was they who had controlled government policy for so long. Edward's Scottish strategy, including the decision to quitclaim the Northerners' Scottish lands, was actually determined by the Despensers. They had helped to kill Lancaster and Harclay, the earl of Carlisle, the only two men with enough regional power to defend the North against the Scots. For Percy, Lancaster had been a cantankerous relic, but now he appreciated the old man's worth, and began to rue the annulment of Lancaster's treasured Ordinances in the Statute of York of 1322, in which he had played a part. Formerly, the Ordinances had prevented the king from appointing his own councillors and surrounding himself with greasy sycophants like Gaveston and Despenser the Younger. Now the lord of Alnwick recognised the dangers of an unstable king manipulated by unscrupulous favourites, like the Despensers, who cared not a fig for the Border and the North – a faraway country of which they knew little and cared even less.

By 26 October Isabella and Mortimer's army had trooped to Bristol, whose garrison handed over the ninety-year-old earl of Winchester, the elder Despenser. The next day, in front of a jerry-rigged court, he was sentenced to be immediately drawn, hanged and decapitated and his head taken to Winchester, 'where you were earl against law and reason'. His torso was suspended by the arms with two strong ropes for four days. It was then chopped up and the pieces thrown to the hounds. One final touch: he was killed wearing a robe decorated with his heraldic arms, but turned inside out so that the arms would be discarded for ever.[101] Nevertheless, they are borne today by earl Spencer.

As for Edward, on 16 November 1326, he was captured by Leicester in Glamorgan, taken to his royal castle of Kenilworth and placed under armed guard until Isabella and Mortimer could decide what to do with him.

In the meantime, the younger Despenser and his father-in-law, the earl of Arundel, had fallen into the queen's hands. This Arundel had, as we saw in previous chapters, been violently against Gaveston and was opposed to the king. However, in 1321, sensing which way the wind was blowing, he married off his eldest son – all of eight years old – to the younger Despenser's daughter (aged seven), and from then on was a resolute royalist. It was to prove an unfortunate calculation, and not only because his son later divorced her after producing a male heir. Apparently, they had been 'forced by blows to cohabit'.[102] Arundel was executed without trial.

Not even Despenser the Younger deserved his fate. He was outfitted in a reversed coat of arms, after which a crown of nettles was jammed onto his head. Scriptural verses denouncing arrogance and hubris were tattooed into his skin. Before a baying crowd, his judgement was read out and he was roughly drawn with four horses, not the usual two. The scaffold, specially constructed, was fifty feet high. After being strung up until unconscious, Despenser was cut down and slapped awake. Then, his intestines were torn out and burnt in front of his eyes. While still alive (timing is everything), he was beheaded, as befitted a 'traitour [and] tyrant'.[103]

The Edwardian regime was dead. Now the de facto rulers had to decide what to do with the *de jure* king at Kenilworth. Isabella and Mortimer wanted to depose him, but the Prince of Wales, and the barons, remained silent. One step too far and the usurpers themselves might be usurped. Whatever was done had to be by the book to lend an ultimately illegal act a reassuring patina of legality. On the other hand, an astounding £60,000 from the royal treasury, if distributed sensibly, might assuage any baronial misgivings. The awesome Despenser and Arundel estates had also fallen into the provisional government's hands.

Edward refused to attend a Parliament, which Percy attended, that was called for 7 January 1327. There, in vaguely Bolshevik style, 'oaths of allegiance to the new regime and noisy public acclamations became the order of the day'. Edward's absence, of course, made the Parliament an illegal convocation, but the prince was created 'Keeper of the Realm', which effectively solved the problem. Over the coming weeks, Mortimer connived to persuade the gathered magnates that Edward II must be formally deposed. Isabella's paramour partly bought Percy's acquiescence by arranging for about £197 to be paid to him, a substantial sum that was owed by Edward I to Percy's father for wages in Scotland and as compensation for horses lost. Its overdue settlement must have eased some tensions, demonstrating that the new regime paid its debts, unlike Edward II.[104]

Mortimer also recruited Thomas Wake, Percy's Northern friend, to stir up the Londoners. In a wonderful piece of stage management, Bishop Stratford told the people outside Westminster that the peers had decided to make the prince a king, but this needed their assent. Then, Wake, theatrically shaking his arms above his head, asked them to give it. A great cry went up, 'Let it be done, Let it be done,' and so it was done on 20 January. One recent historian noted that this strange procedure was 'a precedent for deposition by the magnates with the co-operation, agreement and acclamation of the people'.[105] It should be added here, for future reference, that 'the nation had been called upon to participate in the deposition of Edward II; but it was rather by accepting acts which were performed by the magnates, or a section of them, in its name, than by itself'.[106] Later, in Richard II's reign, it would happen again. Barons, blooded and brutalised by the spate of executions for failure, were rapidly adapting into politically astute creatures. To seal poor Edward's discomfiture, a delegation including Henry Percy (representing the baronage) travelled to Kenilworth to withdraw their homages to him as king of England.[107]

By early summer, a despondent Edward was moved to Berkeley Castle in Gloucestershire. It was announced on 21 September 1327 that he had died, and he was subsequently interred in a magnificent tomb at Gloucester Abbey. In fine *1066 and All That* style, everyone remembers the story about a red-hot poker lodged in an uncomfortable place. According to the *Brut* chronicler, assassins sent by Mortimer entered 'the King's chaumbre ... and laiden an huge table oppon his wombe [stomach], and with men pressede and helde fast adoune the four corners of the table oppon his body: wherewith the gode man awoke, and ... turnede his body opsadoun [upside down]. They tok the false tiraunt, and put [a long horn] into his fundement as depe as thai might, and toke a spete of Copur brennyng [burning copper-spit], and put it through the horne into his body, and oftetimes rollede therewith his bowailes; and so thai quellede [killed] their Lorde, that nothing was perceyuede.'[108]

The choice of method, and subsequently weapon, is odd. Although it would have far easier to kill Edward with a sword, Mortimer was especially concerned to make the death appear a natural one. Crushing him under a table would leave no tell-tale marks ('that nothing was perceyuede'), but when that failed, the assassins improvised with the spit. With the corpse fully clothed for burial the seared wound would be difficult to detect.

The king's death, although a great shock, removed at a stroke any danger to his young successor's rule. The prince, now fourteen, was crowned Edward III on 1 February 1327, ten days after his father's deposition. The king was surrounded by a twelve-man ruling council, which included Henry Percy, Thomas Wake and the former earl of Leicester, now called Henry of Lancaster (the rehabilitation of Earl Thomas in a Parliament held in February meant that he was no longer a traitor, so allowing his brother to assume the title and estates).[109] It did not, however, include Mortimer, who acted as if he were a member of the royal family and was acquiring worryingly Despenser-like habits. Late in 1327, he took the title of earl of March, seized some of Arundel's lands and was dubbed the 'King of Folly' by one of his own sons. Mortimer, however, was but first among equals when it came to the spoils. The earl of Norfolk received great largesse, but Kent was rapidly gaining notoriety for his rapaciousness. Isabella ensured herself a comfortable retirement, receiving an annual endowment of £13,000 (raised from £4,500 during her husband's lifetime).[110]

The three Northern lords, whose swooping intervention had been instrumental in the collapse of Despenser power, were richly rewarded. Percy received a handy 1000 marks (or £666) for 'expenses' and other payments and rewards, whilst Beaumont was given the manors of Whitwick and Loughborough once held by Despenser the Elder.[111]

The Northerners, at last, found themselves in a favourable position with the new administration and lobbied for Edward, Isabella and Mortimer to take an interest in their Scottish claims. Robert Bruce, now suffering from leprosy and increasingly bedridden, similarly felt that the usurpers might be more amenable to recognising his kingship. To aid a quick decision, he embarked on a final campaign to show that an independent Scottish power was a fait accompli. Scottish troops crossed the Tweed and attacked Norham in Northumberland, only a few hours after Edward had been crowned. Although the siege was stoutly baffled, the Scots had tested English mettle for a fight and found it wanting.

What were these Scottish war-bands like? According to a French eyewitness, Jean le Bel:

> These Scottish men are right hardy and sore travailing in harness and in wars. For when they will enter in England, within a day and a night they will drive their whole host twenty-four mile, for they are all a-horseback ... They take with them no purveyance of bread or wine, for their usage and soberness is such in time of war, that they will pass in the journey a great long time with flesh half sodden, without bread, and drink of the river water without wine, and they neither care for pots nor pans, for they seethe beasts in their own skins.[112]

Occasionally, they would eat oatmeal baked into biscuit. As for the English, their rations were slightly richer, but war on the Border sounds pretty miserable. The chivalric chronicler Froissart speaks of 'small poor wine' and 'bread evil baken in panniers' which 'was sore wet with the sweat of horses'. The Englishmen's 'saddles [were] all rotten and broken, and most part of their horses hurt on their backs: nor they had not wherewith to shoe them that were unshod, nor they had nothing to cover themselves withal from the rain and cold but green bushes and armour, nor they had nothing to make fire but green boughs, the which would not burn because of the rain'. Interestingly, the lords on both sides suffered alongside their men, although some, Froissart remarks, brought bottles to fill with river water and used torches for light, but not heat.[113] There would be times when Percy and other wardens would be in the field for months.

Isabella and Mortimer were too busy reordering the realm to fight a war. On 16 February, Strathbogie having died in December, Percy was given a short-term commission as warden of the March, his retinue comprising 159 men-at-arms and 200 hobelars, or mounted infantry. For the nice sum of 1000 marks or £666 he was to serve until Whitsunday (31 May).[114] The orders handed to Percy and his Northern deputy, Lord Neville, were to keep the peace and ensure that no Englishman broke the terms of the 1323 peace treaty.[115]

Appeasement failed. Intelligence from Percy's spies revealed in early April 1327 that Bruce was assembling the entire Scottish host on the Border for a major offensive into Northumberland. Immediately, the commissioners of array were ordered to begin mustering local troops and a general summons went out for mid-May. The earl of Lancaster was made captain of the king's army in the Marches of Scotland, and Lords Wake and Beaumont and others were attached to his command. Isabella even invited her old Hainaulters on behalf of her son, keen to exhibit his prowess to the barons. Soon after, hundreds of veteran Hainaulter men-at-arms became involved in a drunken riot in York sparked by a game of dice. No fewer than 316 Lancashire archers were left dead in the streets.[116]

In early July, warnings were received that Bruce would penetrate Cumbria, not Northumberland, and Edward and his entourage accordingly travelled north-west from York. The place arranged as a rendezvous point for the scattered magnates, barons and men-at-arms to join the king was none other than Percy's manor of Topcliffe – the first time the small castle had been honoured with a royal visit and a mark of Percy's newly exalted status. The king stayed there from 6 to 12 July but the plan changed before most of the army had arrived. On 15 July, the royal train rode instead to Durham, which the Frenchman Jean le Bel called 'the last outpost of civilization'. The Cumbrian approach had been a feint; the smoke from wracked Northumbrian villages alerted the English that three Scottish war-parties under Sir James Douglas and the earls of Mar and Moray were on the rampage.

Three weeks later, Douglas led a bold commando raid into the king's camp at Stanhope Park, one of the bishop of Durham's private hunting preserves. There was not time to capture the king but as Douglas galloped through he slashed the guy-ropes supporting Edward's tent, bringing the lustrous pavilion down on the poor boy's head. When informed that Douglas had reached Scotland safely, the king 'was wonder sory, and ful hertly wepte with his yonge eyne'.

The English army disbanded in disappointment. Rumours of treachery and double-dealing were mostly directed at the Hainaulters, who handed Edward a staggering bill for £55,000 before leaving. The sinews of war were now lubricated by cash on delivery and contracts, although the traditional feudal call-up was retained, in form at least, until 1385, when the last summons of the Middle Ages was issued. The campaign of 1327, however, may be said to mark the last gasp of a Norman feudalism that had lasted for 250 years.

Edward was not quite ready to forsake the North for ever, but he may have entertained the notion after Douglas's latest escapade. He moved the seat of government to York and appointed Percy the chief warden of the East March with plenary powers. Yet Percy's motley collection of demoralised scratch troops – all he could raise – were no match for Scottish war-bands itching to affray.

He must have grumbled loudly to some influential people that he was expected to defend the March on pennies; how could he enforce discipline and stop desertion if his men were not paid? Percy's complaints reached the king, for on 17 August 1327, Edward requested the abbot of St Mary's, York, to pay Percy £142 as a matter of urgency for the arrears due to him.

Bruce now launched a brilliant strike, which came close to conquering Northumberland. Pushing deep into the county, the Scots divided into three forces: the first, under Bruce himself, plundered far and wide; the second, under Moray and Douglas, besieged Percy in Alnwick Castle for a fortnight; and the third, under John 'the Crab', a Flemish pirate who 'was dryuen out of Flaundres for his wickednesse' (we shall meet him again later), besieged Norham. By locking Percy and the garrison in his own castle, fully two bannerets, twenty knights, seventy-seven esquires and a hundred hobelars were taken out of commission. Any English soldiers outside were left isolated and leaderless. Douglas and Moray had given Bruce the run of Northumberland. Fortunately for Percy, the Scots decided to storm Norham, and eventually Moray and Douglas

impatiently broke off the siege and joined Bruce outside Norham.
Indeed, Bruce was so cocksure that Northumberland would fall, he had
even partitioned it by charter between his followers, just as Edward I had
Scotland among his.[117]

Yet, despite these brave appearances, Bruce needed peace. England
had not collapsed into civil war, but he was dying, and he knew it. His
heir, Prince David, was an infant, and there was a significant risk that the
Great Cause of 1291–2 might be replayed. Bruce could trust Douglas and
Moray to look after the child, but Moray was increasingly infirm and
Douglas was unstable, to put it mildly. As for Earl Donald of Mar, like
the late Strathbogie, nobody was ever quite sure whose side he was on
(he had fought alongside Edward II and had even planned to spring him
from Berkeley Castle). When Bruce died, it was possible Scotland would
collapse into an anarchy so total that its nobles might ask the grandson of
Edward the Conqueror to choose their king. The most obvious contender, again, would be a Balliol: namely, Edward Balliol, the son of
Bruce's predecessor. Peace now, in other words, could stave off
catastrophe until David was old enough to take charge of his realm.

The English wanted a break from war as well. Edward's hold on his
troubled realm was not yet secure. To this end, two envoys – Henry
Percy and William Denum, a senior common lawyer – went to see Bruce
on 9 October 1327. Edward had asked them to sound him out about a
lasting peace. Bruce cordially greeted them and laid out his preliminary
terms. First, Edward must grant under his Great Seal that 'Robert shall
have the realm of Scotland free, quit and entire, without any kind of subjection, for himself and his heirs for ever'. Second, Prince David must
marry Edward's sister, Joan, soon fondly nicknamed 'Countess
Makepees' by the Scots. Third, no Englishman might claim lands in
Scotland. Fourth, Edward must give military aid to Scotland if she were
attacked. In return, Bruce relinquished any Scottish claims towards lands
in England and promised aid in the event of a foreign war, *excluding*
France. He would also pay £20,000 over three years as compensation for
his blackmail and raiding.[118]

Percy and Denum brought the terms to Nottingham. Edward eagerly
accepted the proposal of marriage and the offer of compensation. The
question of kingly recognition stuck in his craw but he could negotiate
once the recurring problem of the 'disinherited' lands was settled.
Personally, Edward was not overly exercised about the Scottish properties but Percy, Wake and Beaumont were not allies he wished to lose. For
the moment, however, the terms covered much common ground, and it
was hoped that the quandary would, during negotiations, resolve itself.[119]

Percy and Denum arranged to meet their Scottish counterparts in

Newcastle. Throughout November and the New Year, the two sides, buttressed by clerks, lawyers and diplomats, endeavoured to draft an acceptable treaty of 'Pax et Concordia'. By the early spring, their efforts were reaching fruition. In Parliament at York, on 1 March 1328, Edward III declared,

> We, and certain of our predecessors as kings of England, have tried to assert rights of rule, dominion, or superiority over the realm of Scotland, and in consequence a grievous burden of wars has long afflicted the realms of England and Scotland... [and therefore] we wish, and grant by the present letter, on behalf of ourselves, our heirs, and all our successors... and communities of our realm assembled in our Parliament, that the realm of Scotland, defined by its true Marches as they existed and were maintained in the time of Alexander [III, who died in 1286], of worthy memory, the late king of Scotland, shall remain for ever to the eminent prince Lord Robert, by the grace of God the illustrious king of Scots, our ally and dearest friend, and his heirs and successors.[120]

In this extraordinary document, Edward unambiguously acknowledged King Robert and Scotland's independence. A senior delegation travelled to Edinburgh to settle outstanding points, the question of the men now called the 'Disinherited' being the foremost. This delegation included Lord William la Zouche de Assheby and the most experienced English negotiator, Henry Percy, both detailed to swear to Edward's renunciation of his pretensions to Scottish dominion.[121]

Bruce himself was mostly laid up in bed, but the grandest of Scottish nobles and prelates congregated at Holyrood for the discussions. Within a week, the marriage proposal was formalised, an indenture for £20,000 was drawn up and the Anglo-Scottish military alliance was sealed. Crucially, however, the Disinherited were excluded from the final text of the Treaty of Northampton of 17 March 1328 (so called, confusingly, because it was confirmed there, although it is alternatively termed the Treaty of Edinburgh). Percy's uncontested primacy in the English pecking order may be deduced from the final clause: 'for assurance of the marriage, and for keeping, holding, and accomplishing in good faith, without infringement, each and all of these things, Henry Percy, in the name of the king of England, and by powers specially granted by him, and on his soul, has taken oath upon the Holy Gospels.'[122]

In early July, Queen Isabella and Joan travelled to Berwick for Joan's marriage to David. Despite the lavish celebrations, the omens foretold ill. Edward (recently married to Philippa of Hainault) stayed away; more insultingly, Joan married without a dowry (in 1332 Edward would give another sister £10,000 when she married). Indeed, King Robert personally granted £2000 to Joan, merely to salve her humiliation.[123] Bruce, although ailing, made no attempt to come to Berwick – a fairly short distance from Edinburgh – when he heard that Edward would be absent. The royal *amour propre* must be maintained. Instead, he sent Moray and Douglas.

Whilst chroniclers and contemporaries regarded the Treaty of Northampton as a shameful peace, Edward escaped blame. Rather, it was widely assumed that Isabella and Mortimer had foisted the treaty on the hapless king. According to the *Brut,* 'through false conseile, the Kyng was there [Northampton] falsely disherited' of Scotland.[124] Another chronicler spat darkly at the 'traitors' who controlled the king. Percy, the leading negotiator, was probably identified as one of these false councillors and traitors. His links with Isabella's regime would not have passed unnoticed.

Percy, to put it bluntly, was rapidly dissipating his stock of credit with the baronage. At the time of the coronation and marriage, he had been numbered among the 'tuelf grete Lordes of Engeland' who were ordained to guide the young king. As the *Brut* chronicler noted, however, some councillors had fallen under the malign spell of Isabella and Mortimer, who 'toke unto [themselves] castelles, tounes, Landes and rents, in grete harme and losse unto the croune'.[125] The implication was that some of their tame councillors were also 'taking unto themselves'.

There was one other small problem: the Treaty of Corbeil of 1326, sealed between the French and the Scots. This stipulated that if war broke out between England and France – even if Scotland reached a peaceful concord with England, as in the Treaty of Northampton – the Scots would be obliged to attack England.[126]

Nevertheless, Isabella hoped that the convivial mood and prevailing spirit of *glasnost* would ease Bruce's opposition to restoring the lands of the Disinherited. Two magnanimous gestures by the English helped lessen the tension. Two treasured Scottish relics – one, a piece of the True Cross, which the Scots call the Black Rood – were returned, and Mortimer even suggested returning the Stone of Destiny, but the London mob prevented its removal from Westminster.[127] A little later, Edward ordered that the quarter of the corpse of Harclay, still gruesomely hanging at Carlisle, be removed.[128] Harclay had died because of his 'unofficial' peace treaty and, politically speaking, Edward masterfully demonstrated to the Scots that they were enemies no more.

Their efforts paid off. On the same day that the English and Scottish royal houses were reunited, King Robert by 'our special grace … granted … to Sir Henry Percy, son and heir of the late Sir Henry Percy, all the lands, tenements and rents which belonged to the late Sir Henry his father, or which should have been his by hereditary right... within our realm of Scotland... No forfeiture resulting from war shall impede Henry, or his heirs, in any way.' None other than Moray and Douglas witnessed Percy's grant.[129] Similar, if less formal, concessions – or, more realistically, 'promises' – were made to Wake and Beaumont.[130]

While in Scotland, Percy had taken the opportunity to press his claims with the Bruce himself. Indeed, the rapid progress of the Northampton talks might have been facilitated by King Robert's early acceptance of the chief negotiator's private demands. Some might call this tacit little arrangement an 'abuse of power', or, to paraphrase the *Brut* chronicler, 'taking unto oneself'. As a result, whilst Percy was allowed to take possession of his lands immediately, Wake and Beaumont waited for years before their claims were dealt with. Whether Percy's preferential treatment rankled with his two comrades is unknown; but his lack of energetic exertion on their behalf would have been noted.

Moreover, opposition to the Treaty of Northampton was crystallising around the figure of Henry of Lancaster, whose daughter was married to Thomas Wake. The troublesome Henry Beaumont was already circling the Lancastrians, as was his son-in-law, David of Strathbogie (b. 1309), who after his father's death had revived the family claim to the earldom of Atholl.

The recovery of Percy's Scottish baronies of Urr and Red Castle was relatively straightforward. His father having acquired these over the claims of his Scottish relatives, a branch of the Balliol family, the Scots recognised them as his by descent, even if not *rightful* descent. The surviving lawful heir was one Henry Fishburn, whom Percy pursued relentlessly, desperate to buy his quitclaim to the lands. In 1331, Percy caught up with him and offered him 200 marks (or £132) – probably a fair(ish) figure – to surrender any future claim. The poor man was probably grateful for the money. On 3 June, he accepted the compensation and disappeared from history.[131]

Ideally, Percy would have received Carrick as well. Although the Scots bent over backwards to accommodate him – Moray, for instance, relinquished his half-share of the Urr barony for Percy – Carrick was a lost cause. Bruce had already granted this western principality, a prime strategic asset, to his son, David. 'Before the end of the fourteenth century,' states Professor Barrow, 'it came to be regarded as the peculiar appanage of the heir apparent to the Crown.'[132] Nevertheless, the charter of 28 July specifically granted him 'all the lands, tenements and rents which belonged to his late father'. As Carrick was worth immensely more than Urr and Red Castle combined, Percy felt bitterly short-changed. In the current atmosphere, he could not feud with the son-in-law of the king of England, and his irritation – and frustration – would gnaw at him for years.

CHAPTER NINE

Henry Percy IV and the Conquest of Scotland

For a warrior under Edward III, a contemporary lyricised, 'to fight was to rule, to go forth was to prosper, to contend was to triumph' – a far cry from the young king's ineffectual father.[1] Edward's mighty fulfilment of his kingly office prompted this encomium: 'Against his foes he was grim as a leopard, toward his subjects mild as a lamb.'

Edward III, from his own time to the present day, has been regarded as a Samson and a Solomon in one, the apotheosis of a king who combined wisdom with martial exploit. His tomb in Westminster Abbey supports a gilt-bronze effigy of him taken from a death-mask (making it the first royal 'portrait'), and his epitaph includes the following: 'Here lies the glory of the English, the flower of kings past, the pattern for kings to come, a merciful king, the bringer of peace to his people.' Abroad, his reputation was not quite so adulatory. A French chronicler noted that because of Edward, 'the English, by their very nature, always want to make war on their neighbours without cause'. In person, however, Edward was 'meke and benyne, homely, sobre, and softe to all maner men ... He was devoute and holy ... wyse in counsell, and discrete, soft, meke, and good to speke with.' It was only in his declining years that 'lecchery and ... of his flessh haunted hym'.

The unceasing yearning for martial glory has condemned the third Edward in contemporary eyes as ambitious, selfish, ruthless, unprincipled, unscrupulous and vain, dedicating his life to taking the lives of others, and ignoring the people's welfare. Victorian historians, who preferred to exalt the bourgeois virtues of thrift and caution, were horrified at Edward's personification of such medieval hyper-aristocratic values as lavish magnificence and wanton love- (and war-)making. Until the early nineteenth century, however, historians unanimously considered him the greatest of kings. According to his biographer Joshua Barnes in 1688, Edward was 'the best King, the best Captain, the best Lawgiver, the best Friend, the best Father and the best Husband in his days'.

Yet if there was something ruthlessly one-dimensional about Edward III it must be traced to the circumstances in which he came to power. The deposition and murder of his father mark one of the most momentous ruptures in medieval history since 1066. Kings now were vulnerable, and occasionally dispensable. Throughout his reign Edward III sought to restore royal authority. Authority brought stability, and stability stayed rebellion. Hence his showy emphasis on traditional kingly pursuits and images; the nation expected these of him, and he played to the crowd. War was the great entertainer, satisfying the aristocracy, enriching the common soldier and distracting attention from domestic problems, especially if presented as a national enterprise for the glory of England and her ruler. As the canon of Liège, Jean le Bel, wrote at the time: 'Now, in the time of the noble Edward, who has often put them [the English] to the test, they are the finest and most daring warriors known to man.' Even at home, Northerners were impressed by his attention to the Border – a welcome change from his father.[2]

Unlike his implacable grandfather, Edward won over enemies with rich grants and an amicable, forgiving attitude. Crucially, he abjured favourites like the Despensers and Gaveston until his evening years, and presented himself, as king and defender of the realm, as above petty politicking. Alongside his own growing monarchical prerogatives, an increasingly independent nobility was bound to him by his sharp invigoration of the manners and habits of chivalry. For, according to Ranald Nicholson, '[if] the keynote of Edward I's reign had been *legalitas*, that of Edward III's was to be *militia* or chivalry. Just as an outward respect for legal principles had partly concealed the egotistic ruthlessness of Edward I, so also the panache of chivalry partly concealed the aggressive ambitions of Edward III.'[3] If this was one reason for his invention of the Order of the Garter, another was to replace the factionalism and strife that had ruined the country since Edward II's accession. Who could not feel honoured to join the twenty-five other recipients (including the sovereign, lauded as a second King Arthur) in this charmed circle? Magnates were no longer rivals, but brothers-in-arms.

Just as he freely distributed gifts to his adoring barons, Edward showered huge land grants on his sons to prevent dissension. As a man, Edward is far less interesting than Edward I or II, let alone his grandson Richard II, but he adds up to more than merely a brutal warrior.

The Fall of Mortimer and the Rise of the Disinherited

On 7 June 1329, King Robert of Scotland died at Cardross, aged fifty-five. His heir, by his second marriage, was David, then only a young boy, and his councillors could easily work out the arithmetic of succession. If

David should die without issue, then the throne would descend to his nephew, Robert Stewart, only eight years older than the prince. This Robert was the son of Walter Stewart the High Steward of Scotland and Marjorie, the Bruce's daughter by his first marriage and former prisoner of Edward I's commander Henry Percy. Although there was also a wild card in the shape of King John Balliol's son, Edward Balliol, who had been seen prowling around England, the Bruce dynasty was fortunate in having the loyal earl of Moray as guardian of Scotland.

Edward III had his own problems.[4] Mortimer, who had aggressively grabbed the title of earl of March at a Parliament at Salisbury, was becoming insufferable, and his mother an embarrassment. Although the Scots had, against all expectations, succeeded in paying off the first instalment of the £20,000 stipulated in the Treaty of Northampton, most of it went to Isabella instead of Edward's empty Exchequer. Moreover, the king suspected Mortimer of plotting against him, as he had against his father. Mortimer's daughters had been married off to the heirs of the earldoms of Pembroke and Norfolk. That Mortimer now personally controlled the Welsh border was particularly worrying – had not the younger Despenser attempted the same?

One chronicler despaired of England under Isabella and Mortimer: 'the tresoure that Sir Edward of Carnaryuan [Edward II] hade lefte in meny places of Engelond and in Walyes, were wastede and born away withouten the wille of Kyng Edward his son, in destruccioun of him and of his folc. Also, through whos conseile [Mortimer and Isabella] that the Kyng gaf up the Kyngdome of Scotland, for the whiche reaume the Kyngus ancestres hade ful sore trauaile, and so dede ment a nobleman for her ryght.'[5]

Angered by Mortimer's appeasement of Scotland and by his dangerous pretensions, Lancaster had boycotted the Salisbury Parliament in November 1328. He now arranged secret meetings with the disaffected earls of Kent and Norfolk – as royal uncles, they felt sidelined by Mortimer – and the Disinherited barons Thomas Wake (married to Blanche, Lancaster's daughter; Wake's sister was married to Kent) and Henry Beaumont. The untrustworthy David of Strathbogie, claimant to the earldom of Atholl and Beaumont's son-in-law, also joined the conspirators.

This cabal launched an abortive rebellion, more out of spite than serious intent, which fizzled out when Percy rode to Mortimer and Isabella's aid with a force of six knights and thirty-five esquires just as a skirmish was in the offing. Two key figures, Kent and Norfolk, soon abandoned the Lancastrian cause, and attempts at mediation gradually sapped much of the rebels' rebelliousness. In mid-January 1330,

Lancaster, Strathbogie, Wake and the rest of their followers, such as Henry Ferrers and Hugh d'Audley, sought terms. Their estates and castles were forfeited temporarily; the ringleaders had this commuted to a large fine, which was later cancelled. One rebel remained at large – Henry Beaumont, who fled to France, where he contacted a bored Edward Balliol.

Mortimer chose his next move carefully. The reflected halo of the martyrdom of Thomas, the earl of Lancaster's brother, made him well nigh untouchable, and Norfolk, the elder of the two king's uncles, could be dominated through Mortimer's daughter, but Kent was a soft target owing to the popular hatred caused by his rapaciousness. Early in 1330, he was arrested and forced to confess that he believed Edward II to be still alive[6] and that he had plotted to depose Edward III. On 19 March, Isabella and Mortimer ordered his execution for treason. Even then, the poor man had to wait until the evening before someone could be found to do the deed – a dragooned 'gonge-fermer', medieval slang for a 'shit-scavenger', as it turned out. The earl's assets were immediately transferred into Mortimer's hands.

This act of selective terror backfired. It reminded the baronage of the Despensers' terrible regime and demonstrated that the rebellion that had toppled Edward II had only raised another, equally inequitable, tyranny. Following Kent's death, disgruntled barons beseeched his son to over-throw the usurper and the Dowager, later dubbed the 'She-Wolf of France'.

Their pleas fell on keen ears. Edward was soon turning eighteen, and the father of a baby boy by Philippa. He felt humiliated by Mortimer, who had starved the royal household of money (at this time, there was £41 left in the treasury), executed Kent, Edward's favourite uncle (although no one else liked him much), and planted spies in his court. As early as the winter of 1328 Edward had begun to circumvent Mortimer's authority. He privately arranged with Pope John XXII at Avignon a coded signal so that the Pope could distinguish between requests emanating from Edward and those from Mortimer, so that the latter's could be disregarded. Edward wrote the words, *Pater Sancte*, in his own hand at the foot of letters, one of which survives. It is the only existing specimen of Edward's handwriting – clear and careful but with a nicely decorative capital letter – and the first tangible indication of Edward's broad plan to be rid of the turbulent Mortimer.[7]

Late in 1330 came the last straw. At Nottingham, Mortimer had the weird temerity to interrogate, and then accuse, Edward of complicity in his father's death before a rigged Great Council. Mortimer by this time considered himself the de facto king of England. He affected wondrously tailored clothes, and was 'so ful of pride and wrecchednesse' that he even held a Round Table in Wales in which he 'countrefetede [copied] the maner & doyng of Kyng Arthure'.[8] Lancaster's shadowy movements at this time are instructive. Having avoided the court for nearly a year, he suddenly reappeared on 16 October. Three days later, Edward and several trusted friends stole into Nottingham Castle through a secret underground passage. There they arrested Mortimer, who was dragged to London and executed as a traitor.[9] After arresting his mother, Edward treated her leniently and she lived in retirement for the next twenty-eight years. The she-wolf had been tamed by her cub.

Edward intended to make a fresh start after the ignominious beginnings of his rule, not to mention his ruthless arrest of his mother. Displaying the sureness of touch that characterised Edward's political affairs throughout his life, the king immediately divided Mortimer's empire between his friends and those he wanted to have as friends. Thereafter he drew up a proclamation, which simultaneously announced his 'package of reforms' (in modern parlance) and blamed the previous government for the travails of past years, to be read by his sheriffs throughout the country. Accordingly: 'He wills that all men shall know that he will henceforth govern his people according to right and reason.' Fine words, but a tall order; 'the ineptitude of Edward II and the discord within the ruling elite had left a lasting impression on political society. The fiscal demands of the government, combined with the famines of the early 1320s, had also left the economy, and especially the lower levels of the population, materially weakened.'[10] Edward, bestowed with untrammelled royal power, now decided that a war of some kind would unite the nation.

Heartened by Edward's probable reappraisal of Anglo-Scottish relations, Beaumont and other opponents of Isabella and Mortimer returned home. He and Wake were convinced that Edward intended to make the Disinherited his primary concern. More than compensating for Percy's abandonment of their cause (now that Mortimer, his patron, had fallen, Percy was in some straits himself, although he had cautiously never alienated Edward), the Disinherited were joined by others with various claims. Strathbogie's claim now included half the lands of John Comyn, whom Bruce had murdered in 1306 (Strathbogie's mother was Comyn's daughter); Henry Ferrers sought estates in Galloway and the Lothians; whilst Gilbert Umfraville was determined to regain his father's earldom of Angus, now in the hands of Sir John Stewart. Many others also demanded that insignificant Scottish farms or fields be returned. Sorting out the intricate patchwork of rightful ownership and counter-claims would have taken years. Instead, Edward simply pressed the claims of Wake and

Beaumont, because only they (and Percy) had officially registered their demands during the Treaty of Northampton. Moreover, Bruce had promised restitution.

For almost a year, David and his councillors prevaricated, yet because the Scots faithfully paid their instalments Edward could not use default as an excuse to break off relations and declare war. Impatient, Beaumont then resolved on unilateral action. Although related to the French royal family, this adventurer, according to the well-informed chronicler John Capgrave, sought glory and riches 'through the exercise of arms and warlike events'.[11] In the autumn of 1331, with the clandestine permission of the king, he again travelled to France where Edward Balliol needed little prodding to return to England and raise his standard. King John's son had never forsaken his inheritance, which had been devolved upon his father in a fair and just manner by Edward I. Indeed, he had never married, haughtily judging no French bride worthy of a future king of the Scots.

Balliol's arrival in England provoked consternation across the Border. Hurriedly, a Parliament was summoned at Scone in November 1331 so that David could be anointed and crowned. At the ceremony, according to the Lanercost chronicler, David claimed Scotland 'by no hereditary succession, but in like manner as his father, by conquest alone', a blatant attempt to blunt Balliol's more legitimist pretensions to the throne.[12]

Beaumont next requested Edward's support. After the initial exchanges, Beaumont asked: 'Now, Sir, I praie yow that ye wolde grant him [Balliol] leue [leave] to take unto him soudeoures of Englisshe-men [English soldiers], that thai might safly lede him through your land unto Scotland.' Then, he promised the king that not only he, but all those Disinherited who joined him, would forfeit their English possessions if Balliol failed.[13] At this 'double-or-nothing' offer, Edward relented and allowed Balliol's Disinherited to proceed towards Scotland on the strict condition that he was not giving a royal sanction to a war against his own brother-in-law, who ruled an independent state to boot.[14] Should the private expedition succeed, however, Balliol would be indebted to him and Scotland would revert – unofficially – to its status as an English satellite.

Beaumont and his growing band of compatriots – which included Strathbogie, Umfraville, Wake, Richard Talbot (Strathbogie's uncle), Henry Ferrers and two of his brothers, a number of the Comyn family, and Alexander and John Mowbray – urgently began to raise capital on their lands to pay for their forthcoming adventure. Sometimes the deals they made amounted to little more than gambling; Strathbogie, for instance, rented out his Norfolk manors for five years at one penny annually in return for a lump cash payment immediately. Evidently, the Disinherited felt that any losses on their English lands would be more than recouped when they succeeded to their Scottish estates.

Beaumont had the men and the money, but now he needed the ships too, for he had ambitiously conceived an amphibious campaign launched from the North. Unbeknown to the Disinherited, however, Edward had been having second thoughts about the wisdom of the venture, and he made one last attempt to resolve their claims. He warned the earl of Moray that Beaumont was intent on making mischief. The guardian of Scotland foolishly replied to Edward that if the Disinherited invaded Scotland he would 'let the ball roll'.[15] Despite his bluster, Moray quietly mustered his emergency forces around the Firth of Forth.

He would never see the landing. Moray died at Musselburgh on 20 July (according to unsubstantiated rumours, Beaumont poisoned him), and eleven days later the English set sail in eighty-eight ships from ports on the Humber, far from prying Scottish spies in the Marches. Knowing that Moray was ill, the Disinherited had been biding their time, hoping to catch the Scots in a state of confusion.[16]

There were two notable absences from the expedition: Henry Percy and Thomas Wake, who, despite making provision to sail, had become entangled in an ongoing feud with a petulant Lincolnshire abbot. We shall return to the quest of the Disinherited after turning to Percy's whereabouts and activities.

Henry Percy and the Changing Border

Percy, meanwhile, had kept a very low profile since the fall of Mortimer. His reticence might partially be explained by his mother's death in July 1328, a few months before Lancaster's abortive rebellion. Since her husband's death, she had lived at Seamer, and was buried in Beverley Minster, in the sumptuous 'Percy Shrine', a peerless gem of a tomb whose flowing artistry may have taken her devoted son over a decade to complete and pay for.[17] Percy's closeness to his mother is quite remarkable. Granted, his father died when he was a teenager, but his absence in Percy's memorials strikes a dissonant chord. In 1329, Percy gave a parcel of land at Seamer (revealingly, part of Emma de Port's eleventh-century dower) to two chaplains 'to celebrate divine service daily in the chapel of St Mary within the said manor for the souls of Eleanor, his mother, and his ancestors'. Pride was taken in his forebears, evidently, but not in his father.[18] Reappointed to the keepership and custodianship of

Scarborough Castle on 13 August 1328, Percy also busied himself with restoring it.[19] The houses within the castle, and its turrets, bridge and walls, all needed repair. Work was constantly hampered by lack of funds, and it would not be until Christmas 1336 that Scarborough was ready to withstand a prolonged siege.[20]

Percy's time was also occupied by ingratiating himself with the king and mending fences with the Disinherited leadership, who were still mildly aggrieved at his display of self-interestedness during the Treaty of Northampton negotiations.

Percy appears to have been a natural and charming diplomat. According to the informative chronicler of Alnwick Abbey, he 'demeaned himself so faithfully and prudently in all things and to all, that blame or charge could be laid to him by none, but was beloved by all'.[21] The Lanercost chronicler agreed, and even added a couple of interesting snippets: a 'fine fighter', Percy was 'small of stature but sagacious', implying that he stood below five feet six inches.[22] An exceedingly rare letter written by Percy in later life illuminates his concern with avoiding dissension to maintain general harmony. Writing to the chancellor, Percy pointed out that the former 'sent a commission to the Archbishop of York, Sir Ralph de Nevyll and the writer for keeping the Marches of Northumberland, which the writer does not dare show, because that earl of Angus [Gilbert Umfraville, a Disinherited Northern colleague] was not named in it. He [Percy] believes that, if the earl had seen it, he would not have wished to involve himself to the extent he now has. [Lord Percy] asks that if another commission is sent the earl should be named in it.'[23] Lest we forget, however, much of his friendly emollience instantly dissolved when, as we have seen, it came to defending and advancing his personal and property interests.

Percy was not the dominating leader of men that his father was, at least not until the closing years of his life, as described below; for the most part, he resembled a civil servant, serving whomever was in charge. Careful never to become too closely identified with any one faction, he kept his fingers in as many pies as possible. Revealingly, while relations might on occasion have been strained with particular individuals or groups, they never snapped.

To those close to him, Percy could be remarkably loyal. For instance, he and Lord Neville, like his father and Clifford, stuck together through thick and thin for decades. For his part, Neville was an 'honest and valiant man, bold, wary and greatly to be feared'.[24] No doubt the harrowing nature of Northern defence could raise friendship to the higher level of comradeship. For men who served him, Percy maintained a paternal instinct. He writes to the chancellor of England, no less, on behalf of his valet (a certain 'Aleyn, son of Sir Thomas de Heton') who was in danger of losing his land.[25] Percy's soldiers and knights were generally paid on time and in full out of his own pocket. In return, he continually badgered the Exchequer to reimburse him for wages that had been paid months, and sometimes years, previously. In October 1339 at Newcastle, for instance, Percy and Neville insisted that every hobelar and man-at-arms who had ridden in their company during the recent relief of Perth should be paid immediately.[26] Other barons might not have dipped into their pockets until the Exchequer had shown its cash up front.

Apart from his brief, but crucial, appearance during Lancaster's rebellion, Percy stayed quietly at home – unmarried and alone apart from an obscure younger brother. It was not until the summer of 1329 that he re-emerged. Edward owed homage to the French king Philip VI for Gascony and he required a suitable escort for the journey. One of those austere few invited to join him was Percy – his first trip abroad.[27] The royal retinue included thirteen magnates and prelates and more than forty gorgeously apparelled knights. One of these magnates was Lancaster's remarkable 29-year-old son and heir apparent, Henry of Grosmont, whose military activities, it is said, 'filled his whole life from youth to within a few months of his death'.[28] At Amiens, where they tarried for fifteen days, the English party was received by Philip, the kings of Navarre, Bohemia and Mallorca, dukes, earls and great barons, all 'ready to feast and make cheer'. At one – probably intoxicated – moment, Edward roared that 'there was no realm [that] could be compared to the realm of France'.[29] The atmosphere was later soured when Edward, in a hurry, departed France 'without eny takying leue of the Kyng of Fraunce; wherfore he wonder worth [very wrathful]'.[30]

Having ingratiated himself with the king by keeping up with his companions' drinking prowess, Percy was rapidly promoted in the year or so preceding Mortimer's execution. He was appointed keeper of Bamburgh Castle in April 1330 and, in July, overseer of array throughout the North.[31] Financially, as well, the bounties added up: apart from a debt of £98, which the king rescheduled to half-yearly instalments of £5, 'all other debts, of whatsoever nature, due by him or his ancestors' were pardoned.[32] Next month, he was entrusted with the 'carriage of certain moneys of the king from Scotland to Newerk', which entailed travelling through outlaw-infested badlands.[33] In January 1331, his diplomatic talents having been noted, he was sent to France as an envoy.[34] On his return, he was given the plum post of justiciar of the East March. Part of his duties included a tedious perambulation of the entire Northumberland March to confirm the line of the Border. Whenever a dispute arose over where *exactly* it was, he ordered his clerks to trawl the

Rolls of Henry III and Edward I for affirmation.[35] Such were the dull chores of a Northern administrator in time of peace.

In the autumn of 1331 appear the first glimmerings of Edward's ambitions in Scotland. At the time, Beaumont's invitation to Balliol to return to England (see above) so consternated the Scots that in November they had hurriedly crowned King David. Furthermore, the Scottish magnates would have noted that on 7 October 1331, Percy was, 'for the good service that the said Sir Henry has done to him, and *will do in time to come* [italics added]', granted by Edward the forbidding fortress of Warkworth and the manors of Rothbury, Newburn and Corbridge. These Northumbrian lands were held by the aged Sir John Clavering, who had no sons, and therefore would escheat to the king at his subject's imminent death. What Clavering thought of the arrangement is uncertain, but he caused no dissension (he 'attorned himself to Henry [Percy] and did fealty by the king's order') before he died in early 1332, when Percy took control.[36]

The strategic location of Clavering's estates immensely benefited Percy. Coastal Warkworth, only eight miles south of Alnwick, protected the sea-road to Newcastle and gave Percy a stronger hold on eastern Northumberland. Rothbury, eleven miles south-west, allowed Percy to meld otherwise separate lands into a growing but unified empire and also to watch over Coquetdale. Newburn was just across the river from Berwick, and Corbridge was at the crossroads of Dere Street (running north to Jedburgh – of some importance later) and the main road to Carlisle, running parallel to Hadrian's Wall.

So much regional power suddenly devolving upon a descendant of an infamously martial family alarmed the Scots. More worryingly still, soon after he was granted the Clavering lands in 1332, Percy received full power as warden of the March in August and was instructed to 'keep the peace between the people of the county of Northumberland [also Yorkshire, Lancaster, Cumberland and Westmorland] and the Scots until Michaelmas'.[37] This appointment, made at a time exactly coinciding with Beaumont's invasion of Scotland, suggests that Edward wanted someone experienced on the English side of the Border to cope with any possible 'blowback'. Thus, Percy's secret instructions – as opposed to the official ones above – were rather more robust. Two of his Northumbrian knights on secret service across the Border had informed him and Edward that the Scots were in the midst of 'great preparations' for war, as 'Sir Henry de Beaumont and others with him have set out by sea for Scotland'. It was Percy's responsibility, 'if the Scots enter England in force, to raise the five Northern counties to stop them'.[38]

Henceforth, the Percys were to retain something approaching a hereditary stranglehold on the post of warden of the March until 1559. Forty-four years later, with the Union of the Crowns under King James, the office disappeared. Nonetheless, according to R.R. Reid, 'no office under the Crown has received so much attention from writers of fiction and so little from writers of history as that of Warden of the Marches of England against Scotland.'

In the days of Alexander III and Henry III, the administration of order and (rough) justice on the Border, as well as its defence, was in the hands of local sheriffs. But the outbreak of the Anglo-Scottish wars in 1296 warranted the creation of a military warden. In October 1297, Robert Clifford and two others were appointed *capitaneos custodie partium Marchie Scotie in comitatibus Cumberland et Westmerland*, and three knights were similarly made captains of the March of Scotland in Northumberland. Percy's father, for instance, was termed a king's lieutenant or captain of the Northumberland March. It was only in 1309 that the title 'Warden of the Marches' was first used briefly – of Clifford.

At that time the post was simply a renewable commission revived whenever the Scots were making trouble, but since Edward II's death, it was evolving into a permanent office. To meet the warden's need for an organised staff, the generic 'March' was structured into three regional commands: the West March, Middle March and East March. Cumberland and Westmorland comprised the West, but the third Border shire – Northumberland – was divided into two. The East – the smaller – was a slice running west from the coast along the River Aln (skirting Alnwick itself) and eventually north-west into the Cheviots to the Scottish border. Its first line of defence was the River Tweed, guarded by Berwick, Norham and Wark. If Scots plunderers invaded from the direction of Roxburgh in the west and attempted to cross the River Till after emerging from the Cheviots, the slightly less imposing fortresses of Heton, Ford, Etal and Chillingham acted as gatekeepers. Occupying the rest of Northumberland, the Middle March continued south-west along the hills separating Scotland and England until it reached the boundary of Cumberland.

The Middle had a triple purpose. The castles of Alnwick and Warkworth not only controlled the Great North Road between Newcastle and Roxburgh, and thence Edinburgh, but could also function as a central headquarters on the border of the East and Middle Marches to co-ordinate the English defensive effort. Less heroically, they and their subsidiary castles in Houghton, Langley, Elsdon and Harbottle kept an eye on Tynedale, Redesdale and Coquetdale, all – especially the first two – hotbeds of thievery, cattle-rustling and murder. Supporting these fortresses by the fifteenth century was an impressive crescent of towers running south-west in an arc from Berwick to Cumberland. No longer, it was hoped, would the Scots be able to sneak into the depths of the North without an alarm being sounded.

The powers of the warden expanded over the course of the fourteenth century. Thus, early wardens were merely permitted to array able men between the ages of sixteen and sixty and lead them to the Border. When the enthusiasm of some of these able men was found wanting, the warden was given power to fine, distrain or imprison deserters and evaders of military service. By 1315, the warden had custody of all royal castles in the Marches, except Berwick and Carlisle. Over the next thirty years, the warden became responsible for ensuring that Anglo-Scottish truces were adhered to and for punishing those who broke them *secundum legem et consuetudinem* ('according to the laws and customs of the Marches'). By 1399, the warden had been given authority to grant safe-conducts, receive Scots into the king's peace, make truces of up to two months with the Scots, appoint his own deputies, meet with his Scottish counterparts for the redress of wrongs, and compel military commanders and civil officials in Northumberland, Cumberland and Westmorland to follow his commands.

On the other hand, the warden had no jurisdiction in general civil affairs or 'police' work. He could only intervene if there were a breach – whether perpetrated by Englishmen in Scotland or Scotsmen in England – of military discipline, or a truce, or the ancient Northern customs slowly metamorphosing into the 'Laws of the Marches'. Importantly, these were not offences in the Common Law, so lending the warden a great deal of autonomy and discretion as to how he ran his March.

Given the responsibilities (or opportunities for illicit enrichment) associated with the office, one might have expected the wardenship to be among the most desirable of royal posts. Kings soon learnt, however, that competition for the office was severely limited by the strange political contours of the North. There was a crucial difference between a March and the shire or shires it encompassed. Within these Border counties were huge tracts of land called palatinates, or liberties, in which the king's writ did not run; no sheriff or warden could enter one without its lord's permission. Even if the Scots massed on the Border, if the lord chose not to call out his men they stayed at home, and the warden could do nothing about it. Clearly, appointing a local magnate as warden who also happened to be the lord of a number of liberties prevented such problems arising at inconvenient moments. For this reason, having a Percy (lord of Alnwick and much else in Northumberland besides), a Neville (lord of Raby), a Clifford (lord of Westmorland), a Lucy (lord of Cockermouth), a Dacre (lord of Gilsland) or the Umfravilles (lords of Redesdale) in charge was the king's only option. As these lords combined seignorial and royal power, it was often remarked that the North knew no king but a Percy. That family's quasi-monopoly was affirmed in 1386, when a Percy married an Umfraville heiress, the sister of the current Lord Lucy (see Chapter 13). By such consolidation, 'the Percies became the natural Wardens of the whole March'. Outsiders, however impressive, lacked the personal prestige and the networks of patronage and loyalties assembled over generations by these Northern princes.

Gradually, for efficient defence, most Crown offices in the area also became concentrated in the hands of a few families. The warden, as a matter of course, eventually collected the captaincies of Berwick and Carlisle, the keeperships of Tynedale, Redesdale, Norham, Bamburgh and Dunstanburgh, the stewardships of the bishop of Carlisle, of the abbot of Holme Cultram, and of the priors of Carlisle and Wetheral, and even the shrievalty of Northumberland. Although the appointment of constables, bailiffs and stewards was technically in the king's hand, the warden nominated those best suited to the tasks. Only very rarely was a recommended retainer of the warden not appointed. Borderers depend-ed upon the acumen of their noble protectors to defend them from harm; Southern placemen were regarded as an imposition and frequently provoked a bloody-minded unhelpfulness, among not only the rank and file but their lords as well.

Moreover, as the feudal system of calling out the shire-levies decayed, the power of the Northern magnates increased out of all proportion. Only they, who knew the villages and valleys of the March intimately, could unearth the hundreds, sometimes thousands, of hobelars and archers to man the fortresses and stock the armies. By necessity, wardens had to be men of local and regional importance to attract volunteers from the gentry to serve, as bannerets, knights and esquires in their ret-inues of men-at-arms. In 1336, for example, of fifty-five men-at-arms in Percy's retinue, no fewer than forty hailed from Percy's circle of friends, neighbours and tenants in the Yorkshire gentry.

Horses and wagons had to be requisitioned or bought, as did food, forage and firewood. Wardens were fortunate in that the hardy horses used in the North were cheaper than the fine beasts used down in the more affluent South. Nationally, only 12 per cent of warhorses cost under £5, but in Percy's retinue fully 20 per cent were so priced, the mean value being about £8, and only seven out of 304 horses were worth more than £15 (compared to a quarter in the worldly earl of Salisbury's stables). The chances are that Percy's own warhorse was valued somewhere between £20 and £25. But he in turn could be shamed by the fact that Salisbury had knights in his Southern retinue who could afford to ride magnificent steeds worth £50 each.

The question of money only amplified the warden's influence, for it was his responsibility to pay for the Border's defence. Yet the government could not expect Northern lords to do this out of charity. Hence, the warden's income from his accumulated offices helped offset his personal expenses. There was always, however, a shortfall; by the end of the fourteenth century, it cost £1000 annually in *peacetime* – in wartime, this figure rose to more than £1700 – to maintain the warden, his lieutenants and 500 men. The problem was exacerbated by Parliament – in which the North was barely represented – frequently treating the Border not as a national strategic issue but a local one, and agreeing only to remit to the March shires their share of direct taxation. It was left to the Crown to produce the rest of the money to subsidise the warden. Down South or in Wales, this requirement did not present a problem: those shires were wealthy enough to raise funds on their own account; but in the North, inherently poor and made even poorer by periodic Scottish raids, the Crown would have been hard pressed to raise enough through local taxation.

To square the circle and cut outlay, the Exchequer mandarins persuaded the king to grant swathes of Crown lands in the North to the warden on condition of military service – an anachronistic return to feudal means – in addition to paying him the stipend owing to his various offices. Thus, in exchange for a wage of £330 and the use of his private army, the estates of Warkworth, Corbridge and Rothbury belonging to the extinct Clavering family, which should have reverted to the Crown, had been transferred to Henry Percy. Eventually, Percy acquired all the Crown lands in Northumberland (save the ancient demesne around Bamburgh and Newcastle).

The irony was that whilst the warden would now serve because his financial needs had been met, it was the Exchequer that continued to pay for Border defence. Just as banks cannot afford to alienate their largest debtors for fear of wilful default, for centuries to come the king of England would be obliged to bankroll rebellious 'Warden-Princes' of the North. If the king failed to meet his financial obligations, then his overmighty subjects – made mightier still by the Crown land grants – threatened to withdraw from their posts, or even combine with the Scots, thereby placing the rest of the country in danger. King and warden were mutually dependent, but hatefully so, and not until the late fifteenth century, when Henry VII permanently assigned the income from the forfeited York and Neville lands to the upkeep of the Border, was this vicious circle broken.

In time, these contradictions would become apparent; for the moment, 'this monopoly of control over the Border-service... made the Wardens masters of the only forces in the pay of the Crown that were always under arms, and at the same time drew all the ablest men in the March shires into their personal service as the only road to advancement'. 'To be effective,' writes George MacDonald Fraser, *Flashman*'s creator, the warden 'had to be a mixture of soldier, judge, lawyer, fighting-man, diplomat, politician, rough-rider, detective, administrator, and intelligence agent'.[39]

The chronicler of Alnwick Abbey was certainly convinced of his lord's abilities: Percy 'laboured much by many treaties and truces to keep the country and Marches whole and uninjured'.[40] William Peeris remarked of Percy's wardenship that 'many valiant acts hee did of great noblenesse/ the Castell of Alnewicke hee repaired and made more substantiall'.[41] Peeris was referring to Percy's addition of two enormous octagonal towers flanking the Norman entrance to the keep. Within each tower were guardrooms, below one of which is a bottle-shaped cell measuring nine feet by eight feet. Prisoners taken by Percy in the course of his duties were thrown down by means of a trapdoor. This was modernisation – of a sort.[42]

The Disinherited Return

Following the death of Moray, the Scots magnates were in a quandary over his successor. At the council that met to decide the next guardian, there was 'gret and lang dyssentyown'. Robert Steward was still too young, and the sole candidate worthy of note was Donald, earl of Mar, the only survivor of the great raids of the 1320s. Auspiciously, he was King Robert's nephew; less auspiciously, Mar was not altogether trusted. Formerly a fervent supporter of the Balliols and Edward II,[43] he had met Edward Balliol on a number of occasions and was, moreover, an old acquaintance of several Disinherited. All these factors weighed against Mar, unsurprisingly, yet he persuaded the magnates to take an enormous gamble in electing him guardian on 2 August and moved towards turning over a new leaf by standing close by King David II.

Mar fulfilled his duties patriotically, but unsuccessfully. The Disinherited had disembarked in Scotland and, on 11 August, Mar prepared to fight them at Dupplin Moor, about seven miles south-east of Perth. Despite Mar's large preponderance of Scots, the invaders had several factors in their favour. First, the Scots army relied heavily on unpaid feudal troops, as opposed to Balliol's seasoned professionals and experienced commanders. Second, the English men-at-arms were willing to dismount and fight on foot alongside the massed rows of archers on either flank, whom they defended. Dissension also split the Scots leaders (normally an English failing); before the battle, Lord Robert Bruce, the bastard of King Robert, accused Mar of being in the pay of the English. Mar shouted that he would be the first to come to blows with the enemy and spurred his horse forward. Unfortunately, so did Bruce, and his battalion and followers (including Alexander Fraser and the earls of Moray and Menteith) reached the Balliol lines first. The barrage of the English archers, close enough to aim their bolts directly at their enemies' faces, pushed the Scots flanks inwards towards the centre battalion, whereupon they were all thrown off balance by the line of English pikemen. Mar, accompanied by the great mass of cavalry, now collided with the trapped and disarrayed centre. The heavy horses crushed or suffocated any man unlucky enough to lose his footing. The earl of Fife (the first to sign the Declaration of Arbroath),[44] cooler-headed than his peers, ushered some survivors into a retreat, but those left behind 'composed a little hill a spear's length in height'.

Now, Balliol and Beaumont's remounted cavalry pursued Fife's shaken corps, taking the earl prisoner and killing most of his followers. The English foot contented themselves by jabbing their swords and spears into the twitching pile of bodies before them. Dupplin Moor, although little known, was the Bannockburn of the Scots. For the loss of two English knights, and thirty-three esquires and men-at-arms (no archers were killed), the Scots lost the earls of Mar, Moray and Menteith, Lord Robert Bruce, Nigel Bruce and Alexander Fraser, as well as many other barons and knights. Anywhere between 2000 and 13,000 footmen died. One chronicler, stunned at the reversal, remarked by way of explanation: 'Alle men seide it was Goddis hande, and not mannes hand, for the Scottis were so many, and English so fewe.' Only divine intervention, evidently manifesting itself through Edward Balliol, could explain the massacre and the son of King John's triumphant conquest of Scotland.[45]

Still somewhat shocked by their own victory, Balliol's army invested Perth. There, they were half-heartedly besieged by Sir Archibald Douglas – soon to be appointed Regent of Scotland. This Douglas was the youngest brother of Percy's bugbear, Sir James Douglas, who had recently died in quite bizarre circumstances in Spain.

Diverted from his intended journey to Jerusalem bearing Robert the Bruce's heart, Douglas and his companions volunteered to fight for Castile against the Muslims. Before the battle had officially begun, the Scots impetuously charged forward, much to the bemusement of the ordered Castilians, and were slaughtered. Such was the romantic fate of Sir James Douglas, never wounded in Border fighting but killed in his first skirmish against the Moors when he employed the tactics he learnt during the Anglo-Scottish wars. Just as Bruce, his late master, would have done, he hoped to strike hard and escape before a pitched battle was fought.[46]

Scottish morale experienced a complete collapse when John Crabb, the infamous Flemish pirate (whom we first met in Chapter 8), attacked the Disinheriteds' ships with his squadron and was routed.[47] The panicked Scots now chose as guardian Sir Andrew Moray 'le Riche', the hyperpatriotic uncle of David II – he was married to Bruce's sister, Christina. But the English soon managed to capture Moray the guardian and to take John Crabb prisoner. On 24 September 1332, Balliol was crowned king of the Scots at Scone by the earl of Fife, who had been released after promising to fulfil his hereditary office.

Two months later, on 24 November, Balliol erased three decades of Scottish struggle by setting out his interpretation of the relationship between Scotland and England. He aimed to expunge Bruce from history, so establishing the unbroken rule of the Balliols since the Great Cause. 'Scotland was held of the king of England, its sovereign lord, by homage and fealty,' although Balliol carefully stated that he had already performed his required homage. As sovereign lord, the king of England was to maintain Balliol and his heirs. In return, the Scots would provide an army to aid, if need be, in fighting his battles in England and, crucially, abroad. The de facto king, Balliol, proposed to solve the tricky problem of the deposed King David and his wife Joan, Edward's sister, by regarding their marriage as non-binding and wedding her himself (this was the year before she reached the age of consent).

Next came repayment of debts incurred. Lands worth £2000 per year, all located on the Scottish Border and comprising most of the southern counties, were to be granted to Edward III, including the castle, town and county of Berwick. Tempting though these offers sounded, Edward was toying with the idea of dumping Balliol and, following his grandfather, annexing Scotland to the English Crown. The Disinheriteds' operation had been rather more successful than he had expected. For this reason, he travelled to York but was furious when restrained by an unenthusiastic Parliament from mounting an invasion. One can gauge the tenor of Edward's ugly mood at being denied his war from a letter issued at the time: directed to the mayor and bailiffs of York, 'the king, detesting the abominable smell abounding in the said city more than in any other of the realm from dung and manure and other filth and dirt wherewith the streets and lanes are filled and obstructed, and wishing to provide for the protection of the health ... orders them to cause all the streets and lanes of the city to be cleansed from such filth before St Andrew next, and to be kept clean.'[48]

Balliol may not have realised that, with his usefulness over, the hitherto silent Edward was quite prepared to throw him to the wolves. He also consistently showed himself to be a terrible judge of character. In December 1332, Balliol gladly made peace with Archibald Douglas the Tyneman – the new guardian, the new earls of March and Moray, and Alexander Bruce (b. 1315), King Robert's fiery nephew. He also allowed his English supporters to go home for Christmas. He himself decided to spend Christmas in Annan. On 17 December, the Scots leaders and their followers crept into the castle and slaughtered the sleeping defenders, including Sir John Mowbray, Alexander Mowbray's brother and one of the Disinherited. Balliol, wearing little but his nightclothes, 'brake out through a walle by an Hole in his chambre'.⁴⁹ Riding bareback on an unbridled horse, the bedraggled Scottish king eventually reached Carlisle and safety, the prestige of Dupplin utterly dissipated.⁵⁰

For the moment, seeing as the Bruce faction was stronger than expected, Edward III had to shelve his plan of unseating Balliol and instead combine with him to overthrow the guardian and his allies. Now, Edward, like the apostle, 'put away childish things'.⁵¹

Following Balliol's humiliating arrival in Carlisle, Edward bypassed Parliament and planned an English invasion. The wardens of the March were confirmed, and Henry Percy was one of those appointed to a small, private, five-man council at the end of January 1333. Writs to raise troops were issued, and corn, victuals and silver stockpiled. The Exchequer, the Court of Common Pleas and part of Chancery were removed to York, where they would stay for the next five years. However, as England and Scotland were not at war, Edward required a reason for attacking his neighbour. Here it was the restoration of a crowned king, and Balliol exactly fitted the bill. The Disinherited received Edward's permission for the expedition, as well as substantial financing. Accompanying Balliol, Strathbogie and Beaumont were powerful magnates such as Lancaster, Arundel and Lord Neville: a clear indication that the Disinherited's forces were intended this time as the spearhead of a major campaign rather than a romantic enterprise. Crossing into Roxburghshire, Balliol headed directly for the town and castle of Berwick (the castle lay just outside the town), which was defended by the Scottish earl of March, who had repaired and strengthened the walls. At the end of April, during a brief stay at Alnwick with Percy, Edward III issued the writs for the main body of the army and he decamped to Tweedmouth on 9 May to await it.

Balliol's siege had dragged on for two months by the time Edward arrived on the scene. Percy was immediately appointed as chief liaison between the two forces. On the day he and Edward arrived at Tweedmouth, on English land opposite Berwick, Percy crossed the river and, with Edward's permission, made an agreement with Balliol and the Disinherited. Saving his ultimate allegiance to his sovereign – who now had 'official representation' in the Disinherited's camp, Percy would remain for life in Balliol's service *within* Scotland. In return for a privately funded contingent of either one hundred men-at-arms or thirty knights, he would receive lands in Scotland south of the Forth, annually worth the enormous sum of £1333. As a knight was paid 2 shillings a day, and a man-at-arms 1 shilling, Percy could predict considerable profit.[52] Politically and economically, this was quite a coup for Percy: he was on the right side of both Edward and Balliol; if Balliol's bid for restoration failed – which was highly unlikely now, with Edward's support, Percy had proved to the Disinherited that he too was truly 'one of them'. The shameful peace negotiated at Northampton could be quietly forgotten.

Touring the encampment, Percy would have encountered the indomitable pirate John Crabb, taken prisoner in November 1332 and released on condition that he work for the English. It is said that he now hated the Scots, because they had refused to ransom him and they had killed his son.[53] Crabb was a valuable acquisition: an experienced military engineer, he had helped direct the Scottish defence during Edward II's siege in 1319 and knew every detail of the fortifications. For the next month, Edward's catapults levelled parts of the town, which was razed in a firestorm started accidentally by the Scots. Entertainment for the troops was provided by Turnbull, a gigantic Scottish ruffian, who challenged any Englishman to fight him, Goliath-style. At length, Sir Robert Benhale, an inconspicuous Norfolk knight, marched up to Turnbull, sliced his black mastiff dog in half, then lopped off his left hand and head. In years to come, Benhale would have a distinguished career, becoming Lord Benhale in 1360.[54]

At the end of June, the defenders negotiated a strange truce to last until 11 July 1333; they surrendered twelve hostages and agreed that, if not relieved by that date, the castle and town of Berwick would be Edward's. Edward accepted this peculiar offer because he calculated it would bring Archibald Douglas, the guardian, to a pitched battle on terrain chosen by Edward.

English cunning paid off. On 11 July, Douglas's army crossed the Tweed upriver, intending to draw Edward to the south by besieging Queen Philippa at Bamburgh Castle. The ruse failed. Edward knew that Bamburgh could hold out for weeks (Percy was familiar with the castle's defences and the calibre of the garrison), and he had time on his side. In the meantime, the truce at Berwick had expired and he stayed put.

Because a Scottish army was in the vicinity, the defenders reneged on the agreement. They had ignored, however, Edward's literal and wrathful mind; as the truce had been broken, the hostages were forfeit. The most prominent hostage – Thomas Seton, son of the castle's warden – was hanged in full sight of his parents (who had already lost two sons in the wars) as they stood on the battlements. Henceforth, Edward announced, he would hang two hostages a day until the town surrendered, 'and so he wolde teche ham to breke her couenauntz'.[55] Within days, the defenders agreed that if Berwick were not relieved by 20 July, it would be surrendered. Such were the ways of medieval warfare that knights from Berwick were given safe-conducts to seek out Douglas to tell him of the new arrangement.

The news forced Douglas to cross the Tweed to pin down the English army so that a picked force of 200 men-at-arms could force its way to the gates of Berwick. The new truce technically termed this as 'relief' and the English would be bound to lift the siege. But Douglas was breaking Robert Bruce's cardinal rule: always avoid direct engagements and concentrate on surprise raids to erode morale.

Edward chose to meet Douglas at Halidon, a 500-foot hill two miles north-west of Berwick, which overlooked the overland approaches to the town. On the morning of 19 July Douglas settled down opposite Edward. Each army had three divisions, the Scots relying on their schiltrom-trained pikemen and the English on their archers, who flanked each of Edward's cavalry divisions. Percy's indenture with Balliol required that he serve with the king of Scotland and the Disinherited, not alongside Edward. Edward accepted the advice of Beaumont and other veterans and adopted a defensive formation, the knights and men-at-arms dismounting as usual to protect the archers. Edward, it is said, rode up and down the line addressing his troops before himself dismounting and standing in the very centre of his division. Douglas, however, had also learnt from Dupplin. The Scottish knights and men-at-arms left their horses behind and walked alongside the pikemen; it was the right idea but the wrong time. Edward's position forced the Scots to cross a bog between the armies and attack up a hill, where, according to a chronicler, one defender 'mycht dyscumfyte thre'. Any general worth his salt throughout history has respected the '3 to 1' maxim, but Douglas had no choice: unless 200 men-at-arms reached Berwick by nightfall, Lothian would return into English hands.

As the Scots waded through the marshes and struggled clumsily up the slope, they were lashed with sheets of arrows. Five hundred veterans of Bruce's wars had already fallen by the time the Scots reached Balliol's division on the left, where the earl of Moray's men engaged Percy, Beaumont and their fellow cavalrymen in bitter hand-to-hand combat. In the centre, Edward was holding against David II's nephew, Robert

Stewart, and Douglas was evenly matched against Sir Edward Bohun (representing his brother, the constable of England) and the Earl Marshal's men on the right. Balliol's flank proved crucial. As the first star of the evening appeared, Moray's brigade broke and retreated in great disorder, and the remaining two Scottish divisions scattered. When the Scots lords reached their base they discovered that their grooms had stolen the horses, leaving them to flee on foot. The English remounted, thundered downhill and splashed through the marsh to give chase, slashing at the magnates with their swords and 'iron-shod maces'. Any pikemen still standing were trampled underfoot. The victors refused to take prisoners, so forgoing much potential ransom. As the sun settled below the hills, the knights and men-at-arms returned to Halidon Hill. Edward, who knew how to keep the troops happy, had allowed the English archers to take whatever booty they could from the thousands of dead and wounded (any showing signs of life while their rings were being sawn off were soon turned into corpses) that littered the battlefield. An image from an anonymous poet captures the Scottish nightmare:

> And there her [Scotland's] Baners weren ffounde
> All displayedde on the Grounde,
> And layne starkly on Blode.[56]

For Edward and his barons, Halidon had important implications: yet again, Scotland was leaderless and prey to English domination. Among the dead were Archibald Douglas, the brother of the 'Good Sir James' Douglas, and four earls, as well as Alexander Bruce of Carrick. For the moment, the Douglases were finished as a politico-military force; the new lord of Douglas was Hugh 'the Dull', the surviving half-brother of the Good Sir James and Archibald, 'a cleric without ability or energy', according to Michael Brown. Or so it seemed. Like many of his compatriots, Sir James had left a bastard, named Archibald, a humourless soul nicknamed 'the Grim' for 'both his character and methods'. Over the course of his seventy-year career, he 'was to rise to rule both the house of Douglas and much of southern Scotland' – and emerge as the Percys' nemesis.

Edward's army emerged from the battle with nary a scratch – a worthy revenge for Bannockburn. One knight at most, an esquire and perhaps twelve archers died.[57] Ransom was not a baronial priority because of bonuses promised to them by Edward *and* Balliol in addition to the bestowal of lands formerly belonging to the fallen. The forfeitures of estates held by those who had evaded capture or death, such as the earl of Moray (who had fled to France), began at once. Edward did not disappoint his adoring followers, from highest to lowest. For example, the substantial sums owed by the earl of Surrey and his ancestors to the Crown were cancelled; Sir William Montagu received the rich but possibly dangerous manor of Wark; lower down the scale, Robert Shilvington, a travelling horse-dealer, was, until the day he died, exempt from paying any tolls in the kingdom. For his part, Percy was excused a debt of £263 – a hefty sum.

Percy's real windfall came through Balliol ten days after the battle, but rapidly escalated into a major cause of contention. According to the terms of their contract, Balliol owed Percy land worth £1333, and as part payment duly granted him Bruce's castle at Lochmaben and the whole of Annandale, together worth £666 yearly.[58] Lochmaben, however, was stoutly held by a Scottish garrison loyal to the absent earl of Moray; if Percy wanted it he would have to besiege it at his own expense.

In the meantime, Percy was sidetracked by Edward's ongoing administrative reconstruction. At the end of July Percy was created warden, or *gardeigne*, of the town of Berwick, for which he would receive 40 marks (about £26) per annum – a trifle, but the honour of being in charge of such an important symbol of English lordship over Scotland more than compensated for that.[59] And as the new warden of the castle, his annual stipend amounted to a tidy £100.

While busily ensuring that Edward's administrative capital on the Border could never again fall to the Scots (John Crabb, thankfully, remained faithful to Edward for the rest of his life), Percy was shocked by an insulting interference in his personal business. Lochmaben had surrendered to Edward Bohun and David of Strathbogie, who persuaded the defenders to open the gates on condition that their lives were spared and their lands exempt from forfeiture.

The name 'Bohun' would have rung alarm bells in the heads of any noble familiar with the March. In the time of Edward I, in April 1306, Humphrey de Bohun, earl of Hereford, had been granted the lordship of Annandale, which included Lochmaben. This Hereford later served with Lancaster and died hideously at the battle of Boroughbridge. Like Henry Percy's earldom of Carrick, however, Hereford's lordship was a merely titular title after English power collapsed north of the Border. Sir Edward Bohun was a younger son, and had endeared himself to Edward III – a kinsman, for Bohun's mother was a daughter of Edward I – by helping to overthrow Mortimer and Isabella. After Halidon, Bohun enterprisingly intended to reclaim Annandale, and the Lochmaben incident was a shot across Percy's bows, putting the latter in a quandary. Ever the diplomat, he wished to avoid a 'turf war' with the king's cousin, and Bohun's claim to Annandale was stronger than his own, yet unless he made a stand he would be £666 out of pocket. Indeed, as Percy was very highly ranked in the hierarchy, caving in to the young son of a once-disgraced earl would entail a terrible loss of face.

Although Annandale was worth a respectable amount of money, it was rough, lawless territory permanently divided between Bruce adherents, Balliol loyalists and gangs of robbers. It was also far from Percy's Northumbrian empire. Percy's best alternative, surely, was to keep claiming Annandale for as long as politically possible and to extract as much income as he could before bowing to the inevitable and handing it over to Bohun. If he played his hand well, he would probably be recompensed with less troublesome land nearer Northumberland.

Predictably, Bohun pressed his claim with both Edward and Balliol, who attempted to oust Percy gently from Annandale. Balliol suddenly stipulated that Percy's holding in Annandale could not exceed about £497 annually; any lands worth over and above that figure must revert to him.[60] Percy, with painful good grace, made no bones about the discount and awaited an offer of compensation from Balliol.

The king's next grant doubled as the second instalment of the £1333 of lands owed, and it hinted that Percy should seriously consider relinquishing Annandale. Many Scots had forfeited their estates around Stirling, a strategically crucial area. On 5 September 1333, hoping to flatter Percy that he was the most valued military commander north of the Border, Balliol offered him lands there worth nearly £630 per annum.[61] If Percy graciously stood aside in Annandale, the implication was, other lush lordships would come his way. Still, Percy pocketed the offer and waited for more concessions from Balliol. He did not regard it as 'the second instalment', and he wanted his promised bounty of £1333.

By the autumn of 1333, Bohun and his retainers were conspicuously throwing their weight around Annandale, at which Percy took umbrage. Several drunken brawls between Percy's Northumbrians and Bohun's Welsh Marchers heightened the tension. Edward III, who had returned south, was annoyed at this petty territorial dispute and ordered the two barons to leave off. He commanded that both sides withdraw from Lochmaben and deliver up the castle to Beaumont (now 'restored' to the earldom of Buchan) and Ralph Neville (steward of the royal household) until a compromise could be found at the next Parliament. Nevertheless, Percy's natural hauteur had been pricked and he ignored the order, as did Bohun. On 21 November 1333, Edward, now very angry, ordered both men, at their highest peril and on pain of forfeiture, to give up Lochmaben. The king also made clear to Percy that he was most displeased and warned him against breaking the peace on his own Marches, of which he was warden. This no-nonsense missive rapidly brought

Bohun and Percy to their senses and they accordingly handed Lochmaben to Beaumont and Neville and reined in their troops.[62]

Balliol was secretly advised by Edward to hold a Parliament. There, a solution might be found for Annandale, and Balliol could set his seal as a king. Percy and Bohun were members of the English delegation at Scone, ostensibly to ensure that Balliol kept his promise of donating land worth £2000 to Edward, as he had promised in November 1332.[63] The Disinherited attended the Parliament of 10 February 1334 in force, their paraphernalia of rank glittering; for instance, Strathbogie came dressed as earl of Atholl, Beaumont, as mentioned, as earl of Buchan, and Gilbert Umfraville as earl of Angus, as well as many others. The Scottish lords were there in smaller numbers. Balliol made over Berwickshire to his English patron, although he was reluctant to part with the remainder of the £2000 until he received Edward's unambiguous declaration of support (Balliol might have been tipped off by now about Edward's previous plan to oust him).

Soon afterwards, with Percy and Bohun still quarrelling over Annandale, an English Parliament convened at York on 21 February. However, this time Edward had another grievance that he wished to raise with Percy and other Northern officials. He had received many petitions complaining of the lawlessness rampant in the North and he circulated an annoyed missive, observing that 'notwithstanding the many appointments by the king of Keepers of the Peace felons and transgressors escape punishment because they are maintained by magnates and others, who retain them in their households or in their pay or livery, because gaol deliveries of such felons take place sometimes before they have been indicted, sometimes by surreptitious means, or by dishonest or cowardly jurors.'[64] Edward instilled order by warning those he placed in charge, rather than clamping down harshly on the people below. There were few easy sinecures during Edward's ministry; if a man failed to fulfil his responsibilities, he would be replaced. In 1331, for instance, Percy had testified to the king that three coroners in Northumberland were insufficiently qualified for their positions and their removal was instantly ordered.[65]

Despite this judicial shake-up, still no decision was made on Annandale and royal appointees continued to take care of Lochmaben. More important was Edward's relationship with Balliol. Edward agreed to back Balliol and his heirs as circumstances required, but only if the balance of the £2000 was immediately ceded. Privately, Edward exhorted Beaumont and Strathbogie, as the unofficial guardians of his interests in Scotland, to prevent dispossessed Scottish nobles from influencing Balliol. Furthermore, Edward had received reports that Moray had reappeared from across the Channel to stoke up resistance and to invite the deposed King David to France. It was vital to stop the French resurrecting the Auld Alliance and building up a Bruce pretender across the water.

Apart from these looming dangers, thanks to the efforts of Beaumont (who was now grandiosely calling himself 'earl of Buchan *and Moray*'), Balliol and his quisling government finally ceded the territories owed to Edward on 12 June 1334 in letters patent witnessed by, among others, Beaumont, Strathbogie, Alexander Mowbray and Thomas Wake, who had re-emerged from his interminable feud with the Lincolnshire abbot. The territories comprised Roxburgh, Jedburgh, Selkirk, Ettrick, Peebles, Dumfries, Edinburgh, Haddington and Linlithgow – almost the whole of southern Scotland, an area about 40 per cent the size of Wales.[66]

Edward began moving in his officials and administrators within three days of the grant. Sheriffs, coroners, wardens and tax-collectors as well as a justiciar, a chamberlain and a chancellor were quickly designated and relocated to their new posts. In the rush to bring English administrative efficiency to the provinces, however, Edward failed to provide proper military support; mighty Jedburgh Castle, for instance, was garrisoned with only ten men-at-arms and ten hobelars. Edward, it seems, had been lulled by the apparent strength of Balliol's rule and the weakness of the Scottish nobility after Halidon and the forfeitures.

However, Robert Stewart, whose lands had been bestowed upon David of Strathbogie, resurfaced after having evaded capture. He stirred up nationalist dissension in Clydesdale and the isles in the Clyde estuary, where castles such as Rothesay, Dunoon and Dumbarton were heaving with Stewart adherents. (The former King David had been holed up in Dumbarton since Halidon.) By July 1334, Stewart had joined the earl of Moray and Sir William Douglas of Liddesdale, the late Archibald's kinsman, newly released from an English prison. These two revivified the old Bruce party of Carrick and the Scottish south-west – the very area that had bedevilled the previous Henry Percy and Aymer de Valence in 1306. Alarmingly, the rebel leaders were young (Stewart was eighteen; Moray slightly younger), strongly motivated and highly experienced warriors. Soon afterwards, Moray and Stewart elected themselves joint guardians of Scotland.

Although their rebellion fizzled out next door in traditionally Balliolite Galloway, the guardians established a virtual protection racket throughout Edward's territories to finance their rising. Things became so bad that the chamberlain of Berwick noted that 'all that countryside was in a state of war'. As generally happens with guerrilla resistances 'representing the people', their countrymen's well-being was sacrificed. One pro-

Scottish chronicler felt bound to mention that 'every region which [Moray] traversed in his campaigns he reduced to such desolation and barrenness that more people died of famine and hunger than those who were destroyed by the sword in the fighting'.[67]

Edward at first dismissed the rising as a temporary bother. He appointed Percy and Neville as chief wardens of the Marches and directed them to help Balliol if he needed them. But the ties that had bound the Disinherited together were fraying. Miffed that Balliol had not supported them in a land dispute of some kind, Beaumont and Strathbogie shut themselves up in their private fortresses, while Sir Alexander Mowbray defected to the rebels, happily providing them with details of Balliol's financial and military position.[68]

In late August and September, when Edward realised at last that his hold on Scotland was looking precarious, the Percy–Bohun affair was finally resolved. Percy had been right to hold out. In mid-September, worried about the safety of his territories, Edward persuaded Percy to relinquish Annandale in return for the castle and constabulary of Jedburgh – as well as the forest and other lands – situated on the Scottish March about thirty-five miles west of Alnwick. It was far more convenient than faraway Annandale, currently being torn apart by a very nasty Bruce–Balliol civil war. Moreover, it was one in the eye for Bohun, whose lot it now was to pacify the insurgents. Percy also negotiated an annuity of £333 (in addition to the £266 that Jedburgh was worth) plus custody of relatively civilised Berwick, for which he would receive £66 in peacetime and £200 in time of war. When these sums were added to the £630 worth of land round Stirling granted by Balliol, Percy had emerged with a figure pretty close to the promised £1333.

Edward needed to convert feuding appointees into stakeholders determined to fight for their possessions. Jedburgh was treasured Douglas territory – given to Sir James Douglas by Robert Bruce himself in 1320. Now the wily king gave it to an equally combative dynasty. Hitherto the animosity between Percys and Douglases had been but an impersonal reflection of the wider Anglo-Scottish picture. In the near future, the feud would become intensely personal, with bloody and devastating results.[69]

Family Affairs and Border Relationships

On a happier note, September 1334 would be a kind month for Percy for another reason. His eldest son, Henry, was now aged fourteen, and marriage was on the cards. Although the boy was a little young (only royals traditionally married this early), Percy sought to improve his dynastic connections and had a perfect match in mind. The lady was Mary, second-oldest daughter of Lancaster, who was blessed with five other daughters. The eldest, Blanche, was married to Thomas Wake, whilst Eleanor was betrothed to Henry Beaumont's son John. (Interestingly, she seems to have been involved in an affair with the earl of Arundel at this time.) Another of Lancaster's daughters was the widow of Sir John Mowbray (an original Disinherited and brother of the recent turncoat Alexander Mowbray). Henry of Lancaster's web of ex-Disinherited in-laws was one Percy wanted to join. Together, these men owned most of Scotland, the Midlands and the North. Two other factors whetted Percy's eagerness for the match.

First, Henry, earl of Lancaster and Leicester, former captain general of the king's armies in Scotland and steward of England, was the richest and most powerful man in the kingdom after Edward himself. Second, after he had gone blind in 1330, his son Henry of Grosmont (born in 1300 at Grosmont Castle, Monmouth) had assumed most of his father's duties. This wiry, tight-lipped, high-cheekboned man would become England's foremost general in the first stages of the Hundred Years War, and the Christian world's most renowned knightly exemplar of chivalry – a crusader who would fight for the Faith in Lithuania, Rhodes, Cyprus and the Near East. So immense was his international fame that 'the sons of dukes and lords of France and Germany were wont to serve in his divisions and under his standard'. When Henry travelled to Avignon to see the Pope in 1354, for instance, this medieval superstar was mobbed by awestruck crowds and had to force his way into the city.

Having Henry of Grosmont, Edward III's second cousin, as his brother-in-law could only enhance Percy junior's career and prospects (and those too of his father, no doubt). The marriage took place, with great ceremony, at Lancaster's fortress at Tutbury.[70] It cost a fortune. To pay for it, Percy, determined to impress his grand new in-laws, quietly borrowed more than £2500, a frighteningly large figure, from the bride's father.[71] Fortunately, by drawing on his increased income from Jedburgh and Berwick, he paid off the loan within a year or two.[72]

Percy was not so fortunate with his five other sons, who all died childless. Percy's hopes for an heir and, preferably, a spare, therefore devolved on young Henry. With his four daughters, the indefatigable Percy used all his political skills to forge links with other leading families. Margaret, the oldest, was married to Robert Umfraville, son of Gilbert, the titular earl of Angus, an old Disinherited claimant. On his death, she would marry William Ferrers, son of yet another Disinherited, Henry Ferrers. The alliance between Umfraville and Margaret was not coincidental. As discussed previously, in order to raise money to fund their first expedition in 1332, many of the Disinherited had resorted to unconventional means. Gilbert of Angus had mortgaged many of his Northumberland manors, and it seems that Percy had advanced him money on a number of occasions. Umfraville never forgot this kindness and in 1375, aged sixty and now with all his children dead, he disinherited his half-brothers and entailed his Northumbrian barony of Prudhoe, situated on the Tyne a few miles west of Newcastle, upon his Percy grandson. (This grandson, we shall see, later took Gilbert's widow as his second wife.) So, just as Percy's father and Clifford had married off their children to keep the Northern network tight and clubby, the current Percy and Umfraville did the same, all participants expecting to profit through this wondrous coupling. Maud, Margaret's sister, married John Neville, the son and heir apparent of Percy's trusted comrade on the March, Ralph Neville.[73]

A quick word on the Nevilles. Originally a minor Conquest family with modest Lincolnshire holdings, by the end of the twelfth century they had shifted northwards to Yorkshire. The last direct male descendant died in 1227, some years after his sister and therefore heir, Isabel, had married Robert, lord of Raby and Brancepeth in County Durham. Thereafter, the Nevilles (their son assumed the surname) were almost exclusively concentrated in Yorkshire and south Durham, their *caput* being Raby Castle. In 1399, the family would receive the Honour of Richmond, making its scion 'incomparably the richest and most influential lord in the north-western area of Yorkshire'. The chances are that had the Percys stayed in Yorkshire, they eventually would have been swallowed up into a greater Neville ascendancy. Isabel's descendant, Randolf or Ranulph Neville, was bestowed a barony by writ in 1295, fought in the Scottish wars and generally acted as a reliable public servant (commissioner of array, keeper of the peace, etc., etc.) in the North. He died, aged sixty-nine, in 1331. As his childless heir, Robert (the 'Peacock of the North'), had been slain at Berwick in 1319, Randolf's successor was his oldest surviving son, Ralph, aged over forty in 1331.[74] Owing to the similarity of their Christian names and their simultaneous activities in the 1320s, chroniclers frequently confuse the two men. Ralph, a veteran Marcher throughout the 1320s, was well acquainted with Percy. The latter certainly retained confidence in his colleague's abilities: in 1328, he alienated £100 yearly to Neville for life from his ancient demesne of Pocklington and Topcliffe,[75] probably because he was too occupied with Northumberland and Scotland to properly supervise his Yorkshire properties. This responsibility he passed to Neville, whose own fief was nearby. It was Ralph Neville's son, John, who married Maud Percy.

The fate of his youngest daughter, Isabel, illuminates one of the less salutary aspects of Percy's character. He was diplomatic, canny and silky certainly, but also an obsessive hoarder of property – witness the shower of deeds, writs, letters of attorney and charters from Percy's lifetime and his ruthless disposal of claimants to his estates. His paramount concern was extending and protecting his 'fiefdom' in Northumberland and Scotland. As described earlier, Percy's father had purchased Alnwick under somewhat shady circumstances from Anthony Bek, who was holding it – legally or not – of William Vesci. After the latter died at Bannockburn, his Lincolnshire and Yorkshire lands passed circuitously to a distantly related kinsman, Gilbert Aton. Nothing was heard of Aton until late 1323, when he advanced a claim to Alnwick. Percy was in no real danger of losing Alnwick, but Aton was threatening him with an expensive and embarrassing court case. Percy wanted to make his ownership watertight and struck a bargain with him. In December, Aton permanently renounced his claim, and received 350 marks (about £231) from Percy in consequence. Before he did so, Aton made Percy promise that one of the baron's younger daughters would marry his son, William. Isabel, treated as a mere bargaining counter, was the daughter chosen. Dying in 1389, William outlived Isabel by some twenty years. Although no male heirs survived, their three daughters eventually partitioned the inheritance and that particular line of Atons disappeared.

Isabel is particularly remarkable because of her intellectual attainments. Alone of his children, Percy bequeathed to her a book – *De Natura Animalum* ('On the Characteristics of Animals') – in French.[76] Percy's taste in reading is quite interesting at a time when most others of his class preferred chivalric romances or practical manuals on fox-hunting or swordplay. Henry of Lancaster was a rarity: in a devotional book that he composed, he laid bare his own faults. Although confessedly loathing the stench of the poor and sick, he preferred to mess about with milkmaids rather than ladies of his own class because they were more responsive.[77]

The author of *De Natura Animalium*, Claudius Aelianus (*c.* AD 170–235), collated mariners' yarns, folklore, fantastical tales and superstitions about animals (including the Flesh-Eating Bulls of Ethiopia and the Ants of Babylonia) into a compendium of 225 chapters in which, rather revealingly, given Percy's own faults, 'the folly and selfishness of man are contrasted with the untaught virtues of the animal world'.[78]

The Struggle for Scotland

Heartened by his windfalls, pecuniary, territorial and marital, Percy attended to his duties as warden conscientiously: to Neville's sixty men-at-arms and sixty mounted archers, Percy added his own private force of twenty-three knights, ninety-seven men-at-arms and one hundred mounted archers, a retinue that must have cost no little sum. Although the March was secure, affairs were slipping out of control elsewhere. By now, Beaumont was locked into his Aberdeenshire castle, Dundarg, by Sir Andrew Moray and the turncoat Mowbray. Strathbogie, meanwhile, was chased around the countryside by the earl of Moray. At the end of September, with Moray's sword touching his throat, the duplicitous Strathbogie renounced Balliol and swore allegiance to David Bruce. For this treachery, Balliol seized his English and Irish possessions.

For the remainder of the autumn of 1334 Edward III attempted to gather an army for a winter campaign, but his barons were unenthusiastic. Although they dutifully brought their retinues to serve for pay (interestingly, Percy was accompanied by 120 men-at-arms, more than any other magnate; even Henry of Lancaster only rustled up sixty), Edward mustered a mere 4000 men. Most disappointed, he stationed himself at Roxburgh, which he found in ruins. He ordered it repaired and angrily berated his arrayers for not recruiting enough men. One bright spot amid the royal gloom was that the nucleus of Edward's army comprised exceptionally hardy and loyal soldiers; hardly a man deserted during the 1334–5 Roxburgh campaign. Edward stayed almost the entire winter in Roxburgh, occasionally straying outside for a foray or indulging himself in gambling (he particularly enjoyed throwing dice, once losing £61 in a single session) and growing ever more crotchety. He was especially irritated to hear on 23 December 1334 that Beaumont had capitulated. Thankfully his imprisonment was brief, and by the early summer of 1335, his ransom paid, Beaumont was in England. In February 1335, a very annoyed king disbanded the army, which had been serving on short contracts.

One calamitous decision of Edward's caused the defection to David Bruce of one of Scotland's premier earls, Patrick of March, a man, rather like the Strathbogies, who transferred allegiances as methodically as a modern footballer. After Christmas, Edward had allowed his commanders to pillage indiscriminately. Unfortunately, in their exuberance to burn villages and rape the wives of Scottish tenants, they ruined Earl Patrick's lands as well. In any case, the said earl had perceived it was time to switch partners, and his devastated farmland served admirably as an excuse.

Impressed by Percy's zeal, Edward granted to his faithful warden the substantial Northumbrian barony of Beanley and many other rich manors that had belonged to the disgraced March.[79] Also uppermost in the king's mind was a coup engineered by Percy and Neville in league with Edward's brother, the earl of Cornwall, in early January, when the king was stuck in Roxburgh. While the three lords patrolled south of Roxburgh, local villagers informed them that Thomas Pyngel, a notorious Scot who had been pillaging Redesdale, had recently passed through. Lying in wait for Pyngel's return from across the Border, Percy, Neville and Cornwall encircled him and his 200 horsemen at a nearby ford. Pyngel was slain in the shallows, like many of his men. Such initiatives never failed to please the king.[80]

Located ten miles north-west of Alnwick, Beanley allowed Percy to consolidate his March holdings. Percy probably lobbied hard for that particular tract; it was simply too good an opportunity to miss. Memories of Percy's unceasing opportunism persisted, just as they would among the Douglases following the acquisition of Jedburgh. March's great-nephew, George, would join the English in 1400 and try to influence Henry IV against the Percys 'so that he might dominate more easily in the parts of Northumbria', as one chronicler explained.[81] For every friendship Percy sealed through marriage he confirmed a hereditary enemy across the Border. But if his single-minded territorial jobbery antagonised a few people, in his eyes it was worth it. Since arriving on the scene in 1309, the Percys had risen to become the greatest landholders by far in Northumberland, major players in Scotland and connected with virtually every family of Northern consequence. Small wonder that within two generations the Percys were regarding themselves haughtily – but justifiably – as the Kings in the North.

Percy's ambitions did not stop there: throughout the early 1340s he bought properties in London, York and Newcastle. His London house, according to J.M.W. Bean, was 'an indication of the family's growing importance in national politics'. His son, we know, left the tenement unlet and 'reserved [it] as an inn for himself and his servants', during Parliaments. Like those of other up-and-coming nobles, Percy's London holdings centred on the western end of the City's Aldgate; to this day, tiny Northumberland Alley, named after the house's site, runs off Aldgate and joins Jewry Street near Fenchurch Street station. By his death, Percy had also purchased eight shops with storeys on that street, worth a handy £7 10s 8d yearly in rents. His grandson, however, hankered for more than a mere inn. He would buy a far grander establishment in the fashionable end of town just north of St Paul's on Aldersgate Street.[82]

Although disappointed by the Roxburgh campaign, Edward gamely decided on a summer expedition. The barons were to assemble at Newcastle on 11 June 1335. Perhaps because of less inclement weather or because the Exchequer had recently paid many outstanding balances to them (Percy received £133 6s 8d in the first week of June),[83] the magnates, far more enthusiastic this time, brought three times as many men. No fewer than eight earls and twenty-three bannerets (including Percy, who brought 140 men-at-arms and twenty mounted archers) attended.[84] Allotted persuasive new arrayers, the shires provided much greater numbers than previously, and Edward gathered about 13,000 troops at Newcastle.

At the council of war in mid-June, a striking plan was hatched: Edward's territories in Lowland Scotland were to be squeezed in a pincer movement. The Scots rebels would find it almost impossible not to be caught on open ground with two armies searching the wilderness. Once the rebels had been dealt with, the main Scottish army – which Edward and his commanders were convinced existed – could be found and destroyed. Therefore Edward, accompanied by Beaumont, Henry of Lancaster and three earls, would cross the Solway into Dumfriesshire and Annandale. At the same time Balliol would lead a second group of nobles and magnates – including Percy (called 'a very wealthy baron' by the Lanercost chronicler), the earls of Arundel, Warenne, Oxford, and Angus (Umfraville), and Lords Neville, Thomas Berkeley and William Latimer – from Berwick into Lothian on a pre-arranged date. In the second week of July, the twin arms of the English army invaded, their predetermined junction being near Glasgow.[85]

A raucous and riven Scottish council in Fife (for example, Strathbogie loathed Moray) decided to advise the Lowlanders to seek refuge in the hills while Scots troopers scorched the earth before the English invaders. Meanwhile, the lords would gather their men in the Northern hinterlands. Thus, Edward and Balliol met no resistance on their respective marches north. It is an open question as to who scorched more earth: the retreating Scots or the advancing English. Both took every opportunity to burn villages and waste the countryside.

Passing an emptied Edinburgh, in late July Balliol took Strathbogie's castle of Cumbernauld in north Lothian, midway between the Forth and the Clyde. Among the 200 prisoners was Archibald Douglas's widow, who was spared; the rest were executed on Balliol's orders. In the meantime, Edward had overrun Carrick and the western coast to the Clyde. The king's southern territories had ostensibly been cleansed of rebels, and he and Balliol met at Glasgow to plan the search for the main Scots army.

For once the Bruce's traditional 'scorched earth' strategy had not immobilised an English army: the benefits of a summer campaign combined with better-planned logistics. Both Edward and Balliol agreed that the signs were auspicious and combined to push north-eastwards to Perth. This might have proved a mistake; Edward had still not grasped the verity of Scottish warfare: that the mere passage of an army through

Scotland did not automatically impose control over it; indeed, real control on the ground could only be achieved by the permanent physical presence of experienced (and expensive) garrisons. For instance, some volunteer foreign reinforcements led by the count of Nemurs, a cousin of Edward's queen, had arrived late and tried to make up lost time by riding to Edinburgh. Along the way, they were ambushed by March, Moray and Douglas, and surrendered. Although the English 'cared but little for the capture of the Count of Nemurs', observed the Lanercost chronicler, 'considering it a mighty piece of presumption that he should have dared to enter Scotland in time of war with so slender a force', his surrender was an embarrassment, for the three Scots were not 'supposed' to be in Edward's Lowlands. It was a pointed reminder of the damage that guerrillas could cause behind the lines.[86]

On the other hand, a few days later Edward, and no doubt Percy as well, was cheered to hear that the Scots had been worsted in a skirmish with the constable and garrison of Jedburgh. Humiliatingly, Moray was captured, not by highly trained knights but by Percy's rough Northumbrians. Although Douglas escaped, his brother was killed.

By 7 August, the English arrived in Perth, and settled down for a month, bewildered by their virtually unopposed passage north. Where was the mighty Scottish host? It eventually dawned on Edward that he *had* conquered Scotland in a month; there *was* no Scottish host. All that remained was some isolated bands of guerrillas. The collapse of Scottish morale was borne out to Edward when the earl of Fife, 'a fers [and sterne] man',[87] surrendered Cupar Castle (east of Perth) to a patrol of *fifteen* men-at-arms under Henry Ferrers without firing a bow in anger.

Edward was also informed that the veteran renegade Strathbogie (all of twenty-six years old) and the turncoat Alexander Mowbray had seen the light and wished to renew their friendship. Edward, doubtless with a sense of smug satisfaction, agreed to pardon them for their transgressions. Soon after, the earl of Menteith and rest of the Mowbray family sought, and found, peace with Edward. Now, with the exception of Stewart's strongholds in the Western Isles, Earl Patrick of March's castle of Dunbar and the most distant reaches of the Highlands where no Englishman ever ventured anyway, Edward had pacified the whole of Scotland. (Even Carrick, always a problem, was currently quiescent.) His formerly Disinherited lords again held sway over the entire eastern seaboard (Angus and Buchan) above the Forth; Galloway was happy with Balliol on the throne; efficient warlord-diplomats like Percy governed the Lowlands; Lothian, despite its lurking guerrillas, was overseen by Berwick; Fife and Menteith had accepted English overlordship; and, finally, Strathbogie brought the enormous central area of Atholl under

Edward's watchful eye. Just as satisfyingly, Edward had out-bluffed the French. The Scots had appealed to them in August for aid under the terms of the Treaty of Corbeil. In reply King Philip had suggested to Edward that he submit to arbitration under himself and the Pope, but Edward had reminded him that, at last, peace had been attained. What would the French achieve by intervening now? The Scottish question had vanished – fait accompli. Instead, he proposed that Philip should support *him*, given their kinship through Queen Philippa and his mother, Isabella. And that was that. Thus, by the late summer of 1335, in an almost bloodless offensive, Edward III had not only eclipsed his grandfather's achievements but, to the immense pleasure of his patriotically minded magnates, had also seen off a potential challenge from across the Channel.

In September, Edward disbanded his army (it had so far cost him £25,000) and travelled triumphantly south towards Edinburgh and Berwick, where Balliol joined him. It had been impressed upon Edward during the campaign that refortifying Edinburgh Castle was crucial to maintaining order in Lothian; previously, faraway Berwick had been deemed sufficient. So the king extracted £200 from the community of Lothian to subsidise the building project, thereby shifting the frontier – as opposed to the Border – north to the Forth. As work proceeded, Edward transferred most of the Berwick garrison to Edinburgh, still not quite understanding that successful occupation of Scotland depended on permanent, heavy garrisoning everywhere. Moving troops around the country merely opened gaps in the English defences, which any sharp Scots raider could exploit.

Nevertheless, despite this slip and the cravenly subservient Balliol's meek protestations, Edward was more concerned with pushing the actual Border northwards. On 10 October, he granted to William Montagu the forest of Selkirk and Ettrick along with the town and county of Peebles. With this gift Edward filled in the central space between Percy's Jedburgh lands and Bohun's Annandale territories. He kept hold of the Border strongholds of Berwick in the far east, and Roxburgh in Teviotdale. Looking at a road atlas,[88] it is clear that 'Edward had virtually transformed the south of Scotland into three great marcher lordships'.[89] From Berwick to Jedburgh, Lochmaben and thence to Carlisle, a string of castles protected these lordships and provided a primary defence line before the Border and the fortresses on the English side. In an emergency, Edward's northernmost outposts could support Balliol, but Edinburgh was primarily intended to oversee the Forth region, and Stirling, astride the main route to the south, would give warning of an impending Scottish attack. Strategically, Edward's accessions formed a chunky crescent covering the upper Forth and arcing towards Galloway, boxing any recalcitrant Scots into the Clyde, Cunningham and Kyle, where, hopefully, they could be contained.

While stationed at Edinburgh, overseeing the restoration of order to the shattered provinces, Edward received the honourable surrender and fealty of Stewart. The flames of Scottish nationalism may have abated but its embers smouldered in the form of Sir Andrew Moray, David II's uncle, ex-guardian of Scotland and arch-enemy of Strathbogie. At the end of September, he was re-elected to his post at Dumbarton by the remnants of the uncowed baronage, including the indefatigable William Douglas of Liddesdale, Earl Patrick of March (who had stayed on the same side for once) and the earl of Ross, whose mountainous Highlands fiefdom remained untouched by the English. Trapped in the Clyde, they conducted reprisal raids on those Scottish earls, such as Fife, who had joined Edward.

Their prospects looked so gloomy that Sir Andrew was forced to treat with Edward's representatives in October and November 1335 (the king was enjoying Percy's hospitality at Alnwick), but nothing came of it for reasons explained below. By the end of November, Balliol had appointed Strathbogie his guardian of Scotland north of the Forth and had left to meet Edward at Holy Island. Strathbogie fulfilled his duties over-zealously. He informed Balliol before he left that he intended to crush any flickering resistance to his rule in Moray, Ross and Mar. Any tenant not professing allegiance and paying his taxes would be killed and replaced with one more amenable to the new regime.

Having murdered hundreds, Strathbogie besieged Kildrummy Castle, where Lady Christina Bruce, sister of King Robert and wife of Sir Andrew Moray, was doggedly holding out. Hearing of Strathbogie's audacity, Sir Andrew broke off talks with the English and rushed north with Douglas and Earl Patrick, who both had scores to settle with their treacherous foe. As they made their way across the Mounth, Strathbogie broke off his siege, and camped in the forest covering Culblean Hill about thirty-five miles due west of Aberdeen and twelve miles south of Kildrummy. Here he intended to ambush Sir Andrew as he marched to the castle. Moray, however, was informed of Strathbogie's whereabouts before he reached the fateful pass. In darkness, the Scots quietly circled to the rear of Strathbogie's position, from where the earl would least expect an attack. Warned at the last minute by his scouts, Strathbogie hurriedly lined up his men to face the new danger. Seeing Douglas in front of him, the earl and his cavalry eagerly charged straight into Douglas's row of spears. The two sides were evenly matched, but Strathbogie had not reckoned on Moray's men rushing him from the flank. As his men deserted or were killed, Strathbogie and several of his friends from the old days of Edward II made their last stand around an oak tree. He refused to yield – more out of desperation than heroism, considering that Sir Andrew and Douglas were not in a liberal mood – and he, and all his comrades, were cut down one by one.[90] As a mark of gratitude, Douglas was made earl of Atholl by the Scots, but he never assumed the symbolic title, instead conveying it to Robert Stewart several years later (see Chapter 10).[91]

Strathbogie's death shook Edwardian Scotland and the Marches to the core, but the barons were not saddened by news of the infamous snake's end. Rather, the victory at Culblean destroyed any prospect of a permanent, imposed peace. The terrifying realisation was hammered home that Scotland would be an eternal problem, never to fade away. For every Scottish king, earl, baron or knight who swore fealty to an English king, there would always be brothers, uncles, fathers and sons who continued to fight. There would invariably be yet another guardian or displaced king inspiring resistance, and it was impossible to kill them all.

CHAPTER TEN

The Closing Years of Henry Percy

By the time of Strathbogie's death, the deposed David II was being sheltered by Philip VI of France, who took the Auld Alliance very seriously. His concern with Scottish affairs, especially as they pertained to England, would reveal itself during the Hundred Years War. This Henry Percy, however, took no part in the conflict across the Channel, but, as the next chapter will narrate, his son did. For the moment, however, we shall stay focused on the Border.

Edward diverted his energies down into the south, having effectively reorganised the defences. The Scots beast had been tamed – seemingly for ever – and although the next year or so witnessed the odd Border raid or disturbance, it was nothing his wardens and sheriffs could not handle. For instance, Percy's most onerous task at this time was delineating the Yorkshire–Westmorland border.[1]

Nevertheless, the English had, as always, misunderstood the singular nature of the Anglo-Scottish war; in particular, that small numbers of roving guerrillas could wreak far greater destruction than a cumbersome army designed for European warfare. Sir Andrew Moray and Sir William Douglas, their prestige reaching its zenith in the aftermath of Culblean, remained at large and occasionally evicted Englishmen from Atholl, Buchan and Fife, areas in which, by the end of 1336, Moray and Douglas had razed four minor English-held castles. In dribs and drabs, the subdued Scottish nobles were recovering their battered spirits; the earl of Fife, for instance, discreetly renounced his fealty to Edward and joined the rebels. Meanwhile, owing to the devastation in southern Scotland, hardly any taxes were being collected, and Edward was making a loss on his assets; repairs alone at Edinburgh, Roxburgh, Perth and Stirling castles were costing him £10,000 annually at a time when his total Scottish income amounted to just £2000.[2]

In the winter of 1337, with English power gradually dissipating north of the Forth, the earls of Fife and March joined the two guerrilla leaders and reached the outskirts of Edward's lands in little more than a year. Raids into Galloway, Cumberland and Northumberland inevitably ensued.[3] On the English side, the earl of Warwick (the son of Piers

Gaveston's loathed 'Black Cur', who had been serving on the Border since 1333), Thomas Wake, Anthony Lucy and Lord Clifford headed a private expedition into the west of Scotland. Percy did not participate in this mini-campaign, as he was busy refurbishing the defences in his part of the March. After twelve days of vengeful, but pretty small-scale, plunder and pillage, the barons returned home.[4]

Less than a week later, the Scots returned the compliment in Redesdale and Coquetdale. This raid was in the extreme west of Percy's neck of the woods, but his and lord Neville's response was somewhat desultory. The Lanercost chronicler pointedly noted that the Scots 'would have done much more had not the earl of Angus [Gilbert Umfraville] ... offered them bold resistance with his small force'. About a month later, raiders under the command of Sir William Douglas burnt a number of villages. It was fully three days before Percy and Neville arrived with relief, 'although the leading men had written to them to move with speed', as the Lanercost writer acidly observed.[5]

Edward was too occupied planning his invasion of France to deal with Scottish affairs, but the lackadaisical performance of Percy and Neville was certainly noted in high places because, on the eve of his departure, Edward left the Northern command not to Percy, but to the earls of Arundel and Salisbury; the latter, as William Montagu, had been raised to the peerage a few months earlier for his services, many of a financial nature, to Edward.

A word on Arundel, who assumes considerable importance in the next chapter. Descended from the grand old FitzAlan earls of Arundel, Richard, born in 1313, was the son of the Despensers' hated ally, Edmund of Arundel. Aged eight, in 1321, he was betrothed to Isabel, the seven-year-old daughter of Despenser the Younger, then establishing himself as the king's favourite. This great match came to grief when Despenser and Arundel were executed during Isabella and Mortimer's coup, so leaving Richard with a political liability for a wife and with his inheritance and title passed on to the rapacious earl of Kent. Kent's execution, Mortimer's fall and Edward's rise revived Richard's fortunes. He was restored to the Honour of Arundel and created earl. This was his first real command, and he was keen to impress his royal saviour.

Arundel and Salisbury decided to level the earl of March's Lothian fortress of Dunbar, a bolt-hole for raiders on the run. As Montagu had not ascended to the pinnacle of the political world without cultivating a certain deliberateness of action, the January 1338 siege of Dunbar is remarkable for the presence of a number of skilled sappers and military engineers (such as John Crabb), who were crucial for undermining stout walls impervious to frontal assaults. Percy, whose lands had been wasted by Dunbar-based Scots raiders, joined Salisbury and Arundel soon after the siege had begun in January 1338.[6] His retinue of eighty-three men-at-arms comprised a banneret, sixteen knights and sixty-six esquires, many of whom were members of the Yorkshire gentry.[7] Thus the Percys retained links to their traditional Yorkshire power base, even while their web of patronage and loyalty in the North was expanding.

The English, not expecting an easy time, were not prepared for a difficult one either; March had hightailed it to friendlier quarters, leaving the castle in the capable hands of his wife, 'Black Agnes' Randolph ('be ressone scho was blak skynnit'), the sister of the earl of Moray, who had languished in an English dungeon at Windsor after being captured in 1335. She taunted the besiegers with obscene gestures from the ramparts, giving a show that even attracted Edward III to Dunbar during a flying visit to Scotland. Eventually, diverted by Edward's imminent departure for France, the attackers cut short the siege (whose cost was edging towards £6000).[8] As the chronicler Knighton remarked, Arundel and Salisbury emerged from the Dunbar episode 'to their no small discredit'.[9]

Black Agnes' snub to English military might marked the latest turning-point in English fortunes. Scottish morale was immeasurably boosted, surviving even the retirement of Sir Andrew Moray to his castle at Avoch, where he died in the spring of 1338 – conflicting accounts say of dysentery or, alternatively, mounting an unbroken colt, which threw him, trapping one of his feet in a stirrup and dragging him to death.[10]

A cheerful tale illuminates the rise in Scottish spirits inspired by the defiance at Dunbar: during the siege, the English had threatened to kill Black Agnes' captive brother if she did not surrender, whereupon she caustically replied that 'if ye do that, then shall I be heir to the earldom of Moray', for her brother was childless. This dire counter-threat evidently scared the grizzled English commanders into dropping their plan to execute Moray.[11]

Since 1335, nobles had slowly trickled away from King Edward Balliol's camp to the rebels, but Dunbar exerted an even more powerful magnetism. By this time, Balliol had lost not only Edward III's interest, which was then piqued by his quest for the French Crown (see Chapter 11), but worse, his foremost adviser, Lord Henry Beaumont, who would die in France in 1340.

The rebellion's revival had come about in spite, not because, of King Robert I's grandson and David II's nephew, Robert Stewart, twenty-two years old and heir presumptive of the Crown, a lethargic individual who had been awarded the guardianship of Scotland. William Douglas, however, had expected the post. 'The flail of the English, the wall of the Scots',[12] had he not guarded Scotland while Robert had kept his head down? In a huff, he offered his services in France to the refugee David II and his queen. With funds from David, Douglas hired French pirates to raid England's southern coasts. In April 1341, Douglas was back in Scotland, to be assisted by his able accomplice, the earl of Moray, who at King Philip's urging had been exchanged for the earls of Salisbury and Suffolk, both captured while campaigning with Edward in France.[13]

While Moray created a diversion by ravaging Bohun's Annandale, Douglas – together with a corrupt but militarily effective priest named William Bullock (formerly Balliol's chamberlain until bribed by Douglas) – audaciously captured Edinburgh Castle. When the portcullis was raised to allow in Bullock, who was disguised as an English merchant, he jammed it open and blew his horn, whereupon Douglas and his men rushed the guards. Almost bloodlessly, one of the strongest English fortresses north of Berwick fell. Now, virtually mirroring the reorganisation of the English defences, Douglas and Moray divided the Border into three Marches: Moray held the West; Douglas, the troublesome Middle March (directly opposite Percy's March); and Sir Alexander Ramsay, veteran of Culblean and brother-in-arms of Moray and Douglas, the East. Very soon after their victory, and delighted that Stewart had been shown up as a slothful and indecisive guardian, Moray and Douglas persuaded David II to return to his kingdom in June 1341.

Subsequently, Bullock was rewarded for his bravery at Edinburgh by being appointed royal chamberlain, where he performed sterling service by reducing the deficit from £2881 to slightly more than £1 within a year. (Edward III could have used someone of Bullock's talents, seeing as he then owed the astronomical sum of £400,000 to Italian bankers.) Soon afterwards, Bullock was caught with his hand in the till and thrown into prison, where he died.

In recognition of his heroism at Culblean and elsewhere, Douglas was granted the earldom of Atholl in July 1341, but this Borderer had little desire for Highland honours. An autocratic man of action, Douglas could not change his style to suit the political arena. He spurned Atholl and would settle only for the lordship of Liddesdale (which sat opposite the Yorkshire–Cumbrian border), which he then held in ward for his godson, William, the second son of Sir Archibald Douglas, the guardian who had fallen at Halidon. This, he felt, was his due. Following a year of Douglas's Achilles-like petulance, Robert Stewart was persuaded to take the northern earldom in return for Douglas gaining Liddesdale (hence his famous moniker, the 'Knight of Liddesdale'), thereby defrauding his young godson of his inheritance.

However, Douglas still harboured claims to Roxburghshire, granted to Alexander Ramsay by the Scots despite Henry Percy's insistence that it was his. Scandalously, in June 1342, Douglas and his men kidnapped Ramsay (who had stood loyally by Douglas's side for a decade and more) and took him to Liddesdale's Hermitage Castle where he died, seventeen days later, of starvation.

These developments had occurred under the noses of the English, still ostensibly in command of Scotland. If domestic problems and Edward's preoccupation with France had not intervened, it is unlikely that the Scots would have been granted such a propitious respite. Until mid-1340, Edward's campaign abroad had been gloriously successful – he had defeated the French at sea at Sluys (see Chapter 11) – and was currently starving Tournai into submission. But when forced to make a truce because his officials in England failed to send him the money he required to pay the troops, he laid the blame squarely at the door of John Stratford, archbishop of Canterbury, whom he had made chancellor. Indeed, the king fumed to Pope Benedict XII, 'I believe that the archbishop meant, by lack of money, to see me betrayed and killed.' Pertinent words – Stratford had played a role in deposing Edward's father. Edward had already been warned in France that Stratford was featherbedding, inefficient and, unforgivably, *ambivalent* about the French war. Convinced that maladministration was depriving him of victories, in late autumn 1340, Edward snapped. In one of his occasional bouts of violent indignation, he arrived unannounced at the Tower of London at midnight on 30 November. His anger was not appeased when he discovered that the keeper of the Tower, in direct contravention of orders, was out of town. Edward promptly arrested various justices and merchants, as well as other officials, including the Master of the Rolls, the treasurer and, for good measure, Stratford's cousin, a Chancery administrator. The next day, every sheriff in the land was ordered to investigate local officials' behaviour and financial probity.[14] A great administrative purge was set in motion. Many of the aforementioned sheriffs were dismissed, as were judges, Exchequer bureaucrats, escheators and customs and tax collectors throughout 1340–1. Archbishop Stratford was older, wilier and tougher than his subordinates, and the king failed to get rid of him despite another seven years of political manoeuvring. It was only Stratford's death in 1348 that finally pulled this particular thorn from Edward's flesh.[15]

This cleared out much of the entrenched corruption and incompetence left over from his father's regime, not to mention Isabella and Mortimer's, and it was obviously in the interests of his subjects; nevertheless, Edward's fixation with destroying Stratford provoked a major political crisis. The king almost recreated the coalition of Lords Ordainers of 1311, whose remnants had plagued Edward II until

Lancaster's death in 1322. Again, a Percy was involved, for in 1340 Percy had been appointed to the regency council led by Stratford, which also included Thomas Wake (who had close ties with the archbishop), Lord Neville and the earls of Lancaster, Surrey, Arundel and Gloucester.[16] These men, not amused at being tarred with the same brush of treachery as Stratford, reactively formed a defensive circle around the archbishop. The Northerners' anger was also stoked by the worsening situation in Scotland. Percy, for instance, saw his hold on Jedburgh slipping, which was due in part to Edward's preoccupation with France, and he was worried about the activities of Douglas and Moray. His and Neville's act of insubordination was to register a protest vote at the king's willingness to leave unfinished business unfinished. For Edward, however, most members of this well-knit little group had underperformed, to say the least, in Scotland. Percy and Neville, for instance, had neglected their defensive duties, while Arundel had been partially responsible for the Dunbar debacle.

In April 1341, when Parliament met at Westminster, Edward barred Stratford from attending a regency council meeting. But, confronted with furious opposition, Edward backed down and, momentously, the lords declared that henceforth 'none of their rank [which included prelates] should be arrested, tried or imprisoned except in full parliament and before his peers'. The commoners now raised their voices. Tired of being continually pushed around by obnoxious appointees and being tapped for money, they called for an audit of the royal finances, and demanded that Edward's high officials must be appointed, not by royal whim, but by the king in Parliament, swearing an oath there to uphold the law. Astonished, and probably a little dazed, at being harangued, Edward ill-naturedly gave his assent. Out of the blue, a royal tantrum and a personal feud with an ageing but agile ecclesiastic provoked written legislation, asserting that peers should be tried by their fellows – no longer, it seemed, could a baron who fell foul of the king be punished solely by his command – and that ministers were responsible to the nation, not the king in person. Unwittingly, Edward III had affirmed the integrity of Magna Carta, completed the Montfortian programme of 1258 and fulfilled the Lancastrian policy of 1311, which cumulatively sought to restrict royal autocracy in favour of baronial oligarchy. Remarkably, a Percy was involved in each of these constitutional shifts.[17]

Edward did come to understand the ramifications of this close shave with his frenzied nobles. Given time, frenzies pass (Edward's did, anyway) and this would be the last such test of his kingship. Just as his grandfather would have done in similar circumstances, he eventually reasserted unimpeded royal authority, but henceforth ensured that he reconciled any alienated magnates to his rule. He needed the barons more than they needed him, and he realised that the baronial class far preferred to support the king, as they had done since the Conqueror's time, rather than oppose him.

Seeking to rebuild his baronial bridges, Edward chose his next move carefully. A council convened throughout September and October 1341 to focus on the Scottish problem, which had threatened to worsen following David II's return in June, near the height of the Stratford business. Inviting the dissidents back into his favour, Edward cited the danger to the nation posed by the Scots – a prime concern of the Northern barons. Thus, in July, Percy and Neville, among others, were instructed to 'treat with the King's subjects in the North for the defence of the country against the Scots'.[18] Many magnates, such as Percy and Wake, signalled their peaceful intentions towards Edward by joining Henry, earl of Lancaster – newly appointed captain of the king's army – in Newcastle.[19] Promises were also made that the baronage would be welcomed aboard the French gravy-train. However, Arundel and a number of the earls still stood aloof from the king. At a magnificent tournament at Dunstable, for instance, which Edward organised to please his magnates, Arundel was prominent by his absence, claiming, although only in his mid-thirties, that he was too old and infirm to attend.[20] Yet very soon after, he made his peace with Edward and was created joint warden of the March in Northumberland. Percy could now strengthen their acquaintance and persuade one of the richest and most powerful men in England to take his son into his retinue (see Chapter 11).[21]

Arundel's intransigence aside, Edward felt secure enough in his autumn council to revoke the Statute of 1341, claiming that he had not sworn to it freely, an action to which the magnates present assented. There was to be no automatic right to trial by one's peers and Edward was ostensibly permitted to choose his own councillors, but the magnates saved face by establishing the principle, by custom if not by law, of co-government. Only a very unwise king would act vindictively against one of their number without first seeking their assent.

For the first time, the increasingly confident voice of the third estate was heard during the crisis, marking the emergence of the Commons as a distinct political entity. Their petition of February 1339 audaciously declared that 'no free man should be assessed or taxed without common assent of Parliament'. Although they were somewhat dismayed at Edward's U-turn over the 1341 Statute, their view that the king should not consider them his personal chequebook was duly noted. Edward felt bound to declare that 'it was not his intention to grieve or oppress his subjects but to rule them by lenience and gentleness', a significant pledge of good kingship. By the 1350s, the Commons had secured the right to grant direct and indirect taxation, and, importantly, sometimes linked the reform of grievances to that grant. This was not the Commons gaining power at the expense of the Crown; rather, the two worked smoothly together because Edward was equally interested in introducing reforms such as the Ordinance of Labourers and the uniformity of weights and measures (both of which neatly satisfied the Commons *and* increased royal profits). The results of these events were increased administrative efficiency and Edward's subsequent receipt of the massive sums required for his military campaigns and paying off creditors. For instance, between 1344 and 1357, the Commons granted no less than £418,000, with the Church subscribing another £144,000, swelling the king's total revenue by £562,000 (although not every penny was collected). Additionally, Edward was able to levy an indirect tax of 50 shillings per sack of wool exported from England, which helped the Exchequer rake in an additional £700,000 in less than a decade.[22]

With such a crisis occupying the English government for three years or so, the Scottish question was again put on the back burner. The heat was soon raised. While Percy absented himself up north, in London a war was being urged.[23] At the Westminster Parliament of June 1344, it was feared that, if the French abandoned the truces currently in force, then 'they [the Scots] will not keep them either, but will raid upon England and accomplish as much damage as they can'.

Two years later, the Anglo-French peace talks had indeed collapsed, and by July 1346, Edward had taken the largest army he ever raised, some 32,000 men, to Normandy (see Chapter 11). As every English soldier in France meant one fewer up North, the Scots launched a substantial raid led by the earl of Moray on Cumberland and Westmorland as a cover for an intelligence-gathering operation. David II secretly travelled with the army (under Moray's banner) to assess the Northern defences personally. What he saw must have pleased him. In July, Percy, Neville, Umfraville and others had angrily complained to London that while the council talked tough about beating the Scots, they had not been paid for the defence of the March for many months. 'Certain lords' and the governor of Berwick threatened that unless they were recompensed soon 'they neither could nor would stay any longer'. Lord Segrave, for example, gave the council three weeks to pay up or he would consider himself 'discharged'.[24]

For the Scots, seeing Northern lords and their men seething with discontent while the king was abroad presented too good an opportunity to miss. In addition, there was renewed Franco-Scottish contact throughout this time; under attack by Edward in France, Philip VI requested David to distract Edward in June and July in order to open a second front. But only after Edward had sacked Caen and won the battle of Crécy on 26 August did David – rather tardily – prepare a major autumn campaign. By early September the English were tied up besieging Calais, which might prevent Edward returning in time to save his kingdom.[25]

In late September, some 2000 knights and men-at-arms and perhaps 17,000 spearmen and hangers-on led by David, who was 'stout and right jolly, and desirous to see fighting', crossed the Esk and laid siege to the Pile of Liddell, a small Border fortress captained by Walter Selby. After a four-day siege, all the inmates were put to the sword. David ('being long demented with guile ... goaded to madness worse than Herod the enemy of the Most High', according to the Lanercost chronicler, who was not an altogether impartial observer) is said to have ordered Selby's two sons strangled before his eyes, afterwards beheading Selby without even granting him confession.

The squalid behaviour of Bruce's son cloaks his character in layers of mystery. Generally thought unworthy of his father's mantle, he usually appeared an amiable enough fellow. But according to the sixteenth-century writer George Buchanan, he lacked the harsh, 'character-building' experiences in the wilderness that had strengthened his father; thus, 'tried both by adverse and prosperous circumstances, [David] appears to have been unfortunate rather than incapable'. Now, for the first time tasting the delights of power and bolstered by military success, David childishly believed that his treatment of Selby would impress hardened warhorses like Douglas.

It did not. Immediately afterwards, fearing an English counter-strike, Douglas uncharacteristically advised David not to advance further in England, or tarry there much longer. For this canny counsel, David and the younger barons mocked him. So David pressed on through Cumberland (sacking Lanercost Priory and shattering the crypts, which explains the chronicler's outrage, noted above) and followed the Tyne to Northumberland. Hexham and Corbridge fell and the army turned south-east to rest at Ebchester. Their spirits were buoyant, for, in the words of the medieval historian Wyntoun: 'They said that they might fare well until London, for in England there was no man left of great might, because all were in France except sowers of seed, skinners and merchants.'

But Douglas's antsiness turned out to be correct; suspiciously, there had been no sign of the English wardens. Where were they? Percy, Neville and the archbishop of York had been summoning every available man in the Northern counties to Auckland Park, ten miles south of Durham. In addition to these levies, Percy had amassed an army, originally with the intent of shipping it to Calais, which included 1200 knights, 3000 archers, 7000 spearmen and about 5000 veterans; he now diverted this into Northern service. All told, the Scottish and English forces were evenly matched – numerically, if not in experience. Early on a foggy 16 October, Douglas, sensing that the English were uncomfortably close, rode with his personal escort to Ferryhill, about five miles east of Auckland Park. Surprised by an English cavalry patrol, he lost hundreds of his men. Streaking back to the main Scottish camp, Douglas shouted at David that the English were only a few miles away. Understanding the delicate Anglo-Scottish diplomatic situation, Percy sent a herald to David requesting that he cease pillaging and leave England immediately. Otherwise, he would bring the Scots to battle. This warning was laughed off, and the Scottish king deployed his troops on a moor just outside Durham, where, on elevated waste ground, stood an ancient, weathered cross marking the limit of the palatinate of Durham. The next day, the English army, ordered into four divisions, marched forward to face the Scots, who formed into three divisions.

The Scottish right, or van, was commanded by Douglas and the earl of Moray; David, with most of the high nobility and the great officers of state, captained the middle; Patrick Earl of March and Robert Stewart led the left, which was by far the largest Scottish formation. As David paraded by his troops, pipes and clarions blared martial music, but the din diverted attention from the fact that the Scots were squeezed into a length of land half that occupied by the English. They had formed up in a hurry (David had eaten no breakfast that morning because the servants had allowed the food to fall into the fire) and their jostling, disorderly lines showed it.

Apart from the fourth division – a cavalry reserve under the perennially unfortunate puppet, Balliol, the English right (which faced Stewart and March) was led by Percy, for whom Gilbert Umfraville acted as deputy. Expected to bear the brunt of the fighting, this division principally consisted of Northumbrian veterans of Scottish service. The centre was commanded by Neville and the archbishop, with the left headed by Sir Thomas Rokeby (sheriff of Yorkshire) and John Mowbray; its strength was dependent on Yorkshiremen and Lancashire archers. Interestingly, this is one of the exceedingly rare appearances of Percy's only sibling. Sir William Percy (he died issueless in 1355) served in this division, but he seems to have made 'continual stay...against the invasions of the king's Scottish enemies' for many years. Ten years after the battle, just before he died, he was meanly accused of cowardice. Eventually, it was judged that he was 'present [and] sufficiently furnished at the battle...as the king has learned by trustworthy testimony'.

In front of the English lines, local clerics bore aloft a large crucifix. Behind them, myriad banners and flags signified the presence of the entire Northern ruling class. The battle of the Standard, fought 200 years previously against a similarly named Scottish king who had attacked a forlorn North, would have sprung to the minds of barons with a sense of history. The only real difference now was that the barons and knights dismounted and sent their horses to the rear, to be prepared by their servants for flight or pursuit.

As the two armies glared at each other, and the sun rose slowly, the enterprising monks of Durham, on top of the cathedral tower from where the battlefield was visible, sang hymns and prayers. The eerie interlude did not last long. The trumpets sounded and the English left loosed a storm of arrows into Moray's and Douglas's men, killing many before they had even raised their weapons. Moray was one of the first to fall, and Douglas, who never excelled in pitched battle, was soon captured by Sir Robert Bertram. Those Scots who survived the fusillade joined the king's division, only to suffer more losses as the archers swivelled slightly to the right and fired into the king's right flank. Amazingly, Rokeby and Mowbray, without moving their men, had already smashed the Scots on their side.

Meanwhile, Percy and Umfraville had engaged Stewart and March in hand-to-hand combat. Both sides used knives, daggers, axes and spears. At one point, when Stewart had partly broken Percy's ranks, Percy was only saved by the arrival of a large reserve cavalry detachment, whose men-at-arms dismounted and thrust their spears among the Scots, allowing Percy's men to re-form the line and renew the attack. Robert Stewart's response would damn him for ever in the eyes of King David, and inspired the usually measured Lanercost chronicler to the heights of howling sarcasm. To prevent their demoralised division being massacred, Stewart and March withdrew in fairly good order from the field. According to the Lanercost historian, the earl of March 'hurt no man, because he intended to take holy orders and to celebrate mass for the Scots who were killed, knowing how salutary it is to beseech the Lord for the peace of the departed'. As for Robert Stewart, 'overcome by cowardice, he broke his vow to God that he would never await the first blow in battle ... These two, turning their backs, fought with great success, for they entered Scotland with their division and without a single wound.'

Curiously, Percy and the Northumbrians made no attempt to pursue them; in fact, Percy forbade the men-at-arms to remount. Until the retreat he had 'encouraged all men to take the field by putting himself in the forefront of the battle', according to the Lanercost chronicler. On the other hand, 'he was small of stature but sagacious', and so may have realised that giving chase now would imperil the other English divisions. Nevertheless, it is odd that absolutely nothing was done. The truth, as will be suggested below, was that Percy, in no condition to lead a pursuit, desperately needed to rest, at least for a short while.

After recovering, Percy pushed his troop to the left, onto the right flank of David's division, and hemmed it in. With the English centre and left pressing as well, the Scottish nobles formed a defensive circle around their king. Now, after three hours of combat, the hardest fighting was about to begin. As Percy barred the right's escape route, the archers poured successive volleys into the infantry and the nobles. Many of the royal household fell, and the circle was thinning. David himself was wounded in the leg and face by the bolts. Eventually, to save his own life, Thomas Carre, David's standard-bearer, shouted to John Coupland, a Northumbrian knight with whom he was grappling: 'That is the king: take him!' Coupland plunged into the circle, dashed the king's sword from his hand and attempted to wrestle him to the ground. In response, David struck Coupland so forcibly in the mouth that he knocked out two of his teeth. Well knowing the size of a king's ransom, Coupland and eight companions managed to bundle David away to Ogle Castle, twenty-four miles distant. Soon afterwards, David was taken to Bamburgh, which was under Percy's keeping, and two barbers extracted an arrow-head from his face by drawing it out through his nose. The scar would linger for at least another five years and would need frequent medical attention.

With the king abducted, the battle, but not the killing, was over. As the monks sang the 'Te Deum' from the cathedral tower, the English pursued the broken Scots, slaughtering them as far away as Corbridge and Prudhoe. The number of lives lost on 17 October 1346 is unknown; the chroniclers' estimates unhelpfully range from 1000 to 15,000. For this third Scottish defeat (after Dupplin Moor and Halidon Hill) the Scottish nobility once again paid a high price. The king had been captured, as had Douglas, the earls of Fife, Menteith and Wigton, plus fifty other barons and knights. Douglas did not go quietly into prison; in a cleverly phrased letter the prior of Durham informed Thomas Hatfield, bishop of Durham, that he 'was not so much valiant as malevolent' (*non tamen valentior sed revera malevolentior est*). Menteith and Fife were later tried for treason, with the former being drawn, hanged, beheaded and quartered. Wigton, however, bribed his way free. The earl of Moray was killed (the last male Randolph of his line, he was indeed succeeded in his honours and estates by his sister, the countess of March, 'Black Agnes'). The list of the dead also included the earl of Strathearn, the chancellor, the marshal, and the constable of Scotland. Another thirty-seven nobles were killed, most of them during the battle's final hour. English losses were minimal, with no one of great account (apart from Lord Hastings) losing his life. Three days after the battle, a gracious letter of thanks from the king sped to Northumberland, citing Percy, the archbishop of York, Umfraville, Neville, Mowbray, Thomas de Lucy, Thomas Rokeby and a number of others for their brilliant and heroic victory.

The doughty John Coupland was amply rewarded for his valour; he was made a knight-banneret and given an annuity of £500. In addition he was pardoned for various 'homicides and felonies', received King Edward's thanks, was granted manors throughout the North and would variously hold the shrievalty of Northumberland, the governorship of Berwick and the wardenship of Roxburgh. Occasionally he acted as David's jailer.[26] In 1363 some irate Northumbrians unaccountably murdered him. Shortly after the victory, Lord Neville – more muscular in his Christianity than his fellows – personally paid for an impressive cross (hence, the battle of Neville's Cross) to replace the rickety wooden one already marking the Durham palatinate boundary. Neville's Cross had 'seven steps leading to an eighth, a large thick square stone on whose chamfered corners were the statues of the four evangelists' covered in lead and was three and a half yards high.[27] It was destroyed by Protestants in 1589, and today, Neville's Cross is just a stump protected by a railing. More philanthropically still, Neville donated a choir screen (still known as the Neville Screen) to Durham Cathedral. In return, the bishop and prior permitted their patron and his wife (and later his heir and his wife, as well) to be buried within the cathedral, the first time a layman had been thus honoured. Unfortunately, some Scots prisoners who were impounded in the cathedral in 1651 'utterlye defaced' the Neville tombs in the name of David II.[28]

From our point of view, the Lanercost chronicler ominously ends his long work with the battle of Neville's Cross, noting in his last paragraph that 'my lord Henry de Percy being ill', Umfraville and Neville patrolled the Marches without him.

Knowing for certain what disease or sickness afflicted Percy is impossible, but several clues may point the way: first, he was about forty-five years old, a mature age for the time; second, probably in 1349 and definitely in 1352 (see below), he was again taken ill; third, on all three occasions, it happened during the winter; fourth, he participated in an invasion of Scotland in May 1347, yet he undertook no arduous duties between Neville's Cross (October 1346) and the early summer of the following year, or throughout 1349. Typical of Percy's less strenuous activities during his recuperation was a letter he wrote to Pope Clement VI, on behalf of the prior and convent of Durham, begging His Holiness to allow the prior to take over the church of Hemingbrough and its revenue, as the convent had suffered mightily from warfare since Edward I's death in 1307.[29] By October 1350, he was back on his feet, and for the next year was constantly engaged in negotiations with the Scots.[30]

It is tempting to ascribe Percy's illness to the Black Death, but that plague did not arrive in England until 1348, and 1352 was not a plague year. Moreover, it was the wrong season and there are no reports of people in Percy's circle dying; his was an isolated case. Was he wounded in battle? Perhaps, but would not the chronicler record this as a mark of honour in the defence of England? It is equally unlikely that he suffered a heart attack – medievals always mentioned these frightening 'strokes' and 'shakes'. The chances are, then, that each time a mere cold turned into pneumonia or bronchitis.

The final years of Percy's life were victorious ones for the English, providing some cheering respite from his weakening health. By December 1346, he was able to travel to London with sixteen other Northern lords to discuss Scotland's future with the king.[31] In May 1347, Edward Balliol marched out of Carlisle at the head of 3360 men, including Percy (who, with Neville, had contracted to serve Balliol with 180 men-at-arms and 180 archers in January),[32] and reached Falkirk without encountering any resistance. Neville's Cross had so cowed the Scots that none was to be found. They even bought a truce, to last until September, for the unaffordable price of £9000. Although the Scots still held the castles of Dunbar, Edinburgh and Stirling (whose beleaguered garrison had surrendered in 1342), the sheriffdoms of Roxburgh, Peebles and Dumfries, as well as the forests of Jedburgh (much to Percy's relief, no doubt), Selkirk and Ettrick, all reverted into English hands. Nearly all the Scottish gains of the pre-Neville's Cross years had slipped away.[33]

Scottish weakness may be partially ascribed to Robert Stewart, who was revealingly elected 'king's lieutenant', not the more exalted guardian, by the surviving magnates, owing to his power rather than his military and civil aptitude. The Scottish chroniclers' silence on his accomplishments indicates how he was regarded. For the knights, however, the vacancies in the nobility provided opportunities for advancement; one, Sir Robert Erskine, was propelled upwards to the position of chamberlain, where he played a leading role for the next generation. Another development of Stewart's administration was his appointment of sub-guardians, usually in the Gaelic west and Hebrides, who, over time, would become allied or related to Stewart, giving him a Highland power base for his later manoeuvres with the southern-inclined Balliol and King David.[34]

For the moment, however, the Scots were wise to leave off fighting. A far more virulent enemy had appeared across the Border: the Black Death. London was made a 'Nomanneslond' in 1348.[35] The last words ever written by one Welsh poet afflicted with the plague described the fatal buboes that swelled on the neck, armpits and groin: 'It is of the form of an apple, like the head of an onion, a small boil that spares no one. Great is its seething, like a burning cinder, a grievous thing of an ashy colour.'[36] Within a week this stricken individual would have been dead, unless he had contracted the disease's pneumonic form, in which case a high fever would have killed him off in two days.

Meanwhile, negotiations proceeded fitfully over David, Douglas and other high-ranking figures who were held prisoner. The English Parliament in 1348 made it a condition of granting taxation that 'David Bruce, William Douglas, and the other chief men of Scotland, are in no manner to be set free, either for ransom or upon their word of honour'. Edward, preferring concessions and cash from the Scots, ignored the Parliament and used Neville for some secret diplomacy. Neville was to work on Balliol, the main obstacle (understandably) to the repatriation of David and Douglas, although Stewart was in no hurry to face his royal uncle. If David returned, he would be unceremoniously ejected from power. More compellingly for the cash-strapped Scots, David was suffering grievously from his battle-wounds and might die in the near future. If a kingly ransom was paid and David then died on Scottish soil, the money would have been wasted. For all concerned then, apart from David, patience was the key.

But why was Neville the leading negotiator? By right, seniority and experience, it should have been Percy, but his omission in Edward's memoranda to Neville and his absence from active duty sends a strong signal that the ageing and ailing warlord-diplomat was confined to bed, suffering another serious bout of illness, possibly either bronchitis or pneumonia. It was at this time (13 September 1349) that he drew up his will.

In late 1350, Edward had released Douglas – such were the gentlemanly ways of medieval diplomacy – for a special mission to inform the Scots that David might be released on the payment of £40,000. But Douglas knew nothing of an encrypted protocol in the sealed letter he carried. It stated that Edward would return all his conquered Scottish territory on two main conditions: first, that if David – who must additionally swear that Edward was his feudal superior – died without lawful issue, the Scottish throne would pass to one of Edward's younger sons, probably John of Gaunt. This condition cunningly appealed to David's wish to avenge himself on Stewart, his heir-presumptive, by cutting him out of the will, so to speak. Second, the rights and lands of the New Disinherited – that is those granted Scottish estates since the beginning of David's reign – must be respected. To Edward, the New Disinherited (including Percy again, but not Thomas Wake, who had died in 1349) comprised an emotional point of honour. Throughout 1351, Percy – now recuperated – was involved in the Anglo-Scottish negotiations to thrash out the terms of David's release.[37]

In February 1352, David was paroled to persuade the Scottish Parliament to accept the terms. Here things become extremely murky (see especially Chapter 11). Nobody knows the degree of David's enthusiasm for these demands. He might have been willing to change the line of succession but never would he consider English overlordship. Still reasonably young, he might even himself produce a natural heir. As for Edward, he was hoist by his own petard, for if David was to recognise his lord paramountcy and sign away the line of succession then, of necessity, he must be officially acknowledged as king, something the English Chancery refused to accept. Balliol, as usual, got the short end of the stick; for him, if David was recognised as king, then farewell the throne (again).

The Scottish Parliament convened in late February 1352 to consider the terms. A surprising compact now emerged between Balliol and Stewart, for both realised they would lose equally by an Anglo-Scottish deal returning David. They turned to the French for aid, but received only the promise of men and money should David invade his own kingdom with English backing, a highly unlikely scenario. In the end, the Parliament rejected the proposals and in March David returned to the Tower of London to await further negotiations for his release. He would not leave his gilded prison until 1357.[38]

Douglas, on the other hand, had never ceased raging at his ill luck; he had been cooling his heels in England since 1346 only because David and his friends had ignored his advice about invading Northumbria and meeting the English in battle. On 17 July 1352, Douglas, heartily displeased by David's forced proposal to hand Scotland over to John of Gaunt, came to an agreement with the hated Edward. Once restored to his Liddesdale lands, he would, humiliatingly, allow English forces free passage in the event of war but, never a traitor, he refused to accept Edward's demand that, if necessary, he should fight for England against his countrymen.

And so in mid-July 1352, the grand old man of Scottish resistance returned to what was left of the kingdom and prepared to retire to his estates. During his sojourn in England, however, his godson and namesake, who, it may be remembered, had been cheated by Douglas in 1342 out of his rightful inheritance of the lordship of Liddesdale, had returned from France. A year later, the elder Douglas was travelling alone through Ettrick forest when William Douglas the Younger and some heavily armed toughs ambushed him, leaving the bloodied corpse lying in the dirt. William Douglas had waited ten years for this opportunity, and it glaringly shows the frightful implacability of the Douglas dynasty. Generation after generation of Douglases were lauded by the chroniclers, both for their unswaying loyalty to Scotland and for their fighting prowess; this younger Douglas was called 'exceedingly warlike' by Fordun, while his son was 'a most ferocious knight and a permanent danger to the English'. Another 'indefatigably harried the English as much by land as by sea. This man was black in colour...of gigantic physique...[he] reduced the power and increased the fear of the English that were against him'.[39] Since the Percys doggedly held on to their little isle of Englishness – Jedburgh and its surroundings, which abutted the Douglas patch – until 1403–4, they had clearly not chosen their hereditary and territorial enemies wisely.

Henry Percy was not destined to see his old foe assassinated. Evidently recovered from his most recent sickness, he was staying at Warkworth Castle, where he received his last orders on 1 February 1352: 'to treat with the Scots for the ransom of David II and final peace'.[40] According to the chronicler of Alnwick Abbey, on 26 February 1352, when about to depart on his mission, Percy was 'detained, as though by slight sickness [and] died unexpectedly, and was honourably buried in the said abbey'.[41] He was fifty-one. His stately and solemn burial must have been a moving sight.

According to his will, he left 50 marks (about £33) for wax candles to be burnt around his body, 20 shillings for 200 priests to say Masses (a rather parsimonious sum for one so wealthy) and 100 shillings for oblations at the funeral. A degree of guilt, or remorse, seems to have afflicted Percy in his final years. Many religious establishments were enriched by his bequests, especially Alnwick Abbey, to which he had grown increasingly attached in the later 1340s and early 1350s. He set aside 1000 marks (around £660) in florins – a useful international currency – for a planned pilgrimage to the Holy Land; if his heir went in his stead, the money was to be his. The rest of Percy's children received legacies; his youngest daughter Isabel, as was mentioned earlier, was bequeathed a magnificent copy of Aelianus' *De Natura Animalium*, whose moral was that 'animals are guided by Reason, and from them we may learn contentment, control of the passions, and calm in the face of death' – a prime consideration for Percy, as his will was drawn up when he was very sick and perhaps looked unlikely to recover. Just as touchingly, alongside £20 to be distributed to the poor on the way to his place of burial, Percy established a fund of £200 to reimburse any man who lived in any part of England (not Scotland, be it noted) who had cause to complain of his property ever being seized or stolen by anyone working in Percy's service. It is not known whether this fund was ever drawn upon.[42]

CHAPTER ELEVEN

Adventures Abroad

Henry Percy and the Hundred Years War

In my youth the ... English were taken to be the meekest of
the barbarians. Today they are a fiercely bellicose nation ...
[who] have reduced the entire kingdom of France by fire and
sword to such a state that I, who had traversed it lately on
business, had to force myself to believe that it was the same
country I had seen before.

PETRARCH (1360)

Born about 1319–20, Henry Percy had passed his thirtieth birthday
before gaining control of the family's estates. It had been an aggravating-
ly long wait, and for almost a decade Percy diverted his energies into
foreign adventures, just as nineteenth-century sons sought glory in the
farthermost reaches of the empire. He was the first Percy to spend substantial periods overseas (apart from William Percy's ill-starred Crusade
in the 1090s), departing in 1339 for France, aged about nineteen – the
usual age for a noble to take up arms professionally. Before that date
(apart from his marriage to Mary Plantagenet, daughter of Henry of
Lancaster, in September 1334) we know nothing of his activities.

Much of his time would have been spent training for war or gaining
military experience on the Marches, where he may have imbibed the sort
of advice given to ambitious young knights by Sir Geoffroi de Charny in
1352: 'You will have to put up with great labour before you achieve
honour from this employ: heat, cold, fasting, hard work, little sleep and
long watches, and always exhaustion.' When the battle comes, 'You will
needs be afraid often when you see your enemies bearing down on
you ... and you do not know best how to protect your body. Now you see
men slaughtering one another ... and your friends dead whose corpses lie
before you. But your horses are not killed, you could well get away ... If
you stay, you will have honour ever after: if you flee you dishonour
yourself. Is this not a great martyrdom?'[1]

Handed a sword before he was ten, by the time he was fourteen or
thereabouts Percy would have almost certainly read Vegetius' *Epitoma Rei
Militaris*, a summary of previous Roman writings on war and the medieval

nobility's most authoritative textbook. Vegetius recommended that trainee knights learn how to jump high, run fast, swim powerfully and use heavy weapons to develop strength in the upper torso. As for sword-fighting, knights must understand that thrusts cause more damage than strokes. Participation in tournaments and rigorous practice at the quintain, or target, would have painfully borne out this lesson.

Alongside his military training, Percy would have acquired the learning and bearing expected of a noble. His was the last generation to write, speak and read French naturally from childhood. From the 1350s onward, as the Hundred Years War set in, France was portrayed as England's hereditary enemy and its language was slowly being replaced by English. Indeed, the English were already acquiring a Continental reputation for their bad French, a sort of medieval Franglais. Chaucer, in the final three decades of the fourteenth century, sealed English as the native tongue of royalty, aristocrats and commoners alike, and by the beginning of the fifteenth century the nobility had ceased to speak French at home, or to use it in letters and administrative documents.

From the day he was born, religion permeated Percy's daily life. Even the alphabet was presented with a cross at the beginning and 'Amen' written at the end, children terming it the 'Christ-Cross Row'. Books on courtesy were distributed to boys (girls received similar instructions appropriate to their sex) to teach them how to eat, drink and behave in a polite manner. Hair must be combed, ears cleaned, nails cut, clothes befitting the effeminate or the low-born avoided, juice wiped away before it flowed down the chin and so forth.

Depending on the strength of his devotional convictions, Percy might abstain from meat on Wednesdays, Fridays and Saturdays, and through-out Lent. Instead, he would consume vast quantities of smoked, pickled or salted seafood, especially herring and shellfish. In most noble house-holds, fish (pike, eel, trout, lampreys – a surfeit of which apparently fin-ished off King Henry I – and bream, mostly) featured regularly on the menu. Meat, apart from beef and a few other exceptions, varied with the seasons and the occasion. Tongue was eaten early in the year, lamb in the spring, rabbits in the autumn and winter. Veal, piglets and boar were saved for feasts and special occasions. Birds like duck, woodcock, geese and partridges were frequently eaten by the nobility and gentry. Herons, in particular, were a very upper-class dish. Tripe, offal, hooves of oxen and other monstrosities were regarded as delicacies. Fruit and vegetables were not highly esteemed, although garlic, pears and plums proved tempting. Dairy products, apart from eggs, which everybody liked, were reserved for women and children. Spices were especially useful for disguising English cooking (Scots was famously worse, unless one thrived on oatmeal); the typical noble and gentry household stocks included pepper, sugar, cinnamon, saffron, liquorice, vinegar and mustard. Everyone drank wine each and every day (sometimes all day).

By the time Percy left for the Continent, in the words of Nicholas Orme, his upbringing 'had taught him behaviour appropriate to a wide range of people and circumstances. As occasion demanded he could be deferential, friendly, ceremonious and commanding...[and] was conscious of the need to speak clearly and effectively. He paid attention to his personal health and hygiene, and was careful of his table-manners. He was conventionally devout...[but] he had also been moulded by secular values from his earliest years, and religious teaching had to compete for his allegiance with the dictates of rank, privilege, wealth and power... [He] could dance, sing and sometimes play an instrument...The consciousness of his high birth and resources of men and money could make him jealous of his status and arrogant to others.'[2]

As for the rest of Percy's brothers, Richard was granted Seamer in Yorkshire, but died childless shortly after Henry's marriage. Thomas entered the Church, eventually becoming bishop of Norwich. Another three males were born in the mid-1330s, two of whom died childless twenty years later and the last in infancy. In addition, his uncle, Sir William, died without issue. Unless young Henry produced an heir, then, the Percy estates would be divided between Percy's four sisters and their husbands. Some years later, as we shall see, the desired son was born.

The Hundred Years War: the Early Years

The Anglo-Scottish war, as we have seen, was not merely a bilateral conflict between two states, but it requires knowledge of the civil war between the Bruce and Balliol factions to make it properly comprehensible. Moreover, France's role in this tumultuous period of Anglo-Scottish relations has been reassessed.[3] Similarly, the Hundred Years War was a triangular war in which Scotland formed a vital side. Indeed, Henry Percy *le fitz* provided a perfect microcosm of the Anglo-Franco-Scottish war. Unlike his father, who specialised in March defence, young Percy was active on both fronts with equal tenacity.

As in all wars, the outbreak of the Hundred Years War lacks a single cause, but some fundamental issues do stand out, most prominently the status of English kings as vassals of the French Crown as the condition for holding the duchy of Aquitaine (the English used the term,

'Gascony', almost interchangeably with that of Aquitaine). This arrangement was becoming increasingly tenuous. The 1259 Treaty of Paris had laid down that the English kings enjoyed the title and rights of dukes of Aquitaine in exchange for performing liege service, but English kings, as independent sovereigns in their own country, were understandably reluctant to kneel before another sovereign, just as the French kings were discovering that treating another king, especially Edward III, not as an equal but as a vassal, exacerbated the problem of controlling his behaviour. Similarly, the French Capetians – who were becoming more insistent on centralising power in Paris and upholding their rights as overlords – were exasperated by London's belief that Aquitaine, an autonomous territory, answered only to London.

Edward I and Edward II were consistently reluctant to acknowledge their homage, so provoking the French king into declaring the duchy confiscate in 1294 and 1324, when only Queen Isabella's intervention prevented a full-blown war. Edward III, his attentions occupied by Scotland, had grudgingly paid homage in 1329 and 1331. Ironically, it was the Disinherited's success in the North that relit the Continental fuse. By deposing David II and placing Edward Balliol on the throne, they triggered the Auld Alliance at a time when a virile king of the new Valois dynasty, Philip VI, sought military success to cement his dominance, including a possible invasion of Gascony. It was Philip, after all, who urged David to settle in at Château Gaillard in 1334 and funded his small court. In the 1330s, France had sent secret supplies of arms and food to the beleaguered Scots, and there was once a plan to transport 1200 French men-at-arms and 20,000 serjeants to the Scottish Lowlands. Moreover, aware of the 1326 agreement of mutual aid between Robert I and Charles IV, Philip took up David's cause and began building an armada to batter the English coast. In the meantime, he warned Edward that the issue of the Scottish succession must figure in future Anglo-French negotiations. Thus, every English/Balliol success across the Border in the early 1330s prompted the French to step their military preparations up a gear, as did every failure.

By 1335, when English power in Scotland reached its zenith, Philip's stance became more threatening, increasingly so after the wasteful Roxburgh campaign and the disaster at Culblean highlighted Edward's weakness. In 1336, for instance, shortly after Douglas and Moray had begun razing English castles, Philip agressively sailed his fleet from the Mediterranean to the Normandy ports. A year later, on 24 May 1337, Philip accurately claimed that his English vassal was sheltering his mortal enemy, Robert of Artois,[4] and confiscated the duchy of Aquitaine. As an additional warning, the French fleet raided Southampton, and Philip drew up plans to attack the cross-Channel wine and salt trade. As a result, Edward temporarily forbade wool exports for fear of seizure by the French, and extended royal protection to the worried merchants plying the route between England and Flanders.[5] Philip's aggression stirred up invasion fears as well, and Edward ordered that in Kent and fifteen other maritime counties a special church-bell ringing procedure be implemented, to signal that the French were coming.[6] He also established a commission to investigate those keepers of the coast and arrayers of men who, it was alleged, had basely fled with their men at the time of the Southampton raid – called a 'disgraceful neglect of duty'.[7]

Angered by the French overreaction, Edward decided he would throw off the ancient shackles of homage to Philip and get his lands back. At about this time, one of Edward's learned clerks drew his attention to the twelfth-century chronicle of William of Newburgh, who had written of the reigns of King Stephen and Edward's ancestor Henry II. Seized with admiration at Henry II's acquisition of Aquitaine (actually, he gained it through marriage to Eleanor of Aquitaine) and fascinated by his Normano-English genealogy, Edward III envisaged recreating an empire that, in William of Newburgh's words, had once 'extended from the far border of Scotland to the Pyrenees'. Edward even ordered a special copy of the work for his library, which by the time he died boasted twenty books, thirteen of which recited tales of chivalric romance.

He audaciously drummed up a strong claim to the French throne itself. Through his mother, Queen Isabella, the last Capetian king and Philip's predecessor, Charles IV, was Edward's uncle. Moreover, the great Philip IV was his grandfather, whereas Philip VI was Charles's cousin but, crucially, *through the male line*. That Edward's claim to the throne descended through the weaker female line did not daunt him; on 26 January 1340, he would formally assume the title, 'King of England and France', and ordered letters patent recording so to be affixed to church doors throughout the country.

This was much more than mere empty vanity. As late as 1314, King Louis X had judged that 'reason and natural law instruct us that in default of male heirs females should inherit... in the same way as males'. So if Isabella did not succeed, her right could pass to her son, the nearest male heir to the late Charles IV. So persuasive was Edward's claim that it was supported by a number of French doctors of civil and canon law. Moreover, as duke of Aquitaine and count of Ponthieu, Edward could claim to be just as French as Philip. Crucially, as self-acknowledged king of France, Edward theoretically possessed full sovereign control of French lands, including Gascony, which automatically cancelled out the necessity to pay homage. Moreover, Edward was supported by the Holy

Roman Emperor Ludwig IV and the princes of the Netherlands and Flanders, both cloth-making countries relying on England for wool. In 1338, the Emperor bestowed on Edward the splendid title of 'Imperial Vicar-General', giving him the authority to order Ludwig's vassals to fight against France. Meanwhile, Philip, rapidly finding himself hemmed in from all sides, saw his only real trump card, Scotland, eroding in value during the lackadaisical guardianship of Stewart. Nevertheless, Edward's grand alliances were costing a fortune. As the Emperor and the duke of Brabant were each promised the unaffordable sum of £60,000 for their aid, Edward was obliged to pawn the Great Crown of England to moneylenders, with the earls of Lancaster, Northampton and Warwick standing surety for it.

In 1338, Edward crossed to friendly Flanders, intending to push southward into France. Henry Percy *le fitz* was placed in the king's division, the third, which was the mightiest. The dukes of Gueldres and Brabant commanded the other two. The English tarried in Antwerp, and not until the late summer of 1339 did they besiege the well-victualled fortress of Cambrai with little to show for the effort. Here they employed a strategy from the Scottish wars. Bands of men led by knights like Percy plundered and destroyed every village in the vicinity in an effort to break the enemy's will. In jubilant mood, Edward wrote to his eldest son and the regency council 'that [the] country is clean laid waste [of] corn and cattle and other goods [to a] breadth of ... fourteen leagues of country'. Horrified at his savagery, the Pope intervened and paid 6000 florins to relieve the suffering wrought by the invaders. But Cambrai did not yield.

Breaking off the siege, Edward and his allies marched expectedly to Buironfosse, where the French were actually hoping to meet them in battle – such civilised behaviour made a welcome change from the dastardly guerrilla attacks of the Scots. Both armies formed into their battle order, and then nothing happened until noon when a hare appeared in front of the French lines, causing the ranks to coo and shout. Those at the back, unfortunately, mistook their cries for the signal to attack and hurriedly donned their helms and armed themselves. (The earl of Hainault, panic-stricken, created fourteen knights on the spot, who were afterwards mercilessly teased as the 'Knights of the Hare'.) Meanwhile, Philip's councillors were debating what to do. A messenger from Philip's cousin, the king of Sicily, 'a great astronomer and full of great science', decided the issue. The stars had told the Sicilian that 'if the French king ever fought with King Edward of England, he should be discomfited'. At this heavenly warning, Philip reluctantly withdrew and disbanded his army, but his ministers consoled the miffed king by saying 'how right nobly he had borne himself, for he had valiantly pursued his enemies'. As for Edward, he left a skeleton army under the earl of Salisbury in Flanders and returned home to work on raising the funds for another campaign. And so ended Henry Percy's first experience of abroad.[8]

The following year was far more exciting thanks to the victory at Sluys, the greatest naval battle of the fourteenth century. On 22 June 1340, leaving at 6 a.m. from Orwell, Edward and his barons set sail for Flanders only to find their passage blocked by 'so great a number of ships that their masts seemed to be like a great wood'. It was the French fleet – anchored and chained together. Emerging from his quarters aboard the flagship *Cog Thomas*, Edward declared to his worried admiral, 'I have long desired to fight with the Frenchmen, and now shall I fight with some of them by the grace of God and Saint George.' Ignoring the preponderance of French ships (some 200 against Edward's 150, many of which were transports), he placed his largest galleys in front and ordered his captains to steer with the wind and sun behind them. In the meantime, he packed the decks, the forecastles and aftercastles (literally, simple wooden castles built at the bow and stern) with archers equipped with rapid-firing longbows supported by men-at-arms for close-quarter fighting. Some climbed to the railed crow's nest (topcastle) atop the single mast, winching aloft their weapons and stones to rain down on the enemy. (Cannons were virtually unknown at this time, although the ship *All Hallow's Cog* was armed with a small piece firing lead pellets. The real revolution in artillery would not take place until the early sixteenth century, when just one of Henry VIII's larger ships could have outgunned an entire medieval fleet.)

Closing rapidly on the French 'Great Army of the Sea', as it was known, the archers fired into the dense crowds while the men-at-arms threw grappling hooks over the side and thrust their spears amid the French crossbowmen, who were laboriously firing with the blinding sun in their eyes. 'The battle was right fierce and terrible ... for on the sea there is no recoiling nor fleeing; there is no remedy but to fight and to abide fortune, and every man to show his prowess.' Percy took stout part in the hand-to-hand fighting, a novel and unsettling experience for all concerned (especially for a shipload of English 'countesses, ladies, knights' wives and other damsels', travelling to see the queen at Ghent). When the soldiers and barons boarded, they spared no man; many of the enemy who jumped into the sea drowned or were later clubbed to death by Flemings waiting on the beach. Of the 213 French ships, 190 were captured, and between 16,000 and 18,000 Frenchmen lost their lives, including both their grand admirals. Edward later informed his son that each tide washed ashore a fresh batch of corpses. The killing over and victory sealed, 'the king all night abode in his ship before Sluys, with great noise of trumpets and other instruments'.[9]

His jubilation was short-lived. The land campaign spluttered to a halt outside Tournai, as we saw in the previous chapter, choked by a chronic lack of funds. At one point, the earls of Northampton, Derby and Warwick were arrested and thrown into a debtors' prison. To break the deadlock, Edward challenged 'Philip de Valois' (this was considered an offensive way to refer to a king) to 'decide their quarrel by single combat, by a 100-a-side combat or a general engagement'.[10] Curtly dismissing this approach to one 'Philip de Valois', 'the King of France refuses to acknowledge the challenge as directed to him, considering King Edward's invasion of France as contrary to his duty to him as his liege lord, and intends to drive him out of the kingdom'.[11] And so he did, primarily owing to Edward's worsening domestic problems. Although planning to starve Tournai into submission, Edward's men were mutinous after eleven weeks without pay, and he had to obtain short-term funds at 20 per cent interest. After seeing the country wasted for fifteen miles around, and undergoing a bombardment by slingshot, Tournai, like Cambrai, did not surrender. Following an unsuccessful attack on the city, Edward's allies were prepared to abandon him, with the duke of Brabant's army threatening to walk away. Philip, who wished to avoid a battle, succeeded in extracting a truce to last until 24 June 1341.[12] For this ignoble peace, Edward did not blame his allies, but his ministers and regency council in England (among whom Percy senior was numbered – see the previous chapter – which must have made for some cutting remarks and basilisk stares directed at his embarrassed son). The grand army left for Ghent, where Edward faced his creditors. Insisting on cash, they rejected his offer of 12,000 sacks of wool. With his credit shot, Edward heard of the council's alleged abuses in his absence,[13] flew into one of his rages, and in late November 1340 arrived unannounced as we previously saw at the Tower of London at midnight. Other barons trickled home over the coming months, including Percy, who must have been back in the country by February 1341. Percy's first child, another Henry Percy, was conceived while visiting his wife in the North and was born on 10 November 1341.

Percy's personal happiness was marred by Edward's disastrous fortunes. His fragile alliance with the Low Countries disintegrated, with only Flanders remaining faintly loyal. The Holy Roman Emperor, irritated at not receiving enough of his promised bounty, revoked Edward's imperial vicarship in June 1341.[14] Scotland was falling back into Scottish hands, the return of David II in June making this a very displeasing month. In France, Ponthieu and most of the duchy of Aquitaine had already been lost. To cap it all, Edward had blown about £500,000 so far on his quarrel with Philip, and had borrowed another £400,000. Primarily owing to

Edward's erratic repayments, the Peruzzi and Bardi banks – the ones that had discreetly handled Despenser the Younger's accounts decades before – failed a few years later, breaking the back of the Florentine banking industry. The Hundred Years War might have ended there and then, except that the French were in even worse straits than the English. The richest province, Flanders, had virtually seceded from the kingdom; much of northern France lay wasted; taxes were heavier than ever; and the currency had plummeted to 40 per cent of its pre-war value. Crucially, however, Edward retained the loyalty of his barons, giving him the wherewithal to continue the war if needs be, whereas Philip, conversely, was mistrusted by many of his magnates and knights.[15] Moreover, by mid-1341, despite his continuing financial woes, Edward had brought the half-heartedly rebellious regency council to heel, marking a return to royal authority. Reinvigorated, Edward confidently wrote, 'My power has not been laid so low and the hand of God is not yet so weak that I cannot by His grace prevail over my enemy.' For good measure, he informed Parliament that the next phase of the war would last for many years. Preparations began to amass another army of 13,500 men with 9000 archers.

Archers were to prove Edward's most decisive weapon in the coming conflict. Compared to a Continental crossbowman's two bolts in a minute, a skilled longbowman could release up to *twenty* arrows in the same time. Each archer carried about 100 steel-tipped arrows, replenished by runners when necessary (in 1359, 850,000 arrows were supplied to the Tower). The archers' hierarchy reflected their relative rates of fire and accuracy. At the top were the professional, mounted archers in the elite guards attached to the king, the prince and the magnates. In coloured livery and half-armour (the rustic temporary soldiers wore leather jerkins) and carrying seasoned bows, these well-paid professionals received privileges from their lords like rights of pasture or gifts of timber. During the century, like the diminishing distinction between knight and esquire, the difference between these mounted archers and the men-at-arms faded, as both became drawn from the same social class, that of respectable county yeomen. The indenture system (paid, short-term contracts between commander and volunteer), which had replaced the last vestiges of the feudal summons since the 1320s, professionalised war during the fourteenth century, and in return for faithful and recurring service, a mounted archer might rise to become, ultimately, a knight; in some cases, even a captain.[16]

Of the other, more occasional archers, including the infantry, about one in ten were released felons (three-quarters of whom had been jailed for manslaughter or murder) who hoped to earn their pardon. Percy's

Northumbrian company, however, reflected its Border background and appears to have contained a far greater than average proportion of killers, rapists, thieves and outlaws. The Rolls show Percy's willingness to recommend his men for pardons in return for sterling service in the king's wars across the sea. Northumbrians like Robert atte Kirke of Brantingham (who murdered the cooper Robert Plumton); Richard de Aclyngton (who stoutly served at the 'munition of the king's castle of Rokesburgh' but had killed John Taillour in 'hot conflict and not of malice', according to a defensive Lord Percy); and John Plummer (who killed Robert Epworth and stole his horse, saddle and bridle but did 'good service in the wars of France' for Percy): all these and more received pardons at Percy's request. These, then, were the fine upstanding Englishmen who defended Edward III's honour on the battlefield – but God help the Frenchman whose village they ransacked.[17]

Simply keeping the men in line required fearsome discipline. Yet military life was not altogether a miserable experience. Percy and his ilk may have inflicted fatal punishment on miscreants, but for the rest, they were generally allowed to pillage, drink and rape at will after a successful siege to keep their spirits up. During the campaign, quartermasters strove to prevent unscrupulous innkeepers overcharging the rank and file or watering down the staggering quantity of beer they imbibed. Many men usually ate better than they did at home (beef, pork, mutton, wheat cakes, peas, beans, herrings and cheese were army staples). Indeed, the majority of them returned to their counties safe and sound, laden with loot, and many volunteered for further duty.

The War Continues

On 30 April 1341 John III, duke of Brittany, died, less than two months before the Anglo-French truce expired. Another clash was likely, for the succession was disputed between his half-brother, John de Montfort, and his niece, Joan of Penthièvre, who was married to Philip's nephew, Charles of Blois, a pious, brave soldier in his early twenties. However, John III had also held the English earldom of Richmond since 1335, when his unmarried uncle, John II, had died in England after serving in Scotland and the Marches (Percy's father had served with him at Scawton Moor in 1322). The difficulty was that John III had never specified whom he wished to succeed him (although by the French law of the Crown, which excluded women, Montfort was the duke's closest blood relation); lying on his deathbed and irked by advisers' incessant questions, his last words were: 'For God's sake leave me alone and do not trouble my spirit with such things.'

As soon as the duke had been buried, Montfort arrived in Nantes, the principal city of Brittany, with 200 men. Urged on by his wife, the striking Jeanne, sister of the count of Flanders, he installed himself as duke. According to one chronicler, Jeanne possessed 'the spirit of a man and the heart of a lion'. By the summer of 1341, Montfort controlled eastern Brittany and the southern and western coasts. Edward – advised by his commanders (who knew a bridgehead when they saw one) that 'if he could conquer it, [Britanny] would be the best start that he could have for the conquest of the realm of France' – threw his weight behind Montfort.[18] But in September, Philip declared that Charles of Blois was the rightful heir and summoned an army to expel the pretender. In reply, Edward prepared to send a small expeditionary force to aid Brittany. But it was too late. The French army overwhelmed the Montfortists during the winter of 1341 and John was captured.

By February of 1342, Charles of Blois held all of Brittany apart from Rennes, which was stoutly defended by Montfort's wife. Besieged, she donned armour and rode about the town on a huge charger, prevailing upon the ladies, damsels and other women to hurl paving stones upon the attackers from the battlements. Another time, she led 300 men-at-arms into the French camp and burnt the tents. In the meantime, Jeanne sent the entire ducal treasury to England to reignite the alliance while she played for time. Edward, then engaged in Scotland, dutifully sent a small force under Walter Mauny to aid the countess, who rapturously received him. She 'feasted them the best she might, and thanked them right humbly, and caused all the knights and other to lodge at their ease in the castle and in the town, and the next day she made them a great feast at dinner'. When the French signalled that they were about to abandon the siege, according to Froissart, the countess 'kissed [Mauny] and his companions one after another two or three times, like a valiant lady'.

It was not until October that the main army under Edward arrived in Brittany. With Percy in its ranks, it swept through the south unopposed by the French, who were stuck in the east. In December 1342 Percy, as a junior officer, joined a 400-man expedition against Nantes, and participated in the inevitable raids on the surrounding countryside. Shortly afterwards, a French relief army swatted the besiegers aside and invested Nantes. The English advance team galloped back to Edward without having done much of note, although Edward's aim seems to have been merely to draw the French closer. Although the two armies were only eighteen miles apart, again the French shied away from battle, believing that Edward's army (some 5000 men) was far more powerful than it actually was. Yet another truce, the Truce of Malestroit, was patched together to last until 29 September 1346.

Edward's intervention revived English spirits. Although Montfort remained in prison, large parts of Brittany were satisfyingly reliant on English aid for survival. In return, Edward could establish a residential lieutenant to keep an eye on things and a military governorship in Brest, both paid for by the Bretons. Control of Brest ensured the safety of the trade routes between England and Gascony, and provided a useful jumping-off point for any future invasion. The rest of Brittany, however, had fallen into a civil war crammed with skirmishes and raids between Montfortists and those lords loyal to Charles. Not until 1365 was the succession resolved in favour of Montfort's son, John, who finally defeated an exasperated Charles. As for the redoubtable countess, she departed Brittany in the company of Edward. Within a year, she had gone insane and in October 1343 was removed to Tickhill Castle in Yorkshire, where she died thirty years later. Montfort himself was released and journeyed to England in 1345, eventually acknowledging Edward as king of France and his liege lord for Brittany.[19]

Percy's whereabouts are for the most part unknown at this time. But the scanty evidence suggests he was probably in Northumberland. For one, his wife gave birth to another boy, Thomas, in late 1343 (in December 1342, Percy had been at Nantes so presumably he returned to Northumberland early in the New Year).[20] Second, after the earl of Arundel's appointment as joint warden of the Northumberland March in 1342,[21] Percy senior – a colleague of the earl – successfully persuaded him to take his son into his retinue. Therefore Percy *le fitz* was in Northumberland throughout 1343, learning the ropes with his new master.

Thus it was that in March 1344 young Percy accompanied Arundel abroad on the king's service. Arundel's retinue is interesting for the large number of young Northern knights it contained, evidently a product of his March days. One was Richard Tempest, a Yorkshireman who would become a deputy warden of the Northumberland March, keeper of Berwick and other posts within the Percy sphere of influence. Another was Emericus, son of Sir Thomas Rokeby, the sheriff of Yorkshire who would see service at Neville's Cross (see the previous chapter). Also present was Sir William Percy, Percy *le fitz*'s sole uncle, who would later fight in the same battle. Above all these, as heir presumptive to the pre-eminent Northern dynasty (excepting the Lancasters, whose interests were too thickly spread over thirty English counties, three Welsh counties and twenty-three castles in the North and West to be counted as pure Northerners), young Percy stood imperiously high. All these men had letters of protection for one year.[22]

Arundel's destination was Gascony, which was crying out for an administrative and financial rehauling. 'Ever since the king's return from the continent at the end of 1340 he had been deluged with petitions from damaged towns, dispossessed landowners, unpaid soldiers and disappointed men with grudges and unfulfilled ambitions.'[23] There was enough wrong in Gascony to occupy Arundel and Percy for years, but it was there that Arundel first became enamoured with a woman who would drag him into one of the fourteenth century's nastiest divorce cases. A few months after his arrival, Arundel met Eleanor, widow of Lord John Beaumont (Henry Beaumont's son) and sister of Henry of Grosmont. Unfortunately, Arundel was still married to Isabel, daughter of Despenser the Younger, and had a son and two daughters. Extraordinarily, Arundel began proceedings to annul the marriage. He successfully claimed to the Pope that he and Isabel had married solely because of their families' wishes, and had later renounced their vows 'but were forced by blows to cohabit, so that a son was born'. Arundel obtained the papal mandate on 4 December 1344 and married Eleanor two months later, on 5 February 1345.[24] As the earl attended a tournament at Hereford and a session of the king's council in January 1345, he had clearly left unfinished business in Gascony to be in England.[25] Whither Arundel went, so too did Percy. And it was owing to Arundel's lechery that Percy missed one of the most glorious campaigns of the Middle Ages, a campaign that would have netted him a fortune and made him a warrior of remark.

In May 1345 Henry of Grosmont was commissioned to govern Aquitaine as the king's lieutenant.[26] Invested with full military power and starting with just a skeleton army, Henry subsequently sealed his reputation as Edward's greatest commander. After disembarking in Bordeaux on 9 August 1345, Henry tore through France almost without rest for six months. Bergerac was stormed on 24 August and Henry smashed the French at the battle of Auberoche on 21 October, taking prisoner a count, seven viscounts, three barons, the Seneschals of Toulouse and Clermont, twelve bannerets, a nephew of the Pope and innumerable knights. By the winter of that year, the English and the new earl of Lancaster (Henry of Lancaster, his father, had died in September) had retaken nearly all the territory in the south-west that had been lost earlier in the war. In the spring of 1346, Lancaster pushed northwards with only 1000 soldiers, capping his trek by taking Poitiers.[27]

Although he was Lancaster's brother-in-law (as was Arundel now), Percy was still attached to Arundel's retinue and frustratingly had to cool his heels in England while the earl amused himself. Indeed, Edward was preparing another great expedition to Flanders in the summer of 1345 to present a threat to the French in the north, and among the hundreds of knightly names chosen to go abroad, Percy's was absent.[28]

A son such as Henry Percy, probably kept on a stipend by his father, could only gaze enviously on the riches that those who fought with Lancaster brought home. Lancaster, rich before he started, was a Croesus by the end of it. At Bergerac, his personal cut of the loot came to nearly £35,000, which he subsequently lavished on his palace of the Savoy in London, whilst at Auberoche prisoners worth £50,000 were taken.[29] Gratingly, Arundel had no need for wealth, which may explain his remaining in England while others made fortunes abroad. He was in line to inherit the vast Warenne estates as his uncle, John, the current and last Warenne earl of Surrey and Sussex, was sick and without legitimate issue. (This earl was the grandson of the Earl Warenne – Percy *le fitz*'s grandfather's grandfather, who died in 1304 and was especially fond of the Henry Percy who died in 1314.) John would expire in 1347, leaving his nephew as sole heir, but Arundel only assumed the title of 'earl of Surrey' after John's widow died in 1361. Even without the Warenne bequest, Arundel was extraordinarily rich. Excessively thrifty, he ran a lucrative and politically valuable moneylending business on the side; by the end of his life, his 'clients' included the king (who owed £30,000), the Prince of Wales's widow, Joan of Kent, and twenty-one other men, including abbots and priors. Investing much of his fortune in buying twenty manors in Sussex, the earl ended up with the amazing figure of £60,000 in cash – nearly half of which was stored in cheap sacks – in the high tower at Arundel Castle.[30] To put this figure into perspective, in 1324 the total income received by the Exchequer from the entire country (including Ireland and Wales) was £60,549.[31] Thus one could say that the earl of Arundel's personal savings approached the government's nominal annual budget (not that the Edwards ever bothered balancing the books).

As we saw above, Percy's name was omitted from the list of those heading for Flanders with the king in the summer of 1345. In the event, the expedition came to nothing; just after the English fleet sailed, the pro-English regime there fell in late July. For more than a fortnight in hot weather, thousands and men and horses were stuck on the ships off Sluys. After some diplomatic discussions, Edward sailed his stinking fleet home.[32] Thereupon he calmly fixed a date for another expedition in March 1346, but with one crucial difference. Allies were bothersome, he had learnt; this time his would be a wholly English army. In turn, the invasion logistics became ever more complex: many more ships would be needed; more food, weapons (tens of thousands of sheaves of arrows, for example) and victuals stockpiled; more time allowed for embarkation and disembarkation. Horseshoes, bows, axes, bowstrings, shields, stirrups, portable ovens and mills – all had to be ready. It was once remarked that not until the Egyptian expedition of 1882 would an overseas English army be so lavishly and expertly equipped. The king's insistence on an army of 15,000 to 20,000 men – his largest ever – had worried admirals, who complained that there were insufficient vessels to transport such a force. Edward therefore directed them to amass the 1500 ships required by requisitioning anything larger than a fishing smack, rather like the 1940 withdrawal from Dunkirk in reverse. As it was impossible to organise all this in time for March, especially since the Scots were threatening trouble, the date was postponed to mid-May with the option to depart even later.

For his great invasion, which he hoped would overshadow Lancaster's exploits, Edward developed an almost neurotic mania for secrecy. Spies were sent to ferret out drunken sailors who talked too much; foreign traders were imprisoned; no man, earl or commoner, was to leave England before the fleet's departure; official paperwork was minimised; and regional sheriffs and recruiters were ordered to keep their mouths shut. Only Edward and one or two of his closest advisers knew the expedition's destination, although the smart money said Brittany or Gascony. By June, the fleet was ready (now only 750 ships, carrying between 7000 and 10,000 men, almost half of whom were longbowmen), but contrary winds delayed departure until 11 July 1346.

At dawn on 12 July, the fleet anchored off the large beach at Saint-Vaast-la-Hougue (in 1944, Allied soldiers would land next door at 'Utah Beach') on the northern peninsula of the Cotentin in Normandy. The invasion started badly. As Edward eagerly jumped from the boat, he slipped and fell flat on his face. The knights near him exclaimed that this was an evil omen, but the king, blood issuing profusely from his nose, replied, 'This is a good token for me, for the land desireth to have me.'

The French, like their German counterparts 600 years later, were utterly surprised. Believing Edward would head for Brittany or Gascony, Philip had left Normandy virtually undefended. For five days, the English disembarked the army, with the French host nowhere to be seen.[33] And what of Percy?

Percy's Decision

As late as 6 June 1346 he was numbered among Arundel's retinue, but during the voyage between Portsmouth and La Hougue he intriguingly ceased to be. Clearly, he was chafing under the earl's leadership. So, where did he go? A later memorandum notes that 'Sir Henry Percy ... served in the retinue of the King's *dilectus clericus* [beloved clerk], Philip de Weston, from the date of the disembarkation at Hogges [*sic*] until the King's arrival at Calais, and afterwards before Calais till the following Easter'.[34] Changing one's retinue bore substantial political and military implications. As a small example, it has always been assumed that at the battle of Crécy, Percy fought beside Arundel, whereas, as we shall see, he fought in the King's division.

The retinue, or 'affinity', comprised concentric (but occasionally intertwined) circles of household attendants (generally, full-time, high-level administrators), indentured retainers (usually soldiers under contract available for service abroad or otherwise in time of war) and estate officials. There would also be the usual hangers-on, known in the fifteenth century as 'well-wishers'. Lancaster, for example, retained a wardrober, treasurer, household steward, steward of lands, chamberlain, chancellor and receiver-general, and a host of attorneys-general, auditors, heralds, councillors, minstrels, servants, soldiers and at least fourteen senior valets. The magnate's motive for the retinue was largely display; the numbers signalled his influence and position.

As a body, the retinue had gradually replaced the withered feudal system of military obligation based on land ownership. Cash – in the form of wages, annuities, or rents – governed relations between men. Flexibility – to negotiate contracts, to act as a free agent – superseded stability and loyalty. For the moment, voluntary knightly service was secured through money, hope of preferment and what may be termed *residual loyalty* to certain magnates. Thus, old ties of kinship and acquaintance might produce a place in the retinue of a particular lord. Aggrieved contemporaries considered the system merely wire-pulling, log-rolling jobbery and nepotism, which it certainly was in some cases, but not all. The entire set-up depended on a developed scratch-my-back principle; as a perceptive contemporary advised: 'Accommodate the duke in his request, as you wish him to help you in time to come.'

As regards Percy, his grandfather had married a daughter of a FitzAlan earl of Arundel, his father served with an earl of Arundel on the Border; and Petworth was in Arundel country (although the system of feudal dues was now virtually obsolete, Petworth was held for twenty-two knights' fees at this time). On the other hand, Percy was perfectly willing to leave the earl's employ in search of more sumptuous opportunities with a man with whom he had no familial associations. Although Arundel was astonishingly rich, this was of little consequence to a young knight who had missed Lancaster's campaign owing to his patron's continuing peccadilloes. The split was not necessarily unfriendly; as Percy's original letter of protection had lasted for a year, his was a short-term contract, not a lifetime indenture, and he was now a free agent. It was time to part company.[35]

But who was this Philip Weston? A 'beloved clerk' doesn't sound very exciting, but he is one of the fourteenth century's great forgotten men. A born administrator, at the time, he was a far more important political figure than the earl of Arundel. As the king's confessor – men who 'were often close personal friends of the kings whose sins they absolved' – Weston was one of the eight men who had accompanied Edward on his midnight mission to the Tower of London in November 1340.

Weston would subsequently become prominent in the ministerial revolution that followed. By 1344, he was chief steward of the king's chamber, a position of immense influence. From before the Conqueror's arrival, the Chamber and Wardrobe had held the king's valuables and documents, mainly because a man's private living quarters were the safest place to store them. According to T.F. Tout, the Chamber and Wardrobe needed 'persons of responsibility and trust…If they were honest and able, they were certain, gradually, to become his [the king's] confidants and advisers'. Charged with handling the monarch's private finances, by the fourteenth century the Chamber was a private royal chancery and privy purse, fighting to stay independent of other government departments, particularly the Exchequer Treasury. The steward, especially one who was confessor as well, was the king's trusted confidant and probably knew the private Edward III better than anyone. Ostensibly, Weston audited the royal accounts, and evaluated the king's ships, jewels, armour and so on. But he was also entrusted with secret diplomatic missions, so for a young man like Percy, who wanted to be brought to the attention of the king after being left in the shade for quite a few years, attaching oneself to a leading, if non-aristocratic, bureaucrat was an excellent way of achieving that aim. Furthermore, chief clerks like Weston were granted the status of banneret, so placing them on a par with most lords, and were permitted an escort of men-at-arms and archers, totalling perhaps sixty or seventy. It was noted of Weston, for instance, that he travelled with a 'considerable retinue'.[36]

Now with his foot jammed in the royal door, Percy may have been designated a 'knight of the chamber', a term recently invented for a new class of knight. Until the middle of the fourteenth century, the knights attached to the royal household had been chosen for their fighting abilities. But from about this time, an increasingly clear distinction began to emerge between the warriors present in the great hall (the original meaning of household) and the more literate and mature knights whom the king, ensconced in his private chamber, found useful to have around.

Between 1350 and 1365, this distinction hardened and soon the style of household knight almost disappeared. Administrative matters increasingly dominated the king's time; he required not a horde of fighters, but men equally dextrous with pen and sword to help him with the growing piles of paperwork. He wanted trusted aides who could undertake delicate diplomatic missions, or provide detailed and knowledgeable advice on particular affairs of state. Unfortunately, as the account books listing the chamber knights at this time are incomplete, we cannot be sure that Percy was one.[37] 'Nevertheless, Philip Weston evidently thought him promising enough to be recruited, although far too young to be allowed into the most sensitive councils setting England's foreign and military policy. In future years, Percy's experience would stand him in good stead; after the death of his father, he would be repeatedly employed as a diplomatic envoy and negotiator.

Percy's War

In mid-July 1346, the army moved south down the peninsula and then menacingly east towards Caen, Rouen and Paris. What these barons (the vast majority were of Norman descent) thought as they traversed their ancient homeland is a mystery. Edward had commanded that any man who looted a building or church, or molested any Norman, would be executed or mutilated – an order widely disobeyed by the more unsentimental (Anglo-Saxon) soldiery.

The French were in utter disarray. The duke of Normandy was stuck in the south, and the isolated coastal garrisons were rapidly surrendering to the English. All the while, Edward was closing on Paris. Desperately trying to summon a scratch army, Philip twice implored David II in Scotland to invade the North and draw the English home. By 25 July, Edward had reached Caen, Normandy's second-largest town after Rouen and the site of William the Conqueror's castle. Rejecting calls to surrender, Caen was stormed successfully if bloodily (the archers and spearmen, unleashed, killed 2500 Frenchmen). Afterwards, a number of lords paid homage at the Conqueror's fine tomb, which would be destroyed by Calvinists in 1562. (The replacement memorial housing William's surviving thigh-bone was demolished by the revolutionaries in 1793; today a stone slab marks the site and the bone may or may not be in the grave.)[38]

Tarrying at Caen until 31 July, the English pushed slowly eastwards to Rouen, burning everything for miles on either side of the main army and reaching Lisieux unchallenged on 3 August. They would have passed through, or very close to, the village of Percy-en-Auge,[39] but whether it was damaged or not is unknown. A few days later, two emissaries from Philip offered the return of Ponthieu and Aquitaine to Edward if he held them, like his father and grandfather, as fiefs of the French Crown. This was rejected.

Surprisingly, Edward avoided the obvious plan of attack: namely a time-consuming and wasteful battle of attrition. He bypassed Philip in fortified Rouen and cleverly marched south-east towards Paris, shadowing the Seine and keeping the French on the other side. If Philip stayed where he was, he would lose Paris and be outflanked. If he moved, he would be forced to cross the Seine. On 12 August, Edward was within twenty miles of the capital, with every town and castle lying wrecked behind him. He then finessed the French into a wasteful and exhausting march so that he could cross the Seine unopposed. When Philip learnt that Edward was planning to cross at Poissy, he raced there via Paris, only to find that Edward had destroyed his temporary bridge behind him. Humiliatingly, he had to march back through Paris to cross the Seine in pursuit of Edward, who was now heading towards Flanders and Ponthieu, where reinforcements could be found for a final showdown.

Edward had heard that the duke of Normandy had broken off Lancaster's siege of Alguillon, south-east of Bordeaux, and was hastening north. Lancaster was doggedly following Normandy and hampering his rearguard, but it was inevitable that the duke's seasoned veterans would meet up with Philip's now formidable army, probably equalling Edward's in numbers, if not in experience. While the English wasted time pillaging, Philip was making twenty-five miles a day, hoping to trap Edward at the Somme – the last natural obstacle before the safety of the Low Countries – with the sea to his rear. Edward had waited too long for his battle. His men were without bread, his supply lines from Normandy were severed, his troops were exhausted by constant marching and, worse still, Edward's reinforcements and provisions, which he desperately needed, were in Kent and not waiting offshore.

Fortunately, Edward forded the Somme, guided by a locally transplanted Yorkshireman, just before Philip arrived at the other bank, keen to avenge the Seine debacle. On the night of 25 August, Edward led his men through the great forest, halted outside the village of Crécy and formed up in battle order. The moment had come. By the morning of 26 August, the French van was three miles away and closing. It stopped. Philip's commanders reported that part of the cavalry, the Genoese crossbowmen, and the auxiliaries would only arrive after midday. The infantry and the baggage-train were far behind. The more cautious counselled Philip to wait until the next morning when the entire army would be present and rested. Others, including Philip, feared that Edward would escape yet again. It was time to smash him now. It is worth remembering that when Philip had maintained a stalemate instead of seeking battle, Edward's campaign had collapsed. And each time a campaign collapsed, the cost of its successor spiralled upwards.

The English, surprisingly, were in high spirits. Edward walked among them, joining in their ribald jokes and cracking a few himself, and exhorted them to stand firm in the imminent battle. With the forest of Crécy at their backs, the English had deployed in three battles of dismounted men-at-arms and nobility on a gently sloping hill about sixty metres in height on a front measuring nearly a mile. In front, the teenaged Prince of Wales took command of the first battle (Warwick and Oxford were detailed to look after him), and next to him was the battle overseen by the earls of Northampton and Arundel. Behind them, as a reserve, was the third battle commanded by the king (using a windmill as an observation point) where Percy, attached to Philip Weston, would have taken his place. Between the two front battles was a wedge-shaped formation of longbowmen, ahead of the men-at-arms, with another phalanx on the army's outermost flanks. By jutting forward, these formations could lay down a double crossfire in front of each battle. The English also possessed about 100 small cannon, but these were of little use apart from sowing noise and confusion.

The French formed into three broad lines, one behind the other. In the leading division were about 6000 Genoese crossbowmen paid by Philip. Accompanying them were the blind King John of Bohemia, and 300 Czech and German horsemen. Following them was the 6000-strong primary cavalry division, commanded by the headstrong count of Alençon, the king's younger brother, and comprising the cream of the French nobility, who did not deign to dismount (unlike their English counterparts, who had fought on foot for decades). And lastly, there was the king's division, of possibly 6000 horse, and infantry. Over the course of the afternoon the French army swelled with thousands of late arrivals, deployed haphazardly on the wings of the cavalry.

At five o'clock in the afternoon, rain began to pour down. Philip, bewilderingly, resolved to attack and the trumpets sounded. All the English, who had been sitting down for hours to rest their legs, struggled to their feet and took their positions. The Genoese advanced tentatively, all too aware that the tall shields that protected them while reloading were piled on a faraway cart, still trundling its way towards the battlefield. They bravely advanced, firing as often as they could, but their bolts hardly reached the English lines because the rain had seeped into their bows and slackened the cords. The English archers were ordered to fire directly at the Genoese and the cannons opened up, sending grapeshot, smoke and din in all directions. With waves of arrows piercing their light armour, the Genoese fled towards their own lines.

Confronted with the spectacle of thousands of Italians in headlong flight coming directly towards them, Alençon's cavalrymen assumed the Genoese were either cowards or traitors. Behind him, Alençon could hear Philip shouting, 'Kill this riff-raff! Kill them all!' and he spurred his horse forward with the rest of the division. Philip's division, unwilling to wait, followed Alençon. The Italians were defenceless against this accelerating rush of sword-slashing French horsemen, who now approached the centre of the English line where the Prince of Wales stood with his standard-bearer. Philip and his men seemed unaware of the damage that two wings of long-bowmen can inflict on cavalry funnelling into the gap between them.

As the English men-at-arms waited, hundreds, perhaps thousands, of arrows were being loosed into the sides of the French. Wounded horses threw their riders, who were trampled by those behind. The cannon noise terrified the beasts, which veered away, colliding with each other. The shaken first arrivals crashed into the English front ranks, which didn't break – the goal of any cavalry charge – leaving knights surrounded by spearmen stabbing their mounts and trying to pull them to the ground. Once down, a knight stood no chance. His helmet would be crushed, or his visor levered open, or a sharpened blade would pierce a chink in the plate to gouge the flesh.

Fighting was fiercest near the prince, whose first battle this was. He enjoyed the mêlées and shouted encouragement to those around him. Later, worried they might be overcome, the prince, Warwick and Oxford sent a knight to the king to ask for reinforcements. 'Is my son dead or hurt or on the earth felled?' asked Edward. 'No sir, [but] he hath need of your aid,' was the reply. Edward refused to despatch the reserve; he said that the prince and his companions were on their own, instructing that the knight should 'also say to them that they suffer him this day to win his spurs; for if God be pleased, I wish this day be his and the honour thereof, and to them that be about him'. The Prince of Wales winning his spurs was the first of Crécy's great chivalric tales. Another concerned the blind King John of Bohemia and his horsemen, shouting their war-cry, 'Prague!', as they galloped towards the centre, only for the king to be dragged from his horse and killed.

Until the early evening, the French charged, struck, wheeled and struck again perhaps fifteen times. Only in the battle's fading hours did Edward release the reserve. It is highly likely that Percy saw action, if only at the tail-end of things. He would have been better off sticking with Arundel, in joint command of the second division.

By the end of the day, the French could muster neither the strength nor the morale to hazard another attack. Before them, they could see 1542 knightly corpses, slain horses and hundreds of thousands of arrows protruding at crazy angles (6000 archers could loose half a million during a battle, collectively weighing about twenty tons). Among the slaughtered glinted the heraldry of John of Bohemia and eight princes of the blood, including the counts of Alençon and Flanders, the duke of Lorraine and Philip's nephew Louis, as well as hundreds of sacrificed nobles. Weapons, shields and armour littered the ground. The terrain, sodden by rain, was dyed red. Occasionally, the English infantry had to push the piles of noble and knightly dead over to prevent their view being obscured. The cries of the wounded, lying abandoned in the field for hours, became weaker as the sun went down. Worse still, the French remnants could see the English squires bringing up fresh horses for the inevitable pursuit. The French, their infantry gone, fled. As the English chased the stragglers, they discovered the royal standard where Philip (now recuperating some miles away with an arrow in his face) had stood.

Edward had issued strict orders not to loot the dead – there was plenty of time for that later – to ensure his knights mopped up the survivors. When Percy and others returned from their mission, the supremacy of English arms was blisteringly apparent. Only forty men-at-arms had lost their lives, plus an untold number of archers. The shattered Philip, meanwhile, had reached Amiens, hysterically blaming the Genoese for the disaster. On his orders, all Genoese found in the vicinity were executed.

Local peasants were directed to dig a mass grave for the French dead. On 28 August, Edward and his commanders, clad in black, ceremonially buried the princes in the nearby abbey of Valloires. Two days later, the army marched north, leaving destroyed towns and burnt countryside behind them. As Jonathan Sumption points out, Edward realised that he had beaten the French, but he was no conqueror. His men were too few, and his garrisons too thinly spread, to act as a permanent army of occupation; so this campaign of conquest 'became a *chevauchée*, a great mounted raid passing swiftly through the country before it disappeared'. Edward faced the problem that had beset the Scots for centuries. Raids were easy and caused temporary bother, but ultimately they achieved little of consequence. It was clear now that, for a permanent foothold in France, Calais must be taken.[40]

The Siege of Calais

With the sea to the north, and moats and boggy marshes for miles around, Calais also came replete with modern defences. In English hands, it would be a funnel for troops crossing the Channel. Friendly Flanders was close, and Paris could easily be threatened. On 4 September, Edward and his vanguard encamped half a mile south. A day later, the fleet brought much-needed reinforcements, enlarging the army to between about 10,000 and 12,000 men. The army prepared for a prolonged siege and even began building a town nearby, christened Villeneuve-la-Hardie. Hovels (and brothels), mansions, stables and counting houses all appeared over the following weeks. One observer remarked that this temporary capital's orderly construction reminded him of a 'new London'.[41]

Himself facing a political crisis similar to Edward's in 1340–1, Philip was powerless to relieve Calais. His forces were either in utter disarray or pinned down by Lancaster in the south and Poitou. To make matters worse, David II's audacious gamble in the North had ended inauspiciously at Neville's Cross. There was no prospect now of Edward packing his bags and leaving.

On the other hand, the siege was taking longer than Edward expected. Although blockaded on its three landward sides by the English, Calais was still receiving fresh supplies by sea. Periodic assaults on the walls failed. By the winter, the marshes, combined with the damp and snow, provided an ideal catalyst for disease. Deserters sneaked on board ships arriving to revictual the troops. And so the wait dragged on into the spring of 1347.

In April, Edward's fleet finally managed to isolate Calais from the outside world. Now the noose could be drawn tighter. As the summer lengthened, English spirits revived, fortified by sun and fresh food, while Calais's inhabitants saw their water evaporating and their food-stocks growing rancid. Men consumed their pets and emaciated horses. In late June, the governor informed Philip that unless something was done, 'This is the last letter you will receive from me, for the town will be lost and all of us that are within it.' Unfortunately, the letter fell into English hands; Edward read it, affixed his seal and helpfully forwarded it to Philip.

However valiantly the French tried to force through supplies, they could not break the cordon. The leaders in Calais resorted to expelling 500 of the town's old, infirm, young and sick to fend for themselves. Acting according to the laws of war, the English prevented the refugees from passing through their lines and herded them back towards the town. Finally, the unlucky souls starved in a ditch in no-man's-land. By now, Edward was confident of eventual victory: reinforcements from England had increased his army to some 32,000 men (including 5300 men-at-arms, 6600 infantry and 20,000 archers) – the largest overseas force raised until the sixteenth century. Moreover, 15,000 sailors were engaged in the cross-Channel passages; many could be seconded to the army if necessary, and the Flemings had another 20,000 on the border.

Percy's movements at this juncture are interesting. Sometime in the New Year, Percy was back in England to recruit reinforcements for the Calais garrisons and in early June 1347 he had returned to France. On 20 June he left Philip Weston's retinue and joined Lancaster's glittering affinity. As he was still in his late twenties, there was only so much that Percy could achieve with Weston; over the last year, he had probably done enough poring over account books in Villeneuve-la-Hardie. Now he sought action with his brother-in-law, who was happy to take him on.[42]

Percy would have transferred from Villeneuve to Lancaster's new position at the Nieulay Bridge, a few miles south-west of Calais and the only avenue for a French approach to the town. Lancaster had peppered the ground with palisades, ditches, watchtowers and earthworks. When Philip and his scratch force of between 15,000 and 20,000 men arrived on 27 July at the heights of Sangatte overlooking the English positions, he realised instantly that relief was impossible. The marshes were impassable for cavalry, and archers from their concealed fortifications would pick off the infantry. Some skirmishing occurred between Philip's vanguard and Lancaster's division, but the bridge remained untouched.

Unwilling to risk another Crécy by attacking the entrenched English lines, Philip unsuccessfully sought a local truce to protect the lost souls locked inside Calais. On 1 August 1347, the brave defenders signalled their countrymen on the heights of Sangatte that they were about to surrender. The French army marched away that night, harried all the while by Lancaster and his cavalry.

In the morning, a messenger from Calais offered terms to Edward, who refused them outright; the town had defied him for too long to expect mercy. The governor pleaded that his men [had] 'served their sovereign as loyally as they could and as you yourself would have done in their place'. His logic appealed to the English commanders. It made sense, they told Edward, to be flexible; otherwise every English garrison chief would surrender the moment the vengeful French appeared over the hill. Showing his famed political nous, Edward relented, saying, 'My friends, I do not want to stand alone against all of you.' But someone had to be punished for Calais's intransigence. All were to be spared, but their possessions were forfeit. Furthermore six of the town's most prominent citizens were to 'come before me in their shirtsleeves, with nooses around their necks, carrying the keys of the town and they shall be at my mercy to deal with as I please'.

On 3 August, the exhausted town surrendered, and the six unfortunate 'Burghers of Calais' threw themselves on Edward's mercy. Edward ordered they be beheaded on the spot. Grudgingly dissuaded by the protests of his shocked commanders, Edward's temper was soothed by the calm words of Queen Philippa, who had travelled to France to witness the victory ('Ye make such request to me that I cannot deny you,' he said). The captives were spared, afterwards being clothed and fed at the queen's expense.

Having dispersed the French residents, Edward populated Calais with Englishmen attracted by free grants of land and houses, tax exemptions and iron-clad guarantees of protection against Philip. Within three months, 200 settlers had arrived, and London merchants established branches in the town. Edward had realised that to retain his foothold in France, economic colonisation was as crucial as military domination and administrative order. Berwick, for instance, fulfilled the same task in Scotland. A prosperous and loyal Calais, supplied from England, would act as a depot for forays deeper into the country.

Fearsome examples of what an army could achieve without having to forage for food occurred throughout August. The Prince of Wales raided Artois, and Lancaster, accompanied by his retinue, burnt Fauquembergues, a town thirty miles from Calais, after which the duke and his troops flitted into the night and back to safety. Edward wanted to launch another major invasion, but was concerned for his men, who had campaigned unceasingly for nearly a year and a half. A French pirate named Marant also showed up the weakness of the trans-Channel link. In September, he pounced on an English convoy crossing to Calais, sinking half of it and taking the rest as prize.[43]

With both sides at stalemate, Edward and Philip agreed to a nine-month truce, to last until 7 July 1348. Sometime, then, during the late summer of 1347, Lancaster and Percy sailed for England. According to his indenture, Percy served with the earl from June 1347 'till the following Easter' – in essence, a typical one-year commission, with little prospect for renewal given the new truce. After being released from his duties, at some point between Edward's return from Calais and December 1348, Percy almost certainly attended some of the triumphant victory tournaments held by the king and Lancaster around the country.[44]

The truce's timing was auspicious, in one more sense, at least. The Black Death would hit England in the summer and autumn of 1348, making any resumption of the war impossible. Owing to the fear of contact with the stricken, no Parliaments were held between April 1348 and February 1351, which prevented Edward raising taxes for campaigning. Even if he had declared a general levy, few counties could afford what would be demanded, with thousands of dead labourers rotting in the fields and villages, and the merchants glumly totting up their diminishing receipts in the fetid towns.

To re-instil financial order in the country – the labour shortage inexorably drove up wages and further contributed to a general depression – the council issued an emergency ordinance in June 1349, effectively imposing a wage freeze. In February 1351, following widespread complaints that it was being ignored, the Ordinance of Labourers was enacted as a statute with extra bite. Men would work at pre-1349 wage levels and employers were forbidden to offer more; men under the age of sixty were barred from refusing work. In exchange, prices would be kept 'reasonable'. A month later, commissioners of the peace, including Percy, were appointed in each county to police the Ordinance. His orders were to 'hear and determine trespasses against the ordinance, and continue process against those indicted thereof until they be taken, surrendered or outlawed'. Unfortunately, regulation was of little avail; even the carpenter at Knightsbridge, employed to build the stocks that held offenders against the Ordinance, had to be quietly tipped for his labour.[45]

Even so, some small-scale military operations went ahead. August 1350 saw the second naval battle of Edward's career. Percy and Lord Ralph Neville were aboard the king's ship (the prince and Lancaster commanded their own vessels) as the fleet waited near Calais for the Castilian merchant navy (then in French service). Froissart mentions that the king, in 'a gayer mood than he had ever been seen before', and snappily attired in a black velvet jacket and a matching beaverskin hat, asked for a jaunty German tune to be played so that he and his companions could sing along. When the cry came, 'Ship ahoy! And she looks like a Spaniard,' wine was ordered, singing stopped and battle-helmets donned. Fortified by the liquor, Edward ordered his helmsman to 'steer at that ship straight ahead of us. I want to have a joust at it', an action likened by a modern historian to that of a 'demented ten-year-old on the dodgems'. Ramming the Castilian flagship crippled Edward's vessel, and she began shipping water. So Edward steered alongside another Castilian and boarded it after a ferocious fight. Edward's knights threw the surviving Spaniards into the sea – very chivalrous – and occupied the ship when theirs had sunk. In the course of the day, this Anglo-Spanish running battle ended off Winchelsea, the English sinking or capturing fourteen vessels out of the forty-strong Castilian formation. The stomach-churning experience of bearing down on the enemy whilst gripping the handrails for dear life and crashing directly into his side was probably one Percy never wished to repeat. He did not spend long in Calais after the sea-fight, although he may well have joined the king that night 'in revelry with the ladies, conversing of arms and matters of love'.[46]

We may surmise that he was in England from the winter of 1350, evidently learning about estate management and accustoming himself to the local topography. This was sensible, given his prolonged absence and his father's failing health. He began to assume some of his father's traditional duties, gaining experience of benign public service and good lordship. He was, for instance, appointed to various commissions of oyer and terminer (which empowered its holders to determine indictments on specified offences, such as treasons, felonies and, occasionally, insurrections) in the North. Among the crimes that he and his fellows investigated was the kidnapping of the prebend of Barneby by a 'lay force' (Percy was authorised to 'find by inquisition the names of those who held the prebend... and to remove the lay force by such ways and means as [he] deem[ed] expedient'); the assault by a group of at least twenty-one men on the abbot of Whitby's men and servants; and the knight William Greystoke's complaint that the mayor of York, his brother and a gang of seventeen ruffians 'carried away his goods and £100 of money... and assaulted his men and servants'.[47] (Indeed, York and the surrounding area seem to have seethed with corruption and menace; in 1364, Percy was requested to investigate 'all conspiracies, confederacies, collusions and false alliances' there.)[48]

He also set about balancing the account books, a skill perhaps acquired thanks to Philip Weston. He and John Neville (Lord Ralph Neville's son, who was in his mid-teens and had been contracted to marry Percy's sister Maud since 1344) sent invoices to various knights: four of them owed Percy and (strangely) John Neville a total of 20,000 *French* florins. These debts were paid in full soon after. Why Percy and Neville were owed this respectable sum in a foreign currency is a mystery, although it may have been related to the division of the loot from a recent French campaign.[49] These transactions were probably above board – after all, they were catalogued in the official record – but twenty-five years later, John's involvement in a financial scandal (specifically, the buying up of loans at a discount) ended with his impeachment by the Commons, and dismissal from both his post as steward of the royal household and membership of the council.[50]

The Triangular War

As related in the last chapter, in February of 1352 King David was released from the Tower to present the Scottish Parliament with the latest terms for his release. By May, he was returning to an honourable confinement that would last until 1357. His route is of crucial importance. Normally he would have left Scone (the probable place for Parliament) for Edinburgh and then followed the coastal road to Berwick, Alnwick and Newcastle before setting off for London (on modern maps, the A1 is an accurate guide). Along this road, about ten miles north of Berwick, is Coldingham Priory.

As mentioned in Chapter 10, according to the chronicler of Alnwick Abbey, the elder Lord Percy, then staying at Warkworth Castle, was ordered 'to treat with the Scots for the ransom of David II and final peace'. But as he was preparing to depart at the end of February 1352, Percy unexpectedly succumbed to a 'slight sickness'. This would have been the mission upon which Percy and Lord Ralph Neville, his trusted companion, would have received David and then accompanied him down to London. But Percy's death on 26 February, a few weeks before David's arrival, meant that his son, the presumptive Lord Percy, was appointed in his stead.[51]

Edward III was currently pressing David to relinquish the succession to a Plantagenet and proclaim the English king as his feudal overlord, an age-old English royal obsession. David had no intention of agreeing, although he was more receptive to John of Gaunt succeeding (mainly because David felt a son of his own would arrive in the future). Like his two predecessors, Edward possessed a streak of wiliness, and it would be no surprise to find him fixing the odds by framing David. Percy and Neville would be the instrument, both trusted implicitly to follow orders. Percy, moreover, could utilise his drafting experience, gained under Philip Weston's tutelage.

David made slow progress along the muddy and choked winter roads. Coldingham was a convenient stopover before Berwick, and here, on 19 or 20 March 1352, Percy and Neville met the Scottish king. The result was momentous: 'Letters patent purporting to be granted by David II declaring that on that day [20 March] in the monastery of Coldingham, he had done homage and fealty to Edward III in a form recited before Henry Percy lord of Alnewick and Ranulph Neville lord of Raby, commissioners of England.'[52]

The word 'purporting' is crucial. By modern lights, the letter, including a fake seal of the Scottish royal lion, is a painfully obvious forgery. David never recognised Edward as his lord paramount at Coldingham, but Percy and Neville's being in the right place at the right time meant the forgery could be used in the future, either to blackmail David into concessions or to cause dissension among the Scots. Thankfully, this literary Sword of Damocles was never used, and David was back in the Tower by May 1352, but Percy's part in the murky affair is distinctly unsavoury.

His mission over, and now in control of the family finances and estates, Percy took up his quasi-hereditary post as joint warden of the Eastern March alongside the indestructible Gilbert Umfraville, earl of Angus. Neville, however, although available for Border duty, concentrated on his favoured palatinate of Durham, which was fading from the picture until about 1356. Percy and his old comrade-in-arms, Richard Tempest, principally dealt with the usual run of robberies and assaults.[53] Tempest was currently keeper of the town of Berwick in lieu of Percy, whose father had virtually appropriated the post in the earlier years of the reign.[54] Tempest's relationship with the Percy family was obviously close, although Sir Richard was more a dear right-hand man than a social equal – rather like a canny manservant, who expects to be rewarded richly for extricating his lord from scrapes. In Tempest's instance, in 1358 Percy enfeoffed him in chief with Heiton, the estate lying about six miles from the Border near Kelso in Roxburghshire, the heart of the Percys' Scottish possessions. Interestingly enough, as related in Chapter 2, King David I granted Geffray de Percy and his brothers land in that area prior to 1153.[55] Particularly touching is the two men's respect for Percy's father. In April 1353, Percy alienated the sum of £20 annually 'of land and rent to certain chaplains to celebrate divine service daily for the souls of Henry, his father, and others'.[56] Three years later, near the anniversary of Percy senior's death, Tempest and two parsons collectively gained permission 'to found chantries and other pious works in the abbey [Salley] for the soul of Henry de Percy, deceased'.[57]

Dealing with crime was any Northern notable's bread and butter, but as the most powerful and influential Border lord, Percy, from late 1353 and throughout 1354, was a key participant in the interminable negotiations for King David's release and ransom. A conference held at Newcastle proved abortive; the Scots would not accept David signing away the rights of succession to the Plantagenet dynasty. Indeed, after the conference, the Scots delegates threatened to elect a new king if David continued even to consider this policy. Both sides realised this stalemate would linger until the negotiators simplified matters. Thus, after lengthy discussions, the Scots and English commissioners emerged on 13 July 1354 with what seemed a straightforward ransom agreement: David was to be exchanged for £60,000, payable in nine annual instalments and secured by the periodic release of hostages. In October, David was escorted north for his imminent release. But a series of delays over niggling points of detail prohibited any breakthrough for a month. Moreover, the most serious consideration of all was left unsaid. The real trigger for the July draft treaty had been a proposed peace treaty between Edward III and the new king of France, John II (who succeeded his father, the unlamented Philip VI, in 1350), in

April at Guînes. Edward had pressured for a cancellation of the Franco-Scottish alliance, but John II kept his counsel, hoping to squeeze concessions from Edward in return for accepting English territorial gains on the Continent. Jettisoning David and receiving £60,000 in cash seemed to Edward a fair price for an overseas empire; hence the offer of a surprisingly simple ransom. The Scots, on the other hand, were in a terrible predicament: peace between France and England, and a renunciation of the Auld Alliance, brought diplomatic isolation; the threat of civil war between the Balliol, Stewart and Bruce factions; an English army on the Border released from French duties; and a treasury drained of £60,000. Everything, therefore, hinged on the Anglo-French negotiations. Neither the French nor the English were overly keen on a permanent truce, and John II could utilise the threat of a second front in Scotland if war resumed. As the English saw it, if David were returned as part of an easy deal, John might abandon the peace talks, revivify the Franco-Scottish alliance and urge David to foment trouble on the Border. So, throughout 1354, both sides (but especially the Scots) stalled David's release until the outcome of the Anglo-French discussions was known. By mid-January 1355, however, the negotiations were plainly doomed, and in February poor David was dragged back to Windsor. Like his father, Percy had proved himself an able diplomat throughout a year of prevarication and mounting disappointment.

During the summer of 1355, tensions gradually rose in Scotland. English fears of French interference across the Border were realised by June, when agents reported that the Sire de Garencières had landed with 50 men-at-arms, personally instructed by John II to induce the Scots to rise against the English with the promise of 40,000 *deniers d'or à l'escu* (approximately £7000). The French king was using the Sire's mission to test the effectiveness of his Scottish allies.

Edward reacted exactly as John hoped. Demonstrating English sensitivities about the Border, he summoned an enormous army to Newcastle in July and August on the mere rumour that the Scots nobles were considering a surprise raid into the North. What Edward hadn't realised was that the Scots were divided on whether to attack. William Douglas, slayer of the Knight of Liddesdale, wanted to treat with the English until David could be released, whilst the inveterate troublemaker Patrick, earl of March, and Thomas Stewart, the self-styled earl of Angus (despite Gilbert Umfraville's claim to the title), proposed a more muscular approach. Edward made a truce with Douglas and his allies, mistakenly believing they represented the Scots nation as a whole. Wishing to bloody John II's nose for his knavery, Edward again turned his attention to France.

He hurriedly assembled every Northern lord and their levies, including

Percy, at Calais at the end of September 1355. Percy's success in the King David business was recognised when the king appointed him marshal of the royal army in France. The Prince of Wales, then commanding a small force in Aquitaine, would raid the surrounding area. Lancaster would storm through Brittany, while Edward's ally, Charles of Navarre (the grandson of Louis X, whose claim to the French Crown was nearly as strong as Edward's), was to land in Normandy. Unfortunately, Charles perfidiously came to terms with John at the last moment, forcing Edward to postpone Lancaster's expedition and dashing Percy's hopes of military greatness in his new position. Then, only a month or so later, the king and the Northern complement had to race back to England to face the latest Scottish trouble.

In mid-November, March and Angus joined the Sire de Garencières. Together, they planned to assault Berwick while Edward's back was turned. The town was taken and looted, but the castle held out under the command of Percy's deputy, Sir Richard Tempest. Amazed at the temerity of March and Angus, Edward and Percy (annoyed both for losing his temporary marshalship, and with the Scots for tainting his keepership of Berwick with their antics) flew to Berwick, dispersed the Scots and relieved the castle. The shady Sire de Garencières disappeared back to France, his mission accomplished.

'King' Edward Balliol, however, reappeared after the recovery of Berwick. For the last few years, he had resided in loyal Galloway, ignored by everybody. In 1354, having lost his family's ancestral stronghold of Buittle, he was unofficially homeless. With Edward present in Scotland for the first time in many years – he had brought his teenaged son, John of Gaunt, for his first trip across the Border – Balliol sought an audience. Penniless, humiliated and tired by decades of unceasing struggle stretching back to the 1330s, Balliol met Edward, Percy and several other Northern lords at Roxburgh Castle (Percy, incidentally, had recently been made keeper and sheriff of the county). On 20 January 1356, the king of Scotland pathetically lifted the golden crown from his head, scooped up a handful of Scottish soil and stones, and formally surrendered his kingdom to Edward III, now the pretender to the Scottish throne.

At last, Edward Balliol could enjoy life. Scotland was not his problem any more. As part of the bargain, he received a generous financial settlement from Edward, retired to south Yorkshire and amused himself by poaching in the royal parks. He died at Wheatley, near Doncaster, unmarried and childless, in January 1364, so erasing the Balliol name for ever from the insoluble Scottish dilemma. Seventy years after the Great Cause, the House of Bruce now faced not only the increasingly dangerous House of Stewart, but also the ruling dynasty of England.

Intent on being crowned king of Scotland, Edward set off on his last expedition across the Border. His keenness, however, outweighed his caution; the army he led (which included Percy) relied for its victuals upon the fleet, an imprudent decision owing to the treacherous winter winds. Reaching Edinburgh after a remarkably destructive march (Edward had learnt in France how to burn and travel simultaneously), the campaign of the 'Black Candlemass' sputtered to a halt after only a fortnight. Edward requisitioned the Edinburgh house of an overconfident burgess who had, on the eve of the Neville's Cross venture, beseeched David II to grant him the mayoralty of London. At that moment a sudden north wind, which the Scots attributed to the Virgin's intercession, scattered the victualling ships as they entered the Forth, leaving the army without supplies. The chronicler Knighton says that for a fortnight the English had nothing to drink but rainwater.[58]

The English enjoyed spectacularly better luck in France, although Henry Percy was left yet again on the sidelines. For a warrior, it must have been galling to have missed Lancaster's 1345 campaign, to have been relegated to a minor role at Crécy, to have been abroad during his father's moment of glory at Neville's Cross and then to have hung around at Calais for a year, only, to top it off, to participate in an ignominious retreat from Edinburgh while the prince was rampaging through southern France and, a little later, winning a notable victory at Poitiers.

There was method in the prince's madness. Lancaster, accompanied by 1400 men-at-arms and 1000 archers, had landed in Normandy, seemingly for a *chevauchée*. But there was a broader strategy at work. The prince was currently stationed on the Dordogne with a substantial expeditionary army of about 6000 men. In the high summer of 1356, Lancaster and the prince began to converge on Tours on the River Loire, which was almost equidistant between the northern and southern arms of the English army. If the two armies had met, as planned, they would have sealed off the western strip of France, from Calais to the Spanish frontier. This audacious plan had its essential weakness shown up by King John; he rushed to the Loire and destroyed the bridges. This effectively locked Lancaster into Normandy, and barred the prince's way north when he reached Tours in early September. The prince could only retreat back to Bordeaux, but John II had no intention of letting the English escape so easily, especially when he commanded 16,000 men, including a grand accumulation of dukes and earls and bannerets. Crossing the Loire, he caught up with the prince four miles south-east of Poitiers.

At dawn, on 19 September 1356, the two armies faced each other. King John unfurled the scarlet standard, 'the token of Death, for the French king had issued an order that the life of no Englishman was to be spared except that of the prince himself', according to Henry Knighton. As with Bannockburn, however, at which a Percy wasn't present, little space here will be devoted to the battle, aside from some remarks on a couple of interesting features. First, William Douglas signed on for service in the French army. In fact, Douglas was probably already in France on pilgrimage in expiation for murdering the Knight of Liddesdale, but he quickly abandoned it once he saw a chance to strengthen the Auld Alliance in a personal capacity. Second, for the first time, the French cavalry vanguard under the command of the Dauphin Charles dismounted and sent their horses to the rear. Lessons had been learnt from Crécy; the French, unfortunately, misremembered them. English horsemen dismounted only to *defend* in the initial stages of the battle, and remounted to attack and pursue.

As the French advanced slowly on foot towards the English lines, they were not slaughtered, as their shields protected them from the arrows, nor were they torn apart when they encountered the English men-at-arms; the French were finely trained and this was a clash between dismounted cavalrymen on either side. In the end, the Dauphin retired in good order, and English morale almost collapsed when King John's huge and fresh division appeared over the hill and began to dismount. The battered English men-at-arms could never withstand another assault. One of the prince's staff cried out, 'Alas, we are beaten!' but the prince snapped back: 'Thou liest, fool, if thou sayest that we can be conquered as long as I live!' He came rapidly to the decision that marks him out as one of history's great captains. Ordering the tired men-at-arms to remount, he brilliantly led them on a frontal charge combined with a surprise flank attack into the heart of the French pedestrians. Caught unprotected and horseless in the open, the flower of French knighthood was routed by the waves of cavalry sweeping from all directions through their midst. At this, William Douglas, who had fought valiantly, then withdrew, 'for in no wise he would be taken of the Englishman, he had rather been there slain,' said Froissart. Resoundingly, crashing his way through a doomed circle of noble guardians, Sir Denis Morbeke – a Frenchman who had fled to England during a murder inquiry in his own land – captured King John II alive. Within ten years, almost to the day, English arms had taken prisoner two kings in battle, both times against the odds and both times by mere knights. In the wise words of Froissart, 'Oftentimes the adventures of amours and of war are more fortunate and marvellous than any man can think or wish.'[59]

The fortunes of war were, conversely, catastrophic for the Scots. At a stroke, their foremost ally had been humbled; John II was under armed guard in Bordeaux and, under the Dauphin Charles's regency, France was collapsing into chaos. Now Edward's unsuccessful campaign to Edinburgh in 1356 revealed itself as a sound political move. With no possibility of French intervention, the Scots reflected that the English might reign supreme, as evidenced by the rapid deployment of the army in 1356. They could prevaricate no longer. David II had to be brought home, whatever the financial cost; it was better to act while Edward was still willing to return him. His eyes alight with the promise of France, Edward would far prefer to empire-build there than re-enter the Scottish labyrinth.

Even Robert Stewart had realised the delicacy of the situation; while wanting to retain his regency, he dared not protest for fear of upsetting the nobility. On 17 January 1357, the Scottish council authorised an embassy to treat in London for 'the deliverance of our lord the king and final concord between the kings and their realms'. Edward, in the meantime, had instructed the Prince of Wales to tell the French that any Anglo-French truce must henceforth ignore the Scots; they were now a separate matter. By May, negotiations – in reality, a catalogue of English demands – ensued, and at the end of September the embassy carried north a draft treaty. A few days later, David was brought to Berwick from the Tower of London (to prevent the two men plotting together, Edward kept John II at Windsor) for the final ratification of the document. Henry Percy played a major but unrecorded role in these talks, partially redeeming his own sense of honour for having missed Poitiers by their imminently successful conclusion. Thus, between autumn 1356 and August 1357 he was definitely based in the North, his various duties, including acting as commissioner of the peace, giving him ample time off.

Despite the prospect of peace, Anglo-Scottish Border tension was ever-present. On 6 August 1357, for instance, Percy and Richard Tempest were charged to find – and hang – members of a vicious gang who 'have traitorously adhered to the Scots against the king and have many times perpetrated treasons, plunderings, homicides, felonies and evils in the realm'. Once or twice, however, the cat was bitten by the mice; in 1358, Percy complained that Simon Ward, a knight, and four or five others 'at Topclyf, co. York, broke his houses, carried away his goods and assaulted his men and servants'. Burgling the North's chief policeman seems rather stupid, although this didn't stop a Nicholas Webster swinging from the gallows in 1364 for breaking into and robbing Percy's house at Spofford. The most serious infringement occurred in the winter of 1360, when Richard Tempest and Ralph Neville hunted down a gang of thugs led by one Alan de Heton who had 'carried away the goods of Henry de Percy and divers of his men, tenants and servants, of whom they have beaten many, killed some and robbed some'.[60]

Sealed on 3 October 1357, the treaty released David Bruce from eleven years' imprisonment. His ransom rose to £66,666, to be paid in ten equal instalments. If the Scots fell into arrears, David was to surrender himself. Moreover, a truce was to be observed throughout the decade. To prevent David whipping up an undivided Scots peerage, Edward requested that twenty noble hostages reside in England *at their own expense* on a rotating basis. No Englishmen were to be delivered to the Scots in return. Three 'super-hostages' were additionally demanded from the ranks of the greatest nobles. Eventually, Thomas Moray and the earls of Sutherland and Angus were selected. Crucially, however, despite being an apparent triumph for English diplomacy – after all, Edward made no concessions – the 'Treaty of Berwick' contained two interrelated loopholes: the Scottish succession, and the lord paramountcy of the English Crown in Scotland. Inevitably, the Scottish can of worms could never be sealed tightly shut.[61]

Next on the agenda was the French theatre. By this time, the prince had taken King John to London, there to await the arrival of the French envoys. On 8 May 1358, the two sides came to a preliminary agreement, usually called the first Treaty of London. Edward, at the apex of his powers, had no need to make any concessions; the 'treaty' is really a ransom note similar to the dictate handed to the Scots for the release of David II. Edward obtained from the hapless John II the full sovereignty of all Gascony/Aquitaine up to the Loire, together with Calais and various other places, plus a nightmarish ransom of 4 million *florins d'or à l'ecu* (approximately £700,000), with a first instalment of 600,000 florins due on 1 November and to be paid before release. John, like David, was to go voluntarily into captivity in the event of a default. Finally, Edward stipulated that 'the King of France will altogether abandon the alliance of those in Scotland'. Again, just as in the Scottish negotiations, Edward left his claim to the throne hanging in the air.

The talks broke off when the French were unable to pay the first instalment of the ransom by the agreed date, and Edward accused them of stalling. Nineteen days later, on 20 November, Edward told the French to prepare themselves for war, and on 6 December he ordered the fleet to mobilise. This was no mere sabre-rattling on Edward's part. According to John le Patourel, 'This was to be the final blow, delivered by all his armies acting together as one huge force and culminating in Edward's coronation as king of France in Reims Cathedral,' the birthplace of the French monarchy. Just to underline his warlike intentions, Edward revised the (second) Treaty of London, adding some obviously unacceptable terms, such as the conveyance of Touraine, Maine, Anjou, Normandy and Boulogne (in addition to the areas already agreed) to him in full sovereignty. The terms of the ransom were 'rescheduled', as well; now John II would have to raise three-quarters of the ransom in just four months. Assent to such demands would leave France eternally dismembered, half its former size and bankrupt.

Edward embarked upon the great campaign in the autumn of 1359 after numerous delays. His colossal army was commanded by the best generals in the world – the Prince of Wales and Lancaster – and was staffed by men of Henry Percy's calibre (Percy's son served in the young John of Gaunt's brigade – see Chapter 12). But it all came to naught. No Frenchman would confront him; the troops were demoralised by terrifying tempests of thunder and hail; the country was stripped bare; his siege of Reims failed; and, just as on the ignominious Scottish campaign of 1355, King Edward descended into a broody fury. By March/April 1360, a disillusioned Edward was compelled to order a retreat back to England. In a Dunkirk-style scenario, the English put 'tents, utensils, carts, saddles, and everything else, to fire and flame for want of transport', according to Knighton.[62] The French, under the Dauphin Charles, who had coolly watched Edward's effortless superciliousness slip away, now sought to open negotiations – this time they would have some demands of their own.

Within a few days, on 8 May, agreement was reached in the Treaty of Brétigny. On nearly every point Edward had to climb down until the treaty resembled the original Treaty of London of two years earlier. Edward not only lost his never-owned territorial 'acquisitions' of 1359, but undertook to renounce 'the style, right and crown of the kingdom of France' (one of the causes of the Hundred Years War) if John II renounced his feudal paramountcy in perpetuity of Gascony/Aquitaine, Calais and other territories, as agreed in the first Treaty of London. The French also knocked down the ransom from 4 to 3 million florins, reintroduced the 600,000-florin first instalment and ensured that only 400,000 had to be repaid annually. As for the Franco-Scottish alliance, well, the French demanded that in return Edward must retract his alliance with Flanders.

In principle, the English envoys accepted these demands. Edward, who was not present at the negotiations, travelled to Westminster accompanied by only a few trusted staff – including Percy, arriving on 19 May. On 14 June the two kings promised to ratify the treaty – the delay indicated that Edward had carefully studied the terms. Three weeks later, King John, with Henry Percy as one of his keepers, sailed for Calais, landing on 8 July. Simultaneously the Dauphin set about raising the first ransom instalment. Throughout August, a stream of professional English officials arrived in Calais to prepare the groundwork with their French counterparts and await the arrival of the great magnates (that is, the prince, Lancaster and others) in September.[63] Percy, however, was not among them; he must have tarried in Calais until mid-July before returning for pressing duties in the North. He was definitely there in January 1359, when he and Richard Tempest executed some routine transactions at Topcliffe.[64]

Heartened by Edward's misfortunes in France, King David had been acting up again. In 1358, for instance, Robert Stewart – whose behaviour towards David, who had detested him ever since he ran away at Neville's Cross, was now excessively obsequious – was granted the earldom of Strathearn, and William Douglas the new earldom of Douglas, which raised that peer to a pre-eminent position on the Border. The indefatigable Patrick, earl of March, who nursed a long-standing grudge against the Percys as they currently held his English lands, was also on the prowl. In February 1359, Percy and Neville, as keepers of the truce, were alerted that the earl was planning trouble on the Border. Four months later, David had suggested that France and Denmark attack England, and offered Scottish participation if the French helped out their friend and paid off part of his ransom. Indeed, the Franco-Scottish alliance had technically never been broken, as the Treaty of London had come to naught and Brétigny had not been ratified. After all, Scottish envoys told the Dauphin Charles, the imprisoned David 'was never minded to abandon the French alliance, even although, if he had done so, the king of England would have released him more easily from prison'. Soon afterwards, the dauphin – then faced with the horrific prospect of Edward invading France – offered the Scots about £30,000 to distract him. Subsequently, owing to the dauphin's more immediate concerns, the money was not transferred, leaving the Scots in a financial fix. Only by tripling the duties on wool and every other staple did they manage to pay the second instalment of £6666 due under the Treaty of Berwick on January 1360, but thereafter they annually defaulted on the ransom until Candlemas (2 February) 1366, so triggering the treaty's stipulation that David return to captivity.[65] 'Luckily for them, in January 1360, Edward was too busy with his French campaign to bother with David. Moreover, nobody had ever taken seriously the promise to honour the agreement. From Edward's point of view, the default allowed him to promote an eventual Plantagenet succession; furthermore, he still held the Scottish hostages.

Against this background, Percy's movements in that busy summer of 1360 gain some clarity; in August, after delivering John II to Calais, Percy reported to Edward in England; the king, in turn, appointed him – as a man who understood the Scottish negotiations perhaps better than anyone – his chief plenipotentiary to David II. In Scotland Percy force-fully reminded David about the missed instalments and his promise to submit to English custody, and quietly mentioned that Edward might be mollified if David would hand his throne over after his death. It should be mentioned here (a fuller narrative appears in the next chapter) that from 1359, Percy was related to Edward's third son, John of Gaunt, through marriage. Gaunt was frequently touted as a future king of Scotland if David refused to hand the Crown to Edward but he agreed to devolve it upon the succeeding generation. Percy, therefore, was strongly committed to the success of the negotiations.

Returning to French affairs, Edward arrived in Calais on 9 October for the final stage of the treaty-making: that is, the parallel renunciation of Edward's claim to the French throne and John's surrender of his sovereignty in the English territories. As neither monarch trusted the other, the 'dual renunciation' clauses had been excluded from the treaty, which was now principally concerned with territorial adjustment and the ransom. The two kings essentially wanted to see evidence of progress before renouncing their claims. What followed at Calais is confused, but contemporary accounts speak of 'altercations'. The English complained about the delayed payment of John's ransom, the French about the delayed English withdrawal from the specified areas. While the main treaty was ratified, there was no *formal* dual renunciation; Edward agreed not to style himself 'king of France' (as he had done in Scotland) in exchange for John ceasing to exercise his feudal rights in Aquitaine. This was a temporary compromise that left, in Maurice Keen's words, 'a deli-cate legal question', as both men knew well. The future Charles V's Bolognese legal professors – Bologna was Europe's jurisprudential Mecca – subsequently opined that, as the renunciation claims had not been fulfilled, the treaty was null and void. Thus Gascony and other English possessions were still feudally subservient to the French Crown. Edward's legal team naturally told him the opposite, making continuation of the war almost inevitable in spite of the phoney peace (the territorial exchanges were completed in 1362, but Edward never received the full ransom) engendered by the Treaty of Brétigny. In 1369, Charles V abro-gated the treaty, but with little consequence as the English denied his right to abrogate it at all. Stuck in a legal limbo, the treaty was neither alive nor dead; sovereignty over Aquitaine and the south-west remained the central issue until the reign of Henry V, as we shall see.[66]

As ever, with one problem temporarily resolved, Edward could barely rest before being faced with another, this time in Scotland. Throughout 1362, and into 1363, David faced an insurrection led by the earls of Douglas and March, supported by Robert Stewart. While enjoying David's discomfiture, Edward, as a precaution, ordered the Border defences to be strengthened. For example, noticing that the walls of Berwick Castle needed repairing, Edward authorised Percy to 'arrest as many masons, carpenters and other workmen as are required for the work...and bring them to the castle to stay on the works at the king's wages; and to imprison all those who shall be contrariant or rebellious'.[67]

Ostensibly, the Scottish rebels were protesting that the king was relying on middle-class bureaucrats and churchmen, not them, for advice. However, Stewart's interest (as usual) was more personal. The king had become involved with the widowed, beautiful Dame Margaret Logie, after his barren wife, Queen Joan, grown tired of his womanising (the compiler of the *Book of Pluscarden* referred to David as *fornicator publicus*), had left for England in 1357, there to die in 1362. David, therefore, was a free man; moreover, one seeking to produce a son who would automatically cut Stewart out of the succession and put an end to Edward's constant badgering for a Plantagenet king. The petition, which the rebels laid at David's feet, accordingly demanded that he dismiss his 'evil counsellors' and leave off his amorous liaison with Margaret, which was widely conceived as lascivious and greedy. In the end, David stamped on the ill-organised uprising, and celebrated his victory by marrying the Dame in April 1363. Edward, however, having some sway over Scottish affairs owing to the ongoing default, summoned David and his privy council to Westminster and attempted to clear up the issue of the succession once and for all. The product of this series of meetings was momentous.

In a memorandum of 27 November 1363, David promised to sound out the Scottish estates on the question: should he die childless, would Edward, or perhaps John of Gaunt, accede to the Crowns of England and Scotland? If they agreed to the proposal, Edward would forgo the balance of the ransom, release the hostages, restore to the English the lands once held by the Scottish kings, and relinquish Berwick and the rest of occupied Scotland. Astonishingly, Edward set out firm assurances for his eventual hold of the two Crowns: there would be no 'union'; Scotland's rights, liberties, name and integrity would be preserved; the Stone of Scone would be handed over; and the 'King of England and Scotland' would be crowned both at Westminster and Scone. A less conciliatory second memorandum concerned the possibility of the accession to just the Scottish throne of Gaunt or one of Edward's other sons (if of the heir presumptive, the Crowns on Edward's death would then unite). Nevertheless, according to Ranald Nicholson, the first memorandum 'certainly invites favourable comparison with the terms of the union of 1707'. Finally, Edward III had shown his hand. Great speculation surrounds David's personal views on the subject; he certainly did not reject the proposals out of hand – indeed, he had never done so – but he knew well the kind of man with whom he was dealing (and David was no slouch himself when it came to deviousness) and so he forbore from presenting them as the perfect solution. Indeed, the sixteenth-century Scottish historian John Major made an informed stab at guessing David's mind: perhaps David thought it 'much better for both Englishmen and Scots, to live under one king, provided that the Scots might continue to enjoy their independence'.

David II placed the two memoranda before the Scottish Parliament in March 1364, knowing that the future of Scotland, and England, depended on the Estates' decisions. They could not countenance 'any Englishman's son' (in Wyntoun's words) sitting on the throne, and rejected both memoranda in favour of Robert Stewart's rights. Again, David's disputed reaction to the decision is very interesting. The official record of the Parliament ambiguously says that David 'seems' or is 'presumed to be willing' to accept the terms. On the other hand, David's 'eyes flashed with rage, and his gestures for a moment betrayed the conflict of anger and disappointment which was passing through his mind'. Thus spake P. Fraser Tytler in 1882. But a more perceptive medieval writer suggested that David 'was highly pleased with the answer of the Three Estates, although he made believe otherwise in the presence of the English'.

It seems David maintained an eccentric form of relationship with the English and, in particular, Edward. He had spent, after all, more than ten years in comfortable surroundings there (he was supplied with new outfits every summer and winter, and was allowed luxurious bedlinen). Although those surroundings were suffocatingly boring (his company primarily consisted of an esquire and a chamberlain), he and Edward frequently had audiences and David was allowed to take English mistresses.

Neither firm friends nor bitter enemies, the two men probably developed an amicable working relationship, as modern chairmen of rival companies might. They did share a love of chivalry and heroic deeds, represented in Edward's case by his establishment of the Order of the Garter. They enjoyed tournaments and banquets, admired magnificent suits of armour, and even professed interest in a Crusade, yet showed no compunction about intriguing against each other. As the chronicler Wyntoun noticed: 'thare wes rycht gret specialte betwen hym and the King Edward.'

For the next five years the debate lingered on. To increase the pressure, Edward increased the ransom to £100,000 in 1365; in reply, the Scots managed to get the annual instalment lowered to £4000 and a truce until February 1370 (after that, another, lasting 14 years, was arranged). In May 1366, Edward offered a four-point draft treaty, detailing his views on homage, the succession, territorial swaps and a pact of mutual military aid in the event of a foreign war. The Scots Estates repeatedly declared that they found these proposals 'intolerable and impossible to be observed, and leading to express servitude'.[68]

In 1369–70 it became apparent that Edward had overplayed his hand. Another Continental war was in the offing – Spain providing the backdrop, this time with a revived French state and a bookish, highly capable and wily king, Charles V. (His flamboyant father, John II, had died in London in April 1364, having requested, and received, Edward's forgiveness.) In Castile, the Prince of Wales won the battle of Nájera in 1367 for King Pedro the Cruel against Pedro's half-brother, the French-backed Henry of Trastamara. However, in 1369, Henry invaded, murdered his sibling and allied Castile with the French. To make matters worse, the English army suffered terribly from dysentery and the prince himself 'contracted the debilitating disease that was to leave him a mere husk of the former man'.[69]

In gleeful mood, David travelled to London in June 1369 to discuss the succession and ransom questions with a chastened Edward. To avoid facing a resurgent France with an antagonistic Scotland at his back – the Anglo-Scottish truce would expire the following February – Edward needed to 'relax' his Scottish policy. David obtained significant concessions: the latest £100,000 ransom was reduced to about £38,000. The rescheduled payment rate was now less than £3000 per annum over fourteen years, during which time a truce would be observed. The mooted four-point treaty was also dropped.

Edward's threat to bankrupt Scotland unless his family's succession was granted had visibly failed. No longer could he combine war and statecraft or dextrously juggle France and Scotland in the air at once. His most experienced advisers, such as Lancaster (see below), and the earls of Warwick and Northampton, had died; the moderate if extravagant Queen Philippa passed away in 1369; leaving Edward surrounded by loyal, but 'green', men who lacked the experience of their predecessors. Court whispers had it that the king, who now wasted much of his time with his new, interfering mistress Alice Perrers (who was notorious for using a magician to mix aphrodisiacs), was losing the plot. Worse, his once-sturdy heir was sickening with dropsy and would die before his father in 1376, leaving the prince's only surviving son, Richard, aged nine.

Furthermore, after forty years at the helm, Edward had missed possibly the most dangerous long-term development of all. Thanks, ironically, to his tendency to kick his enemies when they were down, he had left David II the richest medieval king of Scotland, either before that time or after. Worried by Edward's incessant ransom demands, the Scots royal officials had reorganised the country's finances, and had prudently funnelled all sources of national revenue into the king's hand, so enabling accurate budgetary estimates to be made. This gave David a financial footing so sound it shamed Edward III and boded ill for the English Border lords, who might well face a handsomely paid, well-armed Scots army. For the moment, salvation from this dreadful scenario came with the death of the tumultuous and forceful David II, aged forty-seven – still without an heir – on 22 February 1371. The tireless Robert Stewart was crowned at Scone on 26 March 1371 as King Robert II.[70] Edward's stratagem of planting a Plantagenet on the Scottish throne had collapsed.

Percy's Last Years

Where was Henry Percy in the midst of all these great events? After 1362, when he briefly acted for the second time as a negotiator in Scotland to no great effect, Percy performed three final acts of public service (excepting his attendance at three Parliaments between August 1362 and January 1366). First, in December 1363, he and Neville were commissioned to find who 'the malefactors were who killed John de Coupeland... at Belton Mo[o)r... and to follow and arrest all those indicted in respect of this'.[72] It had been Coupland who had captured David II at the battle of Neville's Cross in 1346. The 'malefactors' were never uncovered.

Second, on 19 October 1364 Percy witnessed the marriage treaty between Edward's fourth (reputedly moronic) son, Edmund of Langley (earl of Cambridge) and Margaret, heiress to Flanders and Burgundy. Had the marriage gone ahead, a Plantagenet would have one day ruled those vitally strategic areas in the war against France. But Edward's plan went awry when, under severe pressure from Charles V, Pope Urban V refused to grant the necessary dispensation, and the wedding was cancelled. A few years later Charles secured Margaret for his brother, duke Philip of Burgundy. It was quite a coup.[73]

Percy's last duty was appropriate for his greying years. In February 1367, he was commissioned to delve into a property inquiry raised by the bishop of Durham, who wished to know whether, since lords owned a river adjoining their land up to the halfway point, this rule applied to his lordship of Norham and Tweedmouth, both of which lands abutted the Tweed. He asked because John Bolton, the former chamberlain of Berwick, had for years taken all the bishop's profit for St Cuthbert's, Durham, arising from the fisheries, fixings of weirs, mills and passage tolls.[73]

Thus Percy retired from active military and political life. In his late forties, he was getting long in the tooth and, unlike his father and grandfather, was always a worthy, rather than a great, man. He performed his duties competently, but was incapable of playing a permanent and pivotal role in affairs of state and war like his forebears. Through no real fault of his own, he missed fantastic opportunities for promotion, recognition and gain. His prime chance arrived in 1355 when appointed marshal of the royal army in Calais, but the prospect of military glory disappeared a mere month later when the latest Scottish crisis erupted. This Percy was a product of a medieval Old Boys' network; from birth, he was never required to exert himself strenuously. Married to Lancaster's sister, he had easy access to those of influence and power, and they in turn looked after him, but he never stood out from the crowd of equally blessed nobles and ambitious gentry. Not succeeding to his title and estates until he was thirty or so, Percy was trapped between forging a career and knowing he would inherit in the near future. This may explain his utter lack of his father's and grandfather's territorial drive. The Percy estates swelled not during his lifetime, and he was almost casual about his family's ancestral domains, some of which dated back to the Norman Conquest. He never benefited from the king's largesse. Edward raised eight men to earldoms, and an earl, Henry of Grosmont, to a dukedom; an additional sixty-one were created peers of Parliament. In short, amid this smooth upward mobility, Percy stayed precisely where he was – a senior and respected baron but nothing more. With some perseverance and canny politicking, he might reasonably have expected an earldom.[74] His epitaph? He did a good job, and went thus far and no farther. His son and heir was infinitely more dynamic, able and, regrettably, hubristic. It would be he who would spiral to dizzying heights before crashing into ignominy.

The two years preceding Percy's final retirement were besmirched by the death of his wife, Mary, on 1 September 1362. Her brother, Lancaster, leaving behind no male heirs so extinguishing his title, had preceded her in March 1361, possibly during that year's bubonic plague outbreak or through a particularly vicious strain of influenza, either of which might have killed Mary as well.[75] In less than eighteen months, then, Percy had lost his wife of nearly thirty years, and his foremost patron (although, as a result, Percy's son would be patronised by Grosmont's royal replacement as new duke of Lancaster, John of Gaunt). All his brothers, apart from Thomas, the reclusive bishop of Norwich, had gone, and probably most of his sisters as well. Lord Ralph Neville, the faithful colleague of Percy and his father, died in 1367.

A little-known story speaks volumes of Percy's occasionally tempestuous marriage to Mary in spite of their obvious love for each other. According to Thomas Walsingham, who seems to have been acquainted with the couple, when a monk of great parentage and high connections named Thomas de la Mare became Prior of Tynemouth, he sought to safeguard his priory's finances by recovering the manor of 'Haukeslowe' from Sir Gerard de Wytherington, who claimed it as his own. The consequential bad blood induced Wytherington to try to murder de la Mare, who fell on the mercy of Mary Percy, a 'nobilis et generose' lady. The de la Mares were members of her brother's retinue, so explaining Thomas's easy access to the lady. She pleaded with Percy to bang some sense into Wytherington, but Percy refused; he believed the knight had a case and was unwilling to get involved (there were possibly business dealings between the two men). Mary, however, took de la Mare as her confessor, even sending him jewels to fund his cause. She also may have prevailed upon her brother to mention the problem at court. Soon after, Sir Thomas Colville, a knight close to the Prince of Wales, offered himself as the prior's champion against Wytherington. The prince, moreover, showed great displeasure towards Wytherington, who, seeing that his career and perhaps his life were at stake, humbly asked the pardon of Thomas de la Mare. It is safe to say that some of that princely displeasure was passed in the direction of Percy, who would have been heartily displeased with his interfering wife. Yet their marriage remained stable.[76]

Percy had recovered from his depths of deathly gloom three years later when he married his second wife. She was Joan Orreby, daughter and heiress of John, Lord Orreby, who had died in 1354. Percy married her in May 1365 and later that month she and her husband took possession of her father's lands in Lincolnshire, Essex, Norfolk, Cambridgeshire, Nottinghamshire and Derbyshire.[77] Five months later, Percy received his mother's lands on her death, making 1365 a mixed year, although certainly a financially providential one.[78]

Two aspects of the marriage are especially striking. First, her Anglian-Midlands provenance: for an older man like Percy with deep roots in the North, finding a suitable match above the Humber to whom he was not related might have been difficult. He also did not want to set up a competitor to his eldest son and heir. Should Joan give birth to a son, he could be handed his mother's portion, while Percy's heir would retain control of the Northern estates. Second, her age: Joan was aged four when her father died, making her but fifteen at the time of her marriage to a man who could have been her great-grandfather.

It is possible to paint a far more richly textured picture of this odd marriage. Some background first. The Orrebys first appear in the twelfth and early thirteenth centuries in the service of the earls of Chester. In 1301, after military service in Wales and Scotland, Edward I granted John de Orreby the royal lands in Wales, together with the ancient earldom of Chester. As reward for faithful service, Edward II summoned Orreby to Parliament in 1309 as Lord Orreby. He died at an incredible age (probably in his early eighties) in 1352, the same year as Percy's father. His son and heir presumptive at the time was Philip, who by 1316 was married to Florence de la Mare, a match with obvious financial attractions for two up-and-coming families. Florence was daughter and *heir* of John de la Mare, the scion of a house that had risen from obscurity to become substantial, newly monied landholders. Her father, summoned to Parliament in 1299 as Lord Mare, had also served in Scotland. He died soon after, leaving Florence *suo jure* as Baroness Mare. Both Philip and Florence were dead by 1344 but their son, John Orreby, born in 1318 in Yorkshire, was knighted in 1340. This exact contemporary of Percy was eventually known as Lord Orreby when he reached his majority and then by modern doctrine Lord Mare as well, following the death of his mother. In 1346–7, Lord Orreby served at Crécy and Calais, where he no doubt became acquainted with Percy. In 1350, his daughter, Joan, was born, but Orreby died in 1354 without a male heir, so leaving Joan Orreby a four-year-old heiress blessed by modern doctrine with the titles of Baroness Orreby and Baroness Mare. On 19 May 1365, Joan received her inheritance. That same month, Henry Percy married her.[79]

The de la Mare connection is of central importance because that high-born and turbulent priest who was taken under Mary Percy's wing was named Thomas de la Mare. In the early 1360s, one John de la Mare was extremely close to the Prince of Wales and apparently acted as his unofficial jeweller. In November 1361, for instance, the prince purchased no fewer than 8939 pearls, two brooches worth £130, a 'fine ruby' and a 'ring with a diamond'. Two years later, the royal heir owed £1795 'for divers jewels bought for the prince's use and delivered in the prince's chamber'.[80] All this treasure must have been lavished on the beautiful Joan of Kent, whom he had married in 1361. Now one can understand why Percy's refusal to defend the politically untouchable Thomas de la Mare against the threats of Sir Gerard de Wytherington might have annoyed the prince. Some good, however, might have arisen from this error of judgement: through his wife, perhaps, Percy may have met his future bride, a kinswoman of Mary Percy's confessor, sometime in the early 1360s.

Within a year of her marriage she was pregnant, giving birth to Mary (the choice of name is interesting), who would later marry Lord Roos of Hamlake. A girl would be no rival to Percy's son by his first marriage. Mary eventually became Baroness Orreby and Mare. When she died childless on 25 August 1394 (her husband predeceased her), the titles became extinct. The large Orreby inheritance was broken up, while the Mare properties passed to John de la Mare, 'citizen of London', Florence de la Mare's father's great-grandnephew.[81]

Mary seems to have kept on good terms with her half-siblings. She had inherited from her father a valuable copy of *Le Livre de Seyntz Medicines*, the devotional but racy book written by Henry of Lancaster, Percy's father-in-law, who probably gave it to him around the time of his marriage (in the will it is described as 'uno libro gallico de duce Lancastrie'). Mary evidently possessed a literary bent, for she also owned a 'green primer which once belonged to my lord and father'. On condition that she 'pray for my soul', both of these dear items she bequeathed to her elder half-sister, Isabel, who married Gilbert Aton – another scion of the Aton clan who clung to the Percys after the purchase of Alnwick Castle. Money might have been tight in the Aton household, for alongside Mary's 'mantle and gown of scarlet and fur-lined', Isabel received 20 marks (about £13). The rest of the family were not forgotten: 'my dearest kinsman', Henry Percy, got 'one tablet of gold'; his wife was bequeathed 'one pair of rosaries'; the religiously minded Sir Ralph Percy (a cousin soon after killed in the Holy Land) received 'my best pair of rosaries of gold and one gold ornament'; and her mother-in-law, Lady Roos, garnered two gilt spoons and a diamond ring.[82]

Nevertheless, it is hard not to pity Joan Orreby, fatherless since she was a child, being pursued by a lecherous Henry Percy for her looks and her acres – especially, perhaps, her acres. Percy died in 1368 on Ascension Day (18 May), aged about forty-eight, of unknown causes – possibly plague – although in 1366 one chronicler had observed a strange disease from 'which many men, anon as they were to go to bed whole and in good point, suddenly they died'.[83] Lord Henry Percy elected to be buried in Alnwick Abbey next to his first wife.[84]

After his death, Joan was packed off into the care of Sir Richard Stury, originally of middling gentry stock, who been an esquire of Edward III's in the 1350s. He had fallen in with the Prince of Wales and was familiar with Froissart, as well as being a friend of Chaucer and owning a copy of the *Roman de la Rose*. He seems to have planned to marry Joan himself, but his social standing probably precluded this.

On 6 November 1368, Joan received as part of her dower the ancient Percy heartland of Seamer and significant parts of the family's Northumberland estates on condition that she would not marry again without the king's permission. This was assented to by Percy's heir, who wished to ensure that the lands would come back into his possession once Joan remarried.[85] Soon after, Sir Richard Stury disappeared from the picture and Joan finally married the obscure Sir Constantine Clifton – perhaps for a quieter life? Seven months later she died, possibly in child-birth or in another outbreak of plague. With her early death, the Percy lands were protected for another generation.

CHAPTER TWELVE

Inexorable Ascent

Sir Henry Percy, Marshal of England and Earl of Northumberland (1341–77)

> But I think that the names which move us most by their sound have some sort of thunderous quality. Proust, who was as sensitive to the sound of names as to their history, was never more pleased, so Sir Harold Nicolson has told us, than when he came upon the name of the Duke of Northumberland. It delighted him not only for the echo of its high lineage but also for its sheer sonority. Indeed, there is no other district of England whose name rolls out more tremendously than Northumberland – 'the lordly strand of Northumberland' of which Swinburne sang.
>
> Sir Steven Runciman[1]

Henry Percy's life since his birth on 10 November 1341 until his father's death can be summarised fairly quickly. His famous uncle, earl and later duke of Lancaster, brought him up at the king's court – the first Percy, as far as we know, who matured in such surroundings, where the boy 'was greatly beloved and familiar to him'. The younger Percy and the nineteen-year-old John of Gaunt, the son of Edward III, later travelled to France to fight under Lancaster's mentorship in the embarrassing 1359 campaign, which ended in the Treaty of Brétigny (his father, as mentioned in the previous chapter, served in Lancaster's retinue). A year earlier, mutually sensing dynastic and territorial opportunities, Percy's father and Lord Ralph Neville had arranged a marriage between young Percy and Neville's daughter, Margaret, a widow considerably older than her new husband.

On 4 February 1362 (or thereabouts), Percy was knighted, and in October 1363 he was abroad again. On 20 May 1364, a son and heir presumptive was born, also named Henry. Percy's impressive war record, and connections through his old chief, John of Gaunt – now raised to the dukedom of Lancaster – to Edward III, earned him a Knighthood of the Garter in about 1366, and thereafter he practised Marcher tactics, imbibed Border geography and acted as a trainee warden in Northumberland. On 29 June 1368, aged twenty-six, he inherited the family title and estates.[2]

John of Gaunt

Deserving of scrutiny are Percy's most remarkable connections with a man 'whose territorial power stretched over a third of England, who in a sense may be said to have created the Duchy of Lancaster and founded the Portuguese Alliance [the United Kingdom's oldest partner], who was for fifteen years the titular King of Castile and Leon, and for a dozen years the uncrowned King of England': John of Gaunt.[3] John was the king's third surviving son after the Prince of Wales and Lionel of Antwerp (better known as the duke of Clarence), and was born in Ghent in March 1340, making him a year and a half older than Percy. Two years later, John was invested as earl of Richmond on the death of the childless John III of Brittany. Although Percy junior was already residing at court, his father first became acquainted with Gaunt during the sea battle off Winchelsea in 1350, when the ten-year-old earl had stood alongside the king as he rammed the Castilian ships. As Froissart observed of him: Gaunt was 'too young to bear arms, but he [Edward] had him with him in his ship, because he much loved him'. In 1355, Gaunt attended his first military expedition to France (when Percy senior was briefly made marshal of the royal army in Calais), and this time the teenaged earl was knighted. Shortly afterwards, the army rushed to Berwick and in January 1356 Edward received Edward Balliol's pathetic surrender of his Crown, witnessed by Gaunt and Percy senior.

The depressing 1356 campaign 'was an instructive lesson for Gaunt about England's Scottish problem, whose significance he was never to underestimate as an adult', judges Anthony Goodman. As a test, in 1357 Edward granted him the lordship of Liddel in Cumberland (the late Lord Thomas Wake's stamping ground), which was constantly harassed by cross-Border raids. Gaunt was being groomed for kingship – the negotiations surrounding a Plantagenet successor to David II were begun at this time – and Edward set about establishing his son as a Northern lord without equal. In 1359, therefore, Edward and Lancaster – who lacked sons – arranged for their children to marry. In May of that year, Gaunt wedded Blanche who, with only one sister, Maud, was heiress to 'half of the largest inheritance in England after the Crown'. Just as momentously, during the New Year of 1359, Gaunt was staying at Hatfield in Yorkshire with his brother Lionel and his wife, the countess of Ulster, when he encountered a budding poet in the countess's service named Geoffrey Chaucer. From then on, Chaucer dedicated himself to Gaunt, who acted as his patron. Chaucer leaves us an image of Blanche in *The Boke of the Duchesse*.

And gode faire whyte she hete,
That was my lady name right.
She was bothe fair and bright,
She hadde not hire name wrong.

Froissart describes her as 'frisky, sweet, simple [and] modest of mien'. For the Percys, Blanche's undoubted charms drew them closer to the up-and-coming Gaunt. Blanche, of course, was Percy junior's cousin as his mother was Lancaster's sister. From 1359, then, John of Gaunt was *family*. The Percys unhesitatingly played on this connection. If Gaunt ever became king of Scotland, the return, and even expansion, of the Percys' old lands across the Border were a certainty. Their influence in the North alone would increase unimaginably, especially in tandem with Percy junior's marriage to Neville's daughter. All this doubtlessly added some spice to Percy senior's negotiating technique with David II at this time.

As for Percy junior, he accordingly served alongside Gaunt in France under Lancaster's overall command in late 1359. During that campaign, Lancaster and his two kinsmen fought numerous engagements without loss, although Chaucer was captured at Rethel. Soon afterwards, however, Edward concluded the Treaty of Brétigny. Both men attended Lancaster's burial in Leicester in 1361, with Gaunt appointed temporary custodian of Lancaster's estates. In July, Lancaster's property was divided between his two daughters, Blanche and Maud, with Gaunt receiving through his wife the duke's Northern moiety. Soon afterwards, he was magnificently styled 'John, son of the King of England, earl of Lancaster, Richmond, Derby and Lincoln and High Steward of England'. Within a year, his childless sister-in-law died of the plague (cruelly, it was alleged in some quarters that she had been poisoned) and Gaunt's wealth instantly doubled. Befitting his son's majesty, Edward girded a sword upon Gaunt, bestowed on him a furred cap and circlet of gold and pearls, and entitled him duke of Lancaster. Rumour had it that the tomb of Thomas of Lancaster – Blanche's great-uncle martyred by Edward II – leaked blood at the news.[4]

Maud's death benefited Percy junior immeasurably: his father was edging into retirement, Edward III was getting old, and Gaunt, his brother-in-arms, fellow Northerner, kinsman and potential king of Scotland, was the realm's first subject. The glittering prizes beckoned for a talented young knight. In the mid-1360s, however, the arithmetic of the English succession was transformed by the birth of Edward, the Prince of Wales's son by Joan of Kent, followed by a brother, Richard, in 1367. Although Gaunt had never realistically expected the Crown of England, his chances edged up a notch in 1368 when his elder brother, Lionel of

Antwerp, duke of Clarence, died mysteriously in Italy, leaving one child named Philippa. Percy's mentor was now fifth in line after the Prince of Wales and his two boys, and any male heir of Philippa and a (possible) husband.

Even the most dutiful of sons could calculate that the next few years hinged on fate, perhaps aided by subtle design. Edward III was in his late fifties and growing increasingly corpulent; the Prince of Wales – who called Gaunt his 'very dear and well-beloved brother' – contracted the disease in 1369–70 that would kill him six years later (Gaunt at this time was shocked to find that his heroic brother could no longer mount a horse); and sickness carried away thousands of children annually. Indeed, in 1371, Edward, the six-year-old son of the prince, died, leaving only Richard. If this weakly four-year-old followed his brother to the grave, Gaunt would – literally – be only a heartbeat away from the Crown. Gaunt certainly harboured a quiet (quiet, because the Plantagenets were a close family) ambition on the issue, because some years later he attempted to set aside the right of succession through females, which would have excluded the direct heirs of his niece, Philippa. In decades to come, this attempt would cause untold trouble for Gaunt's son, Henry of Bolingbroke (more on this later). The internal bickering might have been moderated if Edward had been sprightlier, and if Queen Philippa had not died during another visitation of the plague in August 1369. It had been her reproving eye that had always kept her children well behaved; as it was, Edward's delicate web of dynastic loyalty, spun for three decades, was unravelling.[5] Less than a month after the queen's death Gaunt's grief was amplified beyond measure when his beloved Blanche, aged twenty-six or twenty-seven, died, also of the plague (two sons had also died in infancy the year before). According to Chaucer, Gaunt refused to be comforted, mourning that

> *I have of sorwe so gret woon,*
> *That Joye gete I never noon,*
> *Now that I see my lady bright,*
> *Which I have loved with al my might,*
> *Is fro me deed, and is a-goon.*[6]

These grim facets of burgeoning family decay set the scene for the political events of the 1370s, in which Henry Percy (now Lord Percy, following his father's death in 1368) played a conspicuous part. For the moment, however, he was establishing himself as one of Gaunt's right-hand men in the resumption of the Hundred Years War. In 1368–9, Charles V's attorneys produced – in their eyes – irrefutable evidence of the king of England's vassalage to the the royal House of Valois for Aquitaine. Edward's lawyers, of course, presented equally irrefutable evidence for the converse, and, following Charles's obnoxious summons in January 1369 to pay his homage, the Prince of Wales furiously retorted that he would – but with helmet on head and 60,000 Englishmen behind him. His father, on 3 June 1369, accordingly restyled himself as king of France and reissued the seals, abandoned after the Treaty of Brétigny in 1360, displaying the quartered arms of England and France. In the intervening nine years, however, Charles had strengthened his realm's sinews, and now had a serviceable fleet (reinforced by Castilian vessels following the disastrous Spanish episode), an army reinvigorated by close study of English tactics, and a restocked royal arsenal. The French strategy, formulated during the winter of 1368–9, was thus: the duke of Burgundy would destroy English sea power in the Channel, raid the south coast and cut Bordeaux's naval communications with England; as Edward struggled at home, the dukes of Berry and Anjou would drive the English out of Aquitaine. Charles's overall objective was the invasion of England once the Plantagenets had been driven from France.

Feverishly, the English worked to retake the initiative. In late April the earls of Cambridge (Gaunt's younger brother widely regarded as an idiot) and Pembroke (a safe pair of hands) were despatched to Bordeaux to withstand Berry and Anjou. However, the last English holdings in Ponthieu fell at the end of May and intelligence reported a massive French invasion force assembling on the Seine. In a state of panic, Parliament met on 3 June 1369 and hurriedly arranged for a scratch force under Gaunt's command to defend Calais and threaten the French with another front. Over the next three weeks, royal messengers sped throughout the kingdom, delivering privy seal letters to sundry bannerets and knights, ordering them to present themselves at Sandwich. As a banneret, Percy undertook to bring fifty-nine men-at-arms (twelve knights and forty-seven esquires) and a hundred mounted archers, but his contribution, albeit substantial (more than any other banneret apart from the high-flying Lord Latimer), pales beside the awesome retinue of a man like Gaunt, who revelled in the title of duke of Lancaster. Determined to impress his fellows on this, his first independent command, Gaunt took with him 499 men-at-arms (6 bannerets, 130 knights and 363 esquires), 1000 mounted archers, 300 Welsh lances and bowmen, and 30 miners.

Arriving in Calais on 26 July, Gaunt's troops were the advance guard for Edward's main army that would cross the Channel in the coming months. During August, following his father's orders, Gaunt and his company destroyed the countryside to attract the French north from the Seine. The scheme succeeded. Charles V postponed the invasion and detached the duke of Burgundy's divisions to move north to deal with Gaunt. On 23 August, when the English were bivouacking for the night, Burgundy's army was sighted a few miles away. As Gaunt's men deployed in defensive battle array on a nearby hill, so too did Burgundy on an adjacent slope. For the next fortnight, the two armies nervously watched each other with knights occasionally emerging for a spot of skirmishing to break the tedium. By the time Burgundy had decided to attack, the promised reinforcements from England had arrived. Edward, distraught by Queen Philippa's death, handed command over to the earl of Warwick, a fire-eating blowhard who had fought in Scotland and France and gone on crusade with the Teutonic Knights to slay the Baltic pagans. This soldier's soldier took one look at the armies' deployments, barged into Gaunt's tent and, before Percy and other subordinates, tore a strip off the hapless duke. His caution and timidity, Warwick shouted, were a disgrace to English arms and he ought to have smashed Burgundy weeks before. This dressing down was given on the night of 12–13 September – the very day Gaunt's wife died, although he would not have been informed for a week – but word of Gaunt's humbling spread round the troops so quickly that a spy in the camp informed Burgundy that a Warwick-led English attack was imminent. On the morrow, Gaunt and Warwick found that Burgundy had fled in the night. Returning to Calais – where the dreadful news awaited him – Gaunt smothered his sadness and cut a blackened swathe through Normandy with the intention of firing Harfleur, the port from which an invasion of England would come. By the onset of winter, Harfleur had still not fallen, and the English wended their way back to Calais, then gripped by the plague. There, Warwick and many other soldiers succumbed to the disease. Percy was also stricken but managed to fight it off; according to the *Alnwick Chronicle*, 'being seized with sickness, [he] was obliged to return to his country more quickly than he wished'. In hindsight, Gaunt and his staff were right not to force a battle with Burgundy; every day that he wasted the duke's time postponed the invasion and, eventually, Charles disbanded his army. The Prince of Wales in his heyday might have risked a spectacular battle, but Gaunt emerges as 'a sound commander prepared to gamble for lesser objectives, but not for the supreme prizes'.[7]

For the next two years, Percy devoted himself to regional, official and personal affairs in the North and occasionally enjoyed himself at court, perhaps recuperating from his bout with the plague. Gaunt had no such luck. After a few months' rest, he was sent to Aquitaine in 1370 and 1371 to help his ailing older brother in holding back French excursions into the duchy. While he was out there, Gaunt sought to redeem himself from the Warwick-inspired charge of ineptitude. He desperately needed a diplomatic or military coup to impress his detractors at home, and so he schemed to acquire a kingdom: Castile and Leon. In 1369, as we saw in the previous chapter, King Pedro the Cruel had been deposed and assassinated by his half-brother, Henry of Trastamara, but his daughter Constance, his heir, fled to Bordeaux. Gaunt married the princess in September 1371, changed his arms to those of Spain and for the next sixteen years emptily styled himself 'King of Castile and Leon' by right of his wife. If Gaunt thought this would impress the hard-boiled English, he badly miscalculated. Edward III, who backed up his aspirations with armed force, might call himself king of France, but for his son to parade as a Spanish monarch through his wife bespoke unforgivable pompousness and pretentiousness. In the words of Anthony Goodman, 'English folk often expressed disgust at foreigners; the desire of an English magnate to become one puzzled them.'[8]

Gaunt's relationship with his temperamental wife was nowhere near as warm and loving as with Blanche. It was plainly a mutual marriage of convenience. Within a year of the couple's return to England, Gaunt was consorting with Katherine Swynford, the widow of a knight in the late Lancaster's retinue and a former lady-in-waiting to the Duchess Blanche. From Chaucer's point of view, the affair was eminently laudable, for his wife, Philippa, was Katherine's sister. The Lady Swynford produced a number of children – later to play major roles during the reigns of Henry V and VI – whom the duke acknowledged as his own, even bestowing a surname on them: Beaufort (a common nickname for which was 'Fairborn'). In 1396, Gaunt would finally marry his long-standing mistress, but his heart remained with Blanche. Every 12 September, without fail, he and his household attended a solemn celebration at her tomb in St Paul's, and two priests were employed to daily chant Masses for her soul. In his will of 1398, Gaunt specified that his body be buried next to hers in St Paul's.[9]

The early 1370s, likewise, brought Henry Percy marital and martial disaster. In mid-May 1372, Percy's wife, Margaret Neville, of whom he seems to have been genuinely fond, died. She bore him five children – four boys and a girl – and Percy did not remarry for another nine years. Margaret probably died from the unhygienic conditions of childbirth, worsened by having – possibly – twins. Their names were Alan and Margaret, but that apart, we know nothing of them. They too may have died soon afterwards. For his part, Gaunt acted generously and sympathetically, licensing Percy to take some deer in each of his forests 'because of the very great and entire affection and perfect love which we have towards the person of our very dear and well-beloved cousin'.[10]

On the military side, more dreadful news reached the court the next month when the earl of Pembroke's convoy of twenty-odd ships was overwhelmed by Castilian galleys off La Rochelle. In a novel twist, the Castilians sprayed oil onto the decks and rigging and ignited it, burning alive many of the unfortunates aboard. As England's first naval reverse of the Hundred Years War, it must be counted as a first-class rout. Pembroke, travelling to Aquitaine as Gaunt's replacement as lieutenant and accompanied by a substantial retinue, had orders to recruit upwards of 3000 men there to fight off the French, but was captured and imprisoned in very harsh conditions. Three years later, when finally released, he would die at sea on his way back to England. One effect of the La Rochelle disaster was that in the coming months, Charles V successfully conquered Poitou and Saintonge, rendering Aquitaine as good as lost. Another was that in July a furious Edward instructed Gaunt to call off his planned invasion of Castile to aid him instead in avenging Pembroke and re-establishing English mastery in the Channel.

Two months after his wife's death, Percy was summoned to Sandwich with his company to join an impressive roster of notables for the last gasp of Edwardian military showmanship. Edward planned to prowl the Channel in his flagship, *La Grâce de Dieu*, with a large fleet defended by 3000 men-at-arms and 3000 archers, until he could pounce on the Franco-Castilian navies. But from the end of August until early October 1372, contrary winds prevented the fleet from sailing. Edward cancelled the offensive and the retinues went home. 'Thus the powerful expedition and the king's last personal participation in the war ended in complete failure.' All in all, 1372 was a genuine *annus horribilis*.[11]

Percy and Gaunt Return to France

Ascribing his naval setbacks to ill luck, Edward had high hopes for the subsequent year. English arms had been in the doldrums for half a decade, but his armies, comprising some of Europe's keenest soldiers, required only the *opportunity* to fight the French face-to-face to reverse the disappointments of recent years. Gaunt was appointed supreme commander of the English forces. Edward, master of the noble temperament, wished to do his best by his sons; Gaunt had to redeem himself for his perceived clumsiness in 1369 and the Castilian silliness if he was to retain influence within the peerage after his death. With the Prince of Wales weakening, and pale Prince Richard still only six years old, if the Crown fell into Gaunt's hands as a military lame duck resembling Edward II, another ambitious Mortimer or fractious Despenser the Younger might emerge.

In the three months from 1 March 1373, Gaunt and his captains mustered an impressive army of about 6000 men of all ranks. Percy's contribution was even greater than in 1369. He had doubled the number of knights, nearly quadrupled his complement of esquires and tripled the number of Northumbrian mounted archers. Only Lord Despenser, the constable, brought more adherents.[12] To put it bluntly, it was a Percy who consistently raised huge companies for England's later expeditions, and this did not escape Edward III's notice. Such conspicuous loyalty from a family who had supported the Crown since the Conquest (well, for the most part) surely marked out this Percy for stellar promotion.

In late July, Gaunt's magnificent array landed at Calais and on 4 August started south-east through Picardy, Artois and Vermandois, towards Champagne, penetrating the French heartlands to threaten Paris from the east. Charles V, however, copying Robert the Bruce, avoided a battle and ordered his commanders to harass the English day and night. The English response was to burn swathes of countryside and batter small towns to the ground. Inevitably, over the ensuing months, as the English divisions shadow-boxed with invisible French detachments, Gaunt's army's morale was sapped. The pickings in eastern France were easy but not rich, and thousands of pounds were draining away (mostly from Gaunt's deep but not bottomless pockets) while the army stayed in the field. His quandary was unenviable: turn back and face the sneers of his peers, or soldier on. Gambling that Charles V would seek a truce, Gaunt chose the latter. Worse, he inexplicably proceeded south in the direction of Bordeaux through Burgundy and Auvergne rather than turning westwards on Paris, leaving behind the vineyards and harvests of northern France for winter, barren mountains and floods.

Over the coming months, Gaunt's advance began to resemble Napoleon's retreat from Moscow. Food and heat were desperately short; the baggage train was swept away; horses faltered and fell lifeless; illness afflicted the weakened men, and the sick and dying were left behind as this best-equipped of armies clanked indomitably, but miserably, forward. Only at Christmas did it reach friendly Bordeaux, where fewer than half the men answered the roll-call, and half of those were on foot. Following mass desertions, the sheriffs in London were ordered to arrest any man returning without Gaunt's warrant.

Gaunt's march highlighted the intractable nature of the Anglo-French stalemate. Not long after, both sides were seriously considering peace. Gaunt had failed before the entire nation, and despite keeping his army together almost until the end – a prodigious feat in itself – there were bitter whispers in noble circles about his ability. Those, however, who had served under him received no opprobrium among their peers.

Indeed, because they had put up with Gaunt under the worst of conditions, their stock may have risen. If the Alnwick Abbey chronicler is to be believed: 'Percy ... went over the sea with a great army ... and other great men of England, and going through the kingdom of France he behaved himself valiantly, destroying the country, killing those making resistance, burning down towns and cities, and, beyond all others, *governing his army well* [italics added], he returned to his country with the highest honour and noble fame.' After recuperating in Bordeaux, Gaunt abandoned his lieutenancy of Aquitaine and arrived in England in April 1374. He was summoned immediately by his father, who severely reprimanded his errant son, an upbraiding that did not remain a secret for long. Chastened and humbled, the kingdom's mightiest subject locked himself in his Northern estates for nearly a year.[13] When he emerged, with all thoughts of winning glory in France and Castile pushed aside, Gaunt expounded a new policy of peacemaking. Those many months in reflective, brooding seclusion had persuaded the duke that future redemption lay in shedding his tarnished battle-armour and donning the sombre clothes of a statesman.

Gaunt's new policy was strengthened by England's financial exhaustion. He met the dukes of Anjou and Berry at neutral Bruges in the spring of 1375. After initial teething problems, the talks went unusually smoothly and a truce was arranged to last until 1 April 1377. And to cap a better year, the Duchess Constance gave birth to a son, John. Yet even then, Gaunt could do no right. The truce was for a mere two years, and the chroniclers floridly complained of the duke blowing huge sums of public money on high living with his former enemy, the duke of Anjou, during the negotiations. There were rumours that money had changed hands, and that some of the king's ministers and confidants had taken advantage of the ailing Edward III by advocating peace and filling their pockets.

To some extent, these allegations held water. In part-fulfilment of the Treaty of Bruges, Thomas Catterton, captain of the fortress of Saint-Sauveur, handed it to the French in exchange for 53,000 francs. It was all above board, but it was suspected that Catterton kept much of the proceeds for himself. In another instance of featherbedding, the king's chamberlain, Lord Latimer, and the successful merchant, Richard Lyons, had allegedly skimmed money intended for Calais's defence. This was the least of their crimes: under fictitious names, they had lent the Crown 20,000 marks (about £13,300) at 50 per cent interest (including some of the king's own money entrusted to them – hence Edward was unwittingly lending himself his own money at usurious rates!) Worse still, as the Commons was displeased to discover, a group of loyal London merchants had offered the king 15,000 marks (around £9990) for free. Just *how* displeased was the Commons Gaunt would soon discover for himself.

Gaunt, Parliament and the Rabble-Rouser

Complaining during the war about its cost and any consequential corruption would have seemed unpatriotic, but the truce brought grievances to the fore at the famous 'Good Parliament' of spring 1376, the first since 1373. Sidney Armitage-Smith admirably summed up the atmosphere in which this Parliament met: Gaunt

> had impoverished the country and led an English army to ruin, where others had brought back king's ransoms and won victories which stirred the reluctant admiration of Europe. To this must be added the dislike of his countrymen for the Castilian marriage and their fear of the international difficulties which it appeared to involve, and the natural suspicion which they felt for one who, not content with his extraordinary position as the wealthiest subject of the English Crown, surrounded himself with royal state and claimed also the respect due to the King of Castile and Leon.[14]

At the end of April, in the Painted Chamber of Westminster Abbey where Parliament generally met, there was the traditional request for a liberal subsidy to prosecute the war. It was followed by knight after knight lambasting the government for wasting money and harbouring corruption. Finally, one exasperated knight argued that without the support of sympathetic elements in the Lords, all these words were so much hot air. Thereupon, Sir Peter de la Mare, the steward to 24-year-old Edmund, earl of March (the late Lionel of Antwerp's son-in-law and, incidentally, Mortimer's great-grandson), strikingly summed up the Commons' complaints by arguing that taxes had to be raised only because evil ministers were robbing the king blind. As March's wife Philippa had recently given birth to a son, Roger, who arguably held a higher claim to the Crown than even Gaunt, de la Mare represented an extremely powerful patron profoundly dissatisfied with Gaunt's conduct. Furthermore, de la Mare's oratory so impressed the Commons that he was chosen as their emissary to the Lords – the first *recorded* occasion when a Speaker, acting on behalf of the Commons, was employed. Reluctant to appear over-strident when the health of both the king and the Prince of Wales was deteriorating, the gathering proposed an advisory committee of prelates and magnates to transmit their grievances respectfully to the king and to act as an adjudicator.

On 9 May, de la Mare and a small Commons delegation visited the Lords where Gaunt was presiding. According to an eyewitness, a worried Gaunt 'started to speak very uneasily: "which of you has the task of setting out what you have decided among yourselves?"'. De la Mare, having presented himself, refused to speak until Gaunt would permit the Commons delegation to 'intercommune' with the advisory body of the Lords, comprising the equilateral formation – pioneered by the Lords Ordainers under Edward II – of four earls, four prelates and four lords. The most important representatives of the Lords were Percy and Henry Scrope (his cousin was chancellor and a very close acquaintance of Gaunt's). Among the bishops was Bishop Courtenay of London, who had little time for the duke's allies and still less for the duke. As with the Lords Ordainers in Edward II's reign, the earls (March, Warwick, Suffolk and Stafford), their politics and their characters were of prime importance. Most of them would play starring roles during Richard II's reign.

The earl of March, of course, was Gaunt's known enemy, a possible contender for the throne and the greatest landholder in England outside the royal family. He suspected Gaunt's motives, and predicted that his disastrous war leadership would effortlessly translate into equally disastrous peacetime government. March remained intensely annoyed about Gaunt's truce with the French in 1375. It had abruptly halted the earl's military campaign, leaving him saddled with an expensive army that was engaged on a one-year contract, for which Gaunt returned only six months' wages.[15]

March's cousin was Thomas Beauchamp, who had succeeded his father – the grizzled soldier who told off Gaunt during the French campaign of 1369 – as earl of Warwick. Since then he had soldiered in Scotland and France (including acting as marshal on Gaunt's trek to Bordeaux), where he and Percy had become acquainted. Then in his mid-thirties, the conventionally religious Warwick has been described as 'intensely conscious of his rank and rights, brusque and high-handed in defending his interests'.[16] Descended from a long line of notoriously independent-minded Midlands nobles – who else would have berated a king's son? – Warwick was a wild card, likely to sympathise with the Commons' desire for good government while disliking their uppitiness.

Hugh Stafford, earl of Stafford, was a few years older than his kinsman Warwick and had married one of his sisters. He was widely regarded as a braggart; in addition his title was of recent make and was built on providing royal service rather than exhibiting the baronial prowess that had provided the foundation of the old hereditary earls such as Warwick, Oxford and Arundel. Through the female line, the Staffords had been related to the extinct Clare earls of Gloucester. After the death of the last Clare, Gilbert, at Bannockburn in 1314, the subsequent break-up of the awesome Clare estates between Gilbert's three sisters brought great benefits to the Stafford dynasty, and Stafford's father gained a fortune as well as an earldom in 1351.[17]

Finally, there was William Ufford, earl of Suffolk, the last of his name to hold the title, as his only son had died childless. Edward III had given his father the title in 1337 for participating in the palace coup that culminated in the execution of Mortimer and the banishment of his paramour, Queen Isabella. The first earl's two sons followed the family tradition of royal service, and all three were installed as Knights of the Garter. According to the chronicler Walsingham, Suffolk, unlike Stafford, was widely liked by king, nobility, gentry and peasantry; apparently, 'throughout his life he exuded amiability'. He would die suddenly in 1382, collapsing as he left the chapter-house at Westminster.

Blood – whether of kinship or whether spilt – united the earls. March, for instance, was the cousin of Warwick, to whose sister Stafford was married. All four, moreover, had served together in arms in the last few years. Their attitudes towards Gaunt reflected a reasonably balanced mix – March was opposed, Suffolk neutral, Warwick lustily independent and Stafford a strong ally.[18]

Percy, however, held his counsel. Aware of the endemic corruption and sleaze, he knew that the clamour for reform disguised an attack on Gaunt's position. Although he had witnessed Gaunt's failings during the 1373 campaign, he had no desire to bite the hand that had fed him down the years. Percy probably had some sympathy for a governmental housecleaning – after all the Commons had nominated him, and it was said that the 'Prince of Wales', from his sickbed, had expressed support for the reformers – but it was his amiable relationship with Gaunt that chiefly recommended him as an acceptable intermediary.

On 12 May 1376, the intercommuning having taken place and a subsidy sufficient to ease the king's immediate financial difficulties having been agreed, de la Mare confidently levelled the accusation of war-profiteering within the government. Gaunt seethed. The ministers – his *friends* – under attack were ministers of the Crown, and at the moment he was the Crown's representative; ergo, dissent must be crushed. But when Gaunt, expecting to call the other's bluff, 'marvelled and said, "How is that and who are they who have profited?",' de la Mare ignored the sarcasm, took Gaunt's question at face value and launched a diatribe meticulously listing the names and crimes of those involved. That night, thunderstruck at this insolence, the duke bellowed that these mere knights of the shire 'think they are kings or princes of this realm. Have they forgotten how powerful I am?' But the momentum for Latimer and Lyons' impeachment for war-profiteering and money laundering was unstoppable; the official record states they were accused 'by the clamour of the commons',[19] Latimer was sacked as chamberlain and placed under surveillance whilst Lyons was imprisoned, his property forfeit.

Strikingly, Percy at the outset was a central player in the impeachment hearings, although this does not necessarily prove his membership of the coalescing anti-Gaunt faction, given the popular animosity towards Latimer and Lyons. A member of the advisory council, Percy realised that Gaunt's defence of Latimer and Lyons was handing de la Mare and his allies a weapon for attacking the government. The two men must be sacrificed to relieve the pressure on Gaunt's ministry.

Thus, it was Percy who initiated Latimer's fall – the earliest Commons impeachment of a minister of the Crown. Percy, like many others, was party to rumours that a certain unnamed squire had brought a letter from France to the king, apparently detailing Latimer's misdoings. Latimer allegedly had had the squire thrown into jail; the letter, of course, disappeared. Percy raised this new cause célèbre in Parliament and pressed Latimer on the messenger's whereabouts. The people became highly excited and threatened to burn down every sheriff's house unless the boy were produced. Under normal circumstances, some of the Commons might have pooh-poohed this fanciful tale of a missing messenger, but Latimer was unfortunately dogged by a similar story concerning the presumed death of Sir William Elmham. This story was connected with the details of secret negotiations in 1370 in England, at which Lord Latimer had been present, between Edward III and Charles the Bad of Navarre. When Charles, later visiting the French king's court, discovered that the latter knew all about the negotiations, it was said that Elmham, with whom Charles was acquainted, had identified Latimer to Charles as the source of the leak. Latimer then supposedly had had Elmham imprisoned and strangled. In fact, Elmham was alive for many years after 1376, so clearing Latimer of the murder charge, but at the time of the Good Parliament he was abroad on secret state business. In the absence of modern communications, Elmham was effectively incommunicado for years, so engendering the sinister suspicions that he had disappeared.

Eventually the missing messenger was found, and the country breathlessly awaited his testimony. However, he only gave evasive answers as to his recent whereabouts and mission. Naturally, it was rumoured that Latimer's (and Gaunt's) gold had bought his silence, but in the absence of any proper proof, the Commons was forced to examine the meatier, but rather less exciting, financial allegations, some of which would sink him and Lyons.[20]

The Commons turned next to Alice Perrers, the king's mistress, popularly alleged to have manipulated her besotted elderly lover, perverted justice and enriched herself at the public expense. Thomas Walsingham, the chronicler who can usually be counted on to express medieval men-in-the-street sentiments, described her as a 'shameless doxy', an 'infamous whore' and a thoroughly bad influence.[21] Gaunt, who disliked her, allowed the Commons to banish her from the court and confiscate her property (indeed, in 1378, Gaunt picked up the grant to her property, but later had to relinquish it).

On 8 June, in the midst of the furore, Edward, Prince of Wales, died. His corpse was, according to Froissart, 'embalmed and put in lead and kept till the feast of Saint Michael next after, to be interred with the greater solemnity when the parliament should be there'.[22] But Gaunt's hopes of a respite, spurred by sympathy, soon disappeared. Prince Richard was now the royal heir, the king's health was visibly eroding and Gaunt stood as viceroy of England. Even as Gaunt mourned his brother, colourful rumours spread (aided by Charles V of France) that he would assassinate his vulnerable nephew and snatch the Crown. That Gaunt would have attempted a *coup d'état*, when his popularity lay lower than the Dead Sea, is doubtful, the only historical precedents being Henry I's alleged murder of his predecessor William Rufus in 1100 and Prince John's murder of his nephew, Arthur of Brittany. For cultured four-teenth-century *Englishmen*, the uncivilised Normans were best ignored and Prince John was not a man to be emulated. More than mere ambition would be required to usurp a rightful sovereign; twenty years later, such an opportunity would fall to Gaunt's son, Henry of Bolingbroke, who did take the fateful step.

No matter. Before the Good Parliament recessed, it commanded that a permanent council of ten or twelve peers be formed; some of its members were to attach themselves to Richard's person, ostensibly to dispense counsel, but really to ensure his life from Gaunt's predations.

Gaunt's unfortunate propensity to act impetuously when consumed by anger spurred him to declare the Good Parliament, and all its acts, annulled; Alice Perrers returned to court, the new council was dissolved and his friends – Latimer and Lyons – had their impeachments quashed. Most importantly, he hunted down the ringleaders of the Commons rebellion, Sir Peter de la Mare (who was imprisoned in Nottingham Castle) and Bishop Wykeham of Winchester, founder of Winchester College.

The bishop, until recently one of Gaunt's financial confidants, had risen very far, very fast. As England's most politically powerful prelate, his influence was crucial in prosecuting Latimer, a rival during his stint as chancellor. Dead set against allowing Latimer time and counsel for his defence, Wykeham received a taste of his own medicine when Gaunt successfully charged him with buying Crown debts at a discount to gain an illegal profit – the same accusation that had doomed Latimer and Lyons.[23] In November 1376, his fellow bishops stripped Wykeham of his (many) temporalities, much to the chagrin of Gaunt, who had urged imprisonment.

Wykeham's switch to the reformist party – the action of a man previously propelled and protected by courtly connections and royal favour, whom the bishops then refused to jail – formed part of a larger feud between Gaunt and a class of political clerics. The *casus belli* was a turbulent priest, John Wycliffe, whom Gaunt had met during his revel-laden visit to Bruges in the spring of 1375. Historians have wondered why Gaunt, a pious Church benefactor with profoundly orthodox theological views, took under his wing a man counted a heretic and condemned by Pope Gregory XI in 1377. Political expediency? Wycliffe's attacks on the clergy's luxury were a useful battering ram for Gaunt and his allies against the likes of Bishop Wykeham – as Thomas Walsingham acidly observed.[24] Sympathy for Wycliffe's campaign against Church abuses? Henry Knighton, the chronicler (and canon of Leicester Abbey, one of Gaunt's favourite patronages), informedly wrote at the time that the duke 'believed them [Wycliffe's Lollards] to be holy, because of their appealing speech and appearance, but he was deceived, as were many others'.[25]

Both explanations hold water, although this does not detract from Gaunt's essentially conventional religiosity. When Gaunt dropped Wycliffe in the early 1380s, it was mainly because the latter had become too radical theologically for him (and even for many of his followers), but the importance of patching up relations with the prelates also played a role. At heart, however, Gaunt was afflicted by an inner conflict between the era's typically conspicuous consumption (especially in the monasteries) and the asceticism and austerity preached by friars, which compelled him to 'associate himself with holiness, even when it had a dangerously radical edge'.[26]

A Yorkshireman in his forties, Wycliffe was considered the pre-eminent academic theologian at Oxford University, impressing the adequately educated but intellectually unrigorous noble and knightly classes. Wycliffe, a precursor of Luther, stormed at the practical abuses perpetrated by the Church, many of which were exemplified by worldly clerics like Wykeham. By the late 1370s, Wycliffe was fundamentally challenging

Church doctrine and authority, transforming a Lancastrian reformer into the father of English nonconformity, the morning star of the Protestant Reformation. Originally, Wycliffe argued that if the Church shed its luxurious endowments, vulgar ambitions and temporal power, it would be restored to apostolic purity. Then, so-called ecclesiastics who joined the Church for ambition's sake would return to tending the spiritual well-being of their flocks. For a time, Wycliffe gained support from the Commons, which was tired of the Church's resistance to taxation amid an international war, despite holding about a third of the country's land (in 1374, the Prince of Wales had stormed out of a conference shouting that the archbishop of Canterbury was an ass).

Wycliffe believed that invented Church dogma exerted an unhealthy influence on Christians, whom he wanted to discover God's Divine Revelation for themselves. Things, literally, were spiritually deeper than they appeared to the senses, and to penetrate to their core, to grasp their universal essence, was to understand the Divine. The Church, its unrighteous assets, its obscure teaching and its Latin-speaking clerics, were defined as superficial barriers between the believer and his knowledge of God. Only by reading and understanding the Scriptures *in the vernacular* could the truth be found by the common man. And Wycliffe backed up his claim. With his disciples, he supervised the first complete translation of the Bible. In the prologue the translator accused 'covetouse clerkis' of fulfilling the 'develis purpos' by 'stoppen Holi Writ' from being made known to 'symple men'. Indeed, he intended 'with Goddis helpe' to make the English 'more trewe and more open than it is in Latyn' – a goal that in the early fifteenth century spurred the government to condemn the Lollards (Wycliffe's followers) for their propensity to 'make and write books' and 'wickedly instruct and inform people'.

It was not only the outward manifestations of the Church that should be swept away. The visible Church had no automatic claim to divine authority, for the clergy – even the Pope himself – were not guaranteed a place in Heaven. In later years, Wycliffe's more extreme followers would denounce the Pope as Antichrist and his cardinals as agents of Lucifer.

Wycliffe's view – that the external and the superficial must be shed before divine knowledge could be acquired – possessed revolutionary implications not immediately grasped by his rich, propertied, bejewelled, aristocratic and knightly supporters. The same could not be said for the rich, propertied, bejewelled bishops, who sensed precisely where popular Wycliffism was heading.

By the time, however, that Wycliffe had progressed from simply advocating the disendowment of the Church to more complex doctrinal questions, Gaunt had become more than a little wary of the embarrassingly radical Oxford scholar. Being conventionally pious himself, and a man – like everyone else – who believed unquestioningly in the sacred ceremony surrounding the Eucharist, Gaunt once bade Wycliffe to be silent in his presence when the latter told him about his new ideas on the Mass. Wycliffe was angered that people worshipped the bread and wine rather than God. However, he never *completely* denied the miracle of transubstantiation although he was never sure whether the bread remained wholly material, or whether part of it did in fact transubstantiate. Gaunt thought him mad for entertaining such subversive ideas. No wonder the friar Adam Stocton, for whom the Oxford schoolman was once 'venerabilis doctor', angrily dubbed him 'execrabilis seductor' as Wycliffe shifted into heresy.[27]

That rift lay in the future. For the moment, such doubts passed Gaunt by. Wycliffe, after all, was serving him handily. Two months after Bishop Wykeham was imprisoned, a new Parliament met on 27 January 1377. Since it came on the heels of Gaunt's counter-strike on the Good Parliament's ringleaders, he was expecting a smoother ride this time. The new chancellor and Speaker were now solid Lancastrians, and without de la Mare firing them up in righteous indignation, the new shire representatives would be tamer.

Even so, the whispers of possible regicide continued to dog Gaunt and to displease the king. On Christmas day 1376, Edward mounted a public ceremony to show one and all his children's devotion to Prince Richard. After a great feast, at which hundreds of barons, prelates and knights were present, Edward 'caused them all to swear solemnly to maintain him. And on Christmas day the king made him [Richard] sit at his table above all his own children in great estate, representing that he should be king after his decease'.[28]

As with a Hydra, even while one rumour was temporarily suppressed, another grew in its place. Supporters of the imprisoned Wykeham put it about that Gaunt was not the true son of Edward III, but was a changeling – the child of a Flemish woman substituted for Queen Philippa's daughter or dead son. Most listeners heavily discounted such a fanciful tale; rumours of Gaunt's infidelity to his own oath to protect Richard were vastly more entertaining.[29]

To damp them down permanently, during the January 1377 Parliament Gaunt pointedly introduced his royal nephew to the Commons as the king's lieutenant and paid him excessive deference. Gaunt's ecclesiastical ally, the Bishop of St David's (a friend of the late Duchess Blanche) whom he had made chancellor, opened the Parliament in the Painted Chamber with a speech calculated to present Gaunt as a dutiful son and dotingly protective uncle.

These efforts paid off. The committee of lords chosen to deliberate with the Commons by the previous Parliament had swung markedly towards Gaunt. Lords Percy, FitzWalter and Roos, in particular, were distinctly pro-Gaunt.

Lord Roos, scion of a venerable Anglo-Norman Northern family (whose son, John, was to marry Percy's half-sister, Mary), was a senior banneret of Gaunt's retinue; furthermore, his wife was the pro-Gaunt earl of Stafford's sister. He was, moreover, the brother-in-law of Percy's late wife, Margaret Neville, who had perished in 1372 (she had first married Roos's brother, who had died twenty years earlier). The family were originally of similar background and rank to the Percys (one numbered among the twenty-five barons of Magna Carta alongside Sir Richard Percy, and another received his barony from Edward I at about the same time as Henry Percy). Nevertheless, the family, although a power to be reckoned with in the far North, lagged well behind the Percys and the Nevilles. The current Lord Roos, in his forties, had considerable military experience on the Border and in Ireland and France, but lacked Percy's high-powered connections and friendships.[30]

Lord FitzWalter, an ambitious, talented but desperately luckless figure, was a baron of distinctly smaller sway than Roos, let alone Percy. Despite being Percy's cousin (his father, who had been sent to the Tower of London by Edward III for five months for various trespasses and felonies, had married Percy's aunt Eleanor), FitzWalter seems to have nursed a secret — and to us, unfortunately, mysterious — grudge against his wealthier and more influential fellow Northerner — as we shall see. At this time he was heavily indebted, and was attempting to recover his mortgaged castle and lordship of Egremont, in Cumberland. Given command of a naval squadron by Gaunt late in 1377 for a planned French invasion, FitzWalter aided in capturing eight Castilian ships but then suffered the embarrassment of a full-scale mutiny on board his own vessel. During the Peasants' Rebellion, he was hated for his love of attacking peasants. Then, while on campaign in 1386 in Galicia, he died of disease. Not a particularly auspicious career, in other words.

The same could not be said for Lord Percy, whose fortunes markedly improved at the end of 1376 as Gaunt's political position strengthened in the aftermath of the Good Parliament. At the time of the fall of de la Mare and Wykeham, Gaunt sought to chasten the man he considered responsible for his upset: the earl of March, the marshal of England. March was ordered to Calais to take up official duties there, but he refused, believing (accurately) that Gaunt would lay the blame on him for any further reverses against the French. He resigned the marshalcy and stayed in England. In Gaunt's capacity as regent, he bestowed the wooden baton of that office on Henry Percy, who was summoned for the first time as marshal of England on 1 December 1376.

Henry Percy, Marshal of England

A Percy occupied one of the four great offices of state alongside the Lord High Steward (which Gaunt held by hereditary right as earl of Lincoln), the Lord Great Chamberlain and the Lord High Constable. The marshalcy was no empty title: Percy's duties, both civil and military, were onerous. He was to keep the peace and take charge of prisoners within twelve miles of the king's presence, wheresoever he was, a shifting area known as the 'Verge' – no easy task, considering that Percy was expected to pay personally for his enforcers and staff. According to the *Constitutio Domus Regis*, a treatise from Henry II's reign, the marshal had to 'appease and prevent all tumults, noise, and disturbance in the King's Presence. He was also to keep the doors of the great Hall and of all other rooms within the Royal Palace excepting that of the King's Bedchamber'. (The chamberlain jealously guarded the latter.)

In the army, the marshal ranked below the constable, being less concerned with grand strategy and tactics than with organisation and supply. According to a catalogue written during Edward II's reign, the marshal in wartime was charged with recruiting and billeting soldiers, finding lodgings for their commanders, and procuring the huge quantities of beer and ale that kept the men happily sated. He had to organise night watches and drum up a secret watchword each day, catch enemy spies in the camp, administer military justice to misdoers, and keep the accompanying armourers, barbers, tailors, merchants and prostitutes in line and ensure they did not gouge the troops. There was one stricture: 'the marshal ought to be abroad in the field, until the other[s] be lodged, for many considerations; and ought not to come to his own lodging, untill the carriages be come into the said field.' Administrative skills were obviously a prerequisite for these great responsibilities, but there were some advantages. The marshal did not have to stand watch himself, which meant a good night's sleep, and he received the forfeitures of property of those condemned in his court. The aftermath of a successful siege could be lucrative, but not quite on the same scale as that accruing to the constable, who 'in towns taken and surrendered at discretion ... shall have the armour, and all the entire or uncut cloth'. The marshal, however, perhaps befitting his station as quartermaster-general, 'shall have all the vessels of silver, cotes, feathers, sheets, coverlets, table cloths, towels and other kinds of pelf'. The booty could be sold for profit in London or taken to Alnwick to make it more comfortable. As a bonus, the marshal was entitled to all 'spotted beasts, or of divers colours', found within the Verge and, during wartime, to collect fourpence every Saturday from each prostitute following the army.[31]

Aside from his trustworthiness, Gaunt's decision to propel Lord Percy into a role traditionally performed by an earl was carefully calculated. With Edward III's health deteriorating quickly, Gaunt suspected March of plotting a coup against him during the confusion following the king's death. As marshal, March would be perfectly placed to cut off Gaunt's access to the palace and Westminster. Far better to have an ally to do the same to March and Wykeham, if need be.

Gaunt, advised by his number two, Percy, efficiently ran the business of the 1377 Parliament.[32] Few in the heavily Lancastrian Commons dared to enquire of Peter de la Mare's fate, or where Wykeham was (forbidden by Gaunt to come close to the royal person, and watched carefully by Percy, he had to change addresses throughout Surrey and Sussex to keep out of the Verge whenever the king travelled between his nearby palaces).

But the bishop had friends – notably the powerful Bishop of London, William Courtenay – among the lords spiritual, who were angered by Gaunt's flirtation with Wycliffe, currently railing against their worldliness in London's pulpits. Smearing the duke with lies about his parentage and ambitions had failed, but his association with the Oxford scholar was his weakness. How many lords and knights would rally round a heretic who attacked the Church?

First, the bishops secured Wykeham's presence at the Parliament by refusing to discuss business until he was summoned to a convocation. So, says the chronicle, Wykeham 'was joyfully received by his fellow-bishops, and (as became such a person) greatly honoured'. Next, they launched a counter-attack on Gaunt by summoning Wycliffe to answer for his anti-clerical views at St Paul's on 19 February 1377.[33]

The bishops' insolence infuriated Gaunt, and on the morning of the day that Wycliffe was due to appear before them, the duke proposed that henceforth the mayor of London would be permanently replaced by a captain – namely Percy. He was to exercise the marshal's jurisdiction within the city, thereby allowing the power of arrest even if Percy was far outside the twelve-mile Verge.

Word of Gaunt's authoritarianism flew round the city, driving the Londoners into a frenzy about losing their historic liberties. Clearly, Gaunt intended Percy to arrest Courtenay that same afternoon at St Paul's. Furthermore, Gaunt's wish to increase the marshal's powers in London intensified the already overwrought political atmosphere in a city on the edge of vicious infighting between two equally distasteful mayoral candidates – John of Northampton's gang of mercers, weavers and drapers, and Nicholas Brembre's band of victuallers, which included the infamously violent fishmongers. Both wanted to prove their credentials by stirring up passions over the imposition of Lancastrian law.

But most importantly, at that very time Parliament was presented with a public petition protesting against the already wide extent of the marshal's rights and privileges. The main complaint was the status of Southwark in relation to the City. On the south side of the Thames and connected to the growing metropolis by a single bridge, Southwark was a disreputable, filthy warren of gambling dens, taverns, bear-baiting rings, flophouses and brothels, cursed with a rootless population of swindlers, thieves, thugs, felons of varying degrees of criminality, mercenaries, professional false witnesses, quacks, foreign sailors and beggars. It was famed for its exceptionally strong beer made from delicious, if disturbingly brownish, Thames water. The stench and pollution emanating from its numerous lime-burning furnaces contaminated the town and, when the wind blew north, settled on London. Most aggravating for the Londoners, however, was not the lime, but the tradesmen and merchants, who broke City ordinances and escaped London's fiercely independent civic courts by running across the bridge and surrendering themselves to the marshal's men in Southwark, where the Marshalsea prison had been built in 1372 to house those who disturbed the peace within the Verge. But, because Southwark was a separate jurisdiction, the malefactors would often be set free if the king were more than twelve miles away.

A year before, the City aldermen had unsuccessfully petitioned the king to allow them to take control of Southwark. Edward VI would finally give Southwark to London in 1550, but it is easy to see why Gaunt's desire to extend Percy's jurisdiction to encompass the City sparked the aldermen's fury in February 1377. Their ancient privileges would be trampled underfoot; hitherto, no officer of the Crown had power to enter the City of London to arrest someone, to seize forfeited property or to call a jury. Although it was the marshal's right to billet soldiers and members of the court wherever he saw fit, in London the mayor (regarded as being almost equal to an earl), sheriffs and aldermen selected the accommodations and then allowed the marshal to inspect them for suitability.[34] This single act of folly – permanently replacing the mayor with Percy as marshal – instantly dissipated the small stock of goodwill that Gaunt had built up since January, and revived memories of his petulant behaviour during the Good Parliament.

Understandably, then, Wycliffe's summons to St Paul's that afternoon,

19 February, was bound to be fraught with tension, which was heightened by Gaunt's insistence on escorting the cleric to his ecclesiastical trial. Riding with Gaunt, of course, was Percy, who was already loathed by Londoners as their imminent governor. The small, heavily armed procession of Wycliffites reached St Paul's without much incident but the church's forecourt was densely packed with surly citizens who took their time moving out of the way. Percy, brandishing his baton of office, and his beefy Northumbrians began to beat the people down to clear a path into the Lady Chapel. Bishop Courtenay, furious at Percy's rough-handed methods, refused to recognise his marshal's powers, but Gaunt sharply told the bishop that Percy would act like a marshal whether he liked it or not.

Inside, as tempers cooled, Courtenay ordered Wycliffe to stand when facing his interlocutors; Percy, ignoring the insolent bishop's authority, sternly ordered Wycliffe to sit. The packed crowd started taking sides, some cheering on the bishop, others Wycliffe's bolshiness. Succumbing to the sudden, violent anger that occasionally afflicted him, Gaunt leapt up and loudly threatened to drag the bishop outside by his hair. The crowd turned nasty against the duke, and the trial broke up in confusion as the guards pushed onlookers into the cold.[35]

Percy's new enthusiasm for belittling bishops is curious. He seems to have been an opportunist; a political moderate during Gaunt's low days in the Good Parliament, he was now second man to the kingdom's second man. If his superior supported Wycliffe, then so, naturally, did he. With Gaunt's unstinting backing, the title of marshal of England had fallen into his lap; what else might follow? Insulting a bishop to prove one's loyalty to the duke seemed a modest price to pay for being accelerated past the likes of March and the others who had burnt their boats with the next king's uncle by siding with his enemies.

The next morning, London's leading citizens met privately to decide how to react to Gaunt's threat to install Percy as their quasi-military governor. The atmosphere was heated, so much so that when Lord FitzWalter – Percy's own cousin, who had a grudge of some kind against the marshal, the cause of which is unknown – showed up in his capacity as the City's standard-bearer, he was almost ejected. But FitzWalter cried that he had grave news, and told the assembly that Percy had already illegally imprisoned some unfortunate Londoner in the Marshalsea.

FitzWalter was well aware of the electric effect his news would have, but his motives must remain shrouded. The citizens promptly marched across the bridge to the Marshalsea. Breaking down the doors, and overpowering the guards, they descended into the dungeon and released the prisoner from confinement.[36] But there was no sign of Percy. John of

Gaunt's imposing palace of Savoy was the likeliest place to look, and the growing crowd of angry rioters left Southwark and surged back across the river. Encompassing the area now occupied by the Savoy Hotel, the Savoy Theatre, the Strand and Victoria Embankment, the palace had been rebuilt, refurbished and enlarged by Gaunt's father-in-law, the great Henry of Grosmont, who spent the entire proceeds of his French campaigns on the project. This magnificent mansion was equipped with a great hall, stables, chapel, cloister, fortified walls, a river gate, a vegetable garden and a fish pond.[37]

After reaching the Savoy, the enraged crowd was disappointed to find Gaunt and Percy absent. In fact, they were dining at the house of John de Ypres, a rich merchant, an invitation that may well have saved their skins. As the Londoners milled around outside the Savoy, one of Gaunt's retainers disguised himself and rushed to the merchant's mansion. Bursting into the hall, where the first course was being served, he cried that the mob were close by and in murderous mood. Gaunt was so mortified that he painfully cracked his shins against the bench as he jumped up. But fortunately he and Percy did not leave by the front door onto the street, but through the back where there was easy access to the river. The duke's barge took them to Kennington, to seek shelter with Prince Richard and his mother.

Others weren't so lucky. A roving band of Londoners hunting for the elusive Gaunt and Percy happened upon a priest who abused Peter de la Mare and said he should have been hanged long ago; he was beaten to death. One of Gaunt's retainers, Sir Thomas Swinton, still carrying his patron's insignia on his tunic, was pulled from his horse and roughed up, but survived thanks to the mayor's timely intervention. In Cheapside, a shop sign painted with the duke's arms was torn down, reversed – the mark of a traitor – and rehung. Discovering Gaunt's whereabouts, the crowd marched to Kennington, howling that Wykeham and de la Mare deserved fair trials and fruitlessly demanding that Gaunt leave the protection of his sister-in-law. Joan of Kent did, however, send three knights to tell of Gaunt's sorrow for his actions – an act of supplication that went some way to assuaging the Londoners' anger.

The next day, belatedly grasping that the previous night's riot had provided an admirable pretext to impose Percy's law on the City, a deputation of Londoners begged the king's forgiveness but were adamant that it had been Gaunt's high-handed threat to the City's liberties that had caused them to rebel. The old king gracefully accepted these explanations, and promised to uphold London's privileges. Although Gaunt and the Londoners had moved slightly towards a rapprochement, when Percy and the duke came to open Parliament a few days later, they travelled through back streets surrounded by a brigade of heavy cavalry.[38]

Despite being *persona non grata* among most of the bishops owing to the St Paul's episode, Gaunt retained his Commons majority and had lately increased the Lancastrian presence in the government; Percy, of course, remained marshal, but John de Ypres, the accommodating merchant, was promoted to steward of the household, and his old ally, the bishop of St David's, became chancellor. The Commons obediently voted a poll tax of fourpence a head on everyone aged over fourteen; Richard Lyons and (at the king's insistence) even Alice Perrers were restored to their places. Gaunt, however, refused to let Wykeham back into favour, or allow him to be pardoned. In March, he granted Wykeham's substantial temporalities, castles and manors to Prince Richard. This was either to save the Exchequer money or a deft manoeuvre to split the anti-Lancastrians by setting their hero Wykeham against King Edward's heir. It was probably both. Desperate now, Wykeham bribed Alice Perrers to use her undoubted charms to intercede with the king.[39] It took three sleepless months to persuade Edward, but Wykeham's properties were returned to him on 18 June, much to Gaunt's annoyance.

Three days after Wykeham's rehabilitation, and only a day after a grand feast at Windsor where he created Prince Richard a Knight of the Garter, King Edward III, sovereign of England and France for fifty years, died. At the end, he was virtually alone. His only companion was an anonymous local priest who stayed by his deathbed, ministered to the weakening monarch and held the crucifix, which Edward kissed before expiring a few minutes later. Alice Perrers had deserted him, and returned only to pull the rings off his dead fingers. His death was kept a close secret for several days to prevent the French opportunistically launching an attack while the realm was in confusion. In Froissart's words: 'so the body of King Edward the Third with great processions, weepings and lamentations, his sons behind him with all the nobles and prelates of England, was brought along the City of London with open visage to Westminster, and there he was buried beside the Queen his wife.'

The funeral procession was sombre, but spectacular. Broad cloths of gold and red silk and satin covered the carriage and hearse, attended by 400 esquires, dressed in black from head to toe and carrying torches. Before it was lowered into the ground, the corpse was draped in red silk and a white silken cross placed on top. His death mask still survives. Several years later, an epitaph was carved on Edward's monument, which called him 'a ruler triumphant in war' and 'an unconquered leopard, as powerful in arms as the Maccabees'. Could the new king of England – a ten-year-old boy – sustain the reputation of his grandfather?[40]

CHAPTER THIRTEEN

The Fall of the Percys, 1377–1408

On 16 July 1377, a warm Thursday eleven days after Edward III's funeral, the first coronation in over fifty years was held. Very few – probably even no – nobles and prelates could remember the hurried affair that had taken place ten dark days after Edward II's deposition. This coronation's organisers, then, used essentially hearsay and a quickly revised handbook by Abbott Lytlyngton of Westminster – the *Liber Regalis* – on ritual, regalia and procedure; hence the more innovative aspects of Richard II's coronation, which were still used (with some unimportant changes) in Queen Elizabeth's coronation in 1953. The need for future reference resulted, luckily for us, in the first detailed account of an English coronation.

The chief organiser of this most joyous state occasion for decades was John of Gaunt, who petitioned to assume various coronation duties – tasks jealously guarded by the noble families through whom they descended. Gaunt, perfectly reasonably, requested that he be appointed Lord High Steward of England in right of his title as earl of Leicester; as bearer of the king's principal sword, Curtana, a traditional Lancaster honour; and finally, as earl of Lincoln, the carver of the king's meat before him at the feast following the coronation. These were granted, confirming Gaunt's position as ranking peer and beloved protector of Richard. The newly appointed steward began by settling the inevitable disputes over several of the various duties and held a Court of Claims in the royal palace at Westminster, where plaintiffs could present their case to be assigned, say, the coronation services due from the hereditary constableship of England (the 22-year-old Thomas of Woodstock, Richard's uncle and Edward III's fifth son, successfully claimed it because he had married a daughter and heiress of Humphrey de Bohun, late earl of Hereford and hereditary constable).

Some petitions were more obscure; for instance, John Wiltshire, citizen of London, argued that his tenureship of half of the manor of Heyden bestowed on him and his heirs the right to 'hold a towel when our said king shall wash his hands before eating [breakfast] on the day of his coronation'. Upon referring to the Exchequer records, Gaunt found that this was indeed the case and approved Wiltshire's application.

The most colourful service was, of course, the role of king's champion. During the banquet, he rode fully armed and armoured into the hall and challenged anyone who denied the king's legitimacy to the Crown before throwing down his gauntlet. (Interestingly, only once has it been picked up, and that was by an old woman during the coronation of George III, who was worried 'that so finely dressed a gentleman should lose his glove in so great a crowd'.) In 1377, the challenge was planned 'according to the usual custom'; it was first officially mentioned in 1327. How far back this feudalistic Anglo-Norman ritual goes is uncertain, but it is a long way. Gaunt set aside the House of Marmion's hereditary claim in favour of the little-known Sir John Dymoke, lord of Scrivelsby in Lincolnshire, since the duke recalled that Edward III and the late Prince of Wales had once said that the king's champion must be whoever was lord of Scrivelsby at the time. Perhaps so, except that the new champion's background revealed a stolid Lancastrian retainer: that is, someone on Gaunt's payroll to the tune of 20 marks (about £30) a year. Politicking like this made people distrust the duke, and as the Court of Claims proceeded – usually making the legally correct decisions, but sometimes erring in Gaunt's favour, or relying on the duke's 'memory' – some of his enemies justifiably concluded that Gaunt was bringing his own men into government to cement his power. (The Dymoke family kept the championcy until the penny-pinching coronation of William IV. The direct line of the Dymokes would die out in 1875, but a collateral branch have borne the standard of England since Edward VII's coronation.)

The Court of Claims' most politically divisive dispute concerned Henry Percy's status as marshal of England, a hereditary position traditionally accorded the earls of Norfolk. The last Norfolk to hold it, however, had been Edward I's son, Thomas of Brotherton, who died in 1338 without a surviving male heir. As the charter of the marshalcy stated that the office could pass only through his male heirs, it reverted to the Crown. Nevertheless, Margaret, countess of Norfolk, the eldest daughter of Thomas of Brotherton, repeatedly petitioned Gaunt for a deputy chosen by her to act as marshal. Initially, Gaunt dismissed her claim out of hand, but she caused such a clamour that he was obliged to declare 'that a full discussion of the matter was impossible owing to the short space of time before the coronation'. Thus, 'Henry Percy, by the assent and order of the king himself, was appointed to perform the said office.' Whether Percy would 'perform the said office' *after* the ceremonies was left ambiguous, but as the countess's heir was her eleven-year-old grandson, Percy and Gaunt were confident the marshalcy would stay in their hands until the boy reached his majority.

Gaunt's political appointments may have caused grumbles, but not his organisation of a spectacular coronation procession. For the preceding two days, Londoners had enjoyed an unofficial public holiday while the City was repaired and cleaned from top to bottom (it needed it). Musicians and jugglers were stationed at street corners. Huge statues of classical gods and fantastic creatures, large enough to contain a man, stood on the triumphal arches over the main thoroughfares; it was said that when they boomed their greetings as the king passed by, country folk visiting the city for the first time were terrified.

On the morning of the 15th, the procession set out on its lengthy journey from the Tower of London to Westminster – a trip expected to last three or four hours – surrounded by cheering crowds. Richard, clothed in white and riding beneath a canopy, was surrounded by virtually every member of the royal household, his royal uncles, every peer of the realm, and scores of knights in polished armour; before him marched the serjeants-at-arms at the head of armed mounted troops; behind followed esquires dressed in their patrons' livery. Riding alongside were the mayor of London, the aldermen and the sheriffs, together with companies of German mercenaries and delegations of Gascons.

West along Cheapside was the procession's centrepiece: a mock, four-towered castle erected by the Goldsmith's Company, from which flowed free red and white wine. Between the turrets was suspended a golden angel holding a crown, who cleverly descended and offered it to the king when he approached. And from each turret a girl scattered gilt leaves overhead as Richard passed.

When Richard was safely ensconced in Westminster Palace, he drank wine with the nobles, ate dinner and went to bed (another chronicler says he fasted and prayed in a cold cell for most of the night). Early the next morning, Richard heard Mass and met the assembled nobles and prelates in the great hall. Then came the second (short) coronation procession between the palace and the abbey.

Richard, clad in an open heavy velvet surcoat, followed the prelates who carried the consecrated cup and paten to Edward I's throne in the centre of the church, together with those royal uncles and earls bearing the royal regalia. Moving to the altar, Richard took his coronation oath – unchanged since Edward II's day – although the first three clauses were far older: the king would uphold the 'laws and customs granted by the ancient kings of England'; he 'would keep peace and godly agreement [between] God, the holy Church, the clergy and people'; he would 'cause law, justice and discretion in mercy and truth to be executed in all his judgments'; and finally, he would uphold laws and customs 'justly and reasonably' chosen by the people.

After several prayers and hymns (some of which are still used),

Richard was hidden behind a golden tapestry for the coronation's most sacred act. The archbishop of Canterbury touched Richard's palms, breast and the crown of his head with holy oil. Nigel Saul underlines the anointment's significance: 'From this moment he was set apart from other mortals. He was God's anointed ... endowed by the Almighty with special powers, the nature of which was made clear in the next part of the service when he was invested with the insignia of dominion.'

When Richard returned to his wooden throne, he was invested with the sword Curtana to protect his realm, 'do justice, stop the growth of inequity, protect the Holy Church of God'; bracelets and spurs, orb ('the whole world is subject to the Power and Empire of Christ our Redeemer'), his crown and ring ('the ensign of Kingly Dignity, and of Defence of the Catholic Faith'), and the sceptres (one was 'the ensign of Kingly Power and Justice', the other 'the Rod of Equity and Mercy'). There followed a high Mass and the oaths of fidelity ('I do become your liege man of life and limb, and of earthly worship; and faith and truth I will bear unto you, to live and die, against all manner of folks. So help me God.') from his uncles, the earls and the senior lords in close attendance, including Percy.

After the service, the parched and exhausted adolescent king rested in Westminster Palace. There was some confusion when Gaunt's hand-picked champion, resplendent in shining armour atop his charger, mis-timed his entrance by arriving at the abbey door several hours too early. Fortunately Percy, the ever-efficient marshal, had perched himself near the door in case of crowd trouble. Seeing the excited Sir John Dymoke, who may have had too much to drink, Percy firmly bid him to 'take his ease, and rest awhile'.

During the ensuing banquet, this time right on cue, Dymoke charged into the hall and loudly proclaimed that if any man questioned Richard's right to be king, Dymoke was 'redy now till the laste houre of his brethe, with his bodie, to bete him like a false man and a traitor, on what other daie that shal be apoynted'.

At the banquet Richard also created four earls and granted several knighthoods.[1]

Among them, Edward III's youngest son, Thomas of Woodstock, was made earl of Buckingham; the king's friend, John Mowbray, who was about his own age, was promoted to the earldom of Nottingham (it was he who was the grandson of the countess of Norfolk); and lastly, and most importantly, Henry Lord Percy, marshal of England, comrade of John of Gaunt, was created earl of Northumberland. It had taken the family 310 years – eleven generations – to attain this secular pinnacle of English medieval society.[2]

The Earl of Northumberland's Northumbrian Problem

Three days after the coronation, during which old enemies had come together to celebrate (Gaunt and Wykeham – jailer and jailed – had stood near each other during the ceremony), it was back to politicking as usual. In the meantime, the new Parliament had turned anti-Lancastrian, and Peter de la Mare was reinstalled as Speaker. However, Gaunt's recent displays of loyalty made it difficult for the Speaker and his followers to harp upon Gaunt's alleged plots to depose Richard.

For the new earl of Northumberland, there were greater matters afoot; hoping to take advantage of the new king's minority, the Scots were gearing up for a new season of raiding. Mounted bands, charismatically – if competitively – led by George Dunbar, the earl of (Scottish) March, and William, first earl of Douglas and the Scottish warden of the Marches, harassed English outposts in southern Scotland; pirates attacked merchants off Newcastle; and in August, March swooped into English-held Roxburgh on Fair Day, massacring shoppers and refusing quarter to any male. Douglas, meanwhile, occupied himself in Teviotdale, including the area around Jedburgh Forest – where the Percys had held land since the 1330s, and refused to give it up.

Richard and his advisers were rightly outraged by these violations: the current fourteen-year Anglo-Scottish truce was not due to expire until 2 February 1384. On coronation day, Percy had been appointed warden of the East March, and he now rushed north,[3] having resigned his cherished marshal's baton. The redoubtable countess of Norfolk – she would die in 1399 – had exasperatingly resurrected her claim to it, and the new earl and Gaunt were unwilling to keep fending off the dowager.[4]

With mounted archers and men-at-arms, Northumberland headed for Dunbar and wasted the errant earl's lands to avenge the burning of Roxburgh.[5] A letter he sent to King Robert II, complaining that the earl of Douglas, the warden, had ignored his demand for redress for the Roxburgh attack, was fatally compromised by his own raid in retaliation.[6] Thereafter, the Border settled down and in December London's confidence in Northumberland was demonstrated by the earl being given command of the West March to complement his eastern protectorate. Although Lords Clifford, Neville and Greystoke – Northern barons all – were assigned warden's duties on the Marches as equals, Percy, the North's senior policeman/guardian, bore the main responsibilities and duties (and blame).

His primary task was to ensure peace during truces, as well as holding regular March-days with his opposites on the other side, when cross-Border offences would be dealt with by tribunals, with English and Scottish jurors following the odd tenets of Border law – hang 'em high frontier justice mixed with a bit of Common Law – which attempted to regulate traditional Anglo-Scottish pursuits like hostage-taking, raiding and retaliating across what locals regarded as an *imaginary* line. Border law officially did not exist; as long as their wardens safeguarded the Anglo-Scottish *administrative* line, the respective kings and councils generally ignored goings-on in this rough neighbourhood. Indeed, according to J.A. Tuck, 'some of the treaties drawn up between the English and Scottish wardens have as much the character of private agreements between feuding magnates as public treaties between two states.'

Of course, when a truce was in abeyance (that is, in war), Border law was mothballed, as the above felonies were counted as virtues. During a truce, however, lords were responsible for their retainers' actions; the wardens, however, were expected to apprehend suspects whether or not they were in their retinue and also had to ensure they turned up for the March-days. Sometimes the system demanded that old rivalries be laid aside; Percy, for instance, paid £100 to the earl of Douglas because Hugh de Dacre defaulted on a fine for damages for that amount (Northumberland subsequently sued Dacre for the money). Sometimes a hint of menace persuaded suspects to turn up on March-day. In 1381, Northumberland wrote to a Sir William de Swynburn, commanding him 'on behalf of the king our sovereign' to attend a March-day 'to do and receive as right requires'. Finding in the event that Sir William was reluctant to 'do and receive as right requires', Percy added in a second letter: 'And know, indeed in case you are unwilling [to come] that we shall distrain your body and goods to recompense ourself.' Sir William duly turned up – although he had to skip a scheduled court appearance in London on another charge to do it. He later became MP for Northumberland.

A month after the current truce expired in February 1384, Percy introduced a new punishment during the negotiations to renew it: the death penalty for anyone wilfully breaking a truce. Capital crimes included homicide, ransom-taking, seizure of castles or towns, cattle-rustling and armed raids. Restitution was set at double the value of the stolen goods (and if a breach was committed within forty days of a March-day, all the felon's goods were forfeited to the Crown), while 'hand and horn' (the Northern version of hue and cry, when witnesses had to raise a general alarm and give chase when a crime occurred) was legalised to hinder the cross-Border racket in stolen property.[7]

Fine deeds did not always follow fine intentions. Nearing the end of the forty days after a March-day on 22 October 1378, a surprise rogue detachment of Scots took the fortress of Berwick, the key English stronghold in the east. In early December, Percy hurried to Berwick with his recently knighted eldest son, Henry (nicknamed 'Hotspur'), aged fourteen. Retaking Berwick proved straightforward; the castle's defences had been severely weakened during the Scottish attack and there were but fifty morose defenders. After nine days of siege, the English rushed the jerry-rigged barricades and put the garrison to the sword. Meanwhile, the earl of Douglas had stealthily tried to relieve the castle, but arrived too late. Northumberland chased Douglas across the border but halted when his vanguard, under Sir Thomas Musgrave, was ambushed near Melrose by Douglas. Musgrave was taken prisoner.[8]

Though Berwick was recovered, Northumberland was not exactly covered with glory. Musgrave, his hand-picked keeper of Berwick, had first lost the castle to a disorganised gang and had then been captured. Over the next few months, the Marches were rife with Douglas-inspired harrying; a humbled Northumberland reported to Richard that 'the Earls of March and Douglas, and the latter's cousin, Sir Archibald, are harassing the English borderers by imprisonment, ransoms and otherwise'. Northumberland's own unsuccessful raids into Berwickshire in the spring of 1378, which may have prompted the Scots' retorts, were not mentioned.[9]

The king was displeased, and the council decided to reorganise the North's defences, whose state of disrepair, many thought, was owed to the interminable Northumberland and Douglas feud. In February 1379, Richard commissioned John of Gaunt as 'King's Lieutenant in the Marches' to negotiate, approve and enforce treaties, replace inefficient constables of castles and oversee English strategy. On 7 December, Northumberland (and the other Border barons, Clifford, Dacre and Greystoke) were ignominiously replaced by thirteen local wardens (without a title among them). Northumberland would be available as required to Gaunt, who was a great man and Northumberland's friend but who had no roots in the deep North, where land and family reputation were essential for gaining local respect. A Londoner with lands in the Midlands and the South (but only one barony and Dunstanburgh Castle in Northumberland), Gaunt could not grasp peculiar Northern socio-cultural features like the virtually institutionalised banditry, a booty-based economy and the clientage between the old intermarried Border dynasties and the gentry.

Below them, and this must have been incomprehensible to a Southerner accustomed to a centralised and organised justice system, lay a mass of warring gangs identified by the growing use of common surnames, such as the Scottish Armstrongs, Nixons and Grahams, as well as the Charitons and Robsons of Tynedale, and the Reads and Potts of Redesdale. Only a Border magnate familiar with the bizarre geneaologies and stamping grounds of the various gangs, and willing to wield his fearsome reputation rather than apply the 'law' (such as it was), could possibly control the blood-feuds, thieving, arson and skirmishing.

Thus, instead of using Percy's native troopers (120 men-at-arms and 200 archers) to keep the 'peace', Gaunt trundled 2000 retainers – including 14 bannerets, 162 knights, 1492 squires and 1670 archers at a cost of £5000 – to a March-day in 1380. He seemed to envisage it as the prelude to a pitched battle in France rather than an informal working out of who owed what to whom after the latest raiding and robbing. Nevertheless, Gaunt's impressive array and kind words for Douglas and March, the Scottish envoys, confirmed the truce and patched up recent difficulties.

A well-meaning Southerner out of his depth, sacking a new earl from his family's customary post and then promoting his own middle-class retainers, infuriated Northumberland, even though Gaunt gave him a barrel of wine that November in return for his hospitality at Alnwick. Northumberland struck back at Gaunt's high-handedness. Just as Gaunt was interfering in the North, so too could Percy interfere in the South. In 1379, he secured the hand of eight-year-old Elizabeth Mortimer for Hotspur. She was the daughter of Gaunt's old antagonist, the earl of March (her brother would assume the title upon the earl's death in 1381). The Percys, in effect, had married into a royal house that was in direct rivalry with Gaunt, and the Mortimers now had an ally in the North. The Mortimer–Percy connection would be of fateful importance some twenty years later, as we shall see.

The old Percy bloody-mindedness – and a more recent arrogance – surfaced during the great Peasants' Revolt, which erupted in the Home Counties and London in the summer of 1381, leaving the North untouched. At the time, Gaunt – as usual, topping the rebels' hate-list – was in Berwick when he heard rumours of the insurrection in which his magnificent palace of the Savoy had been burnt to the ground by the rebels, who had not even looted it. They had destroyed everything, throwing the gold and silver into the Thames, and using the furnishings for a bonfire. Some had broken into his cellars and got drunk while others in the hall pushed three barrels containing what they thought was gold and silver into the flames. Unfortunately, the barrels held gunpowder, and the explosion blocked off access to the cellar, entombing those downstairs.

On arriving at Alnwick, expecting to lie low for a while, Gaunt was bluntly informed by Sir John Hotham and Thomas Motherby that the earl refused him entry and requested that he go elsewhere. And they added that Gaunt would not be welcome at any castle or manor under Percy's custody until the earl received assurance from the king of Gaunt's trustworthiness. Gaunt was flabbergasted: 'How cometh this to passe? Is there in Northumberland a greater sovereign that I am?' The emissaries sheepishly replied that they merely followed the orders of the earl, 'a principall and sovereigne of all the heads of Northumberland'. Gaunt's chumminess with Douglas and March, and his decision to bypass Percy, had driven the spited earl to deliver what, judging by the space that chroniclers devoted to it, was perhaps the Middle Ages' most spectacular slap in the face. Never before had a recently belted earl (who also owed his title to Gaunt) cast public aspersions on a prince's patriotism and compounded the error by treating him as an inferior.[10]

After a livid Gaunt took shelter with the Scots in Edinburgh, where Douglas was most attentive to his comfort, it was time to settle with Northumberland. In mid-July, Gaunt pointedly refused Northumberland's personal escorts (as ordered by Richard) to accompany him south; instead he took Lord Neville's troop. On 4 August, at a great council attended by the king, Gaunt accused Northumberland of betraying him; and at a feast a fortnight later, the two nobles quarrelled publicly. Mortal combat was averted only when five other earls intervened. Then in October, during a royal council in Berkhampsted, Northumberland answered Gaunt's charges by roundly abusing him 'in the manner of his people' (according to Walsingham, a Southern chronicler, who confused Northumberland's rough accent with that of a Scot), followed by ill-advisedly throwing down his gage as a challenge. After this unprecedented outburst, during which Gaunt stayed impassive, the king ordered Northumberland's arrest. After cooling down, and perhaps sobering up, in his chamber, he was bailed out to await a final decision in Parliament a few weeks later.

In early November, Northumberland, Gaunt and their large armed retinues wended their way through London to Westminster. Gaunt, still loathed by the Londoners – he left the Savoy a black wreck to remind the townspeople of their insolence – was greeted with silence, while Northumberland, the St Paul's contretemps and his term as marshal apparently forgotten, was cheered and he was given citizenship of the city. At Westminster, the king ordered their troops be left at the door. Northumberland produced four letters in which he claimed the king had ordered him to stop anyone entering the castles during the Peasants' Revolt; since Gaunt was not named as an exception, he was merely following orders. After further grievances were aired, Richard ordered a reconciliation and Northumberland humiliatingly acknowledged Gaunt before the peers as 'the greatest lord and the most exalted person in the realm after my liege lord the king'. Northumberland and Gaunt then, awkwardly, exchanged the kiss of peace.

For Gaunt, however, the quarrel was unfinished. In December, he casually sacked Percy as keeper of Berwick and warden of the East March, replacing him with the loyal Lord Neville. Percy, after complaining vociferously, was handed a newly created parcel of land – the Middle March, the most lawless part of the Border, since it encompassed the gang-infested Tynedale and Redesdale. It was a sobering lesson in power-politics for the earl.[11]

The following March the king ended Percy's period of disgrace, for he commissioned Northumberland as joint guardian for both Marches (the Middle was now dissolved) alongside Neville. The two Northerners fell out almost immediately; perhaps Neville, with as much Border experience as Percy, may have envied his title and thought him promoted beyond his abilities, while Northumberland suspected that Neville, whom Gaunt had contracted as a retainer for life in 1370, was Gaunt's spy. Whatever the reason, the prickly relationship between the wardens was possibly exacerbated by their fathers' comradeship. Percy had married Neville's sister; Neville had married Percy's aunt Maud in a match contracted in 1344 (when he was still a child); and in the mid-1370s, when their wives were alive, both lords were among Gaunt's closest confidants. Indeed, the duke had rescued Neville during the 1376 Parliament, when he was charged by the Commons with crooked loan-brokering and misappropriating funds. Soon after, Neville married the daughter of his Lancastrian co-defendant, Lord Latimer.[12]

Northumberland's rehabilitation did not last long. On 20 May 1382, Gaunt, still holding a grudge, was reappointed king's lieutenant and promptly removed Percy from his joint wardenship. Although Gaunt in June avoided *totally* humiliating the poor earl by giving him a new Middle March and the wardenship of Alnwick, Warkworth and their environs, Neville was made warden of the West and the truncated East. Whilst this meant Northumberland personally protected the Percy strongholds, Neville's grip almost everywhere surrounding them was a grave insult.

Although Northumberland could be politically immature, his craftiness shone through when it came to marriage. In 1375, the 65-year-old Gilbert Umfraville (the earl of Angus and a particularly pukka Anglo-Scot) had disinherited his half-brother with whom he was quarrelling, and settled his powerful Northumbrian barony of Prudhoe, near Newcastle, on the children of his wife Maud, sister and heiress of Lord Lucy of Egremont and Cockermouth – both lush Cumbrian baronies – who also owned substantial lands in Northumberland. Now, Maud and

Gilbert were, and would be, childless, leaving Maud as the sole inheritor of the Lucy and Umfraville fortunes. Like his father, Percy had developed a long-term strategic expertise in such matters of the heart; in 1375 he paid the £60 licence fee for Umfraville's settlement – essentially buying an option on Maud's bejewelled hand – while Percy's own first wife was alive and well. No surprise, therefore, that in December 1381, Percy married the thirty-something Maud almost scandalously soon after Gilbert's death, thereby acquiring his lands to reinforce Percy dominance in the North-East. That £60 had evidently been a wise investment. On the Lucy side of the equation, however, if Maud bore Percy children, her property would have been divided among their offspring (and then further subdivided as they married). So, attending strictly to business, Northumberland had no children by his second marriage, allowing Maud's inheritance to pass effortlessly into the Percy family after she died in 1398.

Percy engineered another marriage coup in the 1370s, (when he also, let us recall, nabbed Elizabeth Mortimer for Hotspur). Whilst Gilbert Umfraville had been one of the 'Disinherited' Scottish nobles who had associated with Percy's father in the 1330s, the son of another, David Strathbogie, the titular earl of Atholl, had died in 1369. He left two daughters, Elizabeth and Philippa, both too young to inherit. Percy swiftly bought their marriages for his two other sons, Thomas and Ralph, for the impressive sum of £760. In 1376–7, the girls inherited lands in Tynedale, which had been in the Strathbogie family since 1316 through Robert Bruce's old (murdered) enemy, Comyn of Badenoch, and the area surrounding Mitford, Northumberland, about eighteen miles south of Alnwick. However, because the Strathbogie lands passed downwards through younger sons, Percy's hold on them was not as tight as on the Lucy windfall. It weakened still further when Thomas and Ralph predeceased their father (the former in Spain in 1389; the latter in Palestine a decade later) and the lands were subdivided. By the 1430s, the Percys had lost control over their Strathbogie prize. Even so, in less than one lifetime, amazingly, the Percys had absorbed nearly all the English possessions of the most venerable among Anglo-Scottish Border families – the Umfravilles, the Comyns of Badenoch, the Strathbogies and the Lucys.[13] By the 1380s, the earls of Northumberland counted as princes in the North in anyone's estimation, but it was not too long before they disastrously (over)estimated themselves to be its kings.

For the moment, that other prince of the realm, Gaunt, could not be rid of Percy. He needed him as the countdown began to the end of the fourteen-year truce on 2 February 1384. The tit-for-tat raids brought home to Gaunt the difficulty of running the North without the full co-operation of those who owned it.[14] When, for instance, King Robert II entered into a renewed Franco-Scottish alliance with Charles VI in August 1383, Gaunt was preoccupied (for the next several years) with Castilian and Portuguese affairs. So Gaunt left the Scots to the Northerners, and in December, Neville and the necessarily rehabilitated Percy were again made joint wardens of the East and West Marches.

According to the terms of the alliance, for tying down the English on their northern front, Robert would receive 40,000 gold francs (which would pay off the balance of some £16,000 of David II's ransom, a sum London was beginning to make noises about), 1000 suits of fine French armour and 1000 trained men-at-arms. The aged Robert worried about his legacy; he yearned to regain the parts of southern Scotland that had been lost to the English and, in particular, to the Percys, who had tenaciously held Jedburgh, the stronghold and the surrounding forest since 1334, when they had been granted to Northumberland's father by Edward III.[15] Edward had known that these lands had been bestowed upon the 'Good' Sir James Douglas by Robert Bruce himself in 1320, but shrewdly wanted his Northerners to have a stake in England's Scottish empire so they would fight to keep it. But Earl Douglas's successor in the spring of 1384 was his 26-year-old son, the fiery, fearsome Sir James Douglas, bitter over the theft of his great-uncle's patrimony and hungering to face the usurping Percys in a showdown over Jedburgh. Four years later, near a village called Otterburn in the Percy heartland, he would get it.

Since the end of the truce at Candlemas (2 February) 1384, the Border had witnessed two very brief English campaigns in Scotland. First, Gaunt's gentle jaunt of 1384 was really an attempt to put pressure on the Scots to sign another truce. Remembering his kind treatment at its citizens' hands during the Peasants' Revolt, Gaunt merely held Edinburgh to ransom for a fortnight and forbade looting or razing. It marked the coda of his involvement in Scottish affairs; in his bones, he was a diplomat, not a Border guardian. Indeed, only after Percy then launched a deadly series of raids into southern Scotland in reply to Earl William of Douglas's last success, the conquest of Teviotdale, did the Scots decide to participate in the Anglo-French Treaty of Leulinghen, which carried a truce until May 1385. However, few in England, Scotland or France, apart from Gaunt, truly desired peace on the Border – too many vested interests needed to preserve instability and disorder.

For Percy, for instance, this Cold War was exceptionally lucrative. In the last year of Edward III's reign, when the Border was quiet, annual expenditure on the Marches' defence was less than £1000; but in 1384, Percy was paid £4000 for just forty-two days' worth of wardenship. That was an exceptional figure, but by 1385–6 – when King Richard's income was roughly £125,000 and defending his French possessions consumed £25,000 a year – Percy was taking the lion's share of the annual £16,000 that the Crown spent in time of war, and £8000 during a truce[16] – and this was just the cost of the *garrisons*. Since one of the warden's perks was that you were paid to keep a *private* army loyal to *you* at public expense, Percy was fortifying his fiefdom, enhancing his regional power and protecting his Scottish assets for, essentially, nothing. Indeed, he was turning a handsome profit; contracts left open how many troops the warden must retain, merely stipulating as many as 'necessary', which allowed a discreet skimming of the take. However, if the war ended, or Percy lost the wardenship, those unaffordable costs reverted to him. This strange set-up resulted in a viciously circular process: to keep the peace, the king paid a subject to create an army more loyal to its commander than its benefactor, eventually leading to more turbulence in this remote part of the realm, which necessitated hiring an even larger army to keep the peace.

Hoping to emphasise his role in Northern politics and kick-start his almost non-existent military career, Richard invaded a month after the extended truce expired in May 1385. (Jean de Vienne, admiral of France, had already sailed for Scotland with 1300 men-at-arms and 250 cross-bowmen.) To save £12,000 on the cost of the expedition, and to impress the Northern magnates and their paid soldiers with his royal authority, Richard proclaimed the last feudal summons of the Middle Ages. For the first time since Edward III's (already arachronistic) summons in 1327, virtually all the nobles, tenants-in-chief and bannerets from around the country assembled the fourteenth century's largest army, some 14,000 men – of which Gaunt, displaying his power and influence, provided nearly a third – commanded by the England's greatest lords. But all to little effect.

The Scots, as usual, avoided battle, and the huge army trundled deeper into Scotland. Advancing along a six-mile front, with 'slaughter, rapine and fire raising', the army stopped in a deserted Edinburgh. Gaunt and the other senior commanders argued fiercely about pushing deeper or swinging south towards Cumberland, where it was rumoured the Franco-Scots force was heading. For his part, Gaunt remembered his terrible march through eastern France in 1373 (see Chapter 12) and urged the safer Cumberland option. After Richard had dithered for a week, the English left for Newcastle and thence home, much to the duke's relief.

So did the French, exasperated by the Scots' refusal to fight a battle. Moreover, according to Froissart, the well-bred foreigners quickly lost the romantic urge to help their poor brethren. Scotland lacked the civilised comforts of France, and according to Froissart, they asked the admiral: 'Sir, what pleasure hath brought us hynder? We never knewe what povertie meant tyll nowe.' Relations worsened after a fight over supplies in which 100 Frenchmen, accustomed to commandeering whatever the army needed from the locals, were killed by furious Scots tenants unfamiliar with their foreign ways. At the end of the campaign, the Scots insisted the French pay for all the damage and settle their bills. Froissart reported that before their farewell the visitors told their hosts they hoped England and France would ally and attack Scotland, 'utterly to destroy that realm for ever'.

Horrifyingly, however, in Richard's absence the French had come within an ace of invading England in the south, which was prevented only by the French fleet sailing to the Flemish coast to put down a sudden rebellion. By the ships' return, Richard was in London.[17] That close shave, and his pointless campaign, convinced Richard that the North should be left to Northerners, and hang the cost. Indeed, within days of crossing into England, Richard concluded a valuable indenture with the Percys to secure the North, whereby Northumberland promised 260 men-at-arms and 520 archers for the East March, and Hotspur contracted for 100 men-at-arms and 200 archers.[18]

In the summer of 1388, the new military leader of the Scots, the earl of Fife (Robert II's second son), who was quarrelling with his slightly more dovish older brother, the earl of Carrick (later Robert III), convened with several fellow hawks, including Douglas, to discuss the next round of the Anglo-Scottish war. Richard was then facing a serious crisis in London with the five Lords Appellant – Thomas of Woodstock (now promoted to duke of Gloucester), Richard FitzAlan (earl of Arundel), Thomas Beauchamp (earl of Warwick), the 22-year-old Thomas Mowbray (earl of Nottingham, who had replaced his brother, John, when he died in 1383) and Henry Bolingbroke, the earl of Derby and Gaunt's eldest surviving son – who had launched a charge of treason against five of Richard's favourites.

Since the mid-1380s, in a manner reminiscent of the Lords Ordainers in 1311, there was a growing feeling that Richard, still a minor, was being badly advised on military and fiscal matters by his favourites. In Richard's grandfather's time, the culprit was Piers Gaveston, but now it was Robert de Vere, the 9th earl of Oxford, whose venerable dynasty currently possessed so few lands that it was known as the most insignificant earldom in England. Richard promoted him to the dukedom of Ireland in 1386, so lending him stature equal to that of the king's uncles. Such overt title-inflation prompted the Appellants to defeat de Vere's private army at Radcot Bridge in December 1387 (forcing the duke to flee to the Low

Countries, where he died in 1392 from injuries sustained in boar-hunting) before ordering Richard to rid himself of his 'evil counsel' and submit to a reform-minded council of Appellants. To refuse meant deposition. Richard submitted. On 1 January 1388, the Appellants purged the royal administration, and in the 'Merciless Parliament' that February, thirty-nine charges were read against the favourites. Only one, Nicholas Brembre, a remarkably obese and corrupt former mayor of London, was actually present (the others had escaped the country or taken sanctuary in Westminster). Feelings ran so high that when Brembre offered to clear his name in combat, the assembled lords, knights and even esquires threw down 305 gauntlets. Finally, Brembre and some other favourites were executed. For the next ten years, a bitter Richard would strive to forget the humiliation; his revenge would be equally merciless, and its aftermath would thrust the Percys onto the national stage and into Shakespeare's history plays.

In 1388, however, Northumberland kept studiously neutral. *Knighton's Chronicle* relates that Northumberland's role was limited to advising the king that the Appellants were loyal to the Crown, although he believed the king's favourites were dragging it to the ground. To put it frankly, however, Northumberland remained a bit-player in national politics.[19] He was rather more concerned about the increasingly menacing activity across the Border and ensuring the Exchequer paid his family's bills. In June, with their rival Lord Neville sick – he would die in October – Hotspur was appointed warden of the East March and keeper of Berwick for the princely sum of £12,000 if war broke out.

He was right to watch the Scots. The earls of Fife and Douglas themselves were watching the English and had decided the Appellants' crisis offered a splendid retaliatory opportunity for Richard's 1385 campaign. Together, they planned a three-pronged assault copied from Robert Bruce's invasion of 1327 during the crisis over Edward II's deposition. Sixty years later, the Scottish goals were to eradicate the English pale in southern Scotland and force the English kings to renounce their unending demands for their counterparts' homage (and the balance of David II's ransom). This being the North, personal animosities were naturally involved, most notably those between Percy and Douglas (who a year or two earlier had deliberately devastated Percy's recent Lucy acquisitions in Cumberland, lands that hadn't been raided since the 1320s), but these were part of the larger picture. Thus, the famous ballads of Otterburn and Chevy Chase paint a romantic picture of these two warring Border houses, antagonistic but mutually respectful of each other's martial prowess. But the legendary Percy–Douglas rivalry involved a serious point of principle. Edward III's grant of Jedburgh to the Percys, ignoring

Robert Bruce's gift to Sir James Douglas, symbolised Scottish subordination to the English Crown. Until the English kings were forced to undo their ancestors' deeds, the Scots believed, there could be no permanent peace, only truces.

The Scots chose Cumberland and Westmorland, which were far more weakly defended than Northumberland, for the main brunt of the attack, led by Fife towards Carlisle in early August 1388. Aimed at further stretching the English were two diversionary thrusts into Ireland and Northumberland, the latter led by Douglas. But Fife's expedition faltered; Carlisle did not fall and he retreated across the Border. In contrast, Douglas's luck held and he reached Newcastle, where Hotspur was frantically arranging musters, in mid-August. During the skirmishing, Douglas captured Hotspur's pennon, which the latter vowed to recover before the Scot left England. Northumberland was currently holed up in Alnwick with a large force, but father and son believed Douglas's advance was a feint before the main Scots army arrived. But when Douglas learnt that Fife had failed (which meant he could be trapped between Hotspur and Northumberland), the Percys realised he *was* the main Scots army.

On the morning of 18 August or thereabouts (exact dates are difficult to confirm), the English sentries on Newcastle's walls discovered that Douglas had disappeared. Before noon the next day, Hotspur's scouts reported seeing Douglas racing north-west towards Redesdale, and he urgently set off in hot pursuit. Douglas, however, had paused for the night at the village of Otterburn (intending to attack its tower the next morning) on the River Rede at the south-eastern end of Redesale, equidistant between Alnwick and Newcastle. Instead of waiting for his father, Hotspur – lending credence to his nickname – hared the thirty-two miles to Otterburn, arriving before dusk. Intending to surprise Douglas, he deployed his troops (the size of the armies is unclear, but each side may have numbered several hundred men-at-arms and a few thousand foot) to prepare for a risky night battle under a full moon. Douglas hadn't even assigned sentries and his men were about to bed down when a messenger shouted that a Percy was coming. Douglas was astonished; having decided on a pitched battle, he had not expected Hotspur before the next day at least. With no time to don his armour, he yelled at his men to take positions along a ridge.

Assigning Sir Thomas Umfraville to execute a flank manoeuvre on the enemy camp, Hotspur led a frontal attack against the darkened ridge and fell into Douglas's trap. The earl had taken his best cavalry behind the ridge, circled towards the English right flank, charged, shattered it and pushed the survivors downhill into the roiling centre. Before he could finish off the English, however, Douglas was mortally wounded by an unknown hand. Oblivious to their leader's death, his valiant Scots kept fighting and by dawn had ejected the English from the ridge, even capturing Hotspur (and twenty-one knights) during the night. The next day, both sides withdrew. Today, the Percy Cross – actually an obelisk erected in 1777 – stands at the battlefield. As for the horrendous casualties, chroniclers' estimates vary widely. Certainly, the number of Englishmen killed by their own side had never been higher. According to the Westminster chronicler, when in the darkness the English 'aimed a careless blow at a Scotsman, owing to the chorus of voices speaking a single language it was [often] an Englishman that they cut down'. One reliable indicator might be the 1200 skeletons of young and middle-aged men discovered in the north wall of nearby St Cuthbert's Church in 1877.[20]

Tactically a Scots victory reversing the series of previous English successes, Otterburn was also a strategic draw, the fiery Hotspur's surrender (and subsequent ransoming) being counter-balanced by the death of Douglas, the most hawkish and competent Scots commander. So, we may surmise, the noticeably dovish shift in London and Edinburgh during the coming year was no coincidence.

For Northumberland, however, the aftermath was terrible, even though a royal council, impressed with the hero's derring-do, paid two-thirds of Hotspur's large ransom. The earl's superiors in London, nonetheless, were dissatisfied with Northumberland's lackadaisical performance – Fife's Cumberland raid, while a strategic failure, had been devastating and Otterburn counted as an English defeat. During the next six months, the Appellant earl of Nottingham, a man lacking Northern connections who had publicly disparaged Percy, was sent north as warden of the East March (no special allotment to Percy this time of a Middle March and Alnwick), while the young Lord Beaumont and the Cumbrian Lord Clifford took over the West March. Despite the money saved on Hotspur's ransom, Northumberland's finances were hit hard by his disgrace. With Nottingham's accession, he instantly lost all his huge war subsidies and was ordered to cool his heels at Richard's court when Nottingham and Beaumont raided Scotland the next summer, while Fife and the new earl of Douglas, Archibald the Grim (an illegitimate son of the Good Sir James), invaded Northumberland. In the year following the negotiation of an Anglo-French truce in June 1389, the earl – although not in favour, Percy remained an earl and carried out duties appropriate to his rank – briefly served as captain of Calais and joint ambassador to France.

There was one bright spot, however. Gaunt had been in France and Spain for two years, and during Northumberland's French sojourn the two former companions must have met (Percy's brother, Sir Thomas, was a Gaunt negotiator, and may have acted as a go-between). So, on Gaunt's return to England, he healed the nearly decade-long break between himself and Northumberland before getting to grips with a country cursed by, according to one historian, 'intense political and constitutional conflict, by magnate rebellion, by condemnations for treason and the executions of royal councillors and courtiers'. In the meantime, to keep the Percys onside, the newly released Hotspur was retained in Richard's service for life (at £100 per annum) and given the West March in June 1390, nine months after a new Anglo-Scottish truce, linked to the French one, was concluded.

By the time Northumberland had served his penance and been given the East March again in June *1391* – three years after Otterburn – the Border was quiet. It was little comfort that the Scots were disappointed by the truce; according to Walsingham the chronicler, they had bought weapons in gleeful preparation for the raids to come.[21]

The Fall of Richard II

Between 1389 and 1394, Richard II was preoccupied with negotiating a permanent peace with France. As related in previous chapters, the talks hinged – as they essentially did throughout the Hundred Years War – on the status of the duchy of Aquitaine, held by the English king as a vassal of the French Crown; the actual dukedom was historically held by the king's eldest son.

Richard was not so attached to his hereditary appurtenance. He said himself that he was more concerned with lowering taxes for his subjects, although many were willing to pay those taxes to keep Aquitaine. Richard's proposal, as part of a peace initiative, to divest himself of the title, 'duke of Aquitaine', and give it to Gaunt (so that it would be *his* problem), therefore encountered substantial opposition both at home – in 1392, for example, the Commons said 'it was absurd, beside being extremely damaging to the king and Crown' – and in Gascony, where the Estates of Gascony drew up the 'Instrument of Union', declaring they would consent to be governed only by the Crown of England. There was even a rising in Cheshire, which was traditionally devoted to Richard, in protest. In the face of this opposition and on the advice of his council, Richard eventually withdrew the offer to Gaunt.

An interesting episode involving Hotspur occurred at this time. In 1393, when Gaunt was confident that the plan was still going ahead, he had appointed Hotspur his deputy in Aquitaine. In the spring of that year, perhaps discharging his semi-official duties, Hotspur appears to have travelled to Nicosia in Cyprus, where he met with a convivial King James, king of Jerusalem and Cyprus (who in July sent Richard a letter thanking him for sending Hotspur).[22]

With the status of Aquitaine still unresolved, a new peace treaty was impossible and the Hundred Years War would continue, but a remarkable *twenty-eight-year truce* was agreed in 1396 followed by Richard's betrothal to the six-year-old Princess Isabella of France. Northumberland, whose enforced diplomatic experience was paying dividends, travelled to Calais with Richard to arrange the match and the all-important dowry of £133,333. In the near future, Richard's willingness to give up his 250-year-old Angevin birthright was seen by many as kowtowing to the enemy across the Channel. In reaction, his successors would escalate the Hundred Years War and reclaim their title as king of France.[23]

In January 1397, however, the Commons was again complaining about Richard's excessive spending on his household, and the king's favourites, especially his half-brothers – his mother, Joan of Kent, had first been married to Sir Thomas Holland (died 1360) – 54-year-old Thomas Holland and 47-year-old John Holland (the earls of Kent and Huntingdon respectively), and his cousin the 24-year-old earl of Rutland. Faced with a furious Richard, the Commons apologised. In July, with an ample Exchequer and a Franco-Scottish truce in place, Richard bitterly avenged himself upon the Lords Appellant, by arresting Gloucester (who had been particularly critical of the French negotiations), Arundel and Warwick, for treasonably taking over the government in 1386–8. At his trial, Arundel bravely defended his actions but was executed the same day, 'no more shrinking or changing colour than if [he] were going to a banquet', reported Walsingham. Warwick's 'wailing and weeping and whining' brought merely exile to the Isle of Man (a fate some regarded as worse). As for Richard's most hated foe, it was reported that Gloucester had died in Calais while under arrest. There is, however, exceptionally strong evidence that he was murdered (allegedly smothered by towels in a feather bed by a certain William Serle, a gentlemen of Richard's bedchamber) at Nottingham's instigation. This mercurial former Appellant was captain of Calais at the time and had returned to the king's affinity a while back.

(An interesting footnote: in late 1397, rumours ran around the country that the head and torso of Arundel had miraculously reattached themselves and that he had risen from the grave. After Richard directed Lancaster, Northumberland and three other earls to 'ghostbust' one night to see the truth for themselves, Arundel's corpse was exhumed and reburied under the pavement of an Augustinian friary.)

Next, Richard raised his friends to dukedoms, cheapening the title so much that they were known as 'duketti'. The earls of Rutland, Huntingdon and – extraordinarily – Nottingham were given the dukedoms of Albemarle, Exeter and Norfolk respectively. Kent, however, died of natural causes, so his son, in his late twenties, was created duke of Surrey in his stead.

One former Appellant, however, was untouchable: Henry Bolingbroke, the earl of Derby and Gaunt's heir (loyal to the king since the 1370s, the duke had dutifully followed the royal will that summer). Richard still required Lancastrian support for his policies, and so he also, reluctantly, raised Derby to the dukedom of Hereford.

From Northumberland's point of view, the result of Richard's Anglo-French truce in 1396 was that by 1398 he possessed absolutely no official authority on the Border. The Scots had extended their own truce until 1399, and both sides had mooted the idea of Robert III accepting one of twenty-eight years (like the Anglo-French truce). The earl was well aware that, since 1396, Richard had moved his own men into the Marches – in September, he appointed the duke of Exeter (at the time, earl of Huntingdon) the warden of the West March, followed in 1398 by the duke of Albemarle. Most worryingly, Richard's acquaintance Lord Ralph Neville, son of Percy's late sparring-partner (and also Percy's cousin, since Neville's father had married Maud Percy) was created the earl of Westmorland in 1397 and appointed the next year as 'Guardian of the Truce of the East March'. No longer could Northumberland's own earldom guarantee Percy superiority on the Border, especially in a time of peace and well-connected dukes. Richard was clearly looking towards a permanent Anglo-Scottish peace, when ferocious Border magnates who made their own law would be obsolete. The signs were all there. In Northumberland's personal experience of Richard's diplomacy in the French negotiations, tough talking would be followed by a drastically modified position and then agreement – on the other side's terms. In Scotland's case, Richard had originally asked his diplomats in 1393 to demand (a) homage from the king of Scotland, who held his realm by grace of the king of England; (b) that Scots peers were subjects of the king of England; and (c) that the recaptured lands that Edward Balliol had ceded to England in 1334 be returned, thus following Edward I's traditional policy of the 1290s, later advanced by Edward III. However, since Richard knew the Scots would never agree, he gave his diplomats a fall-back position by secretly instructing them to ignore the 1334 territories and accept whatever the English had held in 1369 – a far smaller area. Northumberland could predict that if the ultimate price of peace was to drop *all* English territorial demands, Richard would do it and his new courtiers on the Border would enforce it. If that happened, Jedburgh and everything that five generations of Percys had wrested from the Scots would be handed over, gratis.

Moreover, there was perhaps a certain element of jealousy involved in Northumberland's disenchantment with Richard, a disenchantment that had been gently brewing for maybe the last twenty years. Since receiving his coveted earldom and the marshal's baton, Northumberland had generally been treated offhandedly by the powers that be. In 1397–8, when those around him were rising fast and he seemed to be standing still, Percy's brother Thomas, described as 'doux, raissonnable, et gracieux' by Froissart, had dutifully fought in France, at sea, and served in a number of administrative and diplomatic positions. Unlike his older brother, Thomas hadn't made too many enemies. Despite lacking assets and territory, Richard granted him the earldom of Worcester, along with property on the Welsh Marches that were forfeited by the late earl of Arundel on the same day that he gave Neville the earldom of Westmorland. This move deliberately rubbed salt, no doubt, into Northumberland's wound, although the two brothers do not appear to have fallen out over the honour even when Thomas was made Steward of the Household.[24]

The same could not be said for the remaining Appellants, Hereford and Norfolk, formerly the earls of Derby and Nottingham. On 30 January 1398, Hereford came before the king at the 'Revenge Parliament' and revealed that the month before a panicked Norfolk had hissed at him, 'We are about to be undone.' Hereford was confused. What did he mean? 'For what was done at Radcot Bridge,' replied Norfolk, referring to the battle between the Appellants and the earl of Oxford in December 1387, which had eventually led to their purge of Richard's administration. But, queried Hereford, they had been pardoned and made dukes; surely they were safe from the king's revenge? To which the cynical Norfolk, who knew a thing or two about cloaks and daggers (he had killed his old friend Gloucester in Calais on Richard's orders), murmured that it was 'un merveillous monde et faux'. Shaken, Hereford asked what was to happen, and Norfolk revealed that he, Worcester, Albemarle and Exeter had quietly foiled a plot by unscrupulous favourites who had been promoted in 1397. It seems that the duke of Surrey, Thomas Despenser (who had been made earl of Gloucester) and others had planned to kidnap and murder Gaunt and Hereford the previous October – with Richard's connivance. Now, of course, added the terrified Norfolk, they were out to get him. In a court feverish with plotting and intrigue, no one was safe. But it was Norfolk's final comment that truly threw Hereford. He had said that the plotters aimed to overturn the judgement concerning Earl Thomas of Lancaster, at which Hereford exclaimed, 'God forbid!' Norfolk was referring to Parliament's 1327 annulment of Edward II's sentence of forfeiture against the rebellious former leader of the Lords Ordainers, who had been beheaded at the king's command and whose estates had escheated to the Crown. After the reversal, the Lancastrian estates were restored to Thomas's brother, Henry, and thence they had passed down the line to Gaunt, who had married into the family. The implication was clear: Richard intended to deprive Hereford of his inheritance when Gaunt died by quashing the 1327 parliamentary annulment. The presence of a direct descendant of the grasping Edwardian opportunist Hugh Despenser among the plotters, as well as Richard's well-known idolisation of Edward II (he repeatedly, if vainly, badgered the Pope to canonise him), could only add to the impression of a wheel turning full circle.

Covetousness of Gaunt's £10,000 net income per annum played only a small role in Richard's calculations (it may have loomed rather larger in those of his acolytes), since the royal finances were excellent. More likely Richard was worried about the succession; he was thirty years old with no heir and a wife who was still a child. His paranoid fears of Gaunt's kingly ambitions had resurfaced; the House of Lancaster under Hereford was in a prime position to usurp him. The only contender was the earl of March – Roger, the son of Lionel of Antwerp and Philippa – who would die in July 1398, aged twenty-four. He left, importantly, a seven-year-old heir, Edmund. About this time, as the king's biographer Nigel Saul has written, Richard was 'a man living increasingly in fear... Wherever he travelled in his realm, he surrounded himself with his Cheshire archers, who ate and slept with him and instilled terror into every community through which they passed.'

Which is why Hereford spoke so frankly at the 1398 'Revenge Parliament' – he needed Richard to deny the rumours of such a plot in front of the Lords and Commons, which the king did. Then, just to make sure, Hereford first obtained an ironclad pardon for all previous crimes (including treason in the 1380s), then written legal confirmation of the Lancasters' lands and titles, so that Richard could never reverse the 1327 annulment – by legal means, anyway.

Richard was in a tricky position as regards Norfolk, who might tell all about Gloucester's death. The king's attempts at reconciliation failed, and after further charges from Hereford, including accusing Norfolk of murdering his uncle, Gloucester, Norfolk insisted on settling the issue by the laws of chivalry – trial by combat. Although Norfolk was a competent jouster, Hereford was the more skilled tourneyer, but no matter who won, Richard would be presented with yet another gnawing problem. A

Norfolk victory would only provide a temporary respite before rumours of Gloucester's death again circulated. But if Hereford triumphed, the king's nemesis would rise even higher in the nobility's estimation – to the detriment of his own.

Just outside Coventry, on 16 September, Hereford, escorted by six esquires and wearing Milanese armour, arrived at nine in the morning for the eagerly awaited tournament, followed by Norfolk (in lavish Bohemian). When the champions exited their pavilions, their lances were measured and they faced each other, with Hereford making the first feint. At that point, the king stood up and cried, 'Halt!', taking, as was his prerogative, the final decision into his own hands. His verdict came two hours later: Norfolk was banished for life, and Hereford exiled for six years, even though no charges had been brought against him. The king did reiterate, however, that if his father died during his exile, Hereford would receive his inheritance abroad.[25]

It was a Solomonic, if inequitable, solution. By the autumn of 1398, therefore, Richard's dominance was unchallenged; the dangerous Hereford was across the water; the sinister Norfolk, who knew too much, wasn't coming back; Arundel had been executed; his chief tormentor, Gloucester, was no doubt rotting in hell; and Warwick was discovering the manifold delights of the Isle of Man.

Almost immediately after Hereford had left England, the 59-year-old Gaunt fell grievously ill most probably from a genital disease contracted during one of his (innumerable) fornicatory bouts. On 3 February 1399, after being visited by his royal nephew, whose newfound deviousness Gaunt still could not fully comprehend, 'time-honoured Lancaster' died. According to Froissart, Richard shed no tears for his departed uncle, even writing to his friend, the king of France, of Gaunt's death 'with a sort of joy'.[26]

The dukedom of Lancaster and all its appurtenances now lay in limbo, presenting Richard with a unique, if risky, opportunity. Confiscating the Lancastrian estates – thereby breaking his promise – might prompt a wrathful Hereford to return illegally to England, whereupon Richard could execute him. But to allow Hereford to inherit *in absentia* – as he had agreed – merely postponed a final reckoning. After six weeks, Richard struck. He confiscated the estates and upped Hereford's banishment from six years to life. If he *ever* set foot on English soil, Hereford was a marked man. However, Richard ignored the peers' discomfort at these arbitrary actions, which were eerily similar to those in King John's and Edward II's final years. If the inherited private property of the greatest prince of all was subject to Richard's wilfulness, what hope had the other peers of justice?

Thus, Richard was indelibly identified in their minds as a tyrant, something widely defined in the Middle Ages as a ruler who arbitrarily disposed of his subjects' property, since this implied that the king acted in his own, not the realm's, interests by imposing Continental forms of royal power on home-grown, Magna Carta-guaranteed liberties and freedoms. Likewise, the foreign cult of obedience to the sovereign as supreme lawgiver was summarised by Richard's chancellor to Parliament in 1397: 'every subject should be duly obedient to the king and his laws.' Previously, the law had existed and the king had lived under it.[27] Such authoritarianism reflected Richard's own character; Adam of Usk, a well-placed chronicler, observed that the chief cause of Richard's ruin was that he confused valid criticism with disloyalty.[28]

To more practically minded men like Northumberland, Richard's behaviour was putting their property, titles and even lives at risk. In the North, moreover, the king's policy of playing the Border barons off against each other to prevent the Percys from becoming too powerful, was weakening. Thus, the Percys' rival, Ralph Neville, earl of Westmorland, who was married to Joan Beaufort, Hereford's half-sister, was alienated from Richard in May 1398, when he was assigned offices and fees belonging to the (under-age) Lord Clifford that were then taken away. In Northumberland's case, his frustration was climbing towards boiling point. After years of exclusion from the Marches, there seemed no prospect of this changing, no matter what he did. Indeed, when Albemarle, then the warden of the West March, asked Richard for permission to give Northumberland the Middle March in July 1398, the king refused.[29] And Percy was given no commission to deal with violators of the Anglo-Scottish truce, further eroding his position as dispenser of Border justice.

Nevertheless, all these lords might have continued to fume in silence had the French duke of Orléans not desired his own kingdom in northern Italy. While Richard was campaigning in Ireland, in 1399, following some complex political manoeuvring in France, the exiled Hereford and the French duke, who was interested in Hereford as a potential pretender to the English throne, came to an agreement. Orléans and the French king would let Hereford 'escape' in return for turning a blind eye to French plans for northern Italy. Shortly after, the duke of Hereford sailed to England with sixty followers to reclaim his inheritance.[30]

On 30 June, Hereford landed at Ravenspur on the Humber estuary. In Yorkshire, the Lancasters would find considerable local support, and Hereford wanted to secure his family's fortresses at Pickering, Knaresborough and, especially, Pontefract, astride the main road to London from the North and the Midlands. Once he was joined by the men of Lancashire, Yorkshire and Lincolnshire, Hereford's route south would pass through the family strongholds of Derby and Leicester. Hereford first received aristocratic backing on 16 July at Doncaster. Unexpectedly, the earl of Northumberland, Hotspur and Westmorland rode up, escorted by their armed Border retinues; the North had risen for Lancaster. Shortly after Hereford's landing, the three magnates must have met secretly, weighed up the chances of success and the penalties for failure, and finally, momentously, resolved to rebel against their lawful king.

Hereford's ultimate goal when he met privately with the Percys that night remains shrouded in mystery. Did Northumberland and Hotspur believe Hereford would be content with regaining his inheritance, or did they suspect he wanted to depose Richard? Most likely the latter, even if Hereford modestly denied such grandiose ambitions so early in the game; why else would they risk a beheading for Lancaster's patrimony? On the other hand, if Hereford's protest turned into a successful revolution, a grateful Lancaster would reward his faithful Percys with – a lavishly endowed dukedom? Undisputed imperial control over Scotland and the Border (excepting Westmorland, of course)? Eventual marriage into the royal house? For the moment, Northumberland was made de facto constable and put in command of the army, while Westmorland was given the marshalcy. Money, of course, was never far from the Percys' minds, and some indication of their usefulness to Hereford – relative to the more compromised Westmorland and others – can be gleaned by their 'wages' for joining him. Whereas Westmorland received £146 for his services, Northumberland negotiated a staggering £1333 for a few months' work, with Hotspur pulling in another £666. Of the £4900 that Hereford spent subsidising his growing forces, the Percys' share approached half.

If Richard had been in England and able to raise support, he still might have saved his Crown, but he was stuck in Ireland and the fleet had already dispersed. His weak royal uncle, Edmund of Langley, the duke of York (and father of the duke of Albemarle), held the keepership of the kingdom, but within weeks thousands had deserted from the army he summoned. By the end of July, even York himself had joined his nephew. Confident that opposition was melting away, Hereford postponed his march on London and moved his growing forces towards Wales, where the king was expected to land to rouse his loyal Cheshire archers. In Bristol, the rebels captured three of Richard's councillors and, under Northumberland's and Westmorland's judgement, executed them, indicating that Hereford and his assistants now intended a *coup d'état*. Indeed, the first Percy prize came on 2 August: Hereford, without formal legal authority, appointed him warden of Carlise and the West March for ten years, and confirmed Hotspur as warden of the East March, Berwick and Roxburgh Castle – showing that Hereford was cognisant of the Percys' Scottish claims. Crucially, by accepting the commission – oddly, there is no mention of Westmorland, who had possibly been shunted subtly aside by the Percys – Northumberland implicitly accepted Hereford's assumption of royal prerogatives. Now he was in up to his neck.

By now, Richard had reached Wales and was lodging at Whitland Abbey, Carmarthen, with the diehard dukes of Exeter and Surrey, three bishops and his steward of the household, Thomas Percy (the earl of Worcester), who had escorted him to Ireland. When Richard secretly fled with fifteen companions to join John Montagu, earl of Salisbury – another favourite promoted to an earldom in 1397 – at Conwy Castle in North Wales, Thomas Percy stayed behind and, weeping, broke his staff of office, telling those remaining that they should disperse for Richard's reign was nearing its end. By this time, it seems clear, Worcester had thrown in his lot with Hereford and Northumberland.

Hereford now faced a problem: from Conwy the king might sail to Scotland, Ireland or even France, and one day return to reclaim his Crown. He had to be flushed out quickly. So on 12 August, Richard received a herald from Northumberland, respectfully requesting a meeting to discuss terms. The king accepted, and Northumberland, accompanied by a small party of his Borderers, entered.

The earl declared that Hereford desired only his inheritance and unblinkingly swore *on the sacraments* that Richard 'would be permitted to retain his royal power and dominion'. (Not that Richard was any less duplicitous; he told friends 'whatever assurances I give [Northumberland], he will be put to bitter death for this outrage'.) On 15 August Richard left Conwy while Northumberland went on ahead, ostensibly to arrange dinner for the royal party at Rhuddlan. When Richard crested a hill about two miles outside Conwy, he saw Northumberland and his entire retinue waiting for him in the valley below. Realising he had been tricked, he tried to turn back to Conwy, but the Borderers surrounded his escort and, acting as constable, the earl took the king into custody. The next day at Flint, halfway between Conwy and Chester, Hereford entered the king's chamber and bowed deeply twice before remarking understatedly: 'My lord, I have come sooner than you sent for me, and I shall tell you why. It is said you have governed your people too harshly, and that they are discontented. If it is pleasing to the Lord, I shall help you govern them better.' Richard was then taken to Chester, where he was locked in the castle tower.

The trickiest part of the coup was to work out a way to depose an anointed, hereditary monarch in favour of an usurper. In September,

Hereford directed all the monasteries in the land, as well as learned doctors and bishops, to search archives dating back to the Conquest to find precedents and tell him 'how it was to be done'.

The obvious example was Edward II, who had been judged 'insufficient to govern', guilty of neglect and losing English possessions abroad. But Edward had voluntarily relinquished power only after the people – well, Londoners anyway – had assented to, and acclaimed, the decision by magnates to depose him and to replace him with his son. Richard, however, might not be amenable to resigning voluntarily, meaning Hereford might need to consider a formal, legal process of deposition, which could be very tricky indeed given Richard's divine appointment. Thankfully for Hereford, his researchers discovered that Pope Innocent IV had formally deposed the Holy Roman Emperor Frederick II in 1245 for tyranny, perjury and sacrilege (Northumberland's own profane oath at Conwy, when he swore on the sacraments that Richard would remain king was conveniently forgotten). Hereford's committee, therefore, listed 33 'crimes' Richard had perpetrated during his reign that could be used against him if necessary. If guilty, he could be dismissed.

What was really needed was Richard's written resignation; he was, after all, appointed by the Grace of God. Time was running out; Hereford had summoned a Parliament for 30 September and he needed that crucial piece of paper from Richard to show the nation's representatives. It was only on 29 September when Hereford himself visited Richard – who by now had almost collapsed under Northumberland's incessant cajoling and threatening throughout September in pursuit of his surrender of the Crown – that the king gave in, on the condition that he keep his inherited lands. Northumberland later confided to the chronicler, John Hardyng, that Richard had resigned 'under dures of prison in the Toure of London in fere of his life'. The king's condition was granted; and Richard 'placed it [the crown] on the ground and resigned his right to God, from whom he had received it'. Soon after, when Adam of Usk, a scholarly chronicler, visited Richard, the despairing king bemoaned the state of England, that 'is ever tainted and toileth with strife and variance and envy' before recalling the travails of his royal predecessors. (Shakespeare paraphrased this lament in *Richard II*, Act III, scene iii.)

Next day, Hereford solemnly asked the Parliament whether those assembled acclaimed his kingship 'with their hearts as well as their mouths', adding with false modesty that if they did not, 'it would not be any great surprise to me'. After they had shouted, 'Yes, yes, yes', Worcester ecstatically cried, 'Long live Henry of Lancaster, King of England!'

At Lancaster's coronation as Henry IV on 13 October 1399, where to signify his status Northumberland proudly bore the Lancaster Sword that Hereford had worn when he had landed at Ravenspur, Sir Thomas Dymoke, the king's champion and son of the John Dymoke who had performed the same service more than twenty years previously, issued the old challenge against those who would deny the king's legitimacy. No one spoke for the now plain 'Sir Richard of Bordeaux'.

The new junta now had to decide what to do with Sir Richard and his adherents. Henry demoted the former dukes of Exeter, Albemarle, Surrey and the earl of Gloucester to their former titles. (However, in 1400, after a chaotic and very short-lived 'rebellion' in which John Montagu, earl of Salisbury, also participated, all apart from Albemarle – who was killed at Agincourt in 1415 – were executed.)

As for other main protagonists, Henry wanted to invite Norfolk back to England, but after making a pilgrimage to the Holy Land, the guilt-ridden duke died in Venice in September, a few weeks before the coronation. Warwick, still languishing in the Isle of Man, was welcomed home by the king.

Richard, in one gilded prison after another, finally came under Henry's custody in Pontefract, but after the failed rebellion by the demoted dukes, Northumberland bloodthirstily urged Henry to have Richard killed to stifle further loyalist disturbances. In the month following Henry's accession, the now-dominant Percys received their just rewards: Northumberland was made constable of England for life, was granted the Isle of Man and arranged a guaranteed annual income for warden work of £1500 in peace and £6000 in war; as befitting the family's blue-chip national status, Hotspur was granted the government of North Wales – never before Percy territory – and an income of £3000 in peace and four times that in war; Thomas Percy, earl of Worcester, was made admiral of England and given an annuity of 500 marks (about £333).

Richard was not so fortunate. Sometime in February 1400, he died, probably chained to the wall and then starved to death at Pontefract by his jailers. When Victorian excavators examined his slender, undermuscled body, nearly six feet tall with a delicate, round face, they found no marks of violence. Henry ordered the corpse to be transported the 200 miles to London for burial with its face uncovered, so that all could see the king was dead.

Richard's deposition broke the hereditary principle for the first time since 1199; on his death, the Plantagenet dynasty became extinct and Henry held power because in 1399 he had meritocratically advanced himself as a better, more popular ruler than Richard. But as Nigel Saul says: 'A dangerous new element of instability had been introduced into politics.'[31] Nevertheless, to instil some stability, Henry stood adamantly on his genealogical legitimacy to the Crown; as he declared in Parliament, 'I am that descendit by right of ye blode comyng from ye god kyng Henry the Thryd.'[32]

Notwithstanding his claims, however, Henry *was* technically a usurper, and was neurotically aware of his potential legitimacy problem; he would deal harshly with those who later claimed Richard was still alive (the first instance occurred in 1402) or questioned his right to govern England. Moreover, with the eight-year-old earl of March (Edmund Mortimer) – whose claim to the Crown was possibly even stronger than Henry's through descent from Edward III's second son, Lionel of Antwerp – in the wings, Henry's hold on the throne depended on a muscular performance. When a man is proclaimed by consent, that consent can also be withdrawn.[33]

Henry IV, the Percys and Scotland

The most effective method, as always, to cement national support is to win a war, preferably against foreigners. The Scots, again as usual, would do. Another quickly arranged Anglo-Scottish truce was expiring that winter, the Scots had already begun raids into the North and, fortuitously, King Robert III in a letter of November 1399 nastily addressed Henry as 'duke of Lancaster, count of Derby and Seneschal of England'.

In Parliament on 10 November, Henry announced an invasion of Scotland in the spring to punish Robert's calculated insult and alluded 'to the great and horrible outrages committed by the sons of Scottish wardens'. Northumberland, knowing the pitfalls of Scottish politics, preferred to strengthen the Border, not launch a full-blown campaign, and he opposed Henry's plan. The king calmed down and ordered negotiations to proceed over the winter while the improvements were under way. Nevertheless, in February 1400, aid came from a wholly unexpected source: George Dunbar, the (Scottish) earl of March, the most experienced general north (maybe south, too) of the Border. Dunbar had paid handsomely to marry his daughter to Robert III's heir, David Stewart, the duke of Rothesay, but his rival, the earl of Douglas, paid still more handsomely to persuade Rothesay to marry Marjorie, his daughter. Working with Rothesay's uncle, Robert of Fife – the duke of Albany – Douglas had the wedding contract annulled, to Dunbar's fury. In consequence the livid earl of March offered to defect, demonstrating he was a worthy descendant of the legendary Earl Patrick of March, who changed sides with bewildering rapidity. (It's worth mentioning that Dunbar's letter was in English, which was slowly displacing Latin and French as the language of choice for official business.) With the disgraced Dunbar out of the frame, the Douglases were granted the lordship of Dunbar, which virtually bordered Percy's Northumberland.

That summer, Henry embarked on the last invasion of Scotland by a reigning king; another eighty-two years would pass before any English army crossed the Border in a major offensive. For his part, Robert III appeared confident that, again, the English would wander around southern Scotland looking fruitlessly for an enemy. Thus, while Henry was at York collecting troops, Robert proposed a full peace based on the 1328 Treaty of Northampton (or Edinburgh), which had explicitly recognised Scottish independence and the renunciation of the English king's feudal overlordship. To accept would have been political suicide for Henry, indebted as he was to the Border barons for his success, and would have signalled a weakness reminiscent of Edward II and Richard II. Instead, on 6 August Henry ordered Robert to acknowledge his feudal master at Edinburgh in a fortnight. The Scots' reply likened Henry to a common thief – another gibe at Henry's legitimacy. But when Henry decided to cross the Border a week later with an enormous army of 13,000 men (only slightly smaller than the expeditions of 1314, 1335 and 1385), Northumberland, unenthusiastic about the expedition's prospects and not wanting to be out of pocket, only brought a mildly respectable 7 men-at-arms and 160 archers – a figure well below the average for earls of 192 men – though this would later increase to 345 men-at-arms and 500 archers as smaller contingents were placed under his command. Crucially, at his insistence, their provisions were directly funded by the Exchequer, not Percy's private account. Northumberland's parsimony and lack of enthusiasm for the venture were financially and militarily wise, but politically foolish. Henry, of course, checked the numbers and gauged loyalty accordingly. He saw the earl of Westmorland voluntarily bringing the largest baronial contingent by far, 200 men-at-arms and 1000 archers. This disparity, combined with Northumberland's incessant badgering for money, did not escape Henry's attention.

In the event, Albany's army shadowed the English, preying on stragglers and burning the countryside ahead of the interlopers. On 29 August, Henry's army straggled back into England, with the embarrassed king scrabbling for funds to pay the £10,000 that the campaign had cost him and no doubt swearing that the North should be left to Northerners, preferably ones like Westmorland.[34]

Instructed by Henry to seek another truce, Northumberland would soon have plenty to occupy him. Archibald the Grim, the earl of Douglas, died in December 1400, and was succeeded by his headstrong son, another Archibald. The new Douglas was Rothesay's brother-in-law, but the two men fell out over Scottish strategy. Douglas, and Rothesay's belligerent uncle Albany, wanted to attack the English, who were currently trying to crush Owen Glendower's rebellion in Wales (see below). Representing the Scottish government (Robert III was feeble and incapable by this time), the more cautious Rothesay arranged with Northumberland to discuss a truce in April 1401. But Rothesay never made it to the rendezvous; ousted in a coup by Albany and Douglas, he later died of starvation in Falkland Castle. Not until November would Northumberland be granted a meeting with Douglas, now Albany's chief negotiator. Douglas haughtily rejected Northumberland's London-authorised suggestion of a marriage alliance between the royal houses, even ignoring the earl's proposal for a one-year truce.

The early summer of 1402 accordingly heralded a fresh round of Border troubles. But Northumberland had recruited the spited Dunbar to help him successfully fight off several waves of marauders, for which he allowed Dunbar to do a little private pillaging on his foes' estates. Infuriated by Northumberland's successes, Douglas massed troops in eastern Scotland for an overwhelming blow, while Dunbar had by now briefed Northumberland on the weaknesses of Scottish strategy. So, when Douglas's army streamed across the Border at harvest time, Northumberland readied his forces at Alnwick, intending to catch him on his return journey, hampered by booty and livestock, but he let Douglas penetrate far south into Durham. In mid-September, having met no resistance – perhaps because of the qualified victory of the Scots at Otterburn in 1388, and with no worries over Northumberland's 'cowardly' vanishing act – Douglas arrived at Wooler, intending to recross the Border later that day. Yet, unbelievably, his scouts reported that an armed force under the command of Northumberland, Hotspur and Dunbar was waiting five miles north-west at Milfield. The Northumbrians, keeping watch on the Scots, must have left Alnwick and marched north on the coastal route towards Berwick (along the modern A1) then circled west (starting on the B6353, perhaps) to cut off Douglas's escape route. Douglas would have to fight his way out.

He chose a position on Homildon Hill (now called Humbledon), fanning his troops out in a crowded phalanx to await the English. Northumberland had to restrain Hotspur, who seemed to have learnt nothing from Otterburn. Brave and gallant, but always a clumsy general, Hotspur urged a frontal assault on his father and Dunbar – exactly as he had done at Otterburn against another Douglas. Dunbar, however, cannily refused, saying that the Scots were deadly at close quarters but lacked skill with the longbow, a long-range weapon with which the

English were particularly potent. Northumberland agreed, despatching a brigade of archers – each carrying twenty-four bolts – to Harehope Hill, a rising just to the north-west of Homildon but separated by a ravine that would be difficult for the enemy cavalry to negotiate. The main body of the army remained deployed directly in front of the Scots, with the men-at-arms mustered behind. At Northumberland's command, thousands of arrows fell upon the Scots in a crossfire from Harehope Hill and the front, as the English longbowmen slowly walked forward. Any Scot who looked upwards risked his face and life, while armour was no protection against the heavier heads on the sheaf-arrows that English bowmen used at shorter ranges (for long-range shooting, they used flight-arrows, longer but lighter for distance). According to one Scots chronicler, the English archers 'made them bristle like hedgehogs, transfixing the hands and arms of the Scots to their own lances'. Apparently, Douglas, frozen with indecision, did not give the order to charge, although his reluctance may be connected with the loss of an eye (he looked up) and five wounds through his plate. Eventually, the Scots rushed forward and the English withdrew in the centre, thereby letting the encircling flanks intensify the crossfire. This proved the end; the Scots cavalry broke and fled, harried by the whooping men-at-arms all the way to the Border. While trying to ford the Tweed another 500 Scots were swept away and drowned. Only five Englishmen are said to have been killed in the battle.[35]

Northumberland had just destroyed a Scottish army and taken the richest haul of noble prisoners in centuries. Douglas, four other earls (including Murdoch of Fife, the eldest son of the duke of Albany), four barons and dozens of knights were together worth a fortune – perhaps tens of thousands of pounds – in ransom. Capturing a Douglas alive – if in delicate condition – was sweet revenge for Hotspur's surrender at Otterburn.

But the innate avarice and growing arrogance of Henry's most powerful subjects coalesced after Homildon Hill; according to Adam of Usk, the Percys became 'too much puffed up' after their victory, adding, from Proverbs 16:18, that 'an haughty spirit goeth before a fall'.[36] Northumberland was consequently stunned, and Hotspur furious, when a week after the battle, Henry, citing mysterious 'urgent reasons', ordered them not to ransom the prisoners. They were to be brought to London instead of remaining with the Percys, to whom, traditionally, the prisoners belonged as private property. The king's decision probably insulted captors and captured equally, for according to Border law (of which Henry had only the haziest notion, if that), which both sides took very seriously, prisoners could expect dignified treatment, occasional cross-Border visits on the honour system and relaxed credit terms for their ransom while in enemy custody. A London imprisonment at the king's pleasure promised to be rather harsher.

This was not the Percys' only money problem, as it was becoming evident that Henry's lavish promises of money were not the same as actually receiving it. The Percys had been complaining that their men were not being paid and that they were owed £20,000 in back payments from 1399 for their services on the Border.[37] Henry retorted that he had, in fact, paid them £60,000 during that time, but the Percys hotly disagreed. In truth, Henry's Exchequer had only authorised £49,390, but of that figure £10,799 was in 'bad tallies', or had been left unpaid, giving the Percys an income of £38,591. The Percys were indeed owed a great deal of money (and had sacrificed a great deal owing to Henry's refusal to let them ransom prisoners), but not as much as £20,000.[38] Still, considering how useful the Percys had been to Henry in 1399, his refusal to 'round up' the figures smacked of ingratitude. The Homildon victors expected their fiscal demands to be met unquestioningly, and grew exasperated when Henry pleaded poverty. He once told the earl directly, 'Aurum non habeo, aurum non habebis' ('I do not have any money, so you won't receive any money'), to which Northumberland starchily countered: 'When you entered the kingdom you promised to rule according to our counsel. You have since, year by year, received great sums from the country; and yet you have nought, and pay nought... God grant you better counsel.' Believing that the king was holding out on him, Northumberland simply did not grasp that Henry was hopeless with money and that the Exchequer was constantly searching for new ways to raise funds. In one year, for example, revenue from taxes (already high) was £16,612; of this £6000 had to be set aside for the king's and queen's expenses, but since Henry's personal slice was a relatively modest £3666, the Percys' wardenship income far surpassed the king's, and Henry must have relied heavily on Lancastrian revenue to subsidise the court and administration. Taking into account the spiralling costs of defending Ireland, Wales and Calais, as well as the expense of paying the enormous royal dowries required for diplomatic reasons, Henry's finances were haemorrhaging alarmingly. The king, whose political antennae were not finely attuned, knew he owed the Percys but he owed money to a lot of people, so Northumberland simply had to take his place in the queue.

There were other grievances that Northumberland repeatedly – and usually respectfully – raised with the king. The earl, for instance, signed his letter to Henry regarding the £20,000 debt, 'Your Mathathias', a reference to the father of the faithful Biblical warriors, the Maccabees. Chief among these grievances was Henry's continued sponsorship of the Neville family on the Border, which the Percys regarded as theirs alone.

In March 1402, for instance, even though Hotspur had been given the captaincy of Roxburgh for ten years, Henry decided that Westmorland ought to have his turn (he also cost less).

Under constant pressure from the Percys, Henry decided on 2 March 1403 to give them land, not money. Aside from a reservation for Westmorland, and royal overlordship of Roxburgh and Annandale, Henry granted to Northumberland the entire south of Scotland (including Douglas's fief), instantly – if theoretically – making the earl one of the top three or four landholders in England. Percys had fought for some of these lands for generations, but although these same lands may have 'belonged' to the English Crown, the Scots, who clearly did not recognise Henry's generosity, currently occupied them. However, for fear of being dragged into an escalating war, Henry would certainly not allow, or finance, a private Percy conquest of southern Scotland. Put simply, the Percys had been granted what they had always wanted, but were powerless to actually get it. Imperceptibly, Northumberland, Hotspur and Worcester (Northumberland's brother Thomas, who by now had been removed from the king's council) were growing alienated from Henry, the king they had made. And to these proud nobles, such a king could also be unmade.

Nevertheless, without the rampant Hotspur egging them on, old hands like Northumberland and Worcester would probably have complained repeatedly but then bitten their tongues. In the end, it would not be the Scots, or the French, or the Nevilles who hastened the Percys' destruction – but the Welsh.

The Downfall

Henry had been fighting a major insurrection in Wales since 1400, sparked by a territorial dispute between Owen Glendower, a northern Welsh landowner, and his neighbour, a Marcher baron named Reginald, Lord Grey of Ruthin, whose intransigence escalated the quarrel into a pro-Richard rebellion. Grey, a great friend of Henry, was an unpleasant Marcher lord who detested Welshmen – in this respect, he was markedly different from the Anglo-Scottish Border lords who lived among their people – and he once deliberately 'lost' Glendower's official summons for military service, so that Glendower missed the call-up and was listed as a traitor. Eventually, Grey got hold of Glendower's lands, turning the once-respectable gentleman into a brigand hiding in the hills, launching raids against Grey's property and English-held towns such as Denbigh.

At this time, Hotspur was chief justice of Chester, North Wales and Flintshire, constable of the major castles and keeper of the lordship of Denbigh. Despite Hotspur's annoying complaints about payment, Henry reckoned the 36-year-old to be his most valiant warrior, and briefly placed the Prince of Wales under his tutelage. At Easter 1401, Hotspur gathered his 120 men-at-arms and 300 archers and raced with the prince to Conwy Castle, which two of Glendower's lieutenants had craftily taken with fewer than forty men. After a siege, Conwy fell. Evidently still accustomed to Anglo-Scottish ways, the admiring Hotspur spared the lives of the two plucky ringleaders (although, having been raised to believe in the firm smack of Percy Border justice, Hotspur beheaded nine of their men, who were wanted as felons). He then blazed through the countryside, chasing bands of Glendower's men, but he never received the £200 Henry owed him for recovering Conwy, let alone anything for his search-and-destroy missions, which he funded personally.

Henry distrusted Hotspur's Border tactics; indeed, he chided him for punishing the rebels too leniently. It also seems that Hotspur had privately met Glendower without arresting him. Annoyed at Henry's lack of confidence in him (such meetings were common in the North; why should the Welsh March be any different?) and his slights, in August 1401 Hotspur returned to Northumberland in a huff. Two months later, Henry's army advanced into Wales to annihilate Glendower's main force in battle. But Glendower was acutely knowledgeable about guerrilla warfare and would never engage the English directly. Having served in Richard II's Scottish campaign of 1385 and possibly in France and Ireland (as a captain), he used his country's hills and valleys to exhaust the lumbering English army as expertly as any Douglas or Bruce. Within weeks, Henry's men straggled back across the Border to Shrewsbury.

By the end of 1401, Glendower captured his enemy, Lord Grey, and another prize – Sir Edmund Mortimer. The 25-year-old Sir Edmund, frequently confused with his nephew and possible contender for Richard's crown, Edmund Mortimer (earl of March, born 1391, who inherited the title when his father, Roger Mortimer, was killed in County Kilkenny seven years later) was Hotspur's brother-in-law. For Henry, Mortimer's capture removed a powerful patron of a potential rival from the picture. The king therefore did not hasten to pay Mortimer's ransom, but instead obtained Grey's release.

Mortimer, like Hotspur, intensely admired Glendower, who was then in his early forties. To rougher-hewn men like Hotspur, Glendower *was* impressive (although Shakespeare's *Henry IV, Part I* inventively portrays Hotspur the Man of Action dismissing the Idealistic Dreamer Glendower: 'O he is as tedious as a tired horse'). Whilst, unlike them,

Glendower had studied law at the Inns of Court, he was also a landowner whose property had been stolen – the nightmare of every baron – and he just wanted it back. He also had an entrancing daughter, who married Mortimer while he was still a prisoner. That December, Mortimer informed his Welsh tenants that he had joined Glendower to restore to the throne either King Richard or, if Richard were dead (rumours abounded in the Ricardian stronghold of North Wales that the king remained a prisoner), the earl of March. Glendower, he said, would be made a prince of Wales.

For the moment, the king appointed the capable Prince Henry to the lieutenancy of the Welsh Marches and ordered him to kill as many rebels as possible. The prince, having learnt his craft from Hotspur and now under Worcester's guardianship, harried and burnt in areas of Glendower support, but begged his father for funds, complaining 'at present we have very great expenses and have made all the pawning we are able of our little jewels to defray them'.

Likewise, at the end of June 1403, Northumberland wrote to Henry, warning that, without money, he could not hold off the Scots, who were reportedly massing for an offensive by August; not only was the chivalry of the realm at stake, but that of the Percys as well. Henry replied that he would not send money (although he gave £1000 to the prince), but would come to the North at the head of an army to deal with the Scots. The earl strangely, even suspiciously, begged him to stay in London, to no avail.

At Nottingham on 13 July, as Henry marched north, he heard the amazing story of a Percy rebellion. Hotspur had raised his banner at Chester three days previously and was recruiting among the loyalist Cheshiremen and the Welsh, saying he would usurp the usurper, whom he called 'Henry of Lancaster', replacing him with Richard or his heir. Worcester, it appeared, had organised funds for the rebellion, including stealing the prince's money from his headquarters in Shrewsbury, and Northumberland was rumoured to be heading south from Alnwick with his Borderers to rendezvous in Wales with his son, Worcester, Glendower and Mortimer. Together, the Percys released a damning manifesto, claiming that at Doncaster in 1399 Henry had sworn to them that he was uninterested in the Crown but wanted only to reclaim his inheritance and lands. They accused him of misleading them and starving Richard to death. The Percys, at least, had admitted Richard was dead, but now proclaimed the earl of March as his rightful successor. In their airbrushed version of events, the Percys were acting as 'Protectors of the Kingdom'.

Pinpointing the genesis or exact cause of the Percy rebellion is almost impossible; Henry had frequently broken his promises, he had upbraided and humiliated Hotspur, he had treated Mortimer shabbily and he had promoted the Nevilles. Northumberland later claimed Hotspur had raised his banner impetuously, thereby forcing him too into rebellion, but although Hotspur often lost his temper and might conceivably have acted alone, the earl had himself been in traitorous contact with Glendower and Mortimer in the summer of 1403. In all likelihood, therefore, Northumberland was not 'forced' to overthrow Henry, but he might have wished for better timing from Hotspur. However, the king's unexpected insistence on raising an army and heading north, rather than paying Northumberland a few thousand pounds in arrears, probably saved his Crown.

As soon as he heard the dreadful news, Henry intuitively wanted to return to London to rally his forces, but the wily old earl of Dunbar advised against this. Why not, he asked, emasculate the rebellion by preventing the Percys from consolidating their forces in Wales, and then destroy them individually? Thus Henry abruptly raced westwards for Shrewsbury in order to beat Hotspur to Wales, frantically ordering county sheriffs to muster troops ahead of him. Hotspur, assuming Henry would wait at Burton to recruit men and believing Glendower's forces would meet him at the 'gentle Severn's sedgy bank' in a few days' time, calmly advanced towards Shrewsbury. Refused entry on 20 July, Hotspur pulled back to a crop-covered plain two miles north-west in front of a village called, auspiciously, Berwick, to await Glendower and Mortimer's reinforcements before striking against Henry.

Henry, arriving at Shrewsbury late that night, prepared for a lightning attack the next morning (Saturday), having discovered that Glendower, Mortimer, Hotspur and Northumberland were to rendezvous on the 23rd. Grouping his army in three divisions under himself, the earl of Stafford and Prince Henry, the king offered the rebels terms if they laid down their arms, and told Worcester, acting as Hotspur's envoy, that he would do his best to remedy the rebels' grievances. But Worcester declared harshly, 'You rob the country every year and always say you have nothing... You are not the rightful heir!' Henry replied that he imposed taxes in good faith and that he had been freely chosen by Parliament to be king. He offered one last time to 'put yourselves in my hand and trust to my favour', but Worcester bitterly retorted, 'We cannot trust you.' 'Then on you must rest the blood shed this day, and not on me,' said Henry as he gave the order to prepare to arms ('En avant baner!').

At midday, the arrows of the Welsh longbowmen, commanded by, of all people, the earl of Douglas (who had stuck by his old adversary, partly because he remained a Border law prisoner, partly because if Henry won he might have to spend the rest of his life in the clink, partly because he relished fighting, and partly because he loathed Dunbar) shattered Henry's infantry, although his archers replied in kind. As the king moved up his main troops, the rebel cavalry charged them twice, crying 'Esperance Percy!' but were bloodily repulsed by the royalist billmen, carrying seven-foot spears fitted with axe-blades, who shouted, 'For St George!' Eager to be participants rather than mere generals, Hotspur and Douglas gathered thirty knights and hacked their way through the enemy lines to kill the king. Making for the royal standard in the middle of Henry's division, they were confused by two knights wearing Henry's arms on their surcoat – another of Dunbar's crafty ideas. After cutting the decoys down, Hotspur and Douglas were pushed backwards towards their own lines. Meanwhile on the left, the division under Prince Henry, who was wounded by an arrow in the face, had outflanked Hotspur's right and was wheeling to the rebels' rear. Disregarding the danger, the buoyant Cheshiremen were crying, 'Henry Percy King!' over and over again. While surveying the situation, Hotspur lifted his visor. Suddenly, a steel-tipped arrow smashed through his eye-socket and he was killed instantly. Seeing him fall, Henry raised a cheer – 'Henry Percy dead, Henry Percy dead!' – that was quickly taken up by his men. Confused and looking around for their leader, the Cheshiremen wavered and broke, leaving thousands of dead and wounded of both sides on the battlefield (the bodies reportedly covered three miles of ground). The other rebel leaders surrendered soon after, with Worcester and Douglas taken alive – although a missing testicle now complemented Douglas's eye lost at Homildon.

Later, touring the field, Henry wept while gazing upon Hotspur's corpse and directed that it be buried respectfully. Acutely aware of his reputation as a usurper, however, Henry heard a rumour circulating among locals that Hotspur had escaped and was raising an army; so, according to the *Chronicle of London*, 'he was taken up ayen out of his grave [that is disinterred], and bounded upright between t[w]o mille stones, that alle men myght se that he was ded.' After a few days, Henry ordered the body salted, quartered and beheaded. To further prove the traitor dead, Hotspur's limbs were divided between Chester, London, Bristol and Newcastle, with his head, jammed onto a spike over the northern gate at York, staring glassily at Percy country. Worcester was 'juged to the deeth. And he was drawe and hanged and his heed smyten of atte Shrowesbury. And his heed sente to London and there sette upon the Brigge.' The indomitable and exquisitely treacherous Douglas was released in 1407 after signing an indenture to remain loyal to Henry IV and his heirs, whereupon he immediately recommenced his Border raids.

After the battle, Henry ordered the earl of Westmorland to capture

Northumberland, who by now knew of the defeat and was heading for Warkworth. Neville was delighted to oblige, knowing that the Percys' fall left him in charge of the North. As Henry marched north he sent letters to the earl promising clemency if he submitted and came to York without armed followers. The broken old man accepted and, on 11 August, saw the rotting head of his favourite son impaled above him. Henry was cold but not unforgiving towards the errant earl, who blamed Hotspur's impetuosity for the uprising. Although he stripped Northumberland of his office of constable and his wardenship of the West March (which was given to Westmorland), and compelled him to resign the trusteeship of Alnwick, Warkworth and Prudhoe to government officers, Henry mercifully decided that Parliament should try him. Henry gave Hotspur's East March and keepership of Berwick to his fourteen-year-old son, Prince John; all Percy lands acquired since the Conquest in Northumberland, Yorkshire, Cumberland, Westmorland and Newcastle, together with their revenues, were entrusted to Lord de Say, the seneschal of the king's household. In less than four years, the earl of Northumberland had fallen from being the king's mightiest and most trustworthy magnate to a disgraced pauper.

At Parliament on 6 February 1404, Northumberland begged forgiveness, admitted his complicity and asked for a royal pardon. The assembled lords determined that he was not guilty of treason – an automatic death sentence – but of aiding it, which brought a fine. On his knees, Northumberland took another oath of unfailing allegiance to his sovereign, adding that if he ever broke it he would accept the harshest of consequences. Henry generously forgave him the fine and returned his lands. He also requested that Northumberland reconcile himself with Westmorland and Dunbar, so the earl humbly shook their hands and kissed them three times each.

There was one other important matter remaining: the loyal Sir William Clifford, the captain of Berwick. Clifford had been appointed the guardian of Hotspur's adolescent son and heir, Henry, before the warrior had headed south to Shrewsbury for the last time. Clifford refused to surrender the castle to the royal officers unless the king promised to restore Hotspur's personal lands which, through his treason, were forfeit to the Crown (as were Worcester's). His demand was granted, partly because Clifford's trump card was that William Serle was in his dungeon. Serle, the most wanted fugitive in the kingdom, had been Gloucester's assassin in Calais in 1397 and had later stage-managed a briefly successful impostor of Richard in Scotland. After being handed over to Henry, he was finally, at Tyburn, hanged, disembowelled as he watched, and then beheaded and quartered.

Northumberland, claiming infirmity, avoided all contact with London or the court for more than a year, despite several summonses to attend the council. At Alnwick, he brooded upon his family's misfortunes, with Hotspur's and Worcester's deaths gnawing at him. Apparently, he and his retainers wished they were dead or banished ('vueillient estre morts s'ils ne se retrehent hors du paiis'), even though Henry returned Berwick and Jedburgh to his safekeeping in November 1404. Unwisely, he remained in touch with Glendower and Mortimer, whose armies were holding their ground in Wales. In February 1405, a trusted deputy of his met secretly with two representatives of Mortimer and Glendower in Bangor. On the last day of the month, after consulting with their masters, the three intermediaries solemnly sealed an agreement known as the Tripartite Indenture. (For dramatic effect in the entirely invented Act III, Scene 1 of *Henry IV, Part I*, Shakespeare set this eighteen months before the battle of Shrewsbury.) In this blatantly treasonous document, the three lords partitioned England and Wales between themselves. Mortimer, as king, would control the South, while Glendower, henceforth Prince of Wales, would be given all territories west of the Severn and south of the Mersey. As for Northumberland, he was allocated everything north of the Trent, as well as the counties of Norfolk, Derbyshire, Leicestershire, Northamptonshire and Warwickshire. Thus, he would dispossess the House of Lancaster and take over its revenues and titles. Since Northumberland's, rather than the king's, writ would run in this colossal princedom, the earl would be King in the North, a deity wielding far vaster power than had even John of Gaunt.

There was an element of fantasy to the whole scheme, but not entirely so. After all, Henry had won at Shrewsbury by good fortune, not skill. He was also vulnerable in London, owing to the unremitting tax burden. One more shove from the sidelines might be sufficient to topple him...

Glendower invoked the Tripartite Indenture two months later, when he appealed to Northumberland to open up a second front in the North in conjunction with his own counter-attacks on the English. With other malcontents who loathed Henry – Archbishop Scrope of York, Lord Bardolph and Thomas Mowbray, the earl of Nottingham and son of Henry's late rival, the duke of Norfolk – Northumberland decided to rouse the North. Luther-like, Scrope nailed the rebels' manifesto to church doors in York and elsewhere, declaring that they were rising against the king because of his extortionate taxes. Further, they said, if taxes were lowered and the Henrician oppression lifted, the Welsh revolt could be solved peaceably. In the light of this populist manifesto, Northumberland's later actions indicate that while retaining in some measure his characteristic ambition, selfishness and thirst for revenge, he genuinely believed Henry to be an avaricious, heartless tyrant oppressing his Northerners.

In the meantime, however, Westmorland had routed a rebel detachment from the North Riding at Topcliffe, the manor of William de Percy that had been owned by the family ever since he joined the Conqueror in harrying the North. Westmorland then faced Scrope's and Nottingham's troops at Shipham Moor, but Westmorland lured the two commanders into his camp, ostensibly to discuss their manifesto, while one of his knights told their army to disperse as an agreement had been reached. As their men disappeared over the horizon, Westmorland arrested the hapless archbishop and his rather dull accomplice. When the king arrived in June, he executed them both, after which the archbishop of Canterbury laid a curse on Henry for his sacrilege regarding Scrope.

Soon after, Northumberland and Bardolph were being chased north by an enraged Henry, who could not rest without screaming in pain (after one of his nightmares at this time, the king awoke crying, 'Traitors! ye have thrown fire over me,' a possible reference to Northumberland and the burning sensation resulting from the gangrenous ergotism in his nose that he caught after Scrope's execution, which some attributed to the curse). One by one, the Percy fortresses fell, even Alnwick. At Warkworth, for instance, Henry used newly invented artillery to batter the walls so effectively that John Middleham, Northumberland's castellan, only held out for seven salvos before surrendering the castle in order to save it. But Northumberland, always one jump ahead of the royal army, evaded capture. Finally, in mid-July, Northumberland found refuge in, of all places, Scotland, with his old friend and adviser to Robert III, Sir David Fleming, who by now was also looking after Hotspur's son. Such were the ways of the Border.

However, in February 1406, Northumberland and Bardolph had to flee, this time to seek shelter with Glendower and Mortimer in Wales when Fleming tipped them off that the duke of Albany – then regent of Scotland as his brother Robert III faded into senility – was quietly negotiating with Henry to exchange them for the imprisoned earl of Douglas, an ally of his. Fleming's warning came only just in time. A few weeks later, while escorting the twelve-year-old Prince James, Robert III's heir, Fleming's party was nearly ambushed by Sir James Douglas, a kinsman of the earl of Douglas who was working for Albany. Although the prince found safety in an East Lothian castle, Fleming was killed on 14 February by Sir James's men. With the power-hungry Albany in the ascendant in Edinburgh, the royalists sent the prince to France aboard a German merchantman to save his life. Unfortunately, just off Flamborough Head in the North Sea, English pirates, led by a certain Hugh atte Fen, boarded the ship. Realising the importance of his captive, the civic-minded Hugh sent the prince to Henry as a hostage. On 4 April, the captive prince became James I, *de jure* king of Scots when his father died and, reminiscent of David II, he remained in English hands for another eighteen years. Albany, wanting time to cement his regency, made friendly overtures to the English on the understanding that he was in no hurry to repatriate James. As part and parcel of the 'understanding', Albany distanced the Scots from the Welsh rebels.

Northumberland and Bardolph only stayed in Wales until the summer, when they sailed for France to obtain the king's support for the Welsh rebellion. Northumberland even went so far as to proclaim himself Charles VI's liege, thereby renouncing his oath of loyalty to Henry. Although the Northern rebellion had ignominiously failed and the Scots were duds, Northumberland's mission to France was not a forlorn one. Indeed, the French king despatched a powerful force of 800 men-at-arms, 600 crossbowmen and 1200 foot to help Glendower. At the beginning of August, the French landed at Milford Haven in Dyfed, to be greeted by Glendower. From the coast, they marched inland to central Wales to await Henry, who was frantically preparing troops in Hereford. There was no battle, as Henry's baggage train was washed away in a terrible September storm, but a great many French knights, unwilling to endure a Welsh winter, left for home in November. By Christmas, a disappointed Charles VI heard from those returning that 'Richard II's friends' were far weaker than Northumberland had led him to believe. He withdrew his support and left Glendower stranded. Henry, well aware of Northumberland's treason, arranged for his trial *in absentia* by the Court of Chivalry, followed by a judgement of Parliament attainting the earl. This meant the forfeit of his titles (including the barony of Percy, which was not regained until 1557), honours, estates and chattels, together with the death sentence for treason. The family's Southern properties were granted to John, Henry's third son (and later the duke of Bedford), while Northumberland House in London's Aldersgate Street fell into the queen's hands, afterwards being dubbed the 'Queen's Wardrobe'.

Northumberland's luck had vanished since the aborted French expedition. In early 1407, he travelled to Flanders, but found the Flemings reluctant to help. By the spring, he and the faithful Bardolph were back in Scotland – this time with the consent of the invariably variable Albany, who thought Northumberland might be a useful pawn to stir up trouble for Henry at inconvenient moments, especially if he was considering repatriating James I. During the summer, reports flooded in that the North and the Midlands were ready to rebel against Henry, but these 'reports' were almost certainly invented by the cunning sheriff of Yorkshire, Sir Thomas Rokeby, and Sir John Skelton of Cumberland.

In July, while one of Bardolph's servants, who had been caught in Yorkshire delivering secret instructions to Percy loyalists, was held in Nottingham Castle, Rokeby apparently designed the plan to coax the wide-eyed Northumberland over the Border. One of Skelton's men, posing as a secret Percy supporter, met Northumberland and told him that the Midlands was crying out for a saviour from the North to save them from Henry's oppressive misrule. Although the canny Albany questioned the man's veracity – he had not heard of tenants smashing up Lancastrian properties in Derby and Stafford, as the spy had told the earl – Northumberland took the bait. Rokeby, a former Percy retainer, had served under him in decades past; there was no reason *not* to trust him.

That December, Northumberland and Bardolph were bowed across the Tweed, determined to rouse popular and armed support as they passed through the Percy heartlands. Winter was the worst possible time for fighting in the North and this was the worst possible winter for such an expedition: throughout Europe, the 'Great Frost and Ice' of 1407–8, as it was dubbed, was the harshest in more than a century. In England, chroniclers, royal clerks and monks could not write or keep records, for the ink froze in their pointels 'every second word', as one of them remembered.

Hugging the coast, Northumberland arrived at his dynasty's ancient bastion of Seamer in the first week of January 1408, intending to move westwards towards Tadcaster, where the perfidious Rokeby had promised to meet him with the men of Yorkshire. Before he departed Seamer on 7 January, Northumberland wrote a letter, signing it 'H', to 'my dearest cousin', John de Clifford, then sheriff of Westmorland and recently married to Hotspur's daughter, Elizabeth – a stirring reminder of the old Percy–Clifford alliance. Although Northumberland hoped to recruit him to the cause, it proved in vain.

Moving slowly westwards from Seamer, Northumberland arrived at the month's end in Thirsk, where he declared himself England's saviour and urged all right-thinking men to join him against the usurper. It was no coincidence that Thirsk was only a few miles north-east of Topcliffe, the *caput* of William de Percy's barony in the eleventh century. Around there, a dozen generations had been Percy tenants since the Conquest; Northumberland could count on their natural loyalty to tide him through. At Thirsk, local clerics and chaplains, whose institutions had been founded and funded by Percys for centuries, rallied to him along with their flocks. Various chroniclers recorded that Percy's pathetic army of liberation comprised no men of note, rank or military experience; its ragtag following, mostly smiths, tailors, falconers, countrymen, mercers and artisans, was drawn from Yorkshire and Northumberland. Few possessed any military experience.

In mid-February, Northumberland's scouts informed him of Rokeby's betrayal; the sheriff had crept north of Tadcaster and was lying in ambush outside Knaresborough with a small force. Northumberland evaded him by skirting cross-country, reaching Wetherby on the night of Saturday, 18 February. From Wetherby, the path to Tadcaster – that great crossroads – and thence the Midlands and the South lay open. Rokeby, however, caught up with Northumberland past Tadcaster the next day. Northumberland chose to fight at Bramham Moor, a couple of miles south-west of Tadcaster where the A1 and A64 intersect, near the south-east corner of Bramham Park. Piled with thick snow and cursed with an icy wind, the moor was not an ideal battlefield. Behind Northumberland to the south, blocking his escape route, was a virtually impenetrable forest of hazelwood, while to his front lay rolling limestone country. At two o'clock, not bothering to ask Northumberland to surrender, Rokeby ordered his forces to attack the scared Northerners. In this messy, nasty skirmish there was none of the initial arrow fusillades or ranks of noble pennons or formations of liveried men-at-arms to which Northumberland was accustomed.

It lasted barely an hour and a half. The elderly Northumberland (who was by now older than Gaunt had been at his death in 1399) was unhorsed underneath his standard halfway through, and sustained a wound to one of his limbs. Quickly, Rokeby's knights cut him down and the attainted earl ignominiously fell face down into the bloodied snow. Although the Northerners held under the trusty Bardolph, towards the end he was wounded in the neck by a lance (he died that night) and they scattered. Rokeby didn't order a cavalry pursuit – they were worthless rabble compared to his prize.

Later that afternoon, Rokeby sliced off Northumberland's head with its grey beard and silver hair, and sent it post-haste to London. There, a pleased Henry paraded it on a pike through the city streets before it was mounted on the middle tower of London Bridge. The earl's corpse was quartered and pickled in a mixture of cloves, cumin and anise, before being thrown into sealed sacks and despatched to the four corners of the Percys' Northern 'kingdom'. On 2 July of that year, all the pieces were taken down and buried in York Minster next to Hotspur's remains.

Henry hurried north to oversee the inevitable division of spoils and executions. Rokeby was rewarded with Northumberland's Norman-era manor and castle of Spofforth, and two other manors, giving him an assured income of £80 annually.

From then until his death in 1413 at the age of forty-six, Henry was left untroubled by wide-scale rebellion. A concerted English offensive from northern Wales along the coast, led by Prince Henry (also enamoured with new-fangled artillery, he carried a frightful cannon called 'The Messenger'), pushed the rebels out of their castles in Anglesey and Aberystwyth – a diehard seat of rebellious sentiment. In January 1409, the Welsh castle of Harlech finally fell to the English. For months, its defenders, without fuel, had survived on practically nothing. The ill-starred Sir Edmund Mortimer had died of starvation during the siege. As for the other Edmund Mortimer, earl of March, he still presented a potential threat; Henry therefore kept a very close eye on him and refused to give him his lands, even when he reached the age of twenty-two by the time of the king's death. He died issueless in 1425 but his nephew, the duke of York, would amount to great things, as we shall see. Glendower, however, escaped into the hills and forests, and continued launching low-level raids despite the capture of his wife, two daughters and three granddaughters at Harlech. Even after Henry V offered him an amnesty, Glendower never surrendered. He died peacefully 'sometime' in 1417 at an unknown location, but probably his son-in-law's manor at Monnington Straddel in the Golden Valley.[39]

The only 'heir', if that is the right word – for in 1408 the Percys were penniless, landless and titleless – was a fifteen-year-old youth named Henry, who was sheltering in Scotland.

CHAPTER FOURTEEN

A Good and Faithful Servant

Percy Resurrected

Young Henry Percy possessed but a dim recollection of England. Shortly after Hotspur's death at Shrewsbury, Northumberland entrusted him to two guardians in Scotland: Sir David Fleming and Bishop Henry Wardlaw of St Andrews, who also had custody of the Scottish heir, Prince James, who was about a year younger than Percy. For a few years the two boys were close companions in Wardlaw's household. Fleming was an influential Borderer and a leading partisan of Scotland's infirm Robert III; he protected Prince James from the predations of the king's brother, the duke of Albany, who was acting as regent and who stood but one life – the prince's – away from the throne.

In the winter of 1406, however, Fleming was killed by the men of Sir James Douglas, a kinsman of the captive earl of Douglas and an ally of Albany. Sir James, as warden of the Marches in the earl's absence, was furious at Fleming's political interference on the Border (the latter was made sheriff of Roxburgh at the king's demand) and his intriguing with Northumberland, the Wales-based rebels and the French. With open Fleming–Douglas civil war roiling in southern Scotland, in March 1406 Prince James was captured by English pirates en route to safety abroad and sent to London. Add this latest catch to the earl of Douglas and Albany's eldest son, Murdoch of Fife – both captured at Homildon Hill in 1402 by Northumberland – and Henry IV could dictate terms to the Scots. After the death of Robert III a month later, Albany assumed the governorship of Scotland in June. The duke showed little enthusiasm concerning the release of the uncrowned king but he did want his son back. His only trump card was a possible exchange involving Henry Percy (for whom Albany had begun to act as 'guardian'), except that Northumberland's treachery, forfeiture and death dropped Percy's stock to zero.

Amicable negotiations continued with Henry IV, who modestly sought a long truce and a large cash payment for the return of Prince James and Murdoch. But his death on 20 March 1413 brought a prince of remarkable diplomatic and military talents to the throne, a man who truly grasped Scotland's place in grander, European affairs.

Immediately after his father's death, demonstrating a new hardline attitude, the 25-year-old Henry V moved his Scottish prisoners to the less-than-luxurious Tower of London (Murdoch complained about his bedding). Following an unostentatious coronation in April, Henry appointed his brother, John (the duke of Bedford), and the loyal Neville, earl of Westmorland, as wardens of the Marches, and he also authorised reinforcements for the Border fortresses. The king also reformed the procedures for wardens' pay – London always suspected the Percys had grossly inflated Border defence estimates – which saved the Exchequer many thousands of pounds a year. In September, alarmed at Henry's seriousness, Albany agreed a truce until 1 June 1414 and sent emissaries to London to discuss James's and Murdoch's release.

Against Albany's expectations, the ruthless, ascetic but charismatic Henry did not intend conquering Scotland and only once resurrected the traditional (but now pointless) English demand for suzerainty. His later victory at Agincourt exaggerates his bellicosity; he preferred elegant diplomacy to military domination to further English interests. For this most ambitious king, Scotland was a sideshow to the main attraction: the entire kingdom of France, not just the Angevin parts in the south. Henry's policy to 'conquer' France was magnificently simple – he wanted to marry Catherine de Valois, the French king's eldest daughter. When mad Charles VI died (he sometimes thought himself made of glass, which would shatter if anyone touched him), Henry would inherit the Crown. To force Charles's hand, Henry undertook simultaneous negotiations with the fiercely competitive Burgundians and Armagnacs, both struggling for mastery as Charles weakened. In return for English support, Henry stipulated to the former, under Duke John the Fearless, that England wanted all her French possessions (and Berry) as laid down in the 1360 Treaty of Brétigny plus recognition of him as king of France. To the more promising Armagnacs, Henry proposed they arrange a marriage with Princess Catherine along with a dowry of 10 million crowns. To back up his intentions, which had enthusiastic parliamentary support, Henry issued summonses for military service in 1414. The French, aware of these preparations, refused to discuss terms unless Henry disbanded his army, which he found unacceptable.

To prevent the French reactivating the Auld Alliance while he was on the Continent, Henry needed a strong Scottish truce. Unfortunately, the current one was nearing its close (1 June 1413), and Albany was annoyed with the lack of progress. To underline this, he authorised Douglas to burn Penmore, an English town, within weeks of the truce's expiry. The chief warden, the pudgy and weak-chinned but capable Bedford, had no real experience of combating raiding. And although he could efficiently strengthen fortresses and pay troops, he was not a Northern magnate with deep regional roots of kinship who could raise garrisons, obtain loyal recruits or outwit Douglas in the hills and valleys of Tynedale or Redesdale.[1] The elderly Westmorland, although, a Northerner, now seemed too much of a courtly yes-man to organise an efficient Border defence. One man, in Henry's eyes, had the potential to quieten the Border: Percy, who was nearing his age of majority. But could he be trusted? Westmorland's immaculately connected second wife, Joan Beaufort, the countess of Westmorland – the king's aunt – who may have originated the idea, thought he could. She seems to have enjoyed a sure eye for the sure thing: of the fourteen children she bore Westmorland – who already had nine by his previous marriage – all married spectacularly, apart from one son, who became bishop of Durham. The youngest daughter, for instance, was mother to two kings, Edward IV and Richard III, and two of her sisters were duchesses. Between 1450 and 1455, five of Westmorland's sons, five of his sons-in-law and several grandsons all sat simultaneously in the House of Lords. Since one could not go wrong with the calibre of advice provided by the countess, Henry alerted Percy that he would look favourably on his petition for the return of his estates and his title as earl.

On 11 November 1414, Percy's petition that 'he be restored to the name, estate and heritage of earl of Northumberland' was discussed in Parliament (which also happily approved the financial arrangements for Henry's imminent French war).[2] Simultaneously, Henry brokered a proxy marriage between Percy and Neville's (and the countess of Westmorland's) daughter, Eleanor, thereby uniting the riven Border houses within (again) the Lancastrian orbit. Bishop Percy's ballad, *The Hermit of Warkworth*, famously presents a picturesque tale of this betrothal.

By the early summer of 1415, Henry had reached a strange agreement with Albany: Murdoch would be exchanged for Percy if Percy advanced Murdoch's ransom money, to be repaid by Albany.[3] The theory was that all three men would be indebted to each other, so preserving Border peace. At the last moment, as Murdoch was being escorted north, he was kidnapped near Leeds by a mysterious band of highwaymen before being rescued a week later. Murdoch's abduction might have been English out-lawry, or just one element in a Byzantine mix of three simultaneous con-spiracies. At the time, three nobles – the 'Southampton Plotters' – were amateurishly conspiring to assassinate Henry and replace him with 'the Mammet', a Scot with an apparent resemblance to Richard II. Unaware of the Anglo-Scottish deal, the highwaymen might have intended swapping Murdoch for Percy, who would then instigate a pro-Ricardian rebellion à la earl of Northumberland. Others have suggested that responsibility lay with rebellious Lollards under Sir John Oldcastle, who were in league with Owen Glendower's Welshmen.[4]

The Scots were outraged at this perceived act of Henrician perfidy, with Albany again unleashing Douglas to attack Penrith. By now, however, Henry was engrossed in the imminent invasion of Normandy (culminating in the battle of Agincourt that October). It was already mid-August; if he postponed the departure of the 1500-vessel fleet any longer, the expedition might be delayed until the following summer. Shortly before he left, Henry despatched ambassadors to Edinburgh to patch together a truce with Albany until a Percy–Murdoch exchange could be rearranged. Not until 9 December did Henry approve the revised protocols, including his instruction not to let Murdoch anywhere near the Border unless 2000 mounted troopers accompanied him.[5] Henry's price for Murdoch's freedom was £10,000 – payable by Percy, who was given the option to repay it in £2000 instalments in lands and rents to the Crown. Finally, on 28 February 1416, Murdoch and Percy crossed the Border into their respective home territories.

Since Percy had only gained royal approval in November 1414 to *pursue* the restoration of his lands, rather than their actual restoration, he was effectively penniless, and needed an emergency grant of £200 to appear at court respectably attired and equipped. The odd arrangement regarding the ransom payment confirms Henry's understandable suspicions over Percy's long-term loyalty; although no evidence linked him to the Southampton Plot, for instance, his name had been implicated in it and his grandfather and father were still regarded by Lancastrians as poisonous traitors. According to one historian, the 'legal doctrine, that treason corrupted the blood of succeeding generations, was introduced in Henry IV's reign ... Only the royal grace and pardon could wash away the guilt which infected the family blood.'[6] By exacting a huge ransom in instalments, Henry ensured Percy was indebted to him; once his loyalty was proved by sterling service, the Exchequer could conveniently forget about the balance. Percy, even if created warden of the March, still relied on Albany to repay him the ransom, so he would work doubly hard to ensure Border peace. Furthermore, the brilliant marriage brokered by Henry between Percy and Eleanor ended the Percy–Neville rivalry and would further pacify the English side of the Border. An additional bonus was Henry's continued possession of James; the mere threat of release might help persuade Albany to hold back Douglas and the war-party. There was a final trump card in Henry's hand. In April 1416, for the first and last time, Henry broached the dread subject of hereditary English paramountcy to one of Albany's envoys, who angrily refused to discuss it. But the warning was unmistakable: once France was dealt with, Henry V might consider emulating Edward I if displeased with Scottish behaviour. Unsurprisingly, throughout 1416, the Scots did not cross the Border in Henry's absence.

On 16 March 1416, Henry created Percy earl of Northumberland, and knighted him. Technically speaking, Percy was not the 2nd earl after his grandfather (although, to avoid confusion, he shall be referred to as such), but the 1st earl. The charter of his creation employed identical language to the one issued to his grandfather in 1377, indicating that Henry intended that the family's original charge of treason should not be erased by the grandson's elevation. In effect, Henry was giving Percy a fresh start, kindly allowing him to take his grandfather's head from London Bridge to York Minster, to be sombrely interred next to Hotspur's remains.[7]

Next on the Percy agenda was to petition for the restoration of his family estates. For the most part, Henry assented. Almost immediately, Percy took back the Northumbrian estates of Alnwick, Warkworth and Langley, the Cumberland and Sussex lands, most of the Yorkshire possessions and parts of the Leicestershire and Lincolnshire properties. However, following Northumberland's attainder, the duke of Bedford had been granted Prudhoe in Northumberland, significant parts of Percy's Yorkshire, Durham, Essex and Lincolnshire inheritance, together with the houses in Newcastle and Aldersgate, London. Although Henry offered Bedford 3000 marks (almost £2000) a year in compensation to surrender the properties, the Exchequer often defaulted on full payments, and Bedford cautiously kept some of the estates as collateral. Only after Bedford's death in 1435 did Percy reacquire nearly all his family's assets.

For most of his life, Northumberland's income covered his expenses with some room to spare. In 1455, for instance, the gross annual revenue from his lands amounted to about £3100, less administrative expenditure, repair costs and partial repayments of Murdoch's ransom, plus, most importantly, the spiralling sums he granted to loyal retainers and soldiers in the increasingly troubled years before the Wars of the Roses. Whenever the Scots wasted Percy lands, once-profitable farms were temporarily turned into 'decayed rents', and from about 1440 onwards, revenue from agrarian rents collapsed – by about 25 per cent on the Percy estates alone. Percy was only saved from severe debt by a £500 annuity paid to his wife from about 1436 onwards and a Crown annuity of £100 for attending the council. In comparison, the duke of Lancaster cleared about £10,000 *net* annually (*after* massive disbursements to his retinue).[8]

In Calais, six months after granting Percy's earldom, Henry met the wily Duke John of Burgundy to arrange an alliance against the Armagnacs surrounding Charles VI, whom Burgundy loathed. Whilst the duke refused to go to war against Charles VI – an act of treason – he simultaneously recognised Henry and his heirs as the rightful kings of France and pledged to become Henry's vassal. Burgundy's friendship however, would only last while Henry's interests served his own: that is, destroying the Armagnacs. Having ensured a friendly welcome from Burgundy when he returned to France, Henry went home in October to prepare his forces for another invasion in August 1417.

Securing the northern border was now essential. Discussions about James's release had made Albany highly apprehensive. Unleashing Douglas across the Border was a sure-fire way to damage the negotiations, and reports of Albany's increasingly frequent meetings with Douglas meant only one thing. Henry suddenly appointed Northumberland warden of the East March on 10 December 1416 with additional authority for the castle and town of Berwick (his father-in-law, Westmorland, remained in his position on the West March). Since Henry was due to leave England the following August, when the raiding season usually commenced, he wanted Northumberland (who officially took office as 'custodia Marchiae Orientalis' – warden of the East March – in March/April) to gain experience in the post before Douglas struck.[9]

In late August 1417, in Henry's absence, the Scots predictably attacked Berwick and Roxburgh, but the wardens were prepared. As Northumberland approached with the first Percy army in the North since Bramham Moor, Albany hastily abandoned his siege of Berwick, while Douglas was forced to stop mining the walls of Roxburgh and had to disappear into the interior. The Scots christened Albany's wasteful *chevauchée* (although it did stop progress on James's release) as the 'Foul Raid', a dual reference to Albany's unwholesome motives and his foolishness.

Aged twenty-four, Northumberland had triumphed in his first major command. With the Border secure, Percy's king could pursue the French Crown without worry – indeed, at this time, Henry was sacking Caen and advancing into undefended Bayeux and Lisieux. Albany was back in Edinburgh with his tail between his legs and the Scots had already dispersed; yet Northumberland hesitated before retaliating. Cautiously, he reinforced the walls of Berwick and Roxburgh, and only then permitted Sir Robert Umfraville, his most ruthless lieutenant, free rein to tear south-eastern Scotland savagely apart *for two years*. The Scots would hesitate before they next harried the East March.

The duke of Bedford, the king's lieutenant in England and a former warden himself, was impressed. He and the new, powerful duke of

Exeter – Thomas Beaufort, the third son of John of Gaunt by Katherine Swynford – had personally witnessed the quality of Northumberland's levies, Exeter remarking that the Northerners had matched the king's warriors seasoned at Agincourt. In December 1417, Bedford appointed Percy to a small but select commission (including Exeter and Westmorland) that convinced a convocation of prelates to make a large contribution towards the king's war finances.[10]

For the next year or so, Northumberland seems to have diligently enforced Border justice alongside his father-in-law.[11] Just as diligently, in 1418 as a commissioner of array he oversaw the recruitment of the contingents Henry needed to conquer France, or as official documents euphemistically put it, 'for the recovery of the inheritance and rights of the Crown'. Thus, in April of that year, he supervised 'the musters of the men at arms, armed men and archers of the retinue of the king's brother Thomas, duke of Clarence'.[12] Whilst many of his fellow peers had left to fight alongside their king in France, Northumberland efficiently and uncomplainingly toiled as Henry's good and faithful servant, his conduct suggesting he wanted to extirpate his family's guilt through penance.

By spring 1418, the English had conquered most of Normandy and now set their sights on Rouen, its capital and the immensely wealthy second city of France after Paris. Rouen's walls extended for five miles, reinforced by sixty watchtowers, six barbicans and a deep ditch. Capturing it would guarantee that the rest of the duchy fell to Henry, who already fancied himself as William the Conqueror in reverse. On 29 July 1418, Henry pitched camp before its mighty gates and, following a beastly siege, entered a shattered Rouen, dressed in black, in mid-January 1419. After banners bearing the arms of England and France were hoisted, Henry provided a hearty meal to every citizen who had heroically defied him for more than six months.

While Henry was besieging Rouen, John of Burgundy had taken Paris and slaughtered thousand of Armagnacs. Yet now, to cement his control as de facto ruler of France, John cynically joined the surviving Armagnacs to hinder the English advance along the Seine. But this was one crooked deal too many; in September, during a meeting on a bridge, a vengeful Armagnac attendant murdered him after he kneeled in mock-homage to the pro-Armagnac French dauphin, the future Charles VII.

It was in mid-1419, however, that the dauphin begged the Scots to send men and arms across the Channel. The Scots did not hesitate, and Douglas's son, Archibald Douglas (earl of Wigtown), and Albany's younger son, the earl of Buchan, were recruited to lead the expeditionary force. Through repeated forays into Scotland, Northumberland delayed the departure of this 6000-man contingent until November 1419.

Immediately afterwards, he was instrumental in organising a much-needed ecclesiastical loan for Border warfare. While his fellows were awash with French gold and were receiving French titles and estates from Henry as they advanced, Percy dutifully slogged away on the godforsaken Border supported by enterprising lieutenants like Umfraville and Sir Robert Ogle. After Sir William Haliburton had sneakily attacked Wark Castle and massacred its garrison, Ogle entered through the sewer and, after a struggle, beheaded Haliburton and the surviving twenty-three Scots. The laws of chivalry, as observed in France, meant little in Border warfare. Interestingly, like the Great Game of the nineteenth century's north-west frontier, the Border also had its share of espionage. John Hardyng, a Percy adherent and future chronicler, was despatched by Northumberland into Scotland in 1418 to spy out the land and sniff out the time and location of the next raid. He stayed there until 1421, surviving several beatings by suspicious (or drunken) Scots.

Although Bedford extended Percy's wardenship for another two years on 21 February 1419, the financial rewards for his uncomplaining Border service were insignificant.[13] But these were also years of tragedy. The Percys lost three boys in infancy, including two in succession named after Eleanor's father.[14] Nevertheless, Percy's sense of loyalty and piety remained unshaken. In 1419 he commissioned two copies of a single book, *De Regimine Principum* (*The Guidance of Princes*), written by Giles of Rome, a pupil of St Thomas Aquinas, in the 1270s. He gave one to his confessor, William de Norham, reserving the other for his personal use. *De Regimine* was one of the Middle Ages' most popular books; in it, Giles insists that rulers be prudent, loved by their people, just, merciful, generous, courageous and humble (but commanding respect). They rule not for themselves, but to advance the people's well-being and prosperity. In return, and for the realm's good, his subjects owe him obedience. Percy's sentiments exactly.[15]

Northumberland's current monarch was close to achieving the very height of his power. On 10 August, the English arrived at the gates of Burgundian-controlled Paris. After six months of complex diplomacy between Henry, the new duke of Burgundy, Philip the Good – who nursed his own ambitions for the French throne – and Charles VI, Philip swung behind Henry, hoping to preserve Burgundian independence from the predations of either the French or the English (or both). The Anglo-French peace would be secured by Henry's marriage to Catherine de Valois – without dowry. Furthermore, Henry was keen to show the French that he was a legitimate claimant, not a usurper (memories of his father's troubles haunted him). Thus Charles VI would keep his crown for life, but his rightful successor would not be the dauphin but Henry and, thereafter, his heirs. England and France would be united under one Crown, and to show good faith, Henry promised the duke that one of his own brothers – perhaps Bedford – would marry one of the duke's sisters, thereby including Burgundy in the Anglo-French empire.

English and French lawyers hurriedly drafted the agreement in which Henry basically renounced the old Plantagenet (and Treaty of Brétigny) claims to south-western France for a marital short cut to the whole country. Crucially, the French insisted – something readily accepted by Henry, with his own red-blooded Englishmen (and Englishness) to consider – on distinguishing between what would be a *union of two crowns* and the (unsuccessful) alternative, a *merger of two kingdoms* into a sort of proto-European Union with identical laws, customs and institutions.[16]

By now, England had heard of the king's imminent nuptials. At Henry's command, the captive King James was asked to attend the wedding and he left Southampton in early May 1420. In the absence of records – he disappears after 24 August 1419, when he was appointed a commissioner of array – Northumberland's movements at this time are mysterious.[17] However, since most of the English baronage (about 400 of all ranks) attended Henry's wedding, logically Northumberland would have accompanied James to Normandy, and thence to Troyes, where Henry – newly named as king-apparent and regent of France in the 21 May Treaty of Troyes – awaited them. During the ceremony, Henry brandished the seal that Edward III had used to finalise the Treaty of Brétigny in 1360. On 2 June, Henry (who was entranced with the eighteen-year-old Catherine, whose funeral effigy at Westminster Abbey depicts a swan-necked, slightly dreamy girl) married her and disinherited the dauphin in one of the greatest dynastic settlements of the Middle Ages. France, soon, would be his.

Northumberland's movements throughout the subsequent summer are unknown. One can, however, calculate by which date he had returned to the North. His son (and heir), also named Henry, was born on 25 July 1421.[18] Assuming a normal pregnancy, Percy must have been reunited with Eleanor in November 1420. We may therefore speculate that, two days after the wedding, Northumberland accompanied Henry to lay siege to Sens, west of Troyes, which fell within the week. The royal army then moved north-west towards Paris (which Henry entered on 1 December), eliminating the remaining dauphinist garrisons along the Seine. During these sieges, news arrived from England in late September of Albany's death and his replacement by his son, Murdoch of Fife, as second duke and governor of Scotland. Murdoch was much weaker than Albany, and Douglas might persuade him to revive the war against England. This unexpected threat prompted Northumberland to race home to buttress the Border's defences – just in case.

On 1 February 1421, Henry and Catherine disembarked at Dover. From there until London, large cheering crowds awaited the conquering hero, suitably impressing Henry's bride, who was due to be crowned queen of England in Westminster Abbey on 23 February, an event to which every noble in the land had been invited the previous month. Within weeks, Catherine was pregnant.

But on 1 April, terrible news arrived from France. The duke of Clarence, Henry's brother, currently in charge of the English occupation, had been slain by a dauphinist-Scottish force in the battle of Bauge a week before. The dauphin had even created the earl of Buchan marshal of France and Wigtown count of Longueville in recognition of the victory. Henry was, obviously, distraught but – marking him as a great statesman – he distinguished between the actions of Wigtown and Buchan in France and the progress of the Scottish negotiations over James whom, on 23 April, Henry made a Knight of the Garter. Within months, Douglas had committed himself to his rightful king and there was, to Northumberland's relief, a halt to Douglas-inspired Border roguery. However, the Franco-Scots were excluded from this neutrality agreement and still resisted in Picardy and Artois. Indeed, as a result, so quiet was the Border that in April, Northumberland managed to raise a large royal loan from 'all persons spiritual and temporal of the West Riding in the county of York'. When the Border was in tumult, there was little chance of raising anything there but troops.[19]

Henry urgently needed to restore the aura of English invincibility after the defeat at Bauge. In June 1421, he again set sail for Calais, leaving Bedford behind as regent. This time Henry brought 5000 men commanded by his younger brother, Gloucester, James and the earls of Warwick and March (he was now twenty-nine, and his estates had finally been restored by Henry). By late autumn, the last major dauphinist outpost was Meaux, a fortified town located strategically 30 miles east of Paris on the Marne, whose garrison commander was a diehard. Meaux, Henry believed, could probably hold out throughout the winter – which was an obstacle but not necessarily an insuperable one. But the awful weather made the siege vastly difficult and the only highlight for both Henry and his sodden, depressed troops was the birth of the 35-year-old king's heir, also named Henry, on 6 December.

For months later, the town of Meaux fell, followed by the fort itself in May 1422. Few, apart from the garrison commander and a trumpeter who had tooted offensive tunes to Henry on the battlements, were executed. Some of the grizzlier English commanders were worried by Henry's uncharacteristic clemency towards an enemy that had held out for so long. But Henry was already sick, a result, no doubt, of living rough for so long. In June, although still lucid and humorous (when James came to his bedside, he remarked: 'I cannot go anywhere without coming face to face with Scots, dead or alive'), he fell into a 'languorem exicialem' (a fatal weariness) and grew hot with fever; he may also have suffered from intestinal problems and dysentery. A king to his boots, however, Henry dictated a codicil to his will on 26 August, detailing his plans for England's future governance. As the first king since Richard I to die abroad, Henry wanted his wishes to be perfectly clear. Gloucester was made regent of England and Bedford of France; Bedford was directed to guard 'that country as well as the remnant of his conquest on the best wise that God would give him grace'. The upbringing and education of his nine-month-old son and future king of England and France, which was of great concern to him, was entrusted to Gloucester, Exeter and two Garter knights. On 31 August 1422, between two and three o'clock in the morning, Henry died at the royal castle of Vincennes. On 7 November, he was buried in Westminster Abbey.

Charles VI followed him some two months later. According to the Treaty of Troyes, Henry's son automatically inherited the throne of France, but the dauphin had no doubts that the English position had dramatically weakened.[20]

CHAPTER FIFTEEN

A Safe Pair of Hands

The Earl of Northumberland and Henry VI

A boy in a cradle, aged barely nine months, ruled England and France. Most of the leading nobles and officials were in France, leaving the late king's youngest brother, Duke Humphrey of Gloucester (aged thirty-two) as keeper of the realm. Owing to the slowness of communications and travel, it was a month after Henry's death before an unimpressive turnout of several bishops and six lords met in London 'for the immediate need of governing the realm, both for the preservation of peace and display of justice and for the exercise of the king's offices'. Northumberland and the aged Westmorland (whose wardenship had been taken over by Sir Richard Neville, one of his sons by the countess, Joan Beaufort, his second wife) remained on the Border, watching for signs of Scottish opportunism. The impromptu governing council, however, did include Joan's brother, the crafty but efficient Henry Beaufort, bishop of Winchester, who soon clashed with Gloucester.

Beaufort and his brother, the duke of Exeter, were John of Gaunt's sons by his long-time mistress and belated third wife, Katherine Swynford. Close to his half-brother (Henry V) when he was still Prince of Wales, Bishop Henry lent the king colossal sums of money for his campaigns while giving well-attended sermons on the theme, 'Let us make war so that we may have peace, for peace is the purpose of war,' at appropriate moments. Whilst the convivial Gloucester enjoyed some popularity among Londoners and in Parliament, Bishop Beaufort, an astute back-room operator, regularly outmanoeuvred him within the council.

There was an informal alliance between the duke of Bedford in France and Beaufort in London; while not antagonistic towards his younger brother, Bedford resented Gloucester's designation as regent simply because he happened to be in England at Henry's death. With Exeter's assistance, in November Bedford arranged for a new council of nobles and prelates to bypass Henry's codicil and create Gloucester the fancy-sounding 'Protector and Defender of England'. Politically speaking, however, the post was far less weighty than regent; essentially Gloucester was only in charge when Bedford was out of the country.

This November council included many fighting in France when Henry V died, as well as such lords as Northumberland, who had come down to London (Westmorland stayed up north).[1] The power-politics within the council were more tussle than vicious struggle, although its tilt against Gloucester subtly reflected Beaufort's string-pulling. Of the seventeen members, five were French veterans and Bedford's eyes and ears (and voting hands), while four others comprised an associated Beaufort faction, including Northumberland and the earl of Norfolk, both of whom married daughters of the elegantly manipulative countess of Westmorland.

Gloucester, probably with little inkling of the 'conspiracy' against him in the council, was shocked when informed that he might not open and close Parliament (his prerogative, as 'regent') without the council's assent. Northumberland's support for Bedford/Beaufort was heartfelt – he had hitherto kept out of high politics – but this did not imply opposition to Gloucester. Moreover, Northumberland had had no dealings with Gloucester in the past, whilst the Beauforts were his in-laws and Bedford had always been cordial, if a little irritatingly tardy, about returning some of Percy's possessions.

The in-built bias against Gloucester aside, the council was essentially a professional governing body designed to look after England's – and Henry VI's – financial, administrative and military interests. According to Ralph Griffiths, 'It is difficult to conceive of a more capable, experienced, or vigorous group of men to exercise the royal authority at the opening of a long minority'.[2] Since Henry was a king, adds another biographer, 'even while still in his cradle the most solemn acts of state had to be performed in his presence; he had to be made available to his subjects; the quarrels of the great had to be resolved before him'.[3] By the time he was two, Henry could lift the golden Great Seal by himself and had even attended Parliament.

Charming as these scenes may have been, Beaufort's preoccupations were maintaining France and improving the Scottish situation. France, generally peaceable under Bedford (who finally conquered Normandy in 1423), was still plagued by the dauphin, who continued to receive Scottish reinforcements. Beaufort, worried about the strain of a French guerrilla war on the royal finances, decided – probably advised by Northumberland – to negotiate with Scotland over the release of James, whom Henry V had carefully cultivated during his long, if comfortable, captivity. The return of a pro-English king, so the thinking went, would weaken the irritating Albany/Buchan/Douglas coalition, and his £40,000 ransom (euphemistically defined as sums owing 'for the maintenance and expenses of the lord King James during the time of his stay in England') would nicely replenish the Exchequer.

In the summer of 1423, Beaufort scouted for a suitable English bride for James whilst authorising English commissioners (including Northumberland) to negotiate with their Scottish counterparts. For his part, Murdoch, the duke of Albany and de facto ruler of Scotland, had no desire to see James return, but could not reveal this to his councillors. Indeed, he was forced to do (or be seen to be doing) his utmost to release James. At York on 10 September, having been directed by Beaufort to settle quickly, Northumberland's embassy reached agreement with the Scots; this was subsequently drafted on 4 December as the Treaty of London. Considering the pressure on Northumberland for quick results, the treaty was not too bad, but far more could have been wrested from the Scots, given time. Thus, the £40,000 ransom was agreed, but it was to be paid in instalments – a condition unhappily familiar to the English, as the money tended to dry up after the first few payments. The Scots promised to stop sending troops to France, but without guaranteeing that those already there would be withdrawn. No permanent peace or declared end to hostilities (Beaufort's preferred policy) were agreed, only a seven-year truce.

Fortunately (if not uncoincidentally), Beaufort's pretty niece, Joan (daughter of the deceased earl of Somerset, the eldest of the Beaufort brothers), married James in February 1424, less than a week after Parliament ratified the Treaty of London.

The only looming fly in the ointment was Walter Stewart, the son of Albany, whose expectations of succeeding his father as governor of Scotland had suddenly been crushed. Finding a willing ally in the virulently anti-English Buchan, both swore on 6 October to 'observe the ancient leagues and confederations' between the French and the Scots; Walter even pledged that Dumbarton could be used to disembark French troops to open a fresh front on the Border.

Despite the opposition of Buchan and Walter, James's return looked inevitable, especially after 28 March 1424, when English negotiators, again including Northumberland, met the Scots in Durham Cathedral to finalise the seven-year truce. James, whom the English had escorted from London, performed his first royal action that day when he sealed the document confirming his own release. On 5 April, James and his queen rode across the Border accompanied by his new relatives, Northumberland and Sir Richard Neville.

Immediately after they deposited James at Melrose, Scotland descended into vicious infighting. James, who had been a prisoner in England for eighteen years, thanks to the Albanys, wanted revenge. On the day he arrived, for instance, James denounced to the assembled lords the 'neglectful government' of Scotland in his absence; although he omitted to name Albany, the implication was clear. A week before his coronation on 21 May, James ordered Walter Stewart's arrest. The two other major offenders, Earl Archibald Douglas and Buchan, were in France. With them and their powerful forces at large, James's ability to avenge himself on the duke of Albany was curtailed, and the former governor and king were coldly polite to each other at the coronation.

James I, Percy and the North

The duke of Bedford's crushing victory over a Franco-Scots army twice the size of his own on 17 August at the battle of Verneuil (known as a 'second Agincourt' for Bedford's brilliant generalship) transformed the Scottish political scene. Thousands of Scots were killed, including doughty old Douglas and the Francophile Buchan. With those trouble-makers and almost all their followers lying dead, James could patch up relations with their heirs and command more weight in the governing councils. Finally, on 21 March 1425 – in the middle of a Parliament – James confidently ordered the arrest of Albany, now in his sixties, and some of his most powerful retainers on charges of fomenting rebellion. On 24 May, Walter Stewart was beheaded, followed the next day by his brother and their father. In little more than a year, the unexpectedly ruthless James had exterminated the Albany Stewarts and brought the eternally fractious Scottish nobility to heel.

During these troubles in Scotland, Northumberland stayed almost permanently in the North. However, the Border remained unusually docile (so much so that in February 1425 London began slowing down repayments to Northumberland for his repairs to Berwick Castle, although on average between 1422 and 1429 most of Percy's fees as warden – that is, £2500 out of his annual salary of £3000 – were paid). The new Earl Douglas, who really ran southern Scotland, was supportive of James, who was in turn not looking for trouble with the English. Even after Westmorland's death in October 1425, and his succession as earl by Ralph Neville, his relatively inexperienced eighteen-year-old grandson – son of Westmorland's eldest son (who predeceased him), by his first marriage – apart from a few minor breaches of the truce, there was no Scots raiding. This was partly owing to the fact that there was no vacuum in the West March; Westmorland's wardenship had been capably handled for the last five years by Sir Richard Neville, the eldest of his fourteen children by his second wife, Joan Beaufort. Even after the old earl had died, his widow, the countess, still strove to bind the Northern baronage tighter; a year after her husband's death, the countess invited Northumberland's only sibling, Elizabeth (recently widowed herself when Lord Clifford died in 1422), to marry the new earl of Westmorland, which she did in 1426. (Sir Richard Neville was married off to Alice Montagu, eldest child of the earl of Salisbury.)

The mid- to late 1420s may have been humdrum in terms of Anglo-Scottish affairs, but Northumberland's family life kept him occupied. In these years, aside from his heir (born 1421), Eleanor bore him eight children (five boys and three girls), probably including a set of twins, or perhaps even triplets in the case of the girls.[4]

He certainly was not required in London for governmental affairs too often, even though the Beauforts' numerical advantage on the council was draining away; first, through Westmorland's death; then the earl of March's; then that of Bishop Wakering of Norwich; then by Exeter's at the end of 1426. Although friendly peers and prelates joined the council – most notably, one of the greatest commanders of the Hundred Years War, Thomas Montagu, earl of Salisbury (one of the few soldiers, apart from Henry V, to appreciate gunnery) – their combined influence could not equal that enjoyed by the late Exeter, and Salisbury was usually in France.

Nevertheless, the council functioned satisfactorily – even after an armed confrontation, and a subsequent reconciliation in 1426 between Gloucester and Beaufort, who was soon to become a cardinal – until 1429, when the English suffered serious reverses in France, and the Scottish frontier almost blew apart. As Bedford recalled to Henry VI five years later, it was the siege of Orléans that sparked the dreadful chain of disasters. In the autumn of 1428, while besieging the city, Salisbury was killed by an iron shard from a cannon ball. Under his replacement, the earl of Suffolk, the siege continued into the spring of 1429. On 29 April, a small lithe girl nicknamed Joan of Arc appeared with a small relief force. A few weeks later, a dejected Suffolk (he would later be captured) lifted the siege, which was followed a week later by a major English defeat at Patay. But the greatest blow to English morale came on 17 July, when the dauphin, on Joan's advice, was crowned Charles VII, king of France, in Reims Cathedral; this was a huge boost to dauphinist spirits.

Joan was wounded in the subsequent struggle for Paris, and Charles VII, obsessed with superstition (he refused to cross wooden bridges, for instance) and perhaps believing Joan was a sorceress, abandoned the Maid of Orléans. Although she recovered, her subsequent attacks on the

Loire failed. In May 1430, she rode to Compiègne in northern France, where she was seized by a Burgundian knight, transferred into Bedford's hands in November and burnt as a heretic in Rouen on 30 May 1431.

During these troubled years, the English were finding James far wilier than expected; Beaufort's gamble in ransoming him had not paid off. James, unwilling to undertake a Border war for the sake of France, still maintained the French connection to obtain the best possible deal from London when the Anglo-Scottish truce expired on 1 May 1431. Thus, in July 1428, James received a proposal that his four-year-old daughter, Margaret, should marry Charles VII's son, Louis. Margaret's dowry would not be money, but some 6000 trained soldiers. James, fearing English retaliation for breaking the terms of the 1424 truce, dithered; the dauphin sweetened the offer with the prospect of French land and a French title, but even after the marriage contract had been signed in November, James, not wanting to antagonise the English while the dauphin was losing the war, avoided sending the 6000 promised reinforcements to France.

Nevertheless, this did not stop Scottish volunteers from fighting there; at Orléans, the garrison included 169 Scots men-at-arms and 400 archers, and Joan of Arc was accompanied to the last by a loyal band of Scotsmen. One colourful event was Charles VII's establishment in 1445 of an elite royal bodyguard – the first in Europe – composed exclusively of 100 Scotsmen, which existed until the late sixteenth century; after that Frenchmen filled the ranks.[5]

James's tilt towards France to pressure the English worked brilliantly. In February 1429, Cardinal Beaufort and Northumberland rushed to meet James at Berwick to discuss the truce and possibly the marriage of Henry VI to Princess Margaret. Nothing was achieved; indeed, the arrears on James's ransom increased as the king realised that he could threaten to send Scots across the Channel if the English tried to enforce payment. Two more missions failed, followed in February 1430 by a high-powered embassy, which included Northumberland and the recently created earl of Salisbury – Sir Richard Neville – who had married, as was mentioned, the late warrior's daughter.

The 'Northumberland Mission', as it could be called after its senior member, was authorised by the English government to negotiate prolonging the truce and, if possible, secure a permanent peace by suggesting (again) a royal marriage. Although the mission ultimately failed, it does provide one striking insight into Northumberland's character. On April 21 at Warkworth Castle, Northumberland was handed a letter by James's envoy, Thomas Roulle, containing the king's reply to an English proposal. But the ever-scrupulous and legalistically minded Northumberland did not open it, since it was addressed not to him but to the commissioners 'all iontly and to gedre' (as they told James). Northumberland then organised a meeting at Newcastle a week hence, where the letter was opened, by which time Roulle had returned to Scotland without any arrangements made for the two sides to meet to discuss the contents. Later – too late to put right the mix-up – the commissioners (including an embarrassed Northumberland) wrote to tell James that they would have accepted the proposals contained in the letter (which has since been lost).[6]

Subsequently, Lord Scrope of Masham travelled to Scotland to discuss the letter's terms with James, a fruitless mission as James prevaricated yet again. Only now did the English grasp the kind of man they themselves had put on the throne; Scrope reported to the council that since 'the king of Scottis is now at hoom in his land', this dangerous, wealthy and sly monarch was also 'a far seeing man, having great experience'. Only in mid-January 1431 – four months before the truce's expiry, and a few months after Bedford had restored English fortunes in France – did James I finally consent to extending the truce for another five years.

To keep the English on their back foot during the truce, James reopened discussions with Charles VII about marrying Margaret off to the Dauphin Louis, and ensured London knew of it. This resulted in a hurried, Beaufort-sponsored embassy in August 1433 led by the cardinal's nephew, Edmund Beaufort, who offered James a full peace treaty if Scotland broke with France. James's reward? The return of Roxburgh and Berwick, the last English possessions in Scotland, and an unconditional retraction of English feudal superiority. James wanted to accept the offer, the most enticing proposal since 1328 – but in October the Scots Estates rejected it in Perth, suspicious that Beaufort's terms were a ruse by the 'artful wolf', as the Scottish chronicler, Walter Bower, who participated in the debate, put it. Given Beaufort's chronic desire for a stable northern border, Scottish suspicions were misplaced, but Scottish reluctance to betray France was crucial to the decision.

Northumberland was hostile to the Beaufort proposal. Although he was a faithful Crown servant, the overly generous terms struck at the heart of Percy tradition. For centuries, his ancestors had fought for Roxburgh and Berwick, which the cardinal proposed selling to the Scots for a scrap of paper. Not only was Northumberland not consulted about the peace deal, he was excluded from the proceedings by the Beaufort clan. For once, Northumberland showed his displeasure at what he regarded as treachery. There are reports of the Berwick garrison – under Northumberland's direct control – raiding the villages of Paxton and Hilton, both several miles east of Berwick. James complained to the council in London, and in the New Year, in Northumberland's absence, a

Scottish raiding party actually reached Alnwick and burnt much of the town. According to official Rolls, a state of 'open werre' and 'misrule' existed on the East March in the winter of 1433–4.

Unable to ignore Northumberland's petulant disobedience, the council withheld payments, expenses and wages owing to him. This was not as damaging as it sounds; the government was technically bankrupt in 1434, and neither Northumberland nor his counterpart in the West had received much money for the past few years.

The Crown's gross annual revenue was £54,000: £31,000 from indirect taxes such as import duties, and the balance from the duchy of Lancaster and other permanent assets. But over half the permanent revenue was funnelled to the king's bloated household, hangers-on, and annuities and fees for Lancastrian loyalists. Worse, the following year's expenses were a projected £57,000, with long-term debt estimated at £165,000 – even before considering the defence of France and the Anglo-Scottish Border. So the warden of the East March's peacetime remuneration of £2500 (up to £5000 in time of war) was ripe for reduction by Exchequer cost-cutters, even without taking Northumberland's misbehaviour into account.

By July 1434, Northumberland could neither afford to pay the Berwick garrison personally (incidentally, he gave charge of the castle in February to the fiery son of the fiery Sir Robert Ogle), nor could he have enjoyed being sent to Coventry by the council, and he sadly resigned the wardenship that he had held continuously since 1417, although dutifully repairing the town of Alnwick's parlous walls before he left office. On 25 July, the diplomatic Salisbury took over, also keeping the wardenship of the West March, which he had held since 1420. The earl gave the council an ultimatum: he would serve for only a year in either post, unless money was forthcoming for him, his men and the reconstruction of the Border fortresses. One year later, having received only £500 of the £2500 promised as the East March warden's salary, Salisbury threatened to resign both offices. This warning went unheeded in London, so he stepped down on 25 July 1435 – only to discover belatedly that Northumberland and the earl of Huntingdon had been secretly commissioned as joint wardens of the East and the West Marches *two weeks* before. How had this happened?

Salisbury's timing was badly off. Gloucester, who, despite his faults, was a long-standing supporter of a tough Border policy as opposed to the views of the Beaufort clique, was back in control of the council. His regulatory-minded elder brother, Bedford, lay ailing in France, eventually dying in September 1435. Cardinal Beaufort, meanwhile, was in Arras, attending an ultimately vain Anglo-Burgundian-French peace congress.

Gloucester enjoyed calling Salisbury's bluff to resign, for the latter was one of the closest political allies of Cardinal Beaufort, as well as his nephew. And since the Neville family was split between its senior (Westmorland) and junior (Salisbury) branches, both the earl of Huntingdon (a well-known crony of Gloucester whose daughter was married to Westmorland's son) and Northumberland welcomed a diminution of Salisbury's influence on the Border.

Between 1430 and 1442–3, a virtual state of war existed between the family stemming from the late Earl Ralph's first wife (Margaret, daughter of the earl of Stafford), and that from his second (Joan Beaufort). Although the current earl of Westmorland was the oldest grandson of Earl Ralph and his *first* wife, and therefore should have inherited everything as he represented the senior Westmorland branch, under the influence of Joan Beaufort his father had tried to provide for the eldest child of *both* marriages. Assuming, perhaps, that his grandson Ralph would get the title and as there were fourteen children by his second marriage but only nine by the first, the earl did not split the Neville assets directly down the middle, but instead granted the family's great estates in Yorkshire to Salisbury, representing the junior branch, and additionally stipulated that a third of the earl of Westmorland's yearly income should go to Joan Beaufort. Of course, Westmorland had a strong legal and moral case against this imposed settlement, which not only made it difficult to maintain the (costly) status of an earl but offended against the laws of primogeniture.

Westmorland loudly complained that the value of his inheritance had been slashed from £2666 to just £400 each year. But it was not until his half-brother became earl of Salisbury in 1429 and came into his wife's inheritance of £665 per annum (which, in combination with other income from offices and holdings, ballooned to about £3000 by 1441) that Westmorland could claim that his sibling was more than capable of taking care of himself (and his mother) financially. Salisbury, however, wanted to usurp his sickly half-brother's position in the North, and was loath to surrender the Yorkshire estates, some of which he was renting out to Cardinal Beaufort for £666 per annum. Relations grew so nasty that London periodically sent letters ordering both sides to refrain from trespassing on each other's land and sending ruffians to vandalise property. In 1438, the two sides actually came to blows 'with grete rowtes and compaignies upon the field' but settled down after the king directed them to keep the peace. Not until 1443 – three years after Joan's death – was a royal settlement made regarding the Neville–Neville feud. Thanks to his friends on the council, Salisbury had successfully persuaded the king that Westmorland was the aggressor and so an additional clause ordered the latter to pay an annual pension of £400 to Salisbury on condition that Salisbury would not claim it unless Westmorland tried to overturn the settlement. Needless to say, the settlement fully satisfied neither branch of the Nevilles, but it was enough to dampen down overt hostility.[7]

Northumberland, with a foot in both camps, was in a tricky position during this long spat; he was married to one of Salisbury's sisters, and his own sister was married to Westmorland. Whilst Salisbury's Beaufort friends were in high places (although Gloucester was then more powerful), the scope of the earl's ambition militated against Northumberland taking his side. Salisbury's opportunistic takeover of the East March and his lavish holdings in Yorkshire, the ancient core of Percy strength, were alarming. Westmorland was the weaker brother, but his consequent lack of aggression weakened the defence of Percy interests. In the mid-1430s, then, Northumberland quietly backed Westmorland to deflect Salisbury's encroachments but did not openly oppose the latter.

Aside from dishing Salisbury, there was another reason for Northumberland to ally with the well-connected Huntingdon as his co-warden: he was more likely to be paid in full for his services. On the other hand, with Huntingdon as his silent partner and middleman with London, more overtly political activities might supersede merely 'keeping the peace'. Thus, by the end of the year, acting on Gloucester's tacit instructions, Northumberland and Huntingdon had helped spark major, if localised, incidents on the Scottish side of the eastern border.

Enter Patrick Dunbar, the eldest son of the (Scottish) earl of March, whose father James had for political and personal reasons been hounding for years, culminating in the earl's forfeiture of his title and estates in January 1435. On the day in July when Northumberland received his warden's commission, Patrick received a safe-conduct to plead for Gloucester's assistance in London; evidently he was successful, given Northumberland's subsequent actions that year. Treating with the English was not new for the Dunbars – Patrick's ancestors, including his father, had changed sides at the blink of an eye (or rather, without blinking an eye). Patrick then met Sir Robert Ogle at Berwick, and slipped across the Border to lie low in the old Dunbar lands in Lothian for the next few months.

But why would Gloucester and the council suddenly approve mischief-making on the Border, in violation of the current truce?

The reason was France. In the late summer of 1435, the congress of Arras, where English, French and Burgundian ambassadors had met to discuss peace terms, ended in a terrible shock for England. After fruitless discussions, the English, under Cardinal Beaufort, walked out. Then, according to Jean de Waurin's *Receuil des croniques*: 'the French and the Burgundians met together in conference … where they had a great discussion together about various matters … and they agreed to make a final peace between King Charles on the one hand and Duke Philip of Burgundy on the other.'[8]

So, in late September, Philip of Burgundy, England's long-time ally and the seemingly implacable foe of Charles VII, treacherously concluded a truce with Charles in return for huge estates in northern France. In a pompous letter to Henry VI attempting to justify his behaviour, Burgundy addressed Henry not as his sovereign lord, but merely as 'king of England'. More than twenty years later, Henry still burnt for vengeance, complaining to a visiting French emissary that 'he [Philip] abandoned me in my boyhood, despite all his oaths to me, when I have never done him any wrong'.

Charles VII had trumped the English in France. Worse still, he was wooing James again by offering the dauphin in marriage to Princess Margaret in exchange for bouts of Border trouble. To his credit (or, more likely, his advantage), James wavered, but in London the council was considering preventive action against James before England was faced with the triple threat of a Franco-Scottish-Burgundian alliance. This is where Patrick Dunbar entered the picture; a Dunbar rebellion, with eastern Scotland behind him, against James (whose predations and taxes were turning noble and popular sentiment against him) would prevent the king involving himself in the Anglo-French war. Furthermore, there was also the more distant, if enticing, prospect of a Dunbar-led coup against James.

Thus, in early September, a medium-sized force consisting of a few thousand irregular Borderers and the Berwick garrison under Sir Robert Ogle headed up the coast to Dunbar, on what is now the A1. James complained to the English government, which affected ignorance, that Ogle was illegally 'meyntenying and suppleying … Paton [Patrick] of Dunbar, the king's rebell'. Some accounts place Northumberland at the head of this force, but for this 'unofficial' covert operation, the warden remained in England – although it was no coincidence that on 12 September he and Huntingdon were appointed to the wardenship of the West March too for a one-year term.[9]

But only eight miles from Dunbar, Ogle was ambushed by James's men; few English were killed, but 'a total of 1500 of their border forces and castle-troops were captured', including the unlucky Ogle.

The gamble had failed. Infuriated, James accepted Charles's offer of a marriage alliance and barred English ambassadors from his court. On 27 March 1436, accompanied by a fleet manned by 1200 sailors and waited on by 140 royal-liveried attendants, the adolescent Princess Margaret sailed for France (the English navy vainly tried to intercept the Scots) to marry her thirteen-year-old husband in June.

In the late winter and spring of 1436, then, England faced the nightmare of a Triple Alliance. Refreshed, resurgent and co-ordinating its attacks surprisingly well, the Alliance set out to break England. In April, Paris fell to Charles VII. In July, Burgundian soldiers arrived to blockade Calais. And on 1 August, a huge Scots army, under James's personal command, appeared outside Roxburgh Castle. This included the latest artillery; according to the contemporary *Book of Pluscarden*, the Scots enjoyed 'fine, large guns, both cannons and mortars', including a splendid piece, the 'Lion', all operated by German gunners who were commanded by one Johannes Paule, the newly appointed 'Master of the King's Engines'.

However, the Roxburgh garrison, owing to Huntingdon's influence with Gloucester, had been properly paid and looked after by Northumberland. The castle's captain, Ralph Grey, and eighty men-at-arms unperturbedly held out against the Scots. Northumberland at the time was in Durham with the archbishop of York and the bishop of Durham – his eastern wardenship had ended on 25 July, and Northumberland was discussing the terrible state of Berwick's walls with the prelates while awaiting a new commission.[10] Although aware on 6 August that the Scots had begun a campaign, not for another four days did the English learn of James's whereabouts. Having assembled the local Northern levies in the interim, Northumberland and the two prelates left for Roxburgh that afternoon. Covering eighty miles in five days, the English hove within sight of the fortress only to see the Scots flee 'wretchedly and for their lives, leaving all the artillery and baggage behind'. As the fifteenth-century writer John Hardyng cheered: 'The erle then of Northumberland throughout raysed up the lands, and when he came it near, the kyng trumped up and went away full clere.' Although the Scots were probably broken more by their own 'detestable schism and most wicked division' (as the *Book of Pluscarden* puts it) rather than dread of Northumberland's relief force, this bloodless victory for Northumberland and catastrophic defeat for James marked a turning-point for English fortunes.[11] That month Gloucester had beaten the Burgundian forces in France and instigated a revolt against Duke Philip in Flanders before relieving Calais. For the next two years, Burgundy was fully occupied in putting down the rebellion and in 1439 he concluded a truce with England. In Normandy and Maine, England's most fearsome commander, Lord Talbot, the 24-year-old duke of York (of whom more later) and Salisbury pushed the French back to the very walls of Paris.

Six months later, James was assassinated. Over the winter of 1436 he had attempted to continue a Border war, but his nobles, shell-shocked after the Roxburgh debacle, were reluctant to endure more taxes to feed James's obsession with participating in the Anglo-French war. At a Parliament in October, the Estates refused to grant any funds after the undaunted James spoke with 'great scorn, imperiousness and proud authority'.

In the end, the plot to kill the king was set in motion by one of James's staunchest allies, Walter, the elderly earl of Atholl, who had backed the king's destruction of the Albany Stewarts, losing two sons in the king's service. By the early 1430s, James was playing off the Atholls against other noble houses to keep them on their toes; for example, by not certifying the family's hold on either the title or the lands that Walter had garnered over half a century. Walter, who had seen James profit from other peers' misfortunes, feared that when he died the king would disinherit his heir and grab the estates. It was either him or James.

The assassins struck while the king was staying in Perth, in the heart of Atholl country. Robert Graham, a retainer of the earl, summoned several old Albany Stewart loyalists, who loathed James for his murderous revenge more than a decade before. After an evening in the company of Atholl and Sir Robert Stewart (an accomplice), James went to bed. The assassins entered the castle, killed James's page and burst into the bedroom. But the king had vanished (in fact, into the sewers by prising up the floorboards), leaving only his queen and several ladies-in-waiting to cover his tracks. Some assassins seized Joan and were about to cut her throat when Thomas Graham cried, 'For shame ... she is bot a woman.' She soon fled the room.

James was eventually discovered in the sewer. Having dealt with two assailants in the narrow passage, he faced Robert Graham. James, now bleeding terribly, 'cried hym mercy' and asked for a priest. Graham snarled, 'Thow shalt never haue other confessore bot this same sword,' and 'smote hym thorogh the body'. Graham and two others then disgraced the corpse by stabbing it sixteen times in the chest. The deed that shocked Europe had been done. But the assassins had erred by letting the queen disappear into the night as they sought the king.[12]

A month later, on 25 March 1437, a six-year-old boy with a vivid, scarlet-coloured birthmark covering the left side of his face was crowned James II, king of Scotland. A later portrait depicts a slim, confident individual, fashionably attired in pointed shoes, shoulder-padded tunic and large hat; belying this picture of innocence is the hand resting warily on the dagger at his side. Within months of her son's accession, Queen Joan had her own vengeance. Robert Graham and the other men whom she recognised were laboriously put to death; Sir Robert Stewart was tortured and executed, and the earl of Atholl was beheaded.

In England, from 13 November 1437 onwards, Henry VI was vested with full kingly powers upon reaching the age of sixteen. His portraits reveal a slim, tall teenager; his washed-out face featured a weak chin (but slightly protruding lower lip) and widely spaced eyes; muscleless arms ended in delicate, pianist's hands. He was good-looking, and even hand-some, with prodigious physical stamina, compared to Charles VII of France, who was described by one horrified French historian as being 'stunted and puny, with a blank face in which scared, shifty, sleepy eyes, peering out on either side of a big, long nose, failed to animate his harsh, unpleasant features'. Intellectually, Henry was precocious and talented (his fluency in French was often noted) while his sobriety and piety dis-guised a credulously loyal yet vacillating and sometimes vindictive nature.

With two such young and inexperienced kings on the English and Scottish thrones, the Border gently simmered down, peppered by the occasional local fracas that was easily dealt with at the next March-day. Indeed, this time a nine-year truce was rapidly arranged, to run from 1 May 1438.

But Border peace spelled trouble for Northumberland. Despite his 'victory' at Roxburgh, his wardenship was not renewed (although he was rewarded with £100 and a special mission to deliver the Order of the Garter to the king of Portugal); in fact, the post was left insultingly vacant until a week after James II's coronation when the duke of Norfolk, with no Border experience, was appointed for a year. Henry VI's assumption of the throne had resulted in Gloucester's influence declining and Cardinal Beaufort's rising. With Salisbury in France (see above) fighting alongside the duke of York and Talbot (Beaufort's kinsman), Norfolk was a temporary stopgap to exclude Northumberland from the East March. In the West March, Beaufort brought in a loosely aligned member of the Beaufort–Salisbury affinity, Marmaduke Lumley, the mild bishop of Carlisle, to keep Salisbury's seat warm. Lumley, however, was not as wide-eyed as Beaufort had first thought; agreeing to a fixed sum of £1050 per annum *in peace or war* (demonstrating just how quiet the Border was) for a seven-year term, the cardinal and Salisbury expected Lumley's resig-nation when the earl himself returned in 1439. But Lumley, enjoying his £1050 for effectively doing nothing, doughtily stuck out his full term – much to his sponsors' annoyance. Not until 1443 did Salisbury resume the wardenship, and even then he had to undercut Lumley's wages by £50 a year. Indeed, the council then bargained down the desperate earl to £983 per annum. In return, Salisbury demanded, and got, a ten-year con-tract and successfully lobbied for his son (Richard, earl of Warwick) to hold the wardenship for *twenty years* after his death. In 1454, Salisbury would manage to extend the contract to 1474 and renegotiate the terms up to £1250 in peace and double that in wartime.

In the meantime, owing to his participation in the Dunbar–Gloucester machinations, Northumberland remained *persona non grata* and was excluded from office. Beaufort pointedly advised the king to give the East March to Northumberland's former deputies, Sir Ralph Grey (the stout captain of Roxburgh during James I's siege) and recently liberated Robert Ogle (the captain of Berwick). Not until April 1440 would Northumberland be partially rehabilitated, when his son and heir, Henry, was appointed warden of the East March for a term of four years. This Henry would also be the first Percy in many a generation to marry outside the Northern nobility.

In 1435, six years after her father's death at Orléans in 1428–9, Henry had wedded Eleanor Poynings. She was the same age as her fourteen-year-old husband, but came from a significantly less exalted family. The Poynings had lived in Sussex since at least 1086, performing services for the earls of Warenne for several generations. Then, from the 1290s, when one of them went to Scotland alongside the first Lord Percy, the Poynings worked as soldiers and diligently accumulated parcels of land in Sussex, Suffolk, Norfolk, Kent and Somerset. Eventually, after they had done much good service in France, Edward III created them barons in 1368. Eleanor, nevertheless, was quite a catch; she was the only heiress of her grandfather's title and estates, *and* her grandmother's dower. The Poynings were worthy people, without political ambitions.

Why Northumberland chose Eleanor as his son's bride is a mystery. Her complete detachment from Northern infighting – then in full swing between Westmorland and Salisbury – may have attracted Northumberland's eye, as may the glint of her money. More practically, once Eleanor's sickly grandfather died in 1446, Henry Percy, now known as Lord Poynings in right of his wife, instantly became a substantial Southern landholder, thereby saving his father a great deal of money by not having to maintain him any longer.[13]

Despite the bitter rapprochement between the two branches of the Neville family in 1442–3, the 1440s marked a growing enmity between the Salisbury and Northumberland dynasties, made more explosive by the coming of age of the earls' turbulent sons. On Percy's side, there was of course the relatively sensible Poynings, but there were also his other sons, Thomas, William, Richard and Ralph. Of Thomas, R.L. Storey has written, 'Quarrelsome violent and contemptuous of all authority, he possessed all the worst characteristics of a Percy for which his grandfather Hotspur [was] still a byword.' In 1447, for instance, he and a gang of ruffians went hell-raising in Yorkshire and landed up in jail. Two years later, in the hope that by making him 'respectable' Thomas would behave (he didn't, as will be seen), the king created him Baron Egremont (in Cumberland), granting him £10 a year but no lands.

William went into the Church and, owing to a special papal dispensation in 1452, was made bishop of Carlisle at twenty-four. Neglecting his flock, he instead helped Egremont to stir up trouble among Salisbury's tenants. In his first year at Rose Castle (the episcopal seat), Cumberland was so riven by 'great dissensions, riots and debates' that 'one half of the shire was divided from that other'. (At one point, Egremont ordered his thugs to beat up the sheriff of Cumberland, a Salisbury follower.) As for Richard and Ralph Percy, although they practised a lower magnitude of villainy than Egremont, the former especially had his genuinely psychotic moments: he once abused the bailiff of Staincliffe at prayer in the local parish church, chased the terrified man to the altar and had drawn his dagger to kill him when the priest, holding the Host aloft, cried at him to stop. Ralph, judging by his later actions, was the son who combined a natural ability for fighting (and violence) with the traditional Percy attributes of dogged loyalty to principle and person. There was one other Percy brother, George, of whom little is known, perhaps because he led a wholly blameless life as a rector in Rothbury. He played no role in the ensuing events.

What their despairing father, who may have heartily disliked Salisbury but was congenitally predisposed towards obedience to due authority, thought of his sons can only be imagined. Northumberland, however, was not entirely innocent. A recently discovered document dating from *circa* 1442 graphically illustrates the widening breach between the two Northern earls. Indeed, it shows Northumberland's concern with *good form*, and how deeply he felt Salisbury was a pushy newcomer who had, to put it bluntly, married his title and shoved Westmorland, his harmless, invalid half-brother – a true Northerner – aside. It was not by chance, perhaps, that the dispute occurred in the aftermath of the touchy Neville–Neville reconciliation, which had clearly left Westmorland unsatisfied. Unfortunately, Northumberland's original letter is missing, but not Salisbury's reply, which directly rebuts Northumberland's allegations.

Apparently, claiming that his own earldom pre-dated Salisbury's, Northumberland accused him of attacking his 'preemynence' on the Border and in the North. He (erroneously) argued that Thomas Montagu's full restoration to the earldom of Salisbury in 1421 (his father, John, had been attainted and executed in the 1400 rebellion against Henry IV) was only, to use an anachronism, a life peerage ('a newe creacion for terme of his life'). Furthermore, he claimed that Neville could not inherit the title through his wife, Montagu's daughter Alice, since everyone knew women could not inherit titles.

In his reply, which snippily addressed Northumberland as 'Henry, pretendyng to bee erl of Northumbrelond', Salisbury reminded the royal council that Northumberland's own title dated only from 1416 (and he was, moreover, the son and grandson of traitors); he demolished the life peerage allegation and he claimed that the title was part of the late Montagu's inheritance, which did descend through his wife.[14] In the end, Salisbury won on points, humiliating Northumberland and publicising his ambition to overtake the earl's pre-eminent Northern position. Soon after, as we have seen, Bishop Lumley was succeeded as warden of the West March by Salisbury, who was granted the position for ten years.

Was it a coincidence, then, that in the following year, Northumberland also fell out with Archbishop Kemp of York, sparking a chain of undefined 'disturbances' in the North? York lay directly between the Percy lands at Spofforth and the Neville lands centred around Sheriff Hutton. Kemp was Cardinal Beaufort's man, and Northumberland believed him biased towards Salisbury in trying to keep the peace in Yorkshire.

It is important to remember that at this time Northumberland was effectively isolated; Westmorland was an exceptionally weak ally, with no influence in London; as for the faithful Lord Clifford, Border barons were small beer compared to the influence that Salisbury wielded through Beaufort. In previous years, Northumberland might have sought help from Gloucester, who was normally interested in anyone (or anything) that obstructed Beaufort, but after 1441 Gloucester was a busted flush. In that year, his rivals raised charges of scorcery against his wife, Eleanor, who had apparently fallen under the sway of a certain Roger Bolingbroke, a fashionable necromancer in Gloucester's household. This Bolingbroke had lured the wide-eyed duchess by casting spells predicting the king's imminent death and his replacement by Gloucester. Eleanor (whom Gloucester could no longer protect, so weak was his political position) was ultimately forced by Cardinal Beaufort and Archbishop Kemp to perform penance by walking through the streets of London – a fate usually reserved for guilty prostitutes. She was then held in custody until she died in 1452. For obvious reasons, then, Gloucester was officially *persona non grata* at the royal court until the death (in very shadowy circumstances) in 1447 of this brother, uncle and son of kings and the very last surviving prince of the Lancastrian blood royal.

Even Northumberland's final trump card failed. His old comrade and co-warden, John Holland, earl of Huntingdon and former crony of Gloucester, had in 1444 been created duke of Exeter, a title stripped from his father (John Holland, Richard II's half-brother) after a clumsy, short-lived rebellion in 1400. Exeter's unfortunate death three years later left the fourteen-year-old Henry Holland as heir. Within a decade, this boy would evolve into one of the Percys' most valued allies, but Northumberland needed his backing now, not later. He was also Henry VI's cousin through his grandmother Elizabeth, John of Gaunt's daughter and Henry IV's sister. Had the crown descended through females, the Holland/Exeter claim would have been far stronger than that of the descendant of Henry IV, whom some still regarded as a usurper.

There was one other potential claimant who would play a major role before too long. In 1403, Hotspur had supported Edmund Mortimer, earl of March, as rightful king owing to his kinship with Edward III's second son, Lionel of Antwerp (also known as the duke of Clarence). But for March's descent through Lionel's only *daughter* – which weakened the royal link – he would have succeeded Richard II. That hereditary claim would have been stronger than Henry IV's (or that of the Hollands/Exeters), both families descended through Lionel's younger brother, John of Gaunt, duke of Lancaster. But in the Lancastrian instance, there were no girls in the way.

March, however, died childless in 1425, ending the direct male link with Lionel of Clarence. (After the deaths of the rebel Northumberland and Hotspur in Henry IV's reign, nobody had overtly championed March's case.) However, his younger sister and heiress, Anne, had the misfortune to marry Richard, earl of Cambridge, her own cousin and the younger son of Edmund duke of York, Edward III's youngest son. Richard foolishly became entangled in the Southampton Plot of 1415 and was executed by Henry V as a traitor, while his elder brother died at Agincourt that same year.

So, it was Cambridge's son, another Richard, who was created duke of York in 1415, and grew up in Salisbury's household until he came of age in 1432. By then, perhaps unsurprisingly, he had married Cicely Neville, *Salisbury's youngest sister*, thereby completing the anti-Percy circle.

This complex dynastic litany can be boiled down to two basic points: (1) in the 1440s, the duke of York was the representative of the March claim to the throne, a connection that was extremely remote but certainly salvageable if (as yet, improbably) the Lancastrian king Henry VI either had no children, was toppled or died; (2) Salisbury closely attached himself to his young brother-in-law, York, cynically seeing this Yorkshire (but also Midlands, Southern, Irish and Welsh) landholder as a priceless asset in his duel with Northumberland.

Salisbury certainly needed a strong patron. Just when Northumberland's two allies, Exeter and Gloucester, both died in 1447, so did old Cardinal Beaufort. After that dire year, Northumberland and Salisbury were suddenly left to their own devices in the North.

In London, the king's new favourite and confidant, the duke of Suffolk (the grandson of Richard II's favourite, Michael de la Pole), ruled the roost, with little time, and even less inclination, for fractious Northerners. His wealth stemmed from holdings in Southern and Eastern England, and it is unlikely that he had ever been further north than the Midlands. Ignoring the complaints of the other councillors, and the intensely annoying York (then governor of Normandy and France), Suffolk barefacedly advanced his friends and interests. He negotiated the Treaty of Tours in 1444, which arranged the betrothal of Charles VII's puppy-fatted but lovely niece, Margaret of Anjou, to Henry; old French hands considered this a sell-out. In exchange, Suffolk agreed a truce, he acquiesced in the return of Maine to Charles and he quietly proposed that Henry renounce his claim to the French throne in return for keeping Normandy and Aquitaine in full sovereignty. When he arrived home, Suffolk was the most hated man in England, for he had betrayed Henry V's legacy.

Worse was to come. While the English Crown's debts had risen to £400,000 and Henry's income had fallen to £30,000 through Suffolk's predations, Charles VII had diligently amassed the resources – including a properly trained and professionally led army – for a major campaign. At the end of July 1449, ignoring Margaret's marriage to Henry, Charles VII launched the great offensive against underfunded, undermanned Normandy. Rouen fell first, and by the early spring of 1450, the Lancastrian empire in northern France had been reduced to only a tip of it – at Cherbourg. On 15 April at Formigny (west of Caen), an English army was defeated for the first time in a major battle since Bannockburn in 1314. Then, in mid-August, Cherbourg itself – where the English put up a last-ditch fight – surrendered, leaving only the Channel Islands and Aquitaine in Henry VI's hands. As one country squire lamented to another in a famous letter of 19 August, 'We have not now a foote of lond in Normandie.'

While Anglo-Norman refugees flowed into Dover, accusations as to 'Who lost France?' swirled around the Commons and the council, and Suffolk was lambasted as a traitor and a bastard when rumours spread that he had taken bribes, skimmed money from our brave boys in Normandy and sold secrets to Charles VII. In April 1450, he was captured at sea by the *Nicholas of the Tower* as he fled for France. A few days later, after the vengeful York had been alerted, Suffolk was thrown onto a rowboat and beheaded (it required six strokes) by an Irishman.

At home, the Kentishmen under Jack Cade, a patriotic lower-class Normandy veteran, rebelled in the spring of 1450, galvanising Southern and Eastern England. Their main grievances were France's fall and the

English misgovernment (meaning Suffolk's) that in their view had caused it. Suffolk had defrauded the king and bankrupted his treasury; Henry should dismiss 'all the false progeny and affinity of the Duke of Suffolk' and replace them with sound patriotic heroes, such as 'the high and mighty prince the Duke of York'. They swarmed into London, sacked the Marshalsea and decapitated the treasurer, Lord Saye and Sele (an accomplice of Suffolk's), in a tavern. Not until 6 July was the rebellion finally broken. Widespread sympathy for the rebels among the gentry and nobles ensured that all were pardoned (except Cade, who was killed) and a commission was sent to Kent to investigate the scale of the abuses perpetrated under Suffolk's leadership.

York quickly established himself among the Commons as the first and best hope for reform. But Suffolk's fall also led to the rise of the duke of Somerset, Edmund Beaufort, as Henry's new confidant. The old Gloucester–Beaufort rivalry of the 1430s had been replaced by that between York and another Beaufort, but after Cade had so publicly endorsed York, Henry was wary of his position as heir apparent to the throne (Prince Edward, Henry's son, would not be born until 1453).

Then in his mid-forties and having inherited his title only two years before when John, his brother, died, Somerset, the third and last surviving son of the eldest Beaufort (another John, who had died in 1410) was very different from the cardinal, his cautious, wily uncle, whose colossal loans had kept the court in his pocket. For one, Somerset would not be lending money to anyone, at least in the short term. Apart from a paltry £300, the Beaufort estates had descended to his late brother's daughter, Margaret. This extremely wealthy great-great-granddaughter of Edward III is perhaps better known as Lady Margaret Beaufort, who, in a few years' time, would marry the earl of Richmond and bear him a posthumous son, later King Henry VII. For the moment, however, with the Beaufort fortunes in the hands of his niece, Edmund's future relied on accumulating mountains of annuities, fees and offices from the king, something at which Somerset was conspicuously successful. Soon, he was living well on a 'salary' of some £3000 a year and his friends at the Exchequer ensured that his expenses and wages were paid on time, in full and sometimes even in advance.

York, although England's wealthiest landowner whose gross income amounted to £7000, had spent huge sums of his own money on defending English interests in Ireland and France and was owed nearly £40,000 by the Crown. Much of his income was spent on servicing his debts and he despised Somerset – a 'Teflon Man' who rose ever higher despite an almost unbroken run of failure and defeats. Furthermore, he had swiped the lieutenancy of France in 1447, a post York had coveted for years.

English rule had then collapsed (Somerset personally surrendered Rouen to Charles VII in 1449), which hadn't hampered Somerset's rise to the top after Suffolk's fall. Having the king's ear, Somerset deftly excluded York from court and military offices (such as the captaincy of Calais, which Somerset grabbed in 1451). Somerset, of course, loathed his rival; according to the contemporary *English Chronicle*, Somerset invariably 'kept near to the king, and dared not depart from his presence, dreading always the power' of York if he were caught straying.

York, impotent with rage, could only watch as Henry and Somerset did little to hinder the French advance towards Gascony in 1451. That summer, Bordeaux surrendered and Charles turned to Calais. In February 1452, York snapped and issued a statement claiming that the disasters in recent years were due to 'the envy, malice and untruth of the said duke of Somerset... who works continually for my undoing'. But after a stand-off at Dartford, York peacefully submitted to Henry, provided that an inquiry be held into Somerset's conduct in Normandy. But Henry, with no intention of honouring the bargain, placed York under Somerset's humiliating wardenship on the ride back to London. Although York's 'rebellion' was technically treason, for Henry it was more like a rush of blood to the head and he released York after making him apologise. Yet York's anger at least provoked government action. In October 1452, a 5000-man force under the venerable lord Talbot (who was now nearly seventy) chased the hated French occupiers out of Gascony.[15]

Less than a year later, however, on 17 July 1453, Charles VII's refurbished grand army, with superb artillery, drove into Gascony and at the climactic battle of Castillon on 17 July 1453 – the last battle of the 'official' Hundred Years War (although Calais, the remaining English toehold on the Continent, held out until 1558) – the English were soundly defeated, and Talbot was killed. Wholly unarmoured (to obtain his release many years before, he had pledged never to wear 'harness' against the French) and swathed in a vivid crimson satin robe, Talbot had led the charge but his horse was wounded. Seeing the struggling old hero trapped beneath the fallen beast, an archer named Michel Perunin cleaved his chest with an axe. It is said that his corpse was so disfigured, his herald could only recognise him by his teeth.

A month later, an easily stressed Henry, whose wife Margaret was carrying his first and only child, received the shocking news of Castillon and Talbot's death, thereby ramming home to the king that he had squandered his father's glorious legacy. He immediately lapsed into what was probably a depressive stupor, a psychotic illness that made him virtually silent and inert for the next eighteen months. He lost his memory and all sense of time, and sat slumped with half-closed eyes, barely able to walk or stand without help. For two months, the king's secret was kept from the Commons, although rumours flew around the peers. Unexpectedly, Somerset, now bereft of his guardian and protector, stood alone in the council, circled by York's angry allies.

Only Bordeaux still held out, but on 19 October, Charles's officials took charge of Bordeaux, effectively bringing the Hundred Years War to a close.[16]

The reverberations of the fall of Bordeaux encouraged York to strike in late November, when he declared to the Lords that 'the losse of ii so noble duchees as Normandie and Guyen' was not simply a forgiveable 'trespasse' on Somerset's part. Accused of treason, Somerset was hauled to the Tower to await his sentence, while his allies (among whom were the Percys – of which more in the next chapter) prepared for civil war over the governance of England. When Queen Margaret dotingly presented Prince Edward to his listless father, hoping to jar him out of his stupor, Henry glanced at him and 'caste doune his eyene ayen'. Without firm royal control, the nobility was cracking apart.

CHAPTER SIXTEEN

Mutual Assured Destruction

The North and the Wars of the Roses

Initium fuit maximorum dolorum in Anglia.
WILLIAM WORCESTER, REFERRING TO THE
FEUD BETWEEN PERCY AND NEVILLE THAT
SPARKED THE WARS OF THE ROSES.[1]

To understand the events leading up to the outbreak of the Wars of the Roses in 1455, we should return to the late 1440s, when the emergency in France, the deaths of Gloucester and Beaufort, the struggle between York and Somerset, and the rebellion in Southern and Eastern England distracted attention from the North, where Salisbury and Northumberland, suddenly left to their own devices, quickly made a hash of things.

The conflict, which would engulf both Percy and Neville, was ignited by the expiry in 1447 of the nine-year truce with Scotland. The new Lord Poynings, itching for some military experience – as warden of the East March since 1440, he hadn't had any – impetuously razed Dunbar in the summer of 1448. In reply, William, the 8th earl of Douglas and Poynings' counterpart on the Scottish March, pointedly burnt Alnwick and Warkworth. So Poynings' dutiful, if unenthusiastic, father prepared to invade with 6000 Northumbrians in October.

Northumberland was less concerned with Douglas than with scoring points off Salisbury, who was still in charge of the West March. Leaving Salisbury spluttering with indignation as the Northumbrians moved west and tramped through his March – a terrible breach of wardenly etiquette – Northumberland crossed the Border near Gretna, and encamped between the River Sark and Kirtle Water, close to the Solway Firth, his strategic intentions unknown.

The Scots quickly mustered an army under the earl of Ormond. Northumberland, inexcusably surprised on 23 October when 4000 well-presented Scots appeared, seems not to have expected a Scottish counter-attack. Nevertheless, the earl quickly divided his numerically superior army into three scratch divisions (*nota bene*: the hot-headed

Poynings was not given a command, but was instead directed to remain at his father's side).

After absorbing the archers' initial salvo, the Scots held, and then their commander, facing the English, astounded Northumberland by rushing the vulnerable archers with his spearmen. Unprotected by the infantry or cavalry in the English centre, the archers were defenceless against the onslaught at close quarters and fled, leaving the other two divisions open to a flank attack when the rest of the Scots charged the useless English cavalry (who, strangely, had not dismounted). By now, the rising tide in the Solway was cutting off Northumberland's retreat, but the English were driven into the marshes and mud behind them. After helping his father escape while hundreds of men drowned, Poynings was captured along with Sir John Pennington, the commander of the English right (both were ransomed shortly after). Total English casualties at the battle of Sark numbered up to 1500, with perhaps another 500 drowned (estimated Scots fatalities vary from 26 to 600). Northumberland had been routed, Sark marking the first major English defeat since Hotspur's surrender at Otterburn in 1388.

Henry ordered Salisbury to respond immediately, whatever the weather. Confidently leaving Carlisle with a large army a fortnight later, Salisbury was bested not by Scots but by impossibly severe conditions and thieves. Within three days, he had lost 2000 horses and had to limp back across the Border, having accomplished nothing. Adding injury to insult, the Scots then attacked the area around Carlisle.

Unsurprisingly, the English sent negotiators to Scotland in 1449 to organise another truce. Northumberland and Salisbury, whose wardens' fees were slashed to signal London's displeasure, were pointedly excluded.

The blazingly hot summer of 1453 witnessed the final, traumatic rupture between the Houses of Percy and Neville, both headed by men in their fifties and squired by resentful, fiery sons. The year before, William Percy (aged only twenty-four) had been appointed bishop of Carlisle – traditionally Neville turf. Within months, William and his turbulent older brother, Lord Egremont, had attracted to their camp any man with an anti-Neville grudge, sparking riots and dissension throughout the West March. Egremont, having loafed around Northumberland's rougher establishments for some years, had the common touch and used it to recruit artisans, tradesmen and the unemployed to his banner. In the winter of 1452–3, he moved to York, which was then struck by a severe recession, and he stoked up resentment against the city aldermen and leading traders, many of whom accepted the Neville shekel.

York was equidistant between a corpus of Neville estates that centred around Sheriff Hutton, with its recently rebuilt castle, and the Percy fief in the west, surrounding Spofforth, where the earl stayed when in Yorkshire. Moreover, only a few miles separated the Percys' Topcliffe cluster near Thirsk and the Neville holdings at Sowerby.[2]

Egremont resided at Healaugh, about seven miles west of York, which had reverted to the Percys after the duke of Bedford's death in 1435. His presence undoubtedly bolstered the tenants' confidence in Percy power; in January 1453, for instance, when three deputy sheriffs came to arrest one Oliver Stockdale, a yeoman-tenant, some 120 locals, claiming that the king's writ did not run in Percy lands, aggressively repulsed the officials. (A year later, Stockdale, having proven his toughness, would enter Egremont's personal service.)

By mid-May, the increasingly insolent Egremont was distributing his distinctive red and black livery to eight former tradesmen from York, who joined his growing private contingent. The king, informed by Salisbury that Egremont was liable to make mischief, summoned the young man and his cohort to London to send them to Gascony. Perhaps foreign martial glory would calm the footloose Egremont. But the landless lord ignored this royal summons, as well as the next on 26 June and a third on 7 July, which promised rapid payment if he turned up. In the end, Gascony fell (on 17 July) before Egremont had bothered to reply.

One reason for his silence was fear. Egremont had lain low and avoided the open road to London because Sir John Neville, Salisbury's third son and, although only in his mid-twenties, an experienced soldier, was looking for him. From about June onwards, Egremont and John Neville played cat and mouse throughout Yorkshire; what animated their personal feud still remains a mystery. Each unleashed their retainers against the other's family properties – smashing windows, making forcible evictions, breaking and entering and generally causing a ruckus. At one point – three days after the government ordered him to desist from disturbing the peace – John Neville threatened to hang the tenants in Topcliffe unless they told him where Egremont was hiding: they didn't know.

By the end of July, following a spate of robberies by Egremont's brother Richard, the king sent identical letters to Salisbury and Northumberland, directing them to control their sons and disband the gangs – to no avail. A commission under Lord Lucy, however, managed to find and reprimand more than a dozen miscreants from both sides, but still John Neville and Egremont evaded capture.

On 24 August, isolated skirmishes escalated into virtual insurrection. The occasion was the marriage between Sir Thomas Neville (John's older brother by a year) and the beautiful, recently widowed Maud Stanhope, the niece and co-heiress of Lord Cromwell, a rich Lincolnshire baron with Beaufort connections. The Percys regarded the match as a slap in the face, for Cromwell had acquired two Percy manors – Wressle in Yorkshire and Burwell in Lincolnshire – in 1438, when Northumberland was still trying to piece the family estates back together. Now the Nevilles had spitefully grabbed them. Perhaps, too, the younger, landless Percys were jealous of the luck of their Neville cousins, and maybe Egremont himself desired Maud's hand.

After the marriage at Tattershall in Lincolnshire, the entire Neville brood wended its way northwards to Sheriff Hutton. At Heworth Moor, to the east of York (but now in the city), the Percys were waiting to assassinate them. The previous day, a Thursday, Egremont and Richard Percy, the second-youngest of the Percy boys and now under his brother's baleful influence, had recruited furiously in York and at home.

The Percy force was considerable; the names, occupations and origins of no fewer than 710 of them have been preserved, and there may have been over 1000 present. They included a 'vagabond', nine labourers, a few hundred yeomen (including the violent Oliver Stockdale), merchants, freemen, a goldsmith who later became mayor of York, tailors, two dyers, five scholars, eight saddlers, two shoemakers, six sailors and, inexplicably, three wandering Scots. In command were knights, bailiffs, clergymen, esquires and younger sons of barons, such as John 'Butcher' Clifford, son of the old Percy adherent, Lord Clifford.

Salisbury and the Nevilles, however, were accompanied by sizeable armed escorts. Mutual fear and the known penalties for staging a pitched battle in Henry's realm prevented a clash; instead, there was name-calling and jostling. Egremont and Richard Percy (Northumberland was absent) glared at the Nevilles and their cavalcade, but the stand-off at Heworth, according to chronicler William Worcester, marked the 'beginning of the greatest sorrow in England': the Wars of the Roses.

Whilst many hoped Heworth would mark the end of the feud, low-intensity warfare continued between the Percys and the Nevilles throughout the autumn of 1453. Indeed, a corps of the Percy 'army' at Heworth was retained, some of whom (including Richard's friend, one John Caterall of Wressle, a man later indicted as one of the North's most notorious 'robbers, ravishers, extortioners and oppressors') accompanied Richard when he broke into a church in Craven and seized Lawrence Caterall, the local bailiff, at his devotions while the vicar said Mass.

In retaliation, two weeks later Sir John Neville and a gang raided the absent Northumberland's house at Catton in Yorkshire, smashing windows, breaking doors and scrawling warnings of dire retribution on the walls. The next day, 25 September, Richard Percy and forty-one drunken rioters (twenty-three of whom were repeat offenders, and nineteen of whom had been at Heworth) crashed into the vicar of Aughton's pleasant house and stole all his wine. More seriously, Egremont beat up Cumberland's deputy sheriff and bailiffs when they came to collect taxes, thereby announcing that the younger Percys did not respect even royal authority.

The Crown, furious at this insult, immediately wrote to Northumberland and Salisbury, reminding them, more harshly this time, that as commissioners of the peace and members of the king's council, their duty and high estate was 'to the service and support of us in keeping of our peace and of our laws'. Unless matters improved, the earls would be degraded in rank. Letters to Egremont and John Neville were blunter still; both had been created barons in the expectation of good service. Unless their 'liegemen' were disbanded and their behaviour modified, they would forfeit their titles.

The Crown's uncompromising warnings compelled the antagonists' attention, but not before one last show of strength – perhaps to prove they weren't avoiding a fight voluntarily. On 20 October, the entire Percy clan (along with Lord Clifford) stayed at Topcliffe with the largest concentration of armed retainers seen so far – up to 10,000 men drawn from throughout the North. The Nevilles gathered at Sand Hutton, a mere four miles north of Topcliffe. If both sides had subsequently clashed with one side decisively losing, the Wars of the Roses would have assumed a very different hue. However, having received the royal warnings, the two earls arranged a truce and disbanded their forces. As Storey observes, however: 'There was no reconciliation; the day of reckoning had merely been postponed.'[3]

Present with the Nevilles at Sand Hutton for the first time was the earl of Warwick, dubbed 'the Kingmaker' in the eighteenth century by David Hume (borrowing from another Scottish historian, John Major, who described the earl as *regum creator* in 1521) – 'thou plucker down and setter up of kings'. (In *1066 and All That*, royal candidates submitted application forms to him, stating their preferred manner of death.) Like Northumberland, we have no pictorial or written evidence of his appearance. Warwick's character is an historical amalgam, dependent on the widely competing opinions held of him by Yorkists and Lancastrians, who described him with words like amoral, generous, gentle, vindictive, cowardly and heroic. His latest biographer's more balanced view is that 'he was the greatest nobleman of the age, the heir to four great families, their estates, connections and traditions.' For the Kingmaker, 'pragmatism and ruthlessness went hand in hand with honour ... An underlying strength of will and determination and an intolerance of opposition and viciousness towards opponents needs to be set against the charm that cajoled, persuaded and won over men of whatever standing.'⁴

As we have seen, Warwick's father, Richard Neville – the eldest son of Westmorland's second marriage to Joan Beaufort (the daughter of John of Gaunt and Katherine Swynford) – had married Alice Montagu, daughter of the feared earl of Salisbury. When the latter died, Richard Neville acquired the title and estates. It was the new Salisbury's son, another Richard (born 1428), for whom he bagged an elephant: Ann Beauchamp, the sister and heiress of the earl of Warwick (who died in 1446). Three years later, Richard Neville was recognised as earl of Warwick.

Normally, the divisions in the North and an ineffective government in London would have presented rich opportunities both to the Scots and the French. But the conclusion of the Hundred Years War, while inglorious for Henry, prevented Charles VII from capitalising on English discomfiture despite the Auld Alliance's re-ratification in 1449.⁵ The Scots, under the young James II, were fighting their own civil war, a sort of mini-Wars of the Roses between the royal house of Stewart and various noble families, particularly the Douglases. In the early 1450s, the 8th earl of Douglas built a power base that made him the mightiest of Scottish earls. He and his allies had seen how James's father had handled nobles whom he paranoically considered threats: divide them against each other, then pick them off individually. At Stirling Castle on 21 February 1452, James asked Douglas to break with his allies. Douglas refused, at which James, in a fit of fury, cried, 'False traitor, sen yow will nocht, I sall!' He then stabbed him repeatedly, after which a courtier struck the fallen earl's skull with a poleaxe. After the murderous orgy, his corpse bore twenty-six wounds and his brains spattered the stone floor. This shocking deed was as criminal as Bruce's sacrilegious murder of John Comyn in a church over a century before, or the assassination of his father James I.

Douglas's heir, previously intent on a clerical career, swore revenge. He and his brothers renounced their feudal fealty to the king and James gathered his forces, including a slew of newly created earls, to offset Douglas's power. In reply, Douglas contacted the English, although refusing to pay homage to Henry. Little came from these semi-treasonous negotiations or the king's attempts to forge an anti-Douglas bloc; instead, over the next few years, Douglas and James interspersed tit-for-tat hostilities with intermittent truces, although, like the Percy–Neville ententes, neither man trusted the other. During Henry's incapacity, for instance, Douglas maintained contact with the English, but subsequently secretly attached himself to York in reaction to James's Somerset leanings (through his mother, Somerset was James's uncle).⁶

The linking of the conflict between James and Douglas to the struggle between York and Somerset was reproduced by Northumberland and Salisbury/Warwick at about the same time. Just after the inconclusive stand-off between the earls on 20 October 1453 – coinciding with Prince Edward's birth and the end of the Hundred Years War – the Nevilles embarked on a radical new strategy. They openly aligned themselves with York, a decision in which the son probably influenced the father: earlier that summer, Warwick had begun a bitter dispute with Somerset over lands in Glamorgan and had swung behind York, his arch-rival. According to the Nevilles' calculations, moreover, York's considerable holdings in Yorkshire would be immensely valuable in the destruction of the Percys. For Northumberland and Poynings, the Nevilles were welcome to take their chances; Somerset, after all, was a Lancastrian in power with the ear of the queen.

The Nevilles' timing was immaculate. Soon afterwards, as related in Chapter 15, following the fall of Bordeaux Somerset was hauled off to the Tower of London and their man came to power. Salisbury's sensitive political antennae highlight Northumberland's clumsiness, for in many respects, a Northumberland alliance with the hitherto unaligned York *against* Salisbury was a natural fit. Northumberland's father and grand-father, for instance, had tried to replace the Lancastrian Henry IV with York's uncle, Mortimer. Salisbury's father and grandfather, on the other hand, had helped to destroy Henry IV's rivals. A nimbler and more flexi-ble operator, like Salisbury for example, would not have let slip such an opportunity. The Percys, however, recovered quickly; many others had also backed Somerset's wrong horse and were willing to confederate. Chief among these was Henry Holland, the duke of Exeter, then in his early twenties.

Northumberland had long known the Hollands, having served as co-warden with his father, John Holland, earl of Huntingdon and duke of Exeter, in the 1430s, when together they arranged Patrick Dunbar's abortive 'covert' Scottish rebellion. Since then, Northumberland had smoothly arranged the marriage of his daughter, Katherine, to Sir Edmund Grey of Ruthin, the current Exeter's cousin.[7] After his father died in 1447, young Henry Holland had been in the care of York, whom he despised for forcing him to marry his ghastly eight-year-old daughter, Anne, just after he turned seventeen.

On 19 January 1454, at Tuxford, south of Doncaster, Egremont and Exeter secretly swore to ally against the Nevilles and York, thereby sub-suming a local family dispute into the greater, national struggle between the houses of Lancaster and York. Exeter as the optimal choice for an ally is questionable: if violent, ambitious, unstable and dull, he was at least militantly pro-Percy, doggedly anti-Neville and, most importantly, he nursed what he believed to be an exceptionally strong claim to the Crown, as we shall see. One historian thinks 'Egremont was exploiting the younger man's vain pretensions for purposes of his own'.[8] Less attention, however, has been paid to the possibility that the singularly adroit Salisbury was similarly manipulating York.

After becoming a duke in his own right, Exeter had been suing numerous lords whom he believed had defrauded his family out of lands. First among these was Lord Cromwell; both Exeter and the Percys, who had never forgiven Cromwell for acquiring their former manors of Wressle and Burwell, were obsessed with him. That Cromwell was married into the gigantic Neville dynasty reinforced Exeter and Northumberland's perception that Salisbury and Warwick were plotting against them (which they were). These mutual enemies made Exeter and the Percys natural allies, with one caveat. With good reason, Somerset and the queen had distrusted Exeter, whose loathing of York did not necessarily make him pro-Somerset. While Northumberland had preferred the fallen Somerset, Exeter always remained staunchly, megalomaniacally pro-Exeter.[9]

Thus, after York's installation as 'Protector and Defender of the Realm' on 27 March, the youthful Exeter believed that the duke, abetted by the malevolent Salisbury, had usurped *his* rightful place. (Only days later, York appointed his brother-in-law Salisbury, a secular peer, chancellor of England, a post traditionally reserved for a prelate.) Truth to tell, Exeter had right, but not might, on his side: his grandmother was John of Gaunt's daughter by his first wife and therefore sister to Henry IV, which made Henry VI his cousin. Had the Crown descended strictly through the female line, Exeter could have been king of England. But it didn't, and York was in charge. More worryingly, York, as protector, could settle disputes between magnates. And Salisbury's malign influence would make it most unlikely that he would decide for the Percys when he inevitably turned his attention to the ongoing quarrel. Already, York had summoned Egremont to London to answer before the council for his and Richard Percy's felonies. But the letter lay undelivered as Egremont had disappeared.

In early May 1454, York and Salisbury directed their fire at Northumberland and Lord Poynings. A statute condemned current and former wardens of the East and West Marches for illegally extending their influence southwards into Yorkshire 'sumtyme for thaire singuler lucre, and sumtyme for malice', a blatant attack on the Percys' traditional influence in the North. Northumberland was, still more ignominiously, ordered to travel to London by 16 May to explain himself, as were Egremont, Poynings and Sir Ralph Percy. No Neville received a similar summons, and appealing to Parliament, Northumberland knew, would be useless. Although everyone understood that York, and behind him Salisbury and Warwick, were pursuing a private vendetta, no man would publicly defend an obscure and troublesome Northerner with few friends at court. Moreover, many would ignore York and Salisbury's violations since, at last, effective government was being delivered. Appealing to the council would be a trap; Cromwell, Warwick, Salisbury and their friends were all members, while Exeter, Somerset, Northumberland, Poynings and Clifford had been excluded. As for Exeter, he was rapidly becoming a duke in name only. On 3 April, as punishment for meeting Egremont in January, he had been replaced as admiral of England by Salisbury, who was to be paid some £1300.[10]

Apart from Bishop William Percy of Carlisle, who, under Church protection, travelled to London to report on developments, no Percy went south by the council's deadline. Instead, Egremont augmented his personal corps of mostly York-based artisans, and was joined by Exeter and the Percy brothers, along with many tradesmen and family tenants from Cumberland. By mid-May, these 'forces' – which Egremont imagined looked impressive when kitted in his livery – had concentrated in York and were holding its mayor hostage. Given his rank and his naive assumption that these were professional soldiers, Exeter addressed the arrayed troops, with banners unfurled and weapons ready (making the gathering a treasonable act of war against the king). Bizarrely, Exeter announced that after ousting York and Salisbury (boos) and claiming the dukedom of Lancaster, he would reward Northerners who were loyal (to him) by exempting them from taxes (cheers). The army marched to Hull, which it failed to take, before pushing west to instigate rebellions throughout Lancashire, Cumberland and Westmorland.

Although intermittently successful in Lancashire, the Exeter– Egremont rebellion fizzled out quickly, especially after York's arrival with a small but efficient body of troops. By early July, the two ringleaders had scarpered; Egremont was holed up in Cockermouth and Exeter had run to seek sanctuary at Westminster. On 23 July, the impatient York had Exeter dragged out, much to the monks' distress. He was handed over to Salisbury and jailed for nine months in Pontefract Castle 'with great heaviness and right chargeable costs'. York, perhaps realising that Exeter was his own worst enemy, had been lenient; execution was the usual punishment in these cases. Thereafter, Salisbury rushed to Yorkshire, whence Egremont was now heading with 200 followers, to join John and Thomas Neville, who were eager to do battle with Egremont. Finally, at the end of October, near the Percy manor of Pocklington at Stamford Bridge, the site of the last victory of Anglo-Saxon England and now Neville territory, the two sides met and the Percy contingent was easily bested. The abject

Egremont, having surrendered to the Neville brothers, was taken to Middleham Castle and cumulatively fined £11,200, payable to Salisbury, his family and various other Nevilles, for all the damage the Percys had inflicted in past years. It was an immense sum considering Egremont's annual income of just £100. Just as the FBI would later charge Al Capone with tax evasion, however, Salisbury continued to hold Egremont on the civil charge of debt. Together with Richard Percy, who by now had also been captured, Egremont was shut into Newgate prison without any prospect of paying his fine.

Two years later, in an inspired feat of bravado, the Percys bribed their warden to allow in arms. Late at night on 13 November 1456, the brothers slipped out of their cell, freed their fellow unfortunates, climbed onto the roof and scaled the wall while the other escapees usefully fought off the wardens. Finding the pre-arranged horses, they scarpered for the Midlands (see next chapter).

Northumberland seems to have been unaware of Exeter and Egremont's plan back in 1454, or at least he kept discreetly aloof from the frenzy, as did the wiser Poynings and Clifford. Nevertheless, on 3 July the duke of York leased the town and borough of Doncaster (originally Percy property, whose return Northumberland sought) from Sir John Salvain for six years. York, who as protector had to stand apart from the grubby Percy–Neville quarrel, was using carrots and sticks to tame the Percys. Losing Doncaster was punishment for losing control of Egremont. But within two months of Stamford Bridge, Poynings, whom York seems to have considered the most sensible Percy, was generously granted custody for seven years of the old Percy lands of Shilbottle, Rennington, Guyzance and Beanley, and he also received £837 for his fees as warden of the East March. Both, clearly, were rewards for keeping clear of Egremont.

During the worsening political crisis of York's protectorate, however, any original criminal charges against the rebels were either forgotten or postponed; for example, by the time proceedings were initiated against Northumberland for his role in the violence of 1453, he had been dead for six years.[11]

The King Returns

On Christmas Day 1454, Henry VI suddenly jolted out of his depressive stupor. By the New Year, his doctors pronounced him fully recovered and capable of making decisions. As Edmund Clere wrote to John

Paston on 9 January, 'Blessed be God, the king is well amended, and hath been since Christmas Day... On Monday afternoon the Queen came to him, and brought my Lord Prince with her. And then he asked what the prince's name was, and the Queen told him Edward, and then he held up his hands and thanked God.'[12] From York's perspective in particular, '[Henry's] recovery was a national disaster' for, 'while he was incapacitated, England had known... the type of government most favoured by general contemporary opinion'.[13]

As the king's faculties returned, so did the queen's influence. Margaret adored Somerset (her 'dear cousin') while detesting York, who, with ill grace, stepped down as protector in late January 1455. Suddenly, Salisbury's personal protector was in a political void. Somerset was released from the Tower on 26 January after being held, as he complained, for a year and ten weeks 'without any reasonable Ground or laweful Process'. Henry immediately absolved him of any treason or incompetence and sent a strong signal to York by replacing him as captain of Calais with Somerset, who was also appointed the leading royal councillor.[14] Pointedly, it was ordered that Exeter – who was not entirely trusted, as was said, by the queen but who had proven anti-York credentials – be removed from Pontefract (Salisbury was the castle's constable) to the rather more luxurious Wallingford Castle, although he remained in custody.

From Northumberland's viewpoint, these were excellent developments. His man was back in office, and the execrable Salisbury was in terrible odour with Henry. The most delicious moment arrived on 7 March, when the council – to which Northumberland, Clifford and William Percy, bishop of Carlisle, had been invited – decided on Salisbury's fate (neither York nor Warwick attended). The earl had refused to release Exeter and was being threatened with a £7000 fine for disobedience. At the meeting, he was dismissed from the chancellorship and replaced by the archbishop of Canterbury. Two weeks later, the universally detested Cromwell and Salisbury's son-in-law, the earl of Worcester, also lost their positions on the council.

On a less personal note, however, these satisfying revenges were unwise. Despite York's private vendettas, he and his government were genuinely popular in the country and with the Commons. Somerset, in particular, was heartily disliked by the Londoners. To those outside noble circles, York's fall smacked of an inside job by a Somerset-led faction.

In mid-April, York, Salisbury and Warwick disappeared. Having been summoned to a great council in Leicester scheduled for 21 May, York suspected – probably rightly – that this was a legalistic tactic by Somerset to put him on trial. Next came news that York was leading an army from the north, presumably heading towards Leicester, but possibly bent on

London, to stage a coup. Panic set in among Somerset's clique, and forces were furiously amassed to intercept York before he reached the capital. Luckily, the major lords were in London, allowing Somerset to enlist the duke of Buckingham, four earls (including Northumberland) and six barons (including Clifford). On Wednesday morning, 21 May, the king and his nobles – accompanied by only one ecclesiastic, William Percy, bishop of Carlisle[15] – left for Leicester, intending to stop that night at Watford (sixteen miles from London), close enough to hurry back to Westminster if required. By now, York, Salisbury and Warwick were clearly heading for London, having travelled along the ancient Ermine Street directly south from Royston to Ware the day before.

The next morning, York decided to see whether Henry would negotiate: raising one's hand towards a king was still a momentous and unforgivable act, and he wanted to make clear that he was rebelling against Somerset, not the monarch. He moved towards St Albans, a natural convergence point midway between the two armies. And Henry did want to talk; to signal his good intentions, he had replaced the inflammatory Somerset as constable of the army with the moderate Buckingham. On 22 May, the armies were stationed at opposite ends of St Albans, the Yorkists to the east along the ridge of the hill on which sits the town. Facing them were the gardens that backed the row of houses along Holywell and St Peter's Street, the main thoroughfares of St Albans. From the ridge through the gardens were two roads – the southernmost being Sopwell Lane and the other Shropshire Lane (now Victoria Street) – leading into central St Albans.[16]

The Lancastrians arrived from the west at 9 a.m., to find the Yorkists already encamped. York had an advantage, not overwhelming, of numbers and experience. The armies, given the significance of the 'battle' of St Albans, were tiny: perhaps 3000 Yorkists and 2000 Lancastrians. Henry, however, was attended by a more distinguished and more numerous bevy of nobles, which might have convinced York that he had exceeded the boundaries of aristocratic behaviour.

After arriving, Henry established himself in the town centre, about where Holywell, St Peter's Street and the market place converge. St Albans was unwalled but not defenceless; the western end of Sopwell and Shropshire Lanes were barricaded, and beyond these the Lancastrians could see the Yorkist positions. York was placed on Shropshire Lane, while Salisbury covered Sopwell; Warwick, commanding the reserves, was between them, directly opposite where the king was sitting (although, owing to the row of houses, he obviously could not see him). Between Warwick and those houses lay the 'towne backsides', mostly open but with some tree cover.

The Lancastrians strengthened the barricades to prevent the Yorkists entering the town. Northumberland took charge of the Shropshire barricade while Clifford (indicating how smoothly the two Northerners worked together) commanded the Sopwell Lane defences. The remaining nobles and their men gathered round the king to await either an attack or York's terms of submission. The latter was more likely; at Dartford in 1452, York had backed away from a fight and might do so again since raising a banner against the king was irrevocable.

York's terms, when they arrived, were autocratic. For a truce, the duke said, all he wanted was Somerset to be turned over to him but Henry, livid at York's presumption, exclaimed: 'By the faith that I owe to St Edward and the crown of England I shall destroy every mother's son and they shall be hanged and drawn and quartered.' There would be no truce. Unfortunately, no one seems to have informed Northumberland or Clifford of the outcome of the parley, such as it was.

At ten o'clock, York and Salisbury sounded the charge and led the assault simultaneously down the two lanes, surprising the defenders. But after the barricades were rapidly reinforced, the Yorkists, caught in the narrow lanes, began to fall. Now Warwick, only in his twenties, came into his own. Seeing that the attacks were occupying the Lancastrians, he quietly led a picked contingent from the reserve through the gardens to the back of the row of houses. There, 'betwene the signe of the Keye and the sygne of the Chekkere' (that is, the Cross-Keys and the Chequers Inns, what is now called 'Battlefield House'), they crashed through the building onto Holywell, directly opposite a startled Henry and his nobles, all without their helmets. As men shouted 'A Warwick! A Warwick!', the young earl was startled by his own success, for he had just split the Lancastrian line. Suddenly looking behind them at the commotion, the Lancastrian defenders on the barricades panicked, thinking Warwick's contingent was the entire reserve, who would attack them from the rear. Apart from a few who stayed with Northumberland and Clifford, the men scattered into the market square, protecting the king but allowing the Yorkists to scale the barricades. By now, Warwick's troops were firing bolts at close quarters at the ill-disciplined crowd in front of them, wounding Henry in the neck, Buckingham in the face and many other senior Lancastrians in the arms or hands. In the lanes, Clifford and Northumberland were still desperately trying to hold back the Yorkists while retreating slowly towards the market square. Clifford reached the main street, but was killed while attempting to relieve those trapped. Northumberland, now in his early sixties, wanted to regroup with the remnants of his guards at the Castle Inn, on the corner of Shropshire and St Peter's. He never made it. Hundreds of Yorkists were streaming over the barricades, and Northumberland was trapped against the wall. He died probably only a few yards from refuge.

Somerset, however, probably in the company of his son, did make it to the Castle Inn; Henry and the other nobles (apart from the earl of Wiltshire, who fled the town disguised as a monk) had surrendered. As for Bishop William Percy, after having his jewels and horses stolen, he escaped on foot to the Percy manor at Isleham in Cambridgeshire.

With several retainers, Somerset held the inn for a short while but – knowing York would never spare him – gallantly rushed into the street and madly slew four soldiers before being cut down by an axe. His son was severely wounded. The entire battle lasted one hour, with only between 60 and 200 fatalities.

Tragically, the deaths of Northumberland and the dogged loyalist Clifford were accidental: York later conceded that his men had acted rashly. Whether Salisbury would have spared Somerset, his old foe, is doubtful. The deliberate shedding of another noble's blood was usually regarded as a sinful act. That would soon change.

As one historian observes, although militarily insignificant, 'the battle proved to be a mile-stone marking the start of the most extended period of civil war in English history'. Thus, 'it constituted a direct assault on the king while journeying … Respect for the Crown, which depended on the personal vigour of its wearer, was violated so flagrantly that the traditional ban on the expression of private enmities in the presence of the king became harder than ever to restore.'[17]

St Albans revived York's supremacy. Although he graciously allowed Henry to appear 'as kynge' on the way back to London by riding on his right, with Salisbury on his left and Warwick ahead bearing the sword, all knew who was in charge. By the end of May, York had appointed himself constable, put Warwick in charge of Calais ('Christendom's finest captaincy', as one chronicler put it) and reconfirmed his joint wardenship of the West March alongside his father until 1475, at rates one-third higher than before. In mid-November, when Parliament convened, York was approved for the second time, as 'Protector and Defender of the Realm'.

With Somerset and Northumberland dead, York could be generous to the defeated. On 12 June 1455, pleased that Lord Poynings had again kept aloof from the fray, York granted the son and heir of the slain earl his rightful inheritance and title as 3rd earl of Northumberland.

CHAPTER SEVENTEEN

Recovery and Disaster, 1455–61

The momentous events in England since Henry VI regained his senses had been carefully watched by James II in Scotland. The same could not be said of Scottish affairs in England. In March 1455, James had suddenly renewed his feud with the Douglases, wasting their lands throughout the south and besieging the earl's castles using his new heavy artillery. On 1 May the two sides clashed at Arkinholm, leaving two of the earl's brothers dead, as well as various kinsmen. Subsequently, the rest of the family were found guilty of treason and forfeited their estates. Douglas himself, however, had escaped across the Border shortly before Arkinholm. In the tumultuous weeks leading up to St Albans, he was ignored in London.

York, in contact with Douglas a few years before, should at least have picked his brains on the kind of king James II was. 'Like [Robert] Bruce he was a talented military leader: he had a remarkable sense of timing and swiftness of decision that verged upon impetuosity . . . he had a clear view of his objectives.' This viper, determined to exterminate the Black Douglases, coldly sparked three civil wars between 1450 and 1455 and, like Robert Bruce, he did not let truces prevent him opportunistically profiting at the expense of the English.[1]

The deaths of Northumberland and Clifford at St Albans, the resulting chaos and the presence of Salisbury, Warwick and the new earl of Northumberland in London, presented too tempting a prospect for James – despite the truce. He marched on Berwick, having been informed by recent Scots visitors that a surprise attack might be successful. But after a tip-off, the defenders were ready for James, who abandoned the enterprise after a few desultory assaults on the walls.

Nevertheless, York was startled into paying some attention to Douglas, who granted the only castle still opposing James, Threave, to Henry VI on 15 July in return for a £500 annuity in expectation of future service until 'he is restored to his heritage . . . taken from him by him who calls himself King of Scots'. Threave fell soon after, but Douglas stayed in England as a potential counterweight to James, a fact that helped moderate the latter's behaviour.

Instead, James turned to diplomacy which, like its king, became 'increasingly far-reaching, complex and devious'. The traditional triangle – Scotland, England and France – was dissolving in the aftermath of the Hundred Years War. Edinburgh's primary politico-military ally, France, was focusing more on its economy and switched its attention to rich Burgundy, leaving James isolated should war break out. It was with mounting concern that he watched France extending support to the Lancastrians while Burgundy guardedly established contacts with the Yorkists. As a back-up, James sought secondary reinforcement outside northern Europe; Castile, Aragon and Naples, and even Ludovico Sforza, duke of Milan, were approached – without much success. In June 1456, James proposed, strangely, an international anti-English crusade. These fanciful designs, however, show that James was considering a renewed Scottish military effort to push the English off-balance. Parliament's meeting in Stirling in October 1455, for instance, was exclusively concerned with military matters. An offensive through Lothian into Northumberland dominated James's thinking; his reforms included permanent guards at fords and lighting beacons to warn of the enemy in the 'est passage betuix Roxburghe and Berwik'. Further, Parliament approved funding three full-time Border garrisons: 400 spearmen and 400 archers in the East and Middle Marches, the combined garrisons forming, not uncoincidentally, the nucleus of a disciplined invasion force. Indeed, to turn the Scots into Spartans, James discouraged the popular pastimes of primitive golf and football in order to promote archery.[2]

These actions might have alarmed London had not Henry lapsed again into inanity in November. Subsequently, Parliament (with Henry's vague blessing) confirmed York as 'Protector and Defender of the Realm'. But the king's physicians promised that the king would recover soon, alerting York that his protectorship was likely to be truncated and that it would be unwise for him to make too many enemies.

Ironically, despite the crushing victory at St Albans, York was in a tricky position: the king, although inert, was sovereign and it behoved the duke to end the aristocratic infighting that pockmarked his first protectorate. To many, the Yorkists had been out of line at St Albans, since the many peers fighting for Henry were implementing their oath of loyalty to him and could not be condemned. Hence York's emphasis on reconciliation following the battle: a general pardon in July for the rebels, and for those rebelled against, encompassing even Exeter, Egremont and Sir Richard Percy (although the latter two, owing to their debts, were not released). Thus, the trust of the Parliament convened after the battle was that the nobles should unite 'to honour, prosperite and welfare of the kyng oure Soveraine Lord, and the politique and restful rule and governaunce of this lande and people'.[3]

In the main, this policy was successful, but whether those whose fathers had been slaughtered – perhaps deliberately – at St Albans, would forgive and forget was questionable. Inheriting his slain father's title, and having recovered from the serious wounds he received at St Albans, the new duke of Somerset, Henry Beaufort, at nineteen was already notorious for his (understandable) hatred of the Nevilles; Lord Clifford, earlier known as John 'Butcher' Clifford, had long associated with the likes of Egremont and the Percy brothers, while the new earl of Northumberland himself was only thirty-four. Even if York made great play that he had graciously allowed them to inherit their titles and estates, they knew that behind his rhetoric of tolerance and togetherness, he and his clique were being disingenuous about ending factionalism. Although not overtly rewarding their supporters, they were subtly ensuring that their rivals were handicapped. For example, Yorkist propaganda, while not directly blaming Somerset's father for 'causing' St Albans, implied that he had exerted a malign and treacherous influence on the king. Clumsily, the Yorkists even tried holding the late Lord Clifford primarily responsible for St Albans, until there were widespread complaints that this was ridiculous. All this did not endear the new Yorkist elite to these men's sons.

Northumberland, in particular, felt that York – through Salisbury – was leashing him. On 20 August, for instance, a court fined him a further £6050 pursuant of the Percys' transgressions before St Albans, a figure suspiciously similar to the £6000 that the Exchequer owed the Percys for years of work for the Crown. This was money Northumberland needed. When he was still plain Lord Poynings, Percy could incur reasonable debts for personal requirements; in 1449, for instance, he owed some merchants in York £30 for cloth of gold used to make a gown for his wife, and Matthew Philip, a London goldsmith, £25 for jewellery – presumably for the same person. (Lady Eleanor seems to have liked finery; she also owned a golden collar and a silver basin.)

While he received his wardenship fees, Poynings' total debt of about £1100 was perfectly reasonable.

But he unexpectedly became earl of Northumberland when those wardenship fees had slipped far into abeyance; moreover, he had inherited his father's debts, which had grown inexorably, owing mainly to the need to maintain ever-larger private armies. Indeed, it was virtually impossible to pare back these expenses as the costs of war continued to rise. A first-class suit of armour, for instance, might cost around £60,000 in today's money. Add to that the cost of weapons, tents, horses, personnel and several other spare suits, and it is easy to understand how expensive war could be.

By 1461, Northumberland's liabilities (including some dating back seventeen years) would exceed £12,000 – or seven times his annual *net* income.[4] By comparison, when he died, the far wealthier duke of York owed around £6000, much of this debt having been contracted in his last year.[5] The Yorkist policy of hurting the Percys financially for their previous misdemeanours – even if they had no intention of ever paying the fines involved – helped to keep them under control.

By late February 1456, Henry had, thankfully, fully recovered and he released York from his protectorship, although retaining him as 'his chief and principal councillor'. To all appearances, England was stable and the conciliatory policy a success; at the end of this protectorate, all those who had been appointed in the past year kept their jobs. Yet, beneath the calm surfaces of the transition lurked signs of imminent turmoil.

Those appointees were all Yorkists and, while the king reigned, York still pulled the levers. Furthermore, Queen Margaret, whose hatred of York was unabated, mistrusted his ambitions. The aloof and reserved York was popular among Londoners, the administration, the Commons and his growing clique. If Henry suffered either a sustained or a serious illness, York might well be installed as protector for life. Margaret worried that York 'would deprive the king of his personal right to govern, and that he would employ its patronage and financial resources for his own ends', which might ultimately include edging out the sickly Prince Edward in a bid for the Crown itself.[6]

Once stricken with smallpox (which had delayed her wedding), the blonde Margaret of Anjou, observed a contemporary witness, is 'a grete and stronge labourid, for she spareth noo peyne to sue hire thinges to an intent and conclusion to hir power' (in modern English, 'a great and intensely active woman, for she spares no pains to pursue her business towards an end and conclusion favourable to her power').[7] To some, Margaret was 'young and fair to see; and her tragic career proved her to be endowed with a spirit of no common order'; to others she was merely 'rash and despotic'.[8]

In the summer of 1456, she began 'pursuing her business to an end' – the formation of her own anti-York party – and, with Prince Edward, she toured the duchy of Lancaster and his earldom of Chester. 'Despotically', she directed that Henry follow her to Kenilworth Castle, near Coventry, in August, and a battery of twenty-six new cannons was ordered for Kenilworth's walls, ostensibly for 'defensive purposes'.

Away from York's intelligence-gatherers in London, and accompanied by the royal court that followed the king, Margaret began slotting into position chosen men, many from her private household. With Henry under her control (observers commented on how long he slept each night), she planned a shadow cabinet to replace the existing administrative machinery of English government. Thus, by October 1456, a new treasurer and chancellor had been appointed. And after the bishop of Durham, Salisbury's brother, died (he was the only Neville child of the 23-strong brood never to marry) his successor was her long-time servant, Laurence Booth, now keeper of the privy seal, the office that, crucially, controlled all branches of the royal administration.

Margaret also approached nobles whom she believed amenable to getting rid of York, Salisbury and Warwick. First was the duke of Exeter, who, although she retained her suspicions as to his stability, was released from prison; next the earl of Shrewsbury; followed by Somerset, who recruited the Percy brothers; and then Northumberland and Clifford.

For a change, the Percys were received with marked favour. In November 1456, suspiciously coinciding with an aborted attempt by Exeter and Somerset to assassinate Warwick, the ruffians Egremont and Richard Percy escaped from Newgate to the Midlands. Another brother, the steady Sir Ralph Percy, was subsequently appointed constable of Dunstanburgh Castle in Northumberland. The altogether more respectable Northumberland was brought into the conspiracy only on 28 February 1457, when he was summoned to court, given a new contract as warden for ten years – the longest indenture he had ever been offered – and promised rapid payment.

His late introduction was caused by James II who, in May 1456, finally renounced the Anglo-Scottish truce, bypassed the English garrison at Roxburgh and halted at Kale Water near the Border. This was an emergency, and Northumberland (the sources are sketchy about his exact movements) must have been on permanent vigil in the North. According to Ranald Nicholson, mistakenly believing that York was actively seeking the throne, James now championed York's claims, and 'thus it was on the basis of an understanding with the Yorkists that James appeared on the water of the Kale'. Interestingly, he was apparently met there 'by mysterious English envoys who induced him to abandon his enterprise'. Had Salisbury, hoping to make trouble for Northumberland, been in secret contact with James and realised that the king had embarrassingly taken matters into his own hands?

For the queen's circle, however, the Scottish action required a robust reply, but, perhaps too preoccupied with outplaying York, they misjudged its tone. Their letter to James on 26 July was clumsily drafted and needlessly antagonistic: addressed to 'James, calling himself King of Scotland', it patronisingly asked if he were 'so ignorant of what penalties await the rebel ... who is so hardy as to deny his homage to his liege superior?' Describing James, an independent sovereign, as a 'rebel' was a major blunder. James, his army ready for battle, knew that Northern forces were disorganised, and he might have wondered just what 'penalties' awaited him. Northumberland, on the Border since the 1440s, would probably not have appreciated this foolish attempt at deterrence.

A fortnight later, immediately after receiving the letter, James struck. Driving twenty miles into Northumberland, he demolished seventeen towers before flaunting his invulnerable army for six days while the local defensive forces made themselves scarce. For James, the hit-steal-and-run raids of Robert Bruce were over. Instead of wasting and looting half of Northumberland, he weakened purely military objectives before returning home with negligible losses.

Humiliatingly, Northumberland had to negotiate a special truce with James, who would only accept one for a meagre six months (that is, until 2 February 1457). Northumberland took it. Immediately the truce had expired, James again assaulted Berwick, but the attack was baffled. Given these events, Margaret's offer to Northumberland of a ten-year wardenship in Coventry in mid-February 1457 was not unexpected. Invested with her full confidence, Northumberland bullied James into a truce on 20 June until 1463, which was later extended for another five years.[9]

Naturally, York and the Nevilles knew what was going on. The duke, for instance, had long been threatened by the belligerent Somerset, who warned him his end was nigh. In September 1456, for example, York discovered the severed heads of five dogs impaled on stakes outside his London house, each with an abusive verse stuffed into its jaws.[10] The culprit was, no doubt, Somerset, who was possibly in London to prepare for the imminent Percy jailbreak. Two weeks after the Percys arrived in Coventry, Somerset attacked York in the street (the duke was saved by the mayor).

Since then, an alarmed York had resided at Sandal in Yorkshire, watching the queen as she watched him. But York and the Nevilles could not prevent the erosion of their power, short of publicly accusing Margaret of manipulating Henry. Their one hope was the duke of Buckingham, who had been commander of the king's forces at St Albans before becoming the most independent upholder of reconciliation.

Buckingham, the third-richest man in England after York and Warwick, was renowned for his rectitude and impartiality. He had stood aloof from the political warfare of the past decade, concentrating on protecting both the authority and the physical safety of the king and his heir (his wife was the prince's godmother). Indeed, as the queen's preparations for a clash with the Yorkists became open knowledge by 1458, only Buckingham's mediation prevented civil war that year.

In one last effort to clear the muggy air, a great council was called in

London in January 1458 to 'set apart such variances as be betwixt divers lords'. Surprisingly well attended, it demonstrated the nobility's traditional aversion to warring among its own. Ominously, however, large and truculent retinues escorted those who came. On strict orders to keep their distance, the two sides avoided clashing in the streets. Even so, Exeter, Egremont and Clifford almost ambushed Salisbury and York when riding through their self-designated turf at Westminster.

Northumberland, Egremont and Clifford brought 1500 rough-hewn Northerners, accommodating them between Temple Bar and Westminster. Somerset and Exeter added another 800 to the Lancastrian complement. The Yorkists, on the other hand, stayed in the City. York was accompanied by 140 cavalrymen and 260 foot, while Salisbury outdid even him by bringing 80 fully armoured knights and 420 foot. The youngest Yorkist, Warwick, made a splash by transporting 600 guards from Calais in scarlet tunics with his emblem of ragged staves embroidered on the front and back.

Soon, the rival magnates could not even bear to sit in the same room. On 9 March Northumberland and Somerset almost assaulted Warwick. Henceforth, negotiators scuttled between York, Salisbury and Warwick at the Blackfriars and Northumberland, Egremont, Clifford and Somerset at the Whitefriars in Fleet Street. Finally, on 24 March came a settlement of sorts. The Yorkists were to endow a chantry at the abbey of St Albans, costing £45 annually, where masses would be celebrated for the souls of the slain; moreover, York and Warwick would forgo a debt of £4000 the Exchequer owed them, of which £3333 would be diverted to the late Somerset's widow and the current duke, with the balance paid to Clifford. As for Northumberland and Egremont, they successfully lobbied to have the damages awarded against them by Salisbury voided. In return, the Yorkists demanded that Egremont be bound over for about £2700 to keep the peace for ten years; to sweeten the burden, the pious Henry kindly offered him Wressle Castle in Yorkshire if he left England on pilgrimage for a while. The settlement was not as onerous on York and the Nevilles as it appeared, however. Under Margaret's regime, none of them would ever have seen a penny of the £4000; more hurtful was the establishment of the chantry, which implicitly acknowledged that York and his allies had brought about the battle at St Albans and the deaths of the lords.

The next morning witnessed the bizarre spectacle of the 'Loveday', in which Henry strode down the steps of St Paul's wearing his crown, preceded by Salisbury and Somerset together, trailed by a grimacing Queen Margaret hand-in-hand with York (the famous picture of Ian Gilmour reluctantly dancing cheek to cheek with Margaret Thatcher comes to mind).

Ominously, Warwick and the Percys did not participate. For the moment, the blood feud was over, but as one William Gregory noticed, 'alle thes lordys departyd from the Parlyment [that is, on Loveday], but they come nevyr all togedr aftyr that tyme to noo Parlyment nor conselle, byt yf hyt were in fylde with spere and schylde.'[11]

If anything, while the Loveday muted overt tensions – bringing to an end the repeated attempted assassinations and assaults on the Yorkists by Somerset, Egremont and co. – it pushed those same tensions underground. The queen merely made her programme to control Henry and the government less obvious. Thus, after Warwick's return to Calais, the subsidies for the fortress's defences were cut, forcing Warwick to pay his garrison out of his own pocket. Warwick went so far as to take to piracy to get his money. With a fleet of five ships, his victims included Spanish, Genoese and Hanseatic League vessels. None of these was an enemy.[12]

His actions brought forth floods of complaints and demands for restitution and threw English foreign policy off the rails. Warwick became highly popular among his men and the English who enjoyed derring-do upon the high seas that entailed dishing Johnny Foreigner. The court, understandably, took a dimmer view. However, there was method in Warwick's piracy: no Burgundian ships were attacked. The Yorkists always viewed Duke Philip of Burgundy as their ally, while the Lancastrians were friendly with Charles VII in France (Henry still remembered Philip's betrayal at Arras in 1435 – see Chapter 15). The queen, after all, was French, and Charles informed her that he had rebuffed James II's recent attempt to renew the Auld Alliance. Despite the Loveday, according to one historian, 'Warwick's naval activity and their [the Yorkists'] secret diplomacy was designed to align England with Burgundy against France: whether with a view to a resumption of war or merely to the creation of a balance of power.'[13]

These implications were not lost on Henry's councillors. Their impressions that Warwick was not honouring either the letter or spirit of the Loveday were confirmed in November 1458 when, recalled to London to answer for his misdeeds, Warwick was involved in a scuffle at Westminster Hall, after one of his retainers struck a menial royal servant – 'itself an offence against the king'. Warwick almost lost his life and fled back to Calais.[14]

When the queen demanded his resignation as captain of Calais, Warwick arrogantly ignored her. By now, Buckingham – whose strict impartiality had always helped the Yorkists – was disgusted by Warwick's behaviour. In mid-1459, he declared his wholehearted support for the king. To all, 'Warwick's Rebellion' – for that is what it represented – was the signal to shrug off the Loveday truce and prepare actively for war. In

May, 3000 bows and sheaves of arrows were ordered for the royal armoury. In the following month a great council, excluding York, Salisbury and, obviously, Warwick,[15] assembled at Coventry to discuss indicting the Yorkists, probably owing to the presumed likelihood of a march on Kenilworth to take the king hostage.

Henry, however, was still conceived to be aloof from his 'evil councillors'. In September, hoping to attract his attention, York, who was then in the Welsh Marches, decided on a war council of his own at Ludlow. He instructed Warwick, still hiding in Calais, to bring his crack soldiery, and Salisbury, who was then in Yorkshire, to do the same with his Northern retainers.

Unsurprisingly, the queen got wind of the Yorkist plan and ordered her available captains to track the three separate armies and eliminate them before they could congregate at Ludlow. The militarily inexperienced Somerset shadowed the veteran Warwick from the moment he landed, but eventually, to Somerset's embarrassment, Warwick arrived safely in Ludlow.

Salisbury's passage was harder. At Blore Heath, between Newcastle-under-Lyme and Market Drayton, he was forced to fight, and defeat, a Lancastrian force under Lord Audley, a local landowner, who died in the battle. After it, Salisbury received a pledge of support from Lord Stanley who was in the vicinity with his Lancashiremen.[16] Salisbury paused to refresh his troops in Market Drayton (he forwarded the letter confirming Stanley's support to Sir Thomas Harington, an ally, exclaiming 'be merry, for yet we have more friends'), but on the following day the royalists captured Harington and Salisbury's sons, Sir Thomas and Sir John Neville, in Cheshire.[17] Worse still, hearing that Henry's main army was approaching Blore Heath, Stanley rescinded his pledge but not before promising to continue as a 'secret' Yorkist sympathiser.

Salisbury had escaped the trap and ran to Ludlow, but more trouble beckoned. The Lancastrian nobles with their retinues were converging on the town. On 7 October, for instance, Northumberland, Egremont, Sir Thomas Percy and even Ralph Neville, the earl of Westmorland – who had been persuaded by the Percys to join the struggle against his much-loathed kinsman – rode through Nottingham escorted by Westmorland's men, Egremont's scratch force of Yorkshiremen and Northumberland's Borderers.[18]

On 12 October, Salisbury and his colleagues sent a manifesto to the king, declaring their dedication to 'the prosperity and augmentation of your common weal of this realm'. One can detect Salisbury's careful hand in the Yorkists wanting to be able to show proof, if any subsequent battle went against them, that they were not rebelling against the king himself, but only against those degrading his realm's 'common weal'. Even after four decades of Henrician rule, the genetically bred respect for monarchy guided noble actions. Salisbury's caution, moreover, was wise; the Yorkists were in a terrible state. Their forces were greatly outnumbered by the encroaching Lancastrians; apart from the flexible Lord Stanley, they had attracted only two minor barons to their banner, the Lords Clinton (known as England's poorest lord) and Grey of Powis, together with a smattering of heirs such as York's two sons, both of whom were really too young to fight; moreover, demoralisation had set in among their contingents, few of whom were enthusiastic about warring with the king.

Henry's offers of pardons for those who laid down their arms must have sorely tempted those sodden Yorkist troops camped on 12 October south of Ludlow at Ludford Bridge. The king and the royal army arrived in the early evening, with banners flying against those who had taken up arms. Any who stood opposite could be charged as traitors.

Flanking the king were Northumberland (and his relatives), Buckingham, Westmorland, Exeter, Arundel, Devon, Shrewsbury, Wiltshire and at least another ten lords. By dribs and drabs, the Yorkist troops deserted (even Warwick's Calais professionals, under the respected Andrew Trollope, defected). So understandably, if not admirably, before midnight York, Salisbury and Warwick left to 'refresh' themselves in the river. With a few companions they unchivalrously deserted the rump of their own army. It surrendered the next morning, but by then the Yorkist leaders had enjoyed half a day's head start.

York fled to Ireland with his second son, Edmund earl of Rutland, entrusting his eldest, the seventeen-year-old Edward earl of March, to Salisbury and Warwick as they raced to the remote safety of Calais. Barring some mopping-up duties, it appeared that Margaret of Anjou and her Lancastrians ruled supreme over England.[19] By the year's end, York, Salisbury, Warwick and twenty-four associates had been legally attainted. Their lands were parcelled out among Margaret's followers, including Egremont, who picked up Conisbrough Castle for his troubles. Northumberland was given virtually regal power in the North, being appointed chief justice north of Trent and constable of Scarborough Castle. Henry committed the government of the North to the earl and his ally Clifford, whom he counted as 'his trusty and most faithful friends'.

'The next eighteen months witnessed more violent swings of the political pendulum than any other period of similar length in English history,' according to John Gillingham. 'First Lancaster was ousted by York, then York by Lancaster and finally Lancaster by York again. Moreover, these were political upheavals brought about by force of arms. This same period saw no less than five battles, culminating in the biggest bloodbath until the seventeenth-century Battle of Marston Moor.'[20]

Despite banishment from English soil, the Yorkists still held some trumps. York and his Neville retainers were untouchable in Ireland;[21] the earl of Wiltshire, appointed as king's lieutenant, never tried to oust him from its wastelands. From Calais, Warwick's pirate fleet attacked French territory and shipping (he had a deal with the Burgundians) to replenish his coffers.[22] In June 1460, Warwick's men established a bridgehead at Sandwich, evidently preparing for a major invasion. The roguish Warwick's piratical exploits had always lent him a certain popularity among Kentishmen and in the South-East, throughout which the Yorkists also circulated pamphlets, detailing their case against the 'evil counsellours' surrounding Henry, and reaffirming their own loyalty to the king's person and authority.[23] Finally, on 26 June, Warwick and Salisbury stepped ashore, busily recruited thousands of Kentishmen and marched to Canterbury, where they knelt piously at the tomb of St Thomas à Becket, who in popular memory had died fighting injustice. By 1 July, they were welcomed into London. The court, then at Coventry, was stunned into a confused sluggishness; in less than a week, the Yorkists had invaded England, reconstituted a popular army of some 20,000 men and now controlled the capital. Moreover, the Yorkists could strike almost anywhere at will, while Margaret's forces simultaneously had to guard against a sea-invasion in the South, a Neville rising in the North and a York-led landing from Ireland in Lancashire or Wales. The Yorkists, the Scots and the Burgundians might even – terrible thought – confederate. Worse, there were hardly any peers at Coventry that summer, so the rebels actually outnumbered whatever forces the Lancastrians could muster at such short notice.

In early July, however, the most dreadfully imminent scenario was a Scottish invasion. Therefore the traditional beginning of the campaigning season was accompanied by summonses to the great magnates, requesting their retinues. While Northumberland was certainly in the North that month, guarding against another Border violation, Egremont remained with the king along with Buckingham, Shrewsbury and Lord Grey or Ruthin (the former Yorkist married to Egremont's younger sister). They then moved to Northampton, closer to London, calling urgently for reinforcements and preparing their defences.

Warwick and young March rushed to Northampton. Although the Lancastrians were outnumbered, there were several factors in their favour. Warwick's performance at Ludlow led to speculation that St Albans had been a fluke; similarly, March had no experience of military command. If Buckingham, who headed the royal forces, could cut off and destroy this Yorkist army, Salisbury, then based in London with 2000 men, could surely not survive. What Buckingham didn't know was that the ruthless Grey of Ruthin – no stranger to controversy: a decade before, he was involved in murdering the Speaker of the House of Commons – had already betrayed them to Warwick, an act one modern historian judged (a touch partially) 'in the sordid annals of even these sterile wars ... no deed of shame so foul'.

On 10 July at two o'clock in the afternoon, the Yorkists attacked – in heavy rain, which ruined the cannons – on a wide front to envelop the defenders. As arranged, Grey's men 'seized [the Yorkists] by the hand and hauled them into the embattled field', and within half an hour the royalist line had broken and fled across the river. The Yorkists had lost almost nobody, but the scale of the Lancastrian defeat was unimaginable. Egremont – disbelieving Grey's treachery; (whatever his faults, this Percy was always studiously loyal) – Buckingham and Shrewsbury made a last-ditch stand in their heavy armour outside the king's tent, desperately trying to ward off Warwick's swarming Kentishmen. As Warwick and Edward had given orders to spare the king and all commoners but to slay any lords, knights and esquires, all three were killed where they stood and the king was captured. It was an ironically heroic end for Lord Egremont.[24]

Northumberland heard probably a few weeks later of his sibling's death, as did James II, for the king launched his expected attack towards the end of July. As usual, he chose Roxburgh, whose garrison, Northumberland had ensured, was adequately paid. James was bullish; England was in a mess after Henry's capture and his new siege guns threatened the castle walls. So bullish, indeed, that he asked his queen, Mary of Guelders, to come and bolster morale. On 3 August, 'on account of joy at the arrival of the queen', James ordered an artillery salute. Curious about the mechanics of gunnery – which one chronicler huffily thought 'did not become the majesty of any king', rather like Edward II's fondness for basket-weaving – James was standing beside a gun that exploded on recoil, hurling a metal fragment into his thigh and sending the king into fatal shock. Just shy of his thirtieth birthday, he left behind an heir, named James, aged only eight.

There was no respite for the English, however. James's civil wars had purged the aristocracy of potential rebels, so the besieging force was cohesive enough under Queen Mary's guidance to continue mauling Roxburgh. A few days later, James's guns broke the defenders' will and Roxburgh fell. Since 1347 and the days of Edward III, this grand fortress had been in English hands, a special charge upon the Percys. Never again would Roxburgh stand as a symbol of English rule in southern Scotland;

the Scots commanders triumphantly ordered the castle to be razed. Thereafter, the only English toehold north of the Tweed was Berwick.[25]

With the luckless Henry in his grasp and with York absent in Ireland, Warwick ruled England – apart from the North, where scattered Lancastrians still lurked. By 10 October, York had wended his way across the Irish Sea and down through Wales. He wanted the Crown. Arriving at Westminster, according to a witness, York 'strode up to the throne and put his hand on its cushion' like 'a man about to take possession of what was rightfully his'. After holding it there for a while, 'he turned to the people and, standing quietly under the canopy of state, waited expectantly for their applause'. None came, just stares of horror at his presumption. The archbishop of Canterbury pointedly asked whether York had come to see the king, ending the duke's hopes of accession by acclamation. Warwick, in particular, was disgusted at York's miscalculation and his Johnny-come-lately attitude. Where had York been while his lieutenants took all the risks?[26]

York eventually grasped that the Commons, remembering the disasters following Bolingbroke's forceful usurpation of Richard II, would never depose a sitting king. Instead he accepted the Act of Accord of 24 October 1460. Recognising York's de facto power, the Commons promised the duke the throne after Henry's death, and its descent to his heirs. The Act seems a moderate piece of statesmanship, yet it stored up problems. Prince Edward's neat exclusion from the succession made it unlikely that his redoubtable mother would roll over and accept the settlement. Many nobles were also alarmed at the Act's implications. Since the twelfth century, their estates, names and titles had descended (with a few exceptions) strictly by inheritance. York had just disinherited the king's son; would he do the same to those who displeased him?

The queen's behaviour was equally startling. Counting on France and Scotland's historic ties, in December she threw herself on the mercy of the dowager Queen Mary of Guelders in Dumfries. Granted, Mary was a Burgundian, but she had no particular truck with the Yorkists. The two queens hit it off. 'And thai said thai war speakand of mariage betuix the forsaid prince [Edward] and King James the thridis sister [the young Princess Mary]'.[27] If Prince Edward were renamed heir to the throne, the sister of James III (who had been crowned in August) would one day be queen of England.

Normally, Northumberland would not have welcomed an imminent Anglo-Scots alliance, or having the Percys' hereditary enemies help him fight his battles. But desperate times required imaginative measures. Following York's arrogance at Westminster, the North in the autumn of 1460 under Northumberland's governorship regarded itself almost as an independent kingdom. Instructions from London were ignored. Northumberland even authorised the wasting of Neville lands through Yorkshire and Cumberland, which must have been satisfying indeed. In Parliament, however, the Percys were damned as ravagers and misdoers.[28]

For Northumberland, the once and future king Henry VI had granted him virtually regal powers everywhere north of the Trent after the 'non-battle' of Ludford Bridge; no jumped-up usurper could rescind that commission. He even assumed martial authority, ordering all men between the ages of sixteen and sixty to arm themselves and help liberate the king. In late November, Somerset (finally back from his repeated attempts to storm Calais in order to flush out Warwick) and Devon arrived at York, where they met the Percys, and pushed south to Hull, to rendezvous with Exeter and Northern landowners like the Lords Clifford, Roos and Greystoke. Credit should be given to Northumberland's administrative ability; according to Anthony Goodman, 'the concentration in Yorkshire of an army from different regions (though mainly from the north) out of the campaigning season was a striking achievement, a measure of the fury caused' by York's Act of Accord.[29]

In early December, unaware of the scale of the forces being mustered against them, York and Salisbury took fewer than 500 men to investigate rumours of Lancastrian activity somewhere in the North. (The paucity of numbers may also be related to the regime's financial difficulties. It was surviving on loans, mostly extended by Exchequer officials.) They stayed at Wakefield, a town held by the duke near his castle at Sandal.

On 30 December, to the Yorkists' horror, Northumberland (after knighting two followers – a glimpse into his newfound belief that he had actually become king in the North) unleashed his relatively enormous army against them.[30] Now based at Sandal, York observed the Lancastrians forming up just north of the castle. Without provisions and undermanned, Sandal could not withstand a siege. One chance remained: breaking the Lancastrian centre with a surprise frontal charge. One problem, also: Sandal's gate on its south side required York to charge out of the gate, cross the moat and wheel around the castle hill to the north, thereby giving the Lancastrians plenty of time to steel themselves. Northumberland's decision to wait to the north was an inspired tactical move. York, escorted by his youngest son, the earl of Rutland, took the initiative and charged directly to the heart of Northumberland's battle. Again, Northumberland must have expected this. His centre easily absorbed the initial blow and the two wings drew inwards, carrying fifteen-foot lances, thereby ensnaring the duke. Fighting bravely, he was dragged down and killed. Rutland and Salisbury managed to escape the noose, but not for long. Clifford caught the fifteen-year-old Rutland, bellowing, 'By God's blode, thy father slew myne and so will I do thee,' before stabbing him to death. That night, Salisbury was captured and hauled to Pontefract to await execution. On the following day he was lynched by a mob, for the 'commune peple of the cuntre loued him nat'. (Others say one of Exeter's bastards decapitated him.) York's severed head was impaled on a spike atop, fittingly, York's gates. Ghoulishly, a paper crown – mocking his kingly aspirations – was placed on it. It was, it appears, a very happy New Year for the Percys.[31] Despite the fact that Warwick and March (York's eldest son) naturally inherited their late fathers' estates, Northumberland ruled the North.

Queen Margaret rushed from the Scottish court to congratulate Northumberland and his fellow commanders at York. When Clifford drew her attention to York's head above the Micklegate, saying, 'Madam, your war is done, here is your king's ransom,' there was 'much joy, and great rejoicing', according to one chronicler. But something was missing. She ordered that a sign, rather cleverly reading 'Let York overlook the town of York', be hung below his head.

The decision was taken to strike south and topple Warwick while the Yorkists were still reeling from Wakefield. As one ballad perceptively rhymed: 'All the lords of the north they wrought by one assent/For to destroy the south country they did all their entent.' Several contemporary observers also noticed that it was now a North versus South conflict. Although York and Salisbury were Northerners, they were Southern in temperament and sympathy. When in London, they had distributed anti-Lancastrian propaganda 'playing the Northern card': that is, issuing bloodcurdling warnings of Northern bestiality and treachery.

Over the next six weeks, the Northern army marched directly towards London. Warwick guessed correctly that St Albans would be its next stop, but he decided against deploying in the town itself à la the first battle of St Albans, partly because the Lancastrians would be unlikely to repeat their previous mistakes. Instead, he formed his lines to the northeast on Barnet Heath, a large, flat field.

Ignorant of Lancastrian plans, Warwick misjudged the direction of their advance on St Albans. He expected it to be from Luton, thus bringing them directly in front of his position for a face-to-face battle. To this end, demonstrating his fascination with military technology, Warwick laid out his defence. He had pavises, which were a kind of 'sandwich board', thickly studded with nails on one side and with a small window near the centre. Propped upright, the pavise provided cover for bowmen, who shot through the window, but it could also be laid flat, nail side up, to cripple horses and unwary soldiers as they ran over it. There were also caltraps – metal starfish hidden in the grass like landmines, with spikes pointing upwards. Revealingly, Warwick also had a contingent of Burgundian mercenaries armed with the latest gadgets, like firearms, that the locals marvelled at.

Had the Lancastrians mounted a frontal assault in the north-east, Warwick's defences would have torn them to shreds. Unfortunately, the Lancastrians came from Dunstable in the north-west. If they overran the town and ran down St Peter's Street, they would collide with Warwick's left flank and rear. Warwick had allowed for this scenario and stationed a small contingent of archers in the market place to keep an eye out.

On 17 February 1461 – Shrove Tuesday – the Lancastrians charged straight into this body of archers, who blunted the attack in the narrow streets. The Lancastrians retreated, but Warwick had too little time to wheel his contingents to face the main Lancastrian force. Furthermore, some intrepid Northerners had discovered a trail that circumvented the town centre and ultimately led via Catherine Lane into St Peter's Street, and Warwick's vulnerable flank and rear. Suddenly, the Lancastrians burst out of Catherine Lane and surprised the Yorkist left, which soon broke. Northern cavalrymen pursued its terrified remnants. Most of Warwick's army ran, leaving a bemused Henry in his tent guarded by a few rather tremulous nobles (they remembered what had happened at Northampton). For the third time, like some toy, the king of England changed hands.[32] He was, however, reunited with the queen and his son.

With Warwick fleeing westwards to the Cotswolds, the road to London was open. Unfortunately, the campaign-weary Lancastrians rested at Dunstable before making their triumphal march into the capital – a fatal pause at the final hurdle. While the Lancastrians had devastated the Yorkists in the North and now in the South, at the beginning of February York's son, the young March, had decisively beaten Lancastrian forces under Wiltshire and Pembroke at Mortimer's Cross, six miles north-west of Leominster. Following St Albans, he rushed to the Cotswolds, to meet a chastened Warwick on 22 February. Together, they force-marched in four days to London, where the citizens happily allowed them in.

Before the Lancastrians knew it, the nineteen-year-old earl of March was at Westminster. In private conference with Warwick the Kingmaker, March boldly chose to mount a coup, as Bolingbroke had done in 1399. He broadcast his claim to Londoners: the Lancastrian kings from Henry IV to Henry VI were usurpers whose rule led to 'unrest, inward war and trouble' among the nobles. March's claim, 'by God's law, man's law and the law of nature', automatically defeated all others. He was descended from both Lionel of Antwerp, duke of Clarence and Edward III's second-eldest son (who died in 1368), and from Edmund, duke of York and Edward III's fourth surviving son (who died in 1402). (Indeed, Northumberland and Hotspur had even championed March's great-uncle, Edmund Mortimer, earl of March (who died in 1425) as king against Henry IV.)

On 4 March 1461, March usurped the usurpers. Postponing the actual coronation, the earl was acclaimed by the people and heard the 'Te Deum' in St Paul's before entering the great hall at the Palace of Westminster. Garbed in the royal robes and invested with the cap of estate, the teenager henceforth known as Edward IV swore the oath and sat on the marble seat called the king's bench. Officially, he had 'taken possession of England'.[33]

Unlike the sickly and stunted Henry VI, Edward looked a king. When his tomb was opened in 1789, his skeleton measured a majestic six foot three and a half inches. To his contemporaries, Edward was toweringly imposing. Many chroniclers, including foreign ones, rhapsodised about his appearance as the handsomest royal in Europe. With the movie-star looks came a certain streak of narcissism; one observer noticed: 'He was wont to show himself to those who wished to watch him, and he seized any opportunity ... of revealing his fine stature more protractedly and more evidently to onlookers.' The household accounts show that Edward spent massively on furs, jewels and clothes expressly designed to show himself off.

His followers forgave him this vanity. This Edward, like his ancestors Edward I and III, was a fighting man and a king; he had little time for artistic foppery, investigating the new humanism or other inferior pursuits. He wasn't even particularly religious (unlike his mother, famed for her piety). What reading he did was confined, in Latin, to official documents or, in English or French for pleasure, determinedly middlebrow and conventional chivalric tales, highlighting the improving 'lessons of history' that nobles must know. His free time was generally spent jousting, hunting, feasting, boozing and impressing females. Neither stupid nor a boor, he was clearly intelligent with an excellent memory for details and was famed for his affability and even-temperedness. Only in his later years did the fatty diet take its toll on his midriff and jowls (the famous picture in the National Portrait Gallery shows him at that stage), but even then he was never uncomely.[34]

Certainly, he was energetic. Two days after his ceremony, Edward issued proclamations to the sheriffs of thirty-three counties: with the exception of those with annual incomes over £66, any adherent of Henry VI who came to him within ten days would be pardoned. Significantly, only one of these proclamations was issued north of the Trent. It was sent to the county of Northumberland itself for Edward and Warwick to test Lancastrian strength in Percy's own backyard. They didn't have much success.

The Trent was not chosen randomly as a boundary. Edward's arrival in London at the head of fresh Welsh and March troops convinced the Lancastrians to fight on. With the 'rightful' king Henry VI and the 'rightful' Prince of Wales, the queen and her nobles hurried past the Trent to their Northern redoubt. Edward and Warwick followed them slowly, amassing money and men from loyal cities all the way up to Pontefract, which the Yorkists reached at the end of March. Somewhere ahead lay the Lancastrian army. In the climactic battle to come, no quarter would be given by either side.

After a bloody skirmish outside Pontefract at Ferrybridge (which crossed the obstacle of the River Aire) with a Lancastrian advance guard led by Somerset, Devon and Exeter, the Lancastrians withdrew to their encampment between the villages of Towton and Saxton, on the Pontefract to Tadcaster road. Despite wounding Warwick with an arrow, the Lancastrians had lost two staunch loyalists, Lord 'Butcher' Clifford and Lord Neville (the earl of Westmorland's brother), in the mêlée.

The next day, as the exhausted Yorkists advanced towards Tadcaster in the freezing rain and ice, they found the well-fed Lancastrians confidently deployed in three battle arrays along a plateau just off to the side with the narrow but deep and steep-sided River Cock to their right. Facing south, Somerset was commanding the right battle; Henry and Exeter were in the rear with the reserves; Northumberland held the left. Edward faced Somerset, with Warwick opposite Northumberland. Both royal standards (treated with paste, to stiffen them) flew.

On 29 March 1461, Palm Sunday, the bloodiest battle in English medieval history began with a fusillade of Lancastrian arrows. But it was snowing, and as the Lancastrians fired, a severe gust of wind blew into their faces and shortened the distance that their arrows flew. Barely hurt by the initial attack, the Yorkists collected the fallen arrows in front of them and, holding to the rhythm shouted out by their captains ('Notch, stretch, loose!'), returned volleys of fire, killing many in the front ranks opposite. Here, the battalion under Somerset – who had under performed in recent years – suddenly surged forward, crying, 'King Henry!' into Edward's unprepared wing, mostly cavalry, which soon broke. Somerset followed in hot pursuit, surprising everyone with his elan. If, at that moment, Northumberland had followed through by immediately charging into Edward's right, it would have finished the Yorkists. But Northumberland was sluggish – the snow forced him, on foot like his heavy infantry, to trudge – and the chance was wasted.

Edward, dismounted and standing by his standard, rallied his remaining knights and men-at-arms and prepared for close combat – always the most confused part of any battle – using maces, swords and axes. Ideally, a noble's retainers would surround him and his banner-bearer and push forward, cutting a swathe through enemy ranks. As the banner advanced, the noble's soldiers were expected to follow it, or at least keep an eye on it so that they could regroup. In reality, amid the blood and noise and bad weather, soldiers would often get cut off or mistakenly fight their own side. Knights were often more at risk than longbowmen and other ranks. Continual bashing by maces or axes on their steel armour made it difficult to move joints; repeated clanging blows on the helmet could render the wearer unconscious. Once a knight's mobility was restricted, he became easier to despatch by inserting daggers or a small sword in the places where the armour was absent (or only partial to permit him to ride, such as the groin, the back of the thighs or the armpit). Add to this the dehydration and exhaustion from being encased in metal, and knights were much more vulnerable than might at first be thought.

Several hours of pitiless fighting ensued, but gradually Northumberland's battle was pushed back, bending the Lancastrian line upon itself. At this point the earl slipped and was struck, leaving him severely wounded. His loyal men dragged his bleeding, stricken body to the rear through the slush. (It was probably here that his signet ring, inscribed 'Nowe ys Thus', which is now in the British Museum, fell from his finger.) The Yorkist duke of Norfolk's reserve then circled and hit the weakened flank, now lacking a commander, which collapsed into panic, scaring Somerset's returned battle, which had been more than holding its own against Edward.

The real bloodbath happened in the panic-stricken aftermath. The Lancastrians were hemmed in by the River Cock, which lay 100 feet down at the bottom of a steep plateau made slippery by the snow and ice. Behind them lay Tadcaster, but they had earlier destroyed its bridge to hamper a Yorkist advance north. Along the banks of the Cock and on the way to Tadcaster, thousands upon thousands of Northumberland's tired Northerners were killed by their mounted pursuers. Bridges of bodies built up across the Cock, allowing some men to tread across them to reach the other side, but falling into the river meant death for any armoured knight or common soldier, dragged down by padded overgarments gorged with water.

Northumberland was one of the slain, although where and when it happened is uncertain. After being dragged to the rear, he may have died of his wounds or of exposure, or alternatively he may have been taken to York where other noble survivors later congregated. Even assuming he survived that journey, the earl certainly perished the next day, perhaps through infection or loss of blood. He was buried in the church of St Denis in Walmgate, York, which was opposite the Percys' palace, and placed 'in the north choir under a large blue marble stone, which had two effigies on it and an inscription on brass around it'. Those two effigies, which would have given us a contemporary likeness of the earl, were destroyed in 1736, along with the tomb.

Towton was the slaughterhouse of the Lancastrians. In an area six miles long and three miles wide, the corpse-littered snow was dyed raw pink. Of the nineteen peers with Henry, at least five were killed in action. Forty-two knights who surrendered were executed the next day. Another two earls – Wiltshire and Devon – were soon captured and beheaded at York (Devon's head replaced York's on the stake). Miraculously, there were few noble Yorkist casualties. Estimates of total fatalities range between 9000 and 28,000, figures that exclude the wounded and the drowned. The overall total might well be double.

A mass grave of soldiers recently discovered at Towton contains invaluable details about medieval warfare. 'Battlefield graves bear silent witness to the ghastly injuries inflicted, primarily on the human skull, from such heavy weapons [as halberds, swords, bills, axes and maces]. A sword thrust to the body might not produce any great pain initially because of the vast amounts of adrenaline pumping through the body at the height of combat, but as the adrenaline subsided, the agony would result in the soldier collapsing, causing a slow death from loss of blood and later hypothermia if he was left out in the field of battle to die. Filthy clothing or stuffing from padded jacks would have been pushed inside wounds, including arrow wounds, which would cause blood poisoning and death from infection ... A heavy blow from a mace, war hammer or axe would, given the right circumstances, be more lethal, as it could penetrate a helmet and shatter the skull, causing massive haemorrhaging.' In the Towton grave, for example, almost every one of the thirty-seven skeletons reveals terrible cranial injuries. One individual was found with five slashes to the side of the head; several others suffered multiple dagger thrusts into the back of the neck, after the helmet had been torn off; another had ten injuries to the skull; one veteran, killed at Towton, had sustained a gaping cut to his face across the mouth and jaw in a previous battle (he had survived, but his face must have been horrifically split in two); and there was a man the back of whose head was superficially slashed by a blade of some sort, penetrated by two dagger wounds and criss-crossed by two smashing blows.

Frustratingly, the War of the Roses was not over. The king, the queen, prince Edward, Somerset and Exeter, as well as numerous Northern stalwarts, escaped to Newcastle and thence to Scotland. Edward did not pursue them. To a Yorkist who had just butchered the earl of Northumberland, the North was a no-go area. One thing Edward realised immediately: Towton, while not decisive, had 'shattered the strength of the great northern lords ... who between them could dominate England north of Trent. The way now lay open for the subjugation of Yorkshire and the regions towards the Scottish Border.' That would come later.[35] One thing he did do, however, was to attaint both Somerset and Exeter.

Edward departed for London in early April and was crowned on 28 June.

CHAPTER EIGHTEEN

Bird in the Bosom

The Lancastrians' Last Stand in the North, 1461–4

Although, according to the fifteenth-century writer John Hardyng, the Percys 'have the hearts of the people of the North and always have had', following St Albans, Northampton and Towton little physical Percy presence remained. The reportedly sick William, bishop of Carlisle, would die the following year. Another brother, George, seems to have been blamelessly respectable; a rector in Rothbury, he would live for another fifteen years. There were only two Percy soldiers left: Sir Ralph Percy, the youngest but the most stable and principled of the brothers, and Sir Richard Percy, the next youngest, who periodically suffered sociopathic bouts. Then there was Henry Percy, aged twelve, the only son of the third earl of Northumberland (the three younger daughters, Elizabeth, Eleanor and Margaret, would marry respectably if not particularly spectacularly).[1]

On 4 November 1461, the boy was disbarred from the title, goods and assets of the late earl, who, along with others at Towton, was attainted for rising against his 'rightwise, true, and natural liege lord, purposing there and then to have destroyed him [Edward IV]'. Attainder for treason – as previous Percys knew – was the law's most solemn penalty, for it not only made inheritances forfeit but presumed that the offender's corrupted (hence, 'attainted') blood had passed to his offspring.[2]

Sir Ralph had not been present at Towton, instead acting as constable of the key fortress of Dunstanburgh, which had been granted to him by the queen in 1456–7. He surrendered it peacefully to Edward IV in September/October. Two factors bore on his decision.

First, as Richard Percy was an irresponsible, boozy no-hoper, it was 36-year-old Ralph's duty to protect his fatherless nephew. These were dark days, but attainders could be reversed, titles and estates restored. Young Henry Percy had been taken to the Tower of London, where he was not mistreated – but that could change should the constable of Dunstanburgh misbehave. And if Sir Ralph himself were attainted for not submitting to the king, the prospects for his wife, three boys and a girl were dire. This necessary submissiveness was not, as later events attest, meek obedience to the regime that the Percys had regarded as illegitimate.

Second, resisting the Yorkist forces was pointless. That autumn Edward's generals finished off Lancastrian resistance in Wales; Lord Herbert heavily defeated Jasper Tudor, earl of Pembroke, and the duke of Exeter – or, more properly, plain old Henry Holland, given that his estates and title had been stripped from him after his flight to take temporary shelter following the battle of Towton – outside Caernarvon, rendering the Lancastrians powerless to field another army. (Only Harlech Castle resisted for several more years.)[3] Even in the North, the Yorkists were slowly taking charge. 'The problem of subduing the hostile county of Northumberland, where the word of a Percy counted for more than the king's command, was left to [Edward's] Neville kinsmen and lieutenants.'[4]

Richard Neville, earl of Warwick, was now the premier English earl; his gigantic estates, almost debtless financial situation and rapid accumulation of royal offices after Towton awed even Continental princes.[5] On 31 July 1461, erasing the Percy grip of the East, he was granted the wardenship of *both* Marches for twenty years, with his uncle, the new earl of Kent (formerly Lord Fauconberg, the Yorkist bowmen's commander at Towton), acting as his lieutenant. Kent died two years later and was replaced by Warwick's third brother, the former John Neville – who had tangled with the late Egremont on several occasions – now raised to the title of Lord Montagu by dint of his excellent service to the House of York.[6]

By mid-September, the Yorkists had effectively chipped away the remaining symbols of Percy dominance. Alnwick Castle submitted peacefully, followed, as we have already seen, by Dunstanburgh. But whilst Alnwick was invested with a Yorkist constable, Edward allowed Ralph Percy to keep his office at Dunstanburgh. This was risky, given the rebellious examples set by other Percys, yet Edward believed that he needed to co-opt the Percys to run the North. Warwick's rule would not last for ever, but the Percys, reconciled with the new regime, could control their followers and persuade the gentry to lay down their arms for ever. 'Reconciliation', however, did not mean restoration to the earldom; the Percys would occupy a subordinate role.[7]

While Ralph Percy performed his duties loyally, Lancastrian diehards demonstrated that Edward could never tame the North. By the year's end, Sir William Tailboys had retaken Alnwick; in Cumberland, Lord Dacre reoccupied his family's castle at Naworth, east of Carlisle. In November, Warwick had to deal with insurrections, albeit small local ones, throughout Northumberland.[8]

The Yorkists quickly detected where these attacks originated and who supported the rebels: Queen Margaret's Lancastrian rump, safe in Scotland. But a military campaign to force the Scots to eject the Lancastrians was out of the question. Edward IV was no Edward I or Edward III; pacifying Wales and the North was hard enough without undertaking the subjugation of Scotland, especially after the humiliating loss of Roxburgh.

Instead, Edward adopted a two-track scheme to pressurise the Scots: one covert, the other diplomatic. A far-fetched enterprise, constructed around Douglas (the earl was still in England since James II drove him south seven years before), to usurp the Stewarts and partition Scotland into three districts loyal to the English Crown, with all southern Scotland falling into Douglas's hands, never got very far. A far more promising approach was to exploit the divisions at the Scottish court over the Lancastrian presence.[9]

With James III a minor, two factions fought for influence over domestic and foreign policy. The first, headed by Bishop James Kennedy, was loyal to the Auld Alliance – now dormant for some years – which entailed maintaining Margaret, Henry and the Lancastrians in Scotland until Edward's overthrow. The Burgundian queen mother, Mary of Guelders, led the faction that naturally inclined to Burgundy (she was Duke Philip's niece), despite her personal liking for the French Queen Margaret. As James II's widow, and queen of the weakest realm, Mary saw the benefits of playing both sides off against one another. James II had considered Duke Richard and the Nevilles a useful Yorkist counterweight against both the ruling Lancastrians *and* the French under Charles VII, who improved ties with Henry VI and Margaret of Anjou after the Hundred Years War. The Yorkists, as befitted their aggressively anti-French policy, were friendly with the Burgundians. Together, these factors might persuade Mary to trade Margaret and Henry for Yorkist concessions in the North and a possible Anglo-Burgundian-Scottish compact against France. On the other hand, Margaret, desperate to buy continued Scottish backing for the Lancastrians, actually signed over Berwick and Carlisle. Although the latter resisted Scottish occupation, Berwick fell into Mary's hands before the end of 1461. Since the thirteenth century, the Scots and the English had fought viciously for Berwick; now it was simply transferred without a shot being fired (so to speak).

Mary, however, wanted to see how high the other side would bid for Scottish support. Hoping to both worry Edward and soothe Bishop Kennedy with the prospect of a revived Franco-Scottish alliance, she financed Queen Margaret's trip to Paris in March 1462 to sound out the new king, Louis XI, who had succeeded the seemingly immortal Charles VII.

In Margaret's absence, Mary's hand weakened when Edward recovered what he had lost the year before in the North: Dacre surrendered Naworth to Montagu; Tailboys was ejected from Alnwick by Lord Hastings, Sir John Howard and Sir Ralph Grey; and even the once-impregnable Bamburgh was captured. But the Scots rebounded in October 1462, when Margaret returned from Louis with a lukewarm Truce of Tours. Under its terms, after Louis occupied Calais – Margaret was basically trading land for war – he would allow the seneschal of Normandy, Pierre de Brézé ('the best warrer of alle that tyme', judged John Warkworth, a well-known chronicler), to take command of a French invasion force.[10] But to take Calais meant crossing Burgundian territory and thereby starting a war, so Louis's interest faded. In the end, a small force of 800 paid for by de Brézé, landed at Bamburgh after collecting Henry in Scotland. Bamburgh and Alnwick opened their gates to Somerset (who boasted that he had seduced Mary during his stay). Believing that the Lancastrians had turned the tide, Sir Ralph Percy threw off his Yorkist cloak and declared for Henry VI.

They hadn't. Without a Percy earl spurring them forward, the Northumbrian gentry awaited Edward's reaction before donning their armour. Only five days after Bamburgh turned Lancastrian, Warwick was racing up from London followed by a commission to raise the Northern levies. Edward sent supplies and ammunition by sea to Newcastle, and authorised the always useful Douglas to raid Lancastrian hideouts.

Hearing that Edward and Warwick were on their way, Margaret and Henry escaped from Northumberland to Scotland (after losing all their ships in a storm). Now the three Lancastrian castles had to resist the Yorkists until reinforcements arrived, perhaps in the spring. By now, however, Margaret had almost exhausted her credibility (let alone credit – she pawned a silver chalice to Mary for about £70) with the Scots, and her 'deals' became more bizarre. She offered the earl of Angus an English dukedom if he helped Henry VI; then promised James III seven English sheriffdoms; and finally proposed Bishop Kennedy as archbishop of Canterbury. The county of Northumberland – ironically, considering all the damage it had suffered since Robert Bruce's day – urgently required significant Scottish aid to save it from the king of England.

There was a brief ray of hope when Edward fell ill with measles in mid-November, but he directed operations from his bed at Warkworth – Hotspur's old haunt. Warwick was his lieutenant[11] and daily undertook the arduous sixty-mile trek around the defences' perimeter to ensure the men received supplies. Faced by Northern veterans like Sir Ralph Grey and Lord (once Sir Robert) Ogle – both had served on the East March with the 2nd earl of Northumberland and knew their way around the fortresses – Bamburgh and Dunstanburgh resisted only until Christmas, whilst Alnwick surrendered on 6 January 1463. Edward was relieved not to employ his great cannons against them, since control of the North hinged on these great strongholds.[12]

Edward's reaction was unexpectedly generous. Somerset's attainder after the battle of Towton was actually reversed between May and June, and the king touchingly tried to ensure the duke's loyalty and friendship, for example by appointing him commander of his bodyguard. Ralph Percy, after swearing fealty to Edward, was granted the constableship of not only Dunstanburgh but Bamburgh as well on 17 March. He could even receive repentant rebels at his own discretion, an honour reserved only for the most loyal of the king's officers.[13] Why was Edward rewarding rebels? Edward considered that he still needed his former enemies to keep the North friendly. Lavishly forgiving Somerset and the others might detach them from Margaret's baleful influence, and thereby isolate her in Scotland, where her welcome was wearing very thin indeed.

But Edward disastrously underestimated their fervent attachment to the *cause* of Lancastrianism – meaning the dynastic legitimacy of Henry VI, weakling though he was.[14] Among medieval nobles, self-interest exacted by violent, mercenary or avaricious means nestled alongside fidelity to principle (Magna Carta being the finest example). Somerset and Percy defected to their de facto king only to survive. Their first loyalties, despite appearances, remained with the battered House of Lancaster.

Edward's trust was soon betrayed. After Warwick returned to London, Ralph Percy turned over his castles to the Lancastrians, as did Sir Ralph Grey – a former Lancastrian now (allegedly) working with the Yorkists – at Alnwick. Yet again, this time after a gruelling winter campaign – even the chroniclers shuddered at the 'fervent colde' – Northumberland remained at heart Lancastrian.[15] Somerset himself would defect (again) sometime between the revocation of his attainder and December 1463.

In Scotland, the tables also unexpectedly turned. Aided by the rise of Bishop Kennedy and the serious illness of Queen Mary, Margaret's position had strengthened. Impressed by her promises of Henry VI's imminent restoration and massive French aid, Kennedy enthused the court and little King James with visions of Scoto-Franco-Lancastrian unity. In July, with Mary's token support, a large Scots army under James III and Henry VI crossed the Border to take Norham Castle. Alnwick, Bamburgh and Dunstanburgh, all in Lancastrian hands, guarded the southern approaches should Warwick try to relieve Norham. But when Warwick and Lord Montagu, recently created warden of the East March, unexpectedly appeared before Norham, the Scots hurriedly retreated, unwilling to risk battle against these two warhorses.

As punishment, the wardens raided sixty-three miles into southern Scotland, burning everything, and Warwick ordered Douglas, lurking in the West March and keen to hurt the Stewarts, to do whatever damage he could across the Border. Even after the Nevilles had returned home, Douglas continued his raids; for Warwick, he dramatically rammed home to his fellow Scots the price of sheltering Henry and Margaret. Nevertheless, although the Yorkists had warded off an invasion, the three castles held out. Since it was summer, their food-stocks would last through the winter, but in any case for the English government three prolonged sieges were too expensive (even one was stretching the budget).

The ingratitude of Percy and the other secret Lancastrians embarrassed Edward. The prospect of a hugely expensive reconquest of the North strengthened calls for the king to pursue the diplomatic track, which had been ignored during the recent military activity.

In August 1463, guided, surprisingly, by Duke Philip of Burgundy (for whom Scotland was a sideshow), English envoys secretly discussed a truce with Louis XI that might lead to a permanent Anglo-Burgundian-French rapprochement. Duke Philip was ageing quickly and with his real enemy, Charles VII, gone, he dreamt of bringing together his Yorkist allies and the new French king. After hearing what had happened at Norham, Louis XI gave up on a Lancastrian restoration, deciding to recognise the Yorkists as England's permanent government. For Edward, like Nixon going to China, a truce was the lesser of two evils. The French presented little danger (especially with Burgundy watching Louis) compared to the recurring menace of Lancastrian revolt. On 8 October 1463, the monarchs undertook a one-year Anglo-French convention. Louis pledged to halt all aid to Henry VI and the Lancastrians, and so cordial was the meeting that Louis sportingly offered to renounce the Auld Alliance for ever.

Queen Margaret was, understandably, devastated. After her final attempt to lure Duke Philip away from the Anglo-French rapprochement – apparently, he listened politely but silently before giving her a little money, a signal that she should leave – Margaret of Anjou and Prince Edward departed for France. She never returned to Scotland, and never saw her husband again.

Margaret's departure, the death of Mary on 1 December and the destruction of his beloved Franco-Scottish-Lancastrian axis persuaded Bishop Kennedy to arrange a truce with Edward on 9 December to run until 31 October 1464. Negotiations for a more permanent peace were scheduled for March of that year. Crucially, in exchange for Edward calling off Douglas, Kennedy sadly withdrew Scottish protection for

Henry VI and the Lancastrian remnants. That Christmas was a miserable one for the bereft Henry, now forced to shelter in Bamburgh Castle, one of a diminishing number of loyal strongholds. Amputated from French and Scottish support, the Lancastrian cause seemed in its death throes.

Yet it still twitched. In late February 1464, the attainted Lord Clifford's son had retaken the family castle at Skipton-in-Craven and declared for Henry. Somerset, now an outlaw, had run from Wales to Bamburgh, including Sir Henry Bellingham and Sir Humphrey Neville, two Lancastrians pardoned by Edward, to turn their coats. The charismatic Somerset's return cheered the Lancastrian ranks into planning a new offensive strategy. Collecting Sir Ralph Percy and Richard Percy, they drove the Yorkist garrisons out of Norham, Langley, Hexham, Bywell and Prudhoe, sealing Lancastrian supremacy from the Border down to Newcastle.

These lightning strikes jeopardised the upcoming Anglo-Scottish talks. Edward postponed them until 20 April and shifted the location from Newcastle to York. In the meantime he despatched Lord Montagu to escort the Scots through what was now enemy territory. Journeying north, Montagu, wary of potential ambushes, avoided a particularly devious one near Newcastle. It was at Hedgeley Moor – about nine miles north-east, revealingly, of Alnwick – that Montagu's troops were assailed by the combined weight of the Lancastrian army, perhaps fewer than 5000 men, commanded by Sir Ralph Percy (Richard Percy was also present), Somerset, Lords Roos and Hungerford, and Sir Ralph Grey. The details of the battle remain unknown, apart from its outcome: another Lancastrian defeat. The turning factor was the death of Ralph Percy, who cried, 'I have saved the bird in my bosom' (a reference to his loyalty to Henry VI) as he fell. His brother was also slain. After Sir Ralph's death, the Lancastrians fled, leaving Montagu free to collect the English envoys on the Border and return to York.[16]

Knowing that Edward intended one final grand assault on the Northern castles, Somerset rushed Henry from Bamburgh to Bywell Castle, and deployed his remaining forces at nearby Hexham. His original mission accomplished, Montagu returned north and attacked the unprepared Lancastrians on 15 May with every man he could muster. Despite Somerset's presence, the Northerners were so disheartened that they seem to have scattered immediately and Montagu, not delayed this time by escorting diplomats, pursued the remnants for miles. Unconcerned with the rank and file, he wanted the ringleaders. The Nevilles, it may be said, were rather less forgiving of erring rebels than their royal master. No reversals of attainder or accepting heartfelt pleas of fealty this time.

Montagu caught Somerset later that day and executed him. Roos and Hungerford followed two days later; by the end of May, another twenty-one had been executed. Sir William Tailboys was discovered on 20 July hiding in a coalpit. The soldiers who found him made their fortunes; he carried the Lancastrian war-funds – some £2000 – in his pockets, which soon made their way into other people's. The only survivors were Sir Ralph Grey and Sir Humphrey Neville, who escaped to Bamburgh.[17]

In his rush, Montagu had forgotten to search Bywell for the king. A few days later, when they broke into the silent castle, his troops found only Henry's crowned helmet and other forlorn pieces of regalia. For the next year, his whereabouts remained a mystery while this refugee in his own realm sheltered in the isolated houses of his few remaining supporters.

Montagu had single-handedly crushed Lancastrianism in a matter of months (Clifford had quickly surrendered Skipton). Apart from young Henry Percy in the Tower (and harmless George Percy at Beverley), there were no Percys left. In the past decade, two earls of Northumberland, and their sons and brothers, had died for the Red Rose. On 27 May Sir John Neville, Lord Montagu, was rewarded with the earldom of Northumberland, and invested with all its titles and lands.[18]

On 11 June, Edward concluded a fifteen-year truce with the Scots at York. Two weeks later, reinforced by the king's three titanic cannons, the 'Newcastle', 'London' and 'Dijon', the new Northumberland and the earl of Warwick bloodlessly achieved Alnwick and Dunstanburgh's surrender. That left Bamburgh, held by Humphrey Neville and Ralph Grey, who spurned a pardon for immediate capitulation. So the two earls glee-fully let loose the cannons on Bamburgh's walls. Grey was knocked unconscious, allowing Neville to arrange a pardon before handing over the keys. He later retired to Yorkshire. Grey was condemned and beheaded.[19]

By the end of June, England was Edward's.

CHAPTER NINETEEN

Percy Restored

An Era of Shifting Alliances

Five years later, on 27 October 1469, twenty-year-old Henry Percy knelt and performed the sacred act of fealty to his overlord, King Edward IV. Six months on, at York on 25 March 1470, Edward graciously restored Percy to his earldom of Northumberland. John Neville immediately became marquess of Montagu, a brand-new degree of peerage, which promoted him above earls but kept him just below the dukes. Nevertheless, the marquessate lacked the traditional social and territorial loyalties, let alone the redolence, of 'earl of Northumberland', which was descended from a pre-Conquest title.

The next day, Northumberland received full custody of all his late father's forfeited estates when Montagu and Edward's brother George, the duke of Clarence (involuntarily) surrendered their claims to them, as we shall see later. Parliament revoked the attainder against the 3rd earl in October 1472, completing the 'rehabilitation process'. The new 4th earl of Northumberland had done well out of his family's second restoration; now only the barest minimum of manors expropriated by Henry IV had not yet been recovered.[1]

Why was Henry Percy favoured so lavishly – and by a Yorkist king! – so soon after his family's disgrace? Charles Ross's comment provides a clue: 'The two years from June 1469 to May 1471 form a period of political instability without parallel in English history since 1066.'[2] This turbulence coincides with Percy's restoration.

What had happened?

Ironically, the five years up to June 1469 had outwardly been the most peaceful for decades. The Yorkist regime was gradually inserting itself into public life and those little areas where Lancastrianism still breathed were successively becalmed. Inwardly, however, the period was marked by Warwick's rising discontent with his master, who seemed to him insufficiently courteous and grateful to the Nevilles, to whom he owed his throne.

As early as the spring of 1464 – when Montagu and Warwick were extinguishing Northern Lancastrian resistance at Hedgeley Moor and Hexham – the king stopped at Stony Stratford on his way to York to conclude the Anglo-Scottish truce. Secretly, very early in the morning of 1 May, Edward rode to Grafton Regis, the home of Richard Woodville, Lord Rivers, and Jaquetta of Luxembourg, his wife. There he married their daughter, Elizabeth Woodville, a young widow.³ After his shotgun wedding, Edward went to bed at the Rivers' house for a short while before returning to his billet at Stony Stratford *sans* Elizabeth. To his retainers, he announced that he had awoken early to go 'hunting' and was now fatigued, so he again retired to bed. Every evening for the three next days, he stayed the night at the Rivers'. Those accompanying the king knew perfectly well Elizabeth was being brought to him – they were all worldly men – but they were wholly unaware that he was *married*.

Edward had a Europe-wide reputation as a (successful) womaniser. Observed Dominic Mancini, who wrote a perceptive memoir of Edward soon after the king's death: 'He pursued with no discrimination the married and the unmarried, the noble and lowly: however, he took none by force.' Possessing a magnetically icy beauty, Elizabeth, rumour had it, had been the only female to refuse his advances. If Edward wanted her, he had to marry her. So he did, and committed a blunder of the first magnitude.⁴

At a time when English envoys were bringing home offers of marriages to nieces of Duke Philip of Burgundy, to Queen Mary of Scotland, and the sister (and eventual heiress) of King Henry the Impotent of Castile, Elizabeth Woodville was dreadfully unsuitable. This was not just because her level of personal warmth matched her looks. Rather, as Edward's stunned council pointed out, 'she was no wife for a prince such as himself; for she was not the daughter of a duke or earl.' 'Daughters of dukes and earls', especially foreign ones with royal connections, bore political, financial and diplomatic implications. Although Elizabeth's mother was the daughter of the French count of St Pol, a descendant of Charlemagne, her husband started married life as the relatively humble Sir Richard Woodville, son of the duke of Bedford's chamberlain. Princes married princesses, in other words, to keep warring kings peaceful.

Diplomatically speaking, the mid-1460s required Edward's full attention,⁵ and his being unmarried would have allowed his diplomats a freer negotiating hand. Within a year of the Anglo-Burgundian-French rapprochement, signed in October 1463, Louis XI's centralising policies had led to a short civil war involving his still technically feudal subjects, the dukes of Burgundy and Brittany. If the tripartite agreement was to be extended beyond its one-year trial period, new negotiations had to take place – if all remained well. Thus, by 1465, London was delicately placed: should she align with Burgundy, England's largest overseas market, or her hereditary enemy, France, which offered significant commercial opportunities in the future?

Edward marginally favoured Burgundy, owing to its long friendship with the Yorkists and Louis XI's shelter of Margaret of Anjou. Warwick was – or rather *thought* he was – Edward's chief foreign affairs adviser. Whilst his father had been strongly anti-French, the earl was the opposite, shrewdly recognising the likelihood of Burgundy's waning influence after the capable – but very ill – Duke Philip died. When Warwick met Philip's tousle-haired, five-o'clock-shadowed heir, Charles of Charolais (the future Charles the Bold), in April 1466, according to one historian, 'at first sight the two men hated each other, politically, viscerally'. In contrast, when Warwick visited Louis in May 1467, he received a 'great jewelled gold cup costing 2000 livres' from the solicitous French king, who sought to secure the English friendship by marrying Edward's nineteen-year-old sister, Margaret of York, to Philip of Savoy, his brother-in-law. So amicable were Warwick and Louis that the latter not only proposed an Anglo-French free-trade zone, but directed the merchants of Rouen to provide the English with silk and velvet gratis, just to show off the superiority of French workmanship over Burgundian products. Little did Warwick know, however, that his embassy was intended to remove him from London while Burgundian envoys were in town.

Charles and Edward had already concluded a symbolic treaty of 'amity and mutual assistance' behind Warwick's back eight months before. Edward and Earl Rivers (his new father-in-law, freshly promoted to an earldom) were quietly colluding with the Burgundians against Louis – and, by extension, Warwick. Thus, while Warwick was getting excited about Louis's marriage proposals, Rivers and Edward were already pondering Margaret's marriage to Charles of Charolais, who on 15 June 1467 became duke of Burgundy after Philip's death.

Thus, in the same month, Edward virtually ignored the French embassy, carrying details of Louis's plans, and announced a strengthened alliance with Burgundy and a pact with Castile – another enemy of France. On 14 July, a humiliated Warwick bade goodbye to the stiff French embassy. This greatest, most loyal of magnates had negotiated in good faith for his king, only to discover, mortifyingly, that the Woodvilles and his own creation, Edward IV, had conspired against him.

Warwick did not return to London, but rode to his estates in the North, and brooded.

In the meantime, the Anglo-Burgundian alliance was bearing a steep price. Edward was forced to postpone the wedding, begging the money for the down payment of the £42,000 dowry that Charles had squeezed from the Exchequer from unenthusiastic (pro-French) London bankers. Furthermore, much to Warwick's horrified chagrin, Edward had become overconfident about his anti-French alliance. In Parliament on 17 May 1468, cheers greeted the announcement of a new series of European truces (including ones with Scotland, Burgundy and Brittany) that would soon permit a full-fledged invasion of France. Edward was immediately voted a substantial tax to this end. However, Louis prevented France's encirclement by making peace with Brittany and Burgundy, but not before Edward had blown £18,000 on a fleet that merely patrolled the Channel against phantom invasion threats.

Exactly when Warwick took the momentous step of breaking with Edward is unknown, but certainly in 1467 and 1468 the earl was in traitorous contact with Louis, who probably then discreetly mooted a rapprochement between Warwick and the indomitable Margaret of Anjou. By mid-1469, Neville agents were agitating in Yorkshire against the 'evildoers' surrounding the king.

Apart from the Woodvilles, chief among these, for Warwick, were the Herberts, who would play a significant role in Percy's life. Sir William Herbert, of fairly middling birth, was the first Welshman to reach the commanding heights of English politics and aristocratic society. He was a moderate Yorkist since the 1450s, but his spectacular rise spurted into life in the early 1460s. After Edward's coronation, almost all of South Wales temporarily fell under royal control, principally owing to the politically convenient attainders of Edward (of Lancaster), the existing Prince of Wales, and Jasper Tudor, earl of Pembroke (an incorrigible rebel). Edward chose Herbert to administer it and, later, parts of North Wales too, as viceroy, chief justice, chamberlain, constable and master-forester. No other man, not even Warwick, received such latitudinous autonomy. After Sir William brought obstinate Harlech Castle to heel, he was promoted to earl of Pembroke in 1468, with the promise of his son's imminent marriage to one of Elizabeth Woodville's sisters. According to T.B. Pugh, 'in less than ten years this grossly ambitious and grasping Welsh country squire had turned himself into an English magnate, with an annual income of some £2400.' Although Pembroke did not yet directly threaten his interests, as earl *primus inter pares* Warwick could not help wanting to retard the Welshman's progress.[6]

Warwick felt stifled by Woodvillian influence both in England's foreign policy and in his own domestic affairs. He exploded in fury on hearing the belated news of Edward's marriage, which was leading to a severe crisis: Elizabeth Woodville's relatives had to command a social and financial position appropriate to a queen's kin. Which is why John Woodville, the queen's twenty-year-old brother, was sent off to marry, as contemporaries sarcastically said, the *juvencula* ('slip of a girl') dowager duchess of Norfolk, then aged sixty-five and the veteran of three marriages. This wealthy dowager also happened to be Warwick's aunt, and he was not altogether pleased that she was being used to pad the Woodville inheritance. (He shouldn't have worried: she outlived John Woodville by fourteen years.) But while two siblings, say, could be easily accommodated, Elizabeth had two sons, five brothers and *seven* unmarried sisters. Warwick had earmarked his two daughters of near-marriageable age, Isabel and Anne, for strategic unions with useful magnates and the royal family, but found the marriage market cornered by the Woodville brothers and sisters. All was not lost, however. There still remained the king's younger brothers, George duke of Clarence, and Richard duke of Gloucester. But, for reasons that Warwick could only believe were related to Edward's desire to match Woodville sisters with royal brothers, the king refused to allow Isabel and Anne to marry them.

False, Fleeting, Perjur'd Clarence

In the absence of any male offspring of Edward and Elizabeth, the duke of Clarence was heir presumptive – a position of understandable substance. That would change in 1470, following the birth of the future Edward V. Money-wise, however, Clarence had few complaints; Edward had carefully given him the earldom of Chester (traditionally the inheritance of the Prince of Wales) and an annual income of about £3700. Yet by the mid-1460s, he was chafing under the controlling hand of his older brother. Clarence was aware that the moment a royal son appeared, his only political and diplomatic importance would lie in marrying some foreign princess Edward had selected for him. Already, Edward was trying to forge a union with Mary of Burgundy, and had forbidden a match with the country's most desirable heiress, Isabel Neville.

Warwick, also annoyed that Isabel was being 'saved' for a Woodville, knew of the unsubtle Clarence's private discontent. Sometime in 1467, the two men secretly agreed a *coup d'état*. According to Jean de Waurin, a Burgundian chronicler, when Warwick complained to Clarence about the parasitic omnipresence of the Woodvilles, the eighteen-year-old duke concurred but was resigned to the prospect of Woodville dominance. Whereupon Warwick grew unexpectedly serious, leant forward and murmured that he could put Clarence on the throne.

What otherwise might have been dismissed as a moment of fantasy was transformed into a bona fide conspiracy over the coming years. The pair made formidable allies: Warwick, the realm's most powerful magnate – militarily experienced, deliriously popular and politically astute, combining with Clarence, who lacked all of these things but possessed the right genes. Clarence, personally, was not unattractive: witty, droll, talented and charming, he had inherited not only the Yorks' handsome looks, but also, unfortunately, their ambition, anger and envy. Young as he was, Clarence was willing prey for Warwick's plots.

In May and June 1469, a time of rising discontent with Edward's tax policies, rebellion broke out in Yorkshire under an individual named Robin of Redesdale (also known as Robin Mend-All). John Neville, then still the earl of Northumberland, easily stamped out the malcontents (who fled into Lancashire), but peace was restored in Yorkshire only briefly. Another insurgence led by 'Robin of Holderness' happened soon after, apparently championing the restoration of a Percy earl. Neville just as easily cracked down on this one, but its harder elements again escaped and joined Redesdale's gang.

Whereas Robin of Holderness's campaign demonstrated a genuine desire for the Percys' return, 'Robin of Redesdale' was the pseudonym of Sir William Conyers, the brother of Sir John Conyers, Warwick's deputy for his Yorkshire estates.[7] The Redesdale commanders were no men of the soil; rather, they included several of Warwick's knightly kinsmen. Clearly, the insurrection was a front for a pro-Warwick force, although in the ranks there existed widespread disillusionment with the current government.

Edward travelled at a leisurely pace to Lancashire to finish off the Redesdalers, seeing this as merely a small-scale disturbance and, perhaps, hoping that the rebellion would burn itself out before his arrival. But in Newark on 10 July, there was worrying news. The Redesdalers had collected three times as many men as the king and were heading towards Coventry, so outflanking Edward. He urgently retreated to Nottingham, ordering Pembroke and Humphrey Stafford, the new earl of Devon and another rising star at court, to summon their Welsh and West Country levies. Now Edward realised he had fallen into Warwick's trap. Not only did the rebels' manifesto contain suspiciously Warwickian demands to rid the court of Woodvilles, Pembroke and Devon, but it menacingly observed that favouritism had caused the depositions of Edward II, Richard II and Henry VI.

Shortly after the king left for the Midlands, Warwick informed his supporters in Coventry that his daughter was to marry Clarence in a ceremony officiated by the archbishop of York, George Neville, Warwick's brother. After sailing to Calais for the hasty ceremony, Warwick and Clarence revealed their colours by reprinting the rebel manifesto and adding their own comments. On 16 July, they returned to Canterbury to be met by legions of their armed followers. They reached London two days later and advanced towards Coventry to rendezvous with the Redesdalers. In this beautifully planned manoeuvre, especially at a time of such slow communications, Warwick had obliged Edward to wait at Nottingham, secured London and threatened to prevent Pembroke and Devon reaching Edward. Coventry stood on the road between South Wales, the West and Nottingham. The two unsuspecting earls would run into the combined rebel forces, which could then surround the king at Nottingham – Warwick country.

On 26 July 1469, at Edgecote (near Banbury in northern Oxfordshire), Warwick and Clarence pounced on Pembroke's cavalry. Devon's archers arrived too late to help and after a brave fight, the Welshmen succumbed. The next day, Warwick vengefully beheaded Pembroke and his brother. Meanwhile, with communications cut off, Edward remained motionless at Nottingham, desperately awaiting reinforcements. Wondering where Pembroke and Devon had got to, he belatedly left Nottingham on 29 July and was deserted by his entire army at Northampton following news of the Edgecote defeat. Friendless and confused, Edward was captured by the Neville archbishop of York and sent to Warwick Castle. Two weeks later, the endgame played out. Warwick ordered the execution of Earl Rivers, John Woodville, the queen's twenty-year-old brother, and the earl of Devon, who had escaped from the aftermath of Edgecote. By mid-August, the 'Kingmaker' was master of England.

Nevertheless, Warwick and Clarence decided not to push their luck by executing Edward. They had won Edgecote without any noble support; moreover, many of the Redesdalers had rebelled against the evil ministers – now lately departed – not Edward himself. It behoved them to treat him with respect and deference. Rather than a kingly usurpation, Warwick's coup was transformed into a temporary usurpation of kingly authority.

Within a few weeks, bowing to political reality, Warwick released Edward. On the surface, Edward was all smiles and was nothing but outwardly courteous towards Warwick and his brother. For their part, Warwick and Clarence claimed they had rebelled for Edward's own good, not their personal betterment. Edward neither exacted, nor did the pair expect, retributive punishment. But inside, Edward burnt. Over the next few months, he subtly shifted powers and responsibilities away from

Warwick and Clarence, especially in the outlying regions. Thus, after Warwick released as a gesture of good faith Pembroke's Welsh offices that he had assumed after the earl's murder, it seemed natural that the king's youngest brother, Duke Richard of Gloucester, should have them. Likewise, it seemed only right to donate the earldom of Wiltshire to John Stafford, the duke of Buckingham's younger son and the brother of the executed earl of Devon.

Young Henry Percy became a pawn in this game between Warwick and Edward. Truth be told, Edward had always kept Percy conveniently around in comfortable if cloistered prisons as insurance against Neville treachery in the North. He had always treated Percy kindly – the two were rather friendly – and no doubt held out the hope of eventual redemption and restoration. Indeed, in 1467–8, Edward started Percy along this road when he placed him in the care of William Herbert, the then earl of Pembroke, who could report on Percy's behaviour; was he a recalcitrant Lancastrian or a stalwart loyalist?[8]

Percy had been six when his grandfather was killed at St Albans, twelve at his father's death and fifteen during the Lancastrian rebellions in Northumberland. He probably barely remembered Ralph Percy, since the two would have been only briefly acquainted before Towton. Of course, he remembered his father, but to any young man, especially one alternately cosseted and buffeted by Yorkist 're-education' for nigh on a decade, fighting and dying for the eccentric Henry VI and his meddlesome French queen would have seemed a trifle quaint. To all intents and purposes, Edward IV was king of England. Thus, he served him.

Even so, perhaps there was something unsettling about this young man, persuading Edward to raise him step by step, so that he could warily watch for signs of imminent danger, instead of handing him the prize in one fell swoop. Whilst outwardly faithful to the regime, Henry Percy, the sole survivor of a massacred dynasty, had been imprisoned for nearly a decade; he had learnt to keep his thoughts to himself and always to be on his best behaviour towards those who held power over him. During his career, Percy would diligently serve his masters – except at the crunch time of having to choose one over the other. Then, it seemed, he froze and adopted an outward neutrality. Privately, he may have favoured one side, but unlike the rest of his family, he did not proudly and obstinately wear his loyalty on his sleeve. Options had to be kept open, especially in an emergency. Whatever the outcome of the power struggle or battle, Percy would not be tagged as a strident partisan.

Betrayed by his closest adviser and his own brother, perhaps Edward was just over-suspicious. No one else felt so. Representatives of the Herberts and their in-laws, the Woodvilles, stood surety for Percy during his performance of fealty on 27 October 1469: 'I faith and truth shall bear to you as my sovereign liege lord … of life and limb and of earthly worship, for to live and die against all earthly people.'[9]

Over the winter, Warwick and Clarence smiled back at Edward through clenched teeth, aware his friendly demeanour was merely skin-deep. According to rumour, men of Edward's household swore at Warwick and Clarence even in the king's presence. Moreover, although not directly punished for their rebellion, they had not been rewarded for saving the king from his evil advisers either. It is likely Warwick and Clarence actually began to believe their own make-believe story.

At the beginning of March 1470, Edward, the earl of Arundel, Lord Hastings and Percy set out for Lincolnshire to put down a low-level disturbance, ignorant of Warwick and Clarence's previous contact with Lord Welles, the instigator of the trouble and one of the country's largest landowners. Welles unsurprisingly proved willing to go along with Warwick; he had, after all, been involved in Robin of Redesdale's uprising.

At Empingham, Edward clashed with the rebel army under Sir Robert Welles, Lord Welles's son. During the brief battle, Edward's suspicions that Warwick and Clarence were behind the uprising were confirmed. On the battlefield, the war-cry 'A Clarence! A Clarence! A Warwick!' had been heard, and Sir Robert Welles was captured wearing Clarence livery. Crucially, a casket found on a ducal envoy contained correspondence between Clarence and Sir Robert, detailing Warwick's fresh plan to trap Edward at Leicester. Before his beheading, Sir Robert confessed that Warwick and Clarence had put him up to it.

Warwick and Clarence ignored the king's subsequent summons on 14 March, and headed north. They traded envoys with Edward, hoping to extract a pardon and safe-conduct. Edward promised to treat them leniently, but would not issue a pardon, which might set a precedent for others who treasonously took up arms against the sovereign. He followed them north, and at York on 22 March offered leniency if Warwick and Clarence came before him before 28 March; if not, they would be considered rebels and traitors. While awaiting Warwick's reply, on 25 March, Edward restored the earldom of Northumberland to Henry Percy, a gift that was not entirely unexpected. A month previously, Edward had arranged the transfer of substantial lands in South-Western England to the current incumbent, John Neville. As we have already seen, when Percy received the title, Neville was granted the marquessate of Montagu and, a day later, the new earl took custody of his father's forfeited estates after Montagu surrendered his claim. Percy also received the family lands held by Clarence, but this was done in the duke's absence and without his

consent. Over the next three months, Montagu stayed in the North clearing up his affairs, so not until 24 June was Percy invested as warden of
the East March for an initial five-year contract.[10] A Percy, after a brief
hiatus, was again King in the North.

Edward's decision, considering John Neville's loyalty during
Warwick's two rebellions, is difficult to explain. Perhaps he genuinely felt
that the ageing Neville wanted to leave behind the rigours of Northern
life – all those rebellious Yorkshiremen and rampaging Scots. On the
surface, Neville's retirement – for that is what the offer of pleasant lands
in South-Western England meant – occasioned no strident complaints,
despite his replacement by the fresh-faced kinsman of rogues like Lord
Egremont and Ralph Percy. Privately, however, Neville felt he had been
coerced into exchanging the princely earldom, wrested from the Percys'
dead fingers, for some baubles like a newfangled marquessate. According
to the Northern chronicler John Warkworth, henceforth 'Montagu
hatyde the Kynge' and complained to sympathetic listeners how Edward
gave him only 'a pyes neste [that is, 'a magpie's nest of lands'] to mayn-
tene his astate with'.[11] Edward seemed blithely unaware of Montagu's
dissatisfaction. His ignorance would cost him dear.

Edward's tarrying inadvertently allowed Warwick, Clarence and their
wives to fly the coop. They sailed for Calais, only to find Warwick's
deputy firing cannons at them. (In fact, he had been warning Warwick
away from Calais, as the duke of Burgundy, who would have turned the
rebels over to Edward, was there.) Eventually, Warwick landed at
Honfleur and was granted refuge by a solicitous Louis XI.

Warwick slotted nicely into Louis's jigsaw puzzle. Chubby, with a
double-chinned neck craning forward, sleepy eyes and a pronounced
overbite, Louis resembled a moron. Yet he was the master manipulator
and diplomatic tactician of the age. From his perspective, only replacing
those in charge could now reorient England's foreign policy towards
France. This entailed putting Henry VI back on the throne.

For a year after his mysterious disappearance from Bywell Castle in
1464, Henry had sheltered with sympathetic, covertly Lancastrian gentry,
in Lancashire, West Yorkshire and Westmorland. But in August 1465,
Yorkist troops captured him crossing the Ribble accompanied only by
two chaplains and a squire. He was taken on horseback to London, his
feet tied to the stirrups; Warwick paraded him through the city to the
Tower, to be held captive for another five years (coinciding with Percy's
imprisonment). Indeed, the prison conditions probably mirrored Percy's
former treatment. He was treated humanely and lived very comfortably.
He was allowed numerous attendants, was supplied with wine from the
royal cellars and velvet for his gowns on occasion and he could see anyone

he chose. If he had so wished, games, books and other amusements could have been supplied, but Henry slipped into lethargy and resigned sadness for his entire time behind bars. His only solace was celebrating Mass each day with his priest, William Kymberley.[12] If Percy had seen the former king in the Tower, 'Henry of Windsor' (as he was now called) would have made a pitiful, if intriguing, sight.

Nevertheless, the old king was still alive, as was his wife, Margaret of Anjou, and even more importantly, his son, the disinherited Prince of Wales, now aged seventeen. In surely a remarkably 'difficult' reconciliation, on 22 July 1470, at Angers, the contrite Warwick begged forgiveness from the queen he had dethroned. She kept him on his knees for fifteen minutes, and made him pledge to do the same publicly in Westminster Abbey. Three days later, the second of Warwick's daughters, Anne, was betrothed to Prince Edward.

The plot to replace Edward with Henry effectively cut Clarence out of the running. On hearing the news of the marriage, and shrewdly predicting what it implied, Edward despatched 'a lady on a secret mission to Clarence, to persuade him not to be the agent of the ruin of his family, to ask him to consider very carefully what room there was for him now that Warwick had married his daughter to the Lancastrian prince of Wales'. To no avail. Clarence remained convinced that Warwick would soon dispose of Margaret and Prince Edward – the union being merely temporary – and place him on the throne. And that was the nub of the Neville–Lancastrian alliance: the desire to usurp Edward IV. Once achieved, however, the natural glue binding the conspirators together would inevitably erode. Every participant was treating the others simply as instruments for his ambitions; after that, they became dispensable. This was Clarence's fate, as Warwick had no further need of him. In the spirit of equity, nonetheless, Margaret planned to ditch Warwick the moment he defeated Edward, and Louis felt no compunction about employing any of these useful idiots to overthrow a foreign government. If the plot failed he could get rid of them. One indication of the alliance's fragility was the refusal of Margaret (and her son) to travel on the same vessel as Warwick in case the earl decided to throw them over the side.

Their plan mirrored Warwick's successful rebellion of 1469: instigate insurrection in the North to draw Edward from London. Then, the rebels could land in the South-West, attract support from those like Jasper Tudor in Wales, and march north-east towards Warwick's Midlands strongholds, while the Northern army drove south. Together they would crush Edward in a vice.

Accordingly, in late July, two of Warwick's associates sparked rebellions in Yorkshire and Cumberland, using veterans of Robin of

Redesdale's campaign. Some, especially from Yorkshire, were former officials of Marquess Montagu, now on their uppers after his replacement. The view in London was that these were indications of a serious uprising. Indeed, Sir John Paston wrote to his brother on 7 August that there were 'so many folks [rebelling] in the north' that he feared Northumberland could not extinguish the danger alone. He had heard that the king himself was coming to do the job.[13]

Paston had heard right. Edward, uncertain whether the Northern uprising was connected to a possible invasion, was determined not to repeat his 1469 mistake of meandering northwards and wasting weeks at Coventry. First he would smash the Northern rebellion and then race south *before* a landing took place (on 7 September, Edward wrote that he expected Warwick somewhere in Kent). After ensuring that the navy watched the Channel for Warwick's fleet, Edward rushed to York and then Ripon. The rebellion instantly dissolved when the royal army came over the hill. With Warwick's fleet still bottled up in port, Edward conceived he had some spare time and stayed in the North for a few weeks to buttress a rather shaken and inexperienced Percy, while ensuring that the rebellion really was extinct.

Percy's rupture from the North in his teens, when traditionally he would be acquainting himself with its topography and inhabitants, made him slightly sheepish regarding his role and position. One has only to compare a letter written by the self-confident Montagu in the late 1460s with one of Percy's a few months after his restoration. Concerning two retainers of Sir John Mauleverer who were beating Sir William Plumpton's servants, Montagu commanded Mauleverer to ensure they 'surcease and leave their said threatenings; and if they have any matters against the said servants lett them complaine unto me thereof, and I shall see that they shall have such a remedy as shall accord with reason'. Percy, on the other hand, wrote a letter full of blandishments and meanderings to Plumpton on a separate matter: 'my welbeloved cossine, I grete you hartily wealle, and desire and pray you that my welbeloved servant Edmund Cape may have and occupie the office of the baliship of Sesey... My trust is in you that, the rather for this mine instance & contemplation, ye will fulfill this my desire, and I will be as well-willed to doe thinge for your pleasure... Written in my manner of Topcliffe, the seventeenth day of August.'[14]

On 9 September a storm allowed Warwick to break out into the Channel. Edward's lookouts were watching Kent; nobody expected Warwick to land near Exeter. Immediately, Warwick, Clarence and the earl of Oxford (John de Vere, another of Warwick's brothers-in-law) set out towards the Midlands, joined by Lord Stanley and the earl of

Shrewsbury. Having protected his rear, Edward confidently plotted a collision course at Nottingham. He counted on Montagu, who had accompanied him from London, to raise the weighty Northern levies (Percy was evidently not performing at peak efficiency, which was forgivable considering his lack of Border experience) and follow him down to meet Warwick in battle.

Montagu did as instructed. But the turncoat declared his support for Warwick, not Edward. The king now faced two considerable Neville armies bearing down on him; Montagu had hidden his disgruntlement well. Edward knew that if he were caught, it meant execution. Sadly, he released his army and absconded east with some of his commanders to King's Lynn. Three ships thence carried him to a Burgundian welcome in Holland. Two weeks later, Edward's queen sought sanctuary in Westminster and gave birth to their first son. On 6 October, the rebels, barely believing it had been so easy, released Henry from the Tower and placed him on the throne.

For Edward, however, this was a strategic retreat. To recover his kingdom, he had to act quickly. Most lords and towns were on his side, but the longer Warwick was able to impose his authority, the less dependable they would become. Edward also knew that the Prince of Wales was preparing to cross the Channel with his mother. As a dynamic, up-and-coming teenager himself when he took the Crown, the usurped king might turn into yesterday's man once the people hailed Prince Edward.

Initially the hard-headed Duke Charles gave Edward the (polite) cold shoulder. His priority was to maintain the Anglo-Burgundian alliance with the king of England – whoever he was. But shortly afterwards, having been rebuffed by the Francophile Warwick, Charles privately began funding Edward's planned expedition. The duke 'unofficially' donated 50,000 florins and outfitted four ships, which came equipped with expert Flemish hand-gunners. Charles wanted 'plausible deniability' should Edward's effort fail, which looked more than likely. As the Milanese ambassador warned his chiefs at the time, 'It is a difficult matter to go out by the door and then try to enter by the windows. [Many] think he will leave his skin there.'[15]

On 2 March 1471, Edward set sail. Twelve days later, with symbolic good fortune, he landed at Ravenspur on the Humber, where Henry Bolingbroke had stepped ashore in 1399. Indeed, Edward had studied his history books in the Low Countries. Like Bolingbroke, he declared that he sought only the duchy held by his father, not the Crown. Edward, however, was keenly aware that he was on the outskirts of Percy country. As the 'official history' of the time, 'Historie of the arrivall of Edward IV. In England and the Finall Recouerye of his Kingdomes from Henry VI,

A.D. MCCCCLXXI', put it: the Northerners 'would not stire with any lorde or noble man other than with the sayde Earle, or at leaste by his commandement'. So, Edward broadcast the fact that he apparently enjoyed the support of the earl of Northumberland by displaying letters, under the earl's seal, inviting him to come to England.

His return was deliberately low-key and cautious. No crowds cheered him and he was heavily outnumbered. Many painfully remembered his recent suppression of Lancastrian dissent, and the massacre at Towton in which 'theyr Maistar, th'Erlls fathar, was slayne, [and] many of theyr fathars, theyr sonns, theyr britherne, and kynsemen'. Had Percy opportunistically turned his coat at this point and summoned the levies, Edward would have been destroyed. Strangely, however, if Northumberland had summoned the levies to *side* with Edward, few (according to the 'Historie of the Arrivall') would have shown up and they would have been, at best, half-hearted. Men naturally looked to the earl for guidance. But Northumberland stayed silent in Alnwick and did nothing. As a result, 'every man in all thos northe partes to sit still also', whilst towns like York were cautiously civil, even though many 'were right evill disposed of them selfe agaynes the Kynge'.

Northumberland and Edward had clearly been in contact before his landing. 'It may be reasonably judged that this was a notable good service, and politiquely done, by th'Erle.'[16] From Percy's shrewd perspective, he lost nothing by sitting idle. If Edward succeeded, he would be rewarded for his loyalty, more so if the Neville brothers were executed; if Edward failed, he could not be punished for sitting on the sidelines. On 25 March Edward crossed the Trent, heading for the Midlands where he expected reinforcements. At Leicester, the faithful Lord Hastings appeared with 3000 soldiers; soon after, two rich knights and 600 heavily armed troops hove into view. At the beginning of April, Edward publicly named himself king.

Warwick had moved to Coventry, awaiting assistance from various supporters, including Montagu and Clarence. But with Henry actually on the throne, Clarence belatedly accepted his exclusion from the succession, and threw in his lot (and the 400 men he commanded) with Edward. Three miles outside Warwick they were reconciled, and there was 'right kind and loving language betwixt them two, with perfect accord knit together for ever hereafter'. Richard of Gloucester also forgave his foolish and errant brother.

Bypassing Warwick and his allies in Coventry, Edward marched on London to get there before Queen Margaret. The irreconcilably Lancastrian duke of Somerset, the grandson of the man killed at St Albans in 1455, was already travelling to the south-west coast to meet her, carrying a commission appointing Prince Edward 'Lieutenant of the Realm of England'. Warwick, grasping Edward's plan, rushed south.

The king reached London and seized Henry. The latter seemed relieved, and even looked forward to returning to his comfortable lodgings in the Tower. He embraced Edward, saying, 'My cousin of York, you are very welcome. I believe that in your hands my life will not be in danger.' Then, at Westminster, Edward greeted his wife and child.

A few days later, he issued forth from London to meet Warwick at Barnet on 14 April. In the battle, Montagu was killed as was Warwick, who was still only forty-three. He was captured and killed by Yorkists before Edward could intervene. Edward was saddened by the deaths of his old mentors and former friends, although their survival would have meant their execution. As a mark of respect, however, he forbore ordering the Nevilles' dismemberment but directed they be buried with their father at Bisham Abbey.[17] The unbalanced former duke of Exeter, Henry Holland, was not treated so respectfully: severely wounded in the battle he was left for dead on the field for several hours, then, after a brief attempt at seeking sanctuary at Westminster Abbey, he was removed and imprisoned in the Tower until he died, broke, broken and forgotten, in 1475. No one seems to have missed him.

A few hours after the Lancastrian rout at Barnet, the former Queen Margaret and the (again, now former) Prince of Wales landed at Weymouth. On 4 May, Edward defeated them at Tewkesbury, the major casualties being Somerset and Prince Edward. The queen was captured, reportedly broken-spirited at her beloved son's death. According to the 'Historie of the arrivall', from then on the House of Lancaster was politically 'extincte and repressed for evar'.[18]

Northumberland played no part in these great events. Instead, on 14 May, the earl, accompanied by a small number of grim-visaged Northern retainers, told a relieved and exhausted Edward in Coventry that, following his suppression of some small insurrections in the North, 'the contrye was in good and sure tranquilitie, without any commotions, or unlawfull gatheryngs'. Revealingly, Northumberland was 'nat arrayed in manar of warr'.[19] For his fidelity, in October 1472 Parliament revoked the attainder against the 3rd earl, symbolically erasing any genetic treachery present in his son.

One final issue needed resolution to ensure the future stability of Edward's reign. A few convenient hours before the king reached London on 22 May 1471, Henry was beaten to death in the Tower. In the discreet words of the 'Historie of the arrivall', however, after hearing of the latest defeat, Henry died of 'pure displeasure and melencoly'.[20] He was buried in the Lady Chapel of the Benedictine abbey at Chertsey. When the king's remains were exhumed in 1910, his hair was matted with blood and the skull was severely damaged. Summarising the political situation for his masters, the Milanese ambassador in France wrote, 'King Edward caused King Henry to be secretly assassinated...He has, in short, chosen to crush the seed' of the last Lancastrian. Overseeing the Tower of London at the time was Duke Richard of Gloucester, later King Richard III.[21]

Tidying Up Loose Ends

Following Henry's death there was, apart from one abortive uprising by the earl of Oxford in 1473, twelve years of domestic peace in Edward's realm. Internationally, Edward had a score to settle with Louis XI of France, who was described by Edward as the 'principal ground, root, and provoker of the King's let and trouble'. On 11 September 1472 Edward reforged an alliance with the dukes of Brittany and Burgundy (despite Charles's initial coldness during his exile in the Low Countries in 1471) in the Treaty of Chateaugiron, which posited an English invasion of France with their support. But Burgundy and Brittany got cold feet and ratified truces with Louis, forcing Edward to postpone his campaign. Burgundy's eyes had now lifted from merely bloodying Louis's nose to the more elevated possibility of being elected Holy Roman Emperor, but his army, Europe's finest, got stuck in Alsace fighting the Swiss; however, by mid-1474 he had again made his peace with Edward. In the Treaty of London, Charles recognised Edward as king of France in return for portions of a dismembered France. Even Francis of Brittany arranged to send 8000 troops to help Edward. Tucking these military-diplomatic successes under his belt, he set about securing his northern border against a Scottish attack aimed at relieving pressure on the French. He proposed that James III's infant son should marry Edward's four-year-old daughter, Cecily. A formal marriage-treaty was drawn up on 26 October and the English negotiated a truce until October 1519. (Anglo-Scottish affairs will be examined more closely in the following chapter.)

Slightly less than a year later, 11,450 English troops had been transported to Calais. Edward was helped by enthusiastic noble support, including that of Percy. This was his first overseas visit, and Edward fortunately gave him a senior commanding role; he seems to have been near the king much of the time and he brought a larger retinue than the dukes of Norfolk and Suffolk.

Leaving Calais on 18 July 1475, the army pushed into France. But Charles of Burgundy treacherously barred English troops from his towns. With summer, and funds, running out, winter and bankruptcy on the horizon and French troops destroying agricultural stocks, Edward feared his army's exposure to freezing weather with few supplies and no pay. Thankfully for public opinion at home, Edward had used his taxes to conquer something – temporarily perhaps – but at least he hadn't been beaten. Some valour had been salvaged; now came discretion. He and his war council decided to negotiate. Luckily, Louis was willing to pay the English to leave as quickly as possible.

From 13 August until the end of the month, representatives shuttled back and forth. Without constitutional or dynastic issues at stake, Edward received nearly everything he requested. He mainly wanted money, with which Louis was liberally endowed; in exchange for taking the next ship home, Edward demanded £15,000 within fifteen days, another £10,000 annually and the dauphin's marriage to one of his two daughters (he didn't care which), additionally giving her an annual income of £6000. Apart from a few nips and tucks, it was a deal. When Charles barged into Edward's tent and started shouting about the agreement, Edward merely informed him that his behaviour disbarred him from further consideration in the Anglo-French treaty.

The kings agreed to meet at Picquigny, three miles downriver from Amiens where the Somme was narrow, but not fordable. Before the talks, apparently unaware of the reputation of Englishmen abroad, Louis hospitably arranged free booze for the troops – as much as they wanted. Before long, genteel Amiens was, predictably, heaving with thousands of drunken men-at-arms and bowmen firing arrows into the air. Edward finally used his bodyguard to clear the city and posted guards at the gates.

On 29 August, the English and French armies waited on opposite sides of the river, fully dressed for battle (to salve English pride). Spanning the river, a specially built narrow bridge was divided in the centre by a wooden screen, which included a trellis to permit conversation (this because Louis remembered the treacherous murder of John, duke of Burgundy, by an attendant of the dauphin on a similar bridge in 1419).

According to Philippe de Commynes, an eyewitness on the bridge with Louis: 'The king of England came along the causeway and was well attended. He appeared a truly regal figure. With him were his brother, the duke of Clarence, the earl of Northumberland, and several lords including his chamberlain, Lord Hastings, his Chancellor and others.' Near the barrier, Edward doffed his black velvet cap decorated with jewels 'and bowed to within six inches of the ground. The King, who was already leaning on the barrier, returned his greeting with much politeness. They began to embrace each other through the holes and the king of England made another even deeper bow.'

After the screen was removed, Edward and Louis got on rattlingly well. The French king slapped his English counterpart on the back, told him to come to Paris and dine with the ladies, 'and [said] that he would give [him] the cardinal of Bourbon as confessor, since the latter would very willingly absolve him from sin if he should have committed any, because he knew the cardinal was a jolly good fellow'.

In the Treaty of Picquigny, signed later that day, Edward got almost everything he had originally wanted. Louis helpfully arranged payment of Edward's annual Danegeld of £10,000 through a Medici bank bond, payable in the City. In return, Louis achieved his aim of free trade; henceforth all tolls and charges upon English and French traders were abolished.

By 18 September 1475, Edward, Northumberland and the army were back in London. Soon afterwards, a secret coda to Picquigny dealt with Margaret of Anjou's ransom. For an extra £10,000, Edward transferred his rights over Margaret to Louis, whose prisoner she became. Before being handed over to the French at Rouen on 22 January 1476, Edward made her renounce her title and claims to the Crown or dower lands in England. Likewise, Louis then instructed Margaret to release all her French claims emanating from her father, King Réné of Anjou, and her mother, Isabel of Lorraine. She was a free woman and, for the first time, harmless. With a modest allowance from Louis, the former queen lived quietly alone for another six years and died on 25 August 1482.[22]

CHAPTER 20

Kings in the North

The Earl of Northumberland and Duke Richard of Gloucester

Aside from his brief campaign in France, Northumberland had little interest or influence in foreign affairs apart from the Scottish question. In the 1470s he stayed in the North, settling domestic issues and looking after the debt-ridden family estates. Fortunately, the 3rd earl's attainder had, like a bankruptcy, quashed some of his inherited liabilities. A certain Henry Thwaites, for example, received only £66 of the £491 owed to him by the earl's father.

Freedom from immediate financial worry did not imply extravagance. Over the decade starting in 1471, the earl husbanded his resources and saved money, particularly by avoiding the potentially expensive diversion of politicking at court. On essentials like armed retinues, however, there could be no cutbacks; armed retainers, for instance, soaked up no less than 27 per cent of his total fixed income, compared to a relatively low 13 per cent spent on the wages and salaries of his estate officials, like secretaries and administrators. By the 1480s, he travelled with no fewer than thirty-three full knights plus hundreds of esquires, yeomen and mounted men-at-arms. In 1475–6, a visit to Hull (he kept a house on Chapel Lane) shows how expensive it was keeping up appearances. In alcohol alone, his men's consumption included thirty-one gallons of Rhenish wine and six and a half gallons of red wine. Nevertheless, within twenty years Northumberland freed the Percy estates from the crushing debt accumulated over the previous century.[1]

Two factors helped him: first, tranquillity on the Border after 1474, when Edward negotiated a truce until 1519; and second, Duke Richard's adoption of the North as his home after Edward IV's recovery of his kingdom.

Despite enjoying a decidedly western title, Duke Richard of Gloucester – the future Richard III – was the only true Northerner among England's late medieval kings. The Tudor chronicler, Edward Hall, believed Richard 'more loved, more esteemed and regarded by the Northernmen than any subjects within his realm'.[2] Oddly, however, he

461

never visited the North before 1465, nor did he reside there, let alone speak with a Northern accent. In 1471, Edward richly rewarded his nineteen-year-old brother, who had been unquestioningly loyal (unlike Clarence). There was plenty of room for expansion in the North, for Warwick's death and forfeiture released his colossal estates to the Crown. These comprised a typical aristocratic accumulation from inheritances and marriages, such as those of the Montagu earls, the Despenser family and the original Beauchamp earls of Warwick. The hereditary kernel, of course, was the Neville possessions, principally in the North. Most families entailed their traditional lands together to bind them into the male line. Thus, only a male Neville could inherit the specifically Neville possessions, whereas the rest of the Warwick's lands descended to his closest relative, his elder daughter, Isabel, who was married to Clarence. The only male Neville alive was George, the attainted marquis of Montagu's son, who was barred from inheriting anything. Edward therefore granted the Neville inheritance to Richard on 29 June 1471, so marking the beginning of his relationship with the North. An additional bauble was Richard's appointment as warden of the West March.

These properties were substantial, but not overwhelming either financially or territorially. Warwick's estates around Middleham in Wensleydale, for instance, were worth about £1000 annually, more than any other Northern lord's income – except that of Northumberland. Although these grants made Richard prominent in Northern politics and his family connections lent him immense status, as regards raw power he was distinctly second to Percy. Only Warwick's other daughter, sixteen-year-old Anne, whose straight blonde hair reached her waist, and who had been widowed after her marriage to the unlucky Edward, Prince of Wales, could escalate Richard past Northumberland and provide him with an income appropriate to his ducal status. Despite Clarence's furious entreaties – he guessed exactly what Richard intended – Richard married Anne between 12 February and 18 March 1472. Immediately after this marriage of convenience, Richard claimed Anne's rightful half-share of the Warwick inheritance, which all the while was fiercely opposed by Clarence. Edward decided in principle on a partition, but unbrotherly legal battles delayed Edward's Solomonic judgement until May 1474. To Richard went the rest of Warwick's lands in the North (and all those in Wales), whilst Clarence kept the Midlands core.

So far, so good, but when Clarence's wife died the following year, he planned to marry Mary, Duke Charles of Burgundy's immensely wealthy heiress. Edward forbade the match. Clarence, now made mad by sheer indignation, foolishly launched a revolt, only to find himself in a minority of one. By compounding the error to include casting aspersions on

Edward's legitimacy, Clarence exhausted his brother's patience. Livid, Edward ordered Clarence's execution for treason. Richard, it seems, interceded on his brother's behalf, but on 18 February 1478, Clarence, held prisoner in the Tower, was drowned in a butt of malmsey wine. It was a somewhat fitting, if perverse, fate; Clarence's favourite drink was malmsey wine.

Richard versus Northumberland

Richard energetically sought to build a stable and suitably majestic estate based on the rump of the Warwick inheritance. He obtained the lordships of Barnard Castle in County Durham, Scarborough and Richmond. Indeed, so 'Northern' was Richard that he disposed of his properties in Wales and the West Country for holdings such as Skipton-in-Craven and Helmsley, the forfeited properties of the Cliffords and the Scropes. In rapid order, numerous offices also came to him: the wardenship in 1470, the chief stewardship of the duchy of Lancaster in 1471, and the keepership of the forests and the stewardship of Ripon a year later. Over the next two years, Richard also became sheriff of Cumberland for life, constable of Bewcastle and justice of the peace in all the Northern counties. There was an element of magpieish hoarding in Richard's zealousness as, owing to the existing ancient networks of patronage and landholding, he was unable to become the majority landholder in any single shire.

Because Richard's lands and responsibilities were so diverse, and his assertion of his rights through the courts so blatant, he inevitably put noses out of joint. Heading the complainants was Northumberland, annoyed that Richard was not only accumulating a clutch of well-paid offices but also poaching men from his retinue, officials and household. Between 1471 and 1473, there was intense – if not aggressively tense – competition between the two nobles for good men. Richard, new to the North, needed baliffs, domestics, foresters, under-sheriffs, constables, stewards, soldiers and the like for his estates, apart from those he 'inherited' by marrying into the Nevilles. Small wonder that Percy, lacking Richard's resources, soon began to find recruitment difficult. Furthermore, during his father's attainder and imprisonment, the Percy affinity had largely evaporated, owing to lack of funds and the absence of an earl.[3] Even the faithful retainers from the 1440s and 1450s were getting too old for active service. Northumberland urgently needed competent younger men. From families who had served the Percys for several decades, he managed to attract back men like Christopher Curwen of

Workington and John Pennington of Muncaster in Cumbria, John Cartington and John Ilderton. But among men without these near-feudal attachments, the earl performed much less well. By 1473, he could compete with the duke only in Northumberland proper. Between 1471 and 1474, for instance, Richard newly employed twenty-eight retainers on his Middleham estate alone.

In May 1473, Northumberland raised Richard's encroachments with the royal council. Although only a newly restored earl, in those days Northumberland enjoyed quite a swing in London. In Michaelmas the year before, he fulfilled what must have been a long-term arrangement with the late earl of Pembroke, William Herbert, by marrying his daughter, Maud. Pembroke's son, now 2nd earl, had married the queen's sister, thereby improving Northumberland's links with the royal Woodvilles. A year later, Northumberland would be made Knight of the Garter, confirming Edward's benevolence towards him.

After Northumberland's protests, Edward promised to have a word with Richard, but to no effect. Verbal cautions could not prevent Richard from outbidding Percy in the job market. The result was a legal indenture, dated 28 July 1474, which essentially signed away the Percys' 'Kingship in the North' to Richard, now regarded as 'Lord of the North'. In it, Northumberland 'promises and grants unto the said duke to be his faithful servant ... to do service unto the said duke at all times lawful and convenient'. In return, Richard 'promises and grants the said earl to be his good and faithful lord at all times; and to sustain him in his right afore all other persons'. Moreover, in the 'anti-poaching' section, 'the said duke shall not accept nor retain into his service any servant or servants that was or any time since has been retained by the said earl of fee, clothing or promise.' In other words, Richard was prohibited from interfering or recruiting in the earl's own county of Northumberland or the East Riding, where he was also strong. Elsewhere, Northumberland had to accept subsidiary status and compete against Richard for men with no historical Percy connections. He rarely did so. He had become one of Richard's retainers – granted, his grandest retainer and one allowed enormous latitude – but a retainer nonetheless. But for Northumberland, signing the contract ensured him dominance on the eastern Border and in the far North without his going bankrupt.

The indenture wasn't an unfriendly or hostile settlement; in fact, Richard and Northumberland got on famously after it, having guaranteed their respective spheres of influence and delineated their borders. Indeed, about this time, Northumberland gave Richard – partly obsequiously, partly to show good faith – his remaining copy of Giles of Rome's masterpiece, *De Regimine Principum* [*The Guidance of Princes*], which his grandfather had commissioned in 1419 (see Chapter 14). Today, a near-illegible inscription, probably written by Percy, reads: 'Egidius de Regimine Liber illustrissimus Principus Ducis Gloucestr' ('The most illustrious book of the prince, the duke of Gloucester').[4]

Relations in the years following the indenture were remarkably tranquil. Both men scrupulously observed the letter and spirit of the contract, giving and taking as required, and often co-operated on an official basis. On a broader level, however, the voluntary suborning of Northumberland was the highest-profile case in Richard's creeping takeover of the North. By the end of the 1470s, all the fine Northern names – like the earl of Westmorland, and Lords Greystoke, Scrope of Masham and Dacre of Gilsland – were members of the duke's retinue.[5] He would need them all for the imminent war with Scotland.

Scotland Again

Following the Anglo-Scottish truce of 1474 (optimistically scheduled to last until 1519), the Border had been quiet. In England, peace with Scotland had been welcomed, mainly because it meant everyone could fight France. Scotland, however, was bitterly divided. North of the Forth, Scots nobles were either too busy feuding to mind what James III did or, like the earls of Crawford and Argyll, they supported the treaty wholeheartedly. Merchants and traders, wherever they were, favoured peace over war for obvious reasons. But in the south, which was dominated by James's brother, Alexander, duke of Albany, earl of March and warden of the Marches, a rabid Scottish patriotism engendered opposition to the marriage proposal. Revealingly, 'Blind Harry's' epic/heroic poem *The [William] Wallace* was composed at this time; indeed, its violently anti-English opening lines attacked the treaty.[6]

By 1479, Alexander's Border raids were spitefully breaking the truce and he was repeatedly sabotaging the scheduled Truce Days held by the various wardens to sort out grievances.[7] James, to maintain his friendly and profitable relationship with an annoyed Edward, needed to demonstrate, by restraining the war party, that he did intend to marry Prince James to Edward's daughter, Cecily, as per the 1474 treaty. Accordingly, Albany was arrested and charged with treason. Edward had religiously paid annual advance instalments of Cecily's dowry to the Scots; six years later, he was wondering whether he would see a return on his money.

These diplomatic tiffs would have passed were it not for Louis XI's handiwork. In 1477, Duke Charles of Burgundy had died in battle at Nancy, leaving his daughter Mary as heir. Louis then invaded Burgundy, to extinguish its independence once and for all. Edward was in a quandary; since the Treaty of Picquigny in 1475, relations between England and France had been amiable, and he still received a substantial pension from Louis. But Burgundy's extinction meant French control over the entire North Sea coast, so endangering Calais and England. How far could he trust Louis's endless protestations of eternal Anglo-French amity? As a test, Edward reiterated his desire to wed his thirteen-year-old daughter, Elizabeth, to the eight-year-old dauphin, but Louis prevaricated. As his own motives were often so suspect, Louis naturally suspected those of others. When Mary of Burgundy married Maximilian of Austria, son of the Habsburg Emperor Frederick III, in August 1477, Louis felt threatened from the east, and believed Edward really intended to marry Elizabeth to one of the Emperor's family, thereby indirectly promoting an Anglo-Burgundian alliance against France. To divert Edward's attention, Louis employed the trusty Scottish tool to stir up trouble. In 1479, a Scottish professor at the Sorbonne, John Ireland, was sent to persuade James to reconcile himself with Albany and make war on England – with full French backing. Accordingly, a Scottish embassy under the earl of Buchan was despatched to France to sound out Louis's terms, which may have included marrying James's sister, Margaret, to the dauphin.

Edward soon had wind of this potential Auld Alliance. In early 1480, advised by Richard, he sent James a harsh ultimatum to bring him to his senses before the war party launched an invasion across the Border. He publicly accused James of illegally possessing Berwick, Roxburgh and other English outposts, refusing to perform homage to his feudal over-lord 'as he oweth to doo and as his progenitours have doon in tyme passed' (the paramountcy issue always set the Scots on the defensive) and allowing his subjects to wreak havoc on the Border. Having poured out money on Cecily's prospective Scottish marriage, Edward, wanted satis-faction, and the restoration of his disinherited colleague, the earl of Douglas. Privately, however, he really only had two objectives; he secret-ly confided to James that if Prince James were handed over to the earl of Northumberland by 1 May 1480 *and* ceded Berwick to its proper owners, England would not declare war.

Neither happened. Edward procrastinated past the deadline until 12 May, when Richard, itching to fight the Scots, persuaded him to place the North on a war footing. He was also appointed 'Lieutenant-General of the North', giving him authority over the wardens allowing him to summon the Northern levies. Crucially, although England and Scotland were at war, Edward held back from invading Scotland and confined Richard to defending the Border and launching raids. While Richard headed north, the earl of Angus – a stalwart ally of Albany – tore across the Border and, to Northumberland's fury, spent three days ravaging the countryside and burning Bamburgh. In early September, to avenge the insult in kind, Richard directed Northumberland and a few others to mount a raid. A letter from Northumberland accordingly summoning his retainers, dated 7 September, has survived:

> Right beloved friend [Robert Plumpton], I greet you well. And whereas the Scotts in great number [have] entred into Northumberland, whose malice, with Gods helpe, I entend to resist; therfore on the king owr soveraigne lords behalfe, I charg you, and also on myne as wardeyn, [that] ye [with] all such personnes as ye may make in there most defensible array, be with me at Topcliff uppon Munday by viii a clocke, as my trust is in you, [signed] Hen: Northumberland.[8]

The raid went ahead, with Richard in charge, and evidently served its purpose. Minor scuffles apart, there were no more Scottish incursions that year. James half-heartedly attempted to persuade Edward to settle the outstanding grievances, but Richard, now effectively in charge of England's war effort, rejected his entreaties. Besides, Edward had already pledged to lead a true assault against Scotland in the summer of 1481 and preparations were well under way. That winter, Richard repaired the walls of Carlisle, stationed men in garrisons along the Border and ordered Northumberland to conduct a military census to determine the availability of soldiers. And it was Richard who travelled down to London to brief Edward on *his* war plan.

Edward was not at all keen. He was accustomed to the brief, one-battle-decides-all warfare of the Wars of the Roses, not the rigorous, extended and expensive campaigning that characterised Anglo-Scottish fighting, let alone the violent subjugation of the populace that a successful conquest demanded. Despite the brutal folk-memory of the Wars of the Roses, for instance, between 1450 and 1485 the sum total of campaigning (including fighting, marching and waiting) was sixty-one weeks, with few battles lasting longer than eight hours. In contrast to the savagery visited upon civilians in Continental wars, for about 97 per cent of the time 95 per cent of the English population lived peacefully.[9]

Understandably, then, the terrible 1481 harvest and the country's financial difficulties which resulted were more important to Edward than Scottish affairs. Furthermore, Continental developments strongly militated against his being isolated for months at a time in Scotland. Indeed, much to Louis's relief, Edward reconfirmed the Anglo-French treaty at Nottingham, provided that Princess Elizabeth's marriage to the dauphin would not be delayed. Tying his hands, as well, was his pension of £10,000 a year, which Edward gravely needed in order to avoid having to ask the Commons to levy taxes. Now getting corpulent and lecherous – tired of Elizabeth Woodville, he called his three current mistresses 'the merriest, the wiliest and holiest harlots in the realm' – Edward ignored appeals for help from Maximilian of Burgundy, who was losing against French forces. Instead, he left the decision to Louis's Maker: the king, after two attacks of apoplexy, was liable to die any moment. His removal, Edward calculated, would end the war with Burgundy. For his part, having received what he wanted from Edward, Louis ignored James's pleas for aid. As the March 1482 Parliament forlornly noted, James had 'divers tymes writtin to the King of France... and gottin nane answer'. The Scots, useful as leverage, could now be put aside. So much for the Auld Alliance.

Thus, despite Richard's tireless organisation, he and Northumberland had to wait for Edward to appear throughout the summer. Finally, in October Richard impatiently rode to Nottingham (as far north as Edward had reached) to complain that the fine weather would soon be over. Infuriatingly, Edward promised to lead the invasion *next* year.

That wasn't good enough for Richard and Northumberland, who together in late October doggedly initiated a siege of Berwick, reinforced by James with an extra 500 men and new artillery. After a few months, pressured by a counter-attack into Northumberland, the English went home and waited for better weather.

In the meantime, his health failing, Edward pursued a subtler approach, one in which the Scots themselves would bring Border peace. In April 1482, he attracted the rogue Albany, then sheltering in France, to England by promising him a Crown. Intrigued, the anti-English Albany met Edward and a rather surprised Richard at Fotheringhay Castle where, on 11 June, Edward unofficially recognised Albany as 'Alexander King of Scotland by the gyfte of the King of England' and asked Richard to help put him on the throne. If successful, 'Alexander R.', as he styled himself, would pay homage to his liege lord, break with France, return Berwick and surrender large areas of south-western Scotland. Neither Richard nor Edward had high hopes for the pretender's chances, but Gloucester travelled north in Albany's cheerful company, knowing that the army he was assembling would be the real arbiter of success.

Not for at least eighty years had the English, through the combined efforts of Richard's Northern lieutenants, amassed so vast an invasion force, possibly numbering up to 20,000 men. Nevertheless, it had one fatal weakness: there was only enough money for, at most, four weeks and no one remembered that most previous campaigns had lasted for several months. Near the end of July, Richard's army crossed the Border at speed – unsurprising, given his tight schedule – and, bypassing Berwick, headed for Edinburgh. James, of course, had frantically mustered his own army at Lauder, but as the English approached, he was arrested by his leading magnates and taken to Edinburgh on 22 July.

Why James was seized is not clear. It may have been connected with his debasement of coin to pay for the war, which antagonised merchants, commoners and nobles alike, and his unpopularity with his half-uncles and much of the assembled nobility. As a result, Richard, Northumberland and Albany entered Edinburgh unopposed, but had to leave almost immediately. The one-month deadline precluded besieging Edinburgh Castle, and tarrying much longer would make storming Berwick impossible. Before they left, the city promised to refund everything Edward had paid towards Cecily's dowry if the marriage did not take place. Honour satisfied, the English hurried to Berwick, which was governed by Lord Gray, an acolyte of Albany's who opened the gates before a shot was fired. (Owing to his propensity to resemble Clarence in a kilt, Albany rebelled in April 1483, allowed an English garrison into his castle in Dunbar and fled to England, where he took up with his fellow exile, Douglas.)

The 1482 campaign was a mitigated success. The Albany coup had failed, but Berwick had fallen (and it would never again be Scottish) and hardly any lives had been lost. Edward, while pleased, was under-impressed: the expedition had spent nearly £100,000 recovering precisely one town and castle. It would have been cheaper to destroy Berwick with artillery and rebuild it in marble.

Henceforth, Edward felt, Richard could bear the burden of indulging his fancy in Scottish affairs himself. Thus, partly as reward and partly as a housewarming gift, in January/February 1483 Edward presented his brother with a private Northern and Border empire – a move cheered by the Commons, who desperately wanted something to cheer following the news after Christmas of Maximilian and Louis's agreement in the Treaty of Arras. Maximilian and Mary's daughter, Margaret, was to marry the dauphin, her dowry being the counties of Artois and Burgundy; Maximilian also withdrew support for English pretensions on the Continent. This must have shaken Edward: his daughter had been humiliatingly spurned, his pension would cease, Burgundy was finished and France ruled supreme. The entire structure of Edwardian diplomacy had just, instantly, collapsed.

Thus, when Parliament disconsolately met on 20 January, it lavished extravagant praise on the great captains – Northumberland was singled out for thanks – of the glorious patriotic war against Scotland. For Richard, the rewards were immense. He was permanently granted the hereditary wardenship of the West March, and the king essentially surrendered all control over him – even of his wartime salary of £1000, which Richard would henceforth raise himself. Throughout Cumberland, the sovereign's customary fees, profits, forfeits, wreck of sea, the right to appoint sheriffs and suchlike were to be diverted to Richard. Most spectacularly, any *Scottish* lands Richard 'intendeth, and with God's grace is like, to get and subdue hereafter' would become his possessions, and Richard was empowered to make Scots living within his empire 'denizens' of England. Although Richard owed the English king ultimate obedience, he had received a palatinate – unlike anything since the days of the Normans – comprising the North-West and whatever parts of Scotland he could conquer. Blessed with regal powers and a hereditary appanage, Richard of Gloucester had truly become King in the North.[10]

Not for long. On 9 April 1483, Edward IV breathed his last, having caught a bad cold while boating. He was only forty-one. (His nemesis, Louis XI, would follow him a few months later.) In a sense, Edward's death was fortunate, as a historian recently pointed out:

> What would have happened – in the *Scottish* context – if Edward IV had survived for several more years? Letting Richard fight his own Scottish war may have made sense in 1482–3 but, judging by past Anglo-Scottish history, it seems safe to conclude that eventually he would have got bogged down, that his own resources would have proved inadequate, and that he would have to have sought help from his brother. So, ultimately, Edward IV would have been sucked into unwinnable and fiscally horrifying Scottish warfare – with potentially disastrous political consequences in England. In his Scottish ambitions of 1482–3, Richard, it would appear, was proposing to bite off more than he could chew.[11]

CHAPTER TWENTY ONE

The Rise and Fall of the North

Born in 1470, Edward V was the uncrowned king of England the moment his father died late at night on 9 April 1483. The next day, a royal messenger sped north to York, five days' hard ride from London, to inform the duke of Gloucester of his brother's death. Meanwhile, the council in London debated the shape of the government during Edward's long minority. The queen's Woodville faction urged a quick coronation on Sunday, 4 May, after which they would surround the young king. Richard, however, was kept abreast of developments thanks to Lord Hastings, a courtier who loathed the Woodvilles, and Henry Stafford, the second duke of Buckingham (and grandson of the Buckingham killed at the battle of Northampton in 1460), who, having been politically obliged to marry one of the queen's ghastly sisters and then excluded from court life, loathed them still more (he thought the Woodvilles were somewhat below-stairs). Together, the three men formed a compact to make Richard the Protector of the Realm.

On 24 April, Edward V and his protective maternal uncle, Earl Rivers, left Ludlow for London. On the way, Richard and Buckingham arranged to meet them on 30 April at Stony Stratford – near the Woodvilles' estate – in Northamptonshire, where, after a convivial evening, Rivers retired rather the worse for wear. The next morning, Richard and Buckingham arrested the surprised Rivers, the king's half-brother Richard Grey and Thomas Vaughn, the chamberlain. To the confused king, Richard showed a 'mournful countenance' and warned of Woodvillian conspiracies to assassinate him before his coronation. The prisoners were despatched to Richard's castles at Middleham and Sheriff Hutton in Yorkshire.

At this point, Richard treated Edward with every respect and soon assured worried Londoners that his palace coup had 'saved' the king from harm. The queen meanwhile sought sanctuary in Westminster with her youngest son, Richard duke of York, and her brother, Lionel Woodville, bishop of Salisbury. The scheduled coronation date passed as the council was bitterly divided over Richard's assertions of sinister Woodvillian plots to ambush Edward. They requested the king be lodged in the Tower of London, as was traditional, pending settlement of the protectorship and, of course, the new date of the coronation. Only between 8 and 13 May did the council finally recognise Richard as Protector after the coronation, which was now set for late June.

Armed with official authority, Richard immediately reconstituted the government by issuing orders under his own signet, slotting his adherents into key positions and rounding up the Woodvilles, who were simultaneously stripped of their offices and grants. For example, Lord Howard became chief steward of the duchy of Lancaster;[1] the odious William Catesby was appointed chancellor of the earldom of March. Orders went out to arrest Sir Edward Woodville, then commanding a fleet at sea, and the marquess of Dorset, the queen's eldest son by her first marriage. However, both were able to flee abroad. On 15 May, Buckingham received virtual viceregal power in Wales and the Marches. As for Percy, still in the North, Richard ensured that 'Edward V' rapidly made two indentures with him: the first, confirming his wardenship of the Marches for five months; and the second, for the captaincy of Berwick until mid-October.

Ominously, after 8 June, entries in the register of grants under the name of 'Edward V' cease.

Two days later, claiming the queen was threatening to murder him and seize the North, Richard sent a message to York, requesting his lieutenants to assemble as many mounted retainers and foot soldiers as possible at Pontefract by 18 June, to march to London under Northumberland. On 13 June, Richard heard that Lord Hastings, one of the original conspirators, had quietly expressed reservations to the archbishop of York, the bishop of Ely and Edward V's private secretary, about the means and methods of Richard's coup. Before a council meeting in the Tower with Richard, Hastings was taken outside and beheaded for 'treason' without warning, let alone a trial. The three men in whom he had confided were arrested and imprisoned.

By this time Northumberland had arrived in York, whose councillors readied 200 men to accompany him to Pontefract. Back in London, Richard's soldiers broke into Westminster and tore the duke of York from sanctuary with the queen to join his brother in the Tower.

On 22 June, the Sunday scheduled for the coronation, Ralph Shaw, a preacher who seems to have been the mayor of London's brother, gave a sermon at St Paul's Cross, arguing that Richard was the only legitimate claimant to the throne since the sons of Edward IV were bastards. Two days later, Buckingham, addressing the mayor and aldermen of London in the Guildhall, revealed a marriage pre-contract between Edward IV and a woman called Lady Eleanor Butler (who had died in 1468), which took place before his wedding to Elizabeth Woodville. Theologically, Richard was plausibly in the right: under canon law, any children conceived before or after Eleanor's death, even if Elizabeth had remained ignorant of the pre-contract, were illegitimate. Even so, it could equally by argued that Lady Butler's death dissolved the pre-contract and therefore Edward V and his brother, both born after 1468, were legitimate. Legally, moreover, such an issue would have to be tried in an ecclesiastical court, which had jurisdiction over matrimonial cases, not before such a secular gathering. And finally, in any case, the cleansing ritual of coronation could erase illegitimacy.[2] But where had this damning knowledge come from? One Bishop Robert Stillington had witnessed this original pre-contract with Edward's then paramour (apparently, the 'pre-contract' ruse succeeded and he had seduced her) and he had kept it hidden for twenty years; in June he had approached Richard with this bombshell. By now, Richard was well on his way to usurping the throne – the pre-contract simply lent a patina of credibility and legality to his *coup d'état*. The ruthlessness of Richard's actions against a boy who was apparently in his trust as Protector and paternal uncle and who was too young to have politically upset anybody is remarkable: '[Edward] could not be accused of tyranny, like Richard II, or gross incompetence, like Henry VI. He had begun to reign, but he had not yet ruled. The usurpation of 1483 was of a fundamentally different order to those of 1399, 1461, or even 1485. Those, whether justifiable or not, were acts of the last resort. In 1483, uniquely, deposition was used as a weapon of first resort.'[3]

The great question is: when did Richard actually decide to steal the throne? Had he hankered for the prize since 1471? It is unlikely. Over the next decade, believing the succession was already determined, he built up his Northern kingdom instead of staying in London to combat the Woodvilles. No, while Richard may have daydreamt occasionally about how nice being king would be, the coup at Stony Stratford was definitely cooked up *after* Edward IV died. Perhaps something Rivers carelessly said during that 'convivial evening' alerted Richard that he was endangered by the Woodville clique after the coronation. Even then, did he imagine the nobility and Commons would readily accept him after ousting the young king? Again, that is unlikely, but anti-Woodville sentiment ran high, and his 'self-defensive' arrests of Rivers and his associates would find widespread sympathy. Sensibly, however, he may have allowed himself room to retreat if things did not pan out, judging by his respectful treatment of Edward V. In London itself, the Woodville purge and his confirmation as Protector (after some turf-battles in the council) proved surprisingly easy. Perhaps it was then that Richard took the irrevocable step of grasping the Crown. So far, opposition had been almost non-existent; once the plan was set into motion, any isolated opposition that did, or was suspected to, exist (like that of Hastings) had to be eliminated immediately before it could coalesce into a coherent force. Although he must have carried a general 'Things to Do' list in his head, Richard proved readily adaptable to changing circumstances and able to exploit unforeseen 'accidents', such as Bishop Stillington's revelation. That quality, such as it was, made Richard of Gloucester truly dangerous.

And what of Northumberland? Percy did not take risks, or even the initiative, without orders from above. As Richard's willing tool, he must have been privy to his ruminations after the death of Edward IV. Early on, even while setting off for Stony Stratford, Richard might have suspected trouble with the Woodvilles and requested that Northumberland be prepared to come to his aid. As the usurpation proceeded, letters would have informed Northumberland about developments in London, with additional flourishes on Richard's brave fight against murderous Woodville conspiracies. Gradually, Northumberland, without knowing all the details, would have become a bona fide member of Richard's plot. (One reason why so much speculation surrounds Richard's motives is precisely that he never put details in writing). Partial proof of this slow immersion is Northumberland's unquestioning supervision of the execution of Rivers, Grey and Vaughn at Pontefract on 25 June. This Percy is hardly likely to have taken the momentous step of murdering the queen's relatives without Richard's prior authority.

Not wholly by coincidence, the next day Richard was enthroned in the marble chair of the Court of King's Bench in Westminster Hall – on which his grandfather had once impetuously placed his hand – and took possession of the royal estate. No one present raised any complaints.

After the executions at Pontefract, Northumberland brought his force of Northerners – some say 4000-strong, but there were undoubtedly far fewer than that – to London for the coronation proper on 6 July. If required, Richard could use them to fend off enemies who might disturb his rule. Believing that Northerners were an alien and backward species, the Londoners proclaimed a ten o'clock curfew and forbade the bearing of arms in the City. In the event, despite some jostling, the Northerners remained peaceful. Indeed, some citizens made nasty jibes about their old-fashioned armour and rusty weapons.

The coronation passed off spectacularly. Granted twelve and a half yards of lustrous scarlet cloth for his gown, Northumberland headed the list of earls and was placed just below the three dukes attending: Norfolk (the newly raised Lord Howard), Suffolk and Buckingham.[4] He bore the sword Curtana before the king.[5] From inglorious attainder, the Percys had again risen to become the highest-ranking earls in England.

No sooner was he king than Richard III toured his realm, presenting this fait accompli to the people. In September, however, a series of small rebellions throughout Southern England broke out, aimed at restoring Edward V – still held in the Tower – to the throne. These involved Margaret Beaufort, countess of Richmond and the mother of Henry Tudor (whom we shall presently meet), and the former queen's brothers, Dorset and the bishop of Salisbury, who had escaped into hiding. Their weirdest convert was Buckingham, whose defection from Richard has never been explained. Some think the weak-minded Buckingham was influenced by his own prisoner, the evidently persuasive Bishop Morton of Ely, or even by some of the late Hastings' retainers, who told him what *really* happened the day he was murdered. Richard robustly believed Buckingham was 'the most untrue creature living'. Together, nonetheless, the isolated revolts in Kent, Wiltshire, Berkshire and Devonshire were coalescing into a pro-Tudor, anti-Richard mutiny.

What had happened to the campaign to put Edward V on the throne? By the late summer, the rebels knew that the two 'Little Princes in the Tower' were dead, most likely by order of Richard soon after the coronation. Indeed, although a 'Ricardian' industry has recently evolved, seeking to exonerate Richard for the crime, from a strictly political-dynastic perspective it would have been remiss of Richard *not* to have had them killed. In charge of the Tower that night in 1471 when Henry VI was murdered, he had matured during the Wars of the Roses – an era dominated by a profusion of rival claimants to the throne – and had seen what had happened to his father and brothers. In a few years, no doubt, an adult Edward V would have found powerful supporters and violently pressed his claim. Perhaps even before then; after all, the Percys had caused Henry IV, another usurper, no end of trouble by supporting the young earl of March less than a century before. If Richard lost the ensuing round, he would lose his head. Nevertheless, Richard's crime crossed moral boundaries, and he continues to be reviled for it.[6]

With the help of Northumberland, Norfolk and Lord Stanley – scion of the most powerful family in Lancashire, who had, like Northumberland, clashed with Richard in the early 1470s over poaching though open resentment died away when the duke backed off – Richard soon had a mostly Northern army in the field and the rebellion collapsed before any battle.[7] The only ranking casualty was Buckingham, who was caught and executed. Most of the leading rebels, however, escaped to Flanders or Brittany with their lives, if not their livelihoods – in Richard's only Parliament, 100 men were attainted (compared to 140 during the whole of Edward IV's troubled era).

In the rebellion's aftermath, and shaken by Buckingham's treachery,

Richard became neurotically insecure about conspiratorial Southerners. Believing that only Northerners were trustworthy, Richard initiated a greatly resented 'colonisation' of the South; dozens of Northern knights and squires were appointed as commissioners, justices of the peace, stewards of confiscated estates, sheriffs, constables and escheators throughout the South. According to the (Southern) Croyland chronicler, writing after the mass attainders, 'What immense estates and patrimonies were collected into this king's treasury in consequence of this measure! All of which he distributed among his northern adherents, whom he planted in every spot throughout his dominions, to the disgrace and lasting and loudly expressed sorrow of all the people in the south.' Some of these Northerners earned the Ricardian regime an unenviable reputation. Sir Ralph Ashton of Redesdale, an adherent from Richard's Northern days, was made vice-constable of England in October 1483 with special instructions to try the survivors of Buckingham's rebellion. Feared as the 'Black Knight', owing to his dyed armour, he possessed a predilection for rolling recalcitrant prisoners down hills in barrels internally studded with spikes. Most Northerners, of course, were perfectly harmless bureaucrats, but Southern resentment was boiling volcanically upwards.[8]

As for Northumberland, he was promoted to the great chamberlainship of England on 30 November, and given the feel-good title of 'Warden-General' of the East March – both empty titles, given Richard's centralising instincts. Despite being lauded and fêted by Richard, Northumberland was sidelined in the North by the king, because Richard, as Lord of the North, retained his keen interest in Northern affairs but didn't delegate his powers to his deputy. Instead, he established a council in York to represent him. In practice, many disputes formerly arbitrated by Northumberland under March law and Northern customs were diverted to the council. For the king, moreover, the 1474 indenture was moot, since the monarch could choose whichever retainers he wanted. During the 'colonisation' many of Percy's men received grants from Richard and headed south. It's hard to tell how bruised and insulted Northumberland felt. He may have grumbled, rather than been overly perturbed. Unlike his predecessors, he wasn't markedly ambitious and generally preferred to follow his superiors' orders. He was still lord of his domain in Northumberland, still warden, still repairing his finances and, most importantly, he still enjoyed unrestricted access to the king, if he needed it.[9]

One Northerner, however, Richard could not be quite sure about – Lord Stanley. Notwithstanding Stanley's exemplary loyalty during Buckingham's rebellion, his wife was the formidable Lady Margaret

Beaufort, who had helped instigate and organise it. She was the only daughter of Margaret Beauchamp and John, duke of Somerset – John of Gaunt's grandson by Katherine Swynford and elder brother of the Lancastrian Somerset, Edmund, killed alongside Northumberland at St Albans in 1455. Her father died within a year of her birth in 1443, leaving her a wealthy heiress. This great-great-granddaughter of Edward III married Edmund Tudor, the young, newly minted earl of Richmond. Tudor was the eldest son of Owain ap Meredith ap Tydier (Anglicised into Owen Tudor), who had married Henry V's French widow, Catherine of Valois. Edmund died in his twenties, of natural causes, in November 1456, leaving a pregnant Margaret, going on 14, to give birth to Henry Tudor three months later on 28 January 1457 in wintry Pembroke Castle. About a year later, Margaret married again, this time to Henry Stafford, a younger son of the first duke of Buckingham (and kinsman to Richard's future accomplice, the second duke). But he died in October 1471, and Margaret, now twice a teenaged widow, married Thomas Lord Stanley, one of Edward IV's favourites, two years later.

Young Henry Tudor had joined Henry Percy in being looked after by William Herbert (soon earl of Pembroke), though Northumberland, being eight years older, considered Tudor something of an irritating younger sibling. All things considered, Margaret was a pukka Lancastrian, but remained in England after the now-attainted Jasper Tudor (the boy's uncle) took Henry into exile after the Barnet and Tewkesbury campaigns. Her marriage to Stanley allowed Margaret to cultivate connections with the new Yorkist regime in order to bring her son home with some sort of inheritance.

Richard III's accession and the princes' murder put Margaret in a bind. Thanks to Stanley's loyalty, Richard had once looked likely to reinstate Henry Tudor, but then she fell in with the Woodvilles and Buckingham, possibly because she was horrified by Richard's barbaric treatment of his nephews. After the rebellion, Richard would have found it difficult to impose attainder, imprisonment or execution on her, 'rememberying the good and feithfull service that Thomas Lord Stanley hath doon … and for his sake'. Instead, she was stripped of her right to all titles and estates, including those destined for Henry Tudor on her death. Richard also ordered Stanley to keep her in 'some secret place' without her servants.[10] Whilst Stanley ostensibly claimed ignorance of his wife's political infidelities because they kept separate households, he was angered at Margaret's forfeiture – by Richard's standards, a fairly lenient punishment. By late 1484, both Stanleys were in treasonous contact with Henry Tudor.

Until the early summer of 1483, we know hardly anything of Henry's intentions, although A.L Rowse has a nice description of his character:

Henry was 'secretive and shrewd, with none of the extrovert Yorkist overconfidence in life, the bonhomie of Edward IV, the blunt impulsiveness of Edward's father, Richard of York. Henry, above all things, kept his own counsel, a rather silent man, an introvert with a far-seeing look in [his] luminous, intelligent, but deep-sunken eyes ... He was made to be a founder of a dynasty.'[11]

It did not seem so in 1483–4. In somewhat straitened exile in Brittany, governed by Duke Francis II, Henry was kept abreast of English politics by his mother and uncle, Jasper Tudor. Soon after Richard's usurpation, the fugitive Sir Edward Woodville, commanding the remnants of his fleet, joined him. Following Buckingham's abortive rebellion, Brittany became a bolthole for the attainted participants, such as Dorset, and a knightly phalanx of Edward IV's former courtiers. To them, Henry was the perfect rival to Richard III; through his mother, he was related to John of Gaunt and the Somersets, those martyrs against Yorkism; through his grandmother, to the martial and heroic Henry V. Moreover, his long absence abroad and isolation from English politics meant Henry could not easily be categorised as either Lancastrian or Yorkist. This ambiguity quickly made him a magnet for disaffected Yorkists, romantic Lancastrians and Woodville adherents (and even Woodvilles themselves), united by their disgust for Ricardian rule. Gratifyingly, then, on Christmas Day 1483 in Rennes Cathedral Henry publicly pledged to marry Edward IV's eldest daughter, the eighteen-year-old, cherubic-faced, slightly tubby Elizabeth of York. To those present, this union would merge – albeit indirectly – the warring houses of Lancaster and York.

Richard was unaware of this coalescence of aggrieved elements. The English navy attacked Breton shipping in the Channel during the winter of 1483–4 to pressure Francis into expelling Henry's court-in-exile. Francis could not shelter Henry should Richard turn truly hostile; his only child was a daughter, Anne of Brittany, and without English support after his death, France would inevitably seek to acquire Brittany. A temporary respite came during the regency of Louis XI's heir, the thirteen-year-old Charles VIII. Without the wily Louis XI at the helm, Francis believed, France might retract her fangs. By June 1484, however, it was clear that the regency council would not alter France's traditional policy and Francis was obliged to attempt Henry's arrest and hold him ready for Richard. Henry, miraculously, heard a whiff of the plan, escaped into France and was welcomed into the French court, which was always aware of the value of a spare pretender to keep the English off balance. If necessary, France could back a Henrician invasion to occupy Richard while Brittany was taken. For the sake of legitimacy, Henry's claim to be the rightful king of England was keenly upheld, particularly after Richard's only son died in April 1484, followed by his queen in March 1485. Unable to marry any of Edward IV's children, especially Elizabeth, in order to outbid Henry's claim since he had declared his own nieces and nephews illegitimate, Richard was in a dynastic impasse by the spring of 1485.

Blocked from out-marrying Henry, a cornered Richard determined to outfight him when the time came. It did on 7 August 1485, when Henry, with about 400 exiled English followers and another 3500 recently recruited Normans, stepped ashore at Milford Haven. The king determined to meet the pretender in battle and slay him. Over the coming weeks, Henry met no resistance (but no real enthusiasm either), as he marched through North and South Wales and thence into the Midlands on his way to Nottingham. Since the 1470s geography had taught that the Crown fell to those victorious in a battle in the Midlands, where the four corners of the kingdom converged. Along the way, he received Lord Stanley's quiet encouragement; Stanley had finally decided to throw in his lot against Richard, although he disguised this from the king, who was already suspicious about where his loyalties lay.

In the meantime, Richard assembled his forces. The duke of Norfolk, with every available able-bodied man, was already making for Nottingham, the royalist mustering-point, before heading for Leicester and Coventry. Northumberland has often been accused of 'gross dereliction' of duty, or at the very least of incompetence, for being slow to summon the Northern levies. Apparently, only when the loyal citizens of York asked on 16 August how they could supplement Richard's military contingents was the earl embarrassed into belated action. The delay could, admittedly, be deemed incompetent or a dereliction of duty, but two other considerations should be factored into any judgement.

First, the time delay and the uncertainty of communications: the news of Henry's landing took four days to reach the king himself – and he was based in Nottingham. Percy, in comparison, was in the deep North, many miles from York, which heard the report only a few days after Richard and only then thanks to good roads. The 'pot luck' aspect of medieval communications additionally means that Percy might have been aware of York's request before he had even heard of Henry's landing. For instance, before he left France Henry had sent letters requesting support from various worthies, including Northumberland, on several occasions. Yet, the earl never saw the letters, as no messenger was able to find him. If he were patrolling the Border, rather than staying at Alnwick, he was effectively incommunicado for months at a time.

Second, Percy was simultaneously coping with a personal tragedy: his wife's death, around 27 July. Organising her funeral arrangements and being expected to raise the levies at short notice would, understandably, have hampered both tasks. In the event, Northumberland appeared more or less on time in the Midlands with a Northern contingent drawn mostly from his fiefdom. Taken together, one chronicler observed, the royal host was the greatest army ever mustered on behalf of one man.

By now, Richard had already spied out the land and determined where to intercept Henry.

> The green, undulating countryside around Bosworth, radiant in summer but bleakly windswept in winter, was scarred by a series of broad thoroughfares ... A league to the south of the battlefield ran the ancient highway known as Watling Street, which linked London with north Wales, and a little to the east was another old road, Fosse Way, which stretched from the southern coast to the north midlands. Along such thoroughfares armies had moved from Roman times ... this part of Leicestershire was no backwater, but a place to feel the pulse of the nation.[12]

Despite the battle of Bosworth's mythical place in English history, supposedly heralding the transition from the Middle Ages to the modern world, very little documentation is available. We are not even quite sure of its exact location.[13] Its participants, while obviously unaware that the Middle Ages were about to 'end', nevertheless recognised something definitive was afoot. Never before had a king and a pretender faced each other in the field, so lending an almost divine finality to the showdown. At the end of the day, England's true king must indisputably be either Richard III or Henry VII.

On the morning of 22 August, the royal army of between 10,000 and 15,000 men deployed atop a hill too cramped for it and divided into the usual three battles: the vanguard in the west under the command of Norfolk, the main body under Richard in the centre and, in the east, the rearguard of Northumberland's contingent.[14] Henry, in contrast, may have only mustered 5000 soldiers, but his force was more mobile. It was divided into two battles. The bulk, including its archers, was given to the earl of Oxford; following him were Henry's small company of well-trained fellow exiles and an elite corps of guardsmen. Behind them, overlooking the field, were Lord Stanley and his 5000 troops whom Henry was desperately counting on – but Stanley remained aloof, remarking simply that he would commit his men at an opportune moment; the wily peer would not burn his Ricardian bridges just yet.

Below the plateau on Ambien Hill, by leaning forward on his horse and straining his head to the right, Richard could see the rebels forming in the south-west, where the wind and sun were behind them. He and Norfolk accordingly strengthened the flanking vanguard, since it was self-evident where Henry would attack. Had they allowed Henry to waste his men's lives on an uphill assault against superior numbers, the battle would have turned out quite differently. As it was, however, Richard and Norfolk decided to take the initiative, charge down the steep hill and smash straight into Oxford's line. As the frontmen rushed forward pell-mell, Oxford shouted that no man should drift more than ten feet from his nearest standard and ordered his adroit brigades to form dense wedges, prickling with their poleaxes' sharp points. In surprise, the royal-ists shied away and lost momentum, whereupon Henry's cavalry wings under Sir John Savage and Gilbert Talbot hacked into them, causing heavy losses and killing Norfolk.

Oxford's stout defence was impressive, but Richard's main army remained untouched on top of the hill. Gathering his household knights and leading retainers around him, Richard was determined to bring the battle directly to his foe, who stood amid a small entourage. In full armour, with colourful banners unfurled, the knightly paladins charged and accelerated down the hill. A cavalry assault so early in the battle was rarity enough; a cavalry assault of elite royal knights commanded by a king (Richard wore the helmet girt by a golden crown) must have pre-sented a stunning, and unique, image. Upon colliding with Henry's troops, Richard skewered the pretender's standard-bearer and pressed inexorably forward, his retinue surrounding him. Henry was his objec-tive, but the charge's initial momentum soon dissipated amid the crowd, and the royalists were cut down or dragged from their horses one by one. The little knot of men around Richard was slowly floating away from Henry. A few fields away, Richard could see Northumberland's battle standing idle and he cried out for reinforcements, reinforcements that if delivered would have overpowered Henry's personal force and won the day. None came. Northumberland stayed on the hill. According to the Crowland Chronicler, 'in the place where the earl of Northumberland stood with a fairly large and well-equipped force, there was no contest against the enemy and no blows were given or received in battle'.[15]

Down below, Sir William Stanley – Lord Stanley's younger brother and the chamberlain of North Wales – agreed with his sibling that the time was 'opportune' for intervention and brought 3000 men into the fray – on Henry's side. There was no escape – the king's horse was taken, possibly after getting stuck in a nearby mire – for the last Plantagenet, who berated the traitors and turncoats on the hill. Even the favoured his-torians of Henry VII's time respected Richard's courage and valiant doggedness after his retainers had all been killed.

Although Shakespeare presented Henry dramatically delivering the fatal blow to Richard, in fact it was probably a humble Welsh footman in Stanley's company who killed the staggering king with a halberd.

> To kill God's anointed took a special kind of resolve, which transcended normal thresholds of human decency. The tyrant must be unkinged by desecration, and all the chroniclers testify to the indignities to which his corpse was subjected. Probably even before Henry Tudor and his companions forced a path through to the site of the last stand, there was no longer any trace of humanity, let alone majesty, in his once handsome face. Besmirched by the mud and dirt, lacerated and mangled in the press, the barely recognisable body was being stripped of its armour and raiment. Naked he would be slung over a horse, his hair hanging down, his shame evident to all.[16]

Surprisingly, overall casualties after the two-hour battle were relatively light, perhaps 1000 all told. William Brandon, Henry's luckless standard-bearer, was the only ranking casualty among Henry's men. After the battle, so the story goes, Richard's coronet was retrieved from under a thorn-bush (perhaps having been secreted there by a solder intending to collect it later) and placed on Henry's head by Lord Stanley, who was soon created earl of Derby for his services – or at least for not doing any for Richard. Northumberland did not escape so lightly, since, unlike Stanley, he was a well-known Ricardian and had obeyed the summons to Nottingham. After he knelt in homage to King Henry VII, he was placed in custody but not, however, attainted. Henry clearly had no real idea why Northumberland had stood impotently aside, but he certainly needed watching for a time. Perhaps he had some fond memories of their time together as boys in Herbert's household. For the moment, Richard's cousin, Lord Fitzhugh (a nephew of Warwick the Kingmaker), was made the king's chief lieutenant in the North and took over the commissions of array in all the Northern counties.

So, the question remains: why did Northumberland not come to the aid of Richard III? His actions, or rather inaction, have historically been attributed to 'betrayal' or even his secret contacts with Henry before the battle.[17] Some, slightly less conspiratorially, believe that 'Northumberland asked to be posted in the rear' because he 'evidently intended to wait and see how things would go'.[18] Others feel that Richard did not trust Northumberland, since his behaviour was 'sullen and unco-operative'.[19]

Perhaps so. But another possible motive for Northumberland's decision that fateful day has gone unnoticed. Apart from the odd minor skirmish, in which he may or may not have participated, Northumberland had never actually *fought* in a battle. He was too young for St Albans, Towton and Hedgeley Moor; he had missed Barnet and Tewkesbury; the 1475 French campaign and the Scottish invasion of 1481–2 had both petered out without a clash; and the Northerners' arrival in London after Buckingham's rebellion in 1483 had been peaceful. Therefore, Bosworth was Percy's first engagement, his sole charge of the reserves requiring a careful judgement of when and where to intervene. Percy was not a risk-taker; when in doubt, perhaps because of spending his early years in prison and relying on the benevolence of the authorities, he simply froze, his seeming neutrality hopefully paying dividends with whoever emerged victorious. In 1471, for example, following Edward's arrival in the North, the earl did nothing to either help or hinder him – which demonstrates political intelligence, not military brilliance. To his inexperienced eye, a charge as fresh reinforcements were arriving and Richard was being swept away was suicidal. So he froze. Northumberland did not betray Richard III; he just didn't come through when Richard needed him most. Indeed, cold feet ruined Richard at Bosworth, not a cold heart. Henry may have recognised this distinction; therefore he briefly imprisoned the earl but did not attaint or execute him.

After Bosworth, the Tudor regime was established remarkably smoothly. In short order, Henry married Elizabeth of York (whom he had never met), became reunited with his mother (whom he hadn't seen in fourteen years) and accepted Charles VIII's recognition and a truce with France. His coronation, owing to the experience gained from Richard's two years before, passed off magnificently.

To be sure, there were hiccups caused by Richard's surviving support-ers. The following year saw risings, 1487 witnessed a battle, and the North in particular missed him and his good lordship. At bottom, however, 'Henry VII was a king elected by proportional representation. He was the first choice of very few, but he had won the first transferable vote of Tudors, Lancastrians, Yorkists, Welshmen and Frenchmen, each with their own axe to grind, who knew nothing substantial against him and hated Richard.'[20]

Four Years Later

Within six months of Bosworth, Northumberland was a freed, and mostly forgiven, man,[21] but no longer an important or influential one. Given the Border disturbances, and Lord Fitzhugh, the chief lieutenant's inexperience with the Scots, Northumberland was admittedly re-granted the wardenship of the East March – but with severely clipped wings. With no more talk of 'warden-generalship', Henry eliminated the tradition of giving each warden a long-term contract for custody of the March with a certain number of men at an agreed – usually exorbitant – price. (Thus, the eastern warden was receiving £3000 in peacetime in 1463, and only £1000 in 1477 owing to the truce, but this was still rather more than normal expenditure, so the warden could skim discreet amounts off the top.) These contracts, when the Exchequer paid them on time, essentially gave the warden total authority over his patch and kept London in the dark. Under Henry, contracts became annually renewable, and royal officials gradually superseded the regional and local magnates. In 1488, for instance, Sir William Tyler, a courtier who had previously been master of the king's jewel house, replaced Northumberland as captain of Berwick. Northumberland and his colleagues were not exactly bypassed, but they were becoming semi-independent contractors. The earl, for example, contracted to supply 200 men – when he was captain, it was 1000 – to defend Berwick if it was attacked after Tyler's arrival.

Indeed, Northumberland was really only a tax collector by 1489 – and a hated one at that. Since 1485, Henry had levied only one general tax, but in November 1487 Parliament voted substantially more, payable within two years, followed by a further £75,000 in January 1489, with the first instalment due as early as May. Historically, the North had been exempt from many taxes or could claim tax allowances, owing to its economically backward nature and the risks associated with Scots raiding. Henry, still annoyed about Richard's popularity in the North, decided against exemptions in these instances. As the king's agent, it was Northumberland's responsibility to collect the money.

The corporation of York, 'in consideration of the said poverte, ruyne, and decae', appealed to Henry for concessions – to no avail. Grudgingly, York coughed up – although the North-East proved recalcitrant. Even the earl tried to intervene, writing to the king that, in words of a later historian, 'The people greatly grudged and murmured, making open Proclamacioun that they have been charged of late years with innumerable incommodities and opressions ... and that nowe there was a houge some requyred of them, which neither they were hable to satesfie ... nor yet would once consent to pay.' Henry, fearing that concessions would spark further unrest in other parts of the country, remained adamant.

Opposition formed at Ayton in Cleveland – a staunchly pro-Richard district – when several yeoman and a local chaplain gathered on 20 April 1489 and decided to march to Thirsk to raise a rebellion against the tax and the Tudor regime. Northumberland had come up from London, where he had attended Parliament. He may have tried to speak to Henry on 14 February about the difficulty of collecting the required instalments, and was staying – for the very first time – at Seamer by Scarborough, the manor that the first William de Percy acquired through his post-Conquest marriage to Emma de Port.

Northumberland heard about the Ayton meeting four days later and began summoning local worthies to help quell the disturbance. In a letter, dated 24 April, he wrote (to Sir Robert Plumpton): '[I] pray you that ye with such a company, and as many as ye may bring with you (with your) ease, such as ye trust, having bowes & arrowes & pryvy harnest, (cum with) my ... nepvew Sir William Gascougne, so that ye may be with me upon Monday (next comeing) at nyght in the towne of Thirsk, not failing herof, as my (special) trust is in you, & as ye love me. Written in my mannor of Seemer, the xxiiii day of Aprill.'

At what is now South Kilvington, about a mile north of Thirsk, and what was then Cocklodge – the earl's sprawling house in the original Percy holding of Topcliffe since William de Percy's castle had fallen into ruin – Northumberland and his retinue met the 700-strong rebel force. Initially, the rebels wanted to press their grievances with the earl, as the royal agent, but for an unknown reason their tempers flared. The earl was dragged from his horse, apparently by one John Chamber, a forester new to Yorkshire but originally from North Wales, which he'd left to join Henry's campaign on its way to Bosworth. It was he, later indicted and executed as the principal assassin, who murdered Northumberland while Percy's retinue looked silently on, doing nothing to aid the stricken earl.

His own Northerners had undone Northumberland. As the earl's corpse lay in the dirt, the rebels grasped the magnitude of their crime and stayed near Thirsk until 9 May fearfully weighing up what to do next. Many would have slunk off home before then but for the mysterious Sir John Egremont, who suddenly appeared and took command.

Egremont, an obscure and dubious character who changed sides whenever it was convenient, appears to have been a Percy in disguise. According to a 1480 deed, which refers to him as 'Johannes Percy miles filius et heres Thome Percy militis Domini dum vixit de Egremond', he was a son of Thomas Percy, better known as the turbulent Lord Egremont killed at the battle of Northampton in 1460. This makes him Northumberland's cousin, and, barring the earl's heirs, his closest relative. At the time of the murder he was bitterly feuding with Northumberland, who was seeking to disinherit him from the late Lord Egremont's estate of Wressle, which if successful would have left him to fend for himself.

Egremont, however, was not present at Cocklodge, but his friends and associates were – in Percy's retinue. Furthermore, the retinue that day was crammed with members of Richard's old affinity, some of whom had witnessed (or had heard about) Northumberland's presumed 'betrayal' at Bosworth of their beloved master and provider. Since the battle and Richard's death, Northumberland had recruited them to flesh out his corps of traditional Percy retainers; a number, like Sir Thomas Broughton and Clement Skelton, even had records of resistance to Henry VII and his Northern policies, but offers of employment were few and far between. Although despising Henry, and by extension Northumberland by dint of his 'betrayal' and co-operation with the Tudor regime, there was nobody else to work for. When the time came for them to help their lord in his travails, the combination of Egremont's clique and Ricardian loyalists hung back and watched him die, just as Northumberland had once done with his royal lord.[22] Upon hearing that the king was sending an army, however, Egremont disappeared and the Northern rebellion of 1489 soon petered out. Its only casualty was Henry Percy, aged forty.

Poignantly, Northumberland had recently commissioned a painstakingly produced family tree, with his dynasty's history haughtily running down the roll parallel to the descent of the kings of England. After his murder, the genealogy stops.[23]

The last King in the North had ignominiously fallen where the first of his dynasty once arose.

Epilogue

The death of this earl of Northumberland is not the end of the saga of the House of Percy. Indeed, a Percy – now exalting in the title of duke – today resides in Alnwick Castle. But the murder that day at Cocklodge did mark the end of their reign as Kings in the North. It also heralded the end of Northern exceptionalism. Henry VII and Henry VIII would henceforth concentrate on suborning the North to the direct, omnipresent control of London.

The assassination of the earl left a minor, another Henry, as his heir, and over the coming decade or so, there was a haemorrhaging of old Northern families from the Percy service to that of the ruling Tudors. They were following the money. The new regime was inserting itself into facets of life that previous ruling houses had left untouched, especially in the Northern backwoods. Henry VII, for instance, sent out bureaucratic commissions to clamp down on the traditional custom of barons and gentry to privately arrange their marriage-alliances and disposal of lands. The king's administrators also pored over the ancient deeds of tenure to reveal whether certain tenancies and rents were actually rightly payable to the Crown, not to the local worthy. Such 'royal commissions of conceal-ment' disrupted the old ways of regionally based personal service and good lordship in the name of centralising, modernising efficiency.

The Tudors also introduced new administrative measures when it came to defence, such as appointing a 'royal lieutenant' working along-side a 'Council of the North', which met regularly to execute London's policies. No more was there the administrative and financial leeway per-mitted to the medieval wardens to run Border affairs in their Northern fiefdoms. In fact, in 1525, when the council was established, Northumberland was not made a member. Even the lieutenants chosen were mostly Southerners, such as the earl of Shrewsbury or the earl of Surrey – victor over the Scots at Flodden in 1513, a time when the 5th earl of Northumberland (who died in 1527) was in France with the king – and they supervised local gentlemen in their tasks. In the late 1520s, owing to continued Northern disturbances and clannish infighting, the new Percy, earl of Northumberland, was made lieutenant, but he was under strict orders to govern in association with the council and act only on London's instructions. During this time, the North's ancient liberties and special exemptions were chipped away, and Henry VIII broke Percy power by enforcing payment of the family's massive debts. But the 6th earl was wholly uninterested in power. Inheriting the vast Percy estates at the age of twenty-five, this childless, chronically ill man loathed his father, his wife and his two brothers. By the time he died ten years later, he had disinherited the family by disposing of pretty much every Percy property south of the Humber (an exception was Petworth which was brought to the dynasty by Joscelin de Louvain in the mid-twelfth century), and he had contracted to donate the rest of the Percy empire – in Northumberland, Cumberland and Yorkshire, the sacred nucleus of William de Percy's holdings after the Conquest – to the Crown in return for the firesale price of a £1000 annuity. He died before the first instalment was due.

Percy power, power that had been assiduously built up over five centuries, had been extinguished in a decade. The king himself directed that 'we will not be bound, of a necessity, to be served there [the North] with lords, but we will be served with such men, what degree soever they be of as we shall appoint to the same'. In 1537, Henry VIII even appointed *himself* warden-general of the Marches, followed by the Midlands-based earl of Rutland five years later. The latter soon fell ill, and was replaced by the earl of Hertford, a man whose experience of the North was restricted to a brief sojourn seventeen years earlier as master of the horse in the earl of Richmond's household. He didn't last long – he loathed the place – and his successors were either dyed-in-the-wool Southerners or men with no Border connections. In the mid-1540s, the Crown resorted to stationing Spanish mercenaries at Alnwick, and Italian soldiers of fortune at Berwick.[1] By the next decade, it was John Dudley, earl of Warwick, and not a Percy, who was made duke of Northumberland.

There were two revolts in the North in the sixteenth century. Neither can be defined as the last romantic gasp of old-time Percyism, although there are instances where the Percy name was shouted by the crowds. The first occurred in 1536, and was harshly put down. 'The Pilgrimage of Grace', as it was called, was mostly a lower-class revolt against high taxation and religious reforms, and it only lasted for a few months. Two of the leaders, however, were the 6th earl's younger brothers, Sir Thomas and Ingram. The former was executed, and the other died a few years later.

Afterwards, the North remained quiescent until 1569, when Thomas Percy, the 7th earl – son of the late Sir Thomas – became fatally involved in the so-called Rising of the Northern Earls. Despite the name, this rebellion had nothing to do with Northernism. Instead, it was a short-lived and clumsily led, if admirably pious, pro-Catholic uprising, which ended in the earl's execution. In 1584, his younger brother, now the 8th earl, whose Catholic sympathies may have led him to participate in a half-baked, anti-Elizabeth conspiracy, was locked in the Tower. A year later, he was found dead with a bullet through the heart and a pistol lying next to him. Officially, it was ruled a suicide, but some nonetheless suspected foul play.

However, the 7th earl had done much to recover the Percy fortunes dissipated by his uncle. While Queen Mary was on the throne in the 1550s, Percy was in good odour and succeeded in reacquiring the Percy properties in Northumberland and Cumberland, some in Yorkshire (Craven was lost), a few Southern manors and Northumberland Place, the Percys' London house. It was originally purchased in 1343, a happier time when the family was on its upward curve. However, Seamer, the dower of Emma de Port, was lost for ever.

Essentially, over the course of a century, the emasculated Percys were completely cut out of playing any significant role in Northern affairs. From 1570 onwards, they did not even live in the North, but moved down to Petworth in Sussex and the newly acquired Syon House in Middlesex. As for Northumberland Place, it was abandoned and used as a gambling dive and, of all things, a bowling alley. The Great Fire of 1666 destroyed it.

In any case, there was little need for Percys in the North any more. The very idea of Kings in the North was obsolete. The Scottish problem, which had transfixed so many English kings, slowly ebbed away over the course of the sixteenth century. Yes, there would be occasional battles and there was constant 'reiving' by outlaws and gangs. For those interested in the New North, the best introductions to this feuding, tribal world are two wonderful books by the creator of Flashman, George MacDonald Fraser, *The Steel Bonnets: the story of the Anglo-Scottish Border reivers*, and his historical novel, *The Candlemass Road* (which cries out to be made into a film).

But the medieval preoccupations with Scottish independence and English paramountcy were dead issues. Independence had been won and, under the influence of the Protestant Reformation, Scotland would be inexorably pulled away from her French orbit into the English system. Henry VII's famous prophecy, that the 'greater would draw the lesser', was fully realised. In any case, the royal houses of England and Scotland began to coalesce into a single dynasty following the Treaty of Perpetual Peace of January 1502, in which it was determined that James IV would marry Margaret Tudor (the marriage took place on 8 August 1503).[2] Despite ups and downs, and tumult, and cross words (and swords), the Anglo-Scottish dynamic had been permanently transformed. If anything, the Scots had redressed some of the balance lost when Edward I asserted his paramountcy; if the Tudor line of succession failed, as it eventually would, none other than a Scottish monarch would probably inherit the throne.

Indeed, 101 years after the Treaty of Perpetual Peace, James VI of Scotland would become James I of England. On 20 October 1604, James proclaimed the existence of 'the blessed Union, or rather Reuniting of these two mightie, famous and ancient Kingdomes of England and Scotland, under one Imperiall Crowne'. In order to reconcile the peoples of this land, James continued, 'it is our dutie, to doe our uttermost endeavour, for the advancement and perfection of that... which God hath put together... an uniformitie of constitutions both of body and minde... A communitie of Language, the principall meanes of Civil societie, An unitie of Religion, the chiefest bande of heartie Union, and the surest knot of lasting Peace.' To further this end, James intended to 'discontinue the divided names of England and Scotland... and take the Name and Stile of KING OF GREAT BRITTAINE'.[3]

And what of the then-current Percy – the 9th earl of Northumberland? He was captain of the gentlemen pensioners, the Praetorian Guard of this Anglo-Scottish sovereign.

On the Percy saga in general, let us turn to the advice of an anonymous fifteenth-century poet, who played on the Percy motto, *Esperance en Dieu* (Hope – or Faith – in God):[4]

> *Esperaunce en dyeu*
> *Trust hym he is moste trewe.*
>
> *En dieu esperaunce*
> *In hym put thyne affiaunce.*
>
> *Esperaunce in the worlde nay.*
> *The worlde variethe every day.*
>
> *Esperaunce in riches nay not so.*
> *Riches slidethe and sone will go.*
>
> *Esperaunce in exaltation of honoure.*
> *Nay it widderethe awaly lyke a floure.*
>
> *Esperaunce en dieu in him is all*
> *Which is above fortunes fall.*

Notes

Introduction, pp. 1–16

1 A. Briggs. 'Themes in Northern history', *Northern History*, I (1966), pp. 1–6.
2 J. Le Patourel, 'Is Northern history a subject?', *Northern History*, XII (1976), pp. 6–7.
3 A. Conan Doyle, M.D., 'On the geographical distribution of British intellect', *Nineteenth Century*, XXIV (1888), August, pp. 184–95.
4 H. Ellis, *A Study of British Genius* (London, 2nd edn, 1927), pp. 1, 41–3.
5 W.E. Kapelle, *The Norman Conquest of the North: the region and its transformation, 1000–1135* (London, 1979), p. 5.
6 Le Patourel, 'Is Northern history a subject?', p. 7.
7 Le Patourel, 'Is Northern history a subject?' p. 8.
8 J.A. Tuck, 'War and society in the medieval North', *Northern History*, XXI (1985), p. 34.
9 Le Patourel, 'Is Northern history a subject?', p. 6, moots eight counties as being in the North, if the Trent is included.
10 F.W. Brooks, *The Council of the North* (London, 2nd edn, 1966), p. 6.
11 R.L. Storey, 'The North of England', in S.B. Chrimes, C.D. Ross and R.A. Griffiths (eds.), *Fifteenth-century England, 1399–1509: studies in politics and society* (Manchester, 1972), pp. 129–30.
12 R.S. Schofield, 'The geographical distribution of wealth in England, 1334–1649', *Economic History Review*, XVIII (1965), pp. 507–9, cited in H.M. Jewell, 'North and South: the antiquity of the great divide', *Northern History*, XXVII (1991), p. 18. I have relied heavily on Jewell's article.
13 Storey, 'The North of England', p. 130.
14 Brooks, *The Council of the North*, p. 7.
15 F. Musgrove, *The North of England: a history from Roman times to the present* (Oxford, 1990), pp. 75–6.
16 H.M. Jewell, 'North and South: the antiquity of the great divide', *Northern History*, XXVII (1991), p. 3.
17 P.H. Blair, 'The Northumbrians and their southern frontier', *Archaeologia Aeliana*, XXVI (1948), p. 117.
18 Blair, 'The Northumbrians and their southern frontier', pp. 120, 126.
19 Jewell, 'North and South', pp. 1–2; P. Salway, *Roman Britain* (Oxford, 1984), p. 23.
20 Blair, 'The Northumbrians and their southern frontier', p. 99; Jewell, 'North and South', p. 2.
21 Blair, 'The Northumbrians and their southern frontier', pp. 112–13.
22 F. Stenton, *Anglo-Saxon England*, p. 32, quoted in Blair, 'The Northumbrians and their southern frontier', p. 115.
23 Le Patourel, 'Is Northern history a subject?', pp. 9–10.
24 Kapelle, *The Norman Conquest of the North*, p. 7.
25 G.W.S. Barrow, 'The Anglo-Scottish border', *Northern History*, I (1966), p. 24.
26 Le Patourel, 'The Norman conquest of Yorkshire', *Northern History*, VI (1971), p. 3.
27 P.H. Blair, 'The Origins of Northumbria', *Archaeologia Aeliana*, XXV (1947), pp. 1–51.
28 Le Patourel, 'The Norman conquest of Yorkshire', p. 4.
29 Barrow, 'The Anglo-Scottish border,' p. 31.
30 Barrow, 'The Anglo-Scottish border,' p. 34.
31 Le Patourel, 'The Norman conquest of Yorkshire', pp. 3–4.

32 Kapelle, *The Norman Conquest of the North*, p. 9.

33 E. Miller, *War in the North: the Anglo-Scottish wars of the Middle Ages* (Hull, 1960), p. 9.

34 *Survey of Possessions of Earl of Northumberland, 1570* (Cumberland), PRO E164/37, f. 3, quoted in A.J.L. Winchester, *Landscape and Society in Medieval Cumbria* (Edinburgh, 1987), p. 1.

35 Quoted in Miller, *War in the North*, p. 10.

36 Quoted in Winchester, *Landscape and Society*, p. 116.

37 Quoted in Winchester, *Landscape and Society*, p. 81.

38 Winchester, *Landscape and Society*, p. 2.

39 Quoted in N. Ridley, *Northumbrian Heritage* (London, 1968), p. 98.

40 Ridley, *Northumbrian Heritage*, p. 161.

41 Quoted in Jewell, 'North and South', p. 5.

42 Quoted in Jewell, 'North and South', p. 9.

43 Quoted in Jewell, 'North and South', p. 16.

44 D. Hay (ed.), *The Anglica Historia of Polydore Vergil, AD 1485–1537*, Camden Society, 3rd series, LXXIV (1950), p. 11.

45 Quoted in Miller, *War in the North*, p. 11.

46 Jewell, 'North and South', p. 19.

47 Jewell, 'North and South', p. 20.

48 R. Vaughn in his introduction to the Latin text, *Camden Miscellany*, XXI, 3rd series, XC (1958), pp. ix–x; Jewell, 'North and South', p. 6.

49 A. Hudson, 'The debate on Bible translation, Oxford 1401', *English Historical Review*, XC (1975), pp. 1–18.

50 G. Chaucer, *The Canterbury Tales*.

51 Geoffrey of Monmouth (ed. L. Thorpe), *The History of the Kings of Britain* (Harmondsworth, 1996), p. 189.

52 Quoted in Jewell, 'North and South', p. 20.

53 C.H. Blair, 'Wardens and Deputy Wardens of the Marches of England towards Scotland in Northumberland', *Archaeologia Aeliana*, XXVIII (1950), p. 32.

54 Jewell, 'North and South', pp. 6–7.

55 F.M. Stenton, *The First Century of English Feudalism* (Oxford, 1932), p. 136, n. 1.

56 Musgrove, *The North of England*, pp. 68–70.

57 Musgrove, *The North of England*, p. 130.

58 Cited in Miller, *War in the North*, p. 6.

59 Tuck, 'War and society', p. 35.

60 Tuck, 'War and society', p. 37.

61 Quoted in Miller, *War in the North*, p. 6; K.

M. Longley, 'The Scottish incursions of 1327: a glimpse of the aftermath', *Transactions of the Cumberland and Westmorland Antiquarian and Archaeological Society*, LXXXIII (1983), pp. 63–72.

62 Miller, *War in the North*, p. 7.

63 Miller, *War in the North*, p. 7.

64 Quoted in P. Dixon, 'Towerhouses, pelehouses and border society', *Archaeological Journal*, CXXXVI (1979), p. 245.

65 Miller, *War in the North*, p. 18.

66 A. Goodman, 'The Anglo-Scottish Marches in the fifteenth century: a frontier society?', in R.A. Mason (ed.), *Scotland and England, 1286–1815* (Edinburgh, 1987), pp. 19, 29.

67 Goodman, 'The Anglo-Scottish Marches', pp. 18–19.

1: The First Northerner, pp. 17–44

1 J.C. Holt, *What's in a name? Family nomenclature and the Norman Conquest* (The Stenton Lecture), (Reading, 1982); B.Z. Kedar, 'Toponymic surnames as evidence of origin: some medieval views', *Viator*, IV (1973), pp. 123–9.

2 G. Brenan, *A History of the House of Percy: from the earliest times down to the present century* (London, 2 vols., 1902), I, p. 3. For exhaustive dissection of the St Lô thesis, see 'G.E.C [okayne]', revised and expanded by V. Gibbs, H.A. Doubleday, G.H. White and Lord H. de Walden, *The Complete Peerage: or a history of the House of Lords and all its members from the earliest times.* (London, 14 vols. In 13, 1910–59), X (1945), pp. 435–6.

3 W. Dugdale, *The Baronage of England* (London, 1675), p. 269; W.P. Hedley, *Northumberland Families* (Newcastle, 2 vols., 1968–70), II, p. 8.

4 W. Peeris (ed. D. Bisley), *Metrical Pedigree of the Percyes* (printed as the '*Metrical Chronicle of the Family of Percy*'), in *Richardson's Reprints of Rare Tracts and Imprints of Antient Manuscripts*, V (Newcastle, 1845); no page numbers.

5 Brenan, *History of the House of Percy*, I, p. 2.

6 Hedley, *Northumberland Families*, I, p. 8.

7 Peeris, *Metrical Pedigree of the Percyes*, in *Richardson's Reprints of Rare Tracts*.

8 *Ibid.*

9 D.C. Douglas, 'Rollo of Normandy'

English Historical Review, LVII (1942), 228, p. 419.

10 Quoted in J. Lindsay, *The Normans and their World* (London, 1973), p. 7.

11 F.M. Stenton, 'The Danes in England', *Proceedings of the British Academy*, XIII (1927), p. 210.

12 Stenton, 'Danes in England', p. 206; R.A. Hall, 'The Five Boroughs of the Danelaw: a review of present knowledge', *Anglo-Saxon England*, XVIII (1989), pp. 149–206.

13 Stenton, 'Danes in England', p. 241.

14 D.M. Hadley, '"And they proceeded to plough and to support themselves": the Scandinavian settlement of England', *Anglo-Norman Studies*, XIX (1996), pp. 69–96.

15 Quoted in Lindsay, *The Normans and their World*, p. 14; Stenton, 'The Scandinavian colonies in England and Normandy', *Transactions of the Royal Historical Society*, 4th series, XXVII (1945), p. 1; G. Fellows Jensen, 'The Vikings in England: a review', *Anglo-Saxon England*, IV (1975), pp. 184–5.

16 D. Bates, *Normandy before 1066* (London, 1982), p. 7 and esp. Map 3, p. 266.

17 S. Runciman, 'Medieval history and the romantic imagination', in J. Richardson (ed.), *Essays by Divers Hands: being the transactions of the Royal Society of Literature*, new series, XXXII (1963), pp. 114–15.

18 E. Searle, 'Fact and pattern in heroic poetry: Dudo of St Quentin', *Viator*, XV (1984), pp. 119–37.

19 Douglas, 'Rollo of Normandy', *English Historical Review*, p. 432.

20 Douglas, 'Rollo of Normandy', *English Historical Review*, p. 434.

21 Douglas, 'Rollo of Normandy', *English Historical Review*, p. 435.

22 R. Allen Brown, *The Normans* (Woodbridge, new edn, 1994), pp. 16–18.

23 L.C. Loyd (ed. C.T. Clay and D.C. Douglas), *The Origins of Some Anglo-Norman Families*, Harleian Society, CIII (Leeds, 1951), pp. 69, 77.

24 Anon., 'The Companions of William the Conqueror, and "The Battle Abbey Roll"', *Herald and Genealogist*, I (1863), 3, pp. 193–208.

25 Anon., 'Companions of William the Conqueror', pp. 193, 202–4.

26 D.C. Douglas, 'The Companions of the Conqueror', *History*, XXVIII (1943), p. 146; J.F.A. Mason, 'The Companions of the Conqueror: an additional name', *English Historical Review*, LXXI (1956), 278, pp. 61–9.

27 William remained duke of Normandy, necessitating his presence there for considerable periods: he spent February to December 1067, early 1072, early 1073, April to December 1075, spring 1076 to autumn 1080, summer and autumn 1082, Easter 1083, summer 1084, and from summer 1086 to his death in 1097, in France. Lindsay, *The Normans and their World*, p. 238.

28 *Ex Registro Cartarum abbatiae de Whitby*, printed in J. Caley, H. Ellis, and the Rev. B. Bandinel, *Monasticon Anglicanum: a history of the abbies and other monasteries, hospitals, frieries, and cathedral and collegiate churches, with their dependencies in England and Wales* (London, 6 vols. in 8), I, p. 409.

29 Searle, 'Dudo of Saint-Quentin', p. 130; Brown, *The Normans*, p. 19.

30 D.P. Kirby, 'Strathclyde and Cumbria: a survey of historical development', *Transactions of the Cumberland and Westmorland Antiquarian and Archaeological Society*, LXII (1962), pp. 77–94.

31 W.E. Kapelle, *The Norman Conquest of the North: the region and its transformation, 1000–1135* (London, 1979), p. 105.

32 A. Williams, *The English and the Norman Conquest* (Woodbridge, 1995), pp. 68–9.

33 Quoted in R. Allen Brown, *The Normans and the Norman Conquest* (Woodbridge, 2nd edn. 1985), p. 167.

34 N. Hooper, 'Edgar the Ætheling: Anglo-Saxon prince, rebel and crusader', *Anglo-Saxon England*, XIV (1985), pp. 197–214; D.N. Dumville, 'The Ætheling: a study in Anglo-Saxon constitutional history', *Anglo-Saxon England*, VIII (1979), pp. 1–34.

35 Quoted in J. Le Patourel, 'The Norman Conquest of Yorkshire', *Northern History*, VI (1971), p. 8.

36 Kapelle, *The Norman Conquest of the North*, p. 119.

37 Kapelle, *The Norman Conquest of the North*, p. 118.

38 C[okayne], *The Complete Peerage*, X, p. 437.

39 Allen Brown, *The Normans and the Norman Conquest*, p. 171, n. 285.

40 G. Washington, 'The Border heritage, 1066–1292', *Transactions of the Cumberland*

and *Westmorland Antiquarian and Archaeological Society*, LXII (1962), p. 102; F. S. Scott, 'Earl Waltheof of Northumbria', *Archaeologia Aeliana*, 4th series, XXX (1952), pp. 149–213.

41 Based on Kapelle, *The Norman Conquest of the North*.

42 F.M Stenton, 'English families and the Norman Conquest', *Transactions of the Royal Historical Society,* 4th series, XXVI (1944), pp. 4–5; J. Godfrey, 'The defeated Anglo-Saxons take service with the eastern Emperor', *Anglo-Norman Studies*, I (1978), pp. 63–74; Hooper, 'Edgar the Ætheling', *Anglo-Saxon England*, pp. 197–214.

43 G. Barraclough, 'The earldom and county palatine of Chester', *Transactions of the Historic Society of Lancashire and Cheshire*, CIII (1951), p. 27; J. Tait, *The Domesday Survey of Cheshire*, Chatham Society, n. s., LXXV (1916), p. 7.

44 G. Barraclough, 'The earldom and county palatine of Chester', p. 26.

45 Tait, *The Domesday Survey of Cheshire*, p. 30; F.M. Stenton, *The First Century of English Feudalism, 1066–1166* (Oxford, 1932), pp. 226–8.

46 Dugdale, *The Baronage of England*, p. 32.

47 Tait, *The Domesday Survey of Cheshire*, p. 8; W.J. Corbett, *Cambridge Medieval History*, V (1929), p. 507.

48 D. Crouch, *The Image of Aristocracy in Britain, 1000–1300* (London, 1992), p. 296.

49 Dugdale, *The Baronage of England*, p. 34.

50 C.T. Clay (ed.), *Early Yorkshire Charters: based on the manuscripts of the late William Farrer*, vol. XI: *The Percy Fee* (Edinburgh, 1963), Chapter 2, pp. 11–19, 334; W.F. Farrer (ed.), *Early Yorkshire Charters* (Edinburgh, 1915), II, Chapter 18, pp. 196–7.

51 H.R. Loyn, *The Norman Conquest* (London, 3rd edn, 1982), p. 111.

52 Stenton, 'English families and the Norman Conquest', *Transactions of the Royal Historical Society*, pp. 1–12.

53 H.M. Thomas, *Vassals, Heiresses, Crusaders and Thugs: the gentry of Angevin Yorkshire, 1154–1216* (Philadelphia, Pennsylvania, 1993), p. 14.

54 Allen Brown, *The Normans and the Norman Conquest*, pp. 183–200; Loyn, *The Norman Conquest,* pp. 111–20; H.M. Chew, 'Scutage', *History*, XIV (1930), pp. 236–9; V.H. Galbraith, 'Nationality and language

in medieval England', *Transactions of the Royal Historical Society*, 4th series, XXIII (1941), esp. pp. 115–16.

55 F. Musgrove, *The North of England: a history from Roman times to the present* (Oxford, 1990), p. 87; C.W. Hollister, 'Magnates and *curiales* in early Norman England', *Viator*, VIII (1977), p. 63.

56 Le Patourel, 'Norman Conquest of Yorkshire', *Northern History*, pp. 20–1.

57 W. Farrer, 'Introduction to the Yorkshire Domesday,' in *Victoria History of the Counties of England: Yorkshire*, II (London, 1912), pp. 133–89. See also the section on William de Percy in the Domesday Survey of Yorkshire printed in I, pp. 259–64; Table I in P. Dalton, *Conquest, Anarchy and Lordship: Yorkshire, 1066-1154* (Cambridge, 1994), p. 298; A.S. Ellis, 'Biographical notes on the Yorkshire tenants named in Domesday Book', *Yorkshire Archaeological and Topographical Journal,* IV (1875–6). Part I, pp. 152–7.

58 See Domesday Survey of Yorkshire, *Victoria History of the Counties of England: Yorkshire*, I, p. 263.

59 W.M. I'Anson, 'The castles of the North Riding', *Yorkshire Archaeological Journal*, XXII (1913), pp. 374–6; J.F. Mason, 'The honour of Richmond', *English Historical Review,* LXXVIII (1963), pp. 703–4; H.M. Thomas, 'Subinfeudation and alienation of land, economic development, and the wealth of nobles on the Honour of Richmond, 1066 to *c.*1300', *Albion*, XXVI (1994), 3, pp. 397–417.

60 Table I, 'The value of the estates of lay Yorkshire tenants-in-chief in Domesday Book', in Dalton, *Conquest, Anarchy and Lordship*, p. 298.

61 Table I, 'Assessment and value of the honour of Chester, 1066–86', in C.P. Lewis, 'The formation of the honour of Chester, 1066-1100', in A.T. Thacker (ed.), *The earldom of Chester and its charters: a tribute to Geoffrey Barraclough*: Special Volume of the *Journal of the Chester Archaeological Society*, LXXI (1991), p. 42.

62 See W.J. Corbett's contribution to *Cambridge Medieval History*, V, Chapter 15 (Cambridge, 1964), pp. 506–11.

63 J.B. Williams, 'Judhael of Totnes: the life and times of a post-Conquest baron', *Anglo-Norman Studies*, XVI (1993), p. 277.

64 Barraclough, 'The earldom and county palatine of Chester', p. 30; Corbett, *Cambridge Medieval History*, p. 508.

65 Corbett, *Cambridge Medieval History*, V, p. 512.

66 For a map of Percy's honour, see Dalton, *Conquest, Anarchy and Lordship*, Map 3, p. 35.

67 Dalton, *Conquest, Anarchy and Lordship*, p. 39.

68 I'Anson, 'The castles of the North Riding', pp. 318–19.

69 J.H. Beeler, 'Castles and strategy in Norman and early Angevin England', *Speculum* XXXI (1956), pp. 581–601.

70 Allen Brown, *The Normans and the Norman Conquest*, p. 186.

71 Kapelle, *The Norman Conquest of the North*, p. 145.

72 Kapelle, *The Norman Conquest of the North*, p. 144.

73 Loyd, *The Origins of some Anglo-Norman families*, p. 79; J.H. Round, 'The families of St John and of Port', *Genealogist*, XVI (1899), pp. 1–13, C[okayne], *The Complete Peerage*, XI (1949), pp. 316–17.

74 Cited in C.P. Lewis, 'The French in England before the Norman Conquest', *Anglo-Norman Studies*, XVII (1994), p. 124.

75 Loyn, *The Norman Conquest*, p. 124; D.R. Bates, 'The character and career of Odo, bishop of Bayeux (1049/50–1097)', *Speculum*, L (1975).

76 According to the Domesday Survey for Hampshire, p. 487 vol. I of *Victoria History of the Counties: Hampshire and the Isle of Wight* (London, 1900).

77 Brenan, *History of the House of Percy*, I, pp. 4–5.

78 'Ex Registro Monasterii de Whitbye' (Harleian MSS 692), contained in J.C. Atkinson (ed.), *Cartularium Abbathiae de Whiteby*, Surtees Society, LXIX (Durham, 2 vols., 1879–81), II, p. 690.

79 Peeris, *Metrical Pedigree of the Percyes* in *Richardson's Reprints of Rare Tracts*.

80 On Emma being Cospatric's daughter, see Ellis, 'Biographical notes on the Yorkshire tenants', p. 156. n. 45, who ridicules the suggestion; Atkinson, *Cartularium Abbathiae de Whiteby*, I, p. 1 and p. 3, n. 2; Hedley, *Northumberland Families*, II, p. 8.

81 Domesday Survey for Hampshire, p. 487 in vol. 1 of *Victoria History of the Counties: Hampshire and the Isle of Wight*.

82 C[okayne], *The Complete Peerage*, X, p. 438.

83 R.H.C. Davis, *The Normans and their Myth* (London, 1976), p. 138, n. 10.

84 Quoted in Davis, *The Normans and their Myth*, p. 124.

85 J.P. Gilson, 'St Julian the Harbinger and the first of the English Percys', *Archaeologia Aeliana*, 3rd series, IV (1908), pp. 304–12.

86 D.C. Munro, 'Did the Emperor Alexius ask for aid at the Council of Piacenza?' *American Historical Review*, XXVII (1922), pp. 731–3.

87 Quoted in R. Payne, *The Crusades: a history* (London, new edn, 1994), p. 34.

88 Fulcher of Chartres (trans. F.R. Ryan and ed. H.S. Fink), *A History of the Expedition to Jerusalem, 1095–1127* (Knoxville, Tennessee, 1969), Book I, pp. 66–7; D.C. Munro, 'The speech of Pope Urban II at Clermont, 1095', *American Historical Review*, XI (1906), pp. 231–42.

89 Appendix D of C.W. David, *Robert Curthose* (Harvard, 1920), pp. 221ff.

90 J. Riley-Smith, *The First Crusaders, 1095–1131* (Cambridge, 1997), pp. 34, 113, 122–3; R. Hill, 'Crusading warfare: a camp-follower's view, 1097–1120', *Anglo-Norman Studies*, I (1978), pp. 75–83.

91 Caley *et al.*, *Monasticon Anglicanum*, pp. 405–6; Ellis, 'Biographical notes on the Yorkshire tenants', pp. 156–7; Williams, *The English and the Normans*, pp. 150-1; J.E. Burton, 'Monasteries and parish churches in eleventh- and twelfth-century Yorkshire, *Northern History*, XXIII (1987), pp. 39–50; C. Tyerman, *England and the Crusades, 1095–1588* (Chicago, Illinois, 1988), p. 15.

92 Riley-Smith, *The First Crusaders*, p. 92.

93 Payne, *The Crusades*, p. 57.

94 *Anonymi Gesta Francorum et aliorum Hierosolymitanorum*, quoted in Fulcher of Chartres, *A History of the Expedition to Jerusalem*, Book I, Part 9, p. 79 n. 1.

95 Fulcher, *A History of the Expedition to Jerusalem*, Book I, Part 17, p. 99.

96 Fulcher, *A History of the Expedition to Jerusalem*, Book I, Part 23, p. 106.

97 B.Z. Kedar, J. Riley-Smith and R. Hiestand (eds.), *Montjoie: studies in Crusade history in honour of Hans Eberhard Mayer* (Aldershot, 1997), p. x.

98 Quoted in Payne, *The Crusades*, pp. 96–7.

99 Atkinson (ed.), *Cartularium Abbathiae de Whiteby,* I, p. 2. On 17 July 1997, I discussed Percy's crusade with Professor Jonathan Riley-Smith of Emmanuel College, Cambridge. On p. 90 of his *The First Crusaders,* he states that Percy 'became lord of a stretch of the Jabal Sumaq in [northern] Syria'. As Percy may have received this land in fief from the prince of Antioch (either Bohemund or Tancred, depending upon the none-too-dependable dates), Professor Riley-Smith told me that his *personal belief* was that Percy had possibly stayed in Syria while the Norman army marched to Jerusalem. A few years later, in the very early twelfth century, he realised he was dying and travelled down to the Holy City for penitence and, subsequently, burial. However, William's son and heir, Alan (see next chapter) inherited the English estates in 1100 – the same time that the news of Percy's death would have reached home.

100 Riley-Smith, *The First Crusaders,* pp. 14–15.

101 Fulcher, *A History of the Expedition to Jerusalem,* Book I, Part 27, p. 122.

102 Atkinson (ed.), *Cartularium Abbathiae de Whiteby,* I, p. 2, n. 1.

2: *When Christ and his Saints Slept,* pp. 44–71

1 R.H.C. Davis, 'What happened in Stephen's reign, 1135–1154', *History,* XLIX (1964), p. 10.

2 S. Painter, *The Reign of King John* (Baltimore, Maryland, 1949), pp. 290–1.

3 E. King, 'The tenurial crisis of the early twelfth century', *Past and Present,* LXV (1974), p. 114.

4 W. Farrer (ed.), *Early Yorkshire Charters: being a collection of documents anterior to the thirteenth century made from the public records, monastic chartularies, Roger Dodsworth's manuscripts and other available sources* (Edinburgh, 1915), II, p. 296, no. 965.

5 Farrer, *Early Yorkshire Charters,* II, pp. 201–5, nos. 856–60.

6 C.T. Clay (ed.), *Early Yorkshire Charters,* XI, *The Percy Fee,* for the Yorkshire Archaeological Society Record Series (Wakefield, 1963), p. 8.

7 C.W. Hollister, 'Magnates and *curiales* in early Norman England', *Viator,* VIII (1977), pp. 63–81; C.W. Hollister, 'Henry I and the Anglo-Norman magnates', in R. A. Brown (ed.), *Proceedings of the Battle Abbey Conference on Anglo-Norman Studies,* II (1980), pp. 93–107; R.W. Southern, 'The place of Henry I in English History', *Proceedings of the British Academy,* XLVIII (1962), pp. 127–69.

8 S.L. Mooers, 'Familial clout and financial gain in Henry I's later reign', *Albion,* XIV (1982), 3–4, p. 270.

9 G.E. C[okayne], revised and expanded by V. Gibbs, H.A. Doubleday, G.H. White and Lord H. de Walden, *The Complete Peerage: or a history of the House of Lords and all its members from the earliest times* (London, 1910–59), XI (1949), p. 318.

10 R.C. De Aragon, 'In pursuit of aristocratic women: a key to success in Norman England', *Albion,* XIV (1982), 3–4.

11 C.A. Newman, 'Family and royal favour in Henry I's England', *Albion,* XIV (1982), 3–4, p. 298; S.L. Waugh, *The Lordship of England: royal wardships and marriages in English society and politics, 1217–1327* (Princeton, New Jersey, 1988), pp. 36–7.

12 M. Abbott, 'The Gant family in England, 1066-1191', unpub. Ph. D. dissertation, Cambridge University (1973), esp. pp. 22–3, 25, 29–31, 76, 110–11, 128.

13 De Aragon, 'In pursuit of aristocratic women', pp, 262–3.

14 I.J. Sanders, *English Baronies: a study of their origin and descent, 1086–1327* (Oxford, 1960), p. 46; C[okayne], *The Complete Peerage,* VII (1929), p. 672.

15 *Victoria History of the Counties of England: Yorkshire,* II (London, 1912), pp. 271–2.

16 Clay (ed.) *Early Yorkshire Charters,* pp. 353–5; C[okayne], *The Complete Peerage,* X (1945), pp. 439–40.

17 S.F.C. Milsom, *The Legal Framework of English Feudalism* (Cambridge, 1976), pp. 142–5; J.C. Holt, 'Feudal society and the family in early medieval England: III – Patronage and politics', *Transactions of the Royal Historical Society,* 5th series, XXXIV (1984), pp. 18–19.

18 There is a small but significant error in J. H. Round's 'The family of Clare', *Archaeological Journal,* LVI (1899), and in his *Feudal England,* p. 472, regarding Adeliza's relationship to Richard, reproduced in J.

C. Ward's 'Royal service and reward: the Clare family and the Crown, 1066–1154', *Anglo-Norman Studies*, XI (1988), p. 262. Round claimed that Adeliza was Richard's *sister*, and therefore a daughter of Gilbert fitz Richard (d. 1117), which would have made her a very old maid indeed. See C[okayne], *The Complete Peerage*, X, p. 441; Clay (ed.), *Early Yorkshire Charters*, XI: *The Percy Fee* (Edinburgh, 1963), p. 3.

19 M. Altschul, *A Baronial Family in Medieval England: the Clares, 1217–1314* (Baltimore, Maryland, 1965), pp. 17–24; Ward, 'Royal service and reward', pp. 261–78.

20 J.C. Ward, 'The lowy of Tonbridge and the lands of the Clare family in Kent, 1066–1217', *Archaeologia Cantiana*, XCVI (1980), pp. 119-26; J.C. Ward, 'The place of the honour in twelfth-century society: the honour of Clare, 1066–1217', *Proceedings of the Suffolk Institute of Archaeology and History*, XXXV (1983), pp. 191–2.

21 R. Mortimer, 'The beginnings of the honour of Clare', *Anglo-Norman Studies*, III (1980), p. 119.

22 Sanders, *English Baronies*, p. 62, n. 5.

23 Ward, 'Royal service and reward', p. 261.

24 G.W.S. Barrow, 'The pattern of lordship and feudal settlement in Cumbria', *Journal of Medieval History*, I (1975), pp. 117–38.

25 H.A. Cronne, 'Ranulf de Gernons, earl of Chester, 1129–1153', *Transactions of the Royal Historical Society*, 4th series, XX (1937), p. 106; Sanders, *English Baronies*, pp. 17–18; P. Dalton, 'Aiming at the impossible: Ranulf II, earl of Chester, and Lincolnshire in the reign of King Stephen', in A.T. Thacker (ed.), *The Earldom of Chester and its Charters*, special volume of *Journal of the Chester Archaeological Society*, LXXI (1991), p. 110.

26 R. Howlett (ed.), *Chronicles of the Reigns of Stephen, Henry II and Richard I*, Rolls Series (London, 4 vols., 1884–9), III, p. 117; G. Barraclough, 'The earldom and county palatine of Chester', *Transactions of the Historic Society of Lancashire and Cheshire*, CIII (1951), p. 30.

27 On the Beaumont family, see L. Fox, 'The honour and earldom of Leicester: origin and descent, 1066–1399', *English Historical Review*, LIV (1939), 215, pp. 385–99. Also, Sanders, *English Baronies*, pp. 61, 93; C[okayne], *The Complete Peerage*, VII, p. 523; L.C. Loyd, 'The Norman earls of

Warwick', in C[okayne], *The Complete Peerage*, XI, Part I, Appendix A.

28 B.S. Bachrach, 'Henry II and the Angevin tradition of family hostility', *Albion*, XVI (1984), 2, pp. 111–30.

29 J.H. Round, 'The counts of Boulogne as English lords', in J.H. Round, *Studies in Peerage and Pedigree* (London, 1910), pp. 147–80.

30 E.J. Kealey, *Roger of Salisbury: viceroy of England* (Berkeley, California, 1972).

31 Richard of Hexham, *The Acts of King Stephen, and the Battle of the Standard*, in J. Stephenson (trans.), *Contemporary Chronicles of the Middle Ages: sources of 12th century history* (Felinfach, 1988), p. 57.

32 T. Forester (ed.), *The Chronicle of Henry of Huntingdon*, (London, 1853, fac. Rep. Felinfach, 1991), p. 264.

33 Richard of Hexham, *The Acts of King Stephen, and the Battle of the Standard*, p. 57.

34 Davis, 'What happened in Stephen's reign, 1135–1154,' p. 7.

35 J. Green, 'William Rufus, Henry I and the royal demesne', *History*, LXIV (1979), 212, p. 342.

36 J.C. Holt, *Magna Carta* (Cambridge, 1965), p. 39.

37 John of Hexham, in T. Arnold (ed.), *Symeonis Monachi Opera Omnia*, II, p. 330; G.W.S. Barrow, *David I of Scotland: the balance of the new and old* (Reading, 1985), pp. 5–7.

38 Southern, 'The place of Henry I', Rolls Series (London, 2 vols., 1882–5); C.W. Hollister, 'Henry I and the Anglo-Norman magnates', *Anglo-Norman Studies* II (1979), esp. p. 93; F.M. Stenton, *English Society in the Early Middle Ages, 1066–1307* (Harmondsworth, 4th edn, 1965), pp. 18–20.

39 Much of the section on the relationship between the two kings is based on J.A. Green, 'David I and Henry I', *Scottish Historical Review*, LXXV (1996), pp. 1–19.

40 G.W.S. Barrow, 'The Scots and the North of England', in E. King (ed.), *The Anarchy of King Stephen's Reign* (Oxford, 1994), p. 245.

41 M.O. Anderson, 'Lothian and the early Scottish kings', *Scottish Historical Review*, XXXIX (1960), pp. 98–112; Barrow, 'The Scots and the North of England', pp. 238–40, 245.

42 J. Green, 'Aristocratic loyalties of the northern frontier of England, *c.*1100–1174', in D. Williams (ed.), *England in the twelfth century: proceedings of the 1988 Harlaxton Symposium* (Woodbridge, 1990), pp. 91–4.

43 Clay (ed.) *Early Yorkshire Charters*, p. 3; P. Dalton, *Conquest, Anarchy and Lordship: Yorkshire 1066–1154* (Cambridge, 1994), p. 201.

44 An impression edited by D. Bisley, vicar of Long Burton, of W. Peeris's manuscript, *Metrical Pedigree of the Percys*, was printed as the *Metrical Chronicle of the Family of Percy* in *Richardson's Reprints of Rare Tracts and Imprints of Antient Manuscripts,* V (Newcastle, 1845).

45 J.C. Atkinson (ed.), *Cartularium Abbathiae de Whiteby*, Surtees Society, LXIX (Durham , 2 vols., 1879–81), I, nos. 57, 59, 60, 61; A.C. Lawrie (ed.), *Early Scottish Charters prior to A.D. 1153* (Glasgow, 1905), Charter nos. 251, 252, 253, 254; Clay (ed.), *Early Yorkshire Charters*, XI, *The Percy Fee*, p. 3; G.W.S. Barrow, *The Anglo-Norman Era in Scottish history: the Ford Lectures delivered to the University of Oxford in Hilary Term 1977* (Oxford, 1980), p. 97, n. 23.

46 J.M.W. Bean, 'The Percies and their estates in Scotland', *Archaeologia Aeliana*, XXXV (1957), 4th series, p. 91.

47 Lawrie (ed.), *Early Scottish Charters*, p. 440.

48 Barrow, *David I of Scotland*, pp. 10–11.

49 Barrow, *The Anglo-Norman Era in Scottish history*, pp. 145–55; W.A. Chaney, *The Cult of Kingship in Anglo-Saxon England* (Berkeley, California, 1970); G. Post, 'Two notes on nationalism in the Middle Ages', *Traditio*, IX (1953), pp. 281–320.

50 Dalton, *Conquest, Anarchy and Lordship*, p. 204.

51 A good source on warfare at this time is M.J. Strickland, 'Securing the North: invasion and the strategy of defence in twelfth-century Anglo-Scottish warfare', *Anglo-Norman Studies*, XII (1990), pp, 177–98.

52 Lawrie (ed.), *Early Scottish Charters*, nos. 50, 54.

53 Aelred of Rievaulx, *Relatio venerabilis Aelredi, abbatis Rievallensis, de Standardo,* in R. Howlett (ed.), *Chronicles of the Reigns of Stephen, Henry II and Richard I* (Rolls Series, 4 vols., 1884–9), III, pp. 192–5, for his attributed speech. Henceforth, referred to as Aelred of Rievaulx, *Relatio de Standardo.*

54 E. Grant, *The Foundations of Modern Science in the Middle Ages: their religious, institutional, and intellectual contexts* (Cambridge, 1996); C.H. Haskins, *The Renaissance of the Twelfth Century* (Cleveland, Ohio, 1957; orig. pub. 1927); C.W. Hollister, 'Henry I and the invisible transformation of medieval England', in *Monarchy, Magnates and Institutions in the Anglo-Norman World* (London, 1986), p. 315; C.R. Young (ed.), *The Twelfth-Century Renaissance* (New York, 1969); J.T. Muckle, 'Greek works translated directly into Latin before 1350', *Mediaeval Studies*, IV (1942), pp. 33–42, and V (1943), pp. 102–14.

55 Gillingham 'Conquering the barbarians', p. 77; S. Painter, *French Chivalry* (Baltimore, Maryland, 1940), pp. 44–5.

56 D. Whitelock (ed. and trans.), *The Anglo-Saxon Chronicle* (London, 1961), p. 159; T. Arnold (ed.), *Historia Regum* of Symeon of Durham, contained in *Symeonis Monachi Opera Omnia*, Rolls Series (London, 2 vols., 1882–5), II, pp. 191–2, cited in J. Gillingham, 'Conquering the barbarians: War and Chivalry in Twelfth-century Britain', *Haskins Society Journal*, IV (1992).

57 Richard of Hexham, *The Acts of King Stephen, and the Battle of the Standard*, in Stephenson (trans.), *Contemporary Chronicles of the Middle Ages*, p. 61.

58 John of Hexham, *Incipit historia Johannis Prioris Hagustaldensis ecclesiae xxv, annorum,* in Arnold (ed.) *Symeonis Monachi Opera Omnia*, II, pp. 293–4. Henceforth referred to as John of Hexham, in *Opera Omnia.*

59 Richard of Hexham, *The Acts of King Stephen, and the Battle of the Standard,* in Stephenson (trans.), *Contemporary Chronicles of the Middle Ages*, pp. 65–6.

60 Strickland, 'Securing the North', p. 194, n. 113.

61 My version of the battle based on A.D.H. Leadman, 'The Battle of the Standard', *Yorkshire Archaeological and Topographical Journal*, X (1889), pp. 377–87, which in turn was collated from the accounts in over twenty contemporary chronicles. John Beeler's *Warfare in England, 1066–1189* (Ithaca, New York, 1966), pp. 86–93, contains an excellent description of the battle.

62 Forester (ed.), *The Chronicle of Henry of*

Huntingdon, pp. 267-9; J.R.E. Bliese, 'Aelred of Rievaulx's rhetoric and morale at the Battle of the Standard, 1138', *Albion*, XX (1980), 4, p. 551–2; R. Rainsford, 'A kind of Noah's Ark: Aelred of Rievaulx and national identity', *Religion and National Identity: Studies in Church History*, XXVIII, pp. 137–46.

63 Aelred of Rievaulx, *Relatio de Standardo*, III, pp. 190–1. A map including the order of battle may be found in K. and D. Guest, *British Battles: the front lines of history in colour photographs* (London, 1996), p.22.

64 F.S. Scott, 'Earl Waltheof of Northumbria', *Archaeologia Aeliana*, 4th series, XXX (1952), p. 175. For a more detailed look at this important man, see A. Young, *William Cumin: Border politics and the bishopric of Durham, 1141–44*, Borthwick Paper no. 54 (York, 1979).

65 Atkinson, *Cartularium Abbathiae de Whiteby*, I, no. 59; Lawrie (ed.) *Early Scottish Charters*, no. 253.

66 Clay (ed.), *Early Yorkshire Charters*, XI, no. 108, p. 124. On William's part in Sallay's foundation, see C[okayne], *The Complete Peerage*, X, p. 441; Clay (ed.), *Early Yorkshire Charters*, XI, no. 12, p. 26.

67 Forester (ed.), *The Chronicle of Henry of Huntingdon*, p. 270.

68 On these aspects, see J.H. Round, in his appendix on 'Fiscal Earls', in *Geoffrey de Mandeville* (London, 1892), pp. 267–77; W.L. Warren, *The Governance of Norman and Angevin England* (London, 1987), pp. 89ff; K.J. Stringer, *The Reign of Stephen: kingship, warfare and government in twelfth-century England* (London, 1993), pp. 50–5; Dalton, *Conquest, Anarchy and Lordship*, pp. 145–52; P. Latimer, 'Grants of *totus comitatus* in twelfth-century England: their origins and meaning', *Bulletin of the Institute of Historical Research*, LIX (1986), pp. 137–46; G.J. White, 'The restoration of order in England, 1153–1165', unpub. Ph. D. diss. (Cambridge University, 1974), p. 163; R.H.C. Davis, *King Stephen, 1135–1154* (London, 3rd edn, 1990), Appendix I, 'Earls and earldoms', esp. pp. 125–8.

69 The following section is heavily based on Paul Dalton's invaluable research in *Conquest, Anarchy and Lordship*, esp. Chapters 4 and 5. For a history of the counts of Aumale, including the earl of York, see B. English, *The Lords of Holderness, 1086–1260: a study in feudal society*

(Oxford, 1979); and J.F. Planché, 'The early lords of Holderness', *Journal of the British Archaeological Association*, XXX (1874), pp. 121–9.

70 'Wapentakes' (the Danelaw equivalent of the southern 'hundreds') were the subdivisions of a shire or county, usually with their own courts. A soke is a type of Danelaw estate where groups of peasants (sometimes encompassing around twenty villages) owed suit of court, rent and often labour service to a local lord. On sokes and sokemen, see F.M. Stenton, 'The Danes in England', *Proceedings of the British Academy*, XIII (1927), pp.215–19.

71 Clay (ed.), *Early Yorkshire Charters*, XI, pp. 353–5; C[okayne], *The Complete Peerage*, X, pp. 439–40.

72 E. Barrington de Fonblanque, *Annals of the House of Percy, from the Conquest to the Opening of the 19th Century*, (London, 2 vols., 1887), I, p. 21. n. 4.

73 Sanders, *English Baronies*, p. 140.

74 Davis, *King Stephen*, Appendix I, 'Earls and earldoms', p. 141.

75 Dalton, *Conquest, Anarchy and Lordship*, pp. 164–5.

76 John of Hexham, in Arnold (ed.), *Opera Omnia*, p. 306.

77 English, *The Lords of Holderness*, p. 21.

78 K.R. Potter (ed.), *Gesta Stephani* (Oxford, 2nd edn, 1976), p. 103; see also Cronne, 'Ranulf de Gernons, earl of Chester, 1129–1153', p. 117.

79 R. Howlett (ed.), 'William of Newburgh', *Historia rerum Anglicarum*, in *Chronicle and Memorials of the Reigns of Stephen, Henry II and Richard I*, (Rolls Series, 4, vols., 1884–9), I, p. 103.

80 See Davis, *King Stephen*, pp. 39–43, for a list of locations.

81 This was the opinion of J.H. Round, in *Geoffrey de Mandeville*, but R.H.C. Davis, in 'What happened in King Stephen's reign, 1135–1154', p. 3, and in 'King Stephen and the earl of Chester revised', *English Historical Review*, LXXV (1960), pp. 654–60, claims it was fewer. A lot depends on whether one counts 'changing sides' as meaning a straight choice between the king and the empress, or whether Ranulf opted for a state of 'armed neutrality'.

82 On the earldom of Cambridge, see Davis, *King Stephen*, Appendix I, p. 135.

83 Orderic Vitalis, V, 125, cited in Davis, *King Stephen*, p. 47.

84 Potter (ed.), *Gesta Stephani*, p. 111.

85 Davis, *King Stephen*, p. 49.

86 Forester (ed.), *The Chronicle of Henry of Huntingdon*, p. 279.

87 Potter (ed.), *Gesta Stephani*, p. 123. See also John of Hexham, in Arnold (ed.), *Opera Omnia*, II, pp. 309–10.

88 John of Hexham, in Arnold (ed.), *Opera Omnia*, II, pp. 310–11. See also S. Painter, 'The Rout of Winchester', in F.A. Cazer (ed.), *Feudalism and Liberty: articles and addresses of Sidney Painter* (Baltimore, Maryland, 1961), pp. 157–64.

89 Potter, *Gesta Stephani*, p. 153.

90 J. Green, 'Earl Ranulf II and Lancashire', in A.T. Thacker (ed.), *The Earldom of Chester and its Charters*, special volume of the *Journal of the Chester Archaeological Society*, LXXI (1991), pp. 101–2.

91 Clay (ed.), *Early Yorkshire Charters*, VII, pp. 44–7.

92 Richard of Hexham, 'The acts of King Stephen, and the Battle of the Standard', in Stephenson (trans.), *Contemporary Chronicles of the Middle Ages*, pp. 63–4.

93 Sanders, *English Baronies*, p. 142; English, *The Lords of Holderness*, p. 22.

94 English, *The Lords of Holderness*, p. 22.

95 Forester (ed.), *The Chronicle of Henry of Huntingdon*, p. 278.

96 J.F.A. Mason, 'Roger de Montgomery and his sons (1067–1102)', *Transactions of the Royal Historical Society*, 5th series XIII (1963), pp. 14–15; Green, 'Earl Ranulf II and Lancashire', p. 104; C.W. Hollister, 'The Anglo-Norman civil war: 1101', *English Historical Review*, LXXXVIII (1973), pp. 315–34.

97 Green, 'Earl Ranulf II and Lancashire', p. 105.

98 H. A. Cronne, 'The Honour of Lancaster in Stephen's reign', *English Historical Review*, L (1935), pp. 670–80.

99 On Ranulf's connection with Coventry, see Davis, *King Stephen*, Appendix VII, 'Ranulf, earl of Chester, and Coventry', pp. 161–5.

100 Cronne, 'Ranulf de Gernons', p. 127.

101 John of Hexham in Arnold (ed.), *Opera Omnia*, II, pp. 322–3, quoted in P. Dalton, '*In neutro latere*: the armed neutrality of Ranulf II, earl of Chester in King Stephen's reign', *Anglo-Norman Studies*, XIV (1991), p. 53. See also Green, 'Earl Ranulf II and Lancashire', p. 106.

102 John of Hexham in Symeon of Durham, Arnold (ed.), *Opera Omnia*, II, p. 323.

103 Dalton, *Conquest, Anarchy and Lordship*, p. 175.

104 Clay (ed.), *Early Yorkshire Charters*, XI, pp. xii, 14, 192: John of Hexham in Symeon of Durham, Arnold (ed.), *Opera Omnia*, II, p. 323.

105 English, *The Lords of Holderness*, pp. 21–22; Dalton, *Conquest, Anarchy and Lordship*, p. 174

106 Gant acquisitions in the East Riding before 1135 are listed in Green, 'William Rufus, Henry I and the royal demesne', p. 344, n. 49.

107 Potter (ed.), *Gesta Stephani*, p. 239.

108 Howlett (ed.), 'The Chronicle of Robert of Torigni', in *Chronicles of the Reigns of Stephen, Henry II and Richard I*, IV, p. 177.

109 Davis, 'What happened in Stephen's reign, 1135–1154', p. 9.

110 The Angevins and heritability have sparked a complex debate. J.C. Holt, 'Politics and property in early medieval England', *Past and Present*, LVII (1972), pp. 3–52; E. King, 'The tenurial crisis of the early twelfth century', *Past and Present*, LXV (1974), pp. 110–17; S.D. White, 'Succession to fiefs in early medieval England,' *Past and Present*, LXV (1974), pp. 118–27; S.E. Thorne, 'English feudalism and estates in land', *Cambridge Law Journal*, VI (1959) new series, pp. 193–209; S.F.C. Milsom, *The Legal Framework of English Feudalism* (Cambridge, 1976); R.C. Palmer, 'The origins of property in England', *Law and History Review*, III (1985), pp. 1–50; J. Hudson, 'Life-grants of land and the development of inheritance in Anglo-Norman England', *Anglo-Norman Studies*, XII (1990), pp. 67–80; R.C. De Aragon, 'The growth of secure inheritance in Norman England', *Journal of Medieval History*, VIII (1982), pp. 381–91.

111 Dalton, *Conquest, Lordship and Anarchy*, pp. 281–95.

112 H.M. Thomas, *Vassals, Heiresses, Crusaders and Thugs: the gentry of Angevin Yorkshire, 1154–1216* (Philadelphia, Pennsylvania, 1993), pp. 33–4.

113 Thomas, *Vassals, Heiresses, Crusaders and Thugs*, pp. 37–9.

114 Thomas, *Vassals, Heiresses, Crusaders and Thugs*, pp. 14–15; see also Painter, *Studies in the History of the English Feudal Barony* (Baltimore, Maryland, 1943), pp. 135–6.

115 'William of Newburgh, *Historia rerum Anglicarum*', in Howlett (ed.), *Chronicles of the Reigns of Stephen, Henry II and Richard I*, pp. 103–4.

116 Dalton, *Conquest, Anarchy and Lordship*, p. 195; P. Dalton, 'William, earl of York, and royal authority in Yorkshire in the reign of Stephen', *Haskins Society Journal*, II (1990), p. 164.

117 For a copy of Percy's actual return, see Clay (ed.), *Early Yorkshire Charters*. XI, no. 88, p. 85, as well as 89, 335, 339, 353–4.

118 A figure based on Table 10, 'The *Cartae Baronum* for Yorkshire: 1166', in Dalton, *Conquest, Anarchy and Lordship*, p. 308.

119 These figures, and the updated Corbett rankings, are taken from Hollister, 'Henry I and the Anglo-Norman magnates', pp. 93–107; and C.W. Hollister, 'The magnates of King Stephen's reign: reluctant anarchists', *Haskins Society Journal*, V (1993), Appendix, 'The upper aristocracy of England in 1135', p. 87.

120 Sanders, *English Baronies*, pp. 52–3; English, *The Lords of Holderness*, p. 151.

121 On Geoffrey, see Clay (ed.), *Early Yorkshire Charters*, XI, p. 180.

3: The End of the Line?, pp. 72–8

1 S.F.C. Milsom, 'Inheritance by women in the twelfth and early thirteenth centuries', in M.S. Arnold, T.A. Green, S.A. Scully and S.D. White (eds.), *On the Laws and Customs of England: essays in honour of Samuel E. Thorne* (Chapel Hill, North Carolina, 1981), p. 69; S.L. Waugh, *The Lordship of England: royal wardships and marriages in English society and politics, 1217–1327* (Princeton, New Jersey, 1988), pp. 15–17.

2 F. Pollock and F.W. Maitland (intro. by S.F.C. Milsom), *The History of English Law before the Time of Edward I* (Cambridge, 2nd edn, 2 vols., 1968), II, p. 275.

3 A.L. Poole, 'England and Burgundy in the last decade of the twelfth century', in H.W.C. Davis (ed.), *Essays in History Presented to Reginald Lane Poole* (Oxford, 1927), p. 267.

4 G. Brenan, *A History of the House of Percy* (London, 2 vols., 1902), I, p. 13.

5 According to the charter reproduced in C.T. Clay (ed.), *Early Yorkshire Charters: based on the manuscript of the late William Farrer* (Edinburgh, 1963), XI: *The Percy Fee*, Charter no. 289, p. 359, which may be dated before 1151, Joscelin donated 100 shillings' rent from his Petworth Honour. See also L.F. Salzman, 'On the early history of the honour of Petworth', *Sussex Archaeological Collections*, LXVIII (1927), pp. 60–66.

6 M.T. Martin (ed.), *The Percy Chartulary*, Surtees Society, CXVII (Durham, 1911), no. CMXIV, p. 391; Clay (ed.), *Early Yorkshire Charters*, Charter no. 288, p. 358.

7 See, for example, Martin (ed.), *The Percy Chartulary*, Charter nos. CM, p. 385, and CMV, p. 387; and Clay (ed.), *Early Yorkshire Charters*, XI, Charter nos. 71, p. 69; and 288–96, pp. 358–63.

8 See J.H. Round, *Studies in Peerage and Family History* (London, 1901), pp. 41–3.

9 W.H.D. Longstaffe, 'The old heraldry of the Percys', *Archaeologia Aeliana*, 2nd series, IV (1860), p. 162.

10 W.S. Ellis, *The antiquities of heraldry, collected from the literature, coins, gems, vases and other monuments of pre-Christian and medieval times: with a catalogue of early armorial seals: tending to show emblems of the heathen deities of antiquity* (London, 1869), pp. 204–5.

11 Longstaffe, 'The old heraldry of the Percys', p. 160.

12 H. Hall (ed.), *The Red Book of the Exchequer* Rolls Series (London, 3 vols., 1896), I, pp. 201, 435.

13 G.E. C[okayne], revised and expanded by V. Gibbs, H.A. Doubleday, G.H. White and Lord H. de Walden, *The Complete Peerage: or a history of the House of Lords and all its members from the earliest times* (London, 1910–59), XII (1959), Part 2, pp. 362–3.

14 The partition is printed in full in *The Percy Chartulary*, no. MXCII, pp. 461–4; and Clay (ed.), *Early Yorkshire Charters*, XI, Charter no. 89, pp. 85–8.

15 R.H.C. Davis, 'What happened in Stephen's reign, 1135–1154', *History*, XLIX (1964), 165, p. 9.

16 Thus, 'pro anima Jocelini mariti mei defuncti', in Clay (ed.), *Early Yorkshire Charters*, XI, Charter no. 78, p. 74. See also Charter nos. 69–77, pp. 68–74.

17 See Clay (ed.), *Early Yorkshire Charters*, XI, Charter nos. 38–67, pp. 45–66. The two charters that refer to William, earl of Warwick, are nos. 50 and 60, the latter being ambiguous as to whether the earl was alive or dead.

18 Clay (ed.), *Early Yorkshire Charters*, XI, Charter no. 74, pp. 71–2.

19 Clay (ed.), *Early Yorkshire Charters*, XI, Charter no. 61, p. 62.

20 Martin (ed.), *The Percy Chartulary*, no. CMLXXI, p. 411; Clay (ed.), *Early Yorkshire Charters*, XI, Charter no. 285, p. 353; C[okayne], *The Complete Peerage*, X (1945), p. 448.

21 Hall (ed.), *Red Book of the Exchequer*, I, p. 434.

22 Martin (ed.), *The Percy Chartulary*, no. CDXXXV, p. 140.

23 W. Farrer (ed.), *Early Yorkshire Charters* (Edinburgh, 4 vols., 1915), II, Charter no. 668, pp. 24–5.

24 E. Barrington de Fonblanque, *Annals of the House of Percy, from the Conquest to the Opening of the 19th Century* (London, privately printed, 2 vols., 1887) I, p. 36.

25 C[okayne], *The Complete Peerage*, X, pp. 448–9. On the fighting in France, see R.V. Turner, *King John* (London, 1994), p. 48.

26 G.D.G. Hall (ed.) with M.T. Clanchy, *Tractatus de Legibus et Consuetudinibus Regni Anglie qui Glanvilla vocatur [The Treatise on the Laws and Customs of the Realm of England commonly called Glanvill]* (Oxford, 1993 edn), VII/3, pp. 77–8.

27 Hall (ed.), *Tractatus de Legibus et Consuetudinibus Regni Anglie qui Glanvilla Vocatur*, VII/3, p. 78.

28 F.M. Powicke, *The Loss of Normandy* (Manchester, 2nd edn, 1960), p. 131.

29 On Briwerre, see I.J. Sanders, *English Baronies: a study of their origin and descent, 1086–1327* (Oxford, 1960), pp. 123, 132–3; J.C. Holt, *The Northerners: a study in the reign of King John* (Oxford, 1961), pp. 218, 234–5.

30 For instance, Barrington de Fonblanque, *Annals of the House of Percy*, I, p. 44; Brenan, *History of the House of Percy*, I, p. 12.

31 T. Duffus Hardy (ed.), *Rotuli Litterarum Clausarum in Turri Londinensi*, Record Commission (London, 2 vols., 1833–4), I, p. 11; C[okayne], *The Complete Peerage*, X, p. 449; Clay (ed.), *Early Yorkshire Charters*, XI, pp. 6–7. It is often claimed that he inherited Maud's half, an unfortunate mistake of the first order, which lends weight to the view that Richard usurped his nephew.

32 Martin (ed.), *The Percy Chartulary*, no. VI, pp. 6–7.

33 Martin (ed.), *The Percy Chartulary*, no. VIII, pp. 8–10.

34 A translation of the litigation is provided in Barrington de Fonblanque, *Annals of the House of Percy*, I, Appendix 2, pp. 482–7.

35 Martin (ed.), *The Percy Chartulary*, no. MXCIII, pp. 464–5.

36 Martin (ed.), *The Percy Chartulary*, nos. XI, p. 11, XLVII, p. 28, CLXIX, p. 73.

37 The details of the feud are multifarious and nefarious. See C[okayne], *The Complete Peerage*, X, p. 450n; Clay (ed.), *Early Yorkshire Charters*, XI, pp. 147–8, 197, 203, 208–11, 275; E.M. Poynton's contribution to 'Notes and Queries', *Genealogist*, XXIV (1908), p. 69; and the relevant charters in Martin (ed.), *The Percy Chartulary*.

38 Pollock and Maitland, *The History of English Law*, II, p. 285–6.

4: Sir Richard Percy, pp. 79–93

1 Quoted in J.C. Holt, 'Magna Carta and the origins of Statute law', *Studia Gratiana*, XV (1972), p. 487.

2 M.J. Vine, 'Two Yorkshire rebels: Peter de Brus and Richard de Percy', *Yorkshire Archaeological Journal*, XLVII (1975), p. 76.

3 J.C. Holt, 'The end of the Anglo-Norman realm', *Proceedings of the British Academy*, LXI (1975), pp. 223–65.

4 H.M. Thomas, *Vassals, Heiresses, Crusaders and Thugs: the gentry of Augevin Yorkshire, 1154–1216* (Philadelphia, Pennsylvania, 1993), pp. 174–83; P.D.A. Harvey, 'The English inflation of 1180–1220', *Past and Present*, LXI (1973), pp. 3–30; F.A. Cazer, Jr., 'The tax of 1185 in aid of the Holy Land', *Speculum*, XXX (1955), pp. 385–92; J.L. Bolton, 'Inflation, economics and politics in thirteenth-century England', *Thirteenth Century England*, IV (1991), pp. 1–14; N.J. Mayhew, 'Money and prices in England from Henry II to Edward III', *Agricultural History Review*, XXXV (1987), pp. 121–32.

5 H. Jenkinson, 'A money-lender's bonds of the twelfth century', in H.W.C. Davis (ed.), *Essays in History Presented to Reginald Land Poole* (Oxford, 1927), pp. 202–4.

6 R.B. Dobson, 'The Jews of medieval York and the Massacre of March 1190', *Borthwick Papers No. 45* (York, 1974), pp. 40–1.

7 S. Menache, 'Matthew Paris's attitudes toward Anglo-Jewry', *Journal of Medieval History*, XXIII (1997), p. 154.

8 William of Newburgh, *Historia rerum Anglicanum*, in R. Howlett (ed.), *Chronicles of the Reigns of Stephen, Henry II and Richard I*, Rolls Series (London, 2 vols., 1884–5), I, p. 313.

9 R. Davies, 'The medieval Jews of York', *Yorkshire Archaeological and Topographical Journal*, III (1873–4) Part I, p. 162. See also J.R. Marcus, *The Jew in the Medieval World: a source book, 1315–1791* (Cincinnati, Ohio, 1990 rep.), p. 132, for a similar explanation.

10 Quoted in F.M. Powicke, *King Henry III and the Lord Edward: the community of the realm in the thirteenth century* (Oxford, 2 vols., 1947), I, p. 125.

11 Dobson, 'The Jews of medieval York', p. 17, n. 60.

12 J.C. Holt, *The Northerners: a study in the reign of King John* (Oxford, 1961), p. 154.

13 Holt, *Northerners*, p. 161.

14 Holt, *Northerners*, pp. 164–5.

15 R.V. Turner, *King John* (London, 1994), p. 98.

16 Turner, *King John*, p. 113; J.C. Holt, 'The origins of the Magna Carta', p. 145, in his collection, *Magna Carta and Medieval Government* (London, 1985).

17 Holt, 'Origins of Magna Carta', p. 136.

18 Holt, *Northerners*, pp. 27, 173.

19 Vine, 'Two Yorkshire rebels', p. 77–8.

20 Holt, 'Origins of Magna Carta', p. 136.

21 Holt, *Northerners*, pp. 79–102.

22 Turner, *King John*, pp. 221–3.

23 J.C. Holt, *Magna Carta* (Cambridge, 1965), p. 96.

24 E. Mason, *Norman Kingship* (Bangor, 1991), p. 25.

25 J.C. Holt, 'The origins of the constitutional tradition in England', p. 13, published in *Magna Carta and Medieval Government*.

26 C.R. Cheney, 'The eve of Magna Carta', *Bulletin of the John Rylands Library*, XXXVIII (1955–6), pp. 312–13.

27 Holt, *Magna Carta*, p. 140.

28 A month after President Kennedy was assassinated, the Crown estates gave an acre of land to the United States at Runnymede, upon which a memorial was built. The Magna Carta memorial itself was paid for by the American Bar Association, a comment on the importance of the charter within the Anglo-American legal tradition. Article by John Lanchester, *Daily Telegraph*, 13 September 1997.

29 A copy is reproduced in Holt, *Magna Carta*, Appendix III, 'The Articles of the Barons', pp. 304–12.

30 Holt, *Magna Carta*, pp. 164–8 (from which the quotation is taken); Cheney, 'The eve of Magna Carta', esp. pp. 324–34; J. Stevenson (ed.), *Radulphi de Coggeshall Chronicon Anglicanum*, Rolls Series (London, 1875), p. 172; H.R. Luard (ed.), *Annales Monastici*, Rolls Series (London, 5 vols., 1864–9), III, p. 43; W. Stubbs (ed.), *Memoriale Fratris Walteris de Coventria*, Rolls Series (London, 2 vols., 1872–3), II, p. 221. On the sealing and signing of documents (including a fascinating discussion of just how it was all done), see G.C. Crump, 'The execution of the Great Charter', *History*, VIII (1928), pp. 247–53.

31 S. Painter, 'Magna Carta', in F.A. Cazel (ed.), *Feudalism and Liberty: articles and addresses of Sidney Painter* (Baltimore, Maryland, 1961), pp. 252–3.

32 H.R. Luard (ed.), *Matthaei Parisiensis, Monachi Sancti Albani, Chronica Majora*, Rolls Series (London, 7 vols., 1872–83), II, p. 604, contains a list of the twenty-five.

33 Holt, *Northerners*, pp. 194–216.

34 E. Miller, 'The background of Magna Carta', *Past and Present*, XXIII (1962), p. 77.

35 As Professor Sir Paul Vinogradoff showed in 'Magna Carta, C. 39: *nullius liber homo, etc.*', esp. pp. 80–2, in H.E. Malden (ed.), *Magna Carta Commemoration Essays* (London, 1917).

36 H.E. Malden, Introduction, p. xxix, to Malden (ed.), *Magna Carta Commemoration Essays*.

37 Turner, *King John*, p. 243.

38 F. Thompson, *Magna Carta: its role in the making of the English Constitution, 1300–1629* (Minneapolis, Minnesota, 1948), p. 92; Turner, *King John*, p. 248.

39 H.D. Hazeltine, 'The influence of Magna Carta on American constitutional development', esp. pp. 209–11, in Malden (ed.), *Magna Carta Commemoration Essays*.

40 Turner, *King John*, p. 247.

41 V.H. Galbraith, 'Runnymede revisited', *Proceedings of the American Philosophical Society*, CX (1966), p. 308.

42 C.R. Cheney and W.H. Semple (eds. and trans.), *Selected Letters of Pope Innocent III concerning England (1198–1216)*, (Walton-upon-Thames, 1953).

43 The treasure, and whether it was really lost, has spurred an interesting debate. See Holt, 'King John's disaster in the Wash', pp. 111–22, in *Magna Carta and Medieval Government*; W. St John Hope, 'The loss of King John's baggage train in the Wellstream in October, 1216', *Archaeologia*, LX (1906), pp. 93–110; G. Fowler, 'King John's treasure', *Proceedings of the Cambridge Antiquarian Society*, XLVI (1952), pp. 4–20; A.V. Jenkinson, 'The jewels lost in the Wash', *History*, VIII (1923).

44 T. Duffus Hardy (ed.), *Rotuli Litterarum Clausarum in Turri Londinensis*, Record Commission (London, 2 vols., 1833–4), I, p. 308.

45 Duffus Hardy (ed.), *Rotuli Litterarum Clausarum*, I, p. 339.

46 Powicke, *King Henry III and the Lord Edward*, I, pp. 1–41.

47 Turner, *King John*, pp. 248–57. A copy of the 1225 version may be found in Holt, *Magna Carta*, Appendix VIII, pp. 350–8. The various changes are discussed in Holt, 'Magna Carta and the origins of Statute law', pp. 289–307, in Holt, *Magna Carta and Medieval Government*.

48 Holt, *Magna Carta*, pp. 275–6.

49 Powicke, *King Henry III and the Lord Edward*, I, p. 148.

50 J.C. Holt, 'Rights and liberties in Magna Carta', pp. 210–13, in *Magna Carta and Medieval Government*. See also Miller, 'The background of Magna Carta', pp. 73–4.

51 Powicke, *King Henry III and the Lord Edward*, I, pp. 147–51.

52 Luard (ed.), *Matthaei Parisiensis, Monachi Sancti Albani, Chronica Majora*, III, pp. 381–2.

53 Vine, 'Two Yorkshire rebels', p. 78.

54 G.E. C[okayne], revised and expanded by V. Gibbs, H.A. Doubleday, G.H. White and Lord H. de Walden, *The Complete Peerage: or a history of the House of Lords and all its members from the earliest times* (London, 1910–59), X (1945), p. 453.

55 M.T. Martin (ed.), *The Percy Chartulary*,

Surtees Society, CXVII (Durham, 1911), no. CDLXI, pp. 148–9.

56 C[okayne] *The Complete Peerage*, X, p. 454 and n. See also Martin (ed.), *The Percy Chartulary*, no. DCCCLXXIX, pp. 375–6.

57 He was last recorded as living in that year, but his date of death is unknown. Martin (ed.), *The Percy Chartulary*, no. CCCCXLII, pp. 142–3.

58 Martin (ed.), *The Percy Chartulary*, no. XLVII, p. 28.

59 Martin (ed.), *The Percy Chartulary*, no. CCXXXV, p. 93.

5: Sir Henry Percy, pp. 94–110

1 G.E. C[okayne], revised and expanded by V. Gibbs, H.A. Doubleday, G.H. White and Lord H. De Walden, *The Complete Peerage: or a history of the House of Lords and all its members from the earliest times* (London, 1910–59), X (1945), p. 455n.

2 M.T. Martin (ed.), *The Percy Chartulary*, Surtees Society, vol. CXVII (Durham/London, 1911), no. LXXVI.

3 C[okayne] *The Complete Peerage*, X, p. 455 and n.

4 C[okayne] *The Complete Peerage*, XII (1953), pp. 503–4.

5 M. Prestwich, *Edward I* (London, 1988), pp. 27–8, based on the Historical Manuscripts Commission, *Report on the Manuscripts of Lord Middleton* (London, 1911), pp. 67–9. Professor Prestwich does not mention Percy in his list of Edward's supporters, but see C[okayne] *The Complete Peerage*, X, p. 455n., which does list him.

6 This 'factional' interpretation is of very recent origin. Previously, the 'Baronial Movement of Reform' was seen as a straightforward and idealistic clash of community and Crown. See R.F. Treharne, *The baronial plan of reform, 1258–1263* (Manchester, 1932), and his *Simon de Montfort and Baronial Reform: thirteenth-century essays* (London, 1986); H.W. Ridgeway, 'The Lord Edward and the Provisions of Oxford (1258): a study in faction', *Thirteenth Century England*, I (1985), pp. 89–99; H.W. Ridgeway, 'King Henry III and the "Aliens", 1236–1272', *Thirteenth Century England*, II (1987), pp. 81–92; H.W. Ridgeway, 'Foreign favourites and Henry III's problems of patronage, 1247–1258', *English Historical Review*, CIV (1989), no. 412, pp. 590–610.

Also, D. Williams, 'Simon de Montfort and his adherents', pp. 166–77, in W.M. Ormrod (ed.), *England in the thirteenth century: proceedings of the 1984 Harlaxton Symposium* (Grantham, 1985).

7 On the Savoyards, see Ridgeway, 'King Henry III and the "Aliens", 1236–1272', p. 84.

8 On the Poitevins, see S. Painter, 'The Houses of Lusignan and Châtellerault, 1150–1250', pp. 73–89, in F.A. Cazel (ed.), *Feudalism and liberty: articles and addresses of Sidney Painter* (Baltimore, Maryland, 1961).

9 Prestwich, *Edward I*, p. 21.

10 *Matthaei Parisiensis, Monachi Sancti Albani, Chronica Majora*, Rolls Series (London, 7 vols., 1872–83), V, pp. 697–8, quoted in Prestwich, *Edward I*, p. 26.

11 For what follows, see mostly D.A. Carpenter, 'King, magnates and society: the personal rule of King Henry III, 1234–1258', pp. 75–106, in Carpenter, *The Reign of Henry III* (London, 1996).

12 R. Stewart-Brown, 'The end of the Norman earldom of Chester', *English Historical Review*, XXXV (1920), 137, pp. 26–53.

13 See Carpenter, 'King, magnates and society: the personal rule of King Henry III, 1234–1258', p. 95, and 'King Henry III's "Statute" against aliens: July 1263', p. 262, both in Carpenter, *The Reign of Henry III*; I.J. Sanders, *English Baronies: a study of their origin and descent, 1086–1327* (Oxford, 1960), pp. 144–5; Ridgeway, 'King Henry III and the "Aliens", 1236–1272', p. 88.

14 In 1774, Edward's tomb in Westminster Abbey was opened. The description in the text is that of a witness in J. Ayloffe, 'An account of the body of King Edward the First, as it appeared on opening his tomb in the year 1774', *Archaeologia*, III (1786), quoted in Prestwich, *Edward I*, pp. 566–7.

15 On Henry's grants to Edward, see Prestwich, *Edward I*, p. 11; on Henry's scrutiny of his son's affairs, see J.R. Studd, 'The Lord Edward and Henry III', *Bulletin of the Institute of Historical Research*, XLX (1977), pp. 4–19. On the royal demesne, see Ridgeway, 'Foreign favourites and Henry III's problems of patronage, 1247–1258', p. 598.

16 Ridgeway, 'The Lord Edward and the Provisions of Oxford (1258)', pp. 91–3.

17 On Sicily, see Carpenter, 'What happened in 1258?', pp. 184–7, in Carpenter, *The Reign of Henry III*; and F.M. Powicke, *King Henry III and the Lord Edward: the community of the realm in the thirteenth century* (Oxford, 2 vols., 1947), I, pp. 343–409.

18 For the 'eyewitness' nature of this account see Carpenter, 'What happened in 1258?', pp. 188–9 and n. 22, in Carpenter, *The Reign of Henry III*. The account I have used in the text is from the 'Annales Monasterii e Theokesberia' (the original of which is kept in the British Library, Cotton MSS Cleopatra A/VII, fos. 1–67v.), printed in H.R. Luard (ed.), *Annales Monastici*, Rolls Series (London, 5 vols., 1864–9), I, pp. 163–5. The translation here is taken from Carpenter, 'What happened in 1258?', pp. 187–8.

19 'Status Regni Nostri Ordinetur', 2 May 1258, no. 2, in R.E. Treharne and I.J. Sanders (eds.), *Documents of the Baronial Movement of Reform and Rebellion, 1258–1267* (Oxford, 1973).

20 R.F. Treharne, 'The personal role of Simon de Montfort in the period of baronial reform and rebellion, 1258–1265', p. 320, in Treharne, *Simon de Montfort and Baronial Reform*. For the text, see 'Provisiones Oxonie', June–July 1258, no. 5, in Treharne and Sanders (eds.), *Documents of the Baronial Movement, 1258–1267*.

21 A.H. Hershey, 'Success or failure? Hugh Bigod and judicial reform during the Baronial Movement, June 1258–February 1259', *Thirteenth Century England*, V (1993), pp. 65–83.

22 'Petitio Baronum', May 1258, no. 3, in Treharne and Sanders (eds.), *Documents of the Baronial Movement, 1258–1267*.

23 'Litera Cuiusdam de Curia Regis de Parliamento Oxonie', c. 18 July 1258, no. 4, in Treharne and Sanders (eds.), *Documents of the Baronial Movement, 1258–1267*.

24 These paragraphs based on Carpenter's, 'What happened in 1258?', pp. 193–7, in Carpenter, *The Reign of Henry III*.

25 Prestwich, *Edward I*, p. 27; also Luard (ed.), *Matthaei Parisiensis, Monachi Sancti Albani, Chronica Majora*, V, pp. 747–8.

26 Luard (ed.), *Matthaei Parisiensis, Monachi Sancti Albani, Chronica Majora*, V, p. 744, translated in Powicke, *King Henry III and the Lord Edward*, I, p. 406.

27 Prestwich, *Edward I*, p. 29; Carpenter, 'The Lord Edward's oath' in Carpenter, *The Reign of Henry III*, pp. 245–6; P. Chaplais, 'The making of the Treaty of Paris (1259) and the royal style', *English Historical Review*, LXVII (1952), pp. 235–53; W. Stubbs (ed.), *The Historical Works of Gervase of Canterbury*, Rolls Series (London, 2 vols., 1879–80), I, pp. 209–10.

28 See *Report on the Manuscripts of Lord Middleton*, Historical Manuscripts Commission (London, 1911), pp. 67–9.

29 Prestwich, *Edward I*, pp. 32–3.

30 *Calendar of Close Rolls of the reign of Henry III* (London, 14 vols, 1902–1938), XI, p. 158.

31 Prestwich, *Edward I*, pp. 34–5.

32 H.W. Ridgeway, 'King Henry III's grievances against the Council in 1261: a new version and a letter describing political events', *Historical Research*, LXI (1988), 145, pp. 227–42; E.F. Jacob, 'The complaints of Henry III against the Baronial Council in 1261', *English Historical Review*, XLI (1926), 164, pp. 559–71.

33 'Grauamina pro quibus Dominus Rex queritur de Consilip suo', 9 March 1261, no. 30, in Treharne and Sanders (eds.), *Documents of the Baronial Movement, 1258–1267*.

34 'Alexander [IV] ... Regi Anglorum', 13 April 1261, no. 32; 'Alexander ... Archiepiscopo Cantuariensi et Aliis', 29 April 1261, no. 33; 'Alexander ... Archiepiscopo Cantuariensi et Aliis', 7 May 1261, no. 34; 'Urbanus [IV] ... Archiepiscopo Cantuariensi et Aliis', 25 February 1262, no. 36, in Treharne and Sanders (eds), *Documents of the Baronial Movement, 1258–1267*.

35 D.A. Carpenter, 'King Henry III and the Tower of London', p. 205, in Carpenter, *The Reign of Henry III*.

36 Luard (ed.), *Matthaei Parisiensis, Monachi Sancti Albani, Chronica Majora*, V, p. 744, quoted in D.A. Carpenter, 'Simon de Montfort: the first leader of a political movement in English history', p. 232, in Carpenter, *The Reign of Henry III*; Stubbs (ed.), *The Historical Works of Gervase of Canterbury*, II, p. 217.

37 M. Howell, 'The children of King Henry III and Eleanor of Provence', *Thirteenth Century England*, IV (1991), p. 61.

38 Prestwich, *Edward I*, p. 38.

39 See Treharne, *Baronial Plan of Reform*, p. 288. However, Martin (ed.), *The Percy Chartulary*, no. DCCCLXXIX, p. 376, n. 1, claims he died overseas.

40 *Calendar of Close Rolls, 1261–64*, p. 249.

41 R.F. Treharne, 'Why the battle of Lewes matters in English history', pp. 150–3, in Treharne, *Simon de Montfort and Baronial Reform*.

42 W.W. Shirley (ed.), *Royal and other historical letters illustrative of the reign of Henry III, from the originals in the Public Record Office*, Rolls Series (London, 2 vols., 1862–6), II, no. DCIX, 16 December 1263, pp. 251–2.

43 'Grauaminia quibus Terra Anglie Opprimebatur', January 1264, no. 37C, in Treharne and Sanders (eds.), *Documents of the Baronial Movement, 1258–1267*. The king's note is 'Per ista Subscripta Grauatur Rex Anglie', January 1264, no. 37A.

44 T. Rymer (ed.), *Foedera, Conventiones, Litterae, et cujuscumque generis Acta Publica*, Records Commission (London, 1816 edn), I, p. 434; W.H. Blaauw, *The Barons' War, including the battles of Lewes and Evesham* (London, 1844), p. 96, n. 1, wherein 'Henry Percy' is called 'Hugh Percy'.

45 'Reformacio Pacis inter Henricum Regem Anglie et Barones Regni sui', 23 January 1264, no. 38, in Treharne and Sanders (eds.), *Documents of the Baronial Movement, 1258–1267*.

46 J.O. Halliwell (ed.), *The Chronicle of William de Rishanger of the Barons' Wars*, Camden Society (London, 1840); C[okayne], *The Complete Peerage*, X, p. 455 n.; R.F. Treharne, 'The battle of Northampton, 5th April 1264', pp. 299–316, in *Simon de Montfort and Baronial Reform*.

47 D.A. Carpenter, *The Battles of Lewes and Evesham, 1264/65* (Keele, 1987), p. 17.

48 Carpenter, *The Battles of Lewes and Evesham*, pp. 19–36.

49 Blaauw, *Barons' War*, p. 175. Regarding Percy's surrender, see H.R. Luard (ed.), *Flores Historiarum*, Rolls Series (London, 3 vols., 1890), II, p. 496.

50 From a contemporary chronicle, quoted in Carpenter, *The Battles of Lewes and Evesham*, p. 33.

51 C[okayne], *The Complete Peerage*, XII, p. 504.

52 Prestwich, *Edward I*, p. 49; and Carpenter, *The Battles of Lewes and Evesham*, p. 38.

53 This account is based on Carpenter, *The Battles of Lewes and Evesham*, pp. 52–66.

54 Halliwell (ed.), *Chronicle of William de Rishanger*, p. 45, quoted in Prestwich, *Edward I*, p. 51. The 'arm of St James' was a Spanish champion's relic recently brought to England (Blaauw, *The Barons' War*, p. 245).

55 Robert of Gloucester, quoted in Blaauw, *The Barons' War*, p. 252.

56 Carpenter, *The Battles of Lewes and Evesham*, pp. 65–6.

57 W. Stubbs, *The Constitutional History of England* (Oxford, 2 vols., 4th edn, 1906), II, p. 103.

58 'Henricus de Percy fuit in prisona inter duo bello de Lewes et Evesham', Martin (ed.), *The Percy Chartulary*, no. DCCCLXVI, p. 368.

59 'Incipit Dictum de Kelenworthe', 30 October 1266, no. 44, in Treharne and Sanders (eds.), *Documents of the Baronial Movement, 1258–1267*.

60 See R. Studd, 'The marriage of Henry of Almain and Constance of Béarn', *Thirteenth Century England*, III (1989), pp. 161–77; Blaauw, *The Barons' War*, pp. 299–311.

61 J.C. Atkinson (ed.), *Cartularium Abbathiae de Whiteby*, Surtees Society, LXIX (Durham, 2 vols., 1879–81), II, p. 686.

62 W.P. Hedley, *Northumberland Families* (Newcastle, 2 vols., 1968–70), II, genealogical table on p. 13 errs uncharacteristically in listing John as 'Joan de Percy, d. in infancy'.

63 C[okayne], *The Complete Peerage*, X, p. 456n.

64 C[okayne], *The Complete Peerage*, X, p. 455.

6: Great Captain, pp. 111–41

1 K.J. Stringer, 'Scottish foundations: thirteenth-century perspectives', in K.J. Stringer and A. Grant (eds.), *Uniting the Kingdom: the making of British history* (London, 1995), pp. 85–6.

2 G.W.S. Barrow, 'The Anglo-Scottish Border', *Northern History*, I (1996), pp. 21–42; and his 'Frontier and settlement: which influence which? England and Scotland, 1100–1300', in R. Bartlett and A. MacKay (eds.), *Medieval Frontier Societies* (Oxford, 1989), pp. 3–21.

3 The text is in E.L.G. Stones (ed.), *Anglo-Scottish Relations, 1174–1328: some selected documents* (Oxford, 2nd edn, 1970), no. 7,

'Carta Convenciones', pp. 38–53. The quotations are from K.J. Stringer, 'Scottish foundations: thirteenth-century prespectives', in Stringer and Grant (eds.), *Uniting the Kingdom*, p. 86.

4 D. Hay, 'England, Scotland and Europe: the problem of the frontier', *Transactions of the Royal Historical Society*, 5th series, XXV (1975), p. 80.

5 Stones, *Anglo-Scottish Relations*, no. 8, 'Marchie Inter Regna', pp. 54–7.

6 A. Goodman, 'The Anglo-Scottish Marches in the fifteenth century: a frontier society?', in R.A. Mason (ed.), *Scotland and England, 1286–1815* (Edinburgh, 1987), p. 19.

7 G.T. Lapsley, 'The problem of the North', in G.T. Lapsley (ed.), *Crown, Community and Parliament in the Later Middle Ages: studies in English constitutional history* (Oxford, 1951), p. 385.

8 D.E.R. Watt, 'The minority of Alexander III of Scotland', *Transactions of the Royal Historical Society*, 5th series, XXI (1971), pp. 10, 14.

9 Watt, 'The minority of Alexander III'; and A. Young, 'The political role of Walter Comyn, earl of Menteith, during the minority of Alexander III of Scotland', *Scottish Historical Review*, LVII (1978), pp. 121–42.

10 G.W.S. Barrow, *Robert Bruce and the Community of the Realm of Scotland* (Edinburgh, 3rd edn, 1988), pp. 1–2.

11 Barrow, *Robert Bruce*, pp. 20–3.

12 G. Stell, 'The Balliol family and the Great Cause of 1291–92', in K.J. Stringer (ed.), *Essays on the Nobility of Medieval Scotland* (Edinburgh, 1985), pp. 150–65; Barrow, *Robert Bruce*, pp. 25–6; I.J. Sanders, *English Baronies: a study of their origin and descent, 1086–1327* (Oxford, 1960), p. 25.

13 A.A.M. Duncan, 'The community of the realm of Scotland and Robert Bruce: a review', *Scottish Historical Review*, XLV (1966), pp. 187–8.

14 G.W.S. Barrow and A. Royan, 'James Fifth Stewart of Scotland', in Stringer (ed.), *Essays on the Nobility of Medieval Scotland*, pp. 166–87, provide the indispensable biography of the man.

15 Duncan, 'The community of the realm', pp. 186–7. See also E.M. Barron, *The Scottish War of Independence: a critical study* (Inverness, 2nd edn, 1934), p. 112; and J.

Stevenson (ed.), *Documents illustrative of the history of Scotland from the death of King Alexander the Third to the accession of Robert Bruce* (Edinburgh, 2 vols., 1870), I, p. 22.

16 Barrow, *Robert Bruce*, p. 28. The Treaty is reproduced in Stevenson (ed.), *Documents illustrative of the history of Scotland*, I, pp. 162–73.

17 Barrow, *Robert Bruce*, p. 29.

18 Stones, *Anglo-Scottish Relations*, no. 14, 'Appellaciones Septem Comitum', pp. 88–101, esp. pp. 98–9 and n. 3.

19 Stones, *Anglo-Scottish Relations*, p. xix.

20 G.W.S. Barrow, 'The reign of William the Lion, king of Scotland', *Historical Studies*, VII (1969), pp. 21–44.

21 Stones, *Anglo-Scottish Relations*, no. 2, 'Carta Regis Ricardi', pp. 13–17.

22 Stones, *Anglo-Scottish Relations*, no. 6, 'Bulla Gregorii Pape Noni', pp. 34–7.

23 Stones, *Anglo-Scottish Relations*, no. 9, 'Bulla Innocencii Pape Quarti', pp. 58–9.

24 Stones, *Anglo-Scottish Relations*, no. 12, 'Homagium Regis Scocie', pp. 80–1.

25 The preceding few paragraphs have been heavily based on the account given in Barrow, *Robert Bruce*, pp. 30–8.

26 G. Neilson, 'Bruce *versus* Balliol, 1291–1292: the model for Edward I's tribunal', *Scottish Historical Review*, XVI (1918) 61, pp. 1–14, contains a good account, as does Barrow, *Robert Bruce*, pp. 39–53.

27 A summary of the arguments is in E.L.G. Stones and G.G. Simpson (eds.), *Edward I and the Throne of Scotland, 1290–1296: an edition of the record sources for the Great Cause* (Oxford, 2 vols., 1978), I, pp. 13–21.

28 See Neilson, 'Bruce *versus* Balliol', pp. 7–8. The quotation is from Barrow, *Robert Bruce*, p. 39.

29 Neilson, 'Bruce *versus* Balliol', p. 11.

30 Stones, *Anglo-Scottish relations*, no. 19, 'Judicium Super Peticionibus', pp. 118–25.

31 Barrow, *Robert Bruce*, p. 50.

32 Stones, *Anglo-Scottish Relations*, no. 20, 'Homagium Regis Scocie', pp. 126–9.

33 J.M.W. Bean, 'The Percies and their estates in Scotland', *Archaeologia Aeliana*, 4th series, XXXV (1957), pp. 92–3.

34 W. Dickson (ed.), 'Cronica Monasterii de Alnewyke ex quodam Libro Cronicarum in Libraria Collegii Regalis Cantabrigiae de dono Regis Henricis VI Fundatoris', in *Archaeologia Aeliana*, 1st series, III (1844), pp. 38–9.

35 N. Denholm-Young, *History and Heraldry, 1254–1310: a study of the historical value of the Rolls of Arms* (Oxford, 1965), pp. 59, 103.

36 W.H.D. Longstaffe, 'The old heraldry of the Percys', *Archaeologia Aeliana*, 2nd series, IV (1860), pp. 163–7; Anon., 'The House of Percy', *Herald and Genealogist*, III (1866), pp. 271–2; J.H. Round, *Studies in Peerage and Family History* (London, 1901), pp. 41–3.

37 Appendix J, 'The Warenne group of checkered shields', in G.E. C[okayne], revised and expanded by V. Gibbs, H.A. Doubleday, G.H. White and Lord H. de Walden, *The Complete Peerage: or a history of the House of Lords and all its members from the earliest times* (London, 1910–59), XII (1953), Part 1, pp. 26–8.

38 *Calendar of Fine Rolls* (London, HMSO, 22 vols., 1911–63), I, p. 346, entry dated 15 October 1294. See also *Calendar of Welsh Rolls, 1277–1294*, in *Calendar of the Various Chancery Rolls, 1277–1326* (London, HMSO, 1912), p. 358.

39 G. Stell, 'The Balliol family and the Great Cause of 1291–92', in Stringer (ed.), *Essays on the Nobility of Medieval Scotland*, p. 160.

40 C[okayne], *The Complete Peerage*, XII, p. 506.

41 Barrow, *Robert Bruce*, p. 59.

42 Barrow, *Robert Bruce*, pp. 62–3.

43 Stevenson (ed.), *Documents illustrative of the history of Scotland*, II, nos. CCCXLIII and CCCXLIV, pp. 8–15.

44 Barrow, *Robert Bruce*, pp. 63–8; Stones (ed.), *Anglo-Scottish Relations*, no. 22, 'Homage e Fealté', p. 139.

45 Stevenson (ed.), *Documents illustrative of the history of Scotland*, II, no. CCCXLII, pp. 7–8.

46 Stones (ed.), *Anglo-Scottish Relations*, no. 23, 'Reddicio Hamgii Regis Scocie', pp. 140–5.

47 For much of what follows, see Barrow, *Robert Bruce*.

48 C[okayne], *The Complete Peerage*, X (1945), p. 456; M. Prestwich, *Edward I* (London, 1988), p. 470.

49 N. Denholm-Young, 'Feudal society in the thirteenth century: the knights', in N. Denholm-Young, *Collected Papers: cultural, textual and biographical essays on medieval topics* (Cardiff, 1969), p. 90.

50 H. Maxwell (ed. and trans.), *The Chronicle of Lanercost 1272–1346* (Glasgow, 1913), p. 134. See also Prestwich, *Edward I*, p. 471.

51 See F. Palgrave, *Documents and records illustrating the history of Scotland (etc.)*, Record

Commission (London, 1837), p. 149; Maxwell, 'The Chronicle of Lanercost', p. 385.

52 Stevenson (ed.), *Documents illustrative of the history of Scotland*, II, nos. CCCLIV (1 April), p. 35; CCCLVI, 'De Operariis Mittendis Domino Regi Usque Berewyke' (4 April), pp. 37–8.

53 G. Washington, 'The Border heritage, 1066–1292', *Transactions of the Cumberland and Westmorland Antiquarian and Archaeological Society*, LXII (1962), pp. 104–5, citing Sir Thomas Grey's *Scalachronica* of 1355–7.

54 Prestwich, *Edward I*, pp. 472–3; Maxwell, *The Chronicle of Lanercost*, p. 387.

55 E.A. Bond (ed.), *Chronica Monasterii de Melsa, a Fundatione usque ad Annum 1396, Auctore Thoma de Burton, Abbate. Accedit Continuatio ad Annum 1406 a Monacho Quodam ipsius Domus*, Rolls Series (London, 3 vols., 1866–8), II, p. 262.

56 Maxwell (ed. and trans.), *The Chronicle of Lanercost*, p. 140. The English soldiery sang to his feats: 'For those Scots,/I rate 'em as sots,/What a sorry shower!/Whose utter lack/In the attack/Lost 'em at Dunbar.' See E.L.G. Stones, 'English chroniclers and the affairs of Scotland, 1286–1296', in R.H.C. Davis and J.M. Wallace-Hadrill (eds.), *The Writing of History in the Middle Ages* (Oxford, 1981), p. 337.

57 C[okayne], *The Complete Peerage*, X, p. 456.

58 Stevenson (ed.), *Documents illustrative of the history of Scotland*, II, no. CCCLXXII, pp. 59–77.

59 Barrow, *Robert Bruce*, pp. 73–4; Anon., 'The Coronation Stone of Scotland', *Scottish Historical Review*, VIII (1911), pp. 223–4. See also E.L.G. Stones and M.N. Blount, 'The surrender of King John of Scotland to Edward I in 1296: some new evidence', *Bulletin of the Institute of Historical Research*, XLVIII (1975), pp. 94–106; J.O. Prestwich, 'The English campaign in Scotland in 1296 and the surrender of John Balliol: some supporting evidence', *Bulletin of the Institute of Historical Research*, XLIV (1976), pp. 135–8; Stones (ed.), *Anglo-Scottish Relations*, no. 25, 'Minimenta Regum Scocie', pp. 150–3; no. 31, 'L'Apostoille et le Droit d'Escoce', p. 233.

60 See Stevenson (ed.), *Documents illustrative of the history of Scotland*, II, no. CCCLII, 'Journal of the movements of King

Edward in Scotland', pp. 25–32; H.G. Richardson and G. Sayles, 'The Scottish Parliaments of Edward I', *Scottish Historical Review*, XXV (1928), p. 309.

61 Stevenson (ed.) *Documents illustrative of the history of Scotland*, II, no. CCCLXXXIX, 8 September 1296, p. 100; Bond (ed.), *Chronica Monasterii de Melsa*, II, p. 263. See also J. Bain (ed.), *Calendar of documents relating to Scotland preserved in Her Majesty's Public Record Office, London* (Edinburgh, 4 vols., 1881–8), II, no. 846, 6 October 1296, pp. 222–3.

62 Stevenson (ed.), *Documents illustrative of the history of Scotland*, II, no. CD, 6 October 1296, p. 110.

63 Sanders, *English Baronies*, pp. 35–6, 103–4; Denholm-Young, *History and heraldry*, pp. 98–9; C[okayne], *The Complete Peerage*, III (1913), p. 290.

64 Barrow, *Robert Bruce*, pp. 73–4.

65 C[okayne], *The Complete Peerage*, XII, p. 506; Barrow, *Robert Bruce*, p. 78.

66 On Wallace, see Barrow, *Robert Bruce*, pp. 90–3. See also E. Ewan's critical review of *Braveheart* and *Rob Roy* in *American Historical Review*, October 1995, pp. 1219–21.

67 Stevenson (ed.), *Documents illustrative of the history of Scotland*, II, no. CDXXXI, 4 June 1297, pp. 170–3.

68 Bain (ed.), *Calendar of documents relating to Scotland*, II, no. 887, 4 June 1297, p. 233.

69 Palgrave (ed.), *Documents illustrative of the history of Scotland*, no. CIX, pp. 197–8, and also p. cxxiii; Stevenson (ed.), *Documents illustrative of the history of Scotland*, II, no. CDXLVII, 7 July 1297, pp. 192–4.

70 Stevenson (ed.), *Documents illustrative of the history of Scotland*, II, no. CDLIII, 23 July 1297, pp. 200–3.

71 Quoted and translated in Barrow, *Robert Bruce*, p. 85.

72 Stevenson (ed.), *Documents illustrative of the history of Scotland*, II, no. CDLV, 24 July 1297, pp. 206–9.

73 Barrow, *Robert Bruce*, p. 86.

74 On Percy's presence at Stirling Bridge see Bond (ed.), *Chronica Monasterii de Melsa*, II, p. 268.

75 Barrow, *Robert Bruce*, pp. 87–8; Barron, *The Scottish War of Independence*, pp. 69–70; T.C.F. Botchie, *The Battlefields of Scotland: their legend and story* (New York, 1913), pp. 60–2. Another note on Wallace and

Braveheart. Even the battle scenes depicted in the film, which garnered admiring reviews for their 'realism', are a damp squib. The film showed two lines of Englishmen and Scotsmen running at each other and colliding. Wallace's Lowlanders would not have worn kilts, and the last Scotsman, or rather Pict, who painted his face blue with woad lived five centuries before Wallace was born. The producers also replaced the Highlander leader, Andrew Murray, with a crazed Irishman acting as Wallace's sidekick.

76 T. Wright (ed.), *The Chronicle of Pierre de Langtoft, in French verse, from the earliest period to the death of King Edward I*, Rolls Series (London, 2 vols., 1866–8), II, p. 301.

77 Barrow, *Robert Bruce*, p. 92; Stevenson (ed.), *Documents illustrative of the history of Scotland*, II, no. CDLXXVII, 21 October 1297, p. 237; Bain (ed.), *Calendar of documents relating to Scotland*, II, no. 954, 21 October 1297, p. 245.

78 Stevenson (ed.), *Documents illustrative of the history of Scotland*, II, no. CDLXXVIII, 23 October 1297, pp. 237–9; no. CDLXXIX, 26 October 1297, pp. 239–40.

79 Prestwich, *Edward I*, p. 479.

80 Contract, dated 19–20 December 1297, reproduced in H. Gough (ed.), *Scotland in 1298: documents relating to the campaign of King Edward in First in that year, and especially to the battle of Falkirk* (Paisley, 1888), p. 65.

81 Stevenson (ed.), *Documents illustrative of the history of Scotland*, II, no. CDLXXXIX, 10 December 1297, pp. 249–50; Gough (ed.), *Scotland in 1298*, p. 66.

82 Stevenson (ed.), *Documents illustrative of the history of Scotland*, II, no. CDLXVI, 5 August 1297, pp. 222–4.

83 'Writ to John de Warenne, earl of Surrey, Captain of the Expedition', 22 January 1298, in Gough (ed.), *Scotland in 1298*, pp. 70–1.

84 Barrow, *Robert Bruce*, pp. 95–9.

85 W. Seymour, *Battles in Britain, 1066–1746* (London, 1997), pp. 76–82; Barrow, *Robert Bruce*, pp. 99–104; Prestwich, *Edward I*, pp. 480–1; Denholm-Young, *History and Heraldry*, pp. 106–7 (see notes below).

86 Gerard Brault's *Rolls of Arms of Edward I (1272–1307)* (London, 2 vols., 1997), I, pp. 404–17, reproduces the complete Falkirk Roll and the divisions between the four brigades.

87 F. Palgrave (ed.), *The Parliamentary writs and writs of military summons, together with the records and muniments relating to the suit and service due and performed to the King's High Court of Parliament and the Councils of the Realm, or affording evidence of attendance given at Parliament and Councils* (London, 2 vols. in 4, 1827–34), I, p. 776.

88 S.L. Waugh, *The Lordship of England: royal wardships and marriages in English society and politics, 1217–1327* (Princeton, New Jersey, 1988), pp. 17–18.

89 Waugh, *The Lordship of England: royal wardships and marriages in English society and politics, 1217–1327* (Princeton, New Jersey, 1988), pp. 17–18.

90 C[okayne], *The Complete Peerage*, III, p. 290.

91 Prestwich, *Edward I*, pp. 436–51.

92 Prestwich, *Edward I*, p. 560.

93 Prestwich, *Edward I*, pp. 436–40.

94 Stevenson (ed.), *Documents illustrative of the history of Scotland*, II, no. DLXXII, 16 July 1299, pp. 379–81.

95 Stevenson (ed.), *Documents illustrative of the history of Scotland*, II, no. DLX, 20 February 1299, p. 367; *Calendar of Fine Rolls*, I, dated 6 March 1299, p. 410.

96 As Edward stated in the grant (Bain (ed.), *Calendar of documents relating to Scotland*, II, no. 1060, 20 February 1299, p. 270), the lands 'which formerly belonged to Ingelram de Balliol, deceased, and now devolving *by hereditary right* on Ingelram de Umfraville the king's enemy and rebel [italics added]'. See also L. Keen, 'The Umfravilles, the castle and the barony of Prudhoe, Northumberland', *Anglo-Norman Studies*, V (1982), pp. 165–84.

97 Bean, 'The Percies and their estates in Scotland', pp. 92–3 (contains a family tree); J. Bain, 'The Percies in Scotland', *Archaeologia Aeliana*, XLI (1884), p. 336. See also Stell, 'The Balliol family and the Great Cause of 1291–2', in Stringer (ed.), *Essays on the Nobility of Medieval Scotland*, p. 154.

98 (London, 1864), Brault (ed.), *Rolls of Arms of Edward I (1272–1307)*, I, 'Caerlaverock Poem', pp. 434–43. Percy is number 18 on the Roll.

99 Palgrave (ed.), *Parliamentary writs and writs of military summons*, I, p. 776, 20 September 1300.

100 *Calendar of Chancery Warrants, 1244–1326* (London, HMSO, 1927), p. 136, 1 October 1301.

101 C[okayne], *The Complete Peerage*, X, p. 459n.

102 Bain (ed.), *Calendar of documents relating to Scotland*, II, no. 1258, 17 November 1301, p. 321.

103 M. Prestwich, *The Three Edwards: war and state in England, 1272–1377* (London, 1980), p. 157.

104 M.T. Martin (ed.), *The Percy Chartulary*, Surtees Society, CXVII (Durham/London, 1911), no. LXXVIII, 31 January 1303, pp. 43–4. See also Bond (ed.), *Chronica Monasterii de Melsa*, II, p. 229; C.T. Clay (ed.), *Early Yorkshire Charters*, XI: *The Percy Fee* (Yorkshire Archaeological Society, 1963), p. 13.

105 Stones (ed.), *Anglo-Scottish Relations*, no. 28, 'Bulla Pape Bonifacii', 27 June 1299, pp. 162–75.

106 Stones (ed.), *Anglo-Scottish Relations*, no. 32, 'Sire Robert de Bruce le Filz', pp. 236–9.

107 Barrow, *Robert Bruce*, pp. 114–27; E.L.G. Stones, 'The submission of Robert Bruce to Edward I, c. 1301–2', *Scottish Historical Review*, XXXII (1953), pp. 122–34; Duncan, 'The community of the realm', pp. 194–8.

108 Palgrave (ed.), *Parliamentary writs and writs of military summons*, I, p. 776, entry dated 20 January 1303.

109 Prestwich, *Edward I*, p. 498; Barrow, *Robert Bruce*, p. 126. See Stevenson (ed.), *Documents illustrative of the history of Scotland*, II, no. DCXXIII, 29 September 1302, p. 448, for the original order made by Edward for a raid under Segrave's command.

110 Prestwich, *Edward I*, pp. 499–500.

111 Bain, 'The Percies in Scotland', p. 337.

112 *Calendar of Chancery Warrants, 1244–1326*, p. 204, entry dated 21 February 1304.

113 Barrow, *Robert Bruce*, pp. 129–30; Prestwich, *Edward I*, p. 500.

114 Palgrave (ed.), *Documents and records illustrating the history of Scotland*, no. CXXV, pp. 262–3; and no. CXXVI, p. 267.

115 Bain (ed.), *Calendar of documents relating to Scotland*, II, p. 672.

116 Stevenson (ed.), *Documents illustrative of the history of Scotland*, II, no. DCXXX, 3 January 1304, pp. 465–6; no. DCXXXIX, 31 March 1304 [Greek Fire], pp. 479–80; no. DCXL, 12 April 1304, p. 481; no. DCXLI, 16 April 1304, pp. 482–3; no. DCXLII, 16 April 1304, pp. 483–4; no. DCXLIII, 30 June 1304, pp. 484–5; *Calendar of Chancery Warrants, 1244–1326*, p. 210, 6 April 1304; Prestwich, *Edward I*, pp. 501–2; Barrow, *Robert Bruce*, pp. 128–9.

117 Barron, *The Scottish War of Independence*, p. 150.

118 C[okayne], *The Complete Peerage*, XII, p. 507.

119 W. Stubbs (ed.), 'Annales Londonienses', in *Chronicles of the Reigns of Edward I and Edward II*, Rolls Series (London, 2 vols., 1882–3), I, p. 133.

120 Prestwich, *Edward I*, p. 503.

121 Barrow, *Robert Bruce*, p. 137; A.A.M. Duncan, *The Nation of Scots and the Declaration of Arbroath (1320)*, Historical Association (London, 1970), p. 17.

122 Palgrave (ed.), *Parliamentary writs and writs of military summons*, I, entry dated 15 September 1305.

123 Duncan, *Nation of Scots and the Declaration of Arbroath*, p. 19.

124 The quotation is taken from Barrow, *Robert Bruce*, p. 135. For the powers of the officials and land reorganisation, see the Ordinance, printed in full in Stones (ed.), *Anglo-Scottish Relations*, no. 33, 'Super Stabilitate Terre Scocie', September 1305, pp. 240–59.

125 Barrow, *Robert Bruce*, pp. 145–6.

126 Palgrave (ed.), *Parliamentary writs and writs of military summons*, I, entry dated 5 April 1306, p. 776; Bain (ed.), *Calendar of documents relating to Scotland*, II, no. 1754, 5 April 1306, p. 473.

127 Barrow, *Robert Bruce*, p. 153.

128 Master John Barbour (ed. W.W. Skeat), *The Bruce; or, the Book of the Most Excellent and Noble Prince, Robert de Broyss, King of Scots*, Early English Text Society Extra Series, XI and XXI (London, 2 vols., 1870–4), I, Book 2, lines 66–7.

129 G.G. Simpson and J.D. Galbraith (eds.), *Calendar of documents relating to Scotland, 1108–1516, preserved in the Public Record Office*, Rolls Series (London, 2 vols., 1862–6), Supplementary (Scottish Record Office, 1988), V, no. 420, 13–15 April 1306, p. 191.

130 Prestwich, *Edward I*, p. 507.

131 Skeat (ed.), Barbour's *Bruce*, I, Book 2, lines 360–1; Simpson and Galbraith (eds.), *Calendar of documents relating to Scotland, 1108–1516*, Supplementary, V, no. 434, June 1306, p. 192.

132 Bain (ed.), *Calendar of documents relating to Scotland*, II, no. 1808, 25 July 1306, p. 485.

133 Barrow, *Robert Bruce*, pp. 161–2; Palgrave (ed.), *Documents and records illustrating the history of Scotland*, no. CLV, pp. 358–9.

134 F.W.D. Brie (ed.), *The Brut, or the Chronicles of England*, Early English Text Society, CXXXI (London, 1906), I, Book 5, lines 107–12.

135 Skeat (ed.), Barbour's *Bruce*, I, Book 5, lines 185–222.

136 Bain (ed.), *Calendar of documents relating to Scotland*, II, no. 1896, 11 February 1307, p. 504.

137 Bain (ed.), *Calendar of documents relating to Scotland*, II, no. 1895, 6 February 1307, p. 504.

138 Skeat (ed.), Barbour's *Bruce*, I, Book 6, lines 476–672; Book 7, lines 1–632; Book 8, lines 1–520; Barrow, *Robert Bruce*, pp. 169–72; A.A.M. Duncan, 'The war of the Scots, 1306–23', The Prothero Lecture, *Transactions of the Royal Historical Society*, 6th series, II (1992), pp. 139–40.

7: The Border Baron, pp. 142–66

1 A general picture from M. Prestwich, *The Three Edwards: war and state in England, 1272–1377* (London, 1980), pp. 137–8, 160–1.

2 W. Dickson (ed.), 'Cronica Monasterii de Alnewyke ex quodam Libro Cronicarum in Libraria Collegii Regalis Cantabrigiae de dono Regis Henrici VI Fundatoris', in *Archaeologia Aeliana*, 1st series, III (1844), p. 38.

3 G.J. Brault (ed.), *Rolls of Arms of Edward I (1272–1307)* (London, 2 vols., 1997), I, p. 436; G.E. C[okayne], revised and expanded by V. Gibbs, H.A. Doubleday, G.H. White and Lord H. de Walden, *The Complete Peerage: or a history of the House of Lords and all its members from the earliest times* (London, 1910–59), XII (1959), Part 2, pp. 370–1.

4 Brault (ed.), *Rolls of Arms of Edward I*, I, pp. 406, 434; C[okayne], *The Complete Peerage*, VII (1929), pp. 681–7.

5 F.W.D. Brie (ed.), *The Brut, or the Chronicles of England*, Early English Text Society, orig. series, CXXXI (London, 1906), pp. 202–3; H. Maxwell (trans.), *The Chronicle of Lanercost, 1272–1346* (Glasgow, 1913), p. 182; M. Prestwich, *Edward I* (London/Yale, 2nd edn, 1997), p. 557.

6 J.S. Hamilton, *Piers Gaveston, Earl of Cornwall, 1307–1312: politics and patronage in the reign of Edward II* (Detroit, Michigan/London, 1988), pp. 19–28.

7 Hamilton, *Piers Gaveston*, pp. 29–34.

8 J.R. Lumby (ed.), *Polychronicon Ranulphi Higden Monachi Cestrensis*, Rolls Series (London, 9 vols., 1865–86, VIII, p. 298; H. Johnstone, 'The eccentricities of Edward II', *English Historical Review*, XLVIII (1933), 190, pp. 264–7.

9 Hamilton, Piers Gaveston, p. 35.

10 C.T. Wood, 'Personality, politics and constitutional progress: the lessons of Edward II', *Studia Gratiana*, XV (1972), p. 522; and C. Robinson's somewhat dated but marvellously titled 'Was Edward II a degenerate?', in the *American Journal of Insanity*, LXVI (1910), pp. 445–64.

11 According to an inquisition taken on the death of Percy, cited in J.M.W. Bean, 'The Percies' acquisition of Alnwick', *Archaeologia Aeliana*, 4th series, XXXII (1957), p. 316.

12 C[okayne], *The Complete Peerage*, III (1913), p. 291; W. Stubbs (ed.), 'Annales Paulini', in *Chronicles of the Reigns of Edward I and Edward II*, Rolls Series (London, 2 vols., 1882–3), I, p. 257; Prestwich, *The Three Edwards*, p. 190. A contemporary treatise on the marshal may be found in F. Grose, *Military antiquities respecting a history of the English army from the Conquest to the present time* (London, new edn, 1801), pp. 193–7.

13 F. Palgrave (ed.), *Parliamentary writs and writs of military summons*, Records Commission (London, 2 vols. in 4, 1827–34), II, p. 1275.

14 The following paragraphs on Bruce's movements are based on G.W.S. Barrow, *Robert Bruce and the community of the realm of Scotland* (Edinburgh, 3rd edn, 1985), pp. 174–82.

15 Palgrave (ed.), *Parliamentary writs and writs of military summons*, II, p. 1275.

16 Barrow, *Robert Bruce*, pp. 190–2.

17 N. Denholm-Young (ed.), *Vita Edwardi Secundi Monachi Cuiusdam Malmesberiensis*

(London, 1957), p. 2; Hamilton, *Piers Gaveston*, pp. 43–5.

18 Hamilton, *Piers Gaveston*, pp. 46–7 and n. 67; J.R.S. Phillips, *Aymer de Valence, earl of Pembroke, 1307–1324* (Oxford, 1972), pp. 26–8; N. Denholm-Young, *History and Heraldry, 1254–1310: a study of the historical value of the Rolls of Arms* (Oxford, 1965), pp. 130–1.

19 T. Rymer (ed.), *Foedera, Conventiones, Litterae, et cujuscumque generis Acta Publica, inter Reges Angliae et alios quosuis Imperatores, Reges, Pontifices, Principes, bel Communitatis ab ingressu Gulielmi I. in Angliam. A.D. 1066*, Records Commission (London, 4 vols., 1816–69), II, Part 1, p. 27.

20 Prestwich, *The Three Edwards*, p. 80.

21 Stubbs (ed.), 'Annales Paulini', I, p. 260; W. Stubbs (ed.), 'Gesta Edwardi de Carnarvon Auctore Canonico Bridlingtoniensi', in the *Chronicles*, II, p. 32.

22 For the following, see Hamilton, *Piers Gaveston*, pp. 47–8; Stubbs (ed.), 'Annales Paulini', I, pp. 261–2; L.E. Tanner, 'Westminster Abbey and the Coronation Service', *History*, XXI (1936–7), pp. 289–301; R.S. Hoyt, 'The Coronation Oath of 1308', *English Historical Review*, LXXI (1956), 280, pp. 353–83.

23 Denholm-Young (ed.), *Vita Edwardi Secundi*, p. 4.

24 Hamilton, *Piers Gaveston*, pp. 48–9.

25 *Calendar of Fine Rolls, 1307–1319* (London, HMSO, 1912), p. 18, entry dated 16 March 1308. Thus, 'Commitment during pleasure to Henry de Percy of the castle of Scardeburgh. Order to the tenants to be intendant to him as constable. *Vacated because surrendered and cancelled.*'

26 Hamilton, *Piers Gaveston*, pp. 50–1 and nn. 103, 104.

27 Hamilton, *Piers Gaveston*, pp. 53–5.

28 Denholm-Young (ed.), *Vita Edwardi Secundi*, p. 6.

29 Palgrave (ed.), *Parliamentary writs and writs of military summons*, II, p. 1275, entry dated 16 June 1308.

30 Palgrave (ed.), *Parliamentary writs and writs of military summons*, II, p. 1275.

31 Denholm-Young (ed.), *Vita Edwardi Secundi*, pp. 6–7.

32 Denholm-Young (ed.), *Vita Edwardi Secundi*, p. 8.

33 Denholm-Young (ed.), *Vita Edwardi Secundi*, p. 87; S.L. Waugh, *The Lordship of England: royal wardships and marriages in English society and politics, 1217–1327* (Princeton, New Jersey, 1988), pp. 219–20.

34 J.H. Trueman, 'The personnel of medieval reform: the English Lords Ordainers of 1310', *Mediaeval Studies*, XXI (1959), pp. 263–4.

35 C[okayne], *The Complete Peerage*, I (1910), pp. 241–2; Trueman, 'Personnel of medieval reform', p. 265.

36 C[okayne], *The Complete Peerage*, X (1945), pp. 219–20.

37 Denholm-Young (ed.), *Vita Edwardi Secundi*, p. 7.

38 Maxwell (trans.), *Chronicle of Lanercost*, p. 234.

39 C[okayne], *The Complete Peerage*, VII, pp. 378–90; Trueman, 'Personnel of medieval reform', pp. 258–9.

40 Denholm-Young, *History and Heraldry*, pp. 101–2; K. Lomas, *North-east England in the Middle Ages* (Edinburgh, 1992), p. 65.

41 W. Dugdale, *The baronage of England, or an historical account of the lives and the most memorable actions of our English nobility in the Saxons time, to the Norman Conquest; and from thence, of those who had their rise before the end of King Henry the Third's reign* (London, 2 vols., 1675), I, p. 273. Previous Percy biographers accept Dugdale's version.

42 Dickson (ed.), 'Cronica Monasterii de Alnewyke', p. 38.

43 M.T. Martin (ed.), *The Percy Chartulary*, Surtees Society, CXVII (Durham, 1911), no. DCCCXXXIV, pp. 349–50.

44 Martin (ed.), *The Percy Chartulary*, no. DCCXXI, p. 266, dated 20 January 1296.

45 Martin (ed.), *The Percy Chartulary*, no. DCCXIX, pp. 265–6, and see n. 11. See also E.S. Scroggs (ed.), *Feet of Fines, Northumberland, 1273–1346* (Newcastle, 1932).

46 Martin (ed.), *The Percy Chartulary*, no. DCXLIII, pp. 219–25, no. DCCLVIII, pp. 290–1; *Calendar of Inquisitions Post Mortem* (London, HMSO, 1908), V, no. 535, p. 312. See also no. 534, pp. 304–10. In 1315, a jury decided that 'Gilbert de Aton is next heir to William de Vescy the elder', citing a complex genealogy to justify the decision.

47 I have relied on J.M.W. Bean's invaluable article, 'The Percies' acquisition of Alnwick', *Archaeologia Aeliana*, 4th series,

XXXII (1954), pp. 309–14, but differ in my conclusions.

48 Bean, 'The Percies' acquisition of Alnwick', p. 317; Martin (ed.), *The Percy Chartulary*, no. CDLXXX, p. 156.

49 Denholm-Young (ed.), *Vita Edwardi Secundi*, p. 63.

50 M. Prestwich, 'Italian merchants in late thirteenth and early fourteenth century England', in (no editor) *The Dawn of Modern Banking* (Yale, 1979), pp. 77–104; T. Blomquist, 'Alien coins and foreign exchange banking in a medieval commune: thirteenth-century Lucca', *Journal of Medieval History*, XX (1994), pp. 337–46.

51 Bean, 'The Percies' acquisition of Alnwick', pp. 316–17 and n. 40.

52 Martin (ed.), *The Percy Chartulary*, no. DCXLIII, p. 221, n. 5; W. Stubbs (ed.), 'Annales Londonienses', in *Chronicles of the Reigns of Edward I and Edward II*, Rolls Series (London, 2 vols., 1882–3), I, p. 176.

53 See C. Hussey, 'Alnwick Castle: the seat of the duke of Northumberland', Part 1, *Country Life*, 22 June 1929, pp. 890–8. I am grateful to Dr John Maddison for this reference. On the changing fashions of castle-building, see Prestwich, *Edward I*, pp. 208–15.

54 Stubbs (ed.), 'Annales Londonienses', I, pp. 168–70.

55 Palgrave (ed.), *Parliamentary writs and writs of military summons*, II, p. 1276; and Stubbs (ed.), 'Annales Londonienses', I, p. 133.

56 F. C. Hingeston (ed.), John Capgrave's *The Chronicle of England*, Rolls Series (London, 1858), p. 178.

57 *Calendar of Chancery Warrants, 1244–1326* (London, HMSO, 1927), p. 360, entry dated 29 April 1311.

58 Denholm-Young (ed.), *Vita Edwardi Secundi*, p. 21.

59 Stubbs (ed.), 'Annales Londonienses', I, p. 202.

60 *Calendar of Fine Rolls, 1307–1319*, p. 127, entry dated 6 March 1312.

61 Palgrave (ed.), *Parliamentary writs and writs of military summons*, II, p. 1276, entries dated 13 and 14 March 1312.

62 Denholm-Young (ed.), *Vita Edwardi Secundi*, p. 22.

63 Stubbs (ed.), 'Annales Londonienses', I, p. 204.

64 Palgrave (ed.), *Parliamentary writs and writs of military summons*, II, p. 1276, entry dated 17 May 1312.

65 Hamilton, *Piers Gaveston*, Appendix 2, pp. 119–26.

66 W. Stubbs (ed.), 'Gesta Edwardi de Carnarvon Auctore Canonico Bridlingtoniensis', in *Chronicles of the Reigns of Edward I and Edward II*, Rolls Series (London, 2 vols., 1882–3), II, pp. 42–3; Maxwell (trans.), *Chronicle of Lanercost*, p. 197.

67 Stubbs (ed.), 'Annales Londonienses', I, pp. 204–6.

68 Denholm-Young (ed.), *Vita Edwardi Secundi*, p. 25.

69 Denholm-Young (ed.), *Vita Edwardi Secundi*, p. 25–6.

70 Denholm-Young (ed.), *Vita Edwardi Secundi*, p. 28.

71 Denholm-Young (ed.), *Vita Edwardi Secundi*, p. 27. See also Stubbs (ed.), 'Annales Londonienses', I, p. 207.

72 Stubbs (ed.), 'Annales Londonienses', I, p. 208; Maxwell (trans.), *Chronicle of Lanercost*, pp. 198–9.

73 Maxwell (trans.), *Chronicle of Lanercost*, pp. 199–205.

74 Denholm-Young (ed.), *Vita Edwardi Secundi*, p. 30–1.

75 *Calendar of Fine Rolls, 1307–1319*, p. 141, entry dated 28 July 1312.

76 Martin (ed.), *The Percy Chartulary*, p. 246, n. 3.

77 Denholm-Young (ed.), *Vita Edwardi Secundi*, p. 33–6.

78 *Calendar of Fine Rolls, 1307–1319*, p. 156, 18 December 1312; also Stubbs (ed.), 'Annales Londonienses, I, p. 225.

79 Hamilton, *Piers Gaveston*, pp. 104–6.

80 Palgrave (ed.), *Parliamentary writs and writs of military summons*, p. 1276, entry dated 16 October 1313; Martin (ed.), *The Percy Chartulary*, no. CDLXIX, p. 151.

81 Martin (ed.), *The Percy Chartulary*, no. DCLXXVIII, p. 246 and n. 3.

82 Much has been written on Bannockburn. The most detailed recent narrative is Barrow, *Robert Bruce*, pp. 203–32. See also Becke's Appendix B in C[okayne], *The Complete Peerage*, XI (1949), pp. 7–38. A lengthy account is given in Master John Barbour (edited by W. W. Skeat), *The Bruce; or, the Book of the Most Excellent and Noble Prince, Robert de Broyss, King of Scots*, Early English Text Society Extra Series, XXI

(London, 2 vols., 1870–4), II, Books 11, 12 and 13.

83 This is a tricky subject. Previous biographers have assumed he was there (as does the *Dictionary of National Biography*, which based its entry on said biographers), but no medieval chronicle of the time that I have consulted mentions his name in its account of the battle, a very odd omission considering Percy's fame and status. The error appears to have first appeared in John Hardyng's *Chronicle from the Firste Begynnyng of England unto the Reigne of Kyng Edwarde the Fourth*, which mentions Percy fleetingly, but this account was written more than a century after Bannockburn. Not only was Hardyng a notorious forger, but he was closely associated with the Percys at the time (and anyone else who paid him).

84 Barrow, *Robert Bruce*, pp. 206–7.

85 Denholm-Young, *History and Heraldry*, p. 142, n. 1. See also *Calendar of Fine Rolls, 1307–1319*, p. 212, entry dated 2 October 1314.

86 Denholm-Young (ed.), *Vita Edwardi Secundi*, p. 49.

87 Denholm-Young (ed.), *Vita Edwardi Secundi*, p. 49.

88 See Palgrave (ed.), *Parliamentary writs and writs of military summons*, II, p. 1276, entries dated 23 December 1313 and 24 March 1314.

89 E.A. Bond (ed.), 'Addition by Adam, Abbas Quartus Decimus' to *Chronica Monasterii de Melsa, a Fundatione usque ad Annum 1396, Auctore Thoma de Burton, Abbate. Accedit Continuatio ad Annum 1406 a Monacho Quodam ipsius Domus*, Rolls Series (London, 3 vols., 1866–8), II, pp. 330–1.

90 Palgrave (ed.), *Parliamentary writs and writs of military summons*, II, p. 1276, entry dated 30 June 1314.

91 Palgrave (ed.), *Parliamentary writs and writs of military summons*, II, nos. 39 and 40, pp. 427–30.

92 Bond (ed.), 'Addition by Adam, Abbas Quartus Decimus', in *Chronica Monasterii de Melsa*, II, pp. 330, 332–3.

93 J. Scammell, 'Robert I and the North of England', *English Historical Review*, LXXIII (1958), 288, esp. pp. 387 (Alnwick figures), 403. See also A.A.M. Duncan, 'The war of the Scots, 1306–23', *Transactions of the Royal Historical Society*, 6th series, II (1992), pp. 147–8.

94 Although the *Dictionary of National Biography* states that he died in 1315, this is incorrect. The date given here is supported by the *Calendar of Fine Rolls, 1307–1319* (London, HMSO, 1912), pp. 212, 214; *Calendar of Inquisitions Post Mortem*, V, no. 536; and the *Calendar of Close Rolls, 1313–1318* (London, HMSO, 1893), p. 125.

8: Outbreak of Peace, pp. 167–97

1 From the Rev. Scott of Satchell's ballad, 'The Armstrongs' quoted in R. Borland, *Border Raids and Reivers* (Dalbeattie, 1898), p. 1.

2 *Calendar of Fine Rolls, 1307–1319* (London, HMSO, 1912), II, p. 219, entry dated 26 November 1314.

3 *Calendar of Fine Rolls, 1307–1319*, II, p. 378, entry dated 13 November 1318.

4 William Peeris, 'Metrical Chronicle of the Family of Percy', in *Richardson's reprints of rare tracts and imprints of antient manuscripts*, V (Newcastle, 1845).

5 *Calendar of Fine Rolls, 1307–1319*, II, p. 378, entry dated 13 November 1318.

6 M.T. Martin (ed.), *The Percy Chartulary*, Surtees Society, CXVII (Durham/London, 1911), no. DXXXIV, 1 July 1335, pp. 176–7; no. DLXXXI, 18 June 1335, pp. 196–7; no. DLXXXII, pp. 197–8; no. DLXXXIV, 18 June 1335, pp. 198–9.

7 K.B. McFarlane, *The Nobility of Later Medieval England: the Ford Lectures for 1953 and related studies* (Oxford, 1973), Appendix B, 'The rate of extinction of noble families', pp. 172–6.

8 J. Scammell, 'Robert I and the North of England', *English Historical Review*, LXXIII (1958), 288, pp. 385–403.

9 E.M. Thompson (ed.), *Adae Murimuth Continuatio Chronicarum*, Rolls Series (London, 1889), p. 24; E.M. Thompson (ed.), *Chronicon Galfridi le Baker de Swynebroke* (Oxford, 1889), p. 9.

10 N. Denholm-Young (ed.), *Vita Edwardi Secundi Monachi Cuiusdam Malmesberiensis* (London, 1957), p. 70.

11 M. Prestwich, *The Three Edwards: war and state in England, 1272–1377* (London, 1980), p. 142.

12 J. Raine (ed.), *Historical Papers and Letters from the Northern Registers*, Rolls Series (London, 1873), no. CLIX, pp. 246–7.

13 Denholm-Young (ed.), *Vita Edwardi Secundi*, p. 75–6.

14 Denholm-Young (ed.), *Vita Edwardi Secundi*, p. 76.

15 *Calendar of Close Rolls, 1318–1323* (London, HMSO, 1895), p. 179, 12 February 1320.

16 J.R.S. Phillips, 'The "Middle Party" and the negotiating of the Treaty of Leake, August 1318: a reinterpretation', *Bulletin of the Institute of Historical Research*, XLVI (1973), p. 16.

17 Denholm-Young (ed.), *Vita Edwardi Secundi*, p. 87; S.L. Waugh, *The Lordship of England: royal wardships and marriages in English society and politics, 1217–1327* (Princeton, New Jersey, 1988), pp. 219–20. The quotation is taken from G.E. C[okayne], revised and expanded by V. Gibbs, H.A. Doubleday, G.H. White and Lord H. de Walden, *The Complete Peerage: or a history of the House of Lords and all its members from the earliest times* (London, 1910–59), VII (1929), p. 687.

18 Denholm-Young (ed.), *Vita Edwardi Secundi*, p. 80–1.

19 Denholm-Young (ed.), *Vita Edwardi Secundi*, p. 82.

20 Denholm-Young (ed.), *Vita Edwardi Secundi*, p. 93.

21 Master John Barbour (ed. W.W. Skeat), *The Bruce; or, the Book of the Most Excellent and Noble Prince, Robert de Broyss, King of Scots*, Early English Text Society Extra Series, XI (London, 2 vols., 1870–4), I, Book 10, lines 275–99. For the description of Douglas as doughty of deed, see *ibid.*, II, Book 11, line 323.

22 H. Maxwell (trans.), *The Chronicle of Lanercost, 1272–1346* (Glasgow, 1913), pp. 219–20.

23 Maxwell (trans.), *Chronicle of Lanercost*, pp. 220–1; Thompson (ed.), *Chronicon Galfridi le Baker de Swynebroke*, p. 10.

24 G.G. Simpson and J.D. Galbraith (eds.), *Calendar of documents relating to Scotland, 1108–1516, preserved in the Public Record Office and the British Library* (Edinburgh, 1988), V, no. 646, p. 246, late 1318.

25 Maxwell (trans.), *Chronicle of Lanercost*, p. 228.

26 A.A.M. Duncan, *The Nation of Scots and the Declaration of Arbroath (1320)*, Historical Association (London, 1970), pp. 34–7.

27 Skeat (ed.), *Barbour's Bruce*, I, Book 1, lines 225–45.

28 Denholm-Young (ed.), *Vita Edwardi Secundi*, pp. 97–104.

29 J. Conway-Davies, 'The Despenser war in Glamorgan', *Transactions of the Royal Historical Society*, 3rd series, IX (1915), p. 21–64.

30 Denholm-Young (ed.), *Vita Edwardi Secundi*, p. 109.

31 W. Stubbs (ed.). 'Gesta Edwardi de Carnarvon Auctore Canonico Bridlingtoniensi', in *Chronicles of the Reigns of Edward I and Edward II*, Rolls Series (London, 2 vols., 1882–3), II, p. 61.

32 Denholm-Young (ed.), *Vita Edwardi Secundi*, p. 111.

33 Denholm-Young (ed.), *Vita Edwardi Secundi*, p. 112.

34 Thompson (ed.), *Adae Murimuth Continuatio Chronicarum*, p. 33; T.F. Tout (ed. H. Johnstone), *The Place of the Reign of Edward II in English History: based upon the Ford Lectures delivered in the University of Oxford in 1913* (Manchester, 2nd edn, 1936), p. 1.

35 Denholm-Young (ed.), *Vita Edwardi Secundi*, pp. 113–14.

36 Denholm-Young (ed.), *Vita Edwardi Secundi*, pp. 115–16.

37 T. Rymer (ed.), *Foedera, Conventiones, Litterae, et cujuscumque generis Acta Publica, inter Reges Angliae et alios quosuis Imperatores, Reges, Pontifices, Principes, bel Communitatis ab ingressu Gulielmi I. in Angliam, A.D. 1066*, Records Commission (London, 4 vols., 1816–69), II, p. 941.

38 N. Fryde, *The Tyranny and Fall of Edward II, 1321–1326* (Cambridge, 1979), p. 51; Thompson (ed.), *Chronicon Galfridi le Baker de Swynebroke*, pp. 10–12.

39 F. Palgrave (ed.), *Parliamentary writs and writs of military summons*, Records Commission (London, 2 vols. in 4, 1827–34), II, p. 1277, 12 November 1321, and Appendix, p. 169.

40 *Calendar of Fine Rolls, 1319–1327*, (London, HMSO, 1912), III, p. 82, 25 December 1321.

41 Thompson (ed.), *Adae Murimuth Continuatio Chronicarum*, p. 35.

42 C.R. Cheney and W.H. Semple (eds. and trans.), *Selected Letters of Pope Innocent III Concerning England (1198–1216)*, (Walton-upon-Thames, 1953).

43 Palgrave (ed.), *Parliamentary writs and writs of military summons*, II, p. 1277, entry dated 14 February 1322.

44 Palgrave (ed.), *Parliamentary writs and writs of military summons*, II, p. 1277, entry dated 26 February 1322.

45 F.W.D. Brie (ed.), *The Brut, or the Chronicles of England*, Early English Text Society, CXXXI (London, 1906), pp. 215–16.

46 Brie (ed.), *The Brut, or the Chronicles of England*, p. 217; Maxwell (trans.), *Chronicle of Lanercost*, p. 232; Skeat (ed.), *Barbour's Bruce*, I, Book 1, line 288.

47 Denholm-Young (ed.), *Vita Edwardi Secundi*, pp. 123–5; J. Mason, 'Sir Andrew de Harcla [*sic*], earl of Carlisle', *Transactions of the Cumberland and Westmorland Antiquarian and Archaeological Society*, XXIX (1929), pp. 98–137; T.F. Tout, 'The tactics of the Battles of Boroughbridge and Morlaix', *English Historical Review*, XIX (1904), no. 76, pp. 711–15. Regarding Hereford's death see Brie (ed.), *The Brut, or the Chronicles of England*, p. 219.

48 Palgrave (ed.), *Parliamentary writs and writs of military summons*, II, p. 1277, 14 March 1322; *Calendar of Fine Rolls, 1319–1327*, III, p. 106, 12 March 1322.

49 Stubbs (ed.), *Gesta Edwardi de Carnarvon Auctore Canonico Bridlingtoniensi*, II, p. 75; M.H. Keen, 'Treason trials under the law of arms', *Transactions of the Royal Historical Society*, 5th series, XII (1962), esp. pp. 102–3; Fryde, *The Tyranny and Fall of Edward II*, pp. 59–61.

50 B.C. Keeney, 'Military service and the development of nationalism in England, 1272–1327', *Speculum*, XXII (1947), pp. 534–49.

51 Denholm-Young (ed.), *Vita Edwardi Secundi*, p. 126.

52 Thompson (ed.), *Adae Murimuth Continuatio Chronicarum*, p. 38.

53 J. Mason, 'Sir Andrew de Harcla, earl of Carlisle', *Transactions of the Cumberland and Westmorland Antiquarian and Archaeological Society*, XXIX (1929), p. 118; K.B. McFarlane, 'Had Edward I a "policy" towards the earls?', in *The Nobility of Later Medieval England: the Ford Lectures for 1953 and related studies* (Oxford, 1973), pp. 247–67.

54 C[okayne], *The Complete Peerage*, X (1945), p. 460.

55 Palgrave (ed.), *Parliamentary writs and writs of military summons*, II, p. 1277, entry dated 1 May 1322.

56 Palgrave (ed.), *Parliamentary writs and writs of military summons*, II, p. 1277, entry dated 11 May 1322.

57 *Calendar of Close Rolls, 1318–1323* (London, HMSO, 1894–5), pp. 547–8, entry dated 1 May 1322.

58 G.W.S. Barrow, *Robert Bruce and the Community of the Realm of Scotland* (Edinburgh, 3rd edn, 1988), p. 243; Maxwell (trans.), *Chronicle of Lanercost*, pp. 238–9.

59 M.R. Powicke, 'The English Commons in Scotland in 1322 and the deposition of Edward II', *Speculum*, XXXV (1960), pp. 556–62.

60 Palgrave (ed.), *Parliamentary writs and writs of military summons*, II, p. 1277, 15 September and 20 September 1322; *Calendar of Patent Rolls, 1321–1324* (London, HMSO, 1904), p. 205.

61 Barrow, *Robert Bruce*, p. 275.

62 J. Bain (ed.), *Calendar of documents relating to Scotland preserved in Her Majesty's Public Record Office, London* (Edinburgh, 4 vols., 1881–8), III, no. 783, pp. 144–5, dated 26 September 1322.

63 C[okayne], *The Complete Peerage*, X, p. 816.

64 Maxwell (trans.), *Chronicle of Lanercost*, p. 240.

65 Brie (ed.), *The Brut, or the Chronicles of England*, pp. 225–6.

66 Palgrave (ed.), *Parliamentary writs and writs of military summons*, II, p. 1277, entry dated 27 November 1322.

67 Palgrave (ed.), *Parliamentary writs and writs of military summons*, II, p. 1277, entry dated 10 December 1322.

68 Maxwell (trans.), *Chronicle of Lanercost*, p. 241.

69 E.L.G. Stones (ed.), *Anglo-Scottish Relations, 1174–1328: some selected documents* (Oxford, 2nd edn, 1970), no. 39, 'Pax cum Scotis', pp. 308–15.

70 Maxwell (trans.), *Chronicle of Lanercost*, p. 242.

71 Maxwell (trans.), *Chronicle of Lanercost*, p. 243.

72 On this extraordinary story, see Professor Münch, 'Concordia Facta inter Anglicos et Scotos, 3 January 1322–3', *Proceedings of the Society of Antiquaries of Scotland*, III (1862), pp. 454–61.

73 Maxwell (trans.), *Chronicle of Lanercost*, p. 245; Mason, 'Sir Andrew de Harcla, earl of Carlisle', pp. 124–7.

74 *Calendar of Patent Rolls, 1321–1324*, p. 278;

Bain (ed.), *Calendar of documents relating to Scotland*, III, no. 809, p. 150, dated 22 April 1323.

75 *Calendar of Close Rolls, 1318–1323*, p. 717, entry dated 5 June 1323; T. Hardy (ed.), *Syllabus of the documents relating to England and other kingdoms contained in Rymer's Foedera* (London, HMSO, 3 vols., 1869–85), I, p. 221, 30 May 1323.

76 Barrow, *Robert Bruce*, pp. 244–5, 249–50; Denholm-Young (ed.), *Vita Edwardi Secundi*, pp. 132–4.

77 Hardy (ed.), *Syllabus*, I, p. 226, entry dated 2 July 1324 (see also 20 August 1324).

78 Fryde, *The Tyranny and Fall of Edward II*, p. 159.

79 Brie (ed.), *The Brut, or the Chronicles of England*, p. 273.

80 Hardy (ed.), *Syllabus*, I, p. 221, 30 May 1323.

81 Fryde, *The Tyranny and Fall of Edward II*, p. 132.

82 *Calendar of Close Rolls, 1323–1327*, p. 264, 30 March 1324; Palgrave (ed.), *Parliamentary writs and writs of military summons*, II, p. 1277, 23 July 1324.

83 Palgrave (ed.), *Parliamentary writs and writs of military summons*, II, p. 1277, 21 December 1324.

84 Palgrave (ed.), *Parliamentary writs and writs of military summons*, II, p. 1277, 17 February 1325.

85 Denholm-Young (ed.), *Vita Edwardi Secundi*, p. 135.

86 Denholm-Young (ed.), *Vita Edwardi Secundi*, pp. 142–3; Thompson (ed.), *Adae Murimuth Continuatio Chronicarum*, p. 45.

87 Hardy (ed.), *Syllabus*, I, p. 234, entry dated 25 March 1326.

88 Thompson (ed.), *Adae Murimuth Continuatio Chronicarum*, p. 40.

89 H. Johnstone, 'Isabella, the she-wolf of France', *History*, XXI (1936–7), pp. 216–17.

90 Fryde, *The Tyranny and Fall of Edward II*, pp. 162–3.

91 Thompson (ed.), *Chronicon Galfridi le Baker de Swynebroke*, p. 20.

92 H.F. Hutchinson, *Edward II: the pliant king* (London, 1971), pp. 132–3.

93 Hardy (ed.), *Syllabus*, I, p. 237, 28 September 1326; Brie (ed.), *The Brut, or the Chronicles of England*, p. 236.

94 Brie (ed.), *The Brut, or the Chronicles of England*, p. 237.

95 *Calendar of Patent Rolls, 1324–1327* (London, HMSO, 1904), p. 228, 27 July 1325.

96 Fryde, *The Tyranny and Fall of Edward II*, pp. 106–18.

97 Fryde, *The Tyranny and Fall of Edward II*, pp. 183–4, on the command structure. On Percy, see Palgrave (ed.), *Parliamentary writs and writs of military summons*, II, p. 1278, entry dated 2 August 1326; and *Calendar of Patent Rolls, 1324–1327*, p. 220, entry dated 24 January 1326.

98 *Calendar of Patent Rolls, 1324–1327*, p. 303, entry dated 2 August 1326.

99 Thompson (ed.), *Adae Murimuth Continuatio Chronicarum*, p. 46.

100 Fryde, *The Tyranny and Fall of Edward II*, p. 190.

101 Fryde, *The Tyranny and Fall of Edward II*, p. 190.

102 C[okayne], *The Complete Peerage*, I (1910), pp. 242–4.

103 Fryde, *The Tyranny and Fall of Edward II*, pp. 192–3; G.A. Holmes, 'Judgement on the Younger Despenser, 1326', *English Historical Review*, LXX (1955), 275, pp. 261–7.

104 *Calendar of Close Rolls, 1327–1330* (London, HMSO, 1896), 28 January 1327, p. 2.

105 This section based on Fryde, *The Tyranny and Fall of Edward II*, pp. 195–200.

106 B. Wilkinson, 'The deposition of Richard II and the accession of Henry IV', *English Historical Review*, LIV (1939), 214, p. 224.

107 Brie (ed.), *The Brut, or the Chronicles of England*, pp. 241–2.

108 Brie (ed.), *The Brut, or the Chronicles of England*, p. 253.

109 Brie (ed.), *The Brut, or the Chronicles of England*, p. 254; L. Fox, 'The honour and earldom of Leicester: origin and descent, 1066–1399', *English Historical Review*, LIV (1939), 215, p. 398.

110 Fryde, *The Tyranny and Fall of Edward II*, pp. 207–8.

111 Hardy (ed.), *Syllabus*, I, p. 239, 13 February 1327; R. Nicholson, *Edward III and the Scots: the formative years of a military career, 1327–1335* (London, 1965), p. 15.

112 Froissart (trans. Lord Berners and ed. G.C. Macaulay), *The Chronicles of Froissart* (London, 1899), p. 17.

113 Froissart (trans. Berners and ed. Macaulay), *The Chronicles of Froissart*, pp. 19–20.

114 On Percy's appointment, see *Calendar of Patent Rolls, 1327–1330* (London, HMSO, 1891), entry dated 16 February 1327, p. 18; on Percy and Neville's orders, see entry dated 15 February 1327, p. 15. For the details of Percy's retinue and expenses, see *Calendar of Patent Rolls, 1327–1330*, entry dated 5 September 1327, p. 163; and also Bain (ed.), *Calender of documents relating to Scotland*, III, no. 934, p. 169, dated 5 September 1327. See also R. Nicholson, 'The last campaign of Robert Bruce', *English Historical Review*, LXXVII (1962), 303, p. 235; C.H. Hunter Blair, 'Wardens and Deputy Wardens of the Marches of England towards Scotland, in Northumberland', *Archaeologia Aeliana*, 4th series, XXVII (1950), p. 40. On hobelars, see J.E. Morris, 'Mounted infantry', *Transactions of the Royal Historical Society*, 3rd series, VIII (1914), pp. 77–102.

115 *Calendar of Patent Rolls, 1327–1330*, 23 April 1327, p. 95.

116 Thompson (ed.), *Adae Murimuth Continuatio Chronicarum*, p. 53.

117 Nicholson, 'The last campaign of Robert Bruce', pp. 242–3; Nicholson, *Edward III and the Scots*, pp. 22–45; Barrow, *Robert Bruce*, p. 254; N.B. Lewis, 'The last medieval summons of the English feudal levy, 13 June 1385', *English Historical Review*, LXXIII (1958), 286, pp. 1–26; E.W.M. Balfour-Melville, 'Two John Crabbs', *Scottish Historical Review*, XXXIX (1960), pp. 31–4; *Calendar of Close Rolls, 1327–1330*, 17 August 1327. On Edward's weeping, see Brie (ed.), *The Brut, or the Chronicles of England*, p. 251.

118 Stones (ed.), *Anglo-Scottish Relations*, no. 40, 'Peticiones Regis Scocie', 30 October 1327, pp. 316–21; Thompson (ed.), *Chronicon Galfridi le Baker de Swynebroke*, p. 216.

119 E.L.G. Stones, 'The Anglo-Scottish negotiations of 1327', *Scottish Historical Review*, XXX (1951), pp. 49–54.

120 Stones (ed.), *Anglo-Scottish Relations, 1174–1328*, no. 41a, 'Pax et Concordia inter Regna', 1 March 1328, pp. 322–5.

121 *Ibid.*, pp. 327–9; Hardy (ed.), *Syllabus*, I, p. 245, 1 March 1328.

122 *Ibid.*, pp. 329–41; Barrow, *Robert Bruce*, pp. 257–9.

123 Hardy (ed.), *Syllabus*, I, p. 247, 21 May 1328.

124 Brie (ed.), *The Brut, or the Chronicles of England*, p. 256; Nicholson, *Edward III and the Scots*, p. 55.

125 Brie (ed.), *The Brut, or the Chronicles of England*, p. 255.

126 Nicholson, *Edward III and the Scots*, pp. 51–2.

127 Maxwell (trans.), *Chronicle of Lanercost*, p. 260.

128 Hardy (ed.), *Syllabus*, I, p. 248, entry dated 10 August 1328.

129 Stones (ed.), *Anglo-Scottish Relations, 1174–1328*, no. 42, 'Concessio Henrico de Percy', 28 July 1328, pp. 342–5.

130 Hardy (ed.), *Syllabus*, I, p. 258, 20 December 1331.

131 Martin (ed.), *The Percy Chartulary*, nos. MLXXVIII–MLXXXIII, 3 June 1331, pp. 453–4; J.M.W. Bean, 'The Percies and their estates in Scotland', *Archaeologia Aeliana*, XXXV (1957), 4th series, p. 96; Nicholson, *Edward III and the Scots*, pp. 57–8.

132 Barrow, *Robert Bruce*, p. 277.

9: Conquest of Scotland, pp. 198–233

1 R. Nicholson, *Edward III and the Scots: the formative years of a military career, 1327–1335* (London, 1965), p. 1.

2 For these quotations and analysis, see D.A.L. Morgan, 'The political after-life of Edward III: the apotheosis of a warmonger', *English Historical Review*, CXII (1997), 448, pp. 856–81. Also crucial is M. McKisack, 'Edward III and the historians', *History*, XLV (1960), pp. 1–15.

3 R. Nicholson, *Scotland: the later Middle Ages* (Edinburgh, 1974), p. 124.

4 The following paragraphs are based on E.M. Thompson (ed.), *Adae Murimuth Continuatio Chronicarum*, Rolls Series (London, 1889), p. 58; *Calendar of Close Rolls, 1327–1330* (London, HMSO, 1896), pp. 528–30; J.R. Lumby (ed.), *Chronicon Henrici Knighton*, Rolls Series (London, 2 vols., 1885), I, pp. 448–50; Nicholson, *Edward III and the Scots*, pp. 61–4; W.M. Ormrod, *The Reign of Edward III: Crown and political society in England, 1327–1377* (New Haven/London, 1990), p. 5; N.B.

Fryde, *The Tyranny and Fall of Edward II, 1321–1326* (Cambridge, 1979), pp. 220–5; G.P. Cuttino and T.W. Lyman, 'Where is Edward II?', *Speculum*, LIII (1978), pp. 522–44; G.A. Holmes, 'The rebellion of the earl of Lancaster, 1328–9', *Bulletin of the Institute of Historical Research*, XXVIII (1955), pp. 84–9; G.E. C[okayne], revised and expanded by V. Gibbs, H.A. Doubleday, G.H. White and Lord H. de Walden, *The Complete Peerage: or a history of the House of Lords and all its members from the earliest times* (London, 1910–59), VII (1929), p. 399; XII (1954), Part 2, pp. 302–4.

5 F.W.D. Brie (ed.), *The Brut, or the Chronicles of England*, Early English Text Society, vol. CXIII (London, 1906), p. 259.

6 See G.P. Cuttino and T.W. Lyman, 'Where is Edward II?', *Speculum*, LIII (1978), pp. 522–43. The authors believe the story that Edward II was alive to be true. Geoffrey le Baker notes the rumours that Edward was still alive in E.M. Thompson (ed.), *Chronicon Galfridi le Baker de Swynebroke* (Oxford, 1889), p. 43.

7 G.C. Crump, 'The arrest of Roger Mortimer and Queen Isabel', *English Historical Review*, XXVI (1911), 102, pp. 331–2.

8 Brie (ed.), *The Brut, or the Chronicles of England*, pp. 262, 269.

9 Brie (ed.), *The Brut, or the Chronicles of England*, pp. 270–2.

10 Ormrod, *The Reign of Edward III*, p. 7.

11 Quoted in Nicholson, *Edward III and the Scots*, p. 80.

12 H. Maxwell (trans.), *The Chronicle of Lanercost, 1271–1346* (Glasgow, 1913), p. 268; Nicholson, *Edward III and the Scots*, p. 73; Brie (ed.), *The Brut, or the Chronicles of England*, p. 274.

13 Nicholson, *Edward III and the Scots*, pp. 77–8.

14 Brie (ed.), *The Brut, or the Chronicles of England*, pp. 274–5.

15 Sir T. Gray (trans. Sir H. Maxwell), *Scalacronica* (London, 1907), p. 159, quoted in Nicholson, *Edward III and the Scots*, p. 77.

16 Nicholson, *Edward III and the Scots*, p. 79.

17 M.T. Martin (ed.), *The Percy Chartulary*, Surtees Society, vol. CXVII (Durham/ London, 1911), no. CDXCIII, 1 July 1328, p. 159; no. DXLI, 21 April 1336, pp. 178–80; W.H.D. Longstaffe, 'The old heraldry of the Percys', *Archaeologia Aeliana*, 2nd series, IV (1860), pp. 167–70.

18 *Calendar of Patent Rolls, 1327–1330* (London, HMSO, 1891), 19 April 1329, p. 383.

19 *Calendar of Close Rolls, 1327–1330* (London, HMSO, 1896), 13 August 1328, p. 484; *Calendar of Fine Rolls, 1327–1337* (London, HMSO, 1913), 13 August 1328, p. 101.

20 See *Calendar of Close Rolls, 1330–1333* (London, HMSO, 1898), 22 March 1331 (p. 214) and 25 May 1331 (p. 235); *Calendar of Close Rolls, 1333–1337* (London, HMSO, 1898), 14 July 1335 (p. 426) and 8 December 1336 (p. 639).

21 W. Dickson (ed.), 'Chronica Monasterii de Alnewyke ex quodam Libro Cronicarum in Libraria Collegii Regalis Cantabrigiae de dono Regis Henrici VI Fundamentoris', *Archaeologia Aeliana*, 1st series, III (1844), p. 39.

22 Maxwell (ed. and trans.), *Chronicle of Lanercost, 1272–1346*, p. 340.

23 G.G. Simpson and J.D. Galbraith (eds.), *Calendar of documents relating to Scotland, 1108–1516, preserved in the Public Record Office and the British Library* (Edinburgh, 1988), no. 801, p. 268, 1 June 1346.

24 Maxwell (ed. and trans.), *Chronicle of Lanercost, 1272–1346*, p. 340.

25 Simpson and Galbraith (eds.), *Calendar of documents relating to Scotland, 1108–1516*, V, no. 801, p. 268, 1 June 1346.

26 Simpson and Galbraith (eds.), *Calendar of documents relating to Scotland, 1108–1516*, V, nos. 780 and 781, p. 266, dated before 15 October 1339.

27 *Calendar of Patent Rolls, 1327–1330*, entry dated 20 May 1329, p. 390.

28 C[okayne], *The Complete Peerage*, VII, p. 403.

29 Froissart (trans. Lord Berners; ed. G.C. Macaulay), *The Chronicles of Froissart* (London, 1899), p. 32.

30 Brie (ed.), *The Brut, or the Chronicles of England*, p. 261.

31 *Calendar of Fine Rolls, 1327–1337*, 4 April 1330, p. 171; *Calendar of Patent Rolls, 1327–1330*, 12 July 1330, pp. 563–4.

32 *Calendar of Patent Rolls, 1327–1330*, entry dated 12 July 1330, p. 541.

33 *Calendar of Close Rolls, 1330–1333*, 24 August 1330, p. 57.

34 T. Rymer (ed.), *Foedera, Conventiones, Litterae, et cujuscumque generis Acta Publica, inter Reges Angliae et alios quosuis Imperatores, Reges, Pontifices, Principes, bel Communitatis ab ingressu Gulielmi I. in Angliam. A.D. 1066*, Records Commission (London, 4 vols., 1816–69), II, Part 1, p. 805.

35 J. Bain (ed.), *Calendar of documents relating to Scotland preserved in Her Majesty's Public Record Office, London* (Edinburgh, 4 vols., 1881–8), III, no. 1032, p. 187, dated 16 May 1331.

36 Martin (ed.), *Percy Chartulary*, no. DCCXXVII, 7 October 1331, pp. 268–9; J. Strachey *et al* (eds.), *Rotuli Parliamentorum ut in Petitiones, et Placita in Parliamento* (London, 6 vols., 1767–77), II p. 62, cited in C. Given-Wilson, *The English Nobility in the Late Middle Ages: the fourteenth-century political community* (London, 1987), pp. 132–3; *Calendar of Close Rolls, 1330–1333*, 23 January 1332, p. 390.

37 *Calendar of Close Rolls, 1330–1333*, 9 August 1332, p. 593; *Calendar of Patent Rolls, 1330–1334* (London, HMSO, 1893), 10 August 1332, p. 326.

38 Bain (ed.), *Calendar of documents relating to Scotland*, III, no. 1057, p. 192, 11 August 1332.

39 This section is based on R.R. Reid's 'The office of Warden of the Marches: its origin and early history', *English Historical Review*, XXXII (1917), no. 127, pp. 479–96; C.H. Hunter Blair, 'Wardens and Deputy Wardens of the Marches of England towards Scotland, in Northumberland'. *Archaeologia Aeliana*, 4th series, XXVIII (1950), pp. 18–95; A. Ayton, *Knights and Warhorses: military service and the English aristocracy under Edward III* (Woodbridge, 1994), pp. 193, 232 n. 169, 247–51. Although it deals with sixteenth-century outlaws, G.M. Fraser, *The Steel Bonnets: the story of the Anglo-Scottish Border Reivers* (London, 1971), pp. 128–48, provides a colourful picture of the wardens.

40 Dickson (ed.), *Cronica Monasterii de Alnewyke*, p. 40.

41 W. Peeris (ed. D. Bisley), *Metrical Chronicle of the Family of Percy*, in *Richardson's reprints of rare tracts and imprints of antient manuscripts*, V (Newcastle, 1845).

42 C. Hussey, 'Alnwick Castle, Northumberland: the seat of the duke of Northumberland', Part 2, *Country Life*, 29 June 1929, pp. 952–4 (see esp. Plate 2).

43 Maxwell (ed. and trans.), *Chronicle of Lanercost, 1272–1346*, p. 268. The quotation referring to the proceedings of the council is from Wyntoun's Chronicle, and cited by B. Webster, 'Scotland without a king, 1329–1341', in A. Grant and K.J. Stringer (eds.), *Medieval Scotland: Crown, lordship and community: essays presented to G.W.S. Barrow* (Edinburgh, 1993), p. 225.

44 Maxwell (ed. and trans.), *Chronicle of Lanercost, 1272–1346*, p. 269, n. 1.

45 Nicholson, *Edward III and the Scots*, pp. 86–90. See also E.M. Thompson (ed.), *Robertus de Avesbury, De Gestis Mirabilibus Regis Edwardi Tertii*, Rolls Series (London, 1889), pp. 296–7.

46 B. Krauel Heredia, 'Sir James Douglas's death in Spain, 1330', *Scottish Historical Review*, LXIX (1990), pp. 84–95; A. Goodman, 'A letter from the earl of Douglas to a king of Castile', *Scottish Historical Review*, LXIV (1985), p. 69.

47 Brie (ed.), *The Brut, or the Chronicles of England*, p. 279.

48 *Calendar of Close Rolls, 1330–1333*, entry dated 28 October 1332, p. 610.

49 Brie (ed.), *The Brut, or the Chronicles of England*, p. 281.

50 Nicholson, *Edward III and the Scots*, pp. 91–104; Nicholson, *Scotland: the later Middle Ages*, pp. 126–8.

51 Thompson (ed.), *Chronicon Galfridi le Baker de Swynebroke*, p. 50.

52 J.M.W. Bean, 'The Percies and their estates in Scotland', *Archaeologia Aeliana*, XXXV (1957), 4th series, p. 97. A defective copy of the indenture is contained in Martin (ed.), *The Percy Chartulary*, no. MLXIV, pp. 447–8.

53 Maxwell (ed. and trans.), *Chronicle of Lanercost, 1272–1346*, p. 274.

54 Thompson (ed.), *Chronicon Galfridi le Baker de Swynebroke*, p. 51.

55 Brie (ed.), *The Brut, or the Chronicles of England*, p. 283.

56 Brie (ed.), *The Brut, or the Chronicles of England*, Appendix A, 'The Romance of the Battle of Halidon Hill', p. 287.

57 Nicholson, *Edward III and the Scots*, pp. 119–38; Brie (ed.), *The Brut, or the Chronicles of England*, pp. 278–86; Maxwell (ed. and trans.), *Chronicle of Lanercost, 1272–1346*, pp. 279–81; Thompson (ed.), *Robertus de Avesbury, De Gestis Mirabilibus Regis Edwardi Tertii*, p. 298.

58 Martin (ed.), *Percy Chartulary*, no. MLXV, 29 July 1333, p. 448.

59 Maxwell (ed. and trans.), *Chronicle of Lanercost, 1272–1346*, p. 282; V.H. Galbraith (ed.), *The Anonimalle Chronicle, 1333 to 1381, from a MS written at St Mary's Abbey, York, and now in the possession of Lieut.-Col. Sir Wiliam Ingilby, Bart., Ripley Castle, Yorkshire* (Manchester, 1927), p. 1.

60 Martin (ed.), *Percy Chartulary*, no. MLXVII, p. 448.

61 Martin (ed.), *Percy Chartulary*, no. MLXIII, 5 September 1333, pp. 446–7.

62 *Calendar of Close Rolls, 1333–1337*, entry dated 21 November 1333, p. 185. See also Bain, 'The Percies in Scotland', p. 341.

63 Bain (ed.), *Calendar of documents relating to Scotland*, III, no. 1094, p. 197, 1 October 1333.

64 *Calendar of Patent Rolls, 1330–1334*, 2 March 1334, p. 573.

65 *Calendar of Close Rolls, 1330–1333*, 16 October 1331, p. 368.

66 This section based primarily on Nicholson, *Edward III and the Scots*, pp. 139–62.

67 John of Fordun, quoted in B. Webster, 'Scotland without a king, 1329–1341', in Grant and Stringer (eds.), *Medieval Scotland*, p. 228.

68 Nicholson, *Edward III and the Scots*, pp. 163–73.

69 Martin (ed.), *Percy Chartulary*, no. MLXX, 20 September 1334, p. 451; no. MLXIX, 23 September 1334, pp. 449–50; Bain (ed.), *Calendar of documents relating to Scotland*, III, no. 1133, p. 205, 20 September 1334; Bain, 'The Percies in Scotland', pp. 339–41; Bean, 'The Percies and their estates in Scotland', pp. 98–9; Nicholson, *Edward III and the Scots*, p. 170.

70 C[okayne], *The Complete Peerage*, X (1945), p. 463; C[okayne], *The Complete Peerage*, VII, p. 401n.; J.T. Rosenthal, 'Aristocratic marriage and the English peerage, 1350–1500: social institution and personal bond', *Journal of Medieval History*, X (1984), pp. 181–94; J. Barnie, *War in Medieval Society: social values and the Hundred Years War, 1337–99* (London, 1974), pp. 58–65; K. Fowler, *The King's Lieutenant: Henry of Grosmont, earl of Lancaster, 1310–1361* (London, 1969).

71 *Calendar of Close Rolls, 1333–1337*, 25 September 1334, p. 335.

72 *Calendar of Close Rolls, 1333–1337*, 28 May 1335, p. 490.

73 C[okayne], *The Complete Peerage*, X, p. 462n.; C[okayne], *The Complete Peerage*, V (1926); W.P. Hedley, *Northumberland Families* (Newcastle, 2 vols., 1968–70), II, p. 10 and family tree, p. 15; J.A. Tuck, 'War and society in the medieval North', *Northern History*, XXI (1985), pp. 49–50.

74 On the early Nevilles of Raby, see C[okayne], *The Complete Peerage*, IX (1936), pp. 491–8. On their lands, see C. Given-Wilson, *The English Nobility in the Late Middle Ages: the fourteenth-century political community* (London, 1987), pp. 105–6, and especially map, 'Yorkshire and Durham: principal holdings of the Nevilles and Mauleys', pp. xii–xiii. The quotation on the Nevilles' power in Yorkshire is from C.D. Ross, 'The Yorkshire baronage, 1399–1435', Oxford D.Phil. (1950), cited in Given-Wilson, p. 106.

75 *Calendar of Patent Rolls, 1327–1330*, entry dated 5 August 1328, p. 308.

76 J.M.W. Bean, 'The Percies' acquisition of Alnwick', *Archaeologia Aeliana*, 4th series, XXXII (1954), pp. 309–14. On Percy's will, see J. Raine (ed.), *Testamenta Eboracensia, or wills registered at York illustrative of the history, manners, language, statistics &c., of the province of York from the year MCCC downwards*, Surtees Society, vol. I (London, 1836), p. 57. On William de Aton, see C[okayne], *The Complete Peerage*, I (1910), p. 325.

77 M. Prestwich, *The Three Edwards: war and state in England, 1272–1377* (London, 1980), p. 159.

78 Aelian (trans. A.F. Scholfield), *On the Characteristics of Animals* (London, 3 vols., 1958), p. xiii.

79 Nicholson, *Edward III and the Scots*, pp. 174–91; Martin (ed.), *Percy Chartulary*, no. DCCLXXVII, 19 February 1335, pp. 302–3; *Calendar of Patent Rolls, 1334–1338* (London, HMSO, 1895), entry dated 19 February 1335, p. 79; Bain (ed.), *Calendar of documents relating to Scotland*, III, nos. 1142 and 1145, pp. 206–7, dated respectively 1 February and 19 February 1335; J.A. Tuck, 'The emergence of a Northern nobility, 1250–1400', *Northern History*, XXII (1986), p. 11.

80 On Pyngel, see W. Stubbs (ed.), *Chronicles of the Reigns of Edward I and Edward II*, Rolls

Series (London, 2 vols., 1882–3), II, p. 121; Martin (ed.), *Percy Chartulary*, no. DCCXCIV, 17 January 1335, p. 322.

81 Quoted in Tuck, 'Emergence of a Northern nobility', p. 9.

82 Martin (ed.), *The Percy Chartulary*, nos. DLXXI, 26 July 1344, p. 194; DLXXII, 31 March 1344, p. 194; DLXXIII, 30 March 1340, pp. 194–5; DCCCXVI, 1 February 1350, pp. 338–9; DCCCXLVIII–DCCCLII, all 18 May 1343, pp. 359–61. Also J.M.W. Bean, *The Estates of the Percy Family, 1416–1537* (Oxford, 1958), p. 7; *Calendar of Inquisitions post Mortem* (London, HMSO, 1938), XII, no. 242, p. 221; *Calendar of Inquisitions post Mortem* (London, HMSO, 1921), X, no. 43, p. 22.

83 Simpson and Galbraith (eds.), *Calendar of documents relating to Scotland, 1108–1516*, no. 738, p. 261, 5–7 June 1335.

84 Nicholson, *Edward III and the Scots*, Appendix IV, pp. 248–9.

85 Nicholson, *Edward III and the Scots*, pp. 192–202. See also Galbraith (ed.), *The Anonimalle Chronicle, 1333 to 1381*, p. 4.

86 Maxwell (ed. and trans.), *Chronicle of Lanercost, 1272–1346*, p. 293.

87 Brie (ed.), *The Brut, or the Chronicles of England*, p. 275.

88 For more detail, see Map 4: 'Physical features, regions, and conjectural linguistic division c. 1400', in Nicholson, *Scotland: the later Middle Ages*.

89 This section based on Nicholson, *Edward II and the Scots*, pp. 203–24. On the treaty of peace between Scotland and England of August 1335, see Thompson (ed.), *Robertus de Avesbury, De Gestis Mirabilibus Regis Edwardi Tertii*, pp. 298–302.

90 Nicholson, *Edward III and the Scots*, pp. 227–36.

91 Maxwell (ed. and trans.), *Chronicle of Lanercost, 1272–1346*, p. 294, n. 9.

10: *The Closing Years, pp. 234–50*

1 G.E. C[okayne], revised and expanded by V. Gibbs, H.A. Doubleday, G.H. White and Lord H. de Walden, *The Complete Peerage: or a history of the House of Lords and all its members from the earliest times* (London, 1910–59), X (1945), p. 461.

2 J. Cambell, 'England, Scotland and the Hundred Years War in the fourteenth century', in J.R. Hale, J.R.L. Highfield and B. Smalley (eds.), *Europe in the Late Middle Ages* (London, 1965), p. 186.

3 H. Maxwell (trans.), *Chronicle of Lanercost, 1272–1346* (Glasgow, 1913), pp. 300–1.

4 Maxwell (trans.), *Chronicle of Lanercost*, p. 306; C[okayne], *The Complete Peerage*, X, p. 461n.; C[okayne], *The Complete Peerage*, XII (1959), Part 2, p. 372.

5 Maxwell (trans.), *Chronicle of Lanercost*, pp. 307–8; V.H. Galbraith (ed.), *The Anonimalle Chronicle, 1333 to 1381* (Manchester, 1927), p. 11.

6 J. Bain (ed.), *Calendar of documents relating to Scotland preserved in Her Majesty's Public Record Office, London* (Edinburgh, 4 vols., 1881–8), III, no. 1268, p. 232, dated 28 April 1338; Maxwell (trans.), *Chronicle of Lanercost*, p. 311.

7 A. Ayton, *Knights and Warhorses: military service and the English aristocracy under Edward III* (Woodbridge, 1994), pp. 172, 193, 246.

8 R. Nicholson, *Scotland: the later Middle Ages* (Edinburgh, 1974), p. 137; Maxwell (trans.), *Chronicle of Lanercost*, pp. 311–13.

9 G.H. Martin (ed. and trans.), *Knighton's Chronicle, 1337–1396* (Oxford, 1995), p. 5.

10 Maxwell (trans.), *Chronicle of Lanercost*, p. 313.

11 Maxwell (trans.), *Chronicle of Lanercost*, p. 314.

12 According to the chronicler Bower, quoted in M. Brown, '"Rejoice to hear of Douglas": the House of Douglas and the presentation of magnate power in late medieval Scotland', *Scottish Historical Review*, LXXVI (1997), p. 170.

13 E.M. Thompson (ed.), *Chronicon Galfridi le Baker de Swynebroke* (Oxford, 1889), p. 67.

14 See T.D. Hardy (ed.), *Syllabus of the documents relating to England and other kingdoms contained in Rymer's Foedera* (London, 3 vols., 1869–85), I, entry dated 30 November 1340, and see also the flurry of memoranda and the letter of indemnity between 2 December 1340 and 1 January 1341, p. 318.

15 N.M. Fryde, 'Edward III's removal of his minister and judges, 1340–1', *Bulletin of the Institute of Historical Research*, XLVIII (1975), pp. 149–61; Thompson (ed.), *Chronicon Galfridi le Baker de Swynebroke*, p. 72.

16 See Hardy (ed.), *Syllabus of the documents*, I, 27 May 1340, p. 315.

17 On the parliament of 1341, see Thompson (ed.), *Chronicon Galfridi le Baker de Swynebroke*, pp. 72–4; E.M. Thompson (ed.), *Adae Murimuth Continuatio Chronicarum*, Rolls Series (London, 1889), p. 118; Fryde, 'Edward III's removal of his minister and judges, 1340–1', *Bulletin of the Institute of Historical Research*, pp. 149–61.

18 Hardy (ed.), *Syllabus of the documents*, I, 27 July 1341, p. 323.

19 Hardy (ed.), *Syllabus of the documents*, I, 10 October 1341, p. 324.

20 E.M. Thompson (ed.), *Adae Murimuth Continuatio Chronicarum*, p. 123; A. Tuck, *Crown and Nobility, 1272–1461: political conflict in late medieval England* (London, 1985), p. 126.

21 Martin (ed. and trans.), *Knighton's Chronicle, 1337–1396*, p. 41; C.H. Hunter Blair, 'Wardens and Deputy Wardens of the Marches of England towards Scotland, in Northumberland', *Archaeologia Aeliana*, 4th series, XXVIII (1950), p. 42.

22 G.L. Harriss, *King, Parliament and Public Finance in Medieval England to 1369* (Oxford, 1976), pp. 270–312; W.M. Ormrod, 'Edward III and the recovery of royal authority in England, 1340–60', *History*, LXXII (1987), pp. 4–19.

23 C[okayne], *The Complete Peerage*, X, p. 461.

24 Bain (ed.), *Calendar of documents relating to Scotland*, III, no. 1463, pp. 266–7, 17 July 1346.

25 Campbell, 'England, Scotland and the Hundred Years War in the fourteenth century', p. 195.

26 R. White, 'The battle of Neville's Cross, fought 17 October 1346', *Archaeologia Aeliana*, 2nd series, I (1857), pp. 271–303; Maxwell (trans.), *Chronicle of Lanercost*, pp. 330–42; E.M. Thompson (ed.), *Robertus de Avesbury, De Gestis Mirabilibus Regis Edwardi Tertii*, Rolls Series (London, 1889), pp. 376–7; Martin (ed. and trans.), *Knighton's Chronicle, 1337–1396*, pp. 69–73; J. Raine (ed.), *Historical Papers and Letters from the Northern Registers*, Rolls Series (London, 1873), no. CCXLIII, 'Litera directa episcopo de conflictu ad Nevile Croys', pp. 387–89; Galbraith (ed.), *The Anonimalle Chronicle, 1333 to 1381*, pp. 26–8; *Calendar of Close Rolls, 1354–1360* (London, 1908), p. 114, 6 February 1355; Nicholson, *Scotland: the later Middle Ages*, pp. 146–7; Hardy (ed.), *Syllabus of the documents*, 20 October 1346, p. 350, and 20 January 1347, pp. 352–3; H. Maxwell, *A History of the House of Douglas: from the earliest times down to the legislative union of England and Scotland* (London, 2 vols., 1902), I, p. 28; C.J. Rogers, 'The efficacy of the English longbow: a reply to Kelly De Vries', *War and History*, V (1998), p. 238. Also, importantly, R. Nicholson, 'David II, the historians and the chroniclers', *Scottish Historical Review*, XLV (1966), pp. 59–78.

27 C.R. Young, *The Making of the Neville Family in England, 1166–1400* (Woodbridge, 1996), p. 117, quoting J.W. Dickenson, *The Battle of Neville's Cross* (Durham, 1991), p. 29.

28 Young, *Making of the Neville Family*, p. 117; C[okayne], *The Complete Peerage*, IX (1936), p. 501n.

29 J. Raine (ed.), *Historical papers and letters from the Northern Registers*, Rolls Series (London, 1873), no. CCXLVII, 'Forma literarum dominorum de Percy et Nevill missa domino Papae pro relavamine post destructionem', pp. 394–5.

30 Hardy (ed.), *Syllabus of the documents*, I, 14 October 1350, p. 367.

31 Hardy (ed.), *Syllabus of the documents*, I, 10 December 1346, p. 351.

32 Galbraith (ed.), *The Anonimalle Chronicle, 1333 to 1381*, pp. 28–9; Hardy (ed.), *Syllabus of the documents*, I, 26 January 1347, p. 353.

33 Nicholson, *Scotland: the later Middle Ages*, pp. 147–8.

34 Nicholson, *Scotland: the later Middle Ages*, pp. 154–5.

35 Thompson (ed.), *Chronicon Galfridi le Baker de Swynebroke*, pp. 98–100.

36 Quoted in M. Prestwich, *The Three Edwards: war and state in England, 1272–1377* (London, 1980), p. 255.

37 Hardy (ed.), *Syllabus of the documents*, I, entries dated 8 March 1351, 28 June 1351, 4 September 1351 and 3 November 1351, pp. 370–1.

38 A.A.M. Duncan, '*Honi soit qui mal y pense*: David II and Edward III, 1346–52', *Scottish Historical Review*, LXVII (1988), 2, pp. 113–41; Nicolson, *Scotland: the later Middle Ages*, pp. 156–9.

39 Brown, '"Rejoice to hear of Douglas"', p. 170.

40 Hardy (ed.), *Syllabus of the documents*, I, 1 February 1352, p. 372.

41 W. Dickson (ed.), 'Cronica Monasterii de

Alnewyke ex quodam Libro Cronicarum in Libraria Collegii Regalis Cantabrigiae de dono Regis Henricis VI Fundamentoris' [Chronicles of Alnwick Abbey], in *Archaeologia Aeliana*, 1st series, III (1844), p. 40.

42 J. Raine (ed.), *Testamenta Eboracensia, or wills registered at York illustrative of the history, manners, language, statistics &c., of the province of York, from the year MCCC downwards*, Surtees Society, vol. 4 (London, 1836), no. XLCVI, 'Testamentum Domini Henrici de Percy', pp. 57–61.

11: *Adventures Abroad, pp. 251–96*

1 Quoted in J. Barnie, *War in medieval society: social values and the Hundred Years War, 1337–99* (London, 1974), p. 74.

2 N. Orme, *From Childhood to Chivalry: the education of the English kings and aristocracy, 1066–1530* (London, 1984), ff; C. Woolgar, 'Diet and consumption in gentry and noble households: a case study from around the Wash', in R.E. Archer and S. Walker (eds.), *Rulers and Ruled in Later Medieval England: essays presented to Gerald Harriss* (London, 1995), pp. 17–31.

3 J. Campbell, 'England, Scotland and the Hundred Years War in the fourteenth century', in J.R. Hale, J.R.L. Highfield and B. Smalley (eds.), *Europe in the Late Middle Ages* (London, 1965), pp. 184–216.

4 T.D. Hardy (ed.), *Syllabus of the documents relating to England and other kingdoms contained in Rymer's Foedera* (London, 3 vols., 1869–85), I, 20 October 1338, p. 306.

5 Hardy (ed.), *Syllabus of the documents*, I, 12 April 1340, p. 314.

6 Hardy (ed.), *Syllabus of the documents*, I, 20 November 1338, p. 307.

7 *Calendar of Patent Rolls, 1338–1340* (London, 1898), 13 October 1338, pp. 180–1.

8 Campbell, 'England, Scotland and the Hundred Years War in the fourteenth century', pp. 187–91; W.M. Ormrod, *The Reign of Edward III: Crown and political society in England, 1327–1377* (New Haven/London, 1990), pp. 7–11; M. Prestwich, *The Three Edwards: war and state in England, 1272–1377* (London, 1980), pp. 165–73; W.M. Ormrod, 'Edward III and his family', *Journal of British Studies*, XXVI (1987), pp. 407–8; R. Howlett (ed.), 'William of Newburgh, Historia rerum

Anglicarum', in *Chronicles and memorials of the reigns of Stephen, Henry II and Richard I*, Rolls Series (London, 4 vols., 1884–9); E.M. Thompson (ed.), *Robertus de Avesbury, De Gestis Mirabilibus Regis Edwardi Tertii*, Rolls Series (London, 1889), pp. 307–8; J. Le Patourel, 'The origins of the Hundred Years War', and 'Edward III and the kingdom of France', both reprinted in his *Feudal Empires: Norman and Plantagenet* (London, 1984); P. Chaplais, 'English arguments concerning the feudal status of Aquitaine in the fourteenth century', *Bulletin of the Institute of Historical Research*, XXI (1948), pp. 203–13; Hardy (ed.), *Syllabus of the documents*, I, 8 February 1340, p. 313, for details of Edward's claim to the title and nailing it to church doors. On the pawning of the Great Crown, see Hardy (ed.), *Syllabus of the documents*, I, 27 February 1339, p. 307; Froissart (trans. Lord Berners and ed. G.C. Macaulay), *The Chronicles of Froissart* (London, 1899), pp. 48–55.

9 Froissart (trans. Berners and ed. Macaulay), *Chronicles of Froissart*, pp. 61–2; J. Sumption, *Trial by Battle*, vol. I of *The Hundred Years War* (London, 1990), pp. 319–29; I. Friel, 'Winds of change? Ships and the Hundred Years War', in A. Curry and M. Hughes (eds.), *Arms, Armies and Fortifications in the Hundred Years War* (Woodbridge, 1994), pp. 183–93.

10 Hardy (ed.), *Syllabus of the documents*, I, 26 July 1340, p. 316.

11 Hardy (ed.), *Syllabus of the documents*, I, 30 July 1340, p. 316; Sumption, *Trial by Battle*, pp. 348–9; Thompson (ed.), *Robertus de Avesbury, De Gestis Mirabilibus Regis Edwardi Tertii*, pp. 314–16.

12 Thompson (ed.), *Robertus de Avesbury, De Gestis Mirabilibus Regis Edwardi Tertii*, pp. 317–23.

13 Sumption, *Trial by Battle*, pp. 348–61.

14 Thompson (ed.), *Robertus de Avesbury, De Gestis Mirabilibus Regis Edwardi Tertii*, pp. 336–7.

15 Sumption, *Trial by Battle*, pp. 362–9.

16 A. Ayton, 'English armies in the fourteenth century', in A. Curry and M. Hughes (eds.), *Arms, Armies and Fortifications in the Hundred Years War* (Woodbridge, 1994), pp. 21–38.

17 *Calendar of Patent Rolls, 1358–1361* (London, 1911), pp. 42–3, 26 February 1358; p. 88, 28 July 1358; p. 367, 28 May 1360; p. 370, 2

June 1360; p. 377, 4 June 1360; p. 521, 10 February 1361.

18 *Chronique de Jean le Bel*, quoted in Prestwich, *The Three Edwards*, p. 174; E.M. Thompson (ed.), *Adae Murimuth Continuatio Chronicarum*, Rolls Series (London, 1889).

19 Sumption, *Trial by Battle*, pp. 370–410; Prestwich, *The Three Edwards*, pp. 174–5; Froissart (trans. Berners and ed. Macaulay), *Chronicles of Froissart*, p. 76–8; Thompson (ed.), *Robertus de Avesbury, De Gestis Mirabilibus Regis Edwardi Tertii*, pp. 340–4; Thompson (ed.), *Adae Murimuth Continuatio Chronicarum*, p. 129; G.E. C[okayne], revised and expanded by V. Gibbs, H.A. Doubleday, G.H. White and Lord H. De Walden, *The Complete Peerage: or a history of the House of Lords and all its members from earliest times* (London, 1910–59), X (1945), p. 462n.

20 C[okayne], *The Complete Peerage*, XII (1959), Part 2, p. 838.

21 G.H. Martin (ed. and trans.), *Knighton's Chronicle, 1337–1396* (Oxford, 1995), p. 41; C.H. Hunter Blair, 'Wardens and Deputy Wardens of the Marches towards Scotland', in Northumberland', *Archaeologia Aeliana*, 4th series, XXVIII (1950), p. 42.

22 T. Rymer (ed.), *Foedera, Conventiones, Litterae, et cujuscumque generis Acta Publica, inter Reges Angliae et alios quosuis Imperatores, Reges, Pontifices, Principes, bel Communitatis ab ingressu Gulielmi I. in Angliam, A.D. 1066*, Records Commission (London, 4 vols., 1816–69), III, p. 10, 'De Protectionibus', 24 March 1344; M.T. Martin (ed.), *The Percy Chartulary*, Surtees Society, vol. CXVII (Durham/London, 1911), no. DCXL, pp. 217–18, 10 april 1351; K. Fowler, *The King]'s Lieutenant: Henry of Grosmont, first duke of Lancaster, 1310–1361* (London, 1969), pp. 172–3.

23 Sumption, *Trial by Battle*, p. 420.

24 C[okayne], *The Complete Peerage*, I (1910), pp. 242–4; Prestwich, *The Three Edwards*, pp. 155–6.

25 Thompson (ed.), *Adae Murimuth Continuatio Chronicarum*, pp. 159, 161.

26 Hardy (ed.), *Syllabus of the documents*, I, p. 341, 10 April 1345.

27 Sumption, *Trial by Battle*, pp. 455–88; Fowler, *The King's Lieutenant*, pp. 53–66; Thompson (ed.), *Robertus de Avesbury, De Gestis Mirabilibus Regis Edwardi Tertii*,

pp. 356–7, 372–6; Martin (ed. and trans.), *Knighton's Chronicle, 1337–1396*, p. 35.

28 Rymer (ed.), *Foedera*, III, pp. 38–53.

29 A. Tuck, *Crown and Nobility, 1272–1461: political conflict in late medieval England* (London, 1985), p. 132.

30 Prestwich, *The Three Edwards*, p. 164; C[okayne], *The Complete Peerage*, I, pp. 242–4; L.F. Salzman, 'The property of the earl of Arundel, 1397', *Sussex Archaeological Collections*, XCI (1953), esp. pp. 32–4.

31 Appendix B, 'Exchequer revenues and expenditure under Edward II and Edward III', in G.L. Harriss, *King, Parliament and Public Finance in Medieval England to 1369* (Oxford, 1975), pp. 523–4.

32 Sumption, *Trial by Battle*, pp. 460–3.

33 Sumption, *Trial by Battle*, pp. 489–502; Prestwich, *The Three Edwards*, p. 195; Froissart (trans. Berners and ed. Macaulay), *Chronicles of Froissart*, p. 94.

34 Major-General the Hon. George Wrottesley, *Crécy and Calais, from the original records in the Public Record Office* (London, 1898), p. 151. For the information that Percy was listed in Arundel's retinue on 6 June, see p. 96.

35 S. Walker, *The Lancastrian Affinity, 1361–1399* (Oxford, 1900), pp. 1–9; N. Saul, 'The Despensers and the downfall of Edward II', *English Historical Review*, XCIX (1984), 390, esp. pp. 6–11; C. Given-Wilson, *The Royal Household and the King's Affinity: service, politics and finance in England, 1360–1413* (London, 1986), pp. 203–4; K.B. McFarlane, *The Nobility of Later Medieval England: the Ford Lectures for 1953 and related studies* (Oxford, 1973), pp. 102–21; Ayton, 'English armies in the fourteenth century', pp. 21–38; Fowler, *The King's Lieutenant*, pp. 175ff; *Calendar of Inquisitions post Mortem* (London, 1921), X, no. 43, p. 22.

36 T.F. Tout, *Chapters in the Administrative History of Medieval England: the Wardrobe, the Chamber and the Small Seals* (Manchester, 6 vols., 1920–33), I, p. 69; II, pp. 314–27; III, p. 120; IV, pp. 266–9, 299–300; Given-Wilson, *The Royal Household and the King's Affinity*, pp. 13, 69.

37 Given-Wilson, *The Royal Household and the King's Affinity*, pp. 203–11.

38 D.C. Douglas, *William the Conqueror: the Norman impact upon England* (London, 1964), p. 363.

39 See Map 24, Sumption, *Trial by Battle*, p. 505.

40 Sumption, *Trial by Battle*, pp. 501–34; R. Hardy, 'The longbow', in A. Curry and M. Hughes (eds.), *Arms, Armies and Fortifications in the Hundred Years War* (Woodbridge, 1994), pp. 161–81; M. Bennett, 'The development of battle tactics in the Hundred Years War', in Curry and Hughes (eds.), *Arms, Armies and Fortifications*, esp. pp. 8–10.

41 Tout, *Chapters in the Administrative History of Medieval England*, III, p. 169.

42 Wrottesley, *Crécy and Calais*, p. 129.

43 Sumption, *Trial by Battle*, pp. 535–86; Fowler, *The King's Lieutenant*, pp. 70–1.

44 Fowler, *The King's Lieutenant*, pp. 104–5.

45 *Calendar of Patent Rolls, 1350–1354* (London, 1907), p. 89, 15 March 1351.

46 Froissart (trans. G. Brereton), *Chronicles* (London, 1968), pp. 114–16; Friel, 'Winds of change? Ships and the Hundred Years War', in Curry and Hughes (eds.), *Arms, Armies and Fortifications*, pp. 187–8; C.R. Young, *The Making of the Neville Family in England, 1166–1400* (Woodbridge, 1996), p. 118; C.F. Richmond, 'The war at sea', in K. Fowler (ed.), *The Hundred Years War* (London, 1971), pp. 98–9.

47 *Calendar of Patent Rolls, 1348–1350* (London, 1905), p. 168, 13 July 1348; *Calendar of Patent Rolls, 1350–1354*, p. 29, 24 November 1350; pp. 78–9, 20 February 1351.

48 *Calendar of Patent Rolls, 1364–1367* (London, 1912), p. 73, 15 November 1364.

49 *Calendar of Close Rolls, 1349–1354* (London, 1906), pp. 404, 464, entries dated, respectively, 21 January 1351 and 28 January 1352.

50 J.S. Roskell, *The Impeachment of Michael de la Pole, earl of Suffolk, in 1386 in the context of the reign of Richard II* (Manchester, 1984), p. 17.

51 Rymer (ed.), *Foedera*, III, p. 241.

52 J. Bain (ed.), *Calendar of documents relating to Scotland, preserved in Her Majesty's Public Record Office, London* (Edinburgh, 4 vols., 1881–8), IV, no. 1844; F. Palgrave (ed.), *Documents and records illustrating the history of Scotland and the transactions between the Crowns of Scotland and England, preserved in the Treasury of Her Majesty's Exchequer*, Record Commission (London, 1837), Appendix, p. 372.

53 *Calendar of Patent Rolls, 1354–1358* (London, 1909), p. 128, 16 October 1354.

54 *Calendar of Patent Rolls, 1348–1350*, p. 582, 12 October 1350; and *Calendar of Patent Rolls, 1350–1354*, p. 131, 4 September 1351.

55 See W. Peeris (ed. D. Bisley), *Metrical Pedigree of the Percyes*, printed as the *Metrical Chronicle of the Family of Percy* in *Richardson's reprints of rare tracts and imprints of antient manuscripts*, vol. V (Newcastle, 1845); J.C. Atkinson (ed.), *Cartularium Abbathiae de Whiteby*, Surtees Society, vol. LXIX (Durham, 2 vols., 1879–81), I, nos. 57, 59, 60, 61; A.C. Lawrie (ed.), *Early Scottish Charters prior to A.D. 1153* (Glasgow, 1905), Charter nos. 251, 252, 253, 254.

56 *Calendar of Patent Rolls, 1350–1354*, p. 431, 16 April 1353.

57 *Calendar of Patent Rolls, 1354–1358*, p. 349, 16 February 1356.

58 R. Nicholson, *Scotland: the later Middle Ages* (Edinburgh, 1974), pp. 160–2; Campbell, 'England, Scotland and the Hundred Years War in the fourteenth century', pp. 198–200; E.M.W. Balfour-Melville, 'The death of Edward Balliol', *Scottish Historical Review*, XXXV (1956), pp. 82–3; C[okayne], *The Complete Peerage*, X, pp. 462–3; Martin (ed. and trans.), *Knighton's Chronicle, 1337–1396*, pp. 121–39.

59 A.H. Burne, 'The battle of Poitiers', *English Historical Review*, LII (1938), no. 209, pp. 21–52; Froissart (trans. Berners and ed. Macaulay), *Chronicles of Froissart*, pp. 119–29; Martin (ed. and trans.), *Knighton's Chronicle, 1337–1396*, pp. 143–9; H. Maxwell, *A History of the House of Douglas: from the earliest times down to the legislative union of England and Scotland* (London, 2 vols., 1902), I, pp. 80–1.

60 *Calendar of Patent Rolls, 1354–1358*, pp. 389, 452, 496, 547, 613, 614, entries dated respectively, 4 September 1356, 15 November 1356, 18 November 1356, 26 January 1357, 3 August 1357, and 6 August 1357; *Calendar of Patent Rolls, 1358–1361*, p. 150, 26 July 1358; *Calendar of Patent Rolls, 1361–1364* (London, 1912), p. 470, 22 February 1364; *Calendar of Patent Rolls, 1361–1364* (London, 1912), p. 470, 22 February 1364; *Calendar of Patent Rolls, 1358–1361*, p. 516, 25 November 1360.

61 Nicholson, *Scotland: the later Middle Ages*, pp. 162–3; Campbell, 'England, Scotland and the Hundred Years War', pp. 200–1; Martin (ed. and trans.), *Knighton's Chronicle, 1337–1396*, p. 153.

62 Martin (ed. and trans.), *Knighton's Chronicle, 1337–1396*, p. 179; Fowler, *The King's Lieutenant*, pp. 197–213.

63 J. Le Patourel, 'The treaty of Brétigny, 1360', reprinted in *Feudal Empires: Norman and Plantagenet* (London, 1984), pp. 19–39.

64 Martin (ed.), *The Percy Chartulary*, no. DCCCXXXVI, p. 351, 14 January 1359.

65 Campbell, 'England, Scotland and the Hundred Years War', pp. 201–2; Nicholson, *Scotland: the later Middle Ages*, pp. 164–8; *Calendar of Close Rolls, 1354–1360* (London, 1908), p. 550, 12 February 1359.

66 Le Patourel, 'The treaty of Brétigny, 1360', pp. 36–9. M. Keen, 'Henry V's diplomacy', in *Nobles, Knights and Men-at-arms in the Middle Ages* (London, 1996), esp. pp. 223–8; Prestwich, *The Three Edwards*, pp. 182–3.

67 *Calendar of Patent Rolls, 1361–1364*, p. 304, 3 February 1363.

68 The above section on Anglo-Scottish relations is based on Nicholson, *Scotland: the later Middle Ages*, pp. 164–74; R. Nicholson, 'David II, the historians and the chroniclers', *Scottish Historical Review*, XLV (1966), pp. 63–70 is especially excellent on David's imprisonment and historians' attitudes over the centuries toward the king. See also A.A.M. Duncan, '*Honi soit qui mal y pense*: David II and Edward III, 1346–52', *Scottish Historical Review*, LXVII (1988), 2, pp. 134–6; L.G. Wickham Legg (ed.), *English Coronation Records* (London, 1901), no. XI, p. 78.

69 Prestwich, *The Three Edwards*, p. 183; Martin (ed. and trans.), *Knighton's Chronicle, 1337–1396*, p. 191.

70 Nicholson, *Scotland: the later Middle Ages*, pp. 175–7, 182–5.

71 *Calendar of Patent Rolls, 1361–1364*, p. 453, 28 December 1363.

72 *Calendar of Close Rolls, 1360–1364* (London, 1909), p. 421, 14 August 1364; *Calendar of Close Rolls, 1364–1368* (London, 1910), pp. 89 and 211, respectively dated 4 December 1364 and 20 January 1366; Ormrod, 'Edward III and his family', pp. 412–13; J.J.N. Palmer and A.P. Wells, 'Ecclesiastical reform and the politics of the Hundred Years War during the pontificate of Urban V (1362–70)', in C.T. Allmand (ed.), *War, Literature and Politics in the Late Middle Ages* (Liverpool, 1976), pp. 169–89.

73 *Calendar of Patent Rolls, 1364–1367*, p. 427, 12 February 1367.

74 J. Bothwell, 'Edward III and the "New Nobility": largesse and limitation in fourteenth-century England', *English Historical Review*, CXII (1997), 449, pp. 1111–40.

75 Martin (ed. and trans.), *Knighton's Chronicle, 1337–1396*, p. 185. See n. 4 for the possibility of influenza.

76 H.T. Riley (ed.), *Gesta Abbatum Monasterii Sancta Albani, by Thomas Walsingham regnante Ricardo Secundo, ejusdem ecclesiae praecentore, copilata*, Rolls Series (London, 3 vols., 1867–9), II, p. 377; Martin (ed.), *The Percy Chartulary*, no. DCCCLXX, pp. 370–1, 1 August 1364; Fowler, *The King's Lieutenant*, p. 178, and p. 287, n. 119; S. Armitage-Smith, *John of Gaunt: king of Castile and Leon, duke of Aquitaine and Lancaster, earl of Derby, Lincoln and Leicester, seneschal of England* (London, 1904), p. 169.

77 *Calendar of Close Rolls, 1364–1368*, p. 107, 19 May 1365.

78 *Calendar of Close Rolls, 1364–1368*, p. 140, 6 October 1365.

79 C[okayne], *The Complete Peerage*, X, pp. 168–74; and VIII (1932), p. 463.

80 *Register of Edward the Black Prince* (London, 1933), Part 4, pp. 389, 403, 476, entries dated 7 August 1361, 5 November 1361, 8 November 1363.

81 C[okayne], *The Complete Peerage*, X, p. 174.

82 J. Raine (ed.), *Testamenta Eboracensia, or wills registered at York illustrative of the history, manners, language, statistics &c., of the province of York, from the year MCCC downwards*, Surtees Society, vol. IV (London, 1836), I, p. 202; J. Ward (trans. and ed.), *Women of the English Nobility and Gentry, 1066–1500* (Manchester, 1995), no. 163, pp. 223–4.

83 J.T. Rosenthal, 'Aristocratic marriage and the English peerage, 1350–1500: social institution and personal bond', *Journal of Medieval History*, X (1984), pp. 181–94; Prestwich, *The Three Edwards*, p. 258.

84 W.H.D. Longstaffe, 'The old heraldry of the Percys', *Archaeologia Aeliana*, 2nd series, IV (1860), pp. 172–3.

85 *Calendar of Close Rolls, 1364–1368*, p. 438, 6 November 1368.

12: Inexorable Ascent, pp. 297–321

1 'Medieval History and the Romantic Imagination', Katja Reissner Lecture,

Essays by Divers Hands: Being the Transactions of the Royal Society of Literature, XXXII (1963), p. 116.

2 G.E. C[okayne], revised and expanded by V. Gibbs, H.A. Doubleday, G.H. White and Lord H. de Walden, *The Complete Peerage: or a history of the House of Lords and all its members from the earliest times* (London, 1910–59), IX (1936), p. 708; W. Dickson (ed.), 'Cronica Monasterii de Alnewyke ex quodam Libro Cronicarum in Libraria collegii Regalis Cantabrigiae de dono Regis Henrici VI Fundamentoris' [Chronicles of Alnwick Abbey], *Archaeologia Aeliana*, 1st series, III (1984), p. 42.

3 S. Armitage-Smith, *John of Gaunt: king of Castile and Leon, duke of Aquitaine and Lancaster, earl of Derby, Lincoln and Leicester, seneschal of England* (London, 1904), pp. xxi–xxii.

4 Gaunt's early years are excellently treated in A. Goodman, *John of Gaunt: the exercise of princely power in fourteenth-century Europe* (London, 1992), pp. 28–43.

5 W.M. Ormrod, 'Edward III and his family', *Journal of British Studies*, XXVI (1987), pp. 398–422.

6 Geoffrey Chaucer, *Boke of the Duchess*, lines 475–9.

7 J. Sherborne, 'John of Gaunt, Edward III's retinue and the French campaign of 1369', pp. 77–97, in A. Tuck (ed.), *War, Politics and Culture in Fourteenth-century England* (London, 1994); Goodman, *John of Gaunt*, pp. 229–32; Dickson (ed.), 'Cronica Monasterii de Alnewyke', p. 43; Froissart (trans. Lord Berners and ed. G.C. Macaulay), *The Chronicles of Froissart* (London, 1899), p. 191; A. Goodman, *The Loyal Conspiracy: the Lords Appellant under Richard II* (London, 1971, pp. 1–2.

8 Goodman, *John of Gaunt*, pp. 48–9.

9 Armitage-Smith, *John of Gaunt*, pp. 77–8, 92–3.

10 C[okayne], *The Complete Peerage*, IX, p. 712; S. Armitage-Smith (ed.), *John of Gaunt's Register*, Camden Series, vols. XXI–XXII (London, 2 vols., 1911), no. 414, quoted in Goodman, *John of Gaunt*, pp. 282–3.

11 J. Sherborne, 'The battle of La Rochelle and the war at sea, 1372–1375', in Tuck (ed.), *War, Politics and Culture*, pp. 41–53; C[okayne], *The Complete Peerage*, IX, p. 709.

12 Table 1.2 in J. Sherborne, 'Indentured retinues and English expeditions to France, 1369–80', in Tuck (ed.), *War, Politics and Culture*, p. 11.

13 Armitage-Smith, *John of Gaunt*, pp. 105–17; Goodman, *John of Gaunt*, pp. 232–4; Dickson (ed.), 'Cronica Monasterii de Alnewyke', p. 43.

14 Armitage-Smith, *John of Gaunt*, pp. 117–22.

15 A. Tuck, *Richard II and the English nobility* (London, 1973), p. 19.

16 Goodman, *The Loyal Conspiracy*, pp. 135–52.

17 C. Given-Wilson, *The English Nobility in the Late Middle Ages: the fourteenth-century political community* (London, 1987), pp. 37–42.

18 S. Walker, *The Lancastrian Affinity, 1362–1399* (Oxford, 1990), pp. 212–14.

19 Quoted in T.F.T. Plucknett, 'The origin of impeachment', *Transactions of the Royal Historical Society*, 4th series, XXIV (1942), p. 70.

20 E.M. Thompson (ed.), *Chronicon Angliae, ab anno Domini 1328 usque ad annum 1388. Auctore Monacho Quodam Sancti Albani*, Rolls Series (London, 1874), pp. 81–4; G. Holmes, *The Good Parliament* (Oxford, 1975), pp. 133–4.

21 Extracts in E. Hallam (ed.), *Chronicles of the Age of Chivalry* (London, 1987), p. 304.

22 Froissart (trans. Berners and ed. Macaulay), *Chronicles of Froissart*, p. 205.

23 V.H. Galbraith (ed.), *The Anonimalle Chronicle, 1333–1381* (Manchester, 1927), pp. 99–100.

24 Thompson (ed.), *Chronicon Angliae, 1328–1388*, p. 117.

25 J.R. Lumby (ed.), *Chronicon Henrici Knighton*, Rolls Series (London, 2 vols., 1895), II, p. 193.

26 Goodman, *John of Gaunt*, pp. 255, 264.

27 M.H. Carré, *Realists and nominalists* (Oxford, 1946); N. Saul, *Richard II* (New Haven/London, 1997), pp. 293–7; P. Vignaux (trans. E.C. Hall), *Philosophy in the Middle Ages* (London, 1959), pp. 52–9, 165–79; G.M. Trevelyan, *England in the Age of Wycliffe* (London, 4th edn, 1909), pp. 169–79; A. Hudson, *Lollards and the Books* (London, 1985); K.B. McFarlane, *John Wyclif and the Beginning of English Nonconformity* (London, 1952); H.T. Riley (ed.), *Thomae Walsingham Historia Anglicana*, vol. I of *Chronica Monasterii Sancti Albani*, Rolls Series (London, 1863–4); W.A.

Pantin, *The English Church in the Fourteenth Century* (Cambridge, 1955).

28 Froissart (trans. Berners and ed. Macaulay), *Chronicles of Froissart*, p. 205.

29 G.H. Moberly, *Life of William Wykeham, sometime bishop of Winchester, and Lord High Chancellor of England* (London, 1887), p. 116.

30 C[okayne], *The Complete Peerage*, XI (1949), pp. 90–102; Walker, *The Lancastrian affinity, 1361–1399*, p. 47n.

31 C[okayne], *The Complete Peerage*, IX, p. 709; Trevelyan, *England in the Age of Wycliffe*, p. 32; F. Grose, *Military antiquities respecting a history of the English army from the Conquest to the present time* (London, 2 vols., new edn, 1801), I, pp. 192–7; J.H. Round, *The King's Serjeants and Officers of State, with their Coronation Services* (London, 1911), pp. 82–92. A useful work is 'The rise of the Marshal', Appendix G, in C[okayne], *The Complete Peerage*, X (1945), pp. 91–9.

32 Thompson (ed.), *Chronicon Angliae, 1328–1388*, p. 108.

33 Moberly, *Life of William of Wykeham*, p. 140.

34 A.R. Myers, *London in the Age of Chaucer* (Oklahoma, 1972), p. 43; T. Baker, *Medieval London* (London, 1970), pp. 91–2; R. Bird, *The Turbulent London of Richard II* (London, 1948), p. 15; C. Pendril, *London life in the Fourteenth Century* (London), pp. 249–77.

35 Thompson (ed.), *Chronicon Angliae, 1328–1388*, pp. 117–21.

36 Thompson (ed.), *Chronicon Angliae, 1328–1388*, pp. 121–3.

37 T. Beaumont Jones, *The Palaces of Medieval England, c.1050–1550: royalty, nobility, the episcopate and their residences from Edward the Confessor to Henry VIII* (London, 1990), p. 114.

38 Thompson (ed.), *Chronicon Angliae, 1328–1388*, pp. 123–30.

39 Moberly, *Life of William of Wykeham*, pp. 142–4; Thompson (ed.), *Chronicon Angliae, 1328–1388*, pp. 136–7.

40 Froissart (trans. Berners and ed. Macaulay), *Chronicles of Froissart*, p. 206; Armitage-Smith, *John of Gaunt*, pp. 184–6; Saul, *Richard II*, pp. 22–3; 357n.

13: *The Fall of the Percys, pp. 322–66*

1 The preceding section based on the following. On Dymoke's status as retainer, see S. Walker, *The Lancastrian affinity, 1361–1399* (Oxford, 1990), pp. 92, 238n., 240n., 268. On the claims to the Coronation services, see L.G.W. Legg (ed.), *English coronation records* (London, 1901), pp. 131–68; and W. Robinson, *Collections relative to claims at the coronations of several of the kings of England, beginning with King Richard II* (London, 1820), pp. 5–6. On the Norfolks' claims, *Complete Peerage*, IX (1936), pp. 596–601. For descriptions of the festivities and ceremony, see W.J. Passingham, *The History of the Coronation* (London, n.d.), pp. 165–8; N. Saul, *Richard II* (New Haven/London, 1997), pp. 24–26; and especially, E.M. Thompson (ed.), *Chronicon Angliae, ab anno Domini 1328 usque ad annum, auctore Monacho quodam Sancti Albani*, Rolls Series (London, 1874), pp. 155–61.

2 *Calendar of Charter Rolls, 1341–1417* (London, HMSO, 1920), 16 July 1377, p. 235.

3 R.L. Storey, 'The wardens of the Marches of England towards Scotland, 1377–1489', *English Historical Review*, LXXII (1957), no. 235, Appendix, 'List of Wardens, 1377–1489', p. 609.

4 Thompson (ed.), *Chronicon Angliae, 1328–1388*, pp. 164–5.

5 Thompson (ed.), *Chronicon Angliae, 1328–1388*, p. 165.

6 J.A. Tuck, 'Richard II and the Border magnates', *Northern History*, III (1968), p. 38.

7 C.J. Neville, 'Keeping the peace on the Northern Marches in the later Middle Ages', *English Historical Review*, CIX (1994), 430, pp. 9–11; Tuck, 'Richard II and the Border magnates', p. 33.

8 Thompson (ed.), *Chronicon Angliae, 1328–1388*, pp. 165–6, 219–20; G.F. Beltz, *Memorials of the most noble Order of the Garter, from its foundation to the present time* (London, 1841), p. 314.

9 Quoted in A. Grant, 'The Otterburn war from the Scottish point of view', in a Goodman and Tuck (eds.), *War and Border Societies in the Middle Ages* (London, 1992), p. 39.

10 G.H. Martin (ed. and trans.), *Knighton's Chronicle, 1337–1396* (Oxford, 1995), pp. 142–48; V.H. Galbraith (ed.), *The Anonimalle Chronicle, 1333–1381* (Manchester, 1927), pp. 152–3; A. Goodman, *John of Gaunt: the exercise of princely power in fourteenth-century Europe* (London, 1992),

pp. 81–2; B. Bevan, *King Richard II* (London, 1990), pp. 29–30.

11 Galbraith (ed.), *The Anonimalle Chronicle, 1333–1381*, pp. 155–6; Thompson (ed.), *Chronicon Angliae, 1328–1388*, pp. 328–30; Goodman, *John of Gaunt*, pp. 89–91; E.C. Lodge, and R. Somerville (eds.), *John of Gaunt's Register, 1379–1383*, Camden Society, 3rd series, vol. LVII (London, 1937), 2, pp. 410–11; Storey, 'Wardens of the Marches of England towards Scotland', p. 596; D. Hay, 'England, Scotland and Europe: the problem of the frontier', *Transactions of the Royal Historical Society*, 5th series, XXV (1975), p. 83.

12 Storey, 'Wardens of the Marches of England', p. 596; C.R. Young, *The Making of the Neville Family in England, 1166–1400* (Woodbridge, 1996), p. 128; C[okayne], *The Complete Peerage*, IX, pp. 502–3; *Complete Peerage*, X (1945), p. 462.

13 J.A. Tuck, 'The emergence of a Northern nobility, 1250–1400', *Northern History*, XXII (1986), pp. 1–17; S. Payling, 'The politics of family: late medieval marriage contracts', in R.H. Britnell and A.J. Pollard (eds.), *The McFarlane Legacy: studies in late medieval politics and society* (Stroud/New York, 1995), pp. 21–47; C[okayne], *The Complete Peerage*, IX, p. 712.

14 A. Tuck, 'The Percies and the community of Northumberland in the later fourteenth century', in Goodman and Tuck (eds.), *War and Border Societies*, pp. 178–95.

15 M.T. Martin (ed.), *The Percy Chartulary*, no. MLXX, 20 September 1334, p. 451; no. MLXIX, 23 September 1334, pp. 449–50; J. Bain (ed.), *Calendar of documents relating to Scotland, preserved in Her Majesty's Public Record Office, London* (Edinburgh, 4 vols., 1881–8), III, no. 1133, p. 205, 20 September 1334; J. Bain, 'The Percies in Scotland', *Archaeological Journal*, XLI (1884), pp. 339–41; J.M.W. Bean, 'The Percies and their estates in Scotland', *Archaeologia Aeliana*, XXXV (1957), 4th series, pp. 98–9.

16 J. Campbell, 'England, Scotland and the Hundred Years War in the fourteenth century', in J.R. Hale, J.R.L. Highfield and B. Smalley (eds.), *Europe in the Late Middle Ages* (London, 1965), p. 211.

17 N.B. Lewis, 'The last medieval summons of the English feudal levy, 13 June 1385', *English Historical Review*, LXXIII (1958),

no. 286, pp. 1–26; Saul, *Richard II*, pp. 145–6; R. Campbell Paterson, *My Wound is Deep: a history of the later Anglo-Scots wars, 1380–1560* (Edinburgh, 1997), pp. 8–11.

18 J.L. Gillespie, 'Richard II: king of battles?', in J.L. Gillespie (ed.), *The Age of Richard II* (Stroud, 1997), pp. 145–6.

19 A. Tuck, *Crown and Nobility, 1272–1461: political conflict in late medieval England* (London, 1985), p. 192; Storey, 'Wardens of the Marches of England towards Scotland', pp. 600, 612; J. Taylor (ed.), *The Kirkstall Abbey Chronicles*, Publications of the Thoresby Society, XLII (Leeds, 1952), pp. 70, 131; A. Goodman, *The Loyal Conspiracy: the Lords Appellant under Richard II* (London, 1971).

20 C. Tyson, 'The battle of Otterburn: when and where was it fought?', in Goodman and Tuck (eds.), *War and Border Societies in the Middle Ages*, pp. 65–93.

21 Tuck, 'Richard II and the Border magnates', pp. 44–5; A. Goodman, 'Introduction', in Goodman and Tuck (eds.), *War and Border Societies in the Middle Ages*, pp. 18–20; C[okayne], *The Complete Peerage*, IX, p. 710; Grant, 'The Otterburn was from the Scottish point of view', in Goodman and Tuck (eds.), *War and Border Societies in the Middle Ages*, p. 52, citing Walsingham; Storey, 'Wardens of the Marches of England towards Scotland', pp. 602, 612; Beltz, 'Sir Henry Percy, called "Hotspur"', *Memorials of the most noble Order of the Garter*, p. 317; Goodman, *John of Gaunt*, pp. 107, 144–5.

22 J. Raine (ed.), *Historical papers and letters from the Northern Registers*, Rolls Series (London, 1873), no. CCLXV, 15 July 1393, pp. 425–6.

23 J.J.N. Palmer, 'The Anglo-French peace negotiations, 1390–1396', *Transactions of the Royal Historical Society*, 5th series, XVI (1966), pp. 81–94, and his 'English foreign policy, 1388–99', in F.R.H. du Boulay and C.M. Barron (eds.), *The Reign of Richard II: essays in honour of May Mckisack* (London, 1971), pp. 75–107; Tuck, *Crown and Nobility*, pp. 200–5.

24 *Calendar of Charter Rolls, 1341–1417*, 29 September 1397, p. 369; Beltz, *Memorials of the most noble Order of the Garter*, pp. 221–7.

25 C. Given-Wilson, 'Richard II, Edward II, and the Lancastrian inheritance', *English*

Historical Review, CIX (1994), 432,
pp. 553–71. Also, Saul, *Richard II*,
pp. 394–402.

26 Goodman, *John of Gaunt*, pp. 166–9.

27 N. Saul, 'The kingship of Richard II', in A.
Goodman and J. Gillespie (eds.), *Richard
II: the art of kingship* (Oxford, 1999),
pp. 37–57.

28 E.M. Thompson (ed.), *Chronicon Adae de
Usk, A.D. 1377–1421* (London, 1904), p. 170.

29 Bain (ed.), *Calendar of documents relating to
Scotland*, IV, no. 506, pp. 106–7.

30 A. Tuck, *Richard II and the English Nobility*
(London, 1973), pp. 212–13; Saul, *Richard
II*, pp. 406–7.

31 Saul, *Richard II*, pp. 405–34; Tuck, *Richard
II and the English Nobility*, pp. 210–25;
J.M.W. Bean, 'Henry IV and the Percies',
History, XLIV (1959), pp. 212–21; Raine
(ed.), *Historical papers and letters from the
Northern Registers*, no. CCLXVII, pp. 427–9;
Appendix B, 'Bolingbroke's army in 1399',
in C. Given-Wilson (ed.), *Chronicles of the
Revolution, 1397–1400: the reign of Richard II*
(Manchester, 1993); P.B. Williams (ed.),
*Chronicque de la Traïson et mort de Richart
Deux roy Dengleterre*, English Historical
Society (London, 1845; rep. 1964); M.V.
Clarke and V.H. Galbraith, 'The
deposition of Richard II', *Bulletin of the
John Rylands Library*, XIV (1930),
pp. 125–81; C. Barron, 'The deposition of
Richard II', in J. Taylor and W. Childs
(eds.), *Politics and Crisis in Fourteenth-century
England* (Gloucester, 1990), pp. 132–49; B.
Wilkinson, 'The deposition of Richard II
and the accession of Henry IV', *English
Historical Review*, LIV (1939), 214,
pp. 215–39; P. McNiven, 'Legitimacy and
consent: Henry IV and the Lancastrian
title, 1399–1406', *Mediaeval Studies*, XLIV
(1982), pp. 470–81.

32 Raine (ed.), *Historical papers and letters from
the Northern Registers*, no. CCLXVII, p. 429.

33 P. McNiven, 'Rebellion, sedition and the
legend of Richard II's survival in the
reigns of Henry IV and Henry V', *Bulletin
of the John Rylands Library*, LXXVI (1994),
pp. 93–117.

34 A.L. Brown, 'The English campaign in
Scotland, 1400', in H. Hearder and H.R.
Loyn (eds.), *British Government and
Administration: studies presented to S.B. Chrimes*
(Cardiff, 1974), pp. 40–54; Campbell
Paterson, *My Wound is Deep*, pp. 21–5.

35 Campbell Paterson, *My Wound is Deep*,
pp. 30–33.

36 Thompson (ed.), *Chronicon Adae de Usk,
A.D. 1377–1421*, p. 256.

37 Copies of these letters may be found in E.
Barrington de Fonblanque, *Annals of the
House of Percy, from the Conquest to the opening
of the 19th Century* (London, privately
printed, 2 vols., 1887), I, pp. 209–10,
522–3, 525–7.

38 Bean, 'Henry IV and the Percies', p. 223.

39 This long section is based on the relevant
chapters of J.H. Wylie, *History of England
under Henry the Fourth* (London, 4 vols.,
1884–98); B. Bevan, *Henry IV* (London,
1994); J.L. Kirby, *Henry IV of England*
(London, 1970); J.D. Griffith Davies, *King
Henry IV* (London, 1935); G. Brenan, *A
history of the house of Percy* (London, 2 vols.,
1902), I; various volumes of *The Complete
Peerage*; J.E. Lloyd, *Owen Glendower*
(Oxford, 1931). Original manuscript
sources are as follows: Thompson (ed.),
Chronicon Adae de Usk, A.D. 1377–1421 (see
p. 257, for the execution of Searle); F.C.
Hingeston, John Capgrave's (ed.), *The
Chronicle of England*, Rolls Series (London,
1858); Taylor (ed.), *The Kirkstall Abbey
Chronicles*; T. Walsingham (ed. H.T. Riley),
*Annales Ricardi Secundi et Henrici Quarti
regum Angliae* (1392–1406), in *Johannis de
Trokelowe et Henrici de Blaneforde*, Rolls
Series (London, 1866); V.H. Galbraith
(ed.), *The St. Albans Chronicle, 1406–1420*
(Oxford, 1937). On the Clifford
connection, see C[okayne], *The Complete
Peerage*, III (1913), p. 293; on a pro-Percy
account of the 1403 Manifesto declaring
that Henry had misled them, see (as usual)
William Peeris's version (ed. by D. Bisley),
Metrical Pedigree of the Percyes, printed as the
Metrical Chronicle of the Family of Percy in
*Richardson's reprints of rare tracts and imprints
of antient manuscripts*, vol. V (Newcastle,
1845). The chronicler John Hardyng's
second-hand description of the manifesto
may be found in A.R. Myers' essay,
'Parliamentary petitions in the fifteenth
century', in the collection edited by C.H.
Clough, *Crown, Household and Parliament in
Fifteenth Century England* (London, 1985),
p. 19. On the subject of Henry VI's
nervousness over being seen as a usuper
and his efforts to show the people that
Richard and the Percys were really dead,

see P. Morgan's important article, 'Henry IV and the shadow of Richard II', in R.E. Archer (ed.), *Crown, Government and People in the Fifteenth Century* (Stroud/New York, 1995), pp. 1–31; and P. Strohm, 'The trouble with Richard: the reburial of Richard II and Lancastrian symbolic strategy', *Speculum*, LXXI (1996), 1, pp. 87–111, which also contains the quotations on the deaths of Hotspur and Worcester.

14: A Good and Faithful Servant, pp. 367–77

1 S.B. Chrimes, 'Some letters of John of Lancaster as Warden of the East Marches towards Scotland', *Speculum*, XIV (1939), pp. 3–27.

2 *Rotuli Parliamentorum ut et Petitiones, et Placita in Parliamento*, Records Commission (London, 6 vols., 1767–77), IV, pp. 36–7; *Calendar of Patent Rolls, 1413–1416* (London, HMSO, 1910), I, 11 May 1415, p. 321.

3 D. MacPherson (ed.), *Rotuli Scotiae in Turri Londinensi et in Domo Capitulari Westmonasteriensi Asservati* (London, 2 vols., 1814–19), II, May 1415, p. 214.

4 T.B. Pugh, *Henry V and the Southampton Plot of 1415* (Southampton, 1988).

5 MacPherson (ed.), *Rotuli Scotiae*, II, 9 December 1415, p. 214.

6 G.L. Harriss, 'The king and his magnates', in G.L. Harriss (ed.), *Henry V: the practice of kingship* (Oxford, 1985), p. 39.

7 *Calendar of Charter Rolls, 1341–1417* (London, HMSO, 1920), V, 16 July 1377 and 16 March 1416, pp. 235, 483.

8 J.M.W. Bean, *The Estates of the Percy Family, 1416–1537* (Oxford, 1958), pp. 81–108; *Calendar of Patent Rolls, 1413–1416*, 27 July 1415, p. 370; A.L. Brown, 'The reign of Henry IV: the establishment of the Lancastrian regime', in S.B. Chrimes, C.D. Ross and R.A. Griffiths (eds.), *Fifteenth Century England, 1399–1509: studies in politics and society* (Manchester, 1972), p. 19.

9 J. Bain (ed.), *Calendar of documents relating to Scotland, preserved in Her Majesty's Public Record Office, London* (Edinburgh, 4 vols., 1881–8), IV, no. 296 (incorrectly dated); MacPherson (ed.), *Rotuli Scotiae*, II, 1 March 1417 and 11 April 1417, pp. 219–21.

10 C. Allmand, *Henry V* (London, 1997 edn), p. 393.

11 *Calendar of Patent Rolls, 1416–1422* (London, HMSO, 1911), II, p. 122; MacPherson (ed.), *Rotuli Scotiae*, II, p. 223.

12 *Calendar of Patent Rolls, 1416–1422*, 1 April 1418 and 11 April 1418, pp. 196, 201.

13 MacPherson (ed.), *Rotuli Scotiae*, II, p. 223.

14 W.P. Hedley, *Northumberland Families* (Newcastle, 2 vols., 1968–70), II, p. 16.

15 A.F. Sutton and L. Visser-Fuchs, *Richard III's Books: ideals and reality in the life and library of a medieval prince* (Stroud, 1997), pp. 107–18.

16 M. Keen, 'Diplomacy', in Harriss (ed.), *Henry V*, pp. 181–99.

17 *Calendar of Patent Rolls, 1416–1422*, p. 271.

18 G.E. C[okayne], revised and expanded by V. Gibbs, H.A. Doubleday, G.H. White and Lord H. de Walden, *The Complete Peerage: or a history of the House of Lords and all its members from the earliest times* (London, 1910–59), IX (1936), p. 716.

19 *Calendar of Patent Rolls, 1416–1422*, 7 April 1421, pp. 384–5.

20 Allmand, *Henry V*; D. Seward, *The Hundred Years War: the English in France, 1337–1453* (New York, 1999 edn); M. Brown, *James I* (Edinburgh, 1994). P.J. Bradley, 'Henry V's Scottish policy: a study in realpolitik', in J.S. Hamilton and P.J. Bradley (eds.), *Documenting the Past: essays in medieval history presented to George Peddy Cuttino* (Woodbridge, 1989), pp. 177–95.

15: A Safe Pair of Hands, pp. 378–99

1 *Rotuli Parliamentorum ut in Petitiones, et Placita in Parliamento* (London, 6 vols., 1767–77), IV, pp. 175, 201 and 399.

2 R.A. Griffiths, *The Reign of King Henry VI: the exercise of royal authority, 1422–61* (London, 1981), p. 23.

3 B. Wolffe, *Henry VI* (London, 1981), p. 33.

4 W.P. Hedley, *Northumberland Families* (Newcastle, 2 vols., 1968–70), II, p. 16.

5 E. Bonner, 'Scotland's "Auld Alliance" with France, 1295–1560', *History*, LXXXIV (1999), pp. 17–18.

6 C. Macrae, 'The English Council and Scotland in 1430', *English Historical Review*, LIV (1939), no. 215, pp. 415–26.

7 J.R. Lander, 'Family, "friends" and politics

in fifteenth-century England', pp. 27–40, in R.A. Griffiths and J. Sherborne (eds.), *Kings and Nobles in the Later Middle Ages: a tribute to Charles Ross* (Gloucester, 1986); M. Hicks, 'Cement or solvent? Kinship and politics in late medieval England: the case of the Nevilles', *History*, LXXXIII (1988), pp. 31–46; R.L. Storey, *The End of the House of Lancaster* (London, 1966), pp. 105–23; M. Hicks, 'The Neville earldom of Salisbury, 1429–71', pp. 353–63, in *Richard II and his Rivals: magnates and their motives in the War of the Roses* (London, 1991); G.L. Harriss, *Cardinal Beaufort: a study of Lancastrian ascendancy and decline* (Oxford, 1988), pp. 267–68.

8 Jean de Waurin (ed. W. and E.L.C.P. Hardy), *Recueil des croniques et anchiennes istories de la Graut Bretaigne à present nommé Engleterre*, Rolls Series (London, 5 vols., 1864–91), IV, pp. 69–87.

9 J. Bellenden (ed.), *The Chronicles of Scotland compiled by Hector Boece*, Scottish Text Society (Edinburgh, 1938–41), Book XVII, Chapter 8.

10 M. Brown, *James I* (Edinburgh, 1994), p. 164.

11 F.J.H. Skene (ed.), *Liber Pluscardensis* (Edinburgh, 2 vols., 1887–80), I, p. 380.

12 Brown, *James I*, pp. 186–8; G. Macintosh (ed.), *The Life and Death of King James the First*, Maitland Club publications (Edinburgh, 1837).

13 G.E. C[okayne], revised and expanded by V. Gibbs, H.A. Doubleday, G.H. White and Lord H. de Walden, *The Complete Peerage: or a history of the House of Lords and all its members from the earliest times* (London, 1910–59), X (1945), pp. 656–65; IX (1936), p. 607.

14 M.W. Warner and K. Lacey, 'Neville *vs.* Percy: a precedence dispute circa 1442', *Historical Research: the Bulletin of the Institute of Historical Research*, LXIX (1996), 169, pp. 211–17.

15 On the Somerset-York rivalry, see M.K. Jones, 'Somerset, York and the Wars of the Roses', *English Historical Review*, CIV (1989), 411, pp. 285–307.

16 D. Seward, *The Hundred Years War: the English in France, 1337–1453* (London, 1978), pp. 253–62.

16: Mutual Assured Destruction, pp. 400–13

1 J. Gairdner (ed.), '*Annales* of William Worcester', contained in *Letters and papers illustrative of the wars of the English in France during the reign of King Henry VI*, Rolls Series (London, 3 vols., 1864), II, Part 2, p. 770.

2 See the map in R.L. Storey, *The End of the House of Lancaster* (London, 1966), p. 128.

3 Storey, *The End of the House of Lancaster*, pp. 124–32; R. Griffiths, 'Local rivalries and national politics: the Percies, the Nevilles and the Duke of Exeter, 1452–1455', *Speculum*, XLIII (1968), pp. 590–605.

4 M. Hicks, *Warwick the Kingmaker* (Oxford, 1998), pp. 1–6.

5 E. Bonner, 'Scotland's "Auld Alliance" with France, 1295–1560', *History*, LXXXIV (1999), p. 19.

6 R. Nicholson, *Scotland: the later Middle Ages* (Edinburgh, 1974), pp. 353–69.

7 G.E. C[okayne], revised and expanded by V. Gibbs, H.A. Doubleday, G.H. White and Lord H. de Walden, *The Complete Peerage: or a history of the House of Lords and all its members from the earliest times* (London, 1910–59), VII (1929), p. 164.

8 Storey, *The End of the House of Lancaster*, pp. 143–4.

9 J. Gillingham, *The Wars of the Roses: peace and conflict in fifteenth-century England* (London, 1981), p. 82; P.A. Johnson, *Duke Richard of York, 1411–1460* (Oxford, 1988), pp. 132–5; B. Wolffe, *Henry VI* (London, 1981), pp. 274–5.

10 Griffiths, 'Local rivalries and national politics', pp. 610–11.

11 Storey, *The End of the House of Lancaster*, pp. 142–9; Griffiths, 'Local rivalries and national politics', pp. 611–24. See also H.T. Riley (ed.), *Registrum Abbatiae Johannis Whethamstede*, Rolls Series (London, 2 vols., 1872–3), II, pp. 303–4; J. Gairdner (ed.), *Three Fifteenth Century chronicles*, Camden Society, vol. XXVIII (London, 2nd series, 1880), p. 149; J.C. Atkinson (ed.), *Cartularium Abbathiae de Whiteby*, Surtees Society, vol. LXXII (Durham, 1881), II, pp. 694–5; J.M.W. Bean, *The Estates of the Percy Family, 1416–1537* (Oxford, 1958), pp. 75, 79n.; *Calendar of Patent Rolls, 1452–1461* (London, HMSO, 1910), p. 584.

12 Quoted in Gillingham, *The Wars of the Roses*, pp. 83–4.

13 Storey, *The End of the House of Lancaster*, p. 159.

14 G.L. Harriss, 'The struggle for Calais: an aspect of the rivalry between Lancaster and York', *English Historical Review*, LXXV (1960), p. 39.

15 Gairdner (ed.), *Three Fifteenth Century Chronicles*, p. 152.

16 See maps in J. Ramsay, *Lancaster and York: a century of English history* (Oxford, 2 vols., 1892), II; and P. Haigh, *The Military Campaigns of the Wars of the Roses* (Stroud, 1995), although any modern street map would do.

17 C.A.J. Armstrong, 'Politics and the Battle of St Albans, 1455', *Bulletin of the Institute of Historical Research*, XXXIII (1960), pp. 1–72; Haigh, *The Military campaigns of the Wars of the Roses*, pp. 8–13; Gillingham, *The Wars of the Roses*, p. 87.

17: Recovery and Disaster, pp. 414–34

1 R. Nicholson, *Scotland: the later Middle Ages* (Edinburgh, 1974), pp. 369–75.

2 Nicholson, *Scotland: the later Middle Ages*, pp. 392–3.

3 Quoted in M.A. Hicks, *Warwick the Kingmaker* (Oxford, 1998), pp. 120–1.

4 J.M.W. Bean, *The Estates of the Percy Family, 1416–1537* (Oxford, 1958), pp. 98–108.

5 J.T. Rosenthal, 'Fifteenth-century baronial incomes and Richard, duke of York', *Bulletin of the Institute of Historical Research*, XXXVII (1964), pp. 233–40.

6 R.L. Storey, *The End of the House of Lancaster* (London, 1966), p. 177.

7 J. Gillingham, *The Wars of the Roses: peace and conflict in fifteenth-century England* (London, 1981), p. 99.

8 J. Ramsay, *Lancaster and York: a century of English history* (Oxford, 2 vols., 1892), II, p. 56; B. Wolffe, *Henry VI* (London, 1981), p. 302.

9 Nicholson, *Scotland: the later Middle Ages*, pp. 394–5.

10 P.A. Johnson, *Duke Richard of York, 1411–1460* (Oxford, 1988), p. 177.

11 C.L. Kingsford (ed.), *The Chronicles of London* (Oxford, 1905), p. 168; R. Flenley (ed.), *Six Town Chronicles of England* (Oxford, 1911), pp. 111–12, 159–60; H.T.

Riley (ed.), *Registrum Abbatiae Johannis Whethamstede*, Rolls Series (London, 2 vols., 1872–3), I, pp. 295–308; J. Gairdner (ed.), 'Gregory's Chronicle, 1189–1469', in *Historical Collections of a Citizen of London*, Camden Society, vol. XVII (London, 1876), pp. 203–4; Hicks, *Warwick the Kingmaker*, pp. 137–8.

12 Hicks, *Warwick the Kingmaker*, p. 147.

13 Hicks, *Warwick the Kingmaker*, p. 150.

14 J.S. Davies (ed.), *An English chronicle of the reigns of Richard II, Henry IV, Henry V, and Henry VI, written before the year 1471*, Camden Series, 1st series, vol. LXIV (London, 1856), p. 78; Flenley (ed.), *Six Town Chronicles*, p. 113; Riley (ed.), *Registrum Abbatiae Johannis Whethamstede*, I, p. 340.

15 G.L. and M.A. Harriss (eds.), 'John Benet's Chronicle for the years 1400 to 1462', in *Camden Miscellany*, Camden Society, 4th series, vol. XXIV (London, 1972), p. 223.

16 A. Goodman, *The Wars of the Roses: military activity and English society, 1452–97* (London, 1981), p. 27, nn. 39–41.

17 Goodman, *The Wars of the Roses*, p. 27.

18 Goodman, *The Wars of the Roses*, p. 28.

19 Harriss (eds.), 'John Benet's Chronicle', p. 224; Riley (ed.), *Registrum Abbatiae Johannis Whethamstede*, I, p. 338.

20 Gillingham, *The Wars of the Roses*, p. 106.

21 Johnson, *Duke Richard of York*, pp. 196–201.

22 C.L. Kingsford, 'The earl of Warwick at Calais in 1460', *English Historical Review*, XXXVII (1922), no. 145, pp. 544–46.

23 Davies (ed.), *An English Chronicle*, pp. 86–90.

24 R.I. Jack, 'A quincentenary: the battle of Northampton, July 10th 1460', *Northamptonshire Past and Present*, III (1960), pp. 21–5; Goodman, *The Wars of the Roses*, 37–40.

25 Nicholson, *Scotland: the later Middle Ages*, p. 396; N. Macdougall, *James III: a political study* (Edinburgh, 1982), p. 46.

26 Gillingham, *The Wars of the Roses*, pp. 116–17; Johnson, *Duke Richard of York*, pp. 211–18.

27 Nicholdon, *Scotland: the later Middle Ages*, p. 400.

28 *Rotuli Parliamentorum ut in Petitiones, et Placita in Parliamento* (London, 6 vols., 1767–77), V, pp. 394–5.

29 Goodman, *The War of the Roses*, p. 42.

30 C.H. Hunter Blair, 'Members of Parliament for Northumberland, 6 October 1399–20 January 1558', *Archaeologia Aeliana*, 4th series, XII (1935), pp. 99, 105.

31 See Ramsay, *Lancaster and York*, II, pp. 237–8; Goodman, *The Wars of the Roses*, pp. 42–3; Hicks, *Warwick the Kingmaker*, p. 214; P.A. Haigh, *The Battle of Wakefield: 30 December 1460* (Stroud, 1996).

32 Ramsay, *Lancaster and York*, II, pp. 245ff.; Gillingham, *The Wars of the Roses*, pp. 125–9.

33 C.A.J. Armstrong, 'The inauguration ceremonies of the Yorkist kings, and their title to the throne', *Transactions of the Royal Historical Society*, 4th series, XXX (1948).

34 C. Ross, *Edward IV* (Yale, 1997 edn; orig. London, 1974), pp. 9–11.

35 Goodman, *The Wars of the Roses*, pp. 50–2; Gillingham, *The Wars of the Roses*, pp. 133–5; Ross, *Edward IV*, pp. 36–8; Ramsay, *Lancaster and York*, II, pp. 270–4; A.W. Boardman, *The Battle of Towton* (Stroud, 1994) and his *The Medieval Soldier in the Wars of the Roses* (Stroud, 1998), pp. 175, 181–6.

18: Bird in the Bosom, pp. 435–42

1 W.P. Hedley, *Northumberland Families* (Newcastle, 2 vols., 1968–70), p. 16.

2 J.R. Lander, 'Attainder and forfeiture, 1453–1509', *Historical Journal*, IV (1961), p. 119; *Rotuli Parliamentorum ut in Petitiones, et Placita in Parliamento* (London, 6 vols., 1767–77), V, pp. 477ff.

3 J.O. Halliwell (ed.), 'Chronicle of the first thirteen years of the reign of King Edward the fourth, by John Warkworth, D.D.', in K. Dockray (intro.), *Three Chronicles of the Reign of Edward IV* (Gloucester, 1988), p. 25.

4 C.D. Ross, *Edward IV* (Yale, 1997 edn; orig. London, 1974), p. 45.

5 M. Hicks, *Warwick the Kingmaker* (Oxford, 1998), pp. 227–8.

6 D. MacPherson (ed.), *Rotuli Scotiae in Turri Londinensi et in Domo Capitulari Westmonasteriensi Asservati* (London, 2 vols., 1814–19), II, p. 402.

7 Ross, *Edward IV*, pp. 41–63; J. Gillingham, *The Wars of the Roses: peace and conflict in fifteenth-century England* (London, 1981), pp. 136–55.

8 J. Gairdner (ed.), 'Annales rerum Anglicarum', in *Letters and papers illustrative of the wars of the English in France during the reign of King Henry VI*, Rolls Series (London, 3 vols., 1864), II, Part 2, p. 779.

9 N. Macdougall, *James III: a political study* (Edinburgh, 1982), pp. 51–69.

10 Halliwell (ed.), 'Chronicle', p. 24.

11 C.L. Kingsford, (ed.), *The Chronicles of London* (Oxford, 1095), p. 178; also, A.H. Thomas and I.D. Thornley (eds.), *The Great Chronicle of London* (London, 1938), p. 200.

12 Halliwell (ed.), 'Chronicle', pp. 24–5.

13 M. Hicks, 'Edward IV, the duke of Somerset and Lancastrian loyalism in the North', in M. Hicks, *Richard III and his Rivals: magnates and their motives in the Wars of the Roses* (London, 1991), p. 150.

14 Hicks, 'Edward IV, the duke of Somerset and Lancastrian loyalism', pp. 160–1.

15 Halliwell (ed.), 'Chronicle', p. 25.

16 J. Gairdner (ed.), 'Gregory's Chronicle, 1189–1469', in *Historical Collections of a Citizen of London*, Camden Society, vol. XVII (London, 1876), pp. 223–4; C.J. Bates, *The History of Northumberland* (London, 1894), p. 201.

17 D. Charlesworth, 'The battle of Hexham, 1464', *Archaeologia Aeliana*, 4th series, XXX (1952), pp. 57–68; Gairdner (ed.), 'Gregory's Chronicle, 1189–1469', pp. 225–6.

18 G.E. C[okayne], revised and expanded by V. Gibbs, H.A. Doubleday, G.H. White and Lord H. de Walden, *The Complete Peerage: or a history of the House of Lords and all its members from the earliest times* (London, 1910–59), IX (1936), p. 717.

19 See 'Anno Edwardi quarti quarto et mensis Maij die xxvij, scilicet in die sancte Trinitatis', reprinted in Halliwell (ed.), 'Chronicle', pp. 58–61.

19: Percy Restored, pp. 443–60

1 J.M.W. Bean, *The Estates of the Percy Family, 1416–1537* (Oxford, 1958), pp. 109–12.

2 C. Ross, *Edward IV* (London, 1977 edn), p. 126.

3 Ross, *Edward IV*, pp. 84–103; J.R. Lander, 'Marriage and politics in the fifteenth century: the Nevilles and the Wydevilles', *Bulletin of the Institute of Historical Research*, XXXVI (1963).

4 J. Gairdner (ed.), 'Gregory's Chronicle, 1189–1469', in *Historical Collections of a Citizen of London*, Camden Society, vol. XVII (London, 1876), p. 226; D. Mancini (ed. and trans. C.A.J. Armstrong), *The*

Usurpation of Richard III (Oxford, 2nd edn, 1969), p. 67.

5 For the following section see Ross, *Edward IV*, pp. 104–25.

6 Quoted in Ross, *Edward IV*, pp. 75–8.

7 J.O. Halliwell (ed.), 'Chronicle of the first thirteen years of the reign of King Edward the Fourth, by John Warkworth, D.D.', in K. Dockray (intro.), *Three Chronicles of the Reign of Edward IV* (Gloucester, 1988), p. 28.

8 G.E. C[okayne], revised and expanded by V. Gibbs, H.A. Doubleday, G.H. White and Lord H. de Walden, *The Complete Peerage: or a history of the House of Lords and all its members from the earliest times* (London, 1910–59), IX (1936), p. 717n.

9 Ross, *Edward IV*, p. 144.

10 R.L. Storey, 'The Wardens of the Marches of England towards Scotland, 1377–1489', *English Historical Review*, LXXII (1957), p. 615.

11 Halliwell (ed.), 'Chronicle', p. 32.

12 B. Wolffe, *Henry VI* (London, 1981), pp. 337–9.

13 Quoted in Ross, *Edward IV*, p. 151.

14 J. Kirby (ed.), *The Plumpton Letters and Papers*, Camden Society, 5th series, vol. VIII (London, 1996), no. 19, 7 December 1464–1469, and no. 21, 17 August 1470, pp. 43–46.

15 Ross, *Edward IV*, pp. 160–62.

16 J. Bruce (ed.), 'Historie of the arrivall of Edward IV. In England and the final recouerye of kingdomes from Henry VI. a.d. MCCCCLXXI', in Dockray, *Three Chronicles*, p. 152. See also Halliwell (ed.), 'Chronicle', p. 36.

17 For a fuller description, see P.W. Hammond, *The Battles of Barnet and Tewkesbury* (Gloucester, 1990), pp. 66–80.

18 Hammond, *The Battles of Barnet and Tewkesbury*, pp. 81–102; Bruce (ed.), 'Historie of the arrivall of Edward IV', p. 184.

19 Bruce (ed.), 'Historie of the arrivall of Edward IV', p. 178.

20 Bruce (ed.), 'Historie of the arrivall of Edward IV', p. 184.

21 Wolffe, *Henry VI*, p. 347.

22 This section mostly based on Ross, *Edward IV*, pp. 204–38.

20: Kings in the North, pp. 461–70

1 J.M.W. Bean, *The Estates of the Percy Family, 1416–1537* (Oxford, 1958), pp. 128–35; R.

Horrox, 'Richard III and the East Riding', in R. Horrox (ed.), *Richard III and the North* (Hull, 1986), p. 91.

2 H. Ellis (ed.), *Edward Hall's Chronicle*, Rolls Series (London, 1809), pp. 426, 442–3.

3 J.C. Hodgson (ed.), *Percy Bailiffs' Rolls of the Fifteenth Century*, Surtees Society, vol. CXXXIV (Durham, 1921).

4 A.F. Sutton and L. Visser-Fuchs, *Richard III's Books: ideals and reality in the life and library of a medieval prince* (Stroud, 1997), pp. 118–19.

5 M. Hicks, 'Dynastic change and Northern society: the career of the fourth earl of Northumberland, 1470–89', *Northern History*, XIV (1978), pp. 78–88; M. Hicks, 'Richard III, duke of Gloucester: the formative years', in J. Gillingham (ed.), *Richard III: a medieval kingship* (London, 1993), pp. 21–23; M. Hicks, 'Richard, duke of Gloucester and the North', in R. Horrox (ed.), *Richard III and the North* (Hull, 1986), pp. 11–26; A.J. Pollard, *Richard III and the Princess in the Tower* (Stroud, 1991), pp. 60–85; E. Barrington de Fonblanque, *Annals of the house of Percy, from the Conquest to the opening of the 19th Century* (London, privately printed, 2 vols., 1887), I, Appendix XLIII, p. 549.

6 N. Macdougall, *James III: a political study* (Edinburgh, 1982), p. 117.

7 A. Grant, 'Richard III and Scotland', in A.J. Pollard (ed.), *The North of England in the Age of Richard III* (Stroud, 1996), p. 118.

8 J. Kirby (ed.), *The Plumpton Letters and Papers*, Camden Society, 5th series, vol. VIII (London, 1996), no. 32, 7 September 1480, pp. 55–6.

9 W.H. Dunham, 'Lord Hastings' indentured retainers, 1461–1483', *Transactions of the Connecticut Academy of Arts and Sciences*, vol. XXXIX (New Haven, 1955), p. 25; A. Goodman, *The Wars of the Roses: military activity and English society, 1452–97* (London, 1981), Appendix, 'Campaigning periods, 1455–85', pp. 227–8.

10 Macdougall, *James III*, pp. 113–83; Grant, 'Richard III and Scotland', pp. 119–27; P.M. Kendall, *Richard the Third* (London, 1955), pp. 137–50; M. Hicks, *Richard III as Duke of Gloucester: a study in character*, Borthwick Papers no. 70 (York, 1986), pp. 22–5; *Rotuli Parliamentorum ut in Petitiones, et Placita in Parliamento* (London, 6 vols., 1767–77), VI, pp. 204–5.

11 Grant, 'Richard III and Scotland', p. 126.

21: *The Rise and Fall of the North,* pp. 471–96

1 A. Crawford, 'The private life of John Howard: a study of a Yorkist lord, his family and household', in P.W. Hammond (ed.), *Richard III: loyalty, lordship and law* (London, 1986), pp. 6–24.

2 M. Levine, 'Richard III – usurper or lawful king?', *Speculum*, XXXIV (1958), pp. 391–401; R.H. Helmholz, 'The sons of Edward IV: a canonical assessment of the claim that they were illegimate', in Hammond (ed.), *Richard III*, pp. 91–103.

3 A.J. Pollard, *Richard III and the Princes in the Tower* (Stroud, 1991), p. 103.

4 'Liberacio Pannorum in Magna Garderoba Domini Regis Erga Coronacionem Domini Henrici Nuper Regis Anglie Quarti', in A.F. Sutton and P.W. Hammond (eds.), *The Coronation of Richard III: the extant documents* (Gloucester, 1983), pp. 92–5, 270.

5 Sutton and Hammond (eds.), *The Coronation of Richard III*, p. 217.

6 P.W. Hammond and W.J. White, 'The sons of Edward IV: a re-examination of the evidence on their deaths and on the bones in Westminster Abbey', in Hammond (ed.), *Richard III*, pp. 104–47.

7 M. Jones, 'Richard III and the Stanleys', in R. Horrox (ed.), *Richard III and the North* (Hull, 1986), pp. 27–50.

8 A.J. Pollard, 'The tyranny of Richard III', *Journal of Medieval History*, III (1977), pp. 147–66; K. Dockray, 'Richard III and the Yorkshire gentry', in Hammond (ed.), *Richard III*, pp. 38–57.

9 M. Hicks, 'Dynastic change and Northern society: the career of the fourth earl of Northumberland, 1470–89', *Northern History*, XIV (1978), pp. 89–92.

10 M. Jones, 'Richard III and Lady Margaret Beaufort: a re-assessment', in Hammond (ed.), *Richard III*, pp. 25–37.

11 A.L. Rowse, *Bosworth Field and the Wars of the Roses* (London, 1966), pp. 205–6.

12 M. Bennett, *The Battle of Bosworth* (Stroud, 1985), pp. 79–80.

13 C. Richmond, '1485 and all that, or what was going on at the battle of Bosworth?', in Hammond (ed.), *Richard III*, esp. pp. 172–7; Bennett, *The Battle of Bosworth*, pp. 141–54.

14 Bennett, *The Battle of Bosworth*, pp. 98–132; P.M. Kendall, *Richard the Third* (London, 1955), pp. 354–69; A. Goodman, *The Wars of the Roses: military activity and English society, 1452–97* (London, 1981), pp. 92–6; M.K. Jones, 'Richard III as a soldier', in J. Gillingham (ed.), *Richard III: a medieval kingship* (London, 1993), pp. 92–112.

15 Quoted in Pollard, *Richard III and the Princes in the Tower*, p. 171.

16 Bennett, *The Battle of Bosworth*, p. 118.

17 See, for instance, J. Gillingham, *The Wars of the Roses: peace and conflict in fifteenth-century England* (London, 1981), p. 241; and Hicks, 'Dynastic change and Northern society', p. 89.

18 Rowse, *Bosworth Field and the Wars of the Roses*, p. 219.

19 Bennett, *The Battle of Bosworth*, p. 114.

20 M. Hicks, *Richard III: the man behind the myth* (London, 1991), p. 151.

21 Goodman, *The Wars of the Roses*, p. 96.

22 J. Kirby (ed.), *The Plumpton Letters and Papers*, Camden Society, 5th series, vol. VIII (London, 1996), no. 74, 24 April 1489; Hicks, 'Dynastic change and Northern society, pp. 78–107; and M. Hicks, 'The Yorkshire rebellion of 1489 reconsidered', *Northern History*, XXII (1986), pp. 39–62; M.E. James, 'The murder at Cocklodge, 28 April 1489', *Durham University Journal*, LVII (1964–5), pp. 80–7; M.J. Bennett, 'Henry VII and the Northern Rising of 1489', *English Historical Review*, CV (1990), pp. 34–59.

23 A.F. Sutton and L. Visser-Fuchs, *Richard III's books: ideals and reality in the life and library of a medieval prince* (Stroud, 1997), pp. 141–2.

Epilogue, pp. 487–90

1 G.T. Lapsley, 'The Problem of the North', in G.T. Lapsley (ed.), *Crown, Community and Parliament in the Later Middle Ages: studies in English constitutional history* (Oxford, 1951), pp. 375–405; M.L. Bush, 'The problem of the far North: a study of the crisis of 1537 and its consequences', *Northern History*, VI (1971), pp. 40–63.

2 D. Dunlop, 'The politics of peace-keeping: Anglo-Scottish relations from 1503 to 1511', *Renaissance Studies*, VIII (1994), 2, pp. 138–61.

3 Quoted in J. Wormald, 'The union of 1603', in R.A. Mason (ed.), *Scots and Britons: Scottish political thought and the Union of 1603* (Cambridge, 1994), pp. 17–18.

4 M.E. James, *A Tudor Magnate and the Tudor state: Henry, fifth earl of Northumberland*, Borthwick Papers, no. 30 (York, 1966), p. 38.

Selected Bibliography

Primary Sources

Abrahams, I., Stokes, H.P. and Loewe, H. (eds.), *Starrs and Jewish Charters Preserved in the British Museum*. Cambridge, 3 vols., 1930–2.

Arnold, T. (ed.), 'Incipit historia Johannis Prioris Hagustaldensis ecclesiae xxv annorum', in *Symeonis Monachi Opera Omnia: Historia Regum eadem historia ad quintum et vicesimum annum continuata, per Joannen Hagulstadensum*. Rolls Series. London, 2 vol., 1882–5.

Atkinson, J.C. (ed.), *Cartularium Abbathiae de Whiteby*, 2 vols. Surtees Society, vols. LXIX and LXXII, Durham, 1879–81. Contained in the second volume is the *Ex Registro Monasterii de Whitbye*.

Bain, J. (ed.), *Calendar of Documents Relating to Scotland, preserved in Her Majesty's Public Record Office, London*. Edinburgh, 4 vols., 1881–8.

[Blind Harry], *The Actis and Deidis of the Illustere and Vailze and Campion Schir William Wallace, Knicht of Ellerslie*. Scottish Text Society. Edinburgh, 1889.

Boece, H. (ed. and trans. J. Bellenden), *The Chronicles of Scotland compiled by Hector Boece*. Scottish Text Society. Edinburgh, 1938–41.

Bond, E.A. (ed.), 'Addition by Adam, Abbas Quartus Decimus', to *Chronica Monasterii de Melsa, a Fundatione usque ad Annum 1396, Auctore Thoma de Burton, Abbate. Accedit Continuatio ad Annum 1406 a Monacho Quodam ipsius Domus*. Rolls Series. London, 3 vols., 1866–8.

Brie, F.W.D. (ed.), *The Brut, or the Chronicles of England*. Original series. Early English Text Society, vols. CXXXI, CXXXVI. London, 1906, 1908.

Bruce, J. (ed.), 'Historie of the arrivall of Edward IV. In England and the final recouerye of kingdomes from Henry VI.

A.D. MCCCCLXXI', in K. Dockray (intro.), *Three Chronicles of the Reign of Edward IV*. Gloucester, 1988.

Calendar of Chancery Warrants, 1244–1326. London, HMSO, 1927.

Calendar of Charter Rolls. London, HMSO, 6 vols., 1903–1927.

Calendar of Close Rolls. London, HMSO, 59 vols., 1892–1954.

Calendar of Fine Rolls. London, HMSO, 22 vols., 1911–1963.

Calendar of Inquisitions Post Mortem. London, HMSO, 18 vols., 1898–1955.

Calendar of Patent Rolls. London, HMSO, 54 vols., 1893–1916.

Calendar of the Various Chancery Rolls, 1277–1326. London, HMSO, 1912.

Caley, J., Ellis, H., and Bandinel, the Rev. B., *Monasticon Anglicanum: a history of the abbies and other monasteries, hospitals, frieries, and cathedral and collegiate churches, with their dependencies in England and Wales*. 6 vols. in 8. London, 1817.

Cheney, C.R. and Semple, W.H. (eds. and trans.), *Selected Letters of Pope Innocent III concerning England (1198–1216)*. Walton-upon-Thames, 1953.

Clay, C.T. (ed.), *The Percy Fee. Early Yorkshire Charters: based on the manuscripts of the late William Farrer*. Vol. XI, Edinburgh, 1963. Alternatively, printed for the Yorkshire Archaelogical Society Record Series. Wakefield, 1963.

C[okayne], G.E., revised and expanded by V. Gibbs, H.A. Doubleday, G.H. White and Lord H. de Walden, *The Complete Peerage: or a history of the House of Lords and all its members from the earliest times*. 13 vols. in 14. London, 1910–59.

Davies, J.S. (ed.), *An English chronicle of the reigns of Richard II, Henry IV, Henry V, and Henry VI, written before the year 1471; with an* appendix, containing the 18th and 19th years of Richard II and the Parliament at Bury St. Edmund's, 25th Henry VI, and the supplementary additions from the Cotton MS. Chronicle called 'Eulogium'. Camden Series, 1st series, vol. LXIV. London, 1856.

Denholm-Young, N. (ed.), Vita Edwardi Secundi, Monachi Cuiusdam Malmesberiensis. London, 1957.

Dickson, W. (ed.), 'Cronica Monasterii de Alnewyke ex quodam Libro Cronicarum in Libraria Collegii Regalis Cantabrigiae de dono Regis Henrici VI Fundamentoris' [Chronicles of Alnwick Abbey], in Archaeologia Aeliana, 1st series, III (1844), pp. 33–45.

Dugdale, W., The baronage of England, or an historical account of the lives and the most memorable actions of our English nobility in the Saxons time, to the Norman Conquest; and from thence, of those who had their rise before the end of King Henry the Third's reign. London, 2 vols., 1675.

Ellis, H. (ed.), Edward Hall's Chronicle. Rolls Series. London, 1809.

Ellis, W.S., The antiquities of heraldry, collected from the literature, coins, gems, vases and other monuments of pre-Christian and medieval times: with a catalogue of early armorial seals: tending to show that modern heraldry embodies or is derived from the religious symbols, the military devices, and the emblems of the heathen deities of antiquity. London, 1869.

Farrer, W. (ed.), Early Yorkshire Charters: being a collection of documents anterior to the thirteenth century made from the public records, monastic chartularies, Roger Dodsworth's manuscripts and other available sources. 4 vols, vol. II. Edinburgh, 1915.

Forester, T. (ed. and trans.), The Chronicle of Henry of Huntingdon, comprising the history of England, from the invasion of Julius Caesar to the accession of Henry II. London, 1853, fac. rep. Felinfach, 1991.

Fraser, C.M. (ed.), Ancient Petitions Relating to Northumberland. Surtees Society, vol. CLXXVI. London, 1966.

Fulcher of Chartres (trans. F.R. Ryan and ed. H.S. Fink), A History of the Expedition to Jerusalem, 1095–1127. Knoxville, Tennessee, 1969.

Gairdner, J. (ed.), Letters and papers illustrative of the wars of the English in France during the reign of King Henry VI. Rolls Series. London, 3 vols., 1864.

Gairdner, J. (ed.), Three Fifteenth-century Chronicles. Camden Society, vol. XXVII. London 2nd series, 1880.

Galbraith, V.H. (ed.), The Anonimalle Chronicle, 1333 to 1381, from a MS written at St Mary's Abbey, York, and now in the possession of Lieut.-Col Sir William Ingilby, Bart., Ripley Castle, Yorkshire. Manchester, 1927.

Galbraith, V.H. (ed.), The St. Albans Chronicle, 1406–1420. Oxford, 1937.

Giles, J.A., The Chronicles of the White Rose of York. A series of historical fragments, proclamations, letters and other contemporary documents relating to the reign of King Edward the Fourth. London, 1845.

Giles, J.A. (trans.), Matthew Paris's English History. 3 vols. London, 1852–4.

Giles, J.A., Roger of Wendover's Flowers of History: formerly ascribed to Matthew Paris. 2 vols. London, 1849; rep. Felinfach, 1994.

Gough, H. (ed.), Scotland in 1298: documents relating to the campaign of King Edward the First in that year, and especially to the battle of Falkirk. Paisley, 1888.

Gray, Sir T. (trans. Sir H. Maxwell), Scalachronica. London, 1907.

Greenway, D.E., Charters of the Honour of Mowbray, 1107–1191. London, 1972.

Grose, F., Military antiquities respecting a history of the English army from the Conquest to the present time. London, 2 vols., new edn, 1801.

Hall, G.D.H. (ed.), Tractatus de Legibus et Consuetudinibus Regni Anglie qui Glanvilla Vocatur [The Treatise on the Laws and Customs of the Realm of England commonly called Glanvill]. Oxford, 1993 edn.

Halliwell, J.O. (ed.), 'Chronicle of the first thirteen years of the reign of King Edward the Fourth by John Warkworth, D.D., in K. Dockray (intro.), Three Chronicles of the Reign of Edward IV. Gloucester, 1988.

Hardy, T.D. (ed.), Rotuli Litterarum Clausarum in Turri Londinensi. Record Commission. London, 2 vols., 1988.

Hardy, T.D. (ed.), Syllabus of the documents relating to England and other Kingdoms contained in Rymer's Foedera. London, 3 vols., 1869–85.

Hardyng, J., The Chronicle from the Firste Begynnyng of Englande, unto the Reigne of Kyng Edwarde the Fourth. London, 1543; facsimile edn published Amsterdam, 1976.

Hingeston, F.C. (ed.), *John Capgrave's The Chronicle of England*. Rolls Series. London, 1858.

Howlett, R. (ed.), 'The Chronicle of Robert of Torigni', in *Chronicles of the Reigns of Stephen, Henry II and Richard I*. Rolls Series. London, 4 vols., 1884–9.

Howlett, R. (ed.), [Richard of Hexham], 'De Gestis Regis Stephani et de Bello Standardi', in *Chronicles of the Reigns of Stephen, Henry II, and Richard I*. Rolls Series. London, 4 vols., 1884–9.

Howlett, R. (ed.), 'Relatio venerabilis Aelredi, abbatis Rievallensis, de Standardo', in *Chronicles of the Reigns of Stephen, Henry II and Richard I*. Rolls Series. London, 4 vols., 1884–9.

Howlett, R. (ed.), 'William of Newburgh, Historia rerum Anglicanum', in *Chronicles of the Reigns of Stephen, Henry II and Richard I*. Rolls Series, 4 vols., 1884–9.

Jacobs, J., *The Jews of Angevin England: documents and records from Latin and Hebrew sources printed and manuscript, for the first time collected and translated*. London, 1893.

Kingsford, C.L., (trans. and ed.), *Song of Lewes*. London, 1890.

Kirby, J. (ed.), *The Plumpton Letters and Papers*. Camden Society. 5th series, vol. VIII. London, 1996.

Lawrie, A.C. (ed.), *Early Scottish Charters, prior to A.D. 1153*. Glasgow, 1905.

Legg, L.G.W. (ed.), *English Coronation Records*. London, 1901.

Luard, H.R. (ed.), *Matthaei Parisiensis, Monachi Sancti Albani, Chronica Majora*. Rolls Series. London, 7 vols., 1872–83.

Luard, H.R. (ed.), *Flores Historiarum*. Rolls Series. London, 3 vols., 1980.

Lumby, J.R. (ed.), *Polychronicon Ranulphi Higden Monachi Cestrensis*. Rolls Series. London, 9 vols., 1865–86.

Lumby, J.R. (ed.), *Chronicon Henrici Knighton*. Rolls Series. London, 2 vols., 1895.

Macintosh, G. (ed.), *The Life and Death of King James the First*, including *Chronicon Jacobi Primi, Regis Scottorum* and *The Dethe of the Kynge of Scotis*. Maitland Club Edinburgh, 1837.

MacPherson, D. (ed.), *Rotuli Scotiae in Turri Londinensi et in Domo Capitulari Westmonasteriensi Asservati*. London, 2 vols., 1814–19.

Martin, G.H. (ed. and trans.), *Knighton's Chronicle, 1337–1396*. Oxford, 1995.

Martin, M.T. (ed.), *The Percy Chartulary*.

Surtees Society, vol. CXVII. Durham/London, 1911.

Maxwell, H. (ed. and trans.), *The Chronicle of Lanercost, 1272–1346*. Glasgow, 1913.

Münch, Professor, 'Concordia Facta inter Anglicos et Scotos, 3rd January 1322–3', *Proceedings of the Society of Antiquaries of Scotland*, III (1862), pp. 454–61.

Nicolas, N.H. (ed.), *The Siege of Carlaverock*. London, 1828.

Palgrave, F. (ed.), *The Parliamentary writs and writs of military summons, together with the records and muniments relating to the suit and service due and performed to the King's High Court of Parliament and the Councils of the Realm, or affording evidence of attendance given at Parliament and Councils*. Record Commission. London, 2 vols. in 4, 1827–34.

Palgrave, F. (ed.), *Documents and records illustrating the history of Scotland and the transactions between the Crowns of Scotland and England, preserved in the Treasury of Her Majesty's Exchequer*. Record Commission. London, 1837.

Potter, K.R. (ed. and trans.), with a new introduction by R.H.C. Davis, *Gesta Stephani*. Oxford, 2nd edn, 1976.

Prestwich, M. (ed.), *Documents Illustrating the Crisis of 1297–98 in England*. Camden Society. 4th series, vol. XXIV. London, 1980.

Raine, J. (ed.), *Testamenta Eboracensia, or wills registered at York illustrative of the history, manners, language, statistics &c., of the province of York, from the year MCCC downwards*. Surtees Society, vol. IV. London, 1836.

Raine, J. (ed.), *Historical Papers and Letters from the Northern Registers*. Rolls Series. London, 1873.

Register of Edward the Black Prince. London, 1938.

Riley, H.T. (ed.), *Gesta Abbatum Monasterii Sancta Albani, by Thomas Walsingham, regnante Ricardo Secundo, ejusdem ecclesiae praecentore, compilata*. Rolls Series. London, 3 vols., 1867–9.

Riley, H.T. (ed.), *Registrum Abbatiae Johannis Whethamstede*. Rolls Series. London, 2 vols., 1872–3.

Robinson, W., *Collections relative to claims at the Coronations of several of the Kings of England, beginning with Richard II*. London, 1820.

Rothwell, H. (ed.), *The Chronicle of Walter of Guisborough*. Camden Society, 3rd series, vol. LXXXIX. London, 1957.

Rymer, T. (ed.), *Foedera, Conventiones, Litterae, et cujuscumque generis Acta Publica, inter Reges Angliae et alios quosuis Imperatores, Reges, Pontifices, Principes, bel Communitatis ab ingressu Gulielmi I. in Angliam, A.D. 1066.* Records Commission. London, 1816–69.

Scroggs, E.S. (ed.), *Feet of Fines, Northumberland, 1273–1346.* Newcastle, 1932.

Shirley, W.W., *Royal and other historical letters illustrative of the reign of Henry III, from the originals in the Public Record Office.* Rolls Series. London, 2 vols., 1862–6.

Simpson, G.G. and Galbraith, J.D. (eds.), *Calendar of Documents Relating to Scotland, 1108–1516, preserved in the Public Record Office and the British Library.* Supplementary. Edinburgh, 1988.

Skeat, W.W. (ed.), *The Bruce; or, the Book of the Most Excellent and Noble Prince, Robert de Broyss, King of Scots: compiled by Master John Barbour, Archdeacon of Aberdeen, A.D. 1375.* Early English Text Society. Extra Series, vols. XI and XXI. London, 2 vols., 1870–74.

Skene, F.J.H. (ed.), *Liber Pluscardensis.* Edinburgh, 2 vols., 1877–80.

Stephenson, J. (trans.), *Contemporary chronicles of the Middle Ages: sources of 12th century history. From the south of England: William of Malmesbury: A history of his own times from 1135 to 1142. From the north of England: Richard of Hexham, 1135 to 1139, and Jordan Fantosme, The war between the English and the Scots in 1173 and 1174.* Felinfach, 1988.

Stevenson, J. (ed.), *Documents illustrative of Sir William Wallace: his life and times.* Maitland Club, 1841.

Stevenson, J. (ed.), *Documents illustrative of the history of Scotland from the death of King Alexander the Third to the accession of Robert Bruce.* Edinburgh, 2 vols., 1870.

Stevenson, J. (ed.), *Radulphi de Coggeshall Chronicon Anglicanum.* Rolls Series. London, 1875.

Stones, E.L.G. (ed.), *Anglo-Scottish Relations, 1174–1328: some selected documents.* Oxford, 2nd edn, 1965.

Stones, E.L.G. and Simpson, G.G. (eds.), *Edward I and the Throne of Scotland, 1290–1296: an edition of the record sources for the Great Cause.* Oxford, 2 vols., 1978.

Strachey, J. *et al.* (eds.), *Rotuli Parliamentorum ut in Petitiones, et Placita in Parliamento.* London, 6 vols., 1767–77.

Stubbs, W. (ed.), *The Chronicle of the Reigns of Henry II and Richard I, AD 1169–92; known commonly under the name of Benedict of Peterborough.* Rolls Series. London, 2 vols., 1867.

Stubbs, W. (ed.), *Chronica Magistri Rogeri de Hoveden.* Rolls Series. London, 4 vols., 1868–71.

Stubbs, W. (ed.), *Memoriale Fratris Walteris de Coventria.* Rolls Series. London, 2 vols., 1872–3.

Stubbs, W. (ed.), 'Annales Londonienses', in *Chronicles of the Reigns of Edward I and Edward II.* Rolls Series. London, 2 vols., 1882–3.

Stubbs, W. (ed.), 'Annales Paulini', in *Chronicles of the Reigns of Edward I and Edward II.* Rolls Series. London, 2 vols., 1882–3.

Stubbs, W. (ed.), 'Gesta Edwardi de Carnarvon Auctore Canonico Bridlingtoniensi', in *Chronicles of the Reigns of Edward I and Edward II.* Rolls Series. London, 2 vols., 1882–3.

Sutton, A.F. and Hammond, P.W. (eds.), *The Coronation of Richard III: the extant documents.* Gloucester, 1983.

Taylor, J. (ed.), *The Kirkstall Abbey Chronicles.* Publications of the Thoresby Society, vol. XLII. Leeds, 1952.

Thomas, A.H. and Thornley, I.D. (eds.), *The Great Chronicle of London.* London, 1938.

Thompson, E.M. (ed.), *Chronicon Angliae, ab anno Domini 1328 usque and annum 1388. Auctore Monacho Quodam Sancti Albani.* Rolls Series. London, 1874.

Thompson, E.M. (ed.), *Adae Murimuth Continuatio Chronicarum.* Rolls Series. London, 1889.

Thompson, E.M. (ed.), *Chronicon Galfridi le Baker de Swynebroke.* Oxford, 1889.

Thompson, E.M. (ed.), *Robertus de Avesbury, De Gestis Mirabilibus Regis Edwardi Tertii.* Rolls Series. London, 1889.

Thompson, E.M. (ed.), *Chronicon Adae de Usk, A.D. 1377–1421.* London, 2nd edn, 1904.

Treharne, R.E. and Sanders, I.J. (eds.), *Documents of the Baronial Movement of Reform and Rebellion, 1258–1267.* Oxford, 1973.

Waurin, J. de (ed. W. and E.L.C.P. Hardy), *Recueil des Croniques et anchiennes istories de la Graut Bretaigne à present nommé Engleterre.* Rolls Series. London, 5 vols., 1864–91.

Williams, P.B., *Chronicque de la Traïson et mort de Richart Deux Roy Dengleterre, mise en lumière d'après un manuscrit de la Bibliothèque Royale de*

Paris, autrefoois conservé dans L'Abbaye de S. Victor; avec les variantes fournies par dix autres manuscrits, des éclaircissements, et un glossaire. English Historical Society. London, 1846, rep. 1964.

Wright, T. (ed. and trans.), *The rolls of arms of the princes, barons, and knights who attended King Edward I to the siege of Caerlaverock.* London, 1864.

Wright, T. (ed.), *The chronicle of Pierre de Langtoft, in French verse, from the earliest period to the death of King Edward I.* Rolls Series. London, 2 vols., 1866–8.

Wrottesley, G., *Crécy and Calais, from the original records in the Public Record Office.* London, 1898.

Secondary Sources

Abbott, M., 'The Gant Family in England, 1066–1191', unpub. Ph.D. dissertation, Cambridge University (1973).

Adams, G.B., 'Innocent III and the Charter', pp. 26–45, in H.E. Malden (ed.), *Magna Carta Commemoration Essays.* London, 1917.

Allmand, C., *Henry V.* London, new edn., 1997.

Altschul, M., *A Baronial Family in Medieval England: the Clare family, 1217–1314.* Baltimore, Maryland, 1965.

Altschul, M., '"Less than I was born to": two studies of King Henry VI', *Medievalia et Humanistica*, XI (1982), pp. 291–7.

Anderson, M.O., 'Lothian and early Scottish kings', *Scottish Historical Review*, XXXIX (1960), pp. 98–112.

Anon., 'Younger branches of the house of Percy', *Collectanea Topographica et Genealogica*, II (1835), pp. 57–66.

Anon., 'Documents relating to the Percy family', *Collectanea Topographica et Genealogica*, VI (1840), pp. 370–80.

Anon., 'The companions of William the Conqueror and the "Battle Abbey Roll"', *Herald and Genealogist*, I (1863), 3, pp. 193–208.

Anon., 'The House of Percy', *Herald and Genealogist*, III (1866), pp. 266–73.

Anon., 'The coronation stone of Scotland', *Scottish Historical Review*, VIII (1911), pp. 223–4.

Appleby, J.C. and Dalton, J. (eds.), *Government, Religion and Society in Northern England, 1000–1700.* Stroud, 1996.

Armitage-Smith, S., *John of Gaunt: king of Castile and Leon, duke of Aquitaine and Lancaster, earl of Derby, Lincoln and Leicester, seneschal of England.* London, 1904.

Armstrong, C.A.J., 'The inauguration ceremonies of the Yorkist kings, and their title to the throne', *Transactions of the Royal Historical Society*, 4th series, XXX (1948).

Armstrong, C.A.J., 'Politics and the Battle of St Albans, 1455', *Bulletin of the Institute of Historical Research*, XXXIII (1960), pp. 1–72.

Aston, M., 'Richard II and the Wars of the Roses', pp. 280–317, in F.R.H. du Boulay and C.M. Barron (eds.), *The Reign of Richard II: essays in honour of May McKisack.* London, 1971.

Ayton, A., 'English armies in the fourteenth century', pp. 21–38, in A. Curry and M. Hughes (eds.), *Arms, Armies and Fortifications in the Hundred Years War.* Woodbridge, 1994.

Bain, J., 'The Percies in Scotland', *Archaeological Journal*, XLI (1884), pp. 335–41.

Balfour-Melville, E.M.W., 'The death of Edward Balliol', *Scottish Historical Review*, XXXV (1956), pp. 82–3.

Balfour-Melville, E.M.W., 'Two John Crabbs', *Scottish Historical Review*, XXXIX (1960), pp. 31–4.

Barnes, P.M. and Barrow, G.W.S., 'The movements of Robert Bruce between September 1307 and May 1308', *Scottish Historical Review*, XLIX (1970), pp. 46–59.

Barnie, J., *War in Medieval Society: social values and the Hundred Years War, 1337–99.* London, 1974.

Barraclough, G., 'The earldom and county palatine of Chester', *Transactions of the Historic Society of Lancashire and Cheshire*, CIII (1951), pp. 23–57.

Barrell, A.D.M., *The Papacy, Scotland and Northern England, 1342–1378.* Cambridge, 1995.

Barrington de Fonblanque, E., *Annals of the house of Percy, from the Conquest to the opening of the 19th Century.* 2 vols., London. Privately printed, limited circulation, 1887.

Barron, C.M., 'The quarrel of Richard II with London', pp. 173–201, in F.R.H. du Boulay and C.M. Barron (eds.), *The Reign of Richard II: essays in honour of May McKisack.* London, 1971.

Barron, C.M., 'The deposition of Richard II', pp. 132–49, in J. Taylor and W. Childs (eds.), *Politics and Crisis in Fourteenth-century England.* Gloucester, 1990.

Barron, E.M., *The Scottish War of Independence: a critical study*. Inverness, 2nd edn, 1934.

Barrow, G.W.S., 'The Anglo-Scottish border', *Northern History*, I (1966), pp. 21–42.

Barrow, G.W.S., 'Northern English society in the twelfth and thirteenth centuries', *Northern History*, IV (1969), pp. 1–28.

Barrow, G.W.S., 'Lothian in the first War of Independence, 1296–1328', *Scottish Historical Review*, LV (1976), pp. 151–71.

Barrow, G.W.S., *The Anglo-Norman era in Scottish History: the Ford lectures delivered to the University of Oxford in Hilary Term 1977*. Oxford, 1980.

Barrow, G.W.S., *David I of Scotland (1124–1153): the balance of new and old*. Reading, 1985.

Barrow, G.W.S., *Robert Bruce and the Community of the Realm of Scotland*. Edinburgh, 3rd edn, 1988.

Barrow, G.W.S., 'Frontier and settlement: which influenced which? England and Scotland, 1100–1300', pp. 3–21, in R. Bartlett and A. Mackay (eds.), *Medieval Frontier Societies*. Oxford, 1989.

Barrow, G.W.S., *Kingship and Unity: Scotland, 1000–1306*. Edinburgh, 2nd edn, 1989.

Barrow, G.W.S., 'The Scots and the North of England', in E. King (ed.), *The Anarchy of King Stephen's reign*. Oxford, 1994.

Bates, D., *Normandy before 1066*. London, 1982.

Bean, J.M.W., 'The Percies' acquisition of Alnwick', *Archaeologia Aeliana*, 4th series, XXXII (1954), pp. 309–19.

Bean, J.M.W., 'The Percies and their estates in Scotland', *Archaeologia Aeliana*, XXV (1957), 4th series, pp. 91–9.

Bean, J.M.W., *The Estates of the Percy Family, 1416–1537*. Oxford, 1958.

Bean, J.M.W., 'Henry IV and the Percies', *History*, XLIV (1959), pp. 212–27.

Bean, J.M.W., *From Lord to Patron: lordship in late medieval England*. Manchester, 1989.

Bellamy, J.G., 'The Northern Rebellions in the later years of Richard II', *Bulletin of the John Rylands Library*, XLVII (1964–5), pp. 254–74.

Bennett, M., *The Battle of Bosworth*. Stroud, 1985.

Bennett, M., 'The development of battle tactics in the Hundred Years War', pp. 1–20, in A. Curry and M. Hughes (eds.), *Arms, Armies and Fortifications in the Hundred Years War*. Woodbridge, 1994.

Bennett, M., 'Edward III's entail and the succession to the Crown, 1376–1471',

English Historical Review, CXIII (1998), 452, pp. 580–609.

Bennett, M.J., 'Henry VII and the Northern Rising of 1489', *English Historical Review*, CV (1990), pp. 34–59.

Bevan, B., *King Richard II*. London, 1990.

Bevan, B., *Henry IV*. London, 1994.

Boardman, A.W., *The Battle of Towton*. Stroud, 1994.

Boardman, A.W., *The Medieval Soldier in the Wars of the Roses*. Stroud, 1998.

Bonner, E., 'Scotland's "Auld Alliance" with France, 1295–1560', *History*, LXXXIV (1999), pp. 5–30.

Bothwell, J., 'Edward III and the "new nobility": largesse and limitation in fourteenth-century England', *English Historical Review*, CXII (1907), 449, pp. 1111–40.

Bradbury, J., 'The early years of the reign of Stephen, 1135–39', in D. Williams (ed.), *England in the Twelfth Century: proceedings of the 1988 Harlaxton Symposium*. Woodbridge, 1990.

Bradley, P.J., 'Henry V's Scottish policy: a study in realpolitik', pp. 177–95, in J.S. Hamilton and P.J. Bradley (eds.), *Documenting the Past: essays in medieval history presented to George Peddy Cuttino*. Woodbridge, 1989.

Brenan, G., *A History of the House of Percy: from the earliest times down to the present century*. London, 2 vols., 1902.

Briggs, A., 'Themes in northern history', *Northern History*, I (1966), pp. 1–6.

Brown, A.L., 'The reign of Henry IV: the establishment of the Lancastrian regime', pp. 1–28, in S.B. Chrimes, C.D. Ross and R.A. Griffiths (eds.), *Fifteenth Century England, 1399–1509: studies in politics and society*. Manchester, 1972.

Brown, A.L., 'The English campaign in Scotland, 1400', pp. 40–54, in H. Hearder and H.R. Loyn (eds.), *British Government and Administration: studies presented to S.B. Chrimes*. Cardiff, 1974.

Brown, M., '"Rejoice to hear of Douglas": the House of Douglas and the presentation of magnate power in late medieval Scotland', *Scottish Historical Review*, LXXVI (1997), pp. 161–84.

Brown, M., *The Black Douglases: war and lordship in later medieval Scotland, 1300–1455*. East Linton, 1998.

Brown, R.A., *The Normans and the Norman Conquest*. Woodbridge, 2nd edn, 1985.

Brown, R.A., *The Normans*. Woodbridge, 2nd edn, 1994.

Burton, J.E., 'Monasteries and parish churches in eleventh- and twelfth-century Yorkshire', *Northern History*, XXIII (1987), pp. 39–50.

Cameron, S. and Ross, A., 'The Treaty of Edinburgh and the Disinherited (1328–1332)', *History*, LXXXIV (1999), pp. 237–56.

Campbell, J., 'England, Scotland and the Hundred Years War in the fourteenth century', pp. 184–216, in J.R. Hale, J.R.L. Highfield and B. Smalley (eds.), *Europe in the Late Middle Ages*. London, 1965.

Carpenter, D.A., *The Battles of Lewes and Evesham, 1264/65*. Keele, 1987.

Carpenter, D.A., *The Reign of Henry III*. London, 1996.

Charlesworth, D., 'The Battle of Hexham, 1464', *Archaeologia Aeliana*, 4th series, XXX (1952), pp. 57–68.

Charlesworth, D., 'Northumberland in the early years of Edward IV', *Archaeologia Aeliana*, 4th series, XXXI (1953), pp. 69–81.

Cheney, C.R., 'The eve of Magna Carta', *Bulletin of the John Rylands Library*, XXXVIII (1955–6), pp. 311–41.

Cheney, C.R., 'The twenty-five barons of Magna Carta', *Bulletin of the John Rylands Library*, L (1968), pp. 280–307.

Chrimes, S.B., *An Introduction to the Administrative History of Medieval England*. Oxford, 1952.

Clanchy, M.T., *From Memory to Written Record: England, 1066–1307*. Cambridge, Massachusetts, 1979.

Clark, G.T., *Medieval Military Architecture*. London, 1884.

Clark, G.T., 'The House of Percy, entitled Barons Lucy of Cockermouth', *Transactions of the Cumberland and Westmorland Antiquarian and Archaeological Society*, XI (1891), pp. 399–432.

Clarke, M.V. and Galbraith, V.H., 'The deposition of Richard II', *Bulletin of the John Rylands Library*, XIV (1930), pp. 125–81.

Clay, C.T., 'A note on the Neville ancestry', *Antiquaries Journal*, XXXI (1951), pp. 201–4.

Clay, C.T., 'The ancestry of the early lords of Warkworth', *Archaeologia Aeliana*, 4th series, XXXII (1954), pp. 64–71.

Collins, A.J., 'The documents of the Great Charter of 1215', *Proceedings of the British Academy*, XXXIV (1948), pp. 233–79.

Collins, S.M., 'The Blue Lion of Percy', *Archaeologia Aeliana*, 4th series, XXIV (1946), pp. 113–18.

Coss, P., *The Knight in Medieval England, 1000–1400*. Gloucester, new edn, 1995.

Cronne, H.A., 'The Honour of Lancaster in Stephen's reign', *English Historical Review*, L (1935), pp. 670–80.

Cronne, H.A., 'Ranulf de Gernons, earl of Chester, 1129–1153', *Transactions of the Royal Historical Society*, 4th series, XX (1937), pp. 103–34.

Crouch, D., *The Image of Aristocracy in Britain, 1000–1300*. London, 1992.

Crump, G.C., 'The arrest of Roger Mortimer and Queen Isabel', *English Historical Review*, XXVI (1911), 102, pp. 331–2.

Cunningham, S., 'Henry VII and rebellion in north-eastern England, 1485–1492: bonds of allegiance and the establishment of Tudor authority', *Northern History*, XXXII (1996), pp. 42–74.

Dalton, P., 'William earl of York and royal authority in Yorkshire in the reign of Stephen', *Haskins Society Journal*, II (1990), pp. 155–65.

Dalton, P., 'Aiming at the impossible: Ranulf II earl of Chester and Lincolnshire in the reign of King Stephen', in A.T. Thacker (ed.), *The Earldom of Chester and its Charters: a tribute to Geoffrey Barraclough*: special volume of the *Journal of the Chester Archaeological Society*, LXXI (1991), pp. 109–32.

Dalton, P., '*In neutro latere*: the armed neutrality of Ranulf II earl of Chester in King Stephen's reign', *Anglo-Norman Studies*, XIV (1991), pp. 39–59.

Dalton, P., *Conquest, Anarchy and Lordship: Yorkshire, 1066–1154*. Cambridge, 1994.

Darby, H.C. and Maxwell, I.S., *The Domesday Geography of Northern England*. Cambridge, 1977.

Davies, R., 'The medieval Jews of York', *Yorkshire Archaeological and Topographical Journal*, III (1873–4), Parts 1 and 2, pp. 147–97.

Davies, R.R., *The Revolt of Owain Glyn Dwr*. Oxford, 1996.

Davis, R.H.C., 'King Stephen and the earl of Chester revised', *English Historical Review*, LXXV (1960), pp. 654–60.

Davis, R.H.C., 'What happened in Stephen's

reign, 1135–1154', *History*, XLIX (1964), 165, pp. 1–12.

Davis, R.H.C., *King Stephen, 1135–1154*. London, 3rd edn, 1990.

De Aragon, R.C., 'The growth of secure inheritance in Norman England', *Journal of Medieval History*, VIII (1982), pp. 381–91.

De Aragon, R.C., 'In pursuit of aristocratic women: a key to success in Norman England', *Albion*, XIV (1982), 3–4, pp. 258–67.

Denholm-Young, N., *History and Heraldry, 1254–1310: a study of the historical value of the Rolls of Arms*. Oxford, 1965.

Dobson, R.B., *The Jews of medieval York and the Massacre of March 1190*. Borthwick Papers no. 45. York, 1974.

Dockray, K., 'The political legacy of Richard III in northern England', in R.A. Griffiths and J. Sherborne (eds.), *Kings and Nobles in the Later Middle Ages: a tribute to Charles Ross*. Gloucester, 1986.

Dockray, K., 'Richard III and the Yorkshire gentry', pp. 38–57, in P.W. Hammond (ed.), *Richard III: loyalty, lordship and law*. London, 1986.

Douglas, D.C., 'The Companions of the Conqueror', *History*, XXVIII (1943), pp. 129–47. See also J.F.A. Mason.

Douglas, D.C., 'The rise of Normandy', *Proceedings of the British Academy*, XXXIII (1947), pp. 101–30.

Douglas, D.C., *William the Conqueror: the Norman impact upon England*. London, 1964.

Duls, L.D., *Richard II in the Early Chronicles*. The Hague, 1975.

Duncan, A.A.M., 'The community of the realm of Scotland and Robert Bruce: a review', *Scottish Historical Review*, XLV (1966), pp. 184–201.

Duncan, A.A.M., *The Nation of Scots and the Declaration of Arbroath (1320)*. Historical Association. London, 1970.

Duncan, A.A.M., *Scotland: the making of a kingdom*. Edinburgh, 1975.

Duncan, A.A.M., 'The Battle of Carham, 1018', *Scottish Historical Review*, LV (1976), 1, pp. 20–8.

Duncan, A.A.M., '*Honi soit qui mal y pense*: David II and Edward III, 1346–52', *Scottish Historical Review*, LXVII (1988), 2, pp. 113–41.

Duncan, A.A.M., 'The war of the Scots, 1306–23', The Prothero Lecture, *Transactions of the Royal Historical Society*, 6th series, II (1992), pp. 125–51.

Ellis, A.S., 'Biographical notes on the Yorkshire tenants named in Domesday Book', *Yorkshire Archaeological and Topographical Journal*, IV (1875–6), pp. 114–157; 214–248; 384–415.

Farrer, W., 'The sheriffs of Lincolnshire and Yorkshire, 1066–1130', *English Historical Review*, XXX (1915), pp. 277–85.

Fenwick, J., 'Notice of the devastations effected by Scottish raids into Northumberland, in the 14th century', *Proceedings of the Society of Antiquaries of Scotland*, I (1855), pp. 118–21.

Fowler, K., *The King's Lieutenant: Henry of Grosmont, first duke of Lancaster, 1310–1361*. London, 1969.

Fox, L., 'The honour and earldom of Leicester: origin and descent, 1066–1399', *English Historical Review*, LIV (1939), 215, pp. 385–99.

Fraser, C.M., *A History of Antony Bek, Bishop of Durham, 1283–1311*. Oxford, 1957.

Fraser, C.M., 'Law and society in Northumberland and Durham, 1290–1350', *Archaeologia Aeliana*, XLVII (1969), pp. 47–70.

Freeman, E.A., 'The Percy castles', in *English Towns and Districts: a series of addresses and sketches*. London, 1883.

Froissart (trans. Lord Berners and ed. G.C. Macaulay), *The Chronicles of Froissart*. London, 1899.

Fryde, N., *The Tyranny and Fall of Edward II, 1321–1326*. Cambridge, 1979.

Gillingham, J., *The Wars of the Roses: peace and conflict in fifteenth-century England*. London, 1981.

Gillingham, J., 'Conquering kings: some twelfth-century reflections on Henry II and Richard I', pp. 163–78, in T. Reuter (ed.), *Warriors and Churchmen in the High Middle Ages: essays presented to Karl Leyser*. London, 1992.

Gillingham J., 'Conquering the barbarians: war and chivalry in twelfth-century Britain', *Haskins Society Journal*, IV (1992), pp. 67–84.

Gillingham, J. (ed.), *Richard III: a medieval kingship*. London, 1993.

Gilson, J.P., 'St Julian the Harbinger, and the first of the English Percys', *Archaeologia Aeliana*, 3rd series, IV (1908), pp. 304–12.

Given-Wilson, C., *The English Nobility in the Late Middle Ages: the fourteenth-century political community*. London, 1987.

Given-Wilson, C., 'Richard II, Edward II, and the Lancastrian inheritance', *English Historical Review*, CIX (1994), 432, pp. 553–71.

Goodman, A., *The Loyal Conspiracy: the Lords Appellant under Richard II*. London, 1971.

Goodman, A., *The Wars of the Roses: military activity and English society, 1452–97*. London, 1981.

Goodman, A., 'The Anglo-Scottish Marches in the fifteenth century: a frontier society?', pp. 18–33, in R.A. Mason (ed.), *Scotland and England, 1286–1815*. Edinburgh, 1987.

Goodman, A., 'John of Gaunt; paradigm of the late-fourteenth century crisis', *Royal Historical Society Transactions*, 5th series, XXXVII (1987), pp. 133–48.

Goodman, A., *John of Gaunt: the exercise of princely power in fourteenth-century Europe*. London, 1992.

Goodman, A. and Gillespie, J. (eds.), *Richard II: the art of kingship*. Oxford, 1999.

Goodman, A. and Tuck, A. (eds.), *War and Border Societies in the Middle Ages*. London, 1992.

Grant, A., 'Earls and earldoms in late medieval Scotland (c.1310–1460), pp. 24–40, in J. Bossy and P. Jupp (eds.), *Essays Presented to Michael Roberts*. Belfast, 1976.

Grant, A., 'Richard III and Scotland', pp. 115–48, in A.J. Pollard (ed.), *The North of England in the Age of Richard III*. Stroud, 1996.

Grant, A. and Stringer, K.J. (eds.), *Medieval Scotland: Crown, lordship and community: essays presented to G.W.S. Barrow*. Edinburgh, 1993.

Grant, A. and Stringer, K.J. (eds.), *Uniting the Kingdom: the making of British history*. London, 1995.

Green, J., 'Anglo-Scottish relations, 1066–1174', pp. 53–72, in M. Jones and M. Vale (eds.), *England and her Neighbours, 1066–1453: essays in honour of Pierre Chaplais*. London, 1989.

Green, J., 'Aristocratic loyalties on the northern frontier of England, c.1100–1174', in D. Williams (ed.), *England in the Twelfth Century: proceedings of the 1988 Harlaxton Symposium*. Woodbridge, 1990.

Green, J., 'Earl Ranulf II and Lancashire', in A.T. Thacker (ed.), *The Earldom of Chester and its Charters: a tribute to Geoffrey Barraclough*: special volume of *Journal of the Chester Archaeological Society*, LXXI (1991), pp. 97–108.

Green, J., 'David I and Henry I', *Scottish Historical Review*, LXXV (1996), pp. 1–19.

Griffith Davies, J.D., *King Henry IV*. London, 1935.

Griffiths, R.A., 'Local rivalries and national politics: the Percies, the Nevilles and Duke of Exeter, 1452–1455', *Speculum*, XLIII (1968), 4, pp. 589–632.

Griffiths, R.A., *The Reign of Henry VI: the exercise of royal authority, 1422–1461*. London, 1981.

Haigh, P.A., *The Military Campaigns of the Wars of the Roses*. Stroud, 1995.

Haigh, P.A., *The Battle of Wakefield: 30 December 1460*. Stroud, 1996.

Hamilton, J.S., *Piers Gaveston, Earl of Cornwall, 1307–1312: politics and patronage in the reign of Edward II*. Detroit, Michigan/London, 1988.

Hammond, P.W., *The Battles of Barnet and Tewkesbury*. Gloucester, 1990.

Hardy, R., 'The longbow', pp. 161–81, in A. Curry and M. Hughes (eds.), *Arms, Armies and Fortifications in the Hundred Years War*. Woodbridge, 1994.

Hay, D., 'Booty and border warfare', *Transactions of the Dumfries and Galloway Natural History and Archaeological Society*, XXXI (1954), pp. 145–66.

Hay, D., 'England, Scotland and Europe: the problem of the frontier', *Transactions of the Royal Historical Society*, 5th series, XXV (1975), pp. 77–91.

Hedley, W.P., *Northumberland Families*, 2 vols. Newcastle, 1968–1970.

Hicks, M., 'Dynastic change and Northern society: the career of the fourth earl of Northumberland, 1470–89', *Northern History*, XIV (1978), pp. 78–107.

Hicks, M., 'Edward IV, the duke of Somerset and Lancastrian loyalism in the North', *Northern History*, XX (1984), pp. 23–37. (Also reproduced, pp. 149–63, in M. Hicks, *Richard III and his Rivals: magnates and their motives in the War of the Roses*. London, 1991.)

Hicks, M., 'Richard, duke of Gloucester and the North', in R. Horrox (ed.), *Richard III and the North* (Hull, 1986), pp. 11–26.

Hicks, M., *Richard III as Duke of Gloucester: a study in character*. Borthwick Papers no. 70. York, 1986.

Hicks, M., 'The Yorkshire rebellion of 1489 reconsidered', *Northern History*, XXII (1986), pp. 39–62.

Hicks, M., 'The Neville earldom of Salisbury, 1429–71', pp. 353–63, in M. Hicks, *Richard III and his Rivals: magnates and their motives in the War of the Roses*. London, 1991.

Hicks, M., *Richard III: the man behind the myth*. London, 1991.

Hicks, M., 'Cement or solvent? Kinship and politics in late medieval England: the case of the Nevilles', *History*, LXXXIII (1998), pp. 31–46.

Hicks, M., *Warwick the Kingmaker*. Oxford, 1998.

Hodgson, J.C. (ed.), *Percy Bailiffs' Rolls of the Fifteenth Century*. Surtees Society, vol. CXXXIV. Durham, 1921.

Hollister, C.W., 'Magnates and *curiales* in early Norman England', *Viator*, VIII (1977), pp. 63–81.

Hollister, C.W., 'Henry I and the Anglo-Norman magnates', in R.A. Brown (ed.), *Proceedings of the Battle Abbey Conference on Anglo-Norman Studies*, (1980), pp. 93–107.

Hollister, C.W., 'Henry I and the invisible transformation of medieval England', in his collection, *Monarchy, Magnates and Institutions in the Anglo-Norman World*. London, 1986.

Holmes, G., *The Estates of the Higher Nobility in the Fourteenth Century*. Cambridge, 1957.

Holmes, G., *The Good Parliament*. Oxford, 1975.

Holmes, G.A., 'Judgement on the younger Despenser, 1326', *English Historical Review*, LXX (1955), 275, pp. 261–7.

Holmes, G.A., 'The rebellion of the earl of Lancaster, 1328–9', *Bulletin of the Institute of Historical Research*, XXVIII (1955), pp. 84–9.

Holt, J.C., 'The barons and the Great Charter', *English Historical Review*, LXX (1955), 274, pp. 1–24.

Holt, J.C., *The Northerners: a study in the reign of King John*. Oxford, 1961.

Holt, J.C., *Magna Carta*. Cambridge, 1965.

Holt, J.C., *Magna Carta and medieval government*. London, 1985.

Horrox, R. (ed.), *Richard III and the North*. Hull, 1986.

Horrox, R., *Richard III: a study of service*. Cambridge, 1989.

Hoyle, R.W., 'Faction, feud and reconciliation amongst the Northern English nobility, 1525–1569', *History*, LXXXIV (1999), pp. 590–613.

Hunter Blair, C.H., 'The sheriffs of Northumberland, Part I, 1076–1602', *Archaeologia Aeliana*, 4th series, XX (1942), pp. 11–89. Also XXII (1944), pp. 11–79.

Hunter Blair, P., 'The origins of Northumbria', *Archaeologia Aeliana*, 4th series, XXV (1947), pp. 1–51.

Hunter Blair, C.H., 'Knights of Northumberland, 1278 and 1324'. *Archaeologia Aeliana*, 4th series, XXVII (1949), pp. 122–75.

Hunter Blair, C.H., 'Wardens and Deputy Wardens of the Marches of England towards Scotland, in Northumberland', *Archaeologia Aeliana*, 4th series, XXVIII (1950), pp. 18–95.

Hunter Blair, C.H., 'Baronys and knights of Northumberland, 1166–1260', *Archaeologia Aeliana*, 4th series, XXX (1952), pp. 1–54.

Hunter Marshall, D.W., 'Two early English occupations of Scotland – the administrative organisation', *Scottish Historical Review*, XXV (1928), pp. 20–40.

Hussey, C., 'Alnwick Castle: the seat of the duke of Northumberland', Part 1, *Country Life*, 22 June 1929, pp. 890–8.

Hutchison. H.F., *Edward II: the pliant king*. London, 1971.

Jack, R.I., 'A quincentenary: the battle of Northampton, July 10th 1460', *Northamptonshire Past and Present*, III (1960), pp. 21–5.

James, M.E. (ed.), *Estate Accounts of the Earls of Northumberland, 1562–1637*. Surtees Society, vol. CLXIII. London, 1955.

James, M.E., 'The murder at Cocklodge, 28 April 1489', *Durham University Journal*, LVII (1964–5), pp. 80–7.

Jewell, H.M., 'North and south: the antiquity of the great divide', *Northern History*, XXVII (1991), pp. 1–25.

Johnson, P.A., *Duke Richard of York, 1411–1460*. Oxford, 1988.

Johnstone, H., 'The eccentricities of Edward II', *English Historical Review*, XLVIII (1933), 190, pp. 264–7.

Johnstone, H., 'Isabella, she-wolf of France', *History*, XXI (1936–7), pp. 208–18.

Jones, M., 'Richard III and the Stanleys', pp. 27–50, in R. Horrox (ed.), *Richard III and the North*. Hull, 1986.

Jones, M.K., 'Somerset, York and the Wars of the Roses', *English Historical Review*, CIV (1989), 411, pp. 285–307.

Jones, M.K., 'Richard III as a soldier', pp. 93–112, in J. Gillingham (ed.), *Richard III: a medieval kingship*. London, 1993.

Jones, M.K., 'Edward IV, the earl of Warwick, and the Yorkist claim to the throne', *Historical Research*, LXX (1997), pp. 342–52.

Jones, R.H., *The Royal Policy of Richard II: absolutism in the later Middle Ages*. Oxford, 1968.

Kapelle, W.E., *The Norman Conquest of the North: the region and its transformation, 1100–1135*. London, 1979.

Keen, M., *Chivalry*. London, 1984.

Keeney, B.C., 'Military service and the development of nationalism in England, 1272–1327', *Speculum*, XXII (1947), pp. 534–49.

Kendall, P.M., *Richard the Third*. London, 1955.

King, E., 'King Stephen and the Anglo-Norman aristocracy', *History*, LIX (1974), 196, pp. 180–94.

King, E., 'The anarchy of King Stephen's reign', *Transactions of the Royal Historical Society*, 5th series, XXXIV (1984), pp. 133–53.

King, E. (ed.), *The Anarchy of King Stephen's Reign*. Oxford, 1994.

Kingsford, C.L., 'The earl of Warwick at Calais in 1460', *English Historical Review*, XXXVII (1922), 148, pp. 544–6.

Kirby, D.P., 'Strathclyde and Cumbria: a survey of historical development to 1092', *Transactions of the Cumberland and Westmorland Antiquarian and Archaeological Society*, LXII (1962), pp. 77–94.

Kirby, J.L., *Henry IV of England*. London, 1970.

Lander, J.R., 'Attainder and forefeiture, 1453–1509', *Historical Journal*, IV (1961), pp. 119–51.

Lander, J.R., 'Family, "friends" and politics in fifteenth-century England', pp. 27–40, in R.A. Griffiths and J. Sherborne (eds.), *Kings and Nobles in the Later Middle Ages: a tribute to Charles Ross*. Gloucester, 1986.

Lapsley, G.T., 'The problem of the north', pp. 375–405, in G.T. Lapsley (ed.), *Crown, Community and Parliament in the Later Middle Ages: studies in English constitutional history*. Oxford, 1951.

Le Patourel, J., 'The Norman conquest of Yorkshire', *Northern History*, VI (1971), pp. 1–21.

Le Patourel, J., *The Norman Empire*. Oxford, 1976.

Le Patourel, J., 'Edward III and the kingdom of France', in *Feudal Empires: Norman and Plantagenet*. London, 1984.

Le Patourel, J., 'The origins of the Hundred Years War', in *Feudal Empires: Norman and Plantagenet*. London, 1984.

Le Patourel, J., 'The treaty of Brétigny, 1360', reprinted in his collection, *Feudal Empires: Norman and Plantagenet*. London, 1984.

Leadman, A.D.H., 'The Battle of the Standard', *Yorkshire Archaeological and Topographical Journal*, X (1889), pp. 377–87.

Levine, M., 'Richard III – usurper or lawful king?', *Speculum*, XXXIV (1958), pp. 391–401.

Lewis, C.P., 'The early earls of Norman England', *Anglo-Norman Studies*, XIII (1991).

Lewis, C.P., 'The formation of the honour of Chester, 1066–1100', in A.T. Thacker (ed.), *The earldom of Chester and its Charters: a tribute to Geoffrey Barraclough*: Special Volume of the *Journal of the Chester Archaeological Society*, LXXI (1991), pp. 37–65.

Lewis, F.R., 'William de Valence', *Aberystwyth Studies*, XII and XIV (1936), Parts 1 and 2, pp. 11–35, 69–92.

Lloyd, J.E., *Owen Glendower*. Oxford, 1931.

Lodge, E.C. and Somerville, R. (eds.), *John of Gaunt's Register, 1379–1383*. Camden Society, 3rd series, vol. LVII. London, 1937.

Lomas, R., *North-east England in the Middle Ages*. Edinburgh, 1992.

Lomas, R., *County of Conflict: Northumberland, from Conquest to Civil War*. East Linton, 1996.

Lomas, R., 'The impact of Border warfare: the Scots and South Tweedside, c.1290–c.1520', *Scottish Historical Review*, LXXV (1996), 200, pp. 143–67.

Longley, K.M., 'The Scottish incursions of 1327: a glimpse of the aftermath', *Transactions of the Cumberland and Westmorland Antiquarian and Archaeological Society*, new series, LXXXIII (1983).

Longstaff, W.H.D., 'The old heraldry of the Percys', *Archaeologia Aeliana*, 2nd series, IV (1860), pp. 157–228.

Loyd, L.C. (ed. C.T. Clay and D.C. Douglas), *The Origins of some Anglo-Norman Families*. Harleian Society, CIII. Leeds, 1951.

Loyn, H.R., *The Norman Conquest*. London, 3rd edn, 1982.

Macdougall, N., *James III: a political study*. Edinburgh, 1982.

McFarlane, K.B., 'The Wars of the Roses', *Proceedings of the British Academy*, L (1965), pp. 87–119.

McFarlane, K.B., *The nobility of later medieval England: the Ford Lectures for 1953 and related studies*. Oxford, 1973.

McGladdery, C., *James II*. Edinburgh, 1990.

McKisack, M., 'Edward III and the historians', *History*, XLV (1960), pp. 1–15.

McNair Scott, R., *Robert the Bruce: king of Scots*. Edinburgh, 1982.

McNiven, P., 'The Scottish policy of the Percies and the strategy of the rebellion of 1403', *Bulletin of the John Rylands Library*, LXII (1979–80), pp. 498–530.

McNiven, P., 'Legitimacy and consent: Henry IV and the Lancastrian title, 1399–1406', *Mediaeval Studies*, XLIV (1982), pp. 470–81.

McNiven, P., 'Rebellion, sedition and the legend of Richard II's survival in the reigns of Henry IV and Henry V', *Bulletin of the John Rylands Library*, LXXVI (1994), pp. 93–117.

Maddicott, J.R., *Simon de Montfort*. Cambridge, 1994.

Mason, J., 'Sir Andrew de Harcla, earl of Carlisle', *Transactions of the Cumberland and Westmorland Antiquarian and Archaeological Society*, XXIX (1929), pp. 98–137.

Mason, J.F.A., 'The honour of Richmond', *English Historical Review*, LXXVIII (1963), pp. 703–4.

Maxwell, H., *A History of the House of Douglas: from the earliest times down to the legislative union of England and Scotland*. London, 2 vols., 1902.

Meehan, B., 'The siege of Durham, the battle of Carham and the cession of Lothian', *Scottish Historical Review*, LV (1976), 1, pp. 1–19.

Miller, E., *War in the North: the Anglo-Scottish wars of the Middle Ages*. Hull, 1960.

Miller, E., 'The background of Magna Carta', *Past and Present*, XXIII (1962), pp. 72–83.

Milsom, S.F.C., *The Legal Framework of English Feudalism*. Cambridge, 1976.

Milsom, S.F.C., 'Inheritance by women in the twelfth and early thirteenth centuries', pp. 60–89, in M.S. Arnold, T.A. Green,

S.A. Scully and S.D. White (eds.), *On the Laws and Customs of England: essays in honour of Samuel E. Thorne*. Chapel Hill, North Carolina, 1981. See also Pollock and Maitland, *The History of English Law*.

Mooers, S., 'Patronage in the Pipe Roll of 1130', *Speculum*, LIX (1984), pp. 282–307.

Moore, J.S., 'Domesday slavery', *Anglo-Norman Studies*, XI (1988), pp. 191–220.

Morgan, D.A.L., 'The political after-life of Edward III: the apotheosis of a warmonger', *English Historical Review*, CXII (1997), 448, pp. 856–81.

Morgan, P., 'Henry IV and the shadow of Richard II', pp. 1–31, in R.E. Archer (ed.), *Crown, Government and People in the Fifteenth Century*. Stroud/New York, 1995.

Musgrove, F., *The North of England: a history from Roman times to the present*. Oxford, 1990.

Myers, A.R. (ed. C.H. Clough), *Crown, Household and Parliament in Fifteenth Century England*. London, 1985.

Myers, H.A., *Medieval Kingship*. Chicago, Illinois, 1982.

Neilson, G., 'Brus *versus* Balliol, 1291–1292: the model for Edward I's tribunal', *Scottish Historical Review*, XVI (1918), 61, pp. 1–14.

Neville, C.J., 'Keeping the peace on the Northern Marches in the later Middle Ages', *English Historical Review*, CIX (1994), 430, pp. 1–25.

Neville, C.J., 'Local sentiment and the "national" enemy in Northern England in the later Middle Ages', *Journal of British Studies*, XXV (1996), pp. 419–37.

Neville, C.J., *Violence, Custom and the Law: the Anglo-Scottish border lands in the later Middle Ages*. Edinburgh, 1998.

Nicholson, R., 'The last campaign of Robert Bruce', *English Historical Review*, LXXVII (1962), 303, pp. 233–46.

Nicholson, R., *Edward III and the Scots: the formative years of a military career, 1327–1335*. London, 1965.

Nicholson, R., 'David II, the historians and the chroniclers', *Scottish Historical Review*, XLV (1966), pp. 59–78.

Nicholson, R., *Scotland: the later Middle Ages*. Edinburgh, 1974.

Norgate, K., *England under the Angevin Kings*. London, 2 vols., 1887.

Ormrod, W.M., 'Edward III and his family', *Journal of British Studies*, XXVI (1987), pp. 398–422.

Ormrod, W.M., 'Edward III and the recovery

of royal authority in England, 1340–60', *History*, LXXII (1987), pp. 4–19.

Ormrod, W.M., *The Reign of Edward III: Crown and political society in England, 1327–1377*. New Haven/London, 1990.

Painter, S., *Studies in the History of the English Feudal Barony*. Baltimore, Maryland, 1943.

Painter, S., *The Reign of King John*. Baltimore, Maryland, 1949.

Painter, S., 'The Houses of Lusignan and Châtellerault, 1150–1250', pp. 73–89, in F.A. Cazel (ed.), *Feudalism and Liberty: articles and addresses of Sidney Painter*. Baltimore, Maryland, 1961.

Painter, S., 'The Rout of Winchester', pp. 157–64, in F.A. Cazel (ed.), *Feudalism and Liberty: articles and addresses of Sidney Painter*. Baltimore, Maryland, 1961.

Palmer, J.J.N., 'The Anglo-French peace negotiations, 1390–1396', *Transactions of the Royal Historical Society*, 5th series, XVI (1966), pp. 81–94.

Palmer, J.J.N., 'English foreign policy, 1388–99', pp. 75–107, in F.R.H. du Boulay and C.M. Barron (eds.), *The Reign of Richard II: essays in honour of May McKisack*. London, 1971.

Palmer, R.C., 'The origins of property in England', *Law and History Review*, III (1985), pp. 1–50.

Passingham, W.J., *The History of the Coronation*. London [n.d.].

Payling, S., 'The politics of family: late medieval marriage contracts', pp. 21–47, in R.H. Britnell and A.J. Pollard (eds.), *The McFarlane Legacy: studies in late medieval politics and society*. Stroud/New York, 1995.

Peeris, W. (ed. D. Bisley), *Metrical Pedigree of the Percyes*, printed as 'Metrical Chronicle of the Family of Percy' in *Richardson's Reprints of Rare Tracts and Imprints of Antient Manuscripts*, vol. V. Newcastle, 1845.

Percy, T. (pref.), *The regulations and establishments of the Household of Henry Algernon Percy, the fifth earl of Northumberland, at his castles of Wresil and Lekinfield in Yorkshire, begun anno Domini M.C.XII*. London, 1770.

Phillips, J.R.S., *Aymer de Valence, Earl of Pembroke, 1307–1324*. Oxford, 1972.

Phillips, J.R.S., 'The "Middle Party" and the negotiating of the Treaty of Leake, August 1318: a reinterpretation', *Bulletin of the Institute of Historical Research*, XLVI (1973), pp. 11–27.

Plucknett, T.F.T., 'The origin of impeachment', *Transactions of the Royal Historical Society*, 4th series, XXIV (1942), pp. 47–71.

Pollard, A., 'Percies, Nevilles and the Wars of the Roses', *History Today*, XLIII (1993), September, pp. 42–8.

Pollard, A.J., 'The northern retainers of Richard Nevill, earl of Salisbury', *Northern History*, XI (1975), pp. 52–69.

Pollard, A.J., *North-eastern England during the Wars of the Roses: lay society, war and politics, 1450–1500*. Oxford, 1990.

Pollard, A.J., 'Fifteenth-century politics and the Wars of the Roses', *Historian*, 57 (1998), pp. 26–8.

Pollard, A.J., (ed.), *The Wars of the Roses*. London, 1995.

Pollard, A.J., (ed.), *The North of England in the Age of Richard III*. Stroud, 1996.

Pollit, R., 'The defeat of the Northern Rebellion and the shaping of Anglo-Scottish relations', *Scottish Historical Review*, LXIV (1985), I, pp. 1–21.

Pollock, F. and Maitland, F.W. (intro. S.F.C. Milsom), *The History of English Law before the Time of Edward I*. Cambridge, 2 vols., 2nd edn, 1968.

Post, G., 'Two notes on nationalism in the Middle Ages', *Traditio*, IX (1953), pp. 281–320.

Powicke, F.M., *King Henry III and the Lord Edward: the community of the realm in the thirteenth century*. Oxford, 2 vols., 1947.

Powicke, M.R., 'The English Commons in Scotland in 1322 and the deposition of Edward II', *Speculum*, XXXV (1960), pp. 556–62.

Prestwich, J.O., 'War and finance in the Anglo-Norman state', *Transactions of the Royal Historical Society*, 5th series, IV (1954), pp. 19–43.

Prestwich, J.O., 'Anglo-Norman feudalism and the problem of continuity', *Past and Present*, XXVI (1963), pp. 39–54.

Prestwich, M., *War, Politics and Finance under Edward I*. London, 1972.

Prestwich, M., *The Three Edwards: war and state in England, 1272–1377*. London, 1980.

Prestwich, M., 'Italian merchants in late thirteenth and early fourteenth century England', pp. 77–104, in (no editor), *The dawn of modern banking*. Yale, 1979.

Prestwich, M., *Edward I*. London/Yale, 2nd edn, 1997.

Rainsford, R., 'A kind of Noah's Ark: Aelred

of Rievaulx and national identity', *Religion and National Identity: Studies in Church History*, XVIII, pp. 137–46.

Ramsay, Sir J., *Lancaster and York: a century of English history*. Oxford, 2 vols., 1892.

Reid, N.H., *Scotland in the Reign of Alexander III*. Edinburgh, 1990.

Reid, R.R., 'The office of Warden of the Marches: its origin and early history', *English Historical Review*, XXXII (1917), pp. 479–96.

Richardson, H.G., 'The English Coronation Oath', *Transactions of the Royal Historical Society*, 4th series, XXIII (1941), pp. 129–58.

Richardson, H.G., 'The morrow of the Great Charter', *Bulletin of the John Rylands Library*, XXVIII (1944), pp. 422–43.

Richardson, H.G. and Sayles, G., 'The Scottish parliaments of Edward I', *Scottish Historical Review*, XXV (1928), pp. 300–17.

Richmond, C.F., 'The war at sea', in K. Fowler (ed.), *The Hundred Years War*. London, 1971.

Ridgeway, H.W., 'The Lord Edward and the Provisions of Oxford (1258): a study in faction', *Thirteenth Century England*, I (1985), pp. 89–99.

Ridgeway, H.W., 'Foreign favourites and Henry III's problems of patronage, 1247–1258', *English Historical Review*, CIV (1989), 412, pp. 590–610.

Ritchie, R.L.G., *The Normans in Scotland*. Edinburgh, 1954.

Robinson, C., 'Was Edward II a degenerate?', *American Journal of Insanity*, LXVI (1910), pp. 445–64.

Roffe, D., 'From thegnage to barony: sake and soke, title, and tenants-in-chief', *Anglo-Norman Studies*, XII (1989), pp. 157–76.

Rogers, C.J., 'Edward III and the dialectics of strategy, 1327–1360', *Transactions of the Royal Historical Society*, 6th series, IV (1994), pp. 83–102.

Rogers, C.J., 'The efficacy of the English longbow: a reply to Kelly DeVries', *War and History*, V (1998), pp. 233–42.

Rogers, C.J. (with an appendix by C.J. Rogers and M.C. Buck), 'The Scottish invasion of 1346', *Northern History*, XXXIV (1998), pp. 51–81.

Rosenthal, J.T., 'Aristocratic marriage and the English peerage, 1350–1500: social institution and personal bond', *Journal of Medieval History*, X (1984), pp. 181–94.

Ross, C., 'Forfeiture for treason in the reign of Richard II', *English Historical Review*, LXXI (1956), 281, pp. 560–75.

Ross, C., *The Wars of the Roses: a concise history*. London, 1976.

Ross, C., *Edward IV*. London, new edn, 1997.

Round, J.H., 'The family of Clare', *Archaeological Journal*, LVI (1899), pp. 221–31.

Round, J.H., 'The families of St. John and of Port', *Genealogist*, XVI (1899), pp. 1–13.

Round, J.H., *Studies in Peerage and Family History*. London, 1901.

Round, J.H., *Studies in Peerage and Pedigree*. London, 1910.

Salzman, L.F., 'On the early history of the honour of Petworth', *Sussex Archaeological Collections*, LXVIII (1927), pp. 60–6.

Sanders, I.J., *English Baronies: a study of their origin and descent, 1086–1327*. Oxford, 1960.

Saul, N., 'The Despensers and the downfall of Edward II', *English Historical Review*, XCIX (1984), 390, pp. 1–33.

Saul, N., *Richard II*. New Haven/London, 1997.

Saul, N., 'The kingship of Richard II', pp. 37–57, in A. Goodman and J. Gillespie (eds.), *Richard II: the art of kingship*. Oxford, 1999.

Scammell, G.V., 'Seven charters relating to the *familia* of Bishop Hugh du Puiset', *Archaeologia Aeliana*, XXXIV (1956), 4th series, pp. 77–89.

Scammell, J., 'Robert I and the north of England', *English Historical Review*, LXXIII (1958), 288, pp. 385–403.

Scammel, J., 'The origins and limitations of the liberty of Durham', *English Historical Review*, LXXXI (1966), pp. 449–71.

Scott, F.S., 'Earl Waltheof of Northumbria', *Archaeologia Aeliana*, 4th series, XXX (1952), pp. 149–213.

Seward, D., *The Hundred Years War: the English in France, 1337–1453*. London, 1978.

Seymour, W., *Battles in Britain and their Political Background, 1066–1746*. London, 1997.

Sherborne, J. (ed. A. Tuck), *War, Politics and Culture in Fourteenth-century England*. London, 1994.

Stell, G., 'The Balliol family and the Great Cause of 1291–92', pp. 150–65, in K.J. Stringer (ed.), *Essays on the Nobility of Medieval Scotland*. Edinburgh, 1985.

Stenton, F.M., 'The Danes in England', *Proceedings of the British Academy*, XIII (1927), pp. 203–46.

Stenton, F.M., 'English families and the Norman Conquest', *Transactions of the Royal Historical Society*, 4th series, XXVI (1944), pp. 1–12.

Stenton, F.M., 'The Scandinavian colonies in England and Normandy', *Transactions of the Royal Historical Society*, 4th series, XXVII (1945), pp. 1–12.

Stenton, F.M., *The First Century of English Feudalism*. Oxford, 2nd edn, 1961.

Stewart-Brown, R., 'The end of the Norman earldom of Chester', *English Historical Review*, XXXV (1920), 137, pp. 26–53.

Stones, E.L.G., 'The Anglo-Scottish negotiations of 1327', *Scottish Historical Review*, XXX (1951), pp. 49–54.

Stones, E.L.G., 'The submission of Robert Bruce to Edward I, c.1301–2', *Scottish Historical Review*, XXXII (1953), pp. 122–34.

Stones, E.L.G., 'The records of the Great Cause of 1291–92', *Scottish Historical Review*, XXXV (1956), pp. 89–109.

Storey, R.L., 'The Wardens of the Marches of England towards Scotland, 1377–1489', *English Historical Review*, LXXII (1957), pp. 593–615.

Storey, R.L., *The End of the House of Lancaster*. London, 1966.

Storey, R.L., 'The North of England', pp. 129–44, in S.B. Chrimes, C.D. Ross and R.A. Griffiths (eds.), *Fifteenth-century England, 1399–1509: studies in politics and society*. Manchester, 1972.

Strickland, M., 'Securing the north: invasion and the strategy of defence in twelfth-century Anglo-Scottish warfare', *Anglo-Norman Studies*. XII (1989), pp. 177–98.

Strickland, M. (ed.), *Anglo-Norman Warfare: studies in late Anglo-Saxon and Anglo-Norman military organisation and warfare*. Woodbridge, 1992.

Stringer, K.J., *The Reign of Stephen: kingship, warfare and government in twelfth-century England*. London, 1993.

Stringer, K.J. (ed.), *Essays on the Nobility of Medieval Scotland*. Edinburgh, 1985.

Stringer, K.J. and Grant, A. (eds.), *Uniting the Kingdom: the making of British history*. London, 1995.

Sumption, J., *The Hundred Years War*. Vol. I, *Trial by Battle*. London, 1990.

Tanner, L.E., 'Westminster Abbey and the Coronation service', *History*, XXI (1936–7), pp. 289–301.

Thomas, H.M., 'Portrait of a medieval anti-Semite: Richard Malebisse, *Vero Agnomine Mala Bestia*', *Haskins Society Journal*, V (1993), pp. 1–15.

Thomas, H.M., *Vassals, Heiresses, Crusaders and Thugs: the gentry of Angevin Yorkshire, 1154–1216*. Philadelphia, Pennsylvania, 1993.

Thomas, H.M., 'Subinfeudation and alienation of land, economic development, and the wealth of nobles on the Honour of Richmond, 1066 to c.1300'. *Albion*, XXVI (1994), 3, pp. 397–417.

Thompson, F., *Magna Carta: its role in the making of the English Constitution, 1300–1629*. Minneapolis, Minnesota, 1948.

Tout, T.F., 'The tactics of the battles of Boroughbridge and Morlaix', *English Historical Review*, XIX (1904), 76, pp. 711–15.

Tout, T.F., *Chapters in the Administrative History of Medieval England: the Wardrobe, the Chamber and the Small Seals*. Manchester, 6 vols., 1920–33.

Tout, T.F., 'The English Parliament and public opinion, 1376–88', rep. in E.B. Fryde and E. Miller (eds.), *Historical Studies of the English Parliament*. Cambridge, 2 vols., 1970.

Tout, T.F., (ed. H. Johnstone), *The Place of the Reign of Edward II in English History: based upon the Ford Lectures delivered in the University of Oxford in 1913*. Manchester, 2nd edn, 1936; rep. Westport, Connecticut, 1976.

Treharne, R.F., *The Baronial Plan of Reform, 1258–1263*. Manchester, 1932.

Treharne, R.F. (ed. E.B. Fryde), *Simon de Montfort and Baronial Reform: thirteenth-century essays*. London, 1986.

Trueman, J.H., 'The personnel of medieval reform: the English Lords Ordainers of 1310', *Mediaeval Studies*, XXI (1959), pp. 247–71.

Tuck, A., 'Richard II and the Border magnates', *Northern History*, III (1968), pp. 27–52.

Tuck, A., 'Northumbrian society in the fourteenth century', *Northern History*, VI (1971), pp. 22–39.

Tuck, A., *Richard II and the English nobility*. London, 1973.

Tuck, A., *Crown and Nobility, 1272–1461: political conflict in late medieval England*. London, 1985.

Tuck, A., 'War and society in the medieval North', *Northern History*, XXI (1985), pp. 33–52.

Tuck, A., 'The emergence of a Northern nobility, 1250–1400', *Northern History*, XXII (1986), pp. 1–17.

Tuck, A., 'Richard II and the Hundred Years War', pp. 117–31, in J. Taylor and W. Childs (eds.), *Politics and Crisis in Fourteenth-century England*. Gloucester, 1990.

Tuck, A. (ed.), [Essays by James Sherborne], *War, Politics and Culture in Fourteenth-century England*. London, 1994.

Tyerman, C., *England and the Crusades, 1095–1588*. Chicago, Illinois, 1988.

Vincent, N.C., 'Simon de Montfort's first quarrel with King Henry III', *Thirteenth Century England*, IV (1991), pp. 167–77.

Vine, M.J., 'Two Yorkshire rebels: Peter de Brus and Richard de Percy', *Yorkshire Archaeological Journal*, XLVII (1975), pp. 69–79.

Walker, S., *The Lancastrian Affinity, 1361–1399*. Oxford, 1990.

Ward, J.C., 'Royal service and reward: the Clare family and the Crown, 1066–1154', *Anglo-Norman Studies*, XI (1988), pp. 261–78.

Warner, M.W. and Lacey, K., 'Neville *vs.* Percy: a precedence dispute circa 1442', *Historical Research: the Bulletin of the Institute of Historical Research*, LXIX (1996), 169, pp. 211–17.

Warren, W.L., *The Governance of Norman and Angevin England*. London, 1987.

Washington, G., 'The Border heritage, 1066–1292', *Transactions of the Cumberland and Westmorland Antiquarian and Archaeological Society*, LXII (1962), pp. 101–12.

Watt, D.E.R., 'The minority of Alexander III of Scotland', *Transactions of the Royal Historical Society*, 5th series, XXI (1971), pp. 1–23.

Waugh, S.L., *The Lordship of England: royal wardships and marriages in English society and politics, 1217–1327*. Princeton, New Jersey, 1988.

Webster, B., 'Scotland without a king, 1329–1341', pp. 223–38, in A. Grant and K.J. Stringer (eds.), *Medieval Scotland: Crown, lordship and community: essays presented to G.W.S. Barrow*. Edinburgh, 1993.

Webster, B., 'Anglo-Scottish relations, 1296–1389: some recent essays', *Scottish Historical Review*, LXXIV (1995), pp. 99–108.

Weiss, M., 'A power in the North? The Percies in the fifteenth century', *Historical Journal*, XIX (1976), pp. 501–9.

White, R., 'The battle of Neville's Cross, fought 17 October 1346', *Archaeologia Aeliana*, 2nd series, I (1857), pp. 271–303.

White, S.D., 'Succession to fiefs in early medieval England', *Past and Present*, LXV (1974), pp. 118–27.

Wilkinson, B., 'The deposition of Richard II and the accession of Henry IV', *English Historical Review*, LIV (1939), 214, pp. 215–39.

Wilkinson, B., 'Northumbrian separatism in 1065 and 1066', *Bulletin of the John Rylands Library*, XXIII (1939), pp. 504–26.

Wilkinson, B., *The Coronation in History*. Historical Association. London, 1953.

Willard, J.F., 'The Scotch raids and fourteenth century taxation of northern England', *University of Colorado Studies*, V (1907–8), pp. 240–2.

Williams, A., *The English and the Norman Conquest*. Woodbridge, 1995.

Wolffe, B., 'The personal rule of Henry VI', pp. 29–48, in S.B. Chrimes, C.D. Ross and R.A. Griffiths (eds.), *Fifteenth-century England, 1399–1509*. Manchester, 1972.

Wolffe, B., *Henry VI*. London, 1981.

Wood, C.T., 'Personality, politics and constitutional progress: the lessons of Edward II', *Studia Gratiana*, XV (1972), pp. 521–36.

Wormald, P., 'The emergence of the Anglo-Saxon kingdoms', in L.M. Smith (ed.), *The Making of Britain: the Dark Ages*. London, 1984.

Wylie, J.H., *History of England under Henry the Fourth*. London, 4 vols., 1884–98.

Young, A., *William Cumin: Border politics and the bishopric of Durham, 1141–44*. Borthwick Paper, no. 54. York, 1979.

Young, C.R., *The Making of the Neville Family in England, 1166–1400*. Woodbridge, 1996.

Index

Aaron of Lincoln, 81

Abernethy, Treaty of (1072), 28–9

Act of Accord (1460), 426

Adam of Usk, 345, 348, 353

Adeliza de Louvain, Queen of Henry I (later d'Aubigny), 49, 61, 72, 119

Aelianus, Claudius: *De Natura Animalium*, 226, 250

Aethelwine, Bishop of Worcester, 25

Agincourt, battle of (1415), 370, 373

Alan the Red, Count, 32, 35

Alan of Thornton, 82

Albany, Alexander, Duke of, 465–6, 468–9

Albany, Murdoch Stewart, 2nd Duke of (earlier Earl of Fife), 353, 367–71, 375, 379–81

Albany, Robert Stewart, 1st Duke of (earlier Earl of Fife), 335–7, 350–2, 362–4, 367–72, 375

Albemarle, Edward, Duke of (earlier Earl of Rutland), 340, 342, 345, 349

Alençon, Charles, Count of, 270–2

Alexander I, King of Scotland, 51

Alexander II, King of Scotland, 88–9, 111–12, 116

Alexander III, King of Scotland, 111–14, 117, 195, 208

Alexander IV, Pope, 98

Alexius I Comnenus, Byzantine Emperor, 38–9

Alfred the Great, King of Wessex, 19–20

Alguillon, siege of (1346), 269

Almain, Henry of see Henry of Almain

Alnwick: burned by Scots (1433), 385

Alnwick Abbey, 250

Alnwick Abbey, Chronicles of, 119, 143, 205, 212, 302

Alnwick Castle: purchased by Percy family, 33, 143, 152–4, 226; John de Vesci owns, 109–10; position and structure, 155; land values decline with Scottish raids, 166; Scots harass and besiege, 171, 193; and control of Marches, 208; Henry Percy IV improves, 212; burnt by 8th Earl of Douglas, 400; submits to Yorkists, 436; Tailboys ejected from, 438; and James III's expedition, 439

Amercham, Walter of, 124

Amiens, Mise of (1264), 105

Anarchy, the, 46, 59, 69

Anglo-Saxon Chronicle, 20, 55

Angus, Archibald Douglas, 5th Earl of, 467

Angus, Gilbert Umfraville, Earl of see Umfraville, Gilbert

Angus, Thomas Stewart, Earl of see Stewart, Thomas

Anjou, Geoffrey V, Count of, 49, 61, 64

Anjou, Louis I, Duke of, 301, 306

Annandale, 13, 114, 219–21, 223, 229, 231, 237

Anne of Brittany, 478

Anne, Queen of Richard III (née Neville; Warwick's daughter), 447, 453, 462, 478

Anselm, Archbishop of Canterbury, 30

Antwerp, Lionel of see Clarence, Duke of

Appellants, 335–6

Aquitaine (Gascony): English hold as fief to French crown, 102, 120, 183, 253–4, 288, 301, 339–40; Anglo-French wars over, 184, 301–2, 304, 398; Edward III loses territories in, 258; 3rd Earl of Arundel in, 263; Edward III offered return of, 269; Black Prince in, 281; Edward III claims full sovereignty in, 285; Henry VI retains, 296; John of Gaunt in, 301–2; Charles V regains, 304; Hotspur in, 340; Charles VII conquers, 398; Egremont ordered to, 403

Arbroath, Declaration of (1320), 171

Arc, Joan of, 382–3

Argyll, 146

Argyll, Colin Campbell, 1st Earl of, 465

Armitage-Smith, Sidney, 307

Arras, Congress of (1435), 387

Arras, Treaty of (1483), 469

Arthur of Brittany, 76–7, 311

Arundel, Sussex, 73

Arundel, Edmund Fitzalan, 2nd Earl of, 150–1, 156–7, 164, 173, 175, 189, 235

Arundel, Isabel, Countess of (née Despenser), 235, 263

Arundel, John Fitzalan (otherwise Mautravers), 21st Earl of, 107

Arundel, Richard Fitzalan, 1st Earl of, 129

Arundel, Richard Fitzalan, 3rd Earl of, 215, 224, 229, 235–6, 239–40, 262–6, 270

Arundel, Richard Fitzalan, 4th Earl of, 335, 340, 344

Arundel, William d'Aubigny, 3rd Earl of, 61, 73, 119

Arundel, William Fitzalan, Earl of, 423, 451

Ashton, Sir Ralph, of Redesdale, 476

Asser, Bishop of Sherborne, 10

Athelstan, King of the English, 20

Atholl, David of Strathbogie, Earl of, 179, 180, 192

Atholl, Ralph de Monthermer, Earl of, 139

Atholl, Walter Stewart, Earl of see Stewart, Walter

Aton, Gilbert, 153–4, 226, 296

Aton, Isabel (née Percy; Henry Percy IV's daughter), 226, 250, 296

Aton, William, 226

Auberoche, battle of (1345), 263–4

Aubigny, William d' see Arundel, 3rd Earl of

Audley, Hugh d' see Gloucester, 1st Earl of

Audley, James Tuchet, 5th Baron, 422

Aymer de Valence see Pembroke, Aymer de Valence, Earl of

Ayton, Yorkshire, 484–5

Badlesmere, Sir Bartholomew, 173

ballads (border), 13–14

Balliol, Agnes de (William Percy III's daughter), 93

Balliol, Bernard of, 54, 56

Balliol, Dervorguilla, 114

Balliol, Edward, King of Scotland: as successor to Bruce, 183, 194, 200–1, 203; Beaumont negotiates with, 203, 207; rebellion, 212–13; crowned, 214, 254; Edward III's relations with, 214–15, 221–3, 236; takes refuge in England, 215; and battle of Halidon Hill, 218; grants lands to Henry Percy IV, 219–21; advised to hold Parliament, 221; cedes territories to Edward III, 222, 341; seizes Strathbogie's possessions, 227; with Edward III's 1335 Scottish expedition, 229, 231; at battle of Neville's Cross, 243; campaign in Scotland (1347), 247; Neville negotiates with over David II, 248–9; death, 281; surrenders crown to Edward III, 281, 298

Balliol, Eustace de, 93

Balliol, Guy de, 7

Balliol, Sir Ingram de, 118, 132

Bamburgh, 12, 467; Castle, 216, 438–9, 442

Bannockburn, battle of (1314), 132, 153, 164–5, 180

Barbour, John, 139–40, 150, 172, 175

Bardi bank, 259

Bardolph, Thomas, 5th Baron, 361–5

Barnard Castle, Co. Durham, 7, 113

Barnes, Joshua, 198

Barnet, battle of (1471), 457

barons (of England): and hereditary succession, 67–8; wealth and properties, 70; and knightly service, 81; rebel against King John, 83–6, 89, 92; and Magna Carta, 86–8, 92; force agreement on Henry III, 99,

103–4; titles and status, 131; families die out, 168; win right to trial by peers, 239; cooperate with Edward III, 240

Barrow, G.W.S., 115, 120, 127, 197

Basset, Gilbert, 92

Basset, Philip, 103

Bates, David, 20

Bauge, battle of (1421), 376

Bean, J.M.W., 228

Beanley, 227–8

Beaufort, Edmund see Somerset, 2nd Duke of

Beaufort, Cardinal Henry, Bishop of Winchester, 378–80, 382–3, 385–6, 391–2, 394, 397, 400

Beaufort, Margaret see Richmond and Derby, Countess of

Beaumont family, 48

Beaumont, Eleanor, Lady (later Countess of Arundel), 224, 263

Beaumont, Henry, Earl of Buchan: surrenders at Scarborough, 159; as 'Disinherited', 183, 185, 200, 215, 221–3; conspires with Queen Isabella, 185, 187–8, 192; Edward III's concessions to, 194, 197; negotiates with Edward Balliol in France, 201, 207; returns to support Edward III in England, 202–4; in wars with Scots, 213, 215, 217, 229; capitulation and ransom (1334), 227; death, 236

Beaumont, John, 4th Baron, 338

Bede, Venerable: Ecclesiastical History, 6

Bedford, John of Lancaster, Duke of (Henry IV's son), 360, 363, 368–9, 371, 372–9, 381–5, 402

Bek, Anthony, Bishop of Durham, 115–16, 123, 128–30, 147, 153–5, 226

Bellardi of Lucca (Lombard bankers), 154–5

Bellingham, Sir Henry, 441

Benedict XII, Pope, 238

Benhale, Sir Robert, 1st Baron, 216

Bergerac, 263–4

Berkeley Castle, 190

Berkeley, Thomas, 229

Bernicia, 8

Berry, Jean de, Duke of, 301, 306

Bertram, Sir Robert, 244

Berwick on Tweed: siege of (1296), 121–2; Bruce threatens, 161; falls to Scots (1318), 170–1; Edward II besieges (1319), 171–2; siege and truce (1333), 216–17; Henry Percy IV made warden of, 219; assaulted by Scots (1355), 281; castle strengthened, 289, 381; fortress captured by Scots renegades (1378), 328; James Douglas besieges, 372; offered to James I, 384; English retain, 426; Queen Margaret signs over to Scots, 437; Richard (Gloucester) besieges, 468; falls to Richard and remains English, 469; Tyler appointed captain, 484

Berwick, Treaty of (1357), 285, 287

Beverley, Yorkshire, 5, 181; Minster, 204

Bigod, Hugh, 50, 99–100

Birgham, Treaty of (1289), 115, 117–18
Bishopthorpe, peace of (1323), 183, 185
'Black Candlemass' campaign, 282
Black Death, 247–8, 275–6
Black Rood (fragment of True Cross), 196
Blacklow Hill, 160, 174, 177
Blair, John, 143
'Blind Harry': *The Wallace*, 465
Blois, Charles of, 260–2
Blore Heath, battle of (1459), 422
Bohemund, Prince of Taranto, 39, 41–2
Bohun, Sir Edward, 219–21, 223, 231, 237
Bohun, Sir Humphrey *see* Hereford, 3rd Earl of
Bolingbroke, Roger, 394
Bolton, John, 292
Boniface VIII, Pope, 134
Boniface, Archbishop of Canterbury, 95, 103
Book of Pluscarden, 289, 389
Booth, Laurence, 418
Bordeaux, 398–9, 406
Boroughbridge, battle of (1322), 175–6, 219
Bosworth, battle of (1485), 480–3
Boulogne Agreement (1308), 147–9
Boulogne, Eustace III, Count of, 49
Bourchier, Thomas, Archbishop of Canterbury, 410, 426
Bouvines, battle of (1214), 84
Bower, Walter, 384
Bowes, Sir Robert, 11
Brabant, Duke of, 256
Brabant, dukedom of, 73–4
Bracton, Henry de, 81
Bramham Moor, battle of (1408), 365
Brandon, William, 482
Brembre, Nicholas, 318, 336
Brenan, Gerald, 17, 72
Brétigny, Treaty of (1360), 186–7, 297, 299, 368, 375
Brézé, Pierre de, seneschal of Normandy, 438
Brice, Edward, 147
Brittany: Edward III in, 261–2; as refuge for attainted exiles, 478
Brittany, Francis II, Duke of, 458, 478
Brittany, Geoffrey, Duke of, 76
Brittany, John II, Duke of, 260
Brittany, John III, Duke of, 260, 297
Briwerre, William, 77, 79–80, 89, 92
Broughton, Sir Thomas, 486
Brown, Michael, 218
Bruce, Edward, 163, 179
Bruce, Isabella (Robert VIII's wife), 139–40, 165
Bruce, Mary de (Robert VIII's sister), 140
Bruce, Nigel, 213
Bruce, Robert VI de ('the Competitor'), 113–15, 118, 120–1
Bruce, Robert VII de, Earl of Carrick, 114
Bruce, Robert VIII, King (Robert I) of Scotland: cross-border raids and expeditions, 12–13, 146, 165–6, 168, 171, 180, 191–4, 336; as Earl of Carrick, 121; as guerrilla fighter, 125, 141, 145; and Wallace, 125, 130;

submits to Edward II, 134; and succession to father, 136; Edward II and, 137, 151, 163; failed rebellion and Methven defeat, 138–40, 145; resumes campaign, 146–7, 149; and Edward II's Scottish campaigns, 156, 179; Edward II consults over Gaveston, 158; and potential English civil war, 161; Bannockburn victory, 165; death, 166, 199, 332; truce with English (1319–21), 171–2, 178; Lancaster's secret agreement with, 175; expedition into Yorkshire (1322), 180–1; Harclay negotiates peace treaty with and recognises kingship, 181; Edward II's peace treaty with (1323), 182; leprosy and decline, 183, 191, 194; hopes for recognition after fall of Edward II, 191; peace terms to Edward III, 194; and son David's marriage to Joan, 196; promises restitution to Disinherited, 203; and murder of Comyn, 405
Bruce, Lord Robert, 213
Bruges, Treaty of (1377), 306–7
Brus, Adam de, 56
Brus, Adam II de, 60
Brus, Agnes de (*earlier* de Roumare; wife of Adam II), 60, 65
Brus, Peter de, 82, 84
Brus, Robert II de, 54, 56
Brut, 190, 196–7
Buchan, Alexander Comyn, Earl of, 114
Buchan, James Stewart, 14th Earl of, 466
Buchan, John Stewart, 1st Earl of, 373, 376, 379–81
Buchanan, George, 242
Buckingham, Henry Stafford, 2nd Duke of, 471–2, 474–5, 477
Buckingham, Humphrey Stafford, 1st Duke of, 411, 419, 421, 423–5
Buckingham, Thomas of Woodstock, Earl of *see* Gloucester, Duke of
Buironfosse, 256
Bullock, William, 347
Burgundy: in Triple Alliance against England, 388–9; contacts with Lancastrians, 415, 421; Yorkists favour, 437, 445; alliances with Edward IV, 445–6, 458; and Louis XI of France, 445; Edward IV flees to, 455; truce with Louis XI, 458; Louis XI invades, 466
Burgundy, Charles the Bold (of Charolais), Duke of, 445–6, 452, 455, 458–9, 466
Burgundy, John the Fearless, Duke of, 368, 372–3, 459
Burgundy, Margaret of Flanders, Duchess of (wife of Philip), 292
Burgundy, Margaret of York, Duchess of (wife of Charles), 445
Burgundy, Philip II, Duke of, 292, 301–2
Burgundy, Philip the Good, Duke of, 374–5, 388–9, 421, 440; death, 445
Burnell, Robert, Bishop of Bath and Wells, 97
Butler, Lady Eleanor, 472–3

Cade, Jack, 396–7

Caen, 242, 268

Caerlaverock Castle, 133, 144

Calais: siege and fall (1346–7), 242–3, 272–5;
John of Gaunt commands force at, 302;
blockaded by Burgundians, 389; holds out
against Charles VII, 398; Warwick
commands, 413, 421, 424; Somerset
attempts to capture from Warwick, 427;
Warwick warned away from, 452; Edward
IV sends troops to, 458

Cambrai, 256, 258

Cambridge, Anne, Countess of, 395

Cambridge, Edmund of Langley, Earl of see
York, 1st Duke of

Cambridge, Richard, Earl of, 395

Camden, William, 9

Canterbury, archbishopric, 6

Canterbury, Archbishops of see Boniface;
Bourchier, Thomas; Courtenay, William;
Kemp, John; Langton, Stephen; Morton,
John; Stratford, John de

Canterbury, Treaty of (1189), 116

Cape, Edmund, 454

Capgrave, John, 203

Carlisle: castle built, 8; David I invests, 50;
Ranulf surrenders to David I, 66; Scots
attack (1296), 122; Henry Percy II's
headquarters in, 124, 128, 133; Edward III
possesses castle, 231; Fife attacks, 337;
Queen Margaret signs over to Scots, 437;
Richard (Gloucester) reinforces, 467

Carlisle, Sir Andrew Carlisle, Earl of see Harclay,
Sir Andrew

Carpenter, D.A., 109

Carre, Thomas, 245

Carrick earldom, 197, 219

Carrick, Alexander Bruce, Earl of, 215, 218

Carrick, Marjorie, Countess of, 114

Cartae Baronum , 69, 74

Cartington, John, 464

Castile and Leon: John of Gaunt claims throne
of, 303

Castilians: defeated in Winchelsea sea battle
(1350), 276

Castillon, battle of (1453), 398

Casus regis , 76, 78–9

Caterall, John, 403

Caterall, Lawrence, 403

Catesby, William, 472

Catherine de Valois, Queen of Henry V, 368,
374, 376

Catterton, Thomas, 306

Cecily, Princess (Edward IV's daughter), 458,
465–6, 469

Chamber, John, 485

Charles II (the Bad), King of Navarre, 281, 310

Charles IV, King of France, 183–4, 186, 254–5

Charles V, King of France (earlier Dauphin): and
ransom for John II, 286; bribes Scots, 287;
abrogates Treaty of Brétigny, 288;

accession, 291; and marriage of Margaret of
Flanders to Philip of Burgundy, 292;
considers Edward III of England a vassal,
300–1; wars with Edward III, 301–2, 304–5

Charles VI, King of France: alliance with Robert
II of Scotland, 333; and death of John of
Gaunt, 344; Northumberland swears
allegiance to, 363; sends force to aid
Glendower, 363; death, 368, 377; Duke of
Burgundy and, 372

Charles VII, King of France (earlier Dauphin):
and death of John of Burgundy, 373; Henry
V disinherits, 375; accession, 377; receives
Scottish reinforcements, 379; crowned,
382; Scots bodyguard, 383; truce with Philip
of Burgundy, 388–9; captures Paris, 389;
appearance, 391; successes against English,
396, 398–9; fails to capitalise on successes,
405; Lancastrians favour, 421

Charles VIII, King of France, 478, 483

Charles the Simple, King of the West Franks, 21

Charny, Sir Geoffroi de, 251

Chateaugiron, Treaty of 1472), 458

Chatham, William Pitt, 1st Earl of, 79

Chaucer, Geoffrey, 11, 252, 298–300, 303

Chaucer, Philippa (Geoffrey's wife), 303

Cheshire: palatine earldom established, 30; under
Henry I, 47–8; rising against proposed
renunciation of Aquitaine, 339; loyalty to
Richard II, 343, 346

Chester, earldom of, 96

Chester, Hugh, Earl of see Hugh d'Avranches

Chester, Lucy, Countess of (Ranulf's wife), 47

Chester, Maud, Countess of (Richard's wife), 47

Chester, Ranulf le Meschin, Earl of, 47–8

Chester, Ranulf II, Earl of, 48, 50, 62–6, 69

Chester, Ranulf III de Blundeville, Earl of, 88, 96

Chester, Richard d'Avranches, Earl of, 47

chivalry, 55

Chronicle of Dover , 107

Chronicle of London , 359

Church: Wycliff challenges doctrines, 312–13

Clare family, 47

Clare, Alice de (née fitz Gilbert), 47

Clare, Gilbert de (son of Richard and Alice) see
Hertford, Earl of

Clare, Gilbert IV de, 96

Clare, Richard fitz Gilbert II de, 47

Clare, Robert de, Earl, 84

Clare, William de, 101

Clarence, George, Duke of, 443, 447–9, 452–3,
456, 459, 462; drowned in malmsey wine,
463

Clarence, Isabel, Duchess of (née Neville), 447,
449, 451, 462

Clarence, Lionel of Antwerp, Duke of, 298–9,
395

Clarence, Thomas, Duke of, 373, 376

Clavering, Sir John, 207

Clement VI, Pope, 246

Clementia, Duchess of Lower Lorraine, 72

Clere, Edmund, 409
Clifford, Isabella de Vipont, 124
Clifford, John ('Butcher'), 13th Baron (and 9th
     Baron Westmorland), 403, 416, 420, 427–8;
     killed, 431
Clifford, John de, 364
Clifford, Robert, 5th Baron (and 1st Baron of
     Westmorland): background, 124; relations
     with 1st Lord Percy, 124–5, 149, 152;
     campaigns against Scots, 125–7, 135, 145;
     ennobled, 131; appearance, 133; pursues
     Bruce, 141, 146; witnesses Edward I's last
     command, 143; made marshal of England,
     146; opposes Gaveston, 148, 159, 161–2;
     border duties, 158, 208; and Gaveston's
     treasure, 159, 163; killed at Bannockburn,
     164–5
Clifford, Roger, 1st Baron, 175–6, 235
Clifford, Roger, 5th Baron, 95, 97, 103–4, 107
Clifford, Thomas, 6th Baron, 326, 328, 345
Clifford, Thomas, 8th Baron, 409–14, 416
Clifford, Sir William, 360
Clifton, Sir Constantine, 296
Clinton, John, 5th Baron, 423
Cobbett, William, 9–10, 70
Cockermouth, 331
Cockodge, near Thirsk, Yorkshire, 485, 487
Coldingham Priory, 278
Colville, Sir Thomas, 294
common law: development of, 90–1
Commoners and Commons: recognised under
     Edward II, 178; demand financial and
     administrative reforms, 239; increasing
     power under Edward III, 240–1; criticise
     John of Gaunt, 307–8; cause Latimer's fall,
     310; support Wycliffe, 313; complain over
     Richard II's spending, 340; decline to
     accept York as king, 426
Commynes, Philippe de, 459
Comyn, Alexander see Buchan, Earl of
Comyn, John, Lord of Badenoch, 114, 134–5,
     138, 202, 332, 405
Constance of Brittany, 76
Constantinople, 40–1
Constitutio Domus Regis, 316
'Contrariants' (rebels), 173, 176, 178–9, 186–8
Conwy Castle, north Wales, 347, 356
Conyers, Sir William see Robin of Redesdale
Copsig, Earl of Northumberland, 24
Coquetdale, 235
Corbeil, Treaty of (1326), 196, 231
Corbridge manor, 207, 211
Cornborough, William, 82
Cornwall, John, Earl of, 228
Cospatric of Bamburgh, Earl of Northumbria
     (later of Dunbar), 23, 25–30
Coupland, John, 245–6, 292
Courtenay, William, Bishop of London (later
     Archbishop of Canterbury), 308, 317, 319
Coventry, 174–5, 449
Cowton Moor see Standard, battle of the

Crabb, John, 193, 214, 216, 219, 235
Crawford, David Lindsay, 5th Earl of, 465
Crécy, battle of (1346), 242, 266, 269–72
Cressingham, Hugh, 124–7
Cromwell, Ralph, 4th Baron, 403, 407–8
Crusade, First (1096–9), 37–43
Culblean, battle of (1335), 232–3, 237, 254
Cumbria: strategic importance, 7; Henry I cedes
     to David I, 48, 50; Scots dispute rights to,
     52, 54, 65, 111
Cumin, William, 58
Cupar Castle, 230
Curwen, Christopher, 463

Dacre, Hugh, 4th Baron, 327–8
Dacre, Humphrey, 2nd Baron, 436, 438, 465
Daliegh, Sir James de, 139
Damory, Roger, 167, 169–70
Danelaw, 19–20
Danes, 19–21, 25–6, 28
Dante Alighieri: Inferno, 110
David I, King of Scots, 48, 50–4, 56–7, 61–2,
     64–6, 69, 279; death, 69
David II (Bruce), King of Scotland: and
     succession, 194, 199–200, 203; marriage to
     Joan, 195–6; granted Carrick, 197; and
     claims of Disinherited, 203; crowned, 207;
     Mar serves, 212; deposed by Edward
     Balliol, 214, 254; in Dumbarton, 222;
     Moray invites to France, 222; Strathbogie
     swears allegiance to, 227; in France, 233,
     237, 254; returns to Scotland, 237, 240;
     campaign against English (1346), 241–3;
     character and qualities, 242; captured at
     Neville's Cross and imprisoned, 244–6, 248,
     273; release, 248–9; ransom and succession
     terms, 249–50, 277–80, 290–1, 298, 333,
     336; returned to Tower of London, 249;
     Philip VI requests to invade North, 268;
     refuses to recognise Edward III as king of
     Scotland, 278, 288–9; return to Scotland,
     284–5; agitates against Edward III, 287;
     Henry Percy V appointed chief
     plenipotentiary to, 287–8; and Robert
     Stewart, 287; Scots earls rise against, 288–9;
     accepts Edward III as king of Scotland,
     289–90; marriage to Margaret Logie, 289;
     profligacy, 289–90; personal relations with
     Edward III, 290; death, 292; financial
     security, 292
David, Earl (grandson of David I of Scotland),
     113
Deddington, Oxfordshire, 159, 161
Deira, 8
de la Mare family, 295
de la Mare, Sir Peter, 307–11, 314–15, 320, 326
de la Mare, Thomas, Prior of Tynemouth, 294–5
Denmark, 287
Denum, William, 194
Derby, Henry, 1st Earl of see Lancaster, Henry,
     Duke of

Despenser, Edward, 305
Despenser, Hugh, the elder, Earl of Winchester, 99, 148–9, 162–3, 173–5, 178, 184–8, 343
Despenser, Sir Hugh, the younger, 167, 169, 172–5, 178, 184–9, 200
Devon, Humphrey Stafford, 1st Earl of, 448–9
Devon, Thomas Courtenay, 6th Earl of, 423, 427, 433
Disinherited, the, 195–6, 202–4, 212, 214–15, 223–5, 230, 254
Domesday Survey, 31, 37, 47, 70
Donald Bane, King of Scots, 29
Doncaster, 409
Doncaster Petition (1321), 174
Dorset, Thomas Grey, 1st Marquess of, 472, 475, 478
Dorylaeum, battle of (1097), 41
Douglas family: as Percys' enemies, 170, 223, 328, 336; implacability, 250; granted lordship of Dunbar, 351; James II's feud with, 414
Douglas, Archibald, 4th Earl of (son of 'the Grim'), 352, 359, 362, 367–70, 372, 376, 379, 381
Douglas, Sir Archibald, 4th Earl of, 213, 215–18, 237, 239
Douglas, Archibald, 5th Earl of, 381
Douglas, Archibald ('the Grim'; illegitimate son of Sir James), 218, 338, 352
Douglas, Hugh, Lord of ('the Dull'), 218
Douglas, James, 9th Earl of, 405, 414, 437–8, 440, 466, 469
Douglas, Sir James ('the Good'): leads cross-border raids, 170–2, 178–80, 193, 196; as Percys' enemy, 170, 175; protects Prince David, 194; witnesses Percy's grants, 197; killed in Spain, 213–14; Bruce bestows land on, 333, 337
Douglas, Sir James, the Younger, 333, 362
Douglas of Liddesdale, Sir William, Earl of Atholl ('Knight of Liddesdale'), 222, 230, 232–8, 242–5, 248–9, 254
Douglas, William, 8th Earl of, 400, 405
Douglas, Sir William, 125
Douglas, William, the Younger, 1st Earl of, 187–8, 237, 249–50, 280, 283, 326–30, 333, 335–7; killed at Otterburn, 338
Doyle, Sir Arthur Conan, 3
Dugdale, Sir William: Baronage of England, 17, 30
Dumbarton, 222
Dunbar, 9th Earl of, 122, 124
Dunbar, 326; battle of (1296), 122–3; siege of (1338), 235–6, 239; 3rd Earl of Northumberland razes, 400
Dunbar, George see March, George Dunbar, 9th Earl of, 392
Dunbar, Patrick (son of James, Earl of March), 387–8, 406
Duncan II, King of Scotland, 28, 116
Dundarg, 227
Dunstable, 240

Dunstanburgh Castle, Northumberland, 175, 328, 435–6, 439
Dupplin Moor, battle of (1332), 212–13, 217, 245
Durham: Treaty of (1139), 61–2, 64; and battle of Neville's Cross, 243–4, 246
Dymoke, Sir John, Lord of Scrivelsby, 323, 325
Dymoke, Sir Thomas, 349

Eadgyth, Queen of Henry I see Matilda
Edgar the Ætheling, 25–6, 28–9
Edgar, King, 8
Edgar, King of Scotland, 29, 51, 116
Edgecote, battle of (1469), 449
Edinburgh: Castle razed by Bruce, 161; Edward III refortifies, 231; William Douglas captures, 237; Richard (Gloucester) reaches, 469
Edinburgh, Treaty of (1328) see Northampton, Treaty of
Edmund, King of Wessex, 7
Edward I, King: Scottish wars and conquests, 11, 111, 121–4, 132, 134–6, 141; birth, 94; relations with Sir Henry Percy III, 95, 103, 110, 142; favours Lusignan party, 97–8, 100, 103; upbringing and marriage, 97; and baronial demands (Provisions of Oxford), 99, 104; pact with Gloucester, 101–3; and Gascon territories, 102–3; swears to support Montfort, 102, 104; defies Council authority, 103; in battle of Lewes, 106–7; escapes from Hereford, 108; at battle of Evesham, 109; annexes Wales, 113; intervenes in Scottish succession question, 114–18; demands homage of Scottish king, 117–18, 120; summons and rebukes John Balliol, 120; wars in France, 124; generalship, 125, 129; and Wallace's rising, 125–6, 128–9; Falkirk victory, 130; awards baronies and knighthoods, 131; and beginnings of Parliament, 131–2; employs siege catapults, 136; death and succession, 137, 141, 143–4; campaign against Bruce, 138–9; punishment for Scottish women, 140; reproaches commanders in Scotland, 141; courtiers, 143–4; attitude to son Edward, 144–6; expels Gaveston, 144–5; character and reign, 199
Edward II, King (Edward of Caernarvon), 115, 120; marriage to Maid of Norway proposed, 115, 120; at Bannockburn, 132; succeeds to throne, 137, 144, 146; and Piers Gaveston, 144–51, 157, 183; character and behaviour, 145–6; marriage to Isabella, 145; Scottish policy, 146–7; opposition to, 147–52, 158–9, 161–3; coronation, 148; agrees to election of Lords Ordainers, 156; accepts 41 Ordinances, 157, 162–4; antagonism to Henry Percy III, 158, 161; and Gaveston's death, 161; defends Gaveston after death, 162–5, 172; leaves for France, 163; forward

policy in Scotland and Bannockburn defeat, 164–5; appoints trustees for Henry Percy IV during minority, 167; hostility to Lancaster, 169–70; besieges Berwick, 171; truce with Bruce, 171–2, 178; Pope John XXII appeals to for peace with Scots, 172; Welsh rebellion against, 172–4; exiles Despensers, 173; claims sole right to summon Parliament, 174; marches against Lancaster, 174–5; condemns defeated Lancaster, 176–7; ennobles Harclay, 177–8; Scottish campaign (1322), 178–9; escapes from Bruce in Yorkshire (1322), 180–1; rebukes Henry Percy IV, 180; peace treaty with Bruce (1323), 182; dispute with Charles IV of France, 183–4; non-recognition of Bruce's kingship, 183; basket-weaving, 185, 425; Isabella conspires against, 185–6; Mortimer's assassination plot against, 186; flight to Wales and capture, 187–8; deposed, violated and killed, 190, 198, 348; Richard II idolises, 343

Edward III, King: clarifies Magna Carta article, 88; born, 162; pays compensation for Despenser's piracy, 173; negotiates peace treaty with France as Prince of Wales, 184; marriage to Philippa, 186, 195; and deposing of father, 189; proclaimed and crowned, 190; campaign against Bruce, 192–3; makes peace with Scots (1328), 194–6; qualities and behaviour, 198–9; opposition to Mortimer, 201; and claims of Disinherited, 203–4; pays homage to French King Philip VI, 206, 254; relations with Edward Balliol, 214–15, 221–2, 236; campaigns and conquests against Scots rebels, 215–19, 227–31, 281, 288–9; and disputes over Annandale, 220; Edward Balliol cedes territories to, 222–9; and costs of Scottish activities, 234; wars in France, 235–8, 239, 241–2, 256–61, 263–74, 280–2, 285–6, 301–2, 304–5; debts, 237, 258; acts against Archbishop Stratford, 238–9; administrative reforms, 239–41; revokes 1341 Statute, 240; revenues, 241; and ransom and succession terms for David II, 248–9, 278, 288–91; claims French throne, 255, 285, 302–3; library, 255; in Brittany, 261–2; invades and campaigns in Normandy (1346), 265, 268–9; household, 267–8; Crécy victory, 270–2; besieges and takes Calais, 272–5; stabilises prices and wages after Black Death, 275–6; truce with Philip VI (1347–8), 275; peace treaty with John II of France (1354), 279–80; reacts to John II's incitement of Scots, 280; Edward Balliol surrenders crown to, 281, 298; and Treaties of London for release and ransom of John II, 285–6; surrenders claim to French throne, 288; claims on Scottish throne, 289–91; Charles V demands vassalage of,

300–1; decline and succession, 300, 317; war with Charles V, 301–2, 304; peace policy, 306; rebukes John of Gaunt for failure in France, 306; favours Richard as successor, 314; and Londoners' anger against John of Gaunt, 320; death and funeral, 321–2; grants Jedburgh to Percys, 336

Edward IV, King (*earlier* Earl of March): and Redesdalers' rebellion, 348; in Wars of Roses, 423–4, 442; usurps Crown, 428–30; appearance and character, 430; Towton victory, 431–2, 434; crowned, 434; attempted control of north, 436, 438–41; avoids involvement in Scotland, 437; truce with Louis XI of France, 440; truces with Scots, 442, 444, 461; 4th Earl of Northumberland swears fealty to, 443; marriage to Elizabeth Woodville, 444, 447; womanising and mistresses, 444, 468; alliances with Burgundy and Brittany, 445–6, 458; Warwick rebels against, 448–9, 451, 453–5; flees to Burgundy, 455; return to England and self-proclamation as king, 455–7; defeats rebels, 457; campaign in France (1475), 458–9; has Henry VI killed, 458; meets Louis XI at Picquigny, 459–60; and Scottish threat and expedition, 466–7, 469–70; finances, 468; French policy collapses, 469; death, 470

Edward V, King: birth, 447; accession, 471–2; sent to Tower, 472; Richard III decides to usurp, 473–4; death in Tower, 475; rebellions in support of, 475

Edward VI, King, 318

Edward the Confessor, King of the English, 11, 24, 85

Edward the Elder, King of Wessex, 19

Edward, Prince of Wales (the Black Prince): at Crécy, 270–1; raids Artois, 275; in Aquitaine, 281; campaigns in France, 282–4, 286; Nájera victory, 291; purchases jewels from John de la Mare, 295; in line of succession, 300; spurns Charles V's demand for English homage, 301; generalship, 302; health decline, 304, 309; supports reforms, 309; death, 311; criticises Archbishop of Canterbury, 313

Edward, Prince of Wales (Henry VI's son): return to England and death at Tewkesbury, 4; born, 397, 399, 406; father welcomes, 410; in mother's care, 417; excluded from succession, 426; flees Edward IV to north, 431; escapes to Scotland, 433–4; settles in France, 440; betrothal to Warwick's daughter Anne, 453; aspires to English throne, 455

Edward, Prince (Black Prince's son): birth and death, 299–300

Egremont, Cumberland, 315, 331

Egremont, Sir John, 485–6

Egremont, Thomas Percy, 1st Baron (2nd Earl of Northumberland's son), 392–3, 401–4, 406–9, 415–16, 418, 420–5, 452, 485

Eleanor of Aquitaine, Queen of Henry II (*earlier* wife of Louis VII of France), 67, 102, 104, 255

Eleanor of Castile, Queen of Edward I, 97

Eleanor of Provence, Queen of Henry III, 94, 96

Elizabeth, Queen of Edward IV (*née* Woodville): marriage, 444, 447, 455, 468; seeks sanctuary after husband's death, 471; Richard III accuses of murder threat, 472; legitimacy of sons questioned, 473

Elizabeth of York, Queen of Henry VII (Edward IV's daughter), 466, 468, 478, 483

Ellis, Henry Havelock, 3

Elmham, Sir William, 310

Emich of Liesingen, 39

Epworth, Robert, 260

Eric II, King of Norway, 113, 115

Erskine, Sir Robert, 247

Eugenius III, Pope, 67

Eustace, Prince, 67, 69

Evesham, battle of (1265), 108–9

Exeter, Anne, Duchess of (wife of 3rd Duke), 406

Exeter, Henry Holland, 3rd Duke of, 395, 406–10, 415, 418, 420, 423, 427, 433–4, 436, 457

Exeter, John Holland, 1st Duke of (*earlier* 1st Earl of Huntingdon), 340–2, 347, 349, 385–9, 394–5, 406

Exeter, John Holland, 2nd Duke of (*earlier* 2nd Earl of Huntingdon), 395, 406

Exeter, Thomas Beaufort, 1st Duke of, 373, 378, 382

Falaise, Treaty of (1174), 116

Falkirk, battle of (1298), 129–30, 144

Falkirk Roll of Arms, 130

Felton, Sir John, 167

Felton, Robert de, 157, 167

Fen, Hugh atte, 362–3

Ferrers, Henry, 202–3, 224, 230

Ferrers, Margaret (*née* Percy; *then* Umfraville; Henry IV's daughter), 224

Ferrers, Robert III de, 96

Ferrybridge, battle of (1461), 431

feudalism, 31–4, 46, 53, 68, 87, 193, 210–11

Fife, Duncan, 8th Earl of, 213, 230, 232, 234, 245

Fife, Murdoch Stewart, Earl of *see* Albany, 2nd Duke of

Fishburn, Henry, 197

FitzAlan, Brian, 128

fitz Duncan, Alice (*earlier* de Rumilly), 64–5

fitz Duncan, William, 64–5, 69

FitzGeoffrey, John, 100

Fitzhugh, Richard, 5th Baron, 482

FitzWalter, Eleanor, Lady, 315

fitz Walter, Robert, 84–5

FitzWalter, Walter, 3rd Baron, 315, 319

Flanders: and Edward III's French wars, 256–8, 263–4, 273–4, 286; revolts against Philip of Burgundy, 389

Fleming, Sir David, 362, 367

Flodden, battle of (1513), 487

food and diet, 252–3

Fordun, John, 250

Formigny, battle of (1450), 396

Forty-one Ordinances, 157, 162–4, 169, 188; annulled, 178

France: dispute with England over Aquitaine/Gascony, 102, 120, 253–4, 269, 288, 301, 339; and 'Auld Alliance' with Scotland, 121, 222, 233, 254, 405, 421, 437; treaties with Scots: (1295), 121; (1326), 196, 231, 254; peace treaty with England (1303), 134; Edward II's relations with, 184; and Edward III's suppression of Scotland, 231; Edward III's wars in, 235–7, 241–2, 256–61, 263–74, 280–6, 301–2, 304–5; peace talks with England collapse (1344), 241; seen as England's enemy, 252; cross-Channel raids on England, 254–5; Edward III claims throne of, 255, 288; Crécy defeat, 270–2; and Treaties of London (1358), 285–6; supports Scots against Richard II, 334–5; threatens invasion of England (1388), 335; truce with England (1389), 338; Richard negotiates permanent peace with, 339, 341; aids Glendower, 363; Henry V campaigns in, 370, 372–3; Henry V claims throne of, 374–5; French volunteers fight in, 383; in Triple Alliance against England, 388–9; truce with England (1463), 440; treaty with England (1475), 459–60, 468

Franco, Archbishop of Rouen, 21

Fraser, Alexander, 213

Fraser, George MacDonald, 212, 489

Fraser, Simon, 134–5, 139

Fraser, William, Bishop of St Andrews, 114, 116

Frederick II, Holy Roman Emperor, 348

Frescobaldi (bankers), 155

Froissart, Jean, 192, 261, 276, 283, 299, 311, 321, 334–5, 344

Galclint Castle, Yorkshire, 60

Galloway, 114, 124, 138, 141, 146–7, 163, 222

Gant, Alice de (*née* de Montfort), 45

Gant, Gilbert de, 45, 46

Gant, Gilbert II de, Earl of Lincoln, 45, 47, 59–60, 63, 66–7, 69

Gant, Walter de, 56

Garencières, Sire de, 280, 281

Garter, Order of the: created by Edward III, 199, 290

Gascony *see* Aquitaine

Gascougne, Sir William, 485

Gaunt, John of *see* Lancaster, John of Gaunt, Duke of

Gaveston, Piers, Earl of Cornwall: as object of antagonism, 144–52, 155, 156–8, 335;

captured and executed, 159–61, 163; treasure, 159, 162–3; Edward defends after death, 162–4, 172
Geoffrey of Monmouth: *History of the Kings of Britain*, 11
Gesta Francorum, 41
Gesta Stephani, 10, 64
Giles of Rome: *De Regimine Principum* (*The Guidance of Princes*), 374, 464
Gillingham, John, 423
Glanvill, Ranulf, 76, 78
Glendower, Owen, 352, 355–8, 361–3, 366, 370
Gloucester, Eleanor, Duchess of, 394
Gloucester, Gilbert de Clare, 8th Earl of, 108
Gloucester, Gilbert de Clare, 9th Earl of, 147, 150, 156–60, 162, 165, 169
Gloucester, Hugh d'Audley, 1st Earl of, 169–70, 201, 239
Gloucester, Humphrey, Duke of, 376–9, 382, 385–7, 389, 391–2, 394–5, 400
Gloucester, Richard de Clare IV, 7th Earl of (and 6th Earl of Hertford), 97–8, 100–7
Gloucester, Richard, Duke of *see* Richard III, King
Gloucester, Robert, Earl of, 61–4, 69–70
Gloucester, Sir Thomas Despenser, Earl of, 342
Gloucester, Thomas of Woodstock, Duke of (*earlier* Earl of Buckingham), 322, 325, 335, 340, 342–3, 349, 360
Godfrey 'Barbatus' VII, Duke of Lower Lorraine, 72–3
Godfrey de Bouillon, Duke (*later* King of Jerusalem), 39, 43
'Good Parliament' (1376), 307, 310–11
Goodman, Anthony, 427
Goodman, John, 298, 303
Graham, Robert, 390
Gray, Andrew, 2nd Baron, 469
'Great Cause' (Scottish succession), 117–18, 194
Great Councils, 90–1, 93, 103
Greenfield, William, Archbishop of York, 205
Gregory IX, Pope, 116
Gregory XI, Pope, 312
Gregory, William, 421
Grelley, Robert, 84
Grey, Sir Edmund, 4th Baron Grey of Ruthin (*later* 1st Earl of Kent), 406, 424–5
Grey, Katherine, Lady (*née* Percy), 406
Grey, Sir Ralph, 392, 438–9, 441–2, 474
Grey, Reginald, 3rd Baron Grey of Ruthin, 355–6
Grey, Richard, 1st Baron Grey of Powis, 423
Grey, Lord Richard (d.1483), 471, 474
Greystoke, Ralph, 5th Baron, 427, 465
Greystoke, Sir William, 277, 326, 328
Griffiths, Ralph, 379
Grosseteste, Robert, Bishop of Lincoln, 80
Gueldres, Duke of, 6
Guiscard, Robert, 39
Guthrum, 19–20

Hainault, 186; troops in England, 192–3

Hainault, William II, Count of, 186
Hainault, William III, Earl of, 256
Haliburton, Sir William, 374
Halidon Hill, battle of (1333), 217–18, 245
Hall, Edward, 461
Hambledon, Hampshire, 37, 74
Harclay, Sir Andrew, Earl of Carlisle, 175–7, 179, 181–2, 188, 196
Hardyng, John, 348, 374, 389, 435
Harfleur, 302
Harington, Sir Thomas, 422
Harlech, 366, 436, 446
Harold Hardrada, King of Norway, 24
Harold, King of the English, 24, 31
Hastings, William, 1st Baron, 438, 456, 459, 471–2, 474–5
Hatfield, Thomas, Bishop of Durham, 245
Healaugh, Yorkshire, 402
Hedgeley Moor, battle of (1464), 441, 444
Henry I, King, 29, 37, 44, 46, 48–51, 55, 59, 72, 311
Henry II (Plantagenet), King: and coalition against Stephen, 66; as Duke of Normandy, 67; marriage to Eleanor, 67, 102; crowned, 69; reign, 71; confirms d'Aubigny's gift of Arundel, 73; succession to, 76; and William the Lion of Scotland, 116; bans usury, 154; and Aquitaine, 255
Henry III, King: intervenes in Percy dispute, 78; succession and coronation, 89; confirms revised Magna Carta, 90; and barons, 91–2, 103–4; son and heir born, 94; court factions, 95–9; 'personal rule', 96–7; offered throne of Sicily, 98–9; and baronial demands for reform (Provisions of Oxford), 99–101, 105; and French possessions, 102, 184; Montfort opposes, 102; and Montfort rebellion, 106; defeated at battle of Lewes, 107; present at battle of Evesham, 108–9; and status of Scotland, 117; and administration of Border, 208
Henry IV, King (Bolingbroke; *formerly* Earl of Derby; *then* Duke of Hereford): wins support, 3; and succession, 300, 343–4; usurps throne, 311, 348–50; in Appellants' charge of treason against Richard II's favourites, 335; made Duke of Hereford, 341; Norfolk confides plot allegations to, 342; Norfolk proposes trial by combat with, 343; Richard II exiles, 344; escapes to England with followers, 345–6; rebellion against Richard II, 346–7; assumes royal prerogatives, 347; coronation, 348; claims legitimacy as king, 350; invades Scotland, 350–1; campaigns in Wales, 352, 355–6; orders Northumberland's Scots prisoners to London, 353–4; financial embarrassment, 354; grants lands to Northumberland, 355; Northumberland rebels against, 357–8, 361–2; Shrewsbury victory, 359, 361; treatment of Northumberland after

Shrewsbury, 360; Wales rebels against, 361–3; and death of Northumberland, 365; death, 367–8; seeks truce with Scotland, 367

Henry V, King (*earlier* Prince): and rights to Aquitaine, 288; campaigns in Wales, 357, 366; wounded at Shrewsbury, 359; accession, 368; character and rule, 368; policy on France, 368; seeks truce with Scotland, 368, 370; reinstates Henry Percy as Earl of Northumberland, 369–71; campaigns in France, 370, 372–4, 376; claim to French throne, 374–5; marriage, 375; death, 377, 379

Henry VI, King: born, 376; regency and council of nobles for, 378–9, 382; revenues, 385, 396; Charles VII of France addresses, 388; achieves full powers on 16th birthday, 391; character and appearance, 391; succession to, 395, 426; marriage, 396; nervous collapses and recoveries, 398–9, 409–10, 415, 417; and wars with Scots, 401; Egremont ignores summons, 402; warns Northumberland and Salisbury against disorder, 404; wounded and surrenders at first battle of St Albans, 411–13; York rebels against, 411; granted Threave Castle, 414; Queen Margaret influences, 417–19; at 'Loveday' in great council (1458), 420; offers Wressel Castle to Egremont, 420; aloofness from council, 422; offers pardon to Yorkists, 423; captured at Northampton, 425–6; taken by Lancastrians at St Albans (1461), 429; flees Edward IV to north, 431; escapes to Scotland after Towton, 433–4; returns from France, 438; continuing support for, 439, 441; in Scotland, 440; isolated in Bamburgh Castle, 441; as refugee, 442, 452; captured and confined in London, 452–3; released and reinstated on throne, 455; killed in Tower, 457–8, 475

Henry VII (Tudor), King: visits York, 10; and financing of border, 211; birth, 397, 475, 477; character, 477–8; in Brittany and France, 478; marriage to Elizabeth, 478, 483; as prospective king, 478–9; lands in Wales and marches against Richard, 479; defeats Richard at Bosworth, 480–2; treatment of Northumberland after Bosworth, 482–3; accession and rule, 483–4, 487–8; suborns North to London control, 487; on Scotland, 489

Henry VIII, King, 487–8

Henry of Almain, 95, 97, 99, 103–6, 110

Henry of Blois, Bishop of Winchester, 49

Henry of Grosmont *see* Lancaster, Henry of Grosmont, 1st Duke of

Henry of Huntingdon, 63

Henry, Prince of Scotland, Earl of Northumberland (David I's son), 1, 50, 53–4, 57–8, 61–2, 64, 66; death, 69

Henry II of Trastamera, King of Castile, 291, 303

Herbert family, 446, 450

Herbert, Sir William, Baron *see* Pembroke, 1st Earl of

Hereford, Humphrey de Bohun IV, Earl of, 96, 99, 102, 107

Hereford, Humphrey de Bohun, 3rd Earl of: provides forces against Scots, 128, 164; military command, 129; advises Edward I, 132; opposes Gaveston, 148, 150–1, 162; in Edward II's Lords Ordainers, 156; and 41 Ordinances, 157; opposes Edward II, 162, 174; and Welsh rebellion, 172; killed at battle of Boroughbridge, 175–6; granted Lordship of Annandale, 219

Hereward the Wake, 28

Hermit of Warkworth, The (ballad), 369

Hertford, 6th Earl of *see* Gloucester, Richard de Clare, 7th Earl of

Hertford, Edward Seymour, 1st Earl of, 488

Hertford, Gilbert de Clare, Earl of, 47, 63

Heton, Alan de, 284

Heton, Aleyn, 206

Hewerth Moor, 403

Higden, Ranulf, 145

'Historie of the Arrivall of Edward IV', 455–7

Holinshed, Raphael, 22

Holland, Henry (2nd Duke of Exeter's son) *see* Exeter, 3rd Duke of

Holland, Sir Thomas, 340

Hollister, C.W., 70

Holy Island, 13, 19

Homildon (Humbledon) Hill *see* Milfield, battle of

Honorius III, Pope, 89

Hotham, Sir John, 329

Hotspur *see* Percy, Sir Henry ('Hotspur')

Howard, Howard, John, 1st Baron *see* Norfolk, 1st Duke of

Howard, Sir John, 438

Hubert de Burgh, 77

Hugh d'Avranches, Earl of Chester, 22, 30–3, 47

Hugh de Lusignan, Lord of Valence, 95

Hugh fitz Baldric, 32

Hume, David, 404

Hundred Years War: involves Scots, 2; and French, 252; outbreak, 253–4; causes, 286; resumes (1368–9), 300; and dispute of English claims in France, 340; final campaigns and conclusion, 398–9, 405

Hungerford, Robert, 3rd Baron, 441–2

Hunmanby, Yorkshire, 45–6, 60, 66

Huntingdon, John Holland, 1st Earl of *see* Exeter, 1st Duke of

Huntingdon, John Holland, 2nd Earl of *see* Exeter, 2nd Duke of

Ilbert de Lacy, 35

Ilderton, John, 464

Innocent III, Pope, 85–6, 88, 174

Innocent IV, Pope, 117, 348

Ireland: Gaveston appointed lieutenant in, 149; Richard II in, 346

Ireland, John, 466

Irvine, Scotland, 125–6

Isabel of Lorraine, 460

Isabella of France, Queen of Edward II: relations with Mortimer, 16, 185–6; marriage to Edward, 145; and Edward's preference for Gaveston, 148, 183; and birth of son (Edward III), 162; taken to Nottingham, 162; Badlesmere refuses entry to Leeds Castle, 173; at Rievaulx, 180; mission to brother Charles IV, 184; conspires against husband and invades England, 185–8; qualities, 185–6; retirement allowance, 191; administration and rule, 192, 200; accompanies Joan to marriage in Berwick, 195; and Treaty of Northampton, 196, 200; and Edward III's reign, 200; unpopularity, 201; arrest and retirement, 202; intervenes over Aquitaine, 254; and Edward III's French kinship, 255

Isabella of France, second Queen of Richard II, 340

James I, King of Scotland (earlier Prince): birth, 362; in English custody, 363–4, 367–8, 370, 372, 375–6; ransom and release, 379–80; return to Scotland and rule, 380–1, 383; Northumberland's mission to, 383–4; relations with France, 383, 388; extends truce with England, 384; unpopularity, 388, 390; failed attack on Roxburgh Castle, 389; assassinated, 390

James II, King of Scotland: crowned, 390; and civil war in Scotland, 405, 414; marches on Berwick, 414; qualities, 414; antagonism towards England, 415, 418–19; invades Northumberland, 419, 425; and French alliance, 421; death, 425

James III, King of Scotland: minority, 437; favours Lancastrian cause, 439; and Scottish unrest, 465–6; threatens invasion of England, 466–7; seeks French help, 468; seized by nobles, 469

James IV, King of Scotland, 458, 465–6, 489

James VI, King of Scotland (James I of England), 208, 490

James, King of Jerusalem, 340

Jassaults, 419

Jean le Bel, 191–2, 199

Jedburgh, 222–3, 228, 231, 239, 250, 333, 336

Jerusalem: captured by crusaders, 43

Jews: moneylending, 80–2; Simon de Montfort attempts to expel from Leicester, 96; revenues from, 104; expelled (1290), 132

Joan of Arc see Arc, Joan of

Joan of Kent (wife of the Black Prince), 264, 295, 299, 320, 340

Joan, Queen of David II of Scotland ('Countess Makepees'), 194–6, 214, 289

Joan, Queen of James I of Scotland, 380, 390

John, King: in line of succession, 76, 79; crowned, 77; and Briwerre, 79–80; loses French possessions, 80, 184; finances, 81–2; barons rebel against, 83–6, 89, 92; and Magna Carta, 86–8; visits to North, 86–7; death, 89; murders nephew Arthur of Brittany, 311

John II, King of France, 279–88, 291

John XXII, Pope, 171–2, 201

John Balliol II, King of Scotland, 113–14, 116, 118, 120–3, 125, 134–6, 138

John of Brittany see Richmond, Earl of

John, King of Bohemia, 270–2

John 'of Gaunt' (elder John of Gaunt's son), 306

John, Prince (Henry IV's son) see Bedford, Duke of

John the Scot, 96

Joscelin de Louvain, 72–5, 119, 488

Judhael of Totnes, 33

Judith, wife of Waltheof, 28

Kapelle, William, 24

Keen, Maurice, 288

Kemp, John, Archbishop of York (later of Canterbury), 394

Kenilworth, battle of (1265), 108

Kenilworth, Dictum of (1266), 109, 135, 176

Kennedy, James, Bishop of St Andrews, 437, 438–40

Kenneth mac Alpin, King of Scots, 8

Kent, Edmund of Woodstock, Earl of, 173, 185, 191, 200–1, 235

Kent, Thomas Holland, Earl of, 340

Kent, William Neville, Earl of (and Baron Fauconberg), 436

Kerbogha, ruler of Mosul, 42

Kildrummy Castle, 232

King's Council, 131–2

kingship (English), 84–5, 90–1, 149

kinship, 46–7

Knighton, Henry, 236, 282–3, 286, 312, 336

Kymberley, William, 453

Labourers, Ordinance of (1351), 241, 276

Lacy, Edmund de, 97

Lacy, John de, 82, 91

Lacy, William de, 58

Lamberton, William de, Bishop of St Andrews, 136, 138

Lancaster family: in Wars of Roses, 406

Lancaster, Alice, Countess of (née de Lacy), 150, 187

Lancaster, Blanche, Duchess of (John of Gaunt's first wife), 298–300, 302–3

Lancaster, Constance, Duchess of (John of Gaunt's second wife), 303, 306

Lancaster, Edmund, Earl of ('Crouchback'), 144

Lancaster, Henry, Duke of (earlier 1st Earl of Derby), 258

Lancaster, Henry, Earl of (earlier Earl of

Leicester): supports Isabella, 185, 187–8; captures Edward II, 188; rehabilitated, 191; border appointment, 192; opposes Treaty of Nottingham, 197; daughters, 224; power and status, 224, 227; preference for lower-class women, 226; accompanies Edward III on Scots expedition, 227, 229; in regency council, 239; Percy and Wake join in Newcastle, 240; death, 263

Lancaster, Henry of Grosmont, 1st Duke of: military qualities, 206, 224, 263; character, 224; connection with Percys, 224; campaigns in France, 263, 269, 273–6, 281–2, 286; wealth and retinue, 264, 266; death, 291, 293, 299; dukedom, 293; enlarges Savoy palace, 320; *Le Livre de Seyntz Medicines*, 296

Lancaster, John of Gaunt, Duke of: in line for Scottish throne, 248–9, 278, 288–9, 298; visits Scotland, 281; in wars against France, 286, 301–2, 304–5; Henry Percy V related to through marriage, 288, 299; patronises Henry Percy VI, 293, 297, 299, 303; achievements and career, 298–9; first marriage (to Blanche), 298; and succession to English throne, 299–300, 395; widowed, 300, 302–3; claims throne of Castile and Leon, 303–4, 307; liaison, children and marriage with Katherine Swynford, 303; failure in France and withdrawal, 305–6; accused of financial misdealings, 306; second marriage and child (with Constance), 306; attacked in Parliament, 307–10; and banishment of Alice of Perrers, 311; represses opposition, 311–12; supposed threat to Richard II, 311, 314, 326; attitude to Wycliffe, 312–14, 317, 319; religious convictions, 312, 314; regains support of Parliament, 315; appoints Henry Percy VI as marshal of England, 316–17; authoritarianism as regent, 317–18; Londoners' hostility to, 317–20, 330; conflict with City of London, 318–19; retains Commons majority, 321; organises Richard II's coronation, 322–3, 326; and disorder in Northumberland, 328–9, 332–3; Henry Percy VI's quarrels and reconciliations with, 329–31; refused entry to Alnwick Castle, 329–30; Savoy Palace destroyed in Peasants' Revolt, 329–30; on Richard II's expedition to Scotland, 334; meets Henry Percy VI in France (1389), 338–9; and rumour of Arundel's resurrection, 340; assassination plot against, 342–3; death, 344

Lancaster, Thomas, Earl of (Edmund's son): royalist sentiments, 148–9, 151–2; hates Earl Warenne, 150, 169; character, 151; and 41 Ordinances, 156–7, 163; leads baronial forces against Gaveston, 158, 161–2; and Gaveston's treasure, 159, 163; and assassination of Gaveston, 160; refuses to back Edward II against Bruce, 164; instructed to provide fighting men, 165; accused of plotting with Scots, 169, 172–3; authority, 169; wife abducted, 169–70; worsening relations with Edward II, 169–71; in coalition against Despensers, 173–4; defeated at Boroughbridge and condemned to death, 176–7, 343; rehabilitated, 191; boycotts Salisbury Parliament, 200; seeks terms with Mortimer and Isabella, 201; and Mortimer's death, 202

Lanerfost Priory, 242

Langtoft, Peter of, 128

Langton, Stephen, Archbishop of Canterbury, 86

La Rochelle, battle of (1372), 304

Latimer, William, 2nd Baron, 149, 158

Latimer, William, 3rd Baron, 229

Latimer, William, 4th Baron, 301, 306, 310–12, 331

Layton, Richard, 10

Leake, Treaty of (1318), 170–1

learning: development of (12th century), 55

le Bel, Jean *see* Jean le Bel

Leconfield, Yorkshire, 134

Leeds Castle, Kent, 173

Leicester, Eleanor, Countess of (Simon de Montfort's wife), 102–3

Leicester, Henry, Earl of *see* Lancaster, Henry, Earl of

Leicester, Simon de Montfort, Earl of *see* Montfort, Simon de

Le Patourel, John, 3, 285

L'Estrange, Hamo, 95, 97, 107

Leulinhen, Treaty of (1384), 333

Lewes, battle of (1264), 106–9

Leyburn, Roger, 97, 104–7

Liddell, Pile of, 242

Liddesdale, 237–8, 249, 298

Lincoln: Ranulf of Chester attacks, 66; battle of (1217), 89, 109

Lincoln, Alice de Lacy, Countess of, 177

Lincoln Castle, 62–3

Lincoln, Henry de Lacy, 3rd Earl of, 97, 129, 132, 143–5, 148–51, 156

Lionel of Antwerp, *see* Clarence, Duke of

Llewelyn ap Gruffydd of Gwynedd, 104, 108

Llywd, Gruffyd, 187

Lochmaben, 219–21, 231

Logie, Dame Margaret *see* Margaret, Queen of David II of Scotland

Lollards, 312–13, 370

London: Percy property in, 228; hostility to John of Gaunt and Henry Percy VI, 317–20; relations with Southwark, 318

London, Treaties of (1358), 285, 287; (1423), 380; (1474), 458

Lords, House of: John of Gaunt attacked in, 307–8

Lords Ordainers, 156–7, 238, 308

Lothian, 8

Loudoun Hill, Kilmarnock, battle of (1307), 141

Louis VI, King of France, 48

Louis IX, St, King of France, 102, 104–5, 108, 116, 174, 184

Louis X, King of France, 255

Louis XI, King of France (*earlier* Dauphin): marriage to Margaret of Scotland, 383–4, 388–9; Queen Margaret's mission to, 437–8; English truces with, 440, 468; and civil war (1463), 445; agreements with Burgundy and Brittany, 446; Warwick negotiates with, 446; harbours Warwick, 452; and succession to Edward IV, 453; meets Edward IV at Picquigny, 458–9; pays Edward IV to quit France, 459; intrigues with Scots, 465–6, 468; invades Burgundy, 466; death, 470

Louis, Prince of France, 89

Lound, Peter de, 135

Loveday (1458), 420–1

Lucy family, 332, 336

Lucy, John Melton, 7th Baron, 402

Lucy, Sir Anthony de, 182, 235

Lucy, Thomas de, 246

Ludford Bridge, 422, 427

Ludlow, 422, 424

Ludwig IV, Holy Roman Emperor, 256, 258

Lumley, Marmaduke, Bishop of Carlisle, 391, 394

Lundie, Sir Richard, 127

Lusignan family and faction, 95, 97–8, 100–3, 108

Lusignan, Geoffrey de, 100

Lusignan, Guy de, 99–100, 107

Luther, Martin, 312

Lyons, Richard, 306, 310–12, 321

Lytlington, Nicholas, Abbot of Westminster: *Liber Regalis*, 322

Magna Carta, 79, 86–93, 174, 239

Mainfred the Dane, 17–18, 20–1

Major, John, 290, 404

Malcolm I, King of Scotland, 7

Malcolm III (Canmore), King of Scotland, 12, 23, 27–9, 48, 55–6

Malcolm IV, King of Scotland ('the Maiden'), 116, 120

Malebisse, Richard, 75

Malestroit, Truce of (1346), 262

Malet, William, 25–7

Malmesbury, Monk of, 148, 154

Mancini, Dominic, 444

Mar, Donald, 12th Earl of, 193–4, 212–13

Marant (French pirate), 275

March, Agnes Randolph, Countess of ('Black Agnes'), 236, 245

March, Edmund Mortimer, 2nd Earl of, 307–8, 315, 317, 319, 329

March, Edmund Mortimer, 3rd Earl of, 329, 395

March, Edmund Mortimer, 5th Earl of, 350, 366, 376, 382

March, Edward, Earl of *see* Edward IV, King

March, George Dunbar, 9th Earl of, 326, 328–30, 350, 352–3, 359–60

March, Patrick Dunbar, 2nd Earl of, 215, 227, 230, 232, 234–6, 243–4, 280–1, 288–9, 351, 357

March, Philippa, Countess of, 300, 307

March, Sir Roger Mortimer, 1st Earl of: relations with Queen Isabella, 16, 185–6; in Isabella's invasion, 187; urges dethroning of Edward II, 189; status and manner, 191, 200–2; governs with Isabella, 192, 200; and Treaty of Northampton, 196; opposition to, 200–1; arrested and executed, 202

March, Roger Mortimer, 4th Earl of, 343

Marchis, Walter, 119

Margaret of Burgundy (daughter of Maxmilian and Mary), 469

Margaret, Queen of Alexander III of Scotland, 112

Margaret, Queen of David II of Scotland (*earlier* Dame Margaret Logie), 289

Margaret, Queen of Eric II of Norway, 113

Margaret of Anjou, Queen of Henry VI: betrothal and marriage, 396; pregnancy and child, 398–9, 410; distrusts Exeter, 407; and Henry's recovery from melancholia, 410; political involvement, 417–23, 438; in Wars of Roses, 423–4; relations with Queen Mary of Scotland, 426, 437; congratulates Northumberland for defeat of Duke of York, 428; flees Edward IV to north, 431; escapes to Scotland after Towton, 433–4; mission to France for Mary of Guelders, 437–8; supports insurrectionists against Edward IV, 437; shelters and plots in Scotland, 438–40; permanent return to France, 440; reaction to 1463 Anglo-French truce, 440; and Warwick's dealings with Louis XI, 446; Warwick submits to, 453; return to England with son Edward, 455–7; ransomed to Louis XI, 460; death, 460

Margaret, Queen of Louis XI of France, 383–4, 388–9

Margaret, Queen of Scotland ('the Maid of Norway'), 113–16, 120

Margaret, St, Queen of Malcolm III, 25

Margaret (sister of James III), 466

Margaret Tudor, Queen of James IV of Scotland, 489

Marmaduke, Sir John, 129

marshal of England: duties, 316–18, 323

Marshal, William, Earl of Pembroke, Regent of England, 76, 89–90

Marshalsea prison, Southwark, 318–19

Mary I (Tudor), Queen, 489

Mary of Burgundy (Duke Charles' daughter), 462, 466

Mary of Guelders, Queen of James II of Scotland, 425–6, 437, 439; death, 440

Mathilda, Queen of William the Conqueror, 26

Matilda, Empress (daughter of Henry I), 49–50, 53, 59, 61–4, 72
Matilda (Maud; *formerly* Eadgyth), Queen of Henry I, 29, 37
Matilda, Queen of Stephen, 49, 63, 67, 69
Mauleverer, Sir John, 454
Mauny, Walter, 261
Maximilian of Austria (and Burgundy), 466, 468–9
Meaux, France, 376
Melton, William, Archbishop of York, 246
Menteith, Sir John, 137
Menteith, John Graham, 9th Earl of, 213, 230, 245
Mercia, 6, 19
Merton, Statute of, 91
Methven, battle of (1306), 139, 141, 145
Middleham, John, 362
Middleton, Sir Gilbert, 168
Milfield (Homildon Hill), battle of (1402), 352–5
moneylending, 80–2, 154–5
Montagu, John Neville, Marquess of: as Yorkist in Wars of Roses, 436, 438–9, 441–2; made Earl of Northumberland, 442; marquessate, 443; stamps out Robin of Redesdale rebellion, 448; loses earldom of Northumberland, 451–2; turns against Edward IV, 452, 454–6; killed at Barnet, 457
Montague, Sir William *see* Salisbury, 1st Earl of
Montague, William, 169–70
Montbegon, Roger de, 86
Montford, John de, 260–2
Montfort, Guy de, 106, 110
Montfort, Henry de (Simon's son), 106
Montfort, Hugh II de, 45
Montfort, Jeanne de, 261–2
Montfort, John, the Younger, 262
Montfort, Peter de, 99–100
Montfort, Robert de, Dean of York, 45
Montfort, Simon de, Earl of Leicester: hostility to Lusignans, 95, 97–8; opposes Henry III, 99, 101, 104–5; Valence accuses, 100; radicalism, 102; and Treaty of Paris, 102–3; retires abroad, 104; Lewes victory, 106–7; rebellion, 106; megalomania, 108; death at Evesham, 109
Montfort, Simon de, Jnr, 106, 108, 110
Montfort, Walter de, 45
Moray, Sir Andrew ('le Riche'), 214, 223, 227, 232–4, 236–7
Moray, Lady Christina (*née* Bruce; Robert VIII's sister), 140, 214, 232
Moray, John Randolph, 3rd Earl of, 215–19, 222, 227, 229–30, 237, 239, 241, 243–5
Moray, Thomas Randolph, 1st Earl of, 170–1, 175, 178, 180, 183, 193–4, 196–7, 200, 204, 212, 254, 285
Morbeke, Sir Denis, 283
Morcar, Earl of Northumbria, 11, 24, 28

Mortimer, Sir Edmund (1376–1409), 356–8, 361–2, 366
Mortimer, Edmund (son of 4th Earl of March), 343
Mortimer, Roger, 1st Earl of March, 16, 107–8
Mortimer, Roger (nephew), 172, 174
Mortimer, Roger (uncle), 172, 174
Mortimer, Sir Roger of Wigmore *see* March, 1st Earl of
Mortimer's Cross, battle of (1461), 429
Morton, John, Bishop of Ely (*later* Archbishop of Canterbury), 475
Motherby, Thomas, 329
Mowbray, Sir Alexander, 203, 222–4, 227, 230
Mowbray, Sir John, 203, 215, 224, 243–4, 246
Mowbray, Robert de, Earl of Northumbria, 29
Mowbray, Roger de, 70
Mowbray, William de, 84, 86
Muntfichet, Richard de, 91
Murray, Andrew, 125–7
Musgrave, Sir Thomas, Baron, 328

Nájera, battle of (1367), 291
nation: as concept, 90–1
Nemurs, Count of, 230
Nennius, 5
Neville family: background, 225; Henry IV sponsors, 355; family quarrels, 386, 392; and Wars of Roses, 400, 406, 408–9; feud with Percys, 401–4; supports York in Wars of Roses, 406; land and possessions, 462
Neville, George, Archbishop of York, 449, 462
Neville, Sir Humphrey, 441–2
Neville, Isabel (Warwick's daughter) *see* Clarence, Duchess of
Neville, Isabel (wife of Robert, Lord of Raby), 225
Neville, John, 6th Baron, 330–1, 333, 336
Neville, Sir John, Baron (Salisbury's son), 402, 404, 408, 422, 431
Neville, John (Ralph's son), 225, 277
Neville, Margaret, 315
Neville, Maud (*formerly* Stanhope), 402–3
Neville, Maud, Lady (6th Baron's wife), 277, 331
Neville, Maud (*née* Percy; Henry Percy IV's daughter), 225
Neville, Ralph de, 4th Baron: in siege of Berwick, 171; maintains peace on border, 192, 205–6; in Disinheriteds' campaign against Scots, 215; and possession of Lochmaben, 220–1; children's marriages, 225, 297; relations with Henry Percy IV, 225; accompanies Edward III into Scotland, 229; and Scots raids, 235, 239–42, 284; at battle of Neville's Cross, 246; in diplomatic negotiations with Scots, 248; in naval battle, 276; negotiates David II's ransom, 278; administration in Durham, 279; commissioned to find Coupland killers, 292; death, 293
Neville, Randolf (or Ranulph), 1st Baron, 225
Neville, Sir Richard *see* Salisbury, 1st Earl of

Neville, Robert, Bishop of Durham, 418

Neville, Robert ('the Peacock'), 225

Neville, Sir Thomas (Salisbury's son), 402, 408, 422

Neville's Cross, battle of (1346), 243–6, 262, 273

Newburn manor, 207

Newcastle: Hotspur defends, 337

Nicholson, Ranald, 199, 289, 418

Nicolson, Sir Harold, 297

Norfolk, Earls of, 323

Norfolk, John Howard, 1st Duke of (earlier Baron Howard), 472, 474–5, 479–81

Norfolk, John Mowbray, 3rd Duke of, 432

Norfolk, John Mowbray, Earl (later 2nd Duke) of, 379, 391

Norfolk, Margaret, Countess of, 323, 326

Norfolk, Roger Bigod, 4th Earl of, 98–100

Norfolk, Roger Bigod, 5th Earl of, 128–9

Norfolk, Thomas of Brotherton, Earl of, 173, 185, 187, 191, 200–1, 323

Norfolk, Thomas Mowbray, 1st Duke of (earlier Earl of Nottingham), 335, 338, 340–4, 349

Norham, Northumberland, 191, 193, 439–40

Norham, William de, 374

Normandy: Norsemen in, 19–21; rebellion against William Rufus, 29; Geoffrey of Anjou captures, 64; King John loses to Philip Augustus of France, 80–1; Edward III invades and campaigns in (1346), 265, 268–9; conquered by Bedford (1423), 379; Charles VII's campaign in, 396

Normans: in England after Conquest, 22–3, 31; castles, 33–5; behaviour, 34; intermarriage with English, 37; and kingship, 53; see also William I (the Conqueror), King

Norsemen (Vikings), 19

North of England: character, 2–4, 9–11; geographical definitions, 4–6, 8–9; speech, 10–11; harried by William the Conqueror, 11–12, 23, 25–7, 30; rebelliousness, 11; Norsemen in, 19–20; Norman castles in, 35; King John visits, 86–7; famine (1315–17), 168; manners and customs in, 328–9; John of Gaunt and disorder in, 329–30, 332; administrative changes under Henry VII, 487–8

Northampton: castle stormed (1264), 105–6; Bruce's expeditions into, 192–3; battle of (1460), 424–5

Northampton, John de, 318

Northampton (or Edinburgh), Treaty of (1328), 195–7, 200, 203, 205, 216, 351

Northampton, William de Bohun, Earl of, 257, 270

Northumberland (county): Scots dispute rights to, 111; Bruce's expedition to, 192–4; and Scottish Marches, 208, 326–7; insurrections against Yorkists, 436–7

Northumberland, Algernon Percy, 9th Earl of, 488

Northumberland, Eleanor, Countess of (née Poynings; 3rd Earl's wife), 392, 416

Northumberland, Eleanor, Countess of (wife of 2nd Earl), 369–70, 375, 382

Northumberland, Henry, 1st Earl of see Henry, Prince of Scotland

Northumberland, Sir Henry Percy, 1st Earl of: born, 258, 297; upbringing and inheritance, 297; serves John of Gaunt, 299–301, 304–6; activities and appointments in north, 302, 326–8, 331; marriages and children, 303, 331–2; and Parliament's criticism and impeachment of John of Gaunt, 308–10; supports John of Gaunt in Parliament, 315; as marshal of England, 316–19, 321, 323; Londoners' hostility to, 318–20; at Richard II's coronation, 323, 325; created Earl of Northumberland, 325; as warden of East March, 326; quarrels and reconciliations with John of Gaunt, 329–30; cross-border raids, 333; income from border activities, 333–4, 346; supports Richard II on border, 335; Douglas harries, 336–7; neutrality in Richard II's reign, 336; as captain of Calais and joint ambassador to France, 338, 340; disgraced over Otterburn defeat, 338; re-established in border offices, 339; and rumours of Arundel's resurrection, 340; loses border offices under Richard II, 341, 345; disenchantment with Richard II, 342; and Richard II's authoritarianism, 345; appointed warden of Carlisle and the West March by Bolingbroke, 346; supports Hereford (Bolingbroke) on return to England, 346; negotiates with Richard II at Conwy Castle and takes into custody, 347–8; at Henry IV's coronation, 349; made constable of England for life, 349; on Henry IV's expeditions against Scots, 351, 357; negotiates with Archibald Douglas, 352; defeats Scots at battle of Milfield, 353; inadequately paid by Henry IV, 354; Henry IV grants lands to, 355; rebels against Henry IV, 357–8, 361–2, 364; granted clemency after Shrewsbury defeat, 360; Tripartite Indenture with Glendower and Mortimer, 361; tried and sentenced for treason and attainted, 363; in Wales, 363; killed, 365

Northumberland, Sir Henry Percy, 2nd Earl of: as Percy heir, 366; upbringing in Scotland, 367; reinstated by Henry V, 369–70; appointments and responsibilities in north, 371–5, 378, 381; earldom, 371; income, 371, 381, 385; lands restored, 371; children, 375, 382, 392–3; on council of nobles, 379; negotiates release of James I, 380; mission to James I of Scotland, 383–5; resigns wardenship of Marches and reinstated, 385, 388; and Neville family feuds, 387; and Ogle/Dunbar rebellion against James I,

388; and James I's attack on Roxburgh, 389; not reappointed to wardenship, 391–2; hostility to Salisbury, 393–4; campaigns across border, 400–1; and Wars of Roses, 400, 406–8; defeated at battle of Sark (1448), 401; warned by Henry VI of feuds and disorder, 404; ordered to London, 407; and Egremont/Exeter rebellion, 409; posthumous proceedings against, 409; regains favour with Henry VI, 410; killed at first battle of St Albans, 412–14

Northumberland, Sir Henry Percy, 3rd Earl of (*earlier* Lord Poynings): born, 375; appointed warden of East March, 392, 409; as Lord Poynings, 392, 400; marriage, 392; captured by Scots at Solway, 401; in Wars of Roses, 406–9, 416, 422–3; granted lease of northern lands, 409; inherits earldom, 413; finances, 416–17, 461; appointments, 418; and James II threat, 418–19, 424, 425; attends great council in London (1458), 420; independence of Duke of York and London, 426–7; raises army against York and Salisbury, 427; and defeat and death of Duke of York at Sandal, 427–8; killed at Towton, 431–4

Northumberland, Henry Percy, 4th Earl of: disbarred from titles and assets after Towton and confined to Tower, 435, 442; swears fealty to Edward IV and restored to earldom, 443, 451–2; in Warwick-Edward IV conflict, 450; and rebellion in north (1469), 454; and Edward IV's return to England and defeat of rebels, 456–7; accompanies Edward IV to France, 458–60; finances, 461; relations with Richard (Gloucester) in North, 463–5, 475; marriage to Maud, 464; and expedition against Scots, 467, 470; confirmed in offices by Edward V, 472; attends Richard III's coronation, 474; and Richard's usurpation plot, 474; appointments under Richard, 476; slow support for Richard against Henry Tudor, 479; and wife's death, 479; at Bosworth, 480–3, 486; submits to Henry Tudor, 482; position under Henry VII, 483–4; tax-collecting, 484–5; murdered, 485–6, 487

Northumberland, Henry Percy, 5th Earl of, 487
Northumberland, Henry Percy, 6th Earl of, 488
Northumberland, Henry Percy, 8th Earl of, 490
Northumberland, Hugh Percy, 1st Duke of (*formerly* Smithson), 74
Northumberland, John Dudley, Duke of (*earlier* Earl of Warwick), 488
Northumberland, John Neville, Earl of *see* Montagu, Marquess of
Northumberland, Maud, Countess of (*earlier* Umfraville; 1st Earl's second wife), 331–2
Northumberland, Maud, Countess of (*née* Herbert; 4th Earl's wife), 464, 479

Northumberland, Thomas Percy, 7th Earl of, 488–9
Northumbria: kingdom of, 5, 7–8, 19; David I claims earldom of, 52
Nottingham: Edward IV in, 448–9
Nottingham, John Mowbray, 1st Earl of, 325
Nottingham, Thomas Mowbray, 3rd Earl of (son of 1st Duke of Norfolk), 361
Nottingham, Thomas Mowbray, Earl of *see* Norfolk, 1st Duke of

Odo, Bishop of Bayeux and Earl of Kent, 23, 25, 36, 40
Ogle, Sir Robert, Baron, 374, 385, 387–8, 392, 438
Old Byland, battle of (1322), 181
Oldcastle, Sir John, 370
Oliphant, Sir William, 136
Orderic Vitalis, 12, 26, 56
Ordinances (41) *see* Forty-one Ordinances
Orkney, Bishop of (1138), 57
Orléans, Louis, Duke of, 345
Orléans, siege of (1428), 382–3
Orme, Nicholas, 253
Ormond, James Butler, 4th Earl of, 400
Orreby family, 294–5
Osulf of Bamburgh, 24–5
Otterburn, battle of (1388), 333, 337–8, 352, 401
Oxford, Provisions of, 99, 101, 104–5, 174
Oxford, John de Vere, 7th Earl of, 229, 270–1
Oxford, John de Vere, 13th Earl of, 454, 458, 480–1
Oxford, Robert de Vere, 6th Earl of, 129, 150–1, 157, 164
Oxford, Robert de Vere, 9th Earl of: influence over Richard II, 335

Paris: Treaty of (1259), 103–4, 254; Henry V reaches, 374; Charles VII captures, 389
Paris, Matthew, 91, 96, 100, 106
Parliament: beginnings under Edward I, 131–2; evolves into Lords and Commons, 178; attitude to Marches, 211; criticises John of Gaunt, 307–8
Paston, Sir John, 409–10, 454
Paule, Johannes, 389
Peasants' Revolt (1381), 315, 329
Pedro the Cruel, King of Castile, 291, 303
Peeris, William, 17–18, 20–1, 52, 167, 212
pele towers, 12
Pembroke, Aymer de Valence, Earl of: background, 129–30; appointments and duties in north, 138–9, 222; in pursuit of Bruce, 141; witnesses Edward I's last command, 143–4; appeals for reinforcements in Galloway, 145; and Edward II's relations with Gaveston, 147, 150–1; and Forty-one Ordinances, 156–7; and capture and killing of Gaveston, 158–60; intercedes in earls' disagreements with Edward II, 162, 170, 173; opposes

Lancastrians at Pontefract, 175; accompanies Edward II to York, 180; death, 184

Pembroke, Jasper Tudor, Earl of (*later* Duke of Bedford), 436, 446, 453, 477

Pembroke, John Hastings, 2nd Earl of, 301, 304

Pembroke, William de Valence, Earl of, 129–30

Pembroke, Sir William Herbert, 1st Earl of, 436, 446, 448–50

Pembroke, William Herbert, 2nd Earl of, 477

Penmore, 368

Pennington, Sir John, 401

Pennington, John, 464

Penthièvre, Joan of, 260

Percy, château, near Villedieu, Normandy, 17

Percy family: northern qualities, 1–2, 4, 9; as warrior leaders, 12; historical sources and interpretation, 14–16; origins and ancestry, 17–18, 20–2; kinship links, 46–8, 52; coat of arms and emblems, 73–4, 119, 143; awarded barony, 131; survival, 168; animosity with Douglas family, 170, 223, 250, 328, 336; and wardenship of Marches, 208–10; as major landowners, 228; acquires northern lands by marriage, 332; arrogance after Homildon Hill (Milfield) victory, 353; alienation from Henry IV, 355; rebellion against Henry IV, 357–8; income from estates, 371; feud with Nevilles, 401–4; decline after Wars of Roses, 436; deaths in Wars of Roses, 442; change of fortune under Tudors, 488–9; motto (*Esperance en Dieu*), 490

Percy, Adeliza de (*née* de Tonbridge; William Percy II's first wife), 46–7, 70–1

Percy, Adeliza (*formerly* de Argentom), 44

Percy, Agnes de (William Percy II's daughter): inherits Topcliffe and marries Joscelin, 72–5, 77, 79, 93

Percy, Alan de (William Percy II's illegitimate brother), 52, 54, 57–8, 132

Percy, Alan de (William Percy II's son), 38, 44–6, 72, 74

Percy Chartulary, The, 134

Percy, Eleanor (3rd Earl of Northumberland's daughter), 435

Percy, Eleanor, Lady (*née* Warenne; 1st Baron's wife), 110, 119, 167–8, 204

Percy, Elizabeth (3rd Earl of Northumberland's daughter), 435

Percy, Elizabeth (*née* Mortimer; Hotspur's wife), 329, 332

Percy, Elizabeth (*née* Strathbogie; Thomas Percy's wife), 332

Percy, Ellen (*née* de Balliol; William Percy III's second wife), 93, 110, 118

Percy, Emma de (*née* de Gant; Alan's wife), 45–6

Percy, Emma de (*née* de Port; William's wife), 36–7, 60, 74, 204

Percy, Geffray (or Gaufrid) de (illegitimate son of William de Percy II), 52, 279

Percy, George (2nd Earl of Northumberland's son), 393, 435, 442

Percy, Sir Henry I (son of Joscelin and Agnes), 75

Percy, Sir Henry II (son of William Percy III and Ellen), 93, 94–5, 97–8, 101–7, 109–10

Percy, Sir Henry III, 1st Baron (Sir Henry/Eleanor's son): relations with Edward I, 93, 103, 110, 142; birth, 110; marriage, 110, 119, 167–8, 204; inheritance on death of parents, 118–19; on campaign in Wales, 119–20; heraldic arms, 119; acquires knightly armour, 122; activities and campaigns against Scots, 122–3, 125–8, 133–7, 139–41, 145–7, 149, 152; barony, 131; earldom of Carrick, 132, 138, 143; Scottish estates, 132, 135, 138, 143; and Warenne's death, 137; as Capitaneus of West March, 139; appearance and character, 142–3; acquires Alnwick Castle, 143, 152–4; and Edward II, 146, 148–9, 152, 157–8; income, 146, 154–5; witnesses Gaveston's appointment to Ireland, 149; command in Perth, 157; reads out 41 Ordinances in London, 157–8; and Gaveston's surrender at Scarborough, 159–61; and Gaveston's treasure, 159; Edward orders arrest and lands seized, 161, 164; freed, 163; loses Scottish lands and Carrick earldom, 163–4, 222; declines service in Scotland under Edward II, 164–5; Edward II summons to Newcastle after Bannockburn, 165; death, 166

Percy, Sir Henry IV, 2nd Baron: marriage and children, 124, 167–8; retains Alnwick Castle, 153–4; under guardianship during minority, 167; harassed by Scots raiders, 168–9, 171, 181, 193, 235; with Edward II at siege of Berwick, 171; attends Lancaster's Pontefract Council, 172–3; avoids Lancaster's Doncaster assembly, 174; custodianship of Scarborough Castle, 174, 204–5; summoned to Coventry, 174–5; given custody of Pickering castle, 176; knighted by Edward II, 178; summoned to Edward II's 1322 Scottish campaign, 178–9; serves under Strathbogie of Atholl, 180; as hostage at Bruce's court, 183; loses Scottish lands, 183, 188; made keeper of Yorkshire coast, 184–5; commissioned to keep peace, 186–7; and Isabella's invasion, 187–8; withdraws homage from Edward II, 190; in Edward III's ruling council, 191; financial reward, 191; life in field, 192; wardenship of the Marches, 192–3, 207, 210–12, 223; negotiates with Bruce for peace, 194–5, 197; recovers Scottish lands, 196–7, 203; supports Mortimer and Isabella against rebels, 200; relations with Edward III, 202, 205; absent from 1331 expedition to Scotland, 204; attachment to mother, 204;

and the Disinherited, 205; qualities and character, 205–6; accompanies Edward III to France, 206; official appointments and duties, 206–7, 219, 223, 226–7; acquires Crown lands in Northumberland, 211, 237; and Edward III's campaigns against Scots, 215–17, 227–9, 340; acquires Scottish lands under Edward Balliol, 216, 219–21, 223; excused debt by Edward III, 219; acquires Jedburgh Castle and constabulary, 223; children's marriages, 224–5; reading and books, 226; extends land and property acquisitions, 228; delineates Yorkshire-Westmorland border, 233; at siege of Dunbar, 236; complains of non-payment, 241; opposes David II, 242; at battle of Neville's Cross, 244–6; illnesses, 246–7; will, 248, 250; in negotiations over David II's release and ransom, 249–50, 278; death, 250, 278; memorial services for, 279

Percy, Sir Henry V, 3rd Baron: first marriage (to Mary), 223–4, 251, 293–4; appointed to regency council (1340), 239; in Arundel's retinue, 240, 262–4; inherits title and estates, 251; military background and service abroad, 251, 253, 256–8, 261–3, 282, 286–7; upbringing, 251–3; Northumbrian troops, 259–60; absent from 1345 Flanders expedition, 264; in Philip Weston's retinue, 266–8, 274; at Crécy, 270–2; serves Henry of Lancaster (1347), 274–5; as commissioner enforcing Ordinance of Labourers, 276; in sea-battle (1350), 276; impeached for financial scandal, 277; takes over management and judicial duties from father, 277; negotiates David II's release terms, 278–80, 284, 287–8, 299; wardenship of Marches, 279; made marshal of royal army in France, 281, 293; and Scots border raids, 284; later public duties and retirement, 292–3; assessed, 293; second marriage (to Joan), 294–6; death, 296

Percy, Sir Henry VI see Northumberland, 1st Earl of

Percy, Henry de (William de Percy II's brother), 52

Percy, Sir Henry ('Hotspur'): Shakespeare depicts, 1, 357; at relief of Berwick (1378), 328; marriage to Elizabeth Mortimer, 329, 332; raises troops to support Richard II on border, 335; positions and appointments on border, 336, 339, 355; captured at Otterburn, 337–8, 353; defends Newcastle against Douglas, 337; retained in Richard II's service for life, 339; as John of Gaunt's deputy in Aquitaine, 340; supports Bolingbroke (Hereford), 346; confirmed in appointments by Bolingbroke, 347; granted government of North Wales, 349, 356; opposes Archibald Douglas at Milfield, 352; campaigns in Wales, 356; rebels against

Henry IV, 357–8; killed at Shrewsbury, 359, 361

Percy, Sir Henry (Richard Percy's illegitimate son), 93

Percy, Idonea (née Clifford; Henry Percy IV's wife), 124, 167

Percy, Ingleram, 104

Percy, Ingram, 488

Percy, Isabel, Lady (née de Brus; Sir Henry Percy I's wife), 75, 77

Percy, Jeffrie (Geoffrey; son of Mainfred), 18, 21

Percy, Joan (née Briwerre; William III's wife), 89, 93

Percy, Joan (née Orreby; later Clifton; Henry Percy V's second wife), 294–6

Percy, Margaret (3rd Earl of Northumberland's daughter), 435

Percy, Margaret (née Neville; Henry Percy VI's wife), 303

Percy, Mary, Lady (née Plantagenet; first wife of Henry Percy V), 224, 251, 293–6

Percy, Maud de (William II's daughter) see Warwick, Maud, Countess of

Percy, Philippa (née Strathbogie; Ralph's wife), 332

Percy, Sir Ralph (2nd Earl of Northumberland's son), 392–3, 407, 418, 435, 438–9, 442, 452

Percy, Sir Ralph (Sir Henry Percy V's cousin), 296

Percy, Ralph (Sir Henry Percy VI's son), 332, 402

Percy, Sir Richard (2nd Earl of Northumberland's son), 392, 403, 407, 409, 415, 418, 435–6, 441

Percy, Richard de, 44

Percy, Richard (Henry Percy IV's son), 253

Percy, Sir Richard (second son of Agnes and Joscelin): in inheritance disputes, 75, 77–80, 89, 92; finances, 83; rebels against King John, 84–6, 88–9; recovers lands, 90; as senior statesman, 91–2; death, 96

Percy, Serlo de, Abbot of Whitby, 18, 22, 40

Percy, Sibyl de (née de Valognes; William Percy II's second wife), 71

Percy, Sir Thomas (2nd Earl of Northumberland's son), 422

Percy, Sir Thomas (1536), 488

Percy, Thomas, Bishop of Norwich (Henry Percy IV's son), 253, 293

Percy, Thomas (Henry Percy VI's son), 332, 339

Percy, Walter de, 44, 64

Percy, William, Bishop of Carlisle (2nd Earl of Northumberland's son), 392–3, 401, 408, 410, 413, 435

Percy, William de, 1st Baron: origins in Normandy, 17, 22–3, 25; refounds Whitby Abbey, 22, 29–40; intercedes for Cospatrick, 27; position in north, 27; and Hugh d'Avranches, 30–1; lands and properties, 32–3, 35, 37, 47, 70, 155; marriage to Emma de Port, 36–7; on crusade, 37–40; properties destroyed, 37–8; death in Holy Land, 43

Percy, William II de, 45–6, 51, 56, 59–61, 64, 66, 68–70, 119; death and succession disputes, 71–2, 74–9
Percy, William III de, 75, 77–9, 89, 92–3; death, 96
Percy, Sir William (Henry Percy IV's brother), 168, 243, 253, 262
Percy-en-Auge, Calvados, Normandy, 22
Perrers, Alice, 291, 311, 321
Perrers, Richard, 187
Perth, 157, 230
Perunin, Michel, 398
Peruzzi bank, 259
Peter the Hermit, 39
Peter of Savoy, 95, 100
Petworth, Sussex, 73, 74–5, 111, 167, 266, 488, 489
Philip IV, King of France, 120, 145, 149
Philip VI, King of France, 206, 231, 233, 237, 241, 254–6, 258–9, 261, 268–75, 279
Philip Augustus, King of France, 80, 84
Philip the Fair, King of France, 134–5
Philip, Matthew, 416
Philip of Savoy, 446
Philippa of Hainault, Queen of Edward III, 186, 195, 201, 216, 231, 275, 302
Philippa, Princess (Lionel of Antwerp's daughter) see March, Countess of
Picquigny, Treaty of (1475), 459–60, 466
Pilgrimage of Grace (1536), 488
Plantagenet dynasty: extinction with death of Richard II, 349
Plummer, John, 260
Plumpton, Robert, 467, 485
Plumpton, Sir William, 454
Plumton, Robert, 260
Poitiers, battle of (1356), 282–3
Pontefract, 34–5, 170, 175–6, 345, 349; Council (1321), 172–3
Port, Henry de, 45
Port, Hugh de, 36–7
Poynings family, 392
Poynings, Henry Percy, Lord see Northumberland, 3rd Earl of
Prestwich, M., 95, 131, 134
Prima Tractorio, 162
Prudhoe, Northumberland, 225, 371
Pugh, T.B., 446
Pyngel, Thomas, 227

Qilij Arslan, Sultan, 39

Raby and Brancepeth, Robert, Baron of, 225
Radcot Bridge, battle of (1387), 335, 342
Ralph de Everley, 40, 43
Ramsay, Sir Alexander, 237–8
Ranulf le Meschin see Chester, Earl of
Redesdale, 235, 331
Reid, R.R., 208
Reinfred (monk), 40

religion see Church
René, King of Anjou, 460
Rere Cross (Ray Cross), 7
retinues, 266
'Revenge Parliament', 342–3
Rhys ap Gruffyd, 187
Richard I (Lionheart), King, 76–7, 81, 84, 116
Richard II, King: creates Earl of Northumberland, 1; in line of succession, 291, 300, 304; born, 299; supposed threat from John of Gaunt, 311, 314, 326; shelters John of Gaunt and Percy from London mob, 320; accession, 321; granted Wykeham's temporalities, 321; coronation, 322–5; and Scots raids across border, 326; income, 334; invades Scotland, 334; Appellants and, 335–6; negotiates permanent peace with France, 339, 341; betrothal to Isabella of France, 340; appoints border officials, 341; seeks peace with Scotland, 341–2; paranoia, 343; succession to, 343; banishes Norfolk and Bolingbroke (Hereford), 344; confiscates Lancastrian estates, 344; accused of tyranny, 345; absence in Ireland, 346; and Bolingbroke's (Hereford's) rebellion, 346–8; taken into custody, 347–8; deposed, 348–9; death, 349; rumoured survival, 350, 357; imposters, 369
Richard III, King (earlier Duke of Gloucester): defeated and killed at Bosworth, 10, 480–2; in Edward IV–Warwick conflicts, 447, 450, 457–8; position and possessions in North, 461–6, 469–70, 484; marriage to Anne (Neville), 462; intercedes for Clarence's life, 463; war with Scotland, 466–70; and Edward IV's death, 471; recognised as Protector, 472; usurpation of throne and coronation, 473–5; and death of Princes in Tower, 475; revolts and rebellions against, 475; rule, 475–6; and Henry Tudor's claim to throne, 479
Richard de Aclyngton, 260
Richard, Duke of York (Edward IV's son): sanctuary at Westminster, 471; Richard III removes to Tower, 472; death in Tower, 475
Richard, Earl of Cornwall, 96, 103, 106–7
Richard fitz Richard, 25
Richard of Hexham, 56, 64
Richard, Prince (son of Edward III), 291
Richmond, Yorkshire, 34–5
Richmond, Alan III, 1st Earl of, 60–1, 63, 65
Richmond and Derby, Margaret Beaufort, Countess of, 397, 475–7
Richmond, Edmund Tudor, Earl of, 477
Richmond, John of Britanny, Earl of, 146, 149–50, 156, 180, 184
Rievaulx Abbey, Yorkshire, 180
Rising of the Northern Earls (1569), 488
Rivers, Anthony Woodville, 2nd Earl, 471, 473–4

Rivers, Jaquetta of Luxembourg, Countess of, 444
Rivers, Richard Woodville, 1st Earl, 444–5, 449
Robert I, King of Scotland *see* Bruce, Robert VIII
Robert II (Stewart), King of Scotland: in Scottish line of succession, 200, 212, 236; at Halidon Hill, 218; rebels with Moray as joint guardian of Scotland, 222, 236; gives fealty to Edward III, 232; indecisiveness, 236–7, 247; at battle of Neville's Cross, 243–4; regency and impending return of David II, 247–9, 284; made Earl of Strathearn, 287; rises against David II, 288; Scots recognise as king, 290; succeeds David II, 292; Henry Percy VI writes to, 326; alliance with Charles VI of France, 333
Robert III, King of Scots (*earlier* Earl of Carrick), 335, 341, 350–2, 362–3, 367
Robert of Artois, 254
Robert atte Kirke of Brantingham, 260
Robert Curthose, Duke of Normandy, 29, 39–43
Robert de Comines, 25, 58
Robert, son of Humphrey of Tilleul-en-Auge, 23
Robin of Holderness, 448
Robin of Redesdale (Sir William Conyers), 448, 453–4
Rochester Castle: besieged (1264), 106
Roger of Salisbury, 49
Rokeby, Emericus, 262
Rokeby, Sir Thomas, 243–4, 246, 262, 364–5
Rollo (Rolf), Duke, 17–19, 21
Romans: in Britain, 5–6
Roos, Beatrice, Lady, 296
Roos, John de, 5th Baron, 315
Roos, Thomas de, 4th Baron, 315
Roos, Thomas de, 9th Baron, 427, 441–2
Roses, Wars of the: origins, 400, 403–4; conduct of, 423–33, 436, 441
Roslin, battle of (1303), 134
Ross, Charles, 443
Rothbury manor, 207, 211
Rothesay, David Stewart, Duke of, 350, 352
Rothesay, Marjorie, Duchess of, 350
Rouen, 19, 21, 373, 398
Roulle, Thomas, 383–4
Roumare, Agnes de *see* Brus, Agnes de
Roumare, William de, 47–8
Roumare, William II de, Earl of Cambridge and of Lincoln, 60, 62
Rowse, A.L., 477
Roxburgh: Earl of March raids, 326; Hotspur granted captaincy, 355; offered to James I, 384; resists attack by James I, 389, 391
Roxburgh Castle, 161, 227–8; James Douglas mines walls, 372; Scots capture and raze, 425–6, 437
Runciman, Sir Steven, 20, 297
Runnymede, 86
Rutland, Edmund, Earl of, 423, 427–8
Rutland, Edward, Earl of *see* Albemarle, Duke of
Rutland, Thomas Manners, 1st Earl of, 488

St Albans: first battle of (1455), 411–13, 415–16, 424; second battle of (1461), 428–9
St David's, Bishop of (1377), 314, 321
St John, Sir Roger, 140
Salibury, Alice, Countess of (*née* Montagu), 382–3, 394, 405
Salisbury, John Montagu, 2nd Earl of, 347, 349, 393
Salisbury, Sir Richard Neville, 1st Earl of: wardenship of Western Marches, 378, 382, 385, 389, 391–2, 400; marriage, 382–3; earldom, 383, 386; mission to James I, 383; takes over Eastern Marches, 385–7; dispute with Westmorland, 386–7, 392; status and finances, 386–7; campaign in France, 389, 391; 2nd Earl of Northumbeland's hostility to, 393–4, 400; defeats Scots after Sark, 401; in confrontation at Heworth Moor, 403; son's marriage and earldom, 405; in Wars of Roses, 405–14, 420, 422–5; captured at Sandal and executed, 427–8
Salisbury, Thomas Montagu, 3rd Earl of, 382, 393–5
Salisbury, Sir William Montague, 1st Earl of, 219, 231, 235–6, 237, 257
Sallust: *Catiline*, 172
Salvain, Sir John, 409
Sand Hutton, 404
Sandal, 427
Sandwich, Kent, 424
Sark, battle of the (1448), 401
Saul, Nigel, 325, 349
Savage, Sir John, 481
Savoy Palace, London, 320, 329–30
Say, William Heron, Baron de, 360
Saye and Sele, James Fiennes, Baron, 397
Scarborough Castle, 158–9, 161, 167, 174, 184, 205
Scotland: part in English history, 2; incursions and raids into England, 7, 12–13, 23, 35, 53, 161, 165, 168–70, 191–3, 235, 241, 326–7, 350, 372, 424, 439; border with England, 8, 111–12, 208–9, 326–7; defences against, 8, 12; Edward I's wars and conquests in, 11, 111, 121–4, 133–5, 138–9; William the Conqueror's expedition to, 28; under David I, 50–3; claim to northern English counties, 52, 54, 65, 111; as kingdom, 53; war with England (1138), 54, 56–7; atrocities, 56; kinships and rivalries in, 113–14; royal succession crisis (1289–92), 114–18; status in relation to England, 116–17; negotiations with Philip IV of France, 120–1; and 'Auld Alliance' with France, 121, 222, 233, 254, 405, 421, 437; treaty with France (1295), 121; regalia and Stone of Destiny removed to London, 123; Wallace's rising in, 125–8; government reforms under Edward I, 137; Robert Bruce resumes offensive in, 146–7; Robert Bruce holds Parliament in, 152; Edward II's campaigns in, 156–7, 164,

178–9; Bannockburn victory, 165; demand for freedom in Declaration of Arbroath, 171–2; truce with English (1319–21), 171–2, 178; expedition into Yorkshire (1322), 180–1; and succession to Bruce, 194, 200, 203, 207; treaty with France (1326), 196, 231, 254; Disinherited claim restitution in, 202–4; concessions to England under Edward Balliol, 214; Edward III's campaigns and conquests in, 215–19, 227–32, 240, 282; rising (1334), 222–3; southern territories ceded to Edward III, 222; continuing resistance to English, 233; guerrilla activities in, 234–5; Neville's Cross defeat, 243–7; in Hundred Years War, 253; Edward III claims crown of, 278, 288–91; John II of France incites to rebel, 280; and French defeat at Poitiers, 283–4; David II released to, 284–5; and David II's ransom, 290–1; reorganises financial arrangements, 292; John of Gaunt's campaign in (1384), 333; French support against Richard II's invasion, 334–5; Otterburn victory, 337–8; truce with Richard II, 341–2; Henry IV invades, 350–1; Henry V negotiates truce with, 368, 370; sends forces to aid Dauphin Charles of France, 373, 376; and release of James I from English custody, 379; and accession of James I, 380–1; under James I, 381; volunteers fight for French, 381, 383; attack and retreat from Roxburgh Castle (1436), 389; nine-year truce ends (1447), 400; civil war under James II, 405; under James II, 414–15; Margaret of Anjou in, 437–40; Kennedy negotiates truce with England (1463), 440–1; Edward IV's truces with, 442, 444, 461, 465; truce with England (1474), 458; Richard (Gloucester) invades, 468–9; Edward IV's policy on, 470; Richard's rights in, 470; decline in unrest (16th century), 489; and Treaty of Perpetual Peace (1502), 489–90

Scrope, Henry, 1st Baron, 308
Scrope, John le Scrope, 4th Baron Scrope of Masham, 384
Scrope, Richard, Archbishop of York, 361–2
Scrope, Thomas le Scrope, 5th Baron Scrope of Masham, 465
Seamer, Yorkshire, 204, 253, 296
Segrave, Johannes de, 2nd Baron, 134–5
Segrave, John de, 4th Baron, 241
Selby, Walter, 242
Sens, siege of (1421), 375
Serle, William, 340, 360
Seton, Thomas, 217
Shakespeare, William: on Northumberland and Hotspur, 1, 357; *Henry IV, Pt.1*, 357, 361; *Richard II*, 348
Shaw, Ralph, 472
Shilvington, Robert, 219
Shrewsbury, battle of (1403), 357–9, 361

Shrewsbury, George Talbot, 4th Earl of, 487
Shrewsbury, John Talbot, 2nd Earl of, 418, 423–5
Shrewsbury, John Talbot, 3rd Earl of, 455
Sicily: Henry III offered throne of, 98–9
Siward, Earl of Northumbria, 23
Skelton, Clement, 486
Skelton, Sir John, 364
Skipton-in-Craven castle, 441–2
Sluys, battle of (1340), 238, 257
Smithson, Sir Hugh *see* Northumberland, Hugh Percy, 1st Duke of
Somerset, Edmund Beaufort, 2nd Duke of: offers James I full peace treaty, 384; character and position, 397–8; surrenders Rouen to Charles VII, 398; accused of treason, 399; in Wars of Roses, 400, 406–8, 421, 431; disliked by Londoners, 410; Queen Margaret's affection for, 410; York's enmity to, 412; at first battle of St Albans, 413, 416; threatens Duke of York, 419; at 1458 great council, 420; shadows Warwick on return from Calais, 422; escapes to Scotland after Towton and attainted, 433–4; claims to seduce Mary of Guelders, 438; enters Alnwick and Bamburgh, 438; attainder reversed, 439; defections, 439; continues support for Henry VI, 441; executed, 442
Somerset, Edmund Beaufort, 4th Duke of, 456
Somerset, Henry Beaufort, 3rd Duke of, 416
Southampton: French fleet raids, 254–5
Southampton Plot (1415), 369–70, 395
Southwark: status, 318
Sowerby, 402
Spalding, Peter de, 170
Spofforth, 366, 402
Stafford, Hugh de, 2nd Earl of, 308–9
Stainmore, Cumberland, 23, 35
Stamford Bridge, battle of (1066), 24
Stamford Bridge, battle of (1454), 408–9
Standard, battle of the (1138), 55–8, 244
Stanhope Park, 193
Stanley, Thomas, 2nd Baron (*later* 1st Earl of Derby), 422–3, 454, 475–7, 479–81
Stanley, Sir William, 481
Stenton, Frank, 20
Stephen of Blois, 70
Stephen, King, 47, 49–51, 53–4, 59–67, 255; death, 69
Stephen (monk of Whitby Abbey), 40, 45
Stewart, James (Bruce's guardian), 114, 123, 125
Stewart, Sir John, 130, 135, 202
Stewart, Marjorie de (*née* Bruce; Robert VIII's daughter), 140, 165, 200
Stewart, Robert *see* Robert II, King of Scotland
Stewart, Sir Robert, 390–1
Stewart, Thomas, Earl of Angus, 280–1, 285
Stewart, Walter, 200
Stewart, Walter, Earl of Atholl, 380–1, 390–1
Stillington, Robert, Bishop of Bath and Wells, 473–4

Stirling Bridge, battle of (1297), 127–8
Stirling Castle, 127–8, 136; Bruce besieges, 161; Scottish lands forfeited, 220
Stockdale, Oliver, 402–3
Stocton, Adam, 314
Stone of Destiny (Stone of Scone), 123, 138, 183, 196, 289
Storey, R.L., 392, 404
Stratford, John de, Bishop of London (later Archbishop of Canterbury), 190, 238–40
Strathbogie, David of see Atholl, David of Strathbogie, Earl of
Strathbogie, David of (son of Earl of Atholl), 197, 200–1, 203, 215, 219, 221–3, 227, 229–30, 332; killed, 232–4
Strathclyde, 7
Strathearn, Malise, 1st Earl of, 57
Strathearn, Maurice Moray, 1st Earl of, 245
Strathord, Perth, 135
Stubbs, William, 109
Stury, Sir Richard, 296
Stuteville, Nicholas de, 82
Suffolk, John de la Pole, 2nd Duke of, 474
Suffolk, Robert de Ufford, 1st Earl of, 237
Suffolk, William de la Pole, 4th Earl (later 1st Duke) of, 382, 396–8
Suffolk, William Ufford, 2nd Earl of, 308–9
Sumption, John, 272
Surrey, John de Warenne, 8th Earl of see Warenne, John, Earl de
Surrey, Thomas Holland, Duke of (earlier Earl of Kent), 341–2, 347, 349
Surrey, Thomas Howard, Earl of, 487
Sutherland, William Sutherland, 5th Earl of, 285
Swein, King of Denmark, 26, 28
Swinburne, Algernon Charles, 10
Swinton, Sir Thomas, 320
Swynburn, Sir William de, 327
Swynford, Katherine, Lady (later Duchess of Lancaster), 303, 373, 378
Symeon of Durham, 27
Syon House, Middlesex, 489

Tadcaster, 364–5, 431–2
Tailboys, Sir William, 436, 438, 442
Taillour, John, 260
Talbot, Gilbert, 481
Talbot, John, Lord (later 1st Earl of Shrewsbury), 389, 391, 398
Talbot, Richard, 203
Tancred, 39
Tempest, Richard, 262, 279, 281, 284, 287
Teviotdale, 333
Tewkesbury, battle of (1471), 457
Thirsk, Yorkshire, 364, 484
Thomas of Woodstock see Gloucester, Duke of
Threave Castle, 414
Thurstan, Archbishop of York, 54, 56
Thwaites, Henry, 461
Tickhill, 174–5
Tinchebrai, battle of (1106), 29

Topcliffe, Yorkshire, 33–5, 72, 74, 77, 152, 155, 180, 192, 402
Torigni, Robert de, 67
Tostig, Earl of Northumbria, 11, 23–4
Toulouse, Raymond IV, Count of, 39
Tournai, 238, 258
Tours, Treaty of (1444), 396
Tours, Truce of (1462), 438
Tout, T.F., 267
Towton, battle of (1461), 431–4
Treaty of Perpetual Peace (Anglo-Scottish, 1502), 489–90
Tripartite Indenture (1405), 361
Triple Alliance (Burgundy-France-Scotland) against England, 388–9
Trollop, Andrew, 423
Troyes, Treaty of (1419), 375
Tuck, J.A., 7
Tudor, Owen, 477
Turnbull (Scottish champion), 216
Tutbury, 224
Tuxford, 406
Tweedmouth, 216
Tyler, Sir William, 484
Tynedale, 331–2
Tytler, P. Fraser, 290

Umfraville, Gilbert, Earl of Angus: provides fighting men, 171; claims earldom with Disinherited, 202–3, 224–5, 280; and Henry Percy IV's diplomacy, 205; Henry Percy IV lends money to, 225; campaigns against Scots, 229, 235; complains of non-payment, 241; at battle of Neville's Cross, 244, 246; as joint warden of Eastern Marches, 279; will and death, 331–2; 1st Earl of Northumberland marries widow, 332
Umfraville, Ingram, 132, 135
Umfraville, Maud, Countess of Angus see Northumberland, Maud, Countess of
Umfraville, Robert, 224
Umfraville, Sir Robert, 372, 374
Umfraville, Sir Thomas, 337
Urban II, Pope, 37–9
Urban V, Pope, 292

Valence, Joan de, 96
Valence, William de, 95, 96–7, 99–100, 103, 106–8, 110
Valognes, Geoffrey de, 71
Vanne, John, 154–5
Vaughn, Thomas, 471, 474
Vegetius: Epitoma Rei Militaris, 251–2
Verneuil, battle of (1424), 381
Vesci, Eustace de, 83–6
Vesci, John de, 97, 109–10
Vesci, William, 152–3, 226
Vesci of Kildare, William (illegitimate son of William), 153, 165
Vienne, Jean de, 334
Vikings see Norsemen

Villeneuve-la-Hardie, 273–4
Vine, M.J., 92

Wake, Blanche, 200, 224
Wake, Thomas, 171, 183, 187, 189–92, 194, 197, 200–4, 222, 235, 239–40, 249, 298
Wakering, John, Bishop of Norwich, 382
Wales: Edward I annexes, 113; Henry Percy II serves in, 119–20; troops in Edward's Scottish wars, 128–9; civil war against Edward II in, 172–4; Henry IV's wars in, 352, 355–6; Prince Henry campaigns in, 357, 366; rebels against Henry IV, 361–3; Edward IV controls south of, 446
Wallace, Sir William, 125–30, 134–7
Wallingford tournament (1307), 147, 150
Walsingham, Thomas, 293, 309, 311–12, 330, 339–40
Walter de Denton, 58
Waltheof, Earl of Northumbria, 28
Waltheof, son of Siward, 23
Ward, Sir Simon, 284
Wardlaw, Henry, Bishop of St Andrews, 367
Warenne, Alice, Countess de, 110–17
Warenne, John, Earl de (and 7th Earl of Surrey): Henry Percy II's friendship with, 95, 98; marriage, 96; loyalty, 98–9; character, 103; split with Edward I, 104–5; at battle of Lewes, 106; commands Dover garrison, 106; escapes to continent, 107; returns to Wales, 108; and Henry Percy III, 118–19; coat of arms, 119; negotiations in Scotland, 120–1, 123; at battle of Dunbar, 121–3; appointed first lieutenant of Scotland, 124; campaigns against Wallace's rebellion, 126–8, 144; praised in 'Song of Caerlaverock', 133; death and burial, 137
Warenne, John, Earl de (and 8th Earl of Surrey and Sussex; William's grandson): unhorsed by Gaveston at tournament, 147; hostility to Gaveston, 148, 150, 158; in Lords Ordainers, 156; besieges Gaveston at Scarborough, 159; and Gaveston's execution, 160; refuses to serve Edward II, 164; opposes Lancaster, 169–70; Edward II wins support of, 173; in campaign against Scots, 179, 229; command in north, 187; debts to Crown cancelled after Halidon Hill, 219; in regency council, 239; dies without issue, 264
Wark Castle, 374
Warkworth Castle, 207, 208, 211, 250, 362, 400
Warkworth, John, 438, 452
Warwick, Ann (née Beauchamp; 'Kingmaker's' wife), 405
Warwick, Guy de Beauchamp, Earl of, 128, 137, 143–4, 148, 151–2, 156–7, 159–60, 162–4, 173
Warwick, Maud, Countess of (William II de Percy's daughter), 72, 74–5, 77, 79, 93

Warwick, Richard de Beauchamp, Earl of, 376, 391
Warwick, Richard Neville, Earl of ('the Kingmaker'): qualities, 404–5; and Wars of Roses, 406, 408, 422; heads for London with Duke of York, 410–11; at first battle of St Albans, 412–13; commands at Calais, 413, 421, 424, 427; and James II, 414; assassination plot against, 418; attends 1458 great council, 420–1; piracy, 421, 424; rebelliousness, 421–2; abandons army at Ludlow, 423–4; lands in Kent, 424; Northampton victory, 425; status and authority, 426, 436; defeated at second battle of St Albans, 428–9; inherits late father's estates, 428; wounded at Towton, 431; campaigns in north, 438–40; bombards Bamburgh, 442; discontent with Edward IV, 444; foreign policy, 445; withdraws from court, 446; intrigues with Clarence over succession, 447–8; and marriage of daughters, 447, 449; rebels against Edward IV, 448–9, 451, 453–5; given refuge by Louis XI, 452; killed at Barnet, 457; estates pass to Crown, 462
Warwick, Thomas Beauchamp, 11th Earl of, 231, 258, 270–1, 291
Warwick, Thomas Beauchamp, 12th Earl of, 302, 308, 335, 340, 344, 349
Warwick, William Newburgh, Earl of, 74
Waurin, Jean de: Receuil des croniques, 388, 447
Webster, Nicholas, 284
Welles, Richard, 7th Baron, 451
Welles, Sir Robert, 451
Wessex: and Danes, 19–20
Westminster Abbey: building of, 104
Westmorland: Scots dispute rights to, 111; Scots attack under Fife, 337
Westmorland, Elizabeth (née Percy; then Clifford; Hotspur's daughter), 364, 382
Westmorland, Joan, Countess of (née Beaufort; 1st Earl's second wife), 345, 369, 378–9, 382, 386, 405
Westmorland, Margaret, Countess of (1st Earl's first wife), 386
Westmorland, Ralph Neville, 1st Earl of, 341, 345–7, 351, 355, 360, 362, 368–9, 372–3, 378–9, 381, 386
Westmorland, Ralph Neville, 2nd Earl of, 381, 386–7, 392–3, 422–3, 465
Weston, Philip, 266–8, 270, 274, 277–8
Whitby Abbey: refounded by William de Percy, 22, 39–40; Hugh d'Avranches discards, 31; William de Percy's heart buried in, 43; Alan de Percy supports, 44, 58
Whitby Chartulary, 73
White Ship: sinks, 48–9
Whitland Abbey, Carmarthen, 347
Wigton, Sir Malcolm Fleming, Earl of, 245
Wigtown, Archibald Douglas, Earl of, 373, 376
William I, Count of Burgundy, 72

William I (the Conqueror), King, 11, 22–31, 33–5, 55, 268

William II (Rufus), King, 8, 29, 39–40, 116, 311

William the Ætheling, 48

William Ciito, Count of Flanders, 48–9

William de Pont d'Arche, 49

William fitz Osbern, 26

William the Lion, King of Scotland, 113, 116

William Longsword, 21

William of Malmesbury, 11, 55

William of Newburgh, 61, 81, 255

Wiltshire, James Butler, Earl of, 413, 423–4, 433

Wiltshire, John, 322

Wiltshire, John Stafford, Earl of, 450

Winchelsea, battle of (1350), 276

Winchester, Hugh Despenser, the elder, Earl of see Despenser, Hugh

Winchester, Treaty of (1153), 67–9

Wishart, Robert, Bishop of Glasgow, 125

Woodville family and faction, 444, 447–8, 450, 471–3, 477

Woodville, Sir Edward, 472, 478

Woodville, John: marries dowager Duchess of Norfolk, 447

Woodville, Lionel, Bishop of Salisbury, 471, 475

Worcester, Thomas Percy, Earl of (Henry Percy V's son), 262, 342, 347, 349, 355, 357–61

Worcester, William, 403

Wycliffe, John, 312–14, 317–19

Wykeham, William, Bishop of Winchester, 311–12, 314–15, 317, 320–1, 326

Wyntoun, Andrew, 242, 290

Wytherington, Sir Gerard de, 294–5

Yolande of Dreux, Queen of Alexander III of Scotland, 113–15

York: provides fighting men, 5; archbishopric, 6; Treaty of (1237), 8, 111; Vikings in, 10; William de Percy in, 23; William the Conqueror in, 25–7; burned (1069), 26; castles rebuilt, 27; threatened by Scots, 56; attacked by Henry Plantagenet, 66; as administrative centre under Edward I, 128;

Statute of (1322), 178, 188; Bruce threatens, 180; Edward III moves government to, 193, 215; Parliament held in (1334), 221; corruption in, 277; Egremont in, 401–2, 408; appeals to Henry VIII for tax concessions, 484

York, Archbishops of see Greenfield, William; Kemp, John; Melton, William; Neville, George; Scrope, Richard; Thurstan; Zouche de Assheby, William la

York, Cecil, Countess of, 65

York, Cicely, Duchess of (née Neville), 395

York, Edmund of Langley, 1st Duke of (earlier Earl of Cambridge), 292, 301, 346

York, Richard, 3rd Duke of: achievements, 366; campaigns in France, 389, 391; background and marriage, 395–6; and Cade's rebellion, 397; finances, 397–8, 417; antagonism to Somerset, 398–9, 400; in Wars of Roses, 405–7, 423; Exeter dislikes, 407; leases Doncaster, 409; leads army on London, 410–11; popularity, 410, 417; Queen Margaret detests, 410, 417; at first battle of St Albans, 411–13; as Protector, 413, 415; and James II of Scotland, 414; power and status, 417, 426; James II supports, 418; and border problems, 419; and London great council (1458), 420; raises troops, 422; flees to Ireland, 423–4; aspires to Crown, 426; killed at Sandal, 427–8

York, William le Gros, Earl of (and Count of Aumale), 56, 59–61, 63, 64–6, 69

Yorkshire: geographical position, 4–5; under William the Conqueror, 12, 26, 28; estates and properties in, 32–3, 59–60; land values, 33; fiefs and landholdings, 70

Ypres, John de, 320–1

Zealand, Maud, Duchess of (sister of Blanche Lancaster), 298–9

Zouche de Assheby, William la (later Archbishop of York), 195